THE ARCHAEOLOGY OF SUSSEX TO AD2000

EDITED BY DAVID RUDLING

UNIVERSITY OF SUSSEX AT BRIGHTON

Heritage

PUBLIISHED BY HERITAGE MARKETING & PUBLICATIONS LTD.
ON BEHALF OF THE CENTRE FOR CONTINUING EDUCATION, UNIVERSITY OF SUSSEX

2003

Published by Heritage Marketing and Publications Ltd on behalf of
The Centre for Continuing Education
University of Sussex

ISBN 0 9544456 1 9

Heritage Marketing and Publications Ltd,
Hill Farm – Unit F, Castle Acre Road, Great Dunham, King's Lynn, Norfolk PE32 2LP

Printed by Olivers Printers,
Cesar House, Eastwood Road, Bexhill-on-Sea, East Sussex TN39 3PS

CONTENTS

CONTRIBUTORS

Luke Barber
Field Archaeology Unit, University College London

Tristan Bareham
East Sussex Archaeology and Museums Project

Martin Brown
Archaeology Division, Transport and Environment, East Sussex County Council

Chris Davenport
Institute of Archaeology, University College London

Peter Drewett
Institute of Archaeology, University College London

Mark Gardiner
School of Archaeology & Palaeoecology, Queen's University Belfast

Paul Garwood
Institute of Archaeology & Antiquity, University of Birmingham

Christopher Greatorex
CG Archaeology

Sue Hamilton
Institute of Archaeology, University College London

Robin Holgate
The Museum of Science and Industry in Manchester

Richard Jones
Centre for English Local History, University of Leicester

Malcolm Lyne
Freelance archaeologist (Roman pottery specialist)

John Manley
Sussex Archaeological Society

Peter Marsden
Shipwreck Heritage Centre (Hastings)

David Martin
Field Archaeology Unit, University College London

Matthew Pope
Institute of Archaeology, University College London

David Rudling
Field Archaeology Unit, University College London *and* Centre for Continuing Education, University of Sussex

Elizabeth Somerville
School of Biological Sciences, University of Sussex

Mark Taylor
Archaeology Division, Environmental and Economic Policy Service, West Sussex County Council

Andrew Woodcock
Archaeology Section, Transport and Environment, East Sussex County Council

PREFACE

The publication in 1978 of the proceedings of a weekend symposium (held at Hassocks in 1977) on the archaeology of Sussex was a landmark in the study of archaeology in the historic county. Fifteen papers provided summaries by period and/or theme concerning *Archaeology in Sussex to AD 1500* (Drewett 1978; http://ads.ahds.ac.uk/catalogue/library/cba/rr29.cfm), and collectively these papers represented the most comprehensive review to date of the county's archaeology, previous overviews having been much more restricted in scope, especially period of coverage (eg Curwen 1930, 1937, 1954; Winbolt 1935; Cunliffe 1973; Aldsworth and Freke 1976). The aims and format of the 1977 Sussex symposium were soon repeated in other counties in the south-east, including Essex (Buckley 1980), Hampshire (Shennan and Schadla-Hall 1981), Kent (Leach 1982) and Surrey (Bird and Bird 1987). The substantial increase in archaeological fieldwork during the 1980s and 1990s, partly linked to major changes in the structure and funding of rescue archaeology in Britain, led to the need to update, revise and expand these county overviews, and to create frameworks for future fieldwork and research. In Sussex a second (but unpublished) weekend symposium (Archaeology in Sussex to AD 1800) was held at the Isle of Thorns, Chelwood Gate in October 1991. Elsewhere there were conferences in Essex (Bedwin 1996) and Hampshire (Hinton and Hughes 1996). In September 1996 there was a two day archaeology conference in Dieppe to "encourage contacts between professional and amateur researchers on either side of the Channel [ie Normandy and Sussex] "(Delestre and Woodcock 1989, 9).

In 1997, twenty years after the first Sussex archaeology symposium, the Centre for Continuing Education at the University of Sussex, in association with the Sussex Archaeological Society, organised a weekend conference at the University which was attended by over 300 people. The main aims of this event were to review some parts of the proceedings of the symposium of 1977, to widen the scope of study, both chronologically (up to, and including, the 20th century) and thematically (eg maritime archaeology), and to produce an up to date volume on the archaeology of Sussex. Such a 'key text' was considered increasingly necessary in order to meet the demands of local and regional archaeologists, expanding numbers of part-time archaeology students at the University of Sussex, and the general public. As the title indicates (ie The Archaeology of Sussex to AD 2000), the conference was designed to cover all periods of archaeology up to the present, which was conveniently close to the end of the millennium! The coverage of very recent archaeology included the study of churchyards (Tristan Bareham) and post-1945 nuclear shelters (Martin Brown). In addition to the nineteen papers presented in 1997, this volume also includes a paper on environmental change and landscape history by Elizabeth Somerville, who chaired part of the conference.

Much of the blame for the long delay in the appearance of these conference proceedings lies with the writer/editor ("pressures of other work, etc") and I apologise to both the contributors and conference delegates for the delay. On the positive side the delay has enabled various contributors to update their papers, including research undertaken as recent as 2002. With the aim of disseminating the information as widely as possible, the main hard-copy proceedings are supplemented by both the availability for purchase of printed individual papers and by an 'E' version of the whole volume.

David Rudling
Convenor for Archaeology
Centre for Continuing Education
University of Sussex

References

Aldsworth, F. and Freke, D. 1976. *Historic Towns in Sussex, an archaeological survey.* London: Institute of Archaeology.

Bedwin, O. (ed). 1996. *The Archaeology of Essex, Proceedings of the Writtle Conference.* Chelmsford: Essex County Council.

Bird, J. and Bird, D. (eds). 1987. *The Archaeology of Surrey to 1540.* Guildford: Surrey Archaeological Society.

Buckley, D.G. (ed). 1980. *Archaeology in Essex to AD 1500,* CBA Res. Rep. **34**.

Cunliffe, B. 1973. *The Regni.* London: Duckworth.

Curwen, C.E. 1930. *Prehistoric Sussex.* 2nd edition. London: The Homeland Association Ltd.

Curwen, E.C. 1937. *The Archaeology of Sussex.* 1st edition. London: Methuen.

Curwen, E.C. 1954. *The Archaeology of Sussex.* 2nd edition. London: Methuen.

Delestre, X. and Woodcock, A. (eds). 1998. *Proximus* **2**, *Publication of the archaeological round-table Dieppe 17th and 18th September.* Rouen: The Association for the Promotion of the Archaeology of Haute-Normandy.

Drewett, P.L. (ed) 1978. *Archaeology in Sussex to AD 1500.* CBA Res. Rep. **29**.

Hinton, D.A. and Hughes, M. 1996. Archaeology in Hampshire: A framework for the future. Hampshire County Council.

Leach, P.E. (ed). 1982. *Archaeology in Kent to AD 1500,* CBA Res. Rep. **48**.

Shennan, S.J. and Schadla-Hall, R.T. (eds). 1981. *The Archaeology of Hampshire, From the Palaeolithic to the Industrial Revolution.* Hampshire Field Club and Archaeological Society Monograph **1**.

Winbolt, S.E. 1935. Romano-British Sussex, in L.F. Salzman (ed), *The Victoria History of the Counties of England, A History of Sussex,* Volume **3**, 1-70.

ACKNOWLEDGEMENTS

The editor would like to thank all the contributors for their co-operation and patience. In addition thanks are due to: Gwen Jones who provided considerable editorial assistance; Susan Rowland who prepared many of the illustrations and also page-set the whole volume; Andy Gammon who designed the cover; Jane and Justin Russell who produced some of the illustrations; Hazel Lintott who scanned the photographs; Helen Dixey for secretarial assistance, and Mary Rudling who read through and checked the final draft. Auriol Griffith-Jones compiled the index.

Abbreviations in this volume

a. Abbreviations in the text

BP Before Present

b. Abbreviations in the references

Most of the abbreviations in the references are based on the recommendations in the third edition (1991) of *Signposts for Archaeological Publication* produced by the Council for British Archaeology. Significant variations from these recommendations include:

BAR	*British Archaeological Reports* (Oxford)
CBA	Council for British Archaeology (once of London, now of York)
EHAR	*English Heritage Archaeological Reports*
OUCA	Oxford University Committee for Archaeology
SAC	*Sussex Archaeological Collections*
SNQ	*Sussex Notes and Queries*

THE ARCHAEOLOGICAL IMPLICATIONS OF COASTAL CHANGE IN SUSSEX

Andrew Woodcock

Abstract

The coastline of Sussex has witnessed enormous changes, since the first human impact on this country over half a million years ago. Inevitably these changes have had a profound effect on the way in which people were able to use, exploit and settle the changing landscape. Only comparatively recently have people taken active measures to reclaim land and build defences against the sea. This article seeks to explain some of the processes involved and document the changes that have led to the Sussex coastline we know today. Only by understanding such events can we adequately interpret the remains that survive in the archaeological record.

Introduction

Coastal environments are, by their very nature, subject to constant change. The present coast of Sussex is extremely varied, encompassing such diverse landforms as the winding creeks of Chichester Harbour (Fig. 1.2), the precipitous cliffs of Beachy Head and Fairlight (Fig.1.4), the reclaimed marshes of the Pevensey and Pett Levels and the shingle beaches of the Crumbles and Rye Bay (Fig.1.5). The appearance of today's coastline owes much to human intervention and efforts to hold back the sea and reclaim the land. The very familiarity of the present coast means that it is often regarded as a natural landform, with the result that it is often difficult for us to imagine how very different it would look if the river embankments and coastal defences were suddenly to be swept away. If this happened, then much of the low-lying pasture and freshwater marsh would be inundated, turning large areas of productive farm-land into salt-marsh. In addition, many areas of modern housing and industrial development would become flooded and have to be abandoned.

This paper will consider six aspects of coastal change, in particular;
• the way in which the coast of Sussex has changed through time,
• the various mechanisms that have caused those changes,
• the nature of the evidence for those changes,
• the manner in which those changes have influenced settlement, communications, trade and the exploitation of the coastal environment,
• the effect that coastal change has had on the nature of the archaeological evidence that is available to us, and arising from that
• the extent to which our archaeological knowledge, and hence the deductions that arise from it, truly reflect the archaeology that once existed, or indeed might still exist and await discovery.

Inevitably, within the constraints of a single paper, it is impossible to cover each of these aspects in great detail and a number of obvious generalisations have had to be made. Although there have been previous assessments of coastal development (Lower 1870, Ballard 1910, Steers 1964, Castleden 1967, Eddison *et al.* 1983, Robinson & Williams 1983, Jennings & Smyth 1987, Eddison & Green 1989, Brandon & Short 1990, Eddison 1998, Jennings & Smyth 1990, Robinson 1999) much new information is now available and few of the earlier papers have put this information in an archaeological context. Hopefully, this paper will establish a basic framework which will allow the reader scope to explore the subject in greater detail, should they wish to do so. This paper would not have been possible without the work of many other researchers, whose contributions and advice is freely acknowledged. Any errors of fact or interpretation that remain are entirely the responsibility of the author. Only principal references have been given as more detailed and site-specific references are to be found within the works cited. In addition, a number of more general and wide-ranging publications have been consulted, which themselves contain relevant bibliographies. These include Reid 1903, Osborne-White 1924, Kirkaldy & Bull 1940, Hodgson 1967, Green 1968, Thompson 1980, Geog. Ed. Com. U. of Sx. 1983, Lake *et al.* 1987, Drewett *et al.* 1988, Young & Lake 1988, Eddison *et al.* 1989, Eddison & Green 1989, Bell & Walker 1992, Jones & Keen 1993, Eddison 1995, Fullford *et al.* 1997, Murton *et al.* 1998.

Setting the scene

If we are to understand the evolution of the Sussex coastline, we must look back at least 500,000 years and at the processes that ultimately produced the familiar coast we see today. During this time there have been vast changes in climate and, in particular, a series of alternating cold glacial and warmer interglacial periods. Although the ice itself never reached as far south as Sussex, its very proximity had a profound effect (Shephard-Thorn 1975). At the height of a glaciation the great volume of water locked up in ice sheets and glaciers around the world would have dramatically reduced sea-levels, at times by over 100 metres, whilst the sheer weight of the ice itself would have caused the land mass, upon which it sat, to be depressed. The extremely cold periglacial conditions, that would have existed in Sussex during a glaciation, would have produced thick sheets of 'soliflucted' gravels. These were laid down as a result of the mass-movement of semi-frozen rock and underlying deposits down the slopes of the Downs onto the coastal plains, into the river valleys and onto the floor of what is now the English Channel.

During the warmer interglacial periods there would have been other effects. With the melting of the ice the sea-level rose, sometimes to levels much higher than today. The evidence for these former sea-levels is preserved in the uplifted fossil cliffs and raised beach deposits of the west Sussex coastal plain. Although the sequence and date of the various stages of these beaches has yet to be worked out in detail, they can be divided into two main series; the higher, delimited by the Goodwood-Slindon raised beach and cliff line, and the lower, delimited by the Brighton-Norton raised beach and cliff line, at altitudes of some 40 metres and 8 metres respectively, above present sea-level (Woodcock 1981, Bates *et al.* 1998, Parfitt 1998, Woodcock 1999).

It is the higher of these raised beaches, and the deposits associated with it (principally the Slindon formation), that is not only the most ancient but the most important, exemplified by the internationally important site at Boxgrove with its ovate handaxes and associated faunal remains, described elsewhere in this volume. The Boxgrove site is believed to predate the Anglian glaciation (OIS 13) and is probably at least 500,000 years old (Roberts 1998, Roberts & Parfitt 1999).

The lower raised beach is much more recent in date and is likely to be pre-Ipswichian (OIS 6 or 7) and probably about 200,000 years old. The most famous exposure of this beach is at Black Rock, near Brighton Marina (Fig. 3) but there are also deposits, thought to be of a similar date, exposed at Selsey (Hutchinson & Millar 1998). Although there are no Palaeolithic tools within these beach sediments that could not have been derived from earlier deposits, this cliff line is nevertheless important, since its presence is suggested by buried landforms beneath the present English Channel (Evans, J. pers. com., Kellaway *et al.* 1975, Jennings & Smyth 1987, 1990).

Prior to the Anglian glaciation, the eastern part of Sussex was joined to the continent by a substantial land-bridge, which was eventually breached by water overflowing from an ice-dammed lake in the southern North Sea. The rivers that cut through the Sussex downland today represent remnants of much larger river systems that originally flowed into an embayment, south-west of this early land bridge, and later into a postulated Channel river, flowing south of the present Sussex coastline (Smith 1989, Hamblin 1992).

The sea advances

The last major cold period to affect this country (the Loch Lomand stadial) was at its height some 13,000 years ago, when an ice sheet over a kilometre thick, would have sat over Scotland and north-west England (Bowen *et al.* 1986).

With ameliorating climatic conditions, Britain once more became habitable and attracted visiting bands of nomadic hunter-gatherers, able to cross the bed of the North Sea, now left largely dry by low sea-levels. As further ice melted and sea-level rose, the river valleys of the North Sea basin began to flood making this access route more difficult. At the same time, the land relieved from the weight of the ice sheet began to rise, leading to a tilting of the British land mass. This effect caused the south-east of England to slowly sink, a process accelerated by the weight of water flooding into the North Sea basin. This adjustment of the land is a long term process, which still continues today. Since the amount of recovery will vary according to location, the pattern of sea-level rise, relative to the land, is therefore highly localised (Long & Roberts 1997).

Several sea-level curves have been produced for the south-east of England. They have been constructed from a detailed study of data from boreholes, sunk in river estuaries, coastal margins and off-shore deposits, palynological and micro-faunal studies and the radio-carbon dating of organic transgressive and regressive indicator horizons (Fig.1.1), (Akeroyd 1972, Devoy 1979, 1982, Jennings & Smyth 1987, Tooley & Switsur 1988, Waller *et al.* 1988, Jennings & Smyth 1990, Tooley 1990, Long 1992, Plater 1992, Long & Innes 1993, Long & Shennan 1993, Long & Hughes 1995, Long & Innes 1995, Plater & Long 1995).

The sea-level curve shows sea-level continuing to rise rapidly throughout the Mesolithic and into the Neolithic, which must have led to a constant readjustment of the coastal environment. Such environments are highly productive and were no doubt attractive to a mobile prehistoric population, only too adept at exploiting the wide range of resources at their disposal. By about 8,000 years ago the sea had re-established itself between Britain and the continent and any contemporary coastal sites, if they survive, must lie far off-shore. Their presence is indicated, however, by finds of flint 'tranchet' axes and barbed harpoon points, dredged from the floor of the North Sea (Clark 1932, Evans 1932, Godwin & Godwin 1933, Louwe Kooijmans 1971).

Whilst rising sea-levels would have flooded the lower reaches of the Sussex rivers, they would also have encouraged wetter fresh-water conditions further up the river valleys, leading to the growth of peat in these locations. The study of these peat deposits not only provides us with a picture of the vegetational history, on and around the sample sites, but also tells us something of the nature and chronology of sea-level rise and coastal change, particularly when the peats are interleaved with inorganic marine silts and clays.

Much of the most recent work has been undertaken in the eastern half of Sussex. Major investigations have taken place in the Ouse (Jones 1971, Thorley 1971, Burrin & Jones 1991, Bates 1998, Waller 1998), Rother (Waller *et al.* 1988) and Brede valleys (Waller 1994), Combe Haven (Jennings & Smyth 1987, Smyth & Jennings 1988) and in the Willingdon (Jennings & Smyth 1987) and Pett Levels (Waller 1993).

One of the deepest sequences, so far investigated, has been at Pannel Bridge (Waller 1993), on the Pett Levels near Winchelsea. Here there are over 11 metres of organic sediments, extending back over 10,000 years, and providing an unparalleled record of the vegetational history of the area. Although it is impossible to make a direct correlation between the growth of peat deposits and the rise in sea-level, the deposits at Pannel Bridge reflect, almost exactly, the generalised sea-level curve established for the south-east of England (e.g. Tooley 1990).

It seems clear that the shape of the early coastline was strongly influenced by the topography of the landscape which the rising sea-level subsequently drowned. However, reconstructing past coastlines is not simply a matter of dropping former sea-levels onto the underlying topography, for a whole series of other factors have to be taken into account. These include: the topography of the landscape prior to recent sea-level rise, the geology and morphology of the coastal environment, the

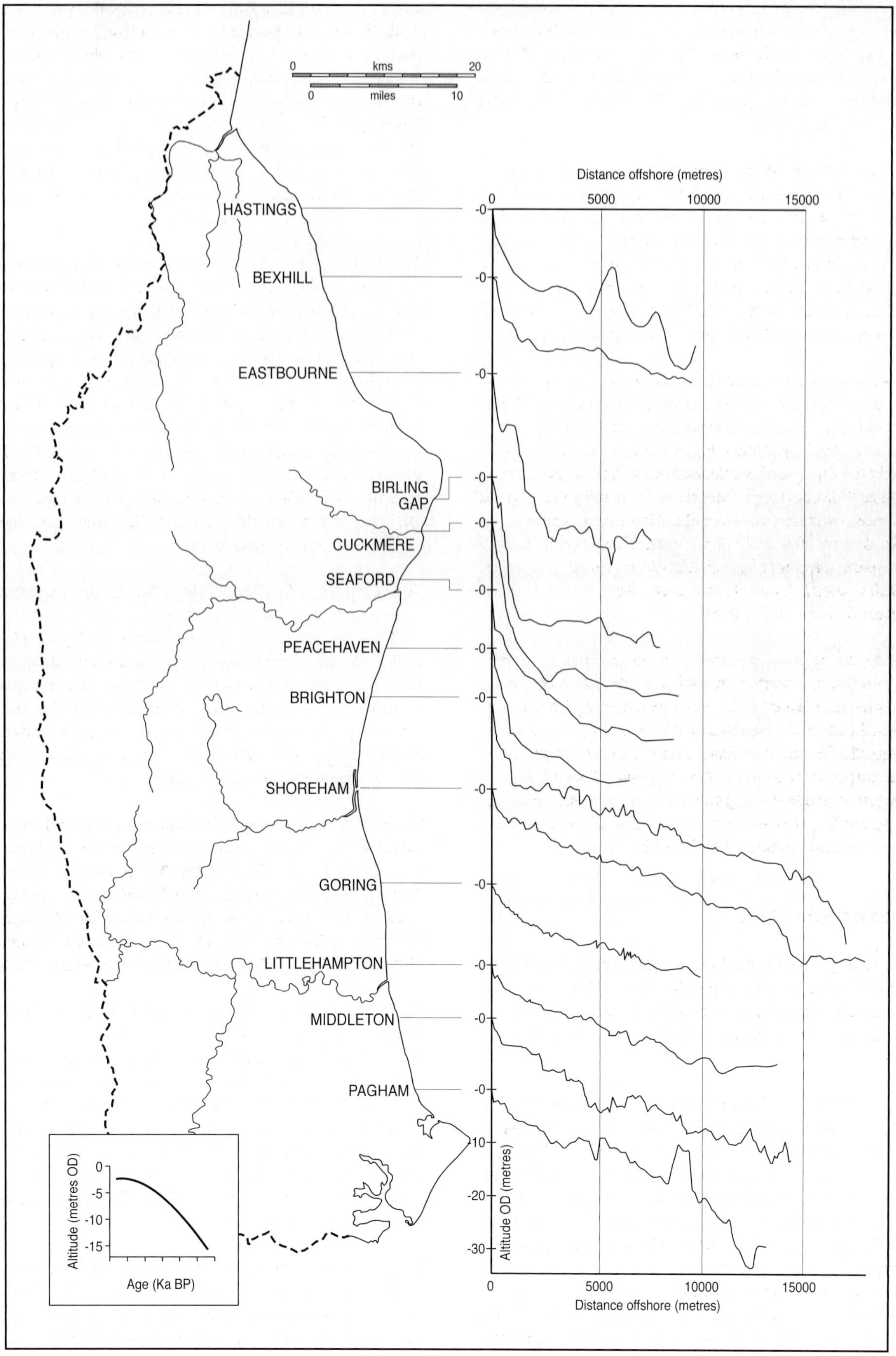

Figure 1.1. *Bathymetric profiles off the coast of Sussex (based on data provided by the British Geological Survey IPR/16-8C © NERC. All rights reserved). Inset, simplified sea-level curve for South-East England (after Long 1992 and Long and Innes 1993).*

availability of gravels and sediments on the floor of the English Channel and their ability to be re-deposited in the coastal zone, the effects of tidal flow and of periods of storms, the re-deposition of coastal sediments by means of longshore drift and the input of river-borne sediments from the land and the effects of human intervention. It is also necessary to estimate the degree to which the former land surface has suffered attrition and erosion, subsequent to its inundation, in turn affected by the 'hardness' of the rocks and the extent to which coastal sediments have been in place to buffer coastal erosion. In addition we must also assume that inter-tidal ranges were not dissimilar to those of the present day and that relative changes in sea-level have been constant across the whole study area.

Whilst the processes of erosion are most obvious at the cliff base and on the inter-tidal shore, there has been little attention paid, until recently, to the extent to which erosion takes place on the sub-tidal continuation of the shore platform, otherwise known as the *shoreface ramp*. Recent studies of the Holderness coast (Wingfield and Evans 1998, Evans *pers. com.*) have shown that whilst cliff erosion produces only 23% of the total sediment flux, the erosion of the shoreface ramp produces substantially more at 33%. This study is of particular relevance to Sussex, since both the gradient and the depth of the foot of the shoreface ramp at Holderness are almost identical to those to the west of Brighton.

New data, collected and collated by the British Geological Survey's Coastal and Off-Shore Geology Group, which shows valleys and other topographic features buried below the sediments on the floor of the present English Channel (Hamblin *et al.* 1992), provides us with an insight into how the prehistoric coast of Sussex might have looked at that time. Particularly interesting is the fact that the BGS data indicates a marked contrast between the form of that coastline to the east and the west of Brighton (Fig. 1.1).

To the east of Brighton, the off-shore sub-surface contours drop steeply and the fact that this feature appears to align with the Brighton raised-beach may not be coincidental (Kellaway *et al.* 1975). At Birling Gap the contours fall over 30 metres within a kilometre of the present coast, and a similar pattern can be seen at Peacehaven and Eastbourne. The steepness and scale of these profiles is such that they are likely to represent a remodelled landscape, rather than an erosional feature formed as a direct consequence of rising sea-level. Thus, it seems probable that this steep change of slope marks the coastal limit of this part of eastern Sussex for much of the prehistoric period and that the present extensive erosion and rapid retreat of the cliff line that is taking place here is a relatively recent phenomenon. This means that the Iron Age hillforts at Hastings and Seaford, although somewhat further inland, would have been sited in prominent positions with commanding views of the English Channel.

To the west of Brighton the off-shore sub-surface profile is markedly different and much shallower. Whilst erosion along this coast is well documented in more recent times, it is not clear how far back in time it is possible to extrapolate this rate of erosion, particularly if the effects of erosion had been attenuated by substantial shingle deposits along the coastal margins.

There seems no doubt, however, that the present Selsey peninsula (which before the construction of a causeway at the north end, was cut off from the mainland at high tide) extended considerably seaward of the present coast. An abundance of later prehistoric and Roman material has been recovered both off-shore and from the eroding cliff (Heron-Allen 1911, Bedwin 1982, Aldsworth 1987, Pitts 1979 & 1980, Wallace 1996) We might even conjecture that, certainly for the later prehistoric and Roman periods, the peninsula extended as far south as the Mixon Reef, some 2 kilometres off-shore. If this were so, then it would help explain the presence of deep hollows on the sea-bed, such as the Mixon and Whirlpool Holes, which lie relatively close to the proposed shoreline. Whilst the mechanism of their formation is still a matter of debate, one suggestion is that they could have been caused as a result of tidal scour, particularly if the shoreline here had remained stable, in its suggested position, for some period of time.

Emerging wetlands

The history of the Sussex coastline is dominated by the formation and migration of coastal and off-shore barriers, whose precise mechanism of formation and chronological development continues to be actively debated (e.g. Jennings & Smyth 1982a & b, Burrin 1982, Jennings & Smyth 1987). It is clear that sand and gravel deposits can migrate landwards under the influence of a rising sea-level to be concentrated in close proximity to the shore (Schwartz 1972, Stanley & Swift 1976, Roy *et al.* 1994). However, the opening up of the Straight of Dover seems to have initiated large scale west-east sand transport (Austin 1991), traces of which have been observed in the Rye (Long *et al.* 1996) and Rye Bay areas (Greensmith & Gutmanis 1990, Dix *et al.* 1998).

The coastline of the early Neolithic would have been deeply indented, possibly with sandy beaches and barriers close inshore. Whilst peat growth was occurring in some favoured locations (Shephard-Thorn 1975), the main phase of peat formation had not yet begun and most river estuaries would have been broad and tidal. As sea-level began to stabilise, long shore drift encouraged the formation of more substantial coastal shingle barriers. Whilst the direction of longshore drift has remained strongly eastward along the majority of the Sussex coast, to the west of the Selsey peninsula the direction is reversed (Hamblin *et al.* 1992). This fact, coupled with the sheltering effect of the Isle of Wight partly explains why Chichester Harbour, and to a lesser extent Pagham Harbour, have a somewhat different evolution to the other Sussex inlets and have managed to escape the most pronounced effects of barrier formation and consequent silting.

In the Rye Bay area, longshore drift seems to have been responsible for the creation of a wide shingle bank extending from the Fairlight Cliffs to beyond Dungeness, causing the rivers to flow eastward and enter the sea near New Romney (Fig. 1.5), (Green 1988). Recent research has documented the spread of peat growth behind these barriers, forming in the higher reaches of the river valleys, as in the Brede at around 6,800 years BP, and spreading eastwards into Walland Marsh between 4,000 to 5,000 years BP (Long *et al.* 1998).

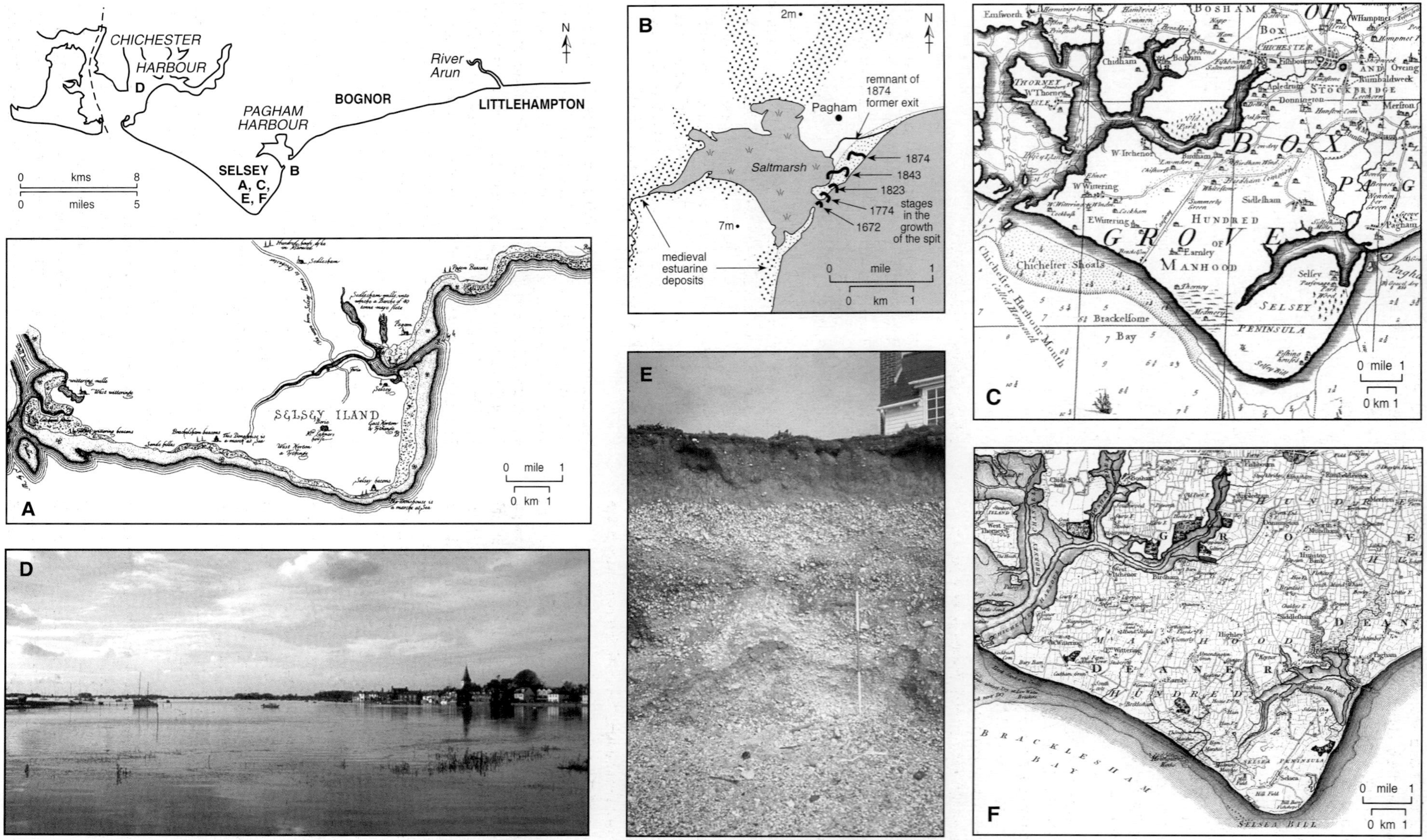

Figure 1.2. *Examples of coastal change in Sussex.*
(a) The Selsey peninsular in 1587, from a survey by Palmer and Covert of the Sussex coast at the time of the Armada. (b) The coastal evolution of Pagham Harbour (after Robinson & Williams 1983 and Robinson 1999). (c) Selsey peninsular in 1724, taken from a map of Sussex produced by Richard Budgen. (d) Chichester Harbour (Photo: Mark Taylor). (e) Pleistocene raised-beach deposits exposed in the cliff face at Selsey. (f) Selsey peninsular in 1795, taken from a map of Sussex produced by William Gardner and Thomas Gream.

Elsewhere, these barriers probably took the form of elongated spits, similar to examples well documented in the medieval and later periods. Their effect would have been to divert the mouths of streams and rivers eastwards, where they entered the sea. This in turn would have impeded drainage and provided a back-barrier environment in which fine grained marine sediments, brought in on the tide, could be deposited. Poor drainage would also have tended to raise the water table further inland, encouraging peat growth in these areas which, as silting increased, was able to spread progressively downstream.

The pattern of sedimentation in those low-lying areas cannot be explained solely as a result of sea-level rise slowing down. Had this been so, changes in the sedimentary sequence would have occurred at roughly the same time in each of the Sussex river valleys and this does not happen. Whilst the same sequence of events can be detected, to a greater or lesser extent, the date at which peat growth is initiated is extremely variable. For example, in the Ouse Valley peat growth commences by 6,000 years BP (Thorley 1971), in the Willingdon Levels, near Eastbourne, by 3,400 years BP (Jennings & Smyth 1987) and at Coombe Haven, near Bexhill, by 6 and 5,000 years BP (Jennings & Smyth 1987). At Worthing, peat had formed behind a shingle ridge, probably sometime before 4,000 BP (Barton 1963). The common link appears to be the mechanism of barrier and spit formation, the timing of which depends on local, rather than regional, circumstances. These include the distribution, thickness and nature of the near-shore and beach sediments and the ease with which they might be moved by longshore drift, in turn influenced by other factors such as the direction and strength of tidal flow, coastal currents and the effects of climatic deterioration and severe storms.

As sea-level stabilised (certainly by the Early to Middle Bronze Age) the peats which had formed in those low-lying areas started to dry out. This allowed Fen Carr to develop and trees to grow on the peat surface. Relics of these trees can be found on the present day on the foreshore at Pett Level, Bexhill and Bognor, as the well known 'submerged forest' deposits (Fig. 1.5), (Godwin 1943, Lake & Shephard-Thorn 1987). Only in the Willingdon Levels, near Eastbourne, where the Shinewater Late Bronze Age platform and trackway were constructed (Woodcock 1996, Greatorex 1995, 1998 and elsewhere in this volume) does the valley floor appear to have remained free of tree cover (Jennings *pers. com.*). Whether this was because of local environmental factors, or for anthropogenic reasons, has yet to be determined.

Lost landscapes

This period of stability was not, however, destined to last. By the end of the Late Bronze Age, we see another dramatic change taking place with marine influence, once more, spreading up the river valleys. It was probably as a direct result of this change that the settlement on the Shinewater Marshes was abandoned and caused the site to be rapidly sealed beneath a thick deposit of silty clay, leading to the anaerobic and waterlogged conditions which have resulted in the site's exceptional preservation.

Again, whilst this marine transgression can be detected in each of the Sussex river valleys, the date at which it occurred is not consistent. In the Ouse Valley, the peat beneath the estuarine deposits was truncated, but dated to about 3,000 years BP (Jones 1971, Burrin & Jones 1991). The marine transgression reached the lower parts of Willingdon Levels, near Eastbourne, by around 3,400 years BP, whilst organic material was growing further up the levels. The occupation of the late Bronze Age site at Shinewater terminated around 2,500 BP, whilst at Mornings Mill, at the head of the levels, peat growth finally ceased at around 2,300 BP (Jennings & Smyth 1987 and *pers. com.*). At Coombe Haven, near Bexhill, peat growth stopped by 2,170 years BP down valley and by 2,930 years BP farther upstream (Jennings & Smyth 1987). This difference of 760 years is accounted for by the influence of forest clearance activities on river discharge and the release of sediment (Smyth & Jennings 1988). On Romney Marsh the earliest dates come from the northern fringes, where peat formation terminated around 3,000 years BP. In Walland Marsh peat cessation happened around 2,000 years BP and at a somewhat later date further inland, for example before 1,700 BP at Old Place in the Brede valley (Long *et al.* 1998).

Thus, just as it was changes in the morphology of the shingle spits and barriers that, either directly or indirectly, provided the conditions responsible for initiating peat growth, it may well have been the erosion or depletion of these barriers that led to the onset of marine conditions. Whether these changes were due to climatic deterioration and increased storminess, or a decrease in sediment supply, or a combination of all these factors, is not clear. What is certain is that the sea flooded right up the lower reaches of the rivers and their estuaries, depositing marine and estuarine sediments on top of the peat. This turned former marsh, meadow and fen into tidal salt-marsh, to produce an environment in many ways similar to that of Chichester Harbour at the present day.

This highly indented coastline remained a consistent feature throughout the Iron Age and Roman periods, with sea-level perhaps 1 to 2 metres lower than the present day (Tooley 1990). Continuing longshore drift may have restarted the process of barrier building that would encourage silting in the back-barrier environment and ultimately enabled land reclamation to take place. Thus, by the time the Roman fort at Pevensey was built, in the earlier part of the 4th century, a substantial shingle spit may have begun to extend eastwards from Langley Point. This would have provided both a safe anchorage close to the Roman fort and shelter from the south-westerly gales. The building of the fort also coincides with a minor marine transgression, noted on Romney Marsh (Tooley & Switsur 1988, Tooley 1990).

This pattern of inlets and tidal estuaries was particularly developed in the eastern half of Sussex, where the Brede, Rother and Tillingham would have flowed eastwards into a broad expanse of small islands and a network of tidal creeks and salt-marsh channels (Fig. 1.5), (Cunliffe 1988, Tooley 1990). The Roman roads, that skirt this area, cross these rivers and their smaller tributaries, at points close to their tidal limit. The siting of the important Roman settlement and river crossing point at Bodiam seems to have been chosen for just these reasons, located as it is at the upstream limit of earlier peats and estuarine deposits. Further upstream there are valley

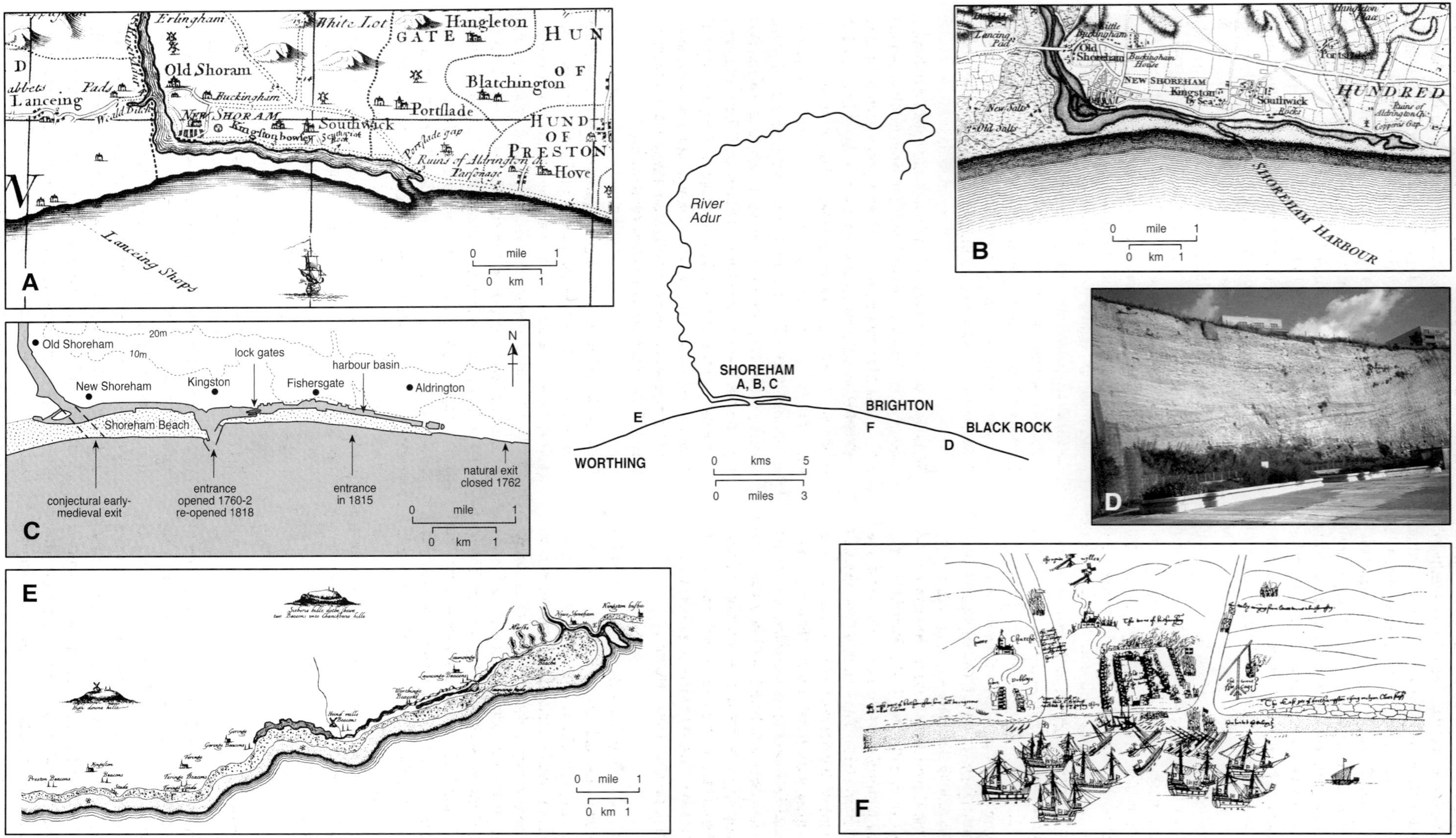

Figure 1.3. *Examples of coastal change in Sussex.*
(a) Shoreham and the mouth of the River Adur in 1724, taken from a map of Sussex produced by Richard Budgen. (b) Shoreham and the mouth of the River Adur in 1795, taken from a map of Sussex produced by William Gardner and Thomas Gream. (c) Coastal evolution at the mouth of the River Adur (after Farrant 1976 and Robinson & Williams 1983). (d) Pleistocene raised-beach deposits exposed in the cliff face at Black Rock, Brighton. (e) The Worthing area in 1587, from a survey by Palmer and Covert of the Sussex coast at the time of the Armada. (f) An attack on Brighton made by the French in 1514 from Horsfield's History, Antiquities and Topography of the County of Sussex (1835).

floor deposits, washed off adjacent hillsides as a result of woodland clearance and farming activities in the prehistoric and Roman periods. Similar deposits have been noted at a number of other sites in East Sussex (Scaife & Burrin 1983, 1985, 1987, Burrin 1988, Burrin & Scaife 1984, Smyth & Jennings 1988). These deposits would have tended to confine and deepen the river here. Downstream, where the river flows through the softer peaty sediments, the river is likely to have been substantially wider. Bodiam then was therefore carefully sited to take advantage of the optimum distance inland that larger ships and barges could travel upstream. The fact that a continuous succession of peats survive at Bodiam illustrates how little the River Rother has deviated from its original position, for if it had meandered back and forth it would surely have destroyed, or at least severely disturbed, these earlier deposits. By the Roman period the Rother must have been confined between banks at this point, for if it were not the settlement at Bodiam would have suffered from severe flooding (Lemmon & Hill 1966).

From this time onwards, the nature of the evidence upon which we have hitherto based our reconstruction of coastal change alters. Because the late Bronze Age marine transgression brought peat growth to a halt on the valley floors, the sedimentary record becomes much more sparse than in the earlier prehistoric period and we have few deposits capable of providing detailed environmental data or radio-carbon dates. However, whilst the sedimentary record may be of less use, we now have documentary and cartographic evidence available to help us reconstruct coastal environments. To this must be added a wealth of archaeological evidence; the saltern mounds, reclaimed fields, sea-walls and dykes, which survive as tangible witnesses in the landscape, not only of the pattern of coastal change, but the reason for and the consequences of that change.

Contesting forces

As we move into the early medieval period, shingle bars would have continued forming at the mouths of the valleys and across the broader embayments of former marshland. This would have encouraged further silting of the former salt-marsh and people were not slow to realise that these areas were ripe for exploitation, at first for the extraction of salt but later, as silting continued, by way of land reclamation.

Salt was only rarely obtained directly from salt-water, although the presence of salt-pans has been claimed on the foreshore at Pett Levels (Lovegrove 1966, Holden 1967). An indirect process was the method most commonly used (Holden & Hudson 1981). The surface of the estuarine silts, which lie between high spring tides and normal high sea-level, are rich in salts. It was these that were raked up and washed to produce a strong brine, which could then be evaporated to form salt crystals. These washings produced the characteristic saltern-mounds that are still prominent features in a number of our marshes and river estuaries (e.g. Pevensey Levels and the Adur estuary). Whilst the date of these mounds is difficult to ascertain, early medieval examples are undoubtedly present. At least 309 salterns were recorded in Sussex in Domesday book (King 1962), the largest number in any English county; 58, and possible c. 78 were in the Adur valley, 34 at Hooe, 16 at Eastbourne and 100 in the marshes near Rye and Old Winchelsea. The distribution of these saltern-mounds is important, for it provides a measure of how far tidal influence was able to spread into the former marshland and up the river valleys. In the Adur valley, for example, saltern-mounds are to be found as far north as Upper Beeding. Records show that whilst Sussex exported considerable quantities of salt to the continent in the early 14th century, by the end of the century most was imported (Pelham 1930). Whether this was because of deteriorating climatic conditions or reclamation of the former salt-marshes is not clear (Brandon 1971b).

The growth of shingle spits at the mouths of the Sussex rivers would have impeded drainage and encouraged the deposition of silts which created conditions favourable for land reclamation. Whilst a number of excellent studies on this subject have been undertaken, there are still many areas where the precise nature of events is poorly understood. On Pevensey Levels there is much visible evidence for attempts at early reclamation; such as the Crooked Ditch, reclaiming land in the early 12th century, and the Mark Dyke, a major drainage feature stretching over two miles across the Pevensey Levels and marking the boundary between the Pevensey and Hastings Rapes (Salzmann 1910, Dulley 1966, Brandon 1971a, 1974). By the time of the early 13th century vast tracts of this marshland, and many others like it, had been reclaimed and become productive, high value agricultural land.

The development of shingle spits played a vital role in determining the location of several early ports. The probable origins of Old Winchelsea, which only assumed importance towards the end of the 12th century, have recently been discussed in detail (Eddison 1998). The location of Old Winchelsea shows a surprising similarity to that of other early ports along the exposed Sussex coast. Many were sited where a river, or tidal embayment, entered the sea and where a developing spit provided shelter from south-westerly storms. Such a combination of circumstances undoubtedly influenced the siting of early ports at Shoreham (Aldsworth & Freke 1987), Seaford (Brookfield 1949, 1951-2), possibly Hastings (Baines 1963, Martin *et al.* 1995) and arguably at Old Winchelsea (Eddison 1998). However, ports situated in such locations are inherently unstable. Should the supply of shingle, deposited as a result of longshore drift, continue, then the Harbour entrance may become silted or migrate eastwards from the port itself, as happened at Shoreham (Fig. 1.3) and Seaford (Fig. 1.4). Conversely, if the supply of shingle fails, or the river breaks through the shingle at its original entrance, or if the shingle bank is weakened by storms, or rendered unstable by the build up of flood water inland, then not only might the protective shingle bar become destroyed and the anchorage become exposed to the south-west storms, but the port itself become endangered. Just such a scenario seems to have happened at Old Winchelsea and possibly also at Shoreham.

Although the ultimate destruction of Old Winchelsea was triggered by a series of great storms in the 1250's, this took several years to accomplish, with the church of St Thomas the Martyr finally being undermined and falling into the sea in 1271. Documentary evidence records the first warning signs in the late 1230's and early 40's. In the end a combination of

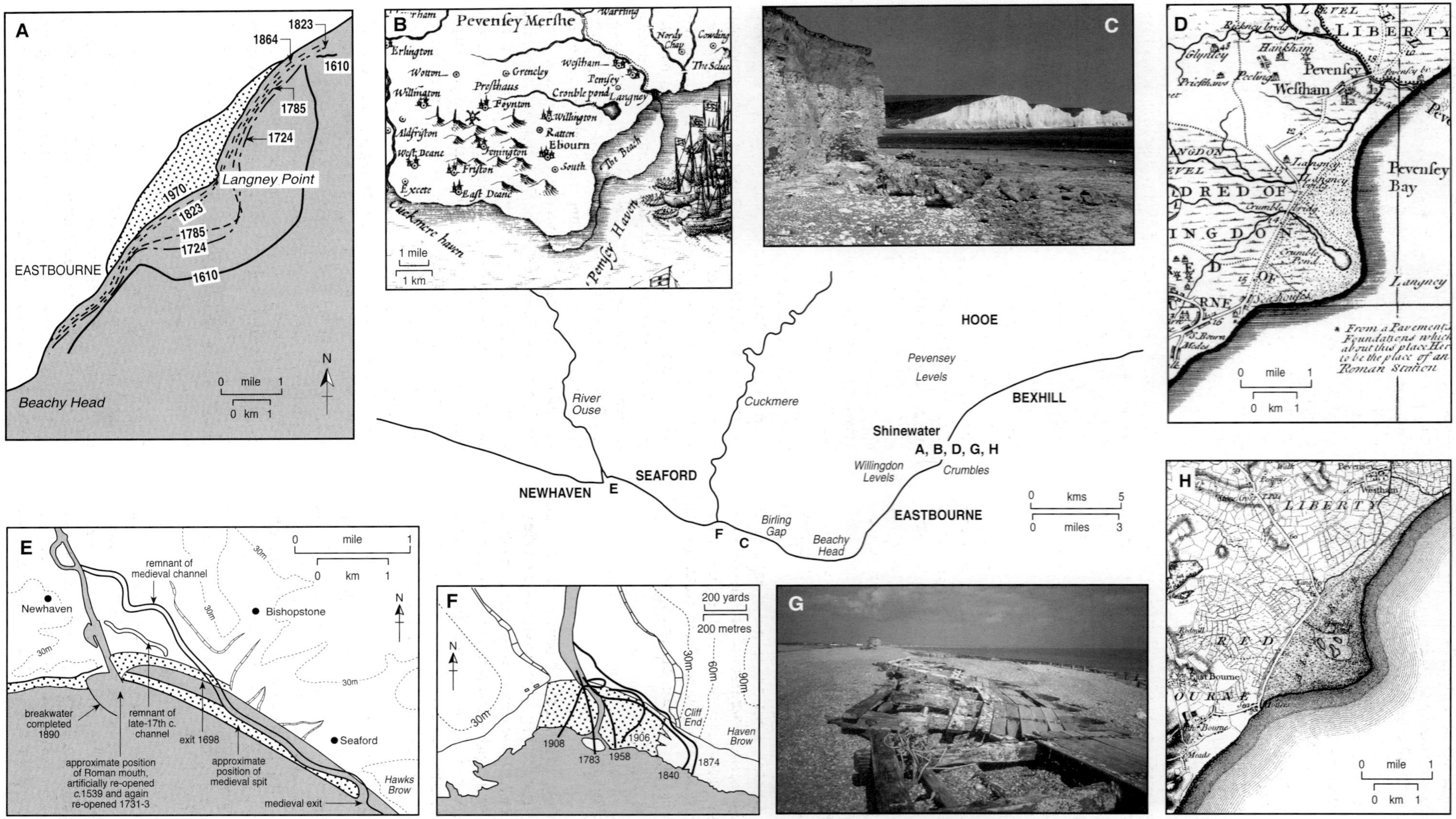

Figure 1.4. *Examples of coastal change in Sussex.*
(a) Coastal evolution of the Crumbles Shingle near Eastbourne (after Jennings & Smyth 1990). (b) Pevensey Bay and the Crumbles Shingle in 1695, taken from a map of Sussex produced by Robert Morden. (c) Cuckmere Haven and the Seven Sisters. (d) Pevensey Bay and the Crumbles Shingle in 1724, taken from a map of Sussex produced by Richard Budgen. (e) Coastal evolution at the mouth of the River Ouse (after Farrant 1976 and Robinson & Williams 1983). (f) Coastal evolution at the mouth of the River Cuckmere (after Robinson 1999). (g) Recent erosion of the Crumbles Shingle, east of Sovereign Harbour. (h) Pevensey Bay and the Crumbles Shingle in 1795, taken from a map of Sussex produced by William Gardner and Thomas Gream.

storms, high spring tides and tidal surges, possibly coupled with an exceptional build up of flood water inland caused the shingle to be breached irrevocably. This ultimately allowed the river Rother to migrate southward, abandoning its previous exit near New Romney, and enter the sea at Rye Bay (Fig. 1.5).

Matthew Paris, although writing somewhat later, gives us a vivid account of these times.

> *'On the first day of October, 1250, the moon upon her change, appearing exceeding red and swelled, began to show tokens of the great tempest of wind that followed, which was so huge and mighty both by land and sea, that the like had not been known, by men then alive. The sea, forced contrary to his natural course, flowed twice without ebbing, yielding such a roaring, that the same was heard (with great wonder) a far distance from the shore. Moreover, the same sea appeared in the dark on the night to burn as it had been on fire, and the waves to strive and fight together after a marvellous sort, so that the mariners could not devise how to save their ships where they lay at anchor. At Winchelsey, besides other hurt that was done in bridges, mills and banks, there were 300 houses and some churches drowned with the rising of the water.'* (Luard 1872-83, 1880)

Recognising that the town of Old Winchelsea was doomed, Edward I took steps in 1280 to buy a new site near the village of Iham and New Winchelsea (the present day Winchelsea) was laid out in 1283 (Aldsworth & Freke 1976).

Throughout the 1280's the sea made increasing inroads up the marshland channels and by 1288 documentary sources record walls broken down and serious flooding in the Brede Valley, possibly as a result of the last of three great sea-floods that are recorded elsewhere on the east coast of Britain (Hallam 1965).

From accounts such as these, and from a wealth of other information, we know that the end of the 13th century marked a period of increased storminess. There might also have been a slight rise in sea-level (Eddison *et al.* 1983). Inevitably these factors gave rise to major changes in coastal morphology. There are numerous documents relating to this time which testify to the difficulty of water control and maintaining the 'walls', which kept the sea at bay.

Such was the case on the Pevensey marshes (Brandon 1971a), where there are a number of charters relating to lands reclaimed by Battle Abbey. The effects of the storms here was to block the Pevensey outfall, probably as a result of drifting shingle. The Pevensey outfall was one of the two tidal channels which drained this area, the other being *Meneflete*, at the head of which stood the minor port of Northey. This exit also seems to have been similarly choked in the early 14th century. Severe storms, with consequent flooding, are recorded at intervals throughout the 14th century (Baker 1966, Brandon 1971b) and this, coupled with flooding resulting from impeded drainage, ultimately led to the abandonment of these areas as highly productive arable fields and their reversion to pasture.

In the Brede valley, near Winchelsea, a major sea-defence, called the *Damme*, was built across the lower reaches of the valley to protect over 1,000 acres of farmland. The wall was over a kilometre long, incorporating a sluice to control water-levels and a dock on its seaward side. Whilst the date of construction is not clear it had been completed by 1309. Unfortunately, whilst the earthwork protected the valley from flooding it also restricted the ebb and flow of the tide up the river. This, in turn, reduced the scouring action of the tide, which had helped prevent the build up of silt at the port of Winchelsea. The result was that the King, who had visited Winchelsea, issued an instruction to repair or construct walls along the Brede valley and remove the 'obstruction', so that the sea could ebb and flow as before (*Cal. Close Rolls 1354-60,* 315). This involved an enormous engineering project and in the early 15th century a new embanked cutting (over 150 metres wide and 7.5 kilometres long) was made for the river, north of and parallel to its old channel. (Gardiner 1995).

Similar problems of flooding occurred in the Ouse valley, much of which is particularly low-lying. At the time of Domesday, the whole width of the valley floor probably formed a tidal inlet with a string of settlements located at its margins. How early reclamation started here is not entirely clear but, by the early 14th century, highly prized meadow land had been inned and embanked. Continuing deposition of shingle at the mouth of the Ouse made accessibility to the port of Seaford, by sea-going ships, difficult. The deposition of shingle also severely impeded drainage, with the result that much of the Ouse valley experienced severe flooding, reaching such an extent that some 400 acres of the Archbishop of Canterbury's land at Southerham was converted into a permanent fishery. By the early 16th century, the extent of land subject to annual inundation exceeded 6,000 acres (Morris 1931, Brandon 1971c).

The solution proposed was to dig a channel through the shingle bar, allowing the Ouse to exit directly into the sea, and create a 'new haven' adjacent to the mouth. The scheme was probably completed by about 1550. The improvement to drainage allowed much of the valley floor to be reclaimed for pasture, but these efforts appear to have been short-lived. Shingle continued to block the river mouth and divert it eastwards. In 1648 the Ouse was reported '*no ways fit to sewe the level or four navigation*' and throughout the 18th century the valley was regularly inundated in winter and often flooded in summer. Matters were not fully rectified until after 1791 when, on the basis of Smeaton's and others proposals, the Ouse was straightened at several points, new drainage dykes dug and a western breakwater constructed to arrest longshore drift (Fig. 1.4), (Brandon 1971c, Farrant 1976a & b). (Smeaton is perhaps better known in connection with the building of the 'new' harbour at Rye and as the architect of the Eddystone lighthouse.)

The later history of the Rye Bay area shows a consistent pattern and it seems clear that after the 13th century no significant new supplies of shingle were reaching this area by longshore drift (either from the east or the west) although reworking of existing deposits undoubtedly occurred (Eddison 1998).

An early map of the decayed harbour at Rye by Philip Symondson, dated to 1594 (E.S.R.O. RYE 132/4-6), is one

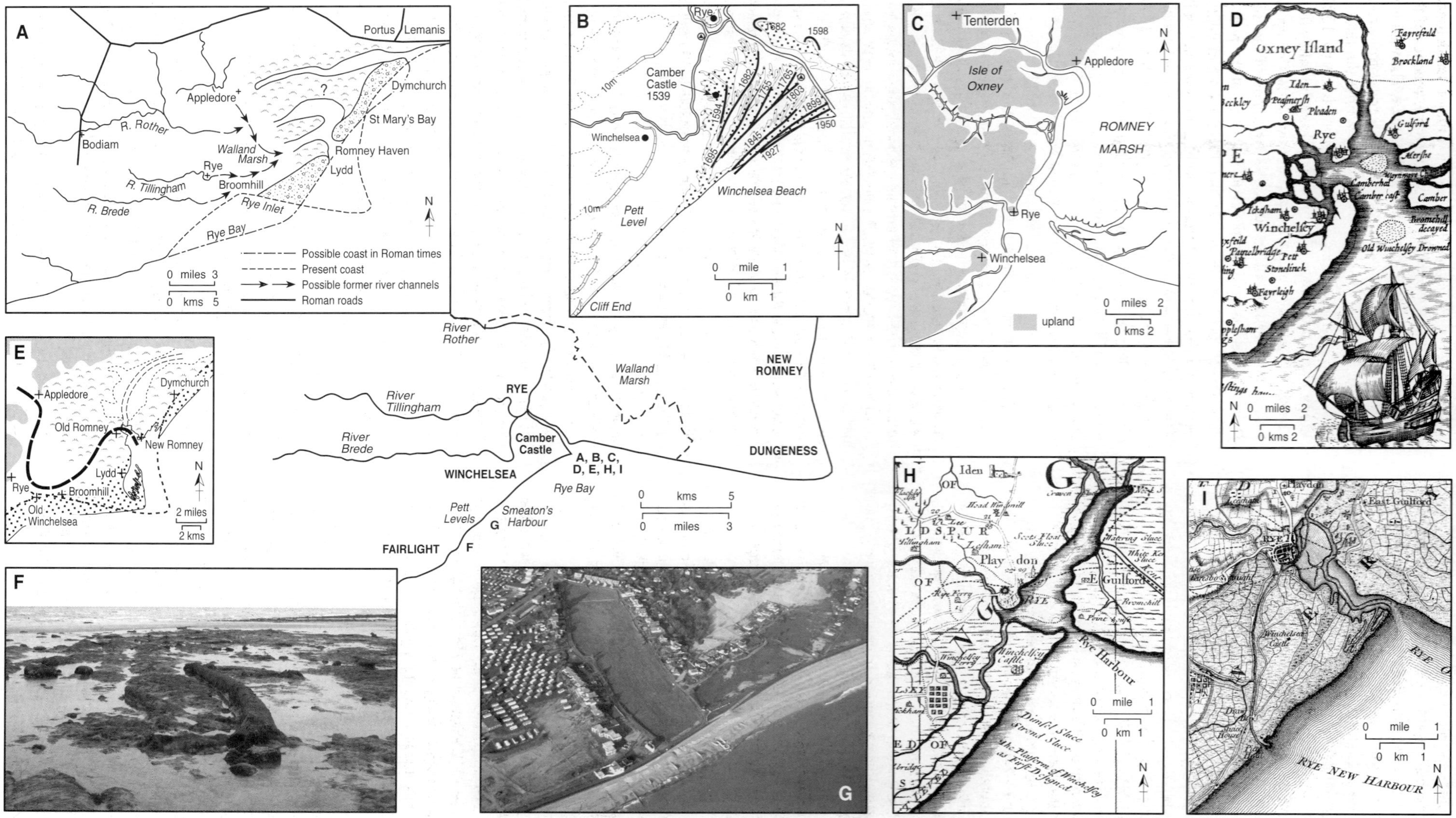

Figure 1.5. *Examples of coastal change in Sussex.*
(a) Conjectural reconstruction of the Rye Bay area during Roman times. (b) Coastal evolution of the Rye Bay area (after Robinson & Williams 1983). (c) An interpretation of Symondson's map of Rye Harbour in 1594. (d) Rye Harbour in 1695, taken from a map of Sussex produced by Robert Morden. (e) Conjectural reconstruction of the Rye Bay area during the early Medieval period, prior to the destruction of Old Winchelsea. (f) Submerged forest off Pett Level. (g) Air photograph of Smeaton's Harbour. (h) Rye Harbour in 1724, taken from a map of Sussex produced by Richard Budgen. (i) Rye Harbour in 1795, taken from a map of Sussex produced by William Gardner and Thomas Gream.

of our earliest pieces of cartographic evidence. The map shows a substantial shingle bank in front of the Pett Levels, in the lee of the Fairlight Cliffs, swinging inland in a series of shingle ridges (Fig. 1.5). A number of reconstructions have been produced to show how Camber Castle, completed around 1540, originally commanded the Rother estuary and the approach to Rye (Lovegrove 1953). Already by 1626, such were the changes in the coastline that the guns of the castle were out of range of the harbour (Salzman 1937). Since that time further shingle deposits have moved the shoreline almost 2 kilometres to the south-east, although largely at the expense of the deposits fronting Pett Levels. In 1873 the beach here was 120 metres wide but by 1931, when the Old Ship Inn was undermined by the sea, it had shrunk to practically nothing (Eddison 1998).

A similar pattern of events is recorded at Shoreham (Fig. 1.3). At the time of Domesday, *Soresham*, with its church, later Old Shoreham, was probably the main harbour (Brookfield 1951-2). By around 1100, silting, perhaps caused by the growth of shingle already being redeposited at the river mouth, had made further use of the harbour impracticable and New Shoreham was established further downstream, perhaps in the lea of the shingle spit. It has been suggested that the southern half of the town was destroyed by the sea before 1410, when Shoreham was reported largely destroyed. The failure of a protective shingle spit would provide an adequate explanation for this destruction in just the same way as has been suggested for the destruction of Old Winchelsea. By the 16th century, the mouth of the river had moved even farther eastward and the port of Shoreham had fallen into comparative obscurity. Much of the remaining trade was concentrated along the waterfronts and creeks to the east, with the River Adur eventually entering the sea near Aldrington, 6 kilometres to the east. In 1760 works were put in hand to create a new entrance at Kingston by cutting through the shingle bank, and to seal the former entrance. By 1815 the river mouth had migrated eastward again, making access to the port difficult. In 1818 the entrance at Kingston was re-cut, and provided with groins and breakwaters as added protection, and in 1850 lock gates built to convert the former channel to the east into a harbour basin (Farrant 1976a & b).

The port at Hastings was always vulnerable to the power of the sea. In 1596, and again in 1597, two unsuccessful attempts were made to build a pier sufficiently robust to withstand the winter weather. The Hundred and Assembly Book of Hastings (Hastings Corporation Records C/A(a)1) records the event vividly:

> *'March 1595 the peere of Hastings was begonne to be re-edified be certain westerne men ...... was built a huge work ...... all of huge rocks but without any timber; yet to mans judgement unremoveable it grew so huge a pile. But notwithstanding, the first wynter flaw overthrew it in a monent and dispersed the huge rocks like thick planks. ...... the next year the like piece of woorke was begon ...... the foundation of this new woorke within the tymber woorke of the old pier and so to continue with tymber braces and barres, crosse dogges and such like up to the top. ...... by all hollautyde 1597 well nere finished, that is to say xxxty foote high and C foot long at least, bewtyfull to behold, huge, invincible and unremoveable in the judgement of all beholders ...... on all saintes daie* [1st November] *appeared the mighty force of god ...... overthrew this huge woorke in lesse then an hower, to the great terrour and abashment of all beholders.'* (Brent 1980)

Further along the coast, at Rye and Winchelsea, there were other problems. Although a number of attempts were made to keep these ports open, by the 17th centuries Winchelsea was virtually cut off and Rye only accessible via the increasingly restricted River Rother (Brent 1980, Hipkin 1995, Collard 1997). In 1698, the Lords of the Admiralty commissioned a report on the Harbour at Rye, which stated '*We take this Harbour to be almost entirely lost, and at best in no condition to be preserved for any purpose of the Navy*' (Sloane MSS 3233 - British Museum).

In response, an ambitious plan was devised to construct a New Harbour on the coast, at what today is Winchelsea Beach (Fig. 1.5), (Farrant 1976a & b, Collard 1997, Eddison 1998). It was served with a system of dams and sluices to maintain water levels and scour out the harbour mouth and keep the entrance open. By 1743 the project was well underway but for various reasons, both political and financial, remained uncompleted. In 1763 Smeaton was commissioned to make recommendations. Although his proposals for an improved harbour were never fully acted upon, the harbour was eventually opened some 25 years later, in June 1787. It had to be abandoned, however, in less than a year, since the movement of shingle had already begun to block the entrance. By 1807 the harbour entrance had been diverted a kilometre to the east, by the formation of a long thin shingle bank.

The Rye Bay area is not the only one where extensive deposits of shingle are recorded in historic times. Early maps also show a substantial shingle accumulation at the Crumbles, just to the east of Eastbourne (Fig. 1.4). The stratigraphic record of the Crumbles shingle has been examined in detail and a relatively recent origin has been proposed, with substantial quantities of gravel being deposited between 800 and 300 BP. The supply of shingle has now dried up and, as a consequence, the coastline has retreated dramatically here, and indeed continues to do so at the present day (Jennings & Smyth 1990).

If we are to seek an origin for the shingle at the Crumbles, and other deposits further east, then we must look at the far western coast of Sussex. We know that the shingle at the Crumbles could not have originated from the erosion of the cliffs, or the shoreline ramp, in the immediate vicinity of Beachy Head. Not only is the erosion here a recent phenomenon, perhaps itself equating with the depletion of the Crumbles shingle, but the cliffs are incapable of yielding substantial quantities of flint nodules, even when eroding at present day rates.

The history of erosion along the west Sussex coast is more difficult to reconstruct, since much less work has been done in this area. There are, however, a number of lines of evidence that can be pursued, if we are to be able to understand what happened here. Initially, as sea-level rose, material originating from the floor of the English Channel would have been swept shoreward and deposited as sand and shingle beaches along the coast, whence it moved eastwards as a result of longshore drift (Schwartz 1972, Stanley & Swift 1976, Roy *et al.* 1994). In addition, gravel deposits would have been available along the west Sussex coastline, both from the eroding cliff and the shoreward movement of the shoreface ramp. This may have been an important factor in the provision of a plentiful supply of shingle, particularly if the sea was eroding substantial earlier quaternary deposits of flint rich coombe-rock gravels. These mechanisms could well account for the volume of shingle necessary to form both the Crumbles Shingle and other extensive gravel deposits along the coast as far as Rye Bay and beyond. As sea-level has been relatively stable, since about 5000 BP, it is unlikely that substantial new material will have been introduced into the system from the floor of the Channel, except in extreme weather conditions.

There are many records of lands lost along the west Sussex coast and of the exceptional rate at which the shore has retreated in historic times (Robinson & Williams 1983, Gifford Associated Consultants 1997). As a consequence, there have been wild estimates as to where the medieval coastline might have lain, based on extrapolating present rates of erosion back in time, without realising just how recent much of this erosion probably is. We do, however, know of a number of medieval villages that have been lost to the sea, such as Charlton, Ilsham and Cudlowe (Brandon 1974).

A consideration of the famous 'Armada' map of the Sussex coastline, made in 1587 by Sir Thomas Palmer and Walter Covert (Lower 1870), shows a coastline fringed by sandy commons and salt-marsh, possible relics of a back-barrier environment such as might be expected behind a coastal barrier or shingle spit (Fig. 1.3). It would not then be unreasonable to suggest that some of these lost villages were either built on land protected by a shingle foreshore or on the shingle accumulations themselves (Wallace 1996).

The history of more recent coastal development illustrates a continuing belief that human intervention and the application of modern engineering techniques can keep the sea at bay, even though the lessons of the past demonstrate otherwise. Often these schemes have been designed to address one localised problem, without due regard for their potential 'knock-on' effects elsewhere. Some 45% of the present Sussex coast has now been provided with a major sea wall against the onslaught of the sea, either attempting to arrest coastal erosion, or to protect low lying agricultural, residential or industrial areas from flooding. In addition, numerous breakwaters have been erected to capture those sediments that are in the process of being transported by longshore drift in an attempt to halt, or even reverse, beach depletion. Where this fails, artificial beach feeding commonly takes place.

Most of these measures are now realised to be only short-term expediencies, not only because the natural supply of shingle has all but run out, but also because most of these schemes only address erosional problems close inshore and ignore the extent to which erosion continues on the shoreface ramp. Only recently has the whole concept of Coastal Zone Management been addressed and the concept of 'managed retreat' even been admitted as a possible management option (Gifford Associated Consultants 1997).

A look to the future

An understanding of the nature of coastal change, through time, is vital in a coastal county such as Sussex, if we are to be able to understand and interpret the County's archaeology. Too often the magnitude of these changes is either misunderstood, underestimated or exaggerated, and this in turn has led to erroneous assumptions regarding settlement, land use, communications, trade and the exploitation of the coastal environment itself. There are enormous differences between the smooth coastline of the present day, the deeply indented inlets of the Neolithic, the fen covered peat filled valleys of the Bronze Age, the inundated coastline of the Iron Age and Roman periods, and the reclaimed coast of the early medieval period. Although most of these aspects have been considered in this paper, there is much that needs further investigation.

Without understanding coastal change we cannot assess the completeness of the archaeological data, that is after all the basis of our attempts to reconstruct, and hence understand, our past. For any particular period, for example, we need not only to be able to estimate the number of sites that might have been lost to coastal erosion and say something of the likely nature of these sites, but also to be able to assess the extent to which today's coastal archaeological sites were 'coastal' within their contemporary environment.

If we understand coastal change then we may also be able to suggest where buried land-surfaces, and the archaeological sites associated with them, might survive, even though they have not yet been detected. Such sites might be well preserved, and hence capable of yielding evidence of a type not readily available elsewhere (as at Shinewater). They might also be relatively common, and hence, have made a much more important contribution to everyday life than hitherto recognised. Too rarely do we question the extent to which our archaeological knowledge, and hence the deductions that arise from it, truly reflect the archaeology that once existed, or indeed might still exist and await discovery.

An understanding of both past and contemporary coastal change, and the processes that affect archaeological sites, is vital to all those involved with the curation of our archaeological heritage. Without such knowledge it is impossible to be able to plan adequately for the future. By initiating surveys to identify archaeological sites under threat, either as a result of coastal erosion or 'managed retreat' or the construction of 'hard' defences, sites can be preserved, either *in situ* or by record, which might otherwise disappear unnoticed.

Whilst archaeologists have only too often failed to recognise the scale or extent of the changes that have affected our coast and its immediate hinterland, similar criticisms can be laid at the feet of those concerned with today's coastal zone management. A study of past environmental changes not only provides a background against which present coastal zone management can be set but also provides a basis for predicting how the Sussex coast might potentially develop in the future, perhaps in ways that are at variance with purely theoretical modelling.

This is an exciting time for all those interested in coastal change. There is much new research underway which will inevitably modify at least some of the arguments presented in this paper. However, significant progress will only be made if we encourage an interdisciplinary approach, such as has happened in the Romney Marsh area. Only by combining the work of archaeologists, ecologists, geographers, geologists, geomorphologists, historians etc. will we eventually come to unravel the evolution of the Sussex coastline and understand something of the impact that those changes had on the generations of men and women whose lives were affected by them.

References

Akeroyd, A. V. 1972. Archaeological and historical evidence for subsidence in southern Britain, *Phil. Trans. Royal Soc. Lond. A. 272, 151-69.*

Aldsworth, F. and Freke, D. 1976. *Historic Towns in Sussex: An Archaeological Survey.* London: Sussex Archaeological Field Unit.

Aldsworth, F. G. 1987. Prehistoric and Roman Selsey, *SAC* **125**, 41-50.

Austin, R. M. 1991. Modelling Holocene Tides on the North-West European Continental Shelf, *Terra Nova* **3**, 276-88.

Baines, J. M. 1986. Historic Hastings. Second edition. St. Leonards-on-Sea: Cinque Port Press.

Baker, A. R. H. 1966. Some evidence of a reduction in the acreage of cultivated lands in Sussex during the early 14th century, *SAC* **104**, 1-5.

Ballard, A. 1910. The Sussex Coast line, *SAC* **53**, 5-25.

Barton, K. J. 1963. Worthing Museum Notes for 1961, *SAC* **101**, 23-25.

Bates, M. 1998. Geoarchaeological Assessment, *in* D. Dunkin, *An Archaeological Assessment (Stage 1) of the Proposed Newhaven Harbour Link Road and Associated Developments, Newhaven, East Sussex*, Archaeology South-East Project 776, 26-35. Unpublished.

Bates, M. R., Parfitt, S. A. and Roberts, M. B. 1998. Later Middle and Upper Pleistocene Marine Sediments of the West Sussex Coastal Plain: a Brief Review, *in* Murton *et al.* (eds) 1998, 151-165.

Bedwin, O. 1982 The Development of Prehistoric Settlement on the West Sussex Coastal Plain, *SAC* **121**, 31-44.

Bell, M. and Walker, M. J. C. 1992. *Late Quaternary Environmental Change: Physical and Human Perspectives.* London: Longman.

Bowen, D. Q., Rose, J., McCabe, A. M. and Sutherland, D. G. 1986. Correlation of Quaternary Glaciations in England, Ireland, Scotland and Wales, *Quat. Sci. Rev.* **5**, 299-340.

Brandon, P. F. 1971a. Late-medieval weather in Sussex and its agricultural significance, *Trans. Inst. Brit. Geog.* **54**, 1-17.

Brandon, P. F. 1971b. Agriculture and the effects of floods and weather at Barnehorne, Sussex, during the late Middle Ages, *SAC* **109**, 69-93.

Brandon, P. F. 1971c. The origin of Newhaven and the drainage of the Lewes and Laughton Levels, *SAC* **109**, 94-106.

Brandon, P. F. 1974. *The Sussex Landscape.* London: Hodder and Stoughton.

Brandon, P. F. and Short, B. 1990. The Medieval Coastline, *A Regional History of England: The South-East from AD 1000,* 74-81. London: Longmans.

Brent, C. E. 1980. *The Maritime Economy of Eastern Sussex 1550-1700,* East Sussex Record Office: Local History Res. Unit Rep. **11**.

Brookfield, H. C. 1949. A Critical Period in the History of Shoreham Harbour, *SAC* **88**, 42-50.

Brookfield, H. C. 1951-2. The Estuary of the Adur, *SAC* **90**, 153-63.

Burrin, P. J. 1982. The coastal deposits of the southern Weald, *Quat. Newslett.* (November), 16-24.

Burrin, P. J. 1988. The Holocene floodplain and alluvial deposits of the Rother valley and their bearing on the evolution of Romney Marsh, *in* Eddison and Green (eds) 1988, 30-52.

Burrin, P. J. and Jones, D. K. C. 1991. Environmental Processes and Fluvial Responses in a Small Temperate Zone Catchment: A Case Study of the Sussex Ouse Valley, Southeast England, in L. Starkel, K.J. Gregory and J.B. Thornes (eds), *Temperate Palaeohydrology,* 217-52. Chichester: John Wiley and Sons Ltd.

Burrin, P. J. and Scaife, R. G. 1984. Aspects of Holocene Valley Sedimentation and Floodplain Development in Southern England, *Proc. Geol. Assoc.* **95**, 81-96.

Castleden, R. 1967. *Classic Landforms of the Sussex Coast.* The Geographical Association.

Clark, J. G. D. 1932. *The Mesolithic Age in Britain.* Cambridge: Univ. Press.

Collard, J. 1997. *A Maritime History of Rye.* Third edition. Rye: John Collard.

Cunliffe, B. W. 1988. Romney Marsh in the Roman Period, *in* Eddison and Green (eds) 1988, 83-7.

Devoy, R. J. N. 1979. Flandrian Sea-Level Changes and Vegetation History of the Lower Thames Estuary, *Phil. Trans. Roy. Soc. London, B,* **285**, 355-407.

Devoy, R. J. N. 1982. Analysis of the geological evidence for Holocene sea-level movements in southern England, *Proc. Geol. Assoc.* **93** (1), 65-90.

Dix, J., Long, A. and Cooke, R. 1998. The Evolution of Rye Bay and Dungeness Foreland: The Offshore Seismic Record, in Eddison *et al.*(eds), 1998, 1-12.

Drewett, P., Rudling, D. and Gardiner, M. 1988. *A Regional History of England: The South-East to AD 1000.* London: Longmans.

Dulley. A. J. F. 1966. The Level and Port of Pevensey in the Middle Ages, *SAC* **104**, 26-45.

Eddison, J. (ed). 1995. *Romney Marsh: The Debatable Ground,* OUCA Monogr. **41**.

Eddison, J. 1998. Catastrophic Changes: the Evolution of the Barrier Beaches of Rye Bay, in Eddison *et al.* 1998, 65-88.

Eddison, J., Carr, A. P. and Jolliffe, I. P. 1983. Endangered Coastlines of Geomorphological Importance, *Geogr. J.* **149**, 39-75.

Eddison, J. Gardiner, M. and Long A. (eds). 1998. *Romney Marsh: Environmental Change and Human Occupation in a Coastal Lowland.* OUCA Monogr. **46**.

Eddison, J. and Green, C. (eds). 1989. *Romney Marsh: Evolution, Occupation, Reclamation* OUCA Monogr. **24**.

Evans, H. M. 1932. The Maglemose Harpoon, *Proc. Prehist. Soc. E. Anglia* **7**, 131-2.

Farrant, J. H. 1976a. The seaborne trade of Sussex 1720-1845, *SAC* **114**, 97-120.

Farrant, J. H. 1976b. *The Harbours of Sussex 1700-1914.* Brighton: J. H. Farrant.

Fulford, M., Champion, T. and Long, A. (eds). 1997. *England's Coastal Heritage.* EHAR **15**.

Gallois, R. W. 1965. *British Regional Geology: The Wealden District.* Fourth edition. London: H.M.S.O.

Gardiner, M. 1995. Medieval Farming and Flooding in the Brede Valley, *in* Eddison (ed), 1995, 127-137.

Geographical Editorial Committee, University of Sussex (ed). 1983. *Sussex: Environment, Landscape and Society.* Alan Sutton.

Gifford Associated Consultants. 1997. *The South Downs Coastal Group, Selsey Bill to Beachy Head: Shoreline Management Plan, June 1997.* Bognor Regis: South Downs Coastal Group.

Godwin, H. 1943. Coastal Peat Beds of the British Isles and the North Sea, *J. of Ecol.* **31**, 199-247.

Godwin, H. and M. E. 1933. British Maglemosian Harpoon Sites, *Antiquity* **7**, 36-48.

Greatorex, G. 1995. *An Archaeological Evaluation at Shinewater Park, Eastbourne, East Sussex.* Archaeology South-East Project 409 for Eastbourne Borough Council and East Sussex County Council. Unpublished.

Greatorex, G. 1998. *The Shinewater Track: An Excavation of a Late Bronze Age Waterlogged Structure on the Willingdon Levels, near Eastbourne, East Sussex.* Archaeology South-East Project 408 for East Sussex County Council. Unpublished.

Green, C. 1988. Palaeogeography of marine inlets in the Romney Marsh area, *in* Eddison and Green (eds), 1988, 167-74.

Green, R. D. 1968. *The Soils of Romney Marsh.* Soil Survey of Great Britain, Bulletin **4**.

Greensmith, J. T. and Gutmanis, J. C. 1990. Aspects of the Late Holocene Depositional History of the Dungeness Area, Kent, *Proc. Geol. Assoc.* **101** (3), 225-37.

Hallam, H. E. 1965. *Settlement and Society: a Study of the Early Agrarian History of South Lincolnshire.* Cambridge: Univ. Press.

Hamblin, R. J. O., Crosby, A., Balson, P. S., Jones, S. M., Chadwick, R. A., Penn, I. E. and Arthur, M. J. 1992. *The Geology of the English Channel,* British Geological Survey, United Kingdom Offshore Regional Report. London: H.M.S.O.

Heron-Allen, E. 1911. *Selsey Bill: Historic and Pre-Historic.* London: Duckworth.

Hipkin, S. 1995. The Impact of Marshland Drainage on Rye Harbour, 1550-1650, *in* Eddison (ed) 1995, 138-147.

Hodgson, J. M. 1967. *Soils of the West Sussex Coastal Plain.* Soil Survey of Great Britain, Bulletin **3**.

Holden, E. W. 1967. Possible medieval salt pans at Pett Level, *SNQ* **16**, 302-4.

Holden, E. W. and Hudson, T. P. 1981. Salt-making in the Adur Valley, Sussex, *SAC* **109**, 117-48.

Hutchinson, J. N. and Millar, D. L. 1998. *in* Murton *et al.* (eds) 1998, 135-68.

Jennings, S. and Smyth, C. 1982a. A preliminary Interpretation of Coastal Deposits from East Sussex, *Quat. Newslett.* (June), 12-19.

Jennings, S. and Smyth, C. 1982b. A Reply to "The coastal Deposits of the Southern Weald", *Quat. Newslett.* (Nov), 24-32.

Jennings, S. and Smyth, C. 1987. Coastal Sedimentation in East Sussex during the Holocene, *Progr. in Oceanography* **18**, 205-41.

Jennings, S. and Smyth, C. 1990. Holocene Evolution of the Gravel Coastline of East Sussex, *Proc. Geol. Assoc.* **101**, 213-24.

Jones, D. K.. C. 1971. The Vale of Brooks, *in* R. B. G. Williams (ed) *Guide to Sussex Excursions,* Institute of British Geographers Special Publication. Sussex: Univ. Press, 43-6.

Jones, R. L. and Keen, D. H. 1993. *Pleistocene Environments in the British Isles.* London: Chapman and Hall.

Kellaway, G. A., Redding, J. H., Shephard-Thorn, E. R. and Destombes, J. P. 1975. The Quaternary History of the English Channel, *Phil. Trans. Roy. Soc. Lond. A.* **279**, 189-218.

King, S. H. 1962 Sussex, *in* H. C. Darby and E. J. Campbell (eds), *The Domesday geography of south-east England.* Cambridge: University Press, 407-82.

Kirkaldy, J. F. and Bull, A. J. 1940. The geomorphology of the rivers of the southern Weald, *Proc. Geol. Assoc.* **51**, 115-50.

Lake, R. D. and Shephard-Thorn, E. R. 1987. *Geology of the country around Hastings and Dungeness.* London: H.M.S.O.

Lake, R. D., Wood., C. J. and Mortimore, R. N. 1987. *Geology of the country around Lewes,* Mem. Geol. Surv. G. B., Sheet 319. London: H.M.S.O.

Lemmon, C. H. and Hill, J. D. 1966. The Romano-British Site at Bodiam, *SAC* **104**, 86-102.

Long, A. J. 1992. Coastal Responses to Changes in Sea-Level in the East Kent Fens and South-East England, UK over the last 7500 years, *Proc. Geol. Assoc.* **103**, 187-99.

Long, A. J. and Hughes, P. 1995. Evolution of the Dungeness Foreland during the last 4000 years, *Marine Geol.* **124**, 253-71.

Long, A. J. and Innes, J. B. 1993. Holocene Sea-Level Changes and Coastal Sedimentation in Romney Marsh, Southeast England, UK, *Proc. Geol. Assoc.* **104**, 223-37.

Long, A. J. and Innes, J. B. 1995. The Back-Barrier and Barrier Developmental History of Romney Marsh, Walland Marsh and Dungeness, Kent, UK, *J. Quat. Sci.* **10**, 267-83.

Long, A. J. and Roberts, D. H. 1997. Sea-Level Change, *in* M. Fulford, T. Champion, and A. Long (eds), *England's Coastal Heritage,* EHAR **15**, 25-49.

Long, A. J. and Shennan, I. 1993. Holocene Relative Sea-Level and Crustal Movements in Southeast and Northeast England, U.K, *Quat. Proc.* **3**, 15-9.

Long, A., Waller, M., Hughes, P. and Long, A. 1998. The Holocene Depositional History of Romney Marsh Proper, *in* Eddison *et al.* (eds) 1998, 65-88.

Louwe Kooijmans, L. P. 1971. Mesolithic Bone and Antler Implements from the North Sea and from the Netherlands, *Berichten van Rijksdienst voor het Oudheidkundig Bodemonderzoek,* 20-21, 27-73. Amersfoort: Rijksdienst voor het Oudheidkundig Bodemonderzoek.

Lovegrove, H. 1966. Possible medieval salt pans at Pett Level, Sussex, *SNQ* **16**, 253-5.

Lovegrove, H. 1953. Old Shore Lines near Camber Castle, *The Geogr. J.* (June), 200-7.

Lower, M .A. 1870. *A Survey of the Coast of Sussex, made in 1587 - with a view to its defence against Foreign Invasion and especially against the Spanish Armada.* Lewes: W. E. Baxter.

Luard, H. R. 1880. *Matthaei Parisiensis Chronica Majora V.* London: H.M.S.O.

Luard, H. R. (ed). 1872-83. 'Matthew Paris', *Chronica Majora,* Rolls Series **57**, i-vii. London: Longmans.

Martin, D., Martin, B. and Whittick C. 1995. *An Archaeological Interpretative Survey of The Old Town Wall, Hastings, East Sussex,* Aarchaeology South-East Project 243 for Hastings Borough Council. Unpublished.

Morris, F. G. 1931. Newhaven and Seaford; a study in the diversion of a river mouth, *Geography* **16**, 28-33.
Murton, J. B., Whiteman, C. A., Bates, M. R., Bridgland, D. R., Long, A. J., Roberts, M. B. and Waller, M. P. (eds). 1998. *The Quaternary of Kent and Sussex: a Field Guide*. Quaternary Research Association.
Osborne-White, H. J. 1924. *The Geology of the country around Brighton and Worthing,* Mem. Geol. Surv. G.B. London: H.M.S.O.
Parfitt, S. A. 1998. Pleistocene Vertebrate Faunas of the West Sussex Coastal Plain: Their Stratigraphic and Palaeoenvironmental Significance, *in* Murton *et al.* (eds) 1998, 121-35.
Pelham, R. A. 1930. Some further aspects of Sussex Trade during the 14th century, *SAC* **71**, 171-204.
Pitts, M. W. 1979. A Gazetteer of Roman Sites and Finds on the West Sussex Coastal Plain, *SAC* **117**, 63-83.
Pitts, M. W. 1980. A Gazetteer of Mesolithic Finds on the West Sussex Coastal Plain, *SAC* **118**, 153-62.
Plater, A. J. 1992. The Late Holocene Evolution of Denge Marsh, Southeast England: A Stratigraphic, Sedimentological and Micropalaeontological Approach, *The Holocene* **2**, 63-70.
Plater, A. J. and Long, A. J. 1995. The Morphology and Evolution of Denge Beach and Denge Marsh, *in* Eddison (ed) 1995, 8-21.
Reid, C. 1903. *The Geology of the country around Chichester,* Mem. Geol. Surv. G.B., explanation of one-inch geological sheet 317 (New Series). London: H.M.S.O.
Roberts, M. B. 1998. Middle Pleistocene Sediments and Archaeology at ARC Eartham Quarry, Boxgrove, West Sussex, *in* Murton *et al.* (eds) 1998, 165-8.
Roberts, M. B. and Parfitt, S. A. 1999. *A Middle Palaeolithic hominid site at Eartham Quarry, Boxgrove, West Sussex*, London, EHAR **17**.
Robinson, D. A. and Williams, R. B. G. 1983. The Sussex Coast Past and Present, in University of Sussex Geography Editorial Committee, *Sussex: Environment, Landscape and Society,* 50-66. Gloucester: Alan Sutton.
Robinson, D. A. 1999. The Coast and Coastal Changes, *in* K. Leslie and B. Short (eds), *An Historical Atlas of Sussex*, 8-9. Chichester: Phillimore.
Roy, P. S., Cowell, P. J., Ferland, M. A. and Thom, B. G. 1994. Wave-Dominated Coasts, *in* R. W. G. Carter and C. D. Woodroffe (eds) *Coastal Evolution: Late Quaternary Shoreline Morphodynamics*, 121-86. Cambridge: University Press.
Salzman, L. F. 1910. The Inning of Pevensey Levels, *SAC* **53**, 32-60.
Salzman, L. F. 1937. *Victoria History of the County of Sussex,* 9. Oxford: Univ. Press.
Scaife, R. G. and Burrin, P. J. 1983. Floodplain Development in and the Vegetational History of the Sussex High Weald and Some Archaeological Implications, *SAC* **121**, 1-10.
Scaife, R. G. and Burrin, P. J. 1985. The Environmental Impact of Prehistoric Man as Recorded in the Upper Cuckmere Valley at Stream Farm, Chiddingly, *SAC* **123**, 27-34.
Scaife, R. G. and Burrin, P. J. 1987 'Further Evidence for the Environmental Impact of Prehistoric Cultures in Sussex from Alluvial Fill Deposits in the Eastern Rother Valley, *SAC* **125**, 1-9.
Schwartz, M. L. 1972. *Spits and Bars*. Stroudburg, Pennsylvania: Dowden, Hutchinson and Ross.
Shephard-Thorn, E. R. 1975. The Quaternary of the Weald - a Review, *Proc. Geol. Assoc.* **86**, 537-47.
Smith, A. J. 1989. The English Channel - Geographical Design or Catastrophic Accident?, *Proc. Geol. Assoc.* **100**, 325-37.
Smyth, C. and Jennings, S. 1988. Mid- to Late-Holocene Forest composition and the Effects of Clearances in the Combe Haven Valley, East Sussex, *SAC* **126**, 1-20.
Stanley, D. J. and Smith, D. J. P. (eds). 1976..*Maritime Sediment Transport and Environment.* London: Wiley-Interscience.
Steers, J. A. 1964. *The Coastline of England and Wales*. Cambridge: University Press.
Thompson, F. H. (ed). 1980. *Archaeology and coastal change, Soc. of Antiq. Occ. Paper* **1**.
Thorley, A. 1971. Vegetational History in the Vale of the Brooks, *in* R. B. G. Williams (ed) *Guide to Sussex Excursions,* Institute of British Geographers Special Publication, 47-50. Sussex: Univ. Press.
Tooley, M. J. 1990. Sea Level and Coastline Changes during the last 5000 years, *in* S. McGrail (ed), *Maritime Celts, Frisians and Saxons,* CBA Res. Rep. **71**, 1-16.
Tooley, M. J. and Switsur, V. R. 1988. Water level changes and sedimentation during the Flandrian Age in the Romney Marsh area, *in* Eddison and Green (eds) 1988, 53-71.
Wallace, H. 1996. *Sea Level and Shoreline between Portsmouth and Pagham for the past 2500 years,* Parts 1 and 2 (Part 1 revised 1999). Chichester: Privately produced.
Waller, M. 1993. Flandrian Vegetational History of Southeastern England. Pollen Data from Pannel Bridge, East Sussex, *New Phytol.* **124**, 345-69.
Waller, M. P. 1994. Flandrian Vegetational History of South-Eastern England. Stratigraphy of the Brede Valley and Pollen Data from Brede Bridge, *New Phytol.* **126**, 369-392.
Waller, M. P. 1998. The Vegetational history of the South Downs: Mount Caburn, *in* Murton *et al.* (eds), 1998, 115-120.
Waller, M., Burrin, P. J. and Marlow, A. 1988. Flandrian Sedimentation and Palaeoenvironments in Pett Level, the Brede and Lower Rother Valleys and Walland Marsh, *in* J. Eddison and C. Green (eds), *Romney, Marsh: Evolution, Occupation, Reclamation* (eds), OUCA Monogr. **24**, 3-30.
Wingfield, R. T. R. and Evans, C. D. R. 1998. The Significance of the Shoreface Ramp for Coastal Development: Holderness, Eastern England, U.K, *Littoral '98: Proceedings of the Fourth International Conference of the European Coastal Association for Science and Technology.* Barcelona: Suport Serveis, 622-678.
Woodcock, A. G. 1981. *The Lower and Middle Palaeolithic Periods in Sussex*. BAR Brit. Ser. **94**.
Woodcock, A. G. 1996. A Late Bronze Age site at Shinewater Park, near Eastbourne, *in* X. Delestre and A. G. Woodcock (eds), *Proximus* **2**, 11-5. Association pour la Promotion de l'Archéologie en Haute-Normandie.
Woodcock, A. G. 1999. Earliest Inhabitants, in K. Leslie and B. Short (eds), *An Historical Atlas of Sussex,* 10-11. Chichester: Phillimore.
Young, B. and Lake, R. D. 1988. *Geology of the country around Brighton and Worthing*. London: H.M.S.O.

THE EARLIEST OCCUPATION OF SUSSEX: RECENT RESEARCH AND FUTURE OBJECTIVES

Matthew Pope

Abstract

The past 20 years has seen Sussex transformed from a backwater of the British Palaeolithic to an area of regional and global significance. This is the result of recent University College London led research programmes aimed at the investigation of the geology and archaeology of the Sussex Coastal Plain. Analysis of raised beach deposits, terrestrial land-surfaces and periglacial gravels has indicated that they may preserve a record of climatic and environmental change over the past 500,000 years. Excavation of the oldest of these deposits has revealed large areas of intact Pleistocene land-surface preserving the traces of hominid tool production, butchery activity and a wide range of palaeo-environmental data. Amongst the faunal finds were those of extinct mammals including a hominid species. Outside of the Coastal Plain, only seven new artefacts have been recovered during this time. Future research must aim to build on these recent advances to improve our understanding of Pleistocene deposits in Sussex river valleys and archaeological material from the Downlands.

Introduction

Descriptions of Palaeolithic archaeology in Sussex have appeared throughout the last century (Grinsell 1929, Woodcock 1978, 1981, 1986) and it is not intended in this paper to attempt yet another summary of Palaeolithic finds in the county. The BAR report produced by Andrew Woodcock (1981) provides an excellent gazetteer of Lower and Middle Palaeolithic sites in Sussex and I would direct anyone requiring a comprehensive survey of the Sussex data for this period to refer to it. More recently, John Wymer (1994) has built on the earlier work of Derek Roe (1968) and Andrew Woodcock to produce an updated listing of Palaeolithic sites in the form of the Southern Rivers Project. This document lists all known find-spots from the river valleys and raised beaches of Sussex alongside summaries of contextual information, as well as geological maps showing the extent of Pleistocene deposits which may contain archaeological remains. In this paper I hope to update these previous accounts by describing, in the brief space available, the results of recent work, some new surface finds and some future directions for research.

Through a summary of geological and archaeological evidence, each of the raised beaches is discussed below. Much of this evidence has been gained from recent research co-ordinated, since 1982, as a series of multidisciplinary projects under the direction of Mark Roberts, Simon Parfitt and Martin Bates. Whilst the excavations at Boxgrove have received much academic and media attention during this time, the analysis of younger deposits at lower elevations on the Coastal Plain is less well-known. These other beaches have yet to produce archaeological remains comparable to those recovered from the Boxgrove excavations. They are, however, no less remarkable in that, taken together, they appear to preserve a unique record of geological and palaeo-environmental processes over the past 500,000 years.

A glossary of some of the technical terms used is located at the end of this paper.

Goodwood-Slindon Raised Beach

The Goodwood-Slindon Raised Beach, which is found at 40m (100ft) above sealevel, is the highest of a series of Pleistocene marine deposits resting on a succession of sea-cut steps which run east-west across the Coastal Plain of Sussex (Fig. 2.1). This raised beach has been effectively traced over 20km between Arundel and Funtington and it is probable that the beach continues beyond this point into Eastern Hampshire, where it is evident at exposures near Portsdown. The Goodwood-Slindon Raised Beach may also be correlated with similar deposits on the Isle of Wight. No evidence exists for the remains of this beach east of the Arun valley, where the fossil cliff-line appears to have been truncated by later marine erosion (Fig. 2.2). Extensive mineral extraction in the vicinity of Chichester during the past century has made numerous exposures of the Goodwood-Slindon raised beach available for investigation. The existence of marine deposits high above the present day sea level was first noted in the 19th century

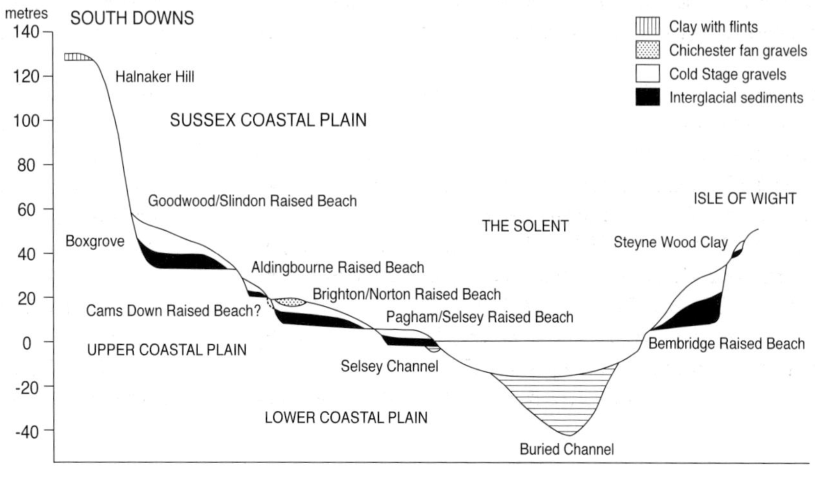

Figure 2.1. *Cross section through the Coastal Plain of Sussex, Hampshire and the Isle of Wight. Five raised beaches can be seen cut into the solid geology at different altitudes above the modern sea level. (Reproduced with the permission of Simon Parfitt).*

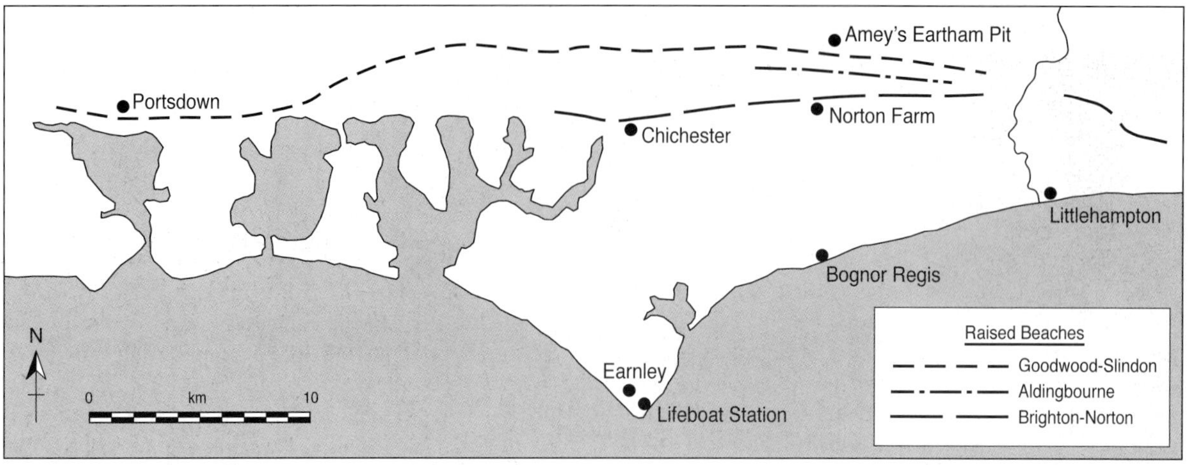

Figure 2.2. *Map showing the position of the Goodwood-Slindon, Aldingbourne and Brighton-Norton raised beaches. Some of the sites mentioned in the text are also shown. (Boxgrove Project).*

(Reid 1892: Prestwich 1892). When stone tools associated with these deposits were subsequently discovered during the first quarter of the 20th century, interest in the 'One Hundred Foot' raised beach increased (Curwen 1925: Fowler 1929; Grinsell 1929). Archaeological interest continued in the quarries around Eartham and Slindon between the wars, largely as a result of extensive collecting by the Revd Joseph Fowler, Bernard Calkin and Dr Eliot Curwen. During this time 14 pits were noted along the line of the '100ft' raised beach. Curwen recovered Acheulean artefacts from the raised beach deposits at Slindon Bottom, all were in a rolled condition suggesting that the archaeology had been disturbed by wave action. Later investigation of the same pit by Calkin produced several unrolled artefacts that, for the first time, indicated the possibility of recovering *in-situ* material from the deposits. Subsequently, Calkin was to discover an undisturbed scatter of handaxes, cores and waste flakes on the surface of the beach. Flakes within this scatter could be refitted, indicating the degree of preservation at the site. Tantalizingly, two collections of burnt flints were also noted and interpreted as hearths (Calkin 1934), unfortunately, no subsequent evidence for fire has been recovered.

The archaeological potential indicated by these early collectors was not fully realized until modern archaeological investigations began in the 1970s. Andrew Woodcock undertook further excavation at Slindon Bottom, but also began to examine exposures made by new gravel extraction at Amey's Eartham Pit, Boxgrove. Here Woodcock, following geological investigations by Shephard-Thorn (1978), documented the presence of fine-grained sediments at the junction between marine and periglacial deposits. At this

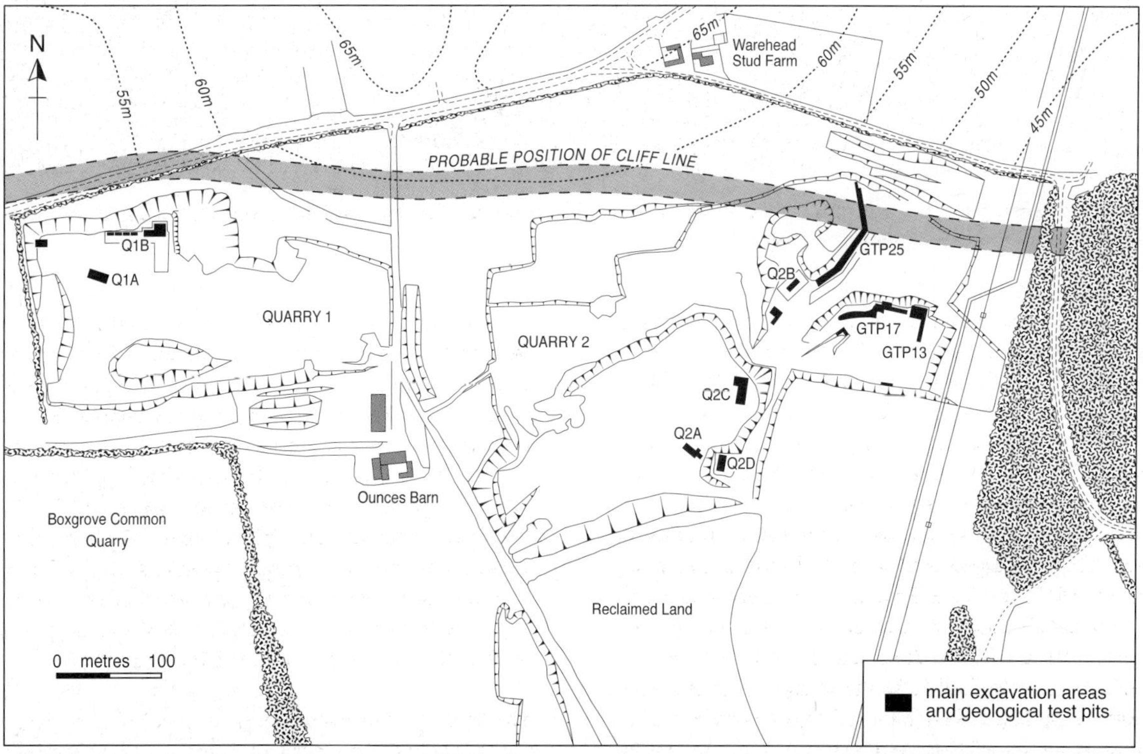

Figure 2.3. *Map showing the main excavation areas and geological test pits at Amey's Eartham Pit* (after *Roberts 1999).*

Figure 2.4. *Photograph of the geological sequence through the deposits of the Goodwood-Slindon Raised Beach and overlying periglacial deposits. (Photograph: Boxgrove Project).*

horizon Woodcock recovered well-preserved mammalian fauna and noted that these remains appeared to be *in-situ* (Woodcock 1981). The more recent history of Palaeolithic research in Sussex has been dominated by the continued investigation of these exceptionally well-preserved deposits at Amey's Eartham Pit. During the last fifteen years a UCL team, led by Mark Roberts and Simon Parfitt, have implemented a comprehensive programme of archaeological research. The investigation of over 90 individual localities within the ARC quarries at Eartham have been undertaken during this time, including area excavations, test-pit sampling surveys and the cutting of deep stratigraphic sections (Fig. 2.3). Between 1993 and 1995, the discovery of human remains at Boxgrove by Roger Pederson led to renewed interest in the site and established Boxgrove as a site of international as well as regional importance. The significance of the ensuing excavation seasons of 1995-1996 was not only due to the provision of early evidence for the hominid occupation of Britain, but to the fact that these finds were associated with well preserved evidence for hominid behaviour and ecology. The results of ongoing research at the site has been reported in a series of reports during the past 15 years (Roberts 1986, 1992, Bergman *et al.* 1990: Roberts *et al.* 1995, 1997). A detailed account of the first two phases of the project is the subject of an English Heritage monograph (Roberts and Parfitt 1999). A further volume on the more recent excavations will appear within the next few years. Only a brief account of the work at this extraordinary site can be provided here.

The deposits of the Goodwood-Slindon Raised Beach record the changing environmental conditions during the last stage of the Cromerian interglacial and the early Anglian glacial.

The geological sequence is shown in Figure 2.4. The marine deposits at the base of the sequence indicate climatic conditions almost identical to those in Britain today. During this stage sea levels were as high as those of today and marine action was leading to the direct erosion of the chalk Downland, forming cliffs identical in origin to those of the modern Sussex coast. At the base of the cliff a shingle beach formed on a wave-cut platform of chalk bedrock; this beach was replaced to the south by sands forming the seabed. Fish bones and molluscs preserved within these deposits indicate that ocean temperatures were similar to those of today and contained species currently present in the English Channel. It is thought that the Straits of Dover had not been breached at this time and thus Britain would have been joined to the Continent as a northerly peninsula of Europe even during inter-glacials. The cliff-line itself would have extended as an embayment around to the north coast of France. Into this bay two large rivers, the Seine and the Solent, would have flowed and many other smaller rivers would have drained the land bridge through gorges cut into the chalk.

Hominids appear to have been active on the beach between the tides. Apart from the possible hearths noted by Calkin, we have abundant evidence for stone tool manufacture at this level. In the absence of well-preserved mammalian fauna from this level it is uncertain whether the manufacture of stone tools was related to the butchery of animals and we have no evidence that the hominids at Boxgrove were exploiting shellfish or other marine resources. Yet, one resource that was undoubtedly exerting a strong pull on hominids was the presence of flint seams running through the chalk cliff as exposures of accessible flint in the parent rock would have been an important and geographically limited resource. Flint in this condition has not been rolled by water, and is less susceptible to the effects of frost; thus it retains good knapping qualities. Whilst variable, most of the seams of flint exposed by the Goodwood-Slindon raised beach are excellent for stone tool production and would have exerted a continued attraction for hominid groups throughout the time-span of the depositional sequence.

Laminated silts indicating a change in the depositional regime to low-energy, quiet water conditions, overlie the marine deposits. One theory is that an offshore shingle bank was exposed during the fall in sea level leading to the formation of a near-shore lagoon. Micro-fauna found within these silts indicate low-energy, brackish-water conditions which would support the idea of a lagoon or enclosed mud-flats. Throughout these deposits are small land-surface horizons which indicate that a mosaic landscape of pools with patches of grassland was beginning to form as sea levels fell. Archaeological remains are found throughout these horizons although they vary in nature from isolated finds disturbed by water flow, to patches of *in-situ* material such as the intact knapping scatter shown in Figure 2.5. One such site, currently under analysis, appears to indicate a short episode of horse butchery. Some seven knapping scatters lie in close proximity to each other alongside the dispersed bones of a single horse individual, (Figure 2.6). The horse itself appears to have suffered an impact injury to its shoulder blade consistent with an impact from a sharp object such as a wooden spear. Spears are known from later sites in Europe (Clacton, Schoningen

Figure 2.5. *Intact knapping scatter from the silts of the Goodwood-Slindon Raised Beach. This scatter appears to preserve the position of the knapper. (Photograph: Boxgrove Project).*

Figure 2.6. *Excavation of an intact knapping scatter from the horse butchery site. (Photograph: Boxgrove Project).*

and Lehringen) and archaeologists are becoming increasingly prepared to accept that hunting had its origins within the Middle Pleistocene. This evidence contradicts theories that interpret Middle Pleistocene hominids as scavengers actively competing with other carnivores for carcasses. At the horse butchery site, however, carnivore gnaw marks always overlie butchery marks made by stone tools. This pattern holds for every observed case in the Boxgrove landscape so that, while the case for direct hunting at Boxgrove is not proven, it would appear hominids at the site were consistently getting primary access to carcasses over and above other predators.

With the continued fall of sea level, the silts filling the lagoon began to dry out and were colonized by grassland vegetation. During this time a rich fauna of large mammals existed within the landscape, including familiar European fauna (red deer, roe deer, horse, boar, bear and wolf) alongside extinct relatives of animals currently restricted to Africa and Southern Asia (elephant, rhinoceros, lion and hyaena). No woodland formed during this time, probably as a result of overgrazing. At this level, artefacts were discarded throughout the landscape, although generally at low densities. These dispersed scatters of artefactual material are composed mainly of handaxe trimming flakes and appear to relate to the modification and resharpening of tools carried by hominids in the landscape. The handaxe shown in Figure 2.7 has three such flakes refitted to its tip. Several areas with dense concentrations of artefacts and animal bone have been located and these have been interpreted as areas where handaxes were manufactured and used in the butchery of large mammals. These assemblages

Figure 2.7. *Handaxe from the excavations at Boxgrove. Three flakes removed during the preparation of the handaxe tip have been refitted to the tool. (Photograph: Boxgrove Project).*

sometimes contain large quantities of debitage from the early stages of handaxe manufacture, suggesting that large blocks of raw material were sometimes carried from the cliff to the butchery sites. Conversely, some scatters just contain debitage from the later stages of handaxe manufacture, suggesting the knapping of previously prepared blanks or the modification/ resharpening of finished tools.

Flake tools and hammer stones also form part of these assemblages and sometimes such patches seem to have become the focus for handaxe discard. Where these tools are found alongside butchered animal bones from many individuals, it would appear that hominids were favouring particular locations for the butchery of large mammals. The site of Quarry 1B (Fig. 2.3), which was excavated between 1995-96, appears to have been one such focus for hominid activity. The geology of the site is complex and appears to represent a body of fresh water that formed either at the same time as the soil horizon or within the earlier lagoonal phase. Interpretation of this site is at an early stage, but it appears that over a period of time this site exerted a particular focus for hominid activity within the landscape, possibly because the fresh water source attracted large concentrations of herbivores. At the site a large assemblage of flint tools was recovered including 450 handaxes, numerous flakes tools, percussors and debitage. Amongst the percussors were two manufactured from the antlers of the giant deer *megaloceros dawkinsi* (now extinct) and red deer. Each percussor exhibited damage from its use in the manufacture of flake tools and even exhibited traces of flint debitage embedded in the surface of the hammer. It had long been suspected that this type of soft hammer was used in the manufacture of Middle Pleistocene tools owing to the degree of finesse in the production of some tools from this period. Such fine flaking is only obtainable through the use of a flexible material such as antler. These two antler soft hammers appear to be the first unequivocal record of such tools anywhere in the world prior to the Upper Palaeolithic. They are also important in that they required extensive modification of the large antler to produce a usable tool. First the antler beam had to be smashed close to the point where it had joined the animal's skull and then the antler base had to be shaped to produce a suitable surface for knapping. The degree of investment in these tools shows how much this material was valued by Middle Pleistocene hominids when compared to the relative ease with which unmodified bone was also often employed in this task.

The site produced a rich assemblage of fauna dominated by rhinoceros, horse and red deer. Much of the animal bone had been butchered showing that this was an important site for food acquisition. The presence of lion, wolf and hyaena remains indicated that hominids were not the only predator/ scavengers to be drawn to the location. It also reminds us that our ancestors were only one of numerous carnivores competing for carcasses in Middle Pleistocene Britain. Amongst the remaining fauna are numerous extinct species that allow some indication of the age of the Goodwood-Slindon raised beach. The animals, which include an extinct deer (*Megaloceros dawkinsi*), a bear (*Ursus denigeri*) and a rhino (*Stephanorhinus hundsheimensis*), have never been found at sites securely dated to after Oxygen Isotope Stage (OIS hereafter) 12 (Anglian glacial). The site is also unlikely to be older than OIS 13 (Cromerian IV) as water voles from the sites appear to have unrooted molars, a characteristic which appeared around 600,000 years ago.

The Quarry 1B site is also unique in that it is the only excavated area from the Goodwood-Slindon raised beach yet to produce hominid remains. Two teeth (both lower incisors) and a tibia (shin-bone) have been recovered from the locality. Whilst the two teeth appear to have come from the same individual, the tibia was excavated from a higher stratigraphic level and may belong to another hominid. The tibia is from a tall, robust individual standing 1.8m high and possibly weighing 90 kilos (Roberts *et al.* 1994). The remains are not sufficient to be firmly assigned to any species, but it is reasonable to expect that the Boxgrove hominds were similar to *Homo heidelbergensis*, a Middle Pleistocene relative of *Homo erectus*. This species is known from numerous fragmentary remains recovered across Europe and Africa. It is named after the famous Mauer jaw that was recovered from a gravel quarry near Heidelberg. The Boxgrove incisors are similar to those from the Mauer jaw, although slightly smaller in size. The teeth had been heavily decayed around the roots by gum disease and preserved the traces of numerous cut-marks across the front surface of the enamel. Similar striations are well documented in Middle and Late Pleistocene hominids, and form a common feature of *Neanderthal* teeth. Such damage may have originated from an unknown but repetitive activity that involved clamping material between the teeth whilst simultaneously cutting it.

The Boxgrove excavations have shown that, through small-scale exposures of paleo-landsurface along a one kilometre stretch of the fossil cliff-line, we can recover a combination of *in-situ* archaeology and palaeontological remains unparalleled for this period outside of Africa. However, a strip of this land-surface some 10-20km long may well be equally preserved between Portsmouth and Arundel. If we assume the deposits remain similar in character and that the archaeological remains are similarly consistent, then we must accept that the Sussex Coastal Plain may well preserve numerous hominids and hundreds of thousands of large mammal remains and stone tools. Research is currently focusing on the results of the latest excavations and it is hoped that, when complete, the data will provide a series of archaeologically derived models of hominid behaviour and ecology for Middle Pleistocene Europe.

Aldingbourne Raised Beach

Deposits of a marine and intertidal nature are also found between Fontwell and Westhampnett along the line of the A27 road. Known as the Aldingbourne formation, these high-energy beach sediments and associated cliff-line run parallel to the Goodwood-Slindon raised beach and about one kilometre to the south. The deposits rest on a wave-cut platform at between 24 and 27.5m OD, some 10m lower than the Goodwood-Slindon raised beach. Overlying the marine/ intertidal deposits are angular gravels deposited under periglacial conditions. The contact between the cold stage deposits and the interglacial sediments is erosive, this allows the possibility that there was once a longer sequence of warm stage sediments which may have included terrestrial surfaces.

The interpretation of the Aldingbourne raised beach, its age and geo-chronological significance, has changed dramatically during the past 150 years. Early investigators of the Sussex Coastal Plain, including Prestwich (1892) and Reid (1892), suggested that all deposits related to a single episode of high sea level. Calkin, however, was subsequently to draw attention to another series of marine deposits at 24-27m O.D. and this fuelled the growing suspicions of Fowler and other investigators that more than one stage of high sea level was responsible (Fowler 1932; Calkin 1934; Woodcock 1981). Woodcock suggested that the Aldingbourne formation related to fluctuations in sea level at the end of the Hoxnian and that the beach deposits formed an offshore bar that might be contemporary with the regressional lagoonal silts of the Slindon formation. Such an interpretation, which was also postulated by Shephard-Thorn *et al.* (1982), owes its origin to the theory prevalent at the time that the earliest human occupation of Britain occurred during the Hoxnian. In this scheme there simply were not enough glacial/interglacial cycles to account for more than three separate beach lines. Recent investigation of these deposits could find no stratigraphic link between the Aldingbourne deposits and those of the Goodwood-Slindon raised beach (Bates *et al.* 1997). That the deposits occur at a lower elevation and contain clasts with exotic lithologies led the authors to suggest that the two deposits represent separate stages. The Aldingbourne sediments cannot be directly dated but recent research suggests that it may have been formed during Oxygen Isotope Stage 11 (Roberts *et al.* 1997; Bates *et al.* 1997).

The lack of unequivocally *in-situ* remains from the Aldingbourne Raised Beach probably reflects the nature of the deposits in the formation. Handaxes and cores have been recovered from both the raised beach deposits and the overlying angular gravels. Find-sites include Aldingbourne, Easthampnett, Pear Tree Knap and Aldingbourne Park Gravel Pit. With the exception of one flake from the A27/A2024 junction that appeared fresh, the archaeological material from the Aldingbourne deposits tends to be rolled and patinated, contrasting with the excellent condition of the remains from the Goodwood-Slindon deposits. Given the condition and context of the Aldingbourne material, it is impossible to make behavioural interpretations of hominid behaviour. Some artefacts may have been derived from older deposits, having been incorporated into the solifluxtion and marine deposits during subsequent erosive episodes.

Brighton-Norton Raised Beach

The oldest deposits on the Sussex Coastal Plain to be traced east of the Arun valley are those associated with the raised beach deposits and cliff-line at Black Rock, Brighton. This series of marine sediments has been traced by geological survey through Arundel, Chichester and possibly as far as Hayling Island. Across this area they are associated with the 15 metre contour line, which traces the approximate line of the fossil cliff. As a result of recent investigations by Bates *et al.* (1997) these deposits are best understood from exposures at Norton Farm and Westhampnett East (Portfield Pit). At these sites, marine gravels replaced by sand to the south are overlain, in turn, by sediments of a terrestrial nature. The depositional sequence ends with solifluxtion gravels. Channel deposits associated with the terrestrial horizon were located at Portfield Pit and were found to contain organic material including plant and insect remains (Bates *et al* 1997). The deposits of the Brighton-Norton raised beach have been assigned to OIS 7 on the basis of amino acid ratios and the characteristics of the mammalian fauna (Bates *et al.* 1997).

Commercial gravel extraction at Portfield Pit exposed one of the terrestrial land-surfaces to erosion during 1995. After the particularly dry summer that year it was possible to field walk a large area of land-surface. Remains of mammoth and horse were abundant but, conspicuously, no stone tools were recovered, despite the excellent chances for their discovery. Whilst a human presence cannot be ruled out on this basis, it is useful to compare the apparent absence with the abundant quantities of stone tools recovered from comparable horizons of the Goodwood-Slindon raised beach.

Possible evidence for a human presence in OIS 7 has emerged from freshwater deposits on the Selsey peninsula. Artefacts previously thought to date to the last interglacial were found at the Selsey lifeboat station (West and Sparks 1960). The assemblage consisted of a few flakes, some with possible Levallois characteristics, which were examined by Nick Ashton of the British Museum. The artifacts were recovered from channel deposits found near the Selsey lifeboat station and were originally thought to be associated with the marine gravels of the Pagham formation (West and Sparks 1960) and OIS 5e. Recent dates provided by amino acid ratios, molluscan and faunal assemblages all indicate an OIS 7 age for this channel (Bowen 1992; Sutcliffe 1995) and would make them broadly contemporary with the deposits of the Brighton-Norton Raised Beach. This reassessment of the Selsey artefacts is consistent with the proposed hiatus of human occupation in Britain during OIS 5e.

Pagham Raised Beach and Summary

Marine deposits have been traced through Brighton, Portslade Worthing, Bognor and Pagham around 3m O.D. (Young and Lake 1988; Bates *et al.* 1997), indicating the most recent of the Sussex raised beach deposits. This sedimentary sequence, designated the Pagham Formation, appears to relate to high sea levels associated with the interglacial of OIS 5e. This date has also been indicated by amino acid ratios (Bowen and Sykes 1994) and thermoluminescence dates from the overlying brickearth deposits (Parks and Rendell 1992). A series of channel deposits underlie the Pagham Formation, including the Earnley Channel (which has not been firmly dated) and the channel deposits from the lifeboat station at Selsey, now dated to OIS 7. The absence of *in-situ* remains from the Pagham raised beach appears to be consistent with the proposed hiatus in the human occupation of Britain during this time.

The Pagham Raised Beach deposits represent the most recent of the four separate high sea level events recognized in the geology of the Coastal Plain. A further raised beach has been recorded outside Sussex at Cams Down and Cams Bridge in Hampshire (ApSimon *et al.* 1977; Palmer and Cooke 1923) and it has been suggested that these deposits can be traced into the west of Sussex (Shephard-Thorn *et al.* 1982; Bates *et al.* 1997). Current interpretations of the Goodwood-Slindon

Raised Beach seem to indicate an OIS 13 date for the base of the sequence. If this interpretation is correct, then it is possible that sedimentary formations from each of the subsequent interglacials indicated by the Oxygen Isotope curve are preserved in Sussex. The result has been to create a series of wave-cut steps that form the coastal plain at the foot of the South Downs. The deposits from each phase of the interglacial/glacial cycle have been raised owing to constant isostatic uplift during the past 500,000 years, preserving them from future marine erosion. This geological sequence in turn preserves a wealth of archaeological, environmental and palaeontological remains in a virtually undisturbed condition. This provides us with a record of ecological and climatic change during the past half million years, as well as an insight into the earliest human presence in the county. It distinguishes the Sussex Coastal Plain as an area of worldwide archaeological importance.

Recent finds and Future research

Aside from the large volume of material recovered in the course of excavation at Amey's Eartham Pit, only seven other artefacts appear to have been found in Sussex during the past 20 years. While lamentable, the paucity of new material is hardly surprising. Historically, the majority of such finds in Sussex have been due to the energies of individual flint collectors, such as Garraway-Rice (1905; 1911; 1920), Grinsell (1929) or Calkin (1934), either by direct hunting or through close contact with the labourers who worked the gravel pits in the county. Today there are few exposures of Pleistocene sediments open to the amateur collector and the mechanization of mineral extraction during this century has effectively ended the discovery of artefacts by quarry workers. These factors, however, do not account for the lack of new finds from the chalk Downlands, despite numerous fieldwalking exercises in the county. With the exception of the Barcombe and Culvers Mead artefacts, none of the finds listed below were recovered by professional archaeologists, instead they were either found by collectors or by observant members of the public. For an updated distribution map of Palaeolithic finds in Sussex *see* Figure 2.8.

1. Gay Street (TQ 0826 1860)

This find was of a single sub-rectangular handaxe, with tranchet removal across the tip, and described as a cleaver. It was found by Mrs Archer-Wills of Gay Street, near Pulborough, whilst weeding a mound of earth derived from the excavation of a nearby pond and was kindly brought to my attention by Mrs Caroline Wells. Whilst not technically in primary context, we can attribute its geological origins to the head deposits overlying the Hythe Beds of the Lower Greensand. The artefact was quite fresh and unpatinated indicating that it was buried quickly after discard.

2. Storrington (TQ 0790 1270)

Mr Layzell of West Grinstead, recovered this handaxe from the scarp slope of the Downs, north of Kithurst Hill. The artefact is cordate and manufactured on flint gravel. This find was recently published by the author (Pope 2000).

3. Storrington (TQ 0705 1256)

Mr Layzell also recovered this handaxe. As with the above find, it too came from the scarp slope of the Downs to the west of the Kithurst Ranges. The handaxe is an ovate manufactured on yellow-brown gravel. This find was also recently published by the author (Pope 2000).

4. Culvers Mead (TQ 4246 1472)

A bifacially worked core (Fig. 2.9) was recovered from a ploughed field at Culvers Mead, Barcombe Mills, through field walking by the Mid Sussex Field Archaeological Team under the direction of Chris Butler. In addition, a number of flakes with a similar ochreous patination were also recovered. From the condition and colour of the artefacts it would appear that they derive from locally outcropping terrace deposits of

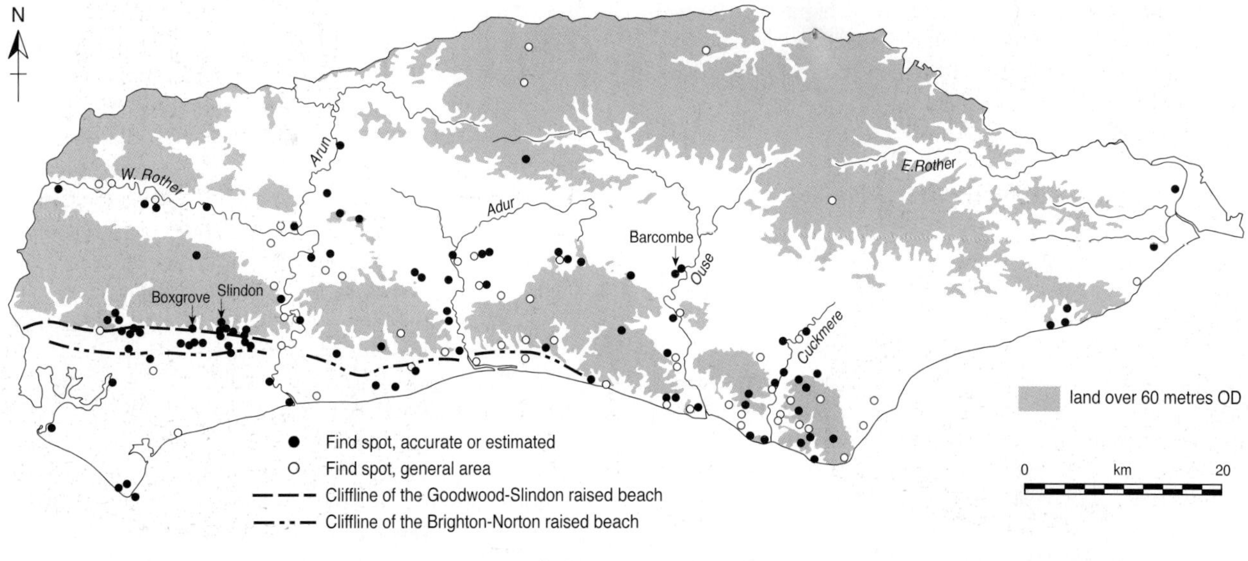

Figure 2.8. *Distribution map showing the position of Palaeolithic find spots in Sussex. (Reproduced with the kind permission of Andrew Woodcock).*

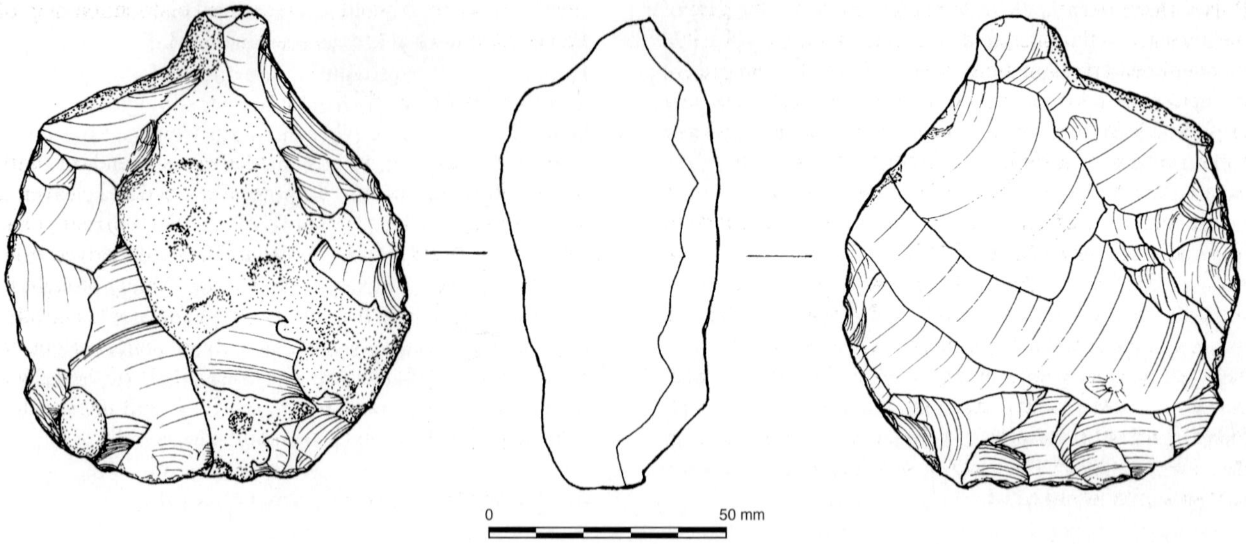

Figure 2.9. *Bifacially worked core from Culvers Mead near Barcombe. (Drawing: Claire Goodey).*

the River Ouse. As such they appear to be the first recorded genuine finds from these gravels, which notably form part of the series of deposits from which it was claimed the Piltdown finds were recovered. Further work now needs to be undertaken to establish whether these finds are being brought up from underlying Pleistocene sediments by the plough, or from 19th century quarrying at the site.

5. Barcombe Roman Villa (TQ4169 1413)

An incomplete handaxe (Fig. 2.10) was recovered during the course of excavations at Barcombe Roman Villa being carried out jointly between the University College London Field Archaeology Unit and the Mid Sussex Field Archaeological Team (Rudling and Butler 2001). The handaxe was found within sediment filling a small palaeo-channel beneath a roundhouse. The handaxe is 15.1 cm long, finely flaked and patinated to an ochreous hue similar to those recovered from Culvers Mead, which lies only one kilometre to the north. Apart from the fact that the object suffered end-shock, perhaps during manufacture, it is in remarkably fresh condition, exhibiting sediment polishing but little actual abrasion. Further work is planned to investigate the context of this find and to try to establish its relationship to nearby terrace deposits. I am grateful to the excavators for allowing me to view these Barcombe finds and to report on them here.

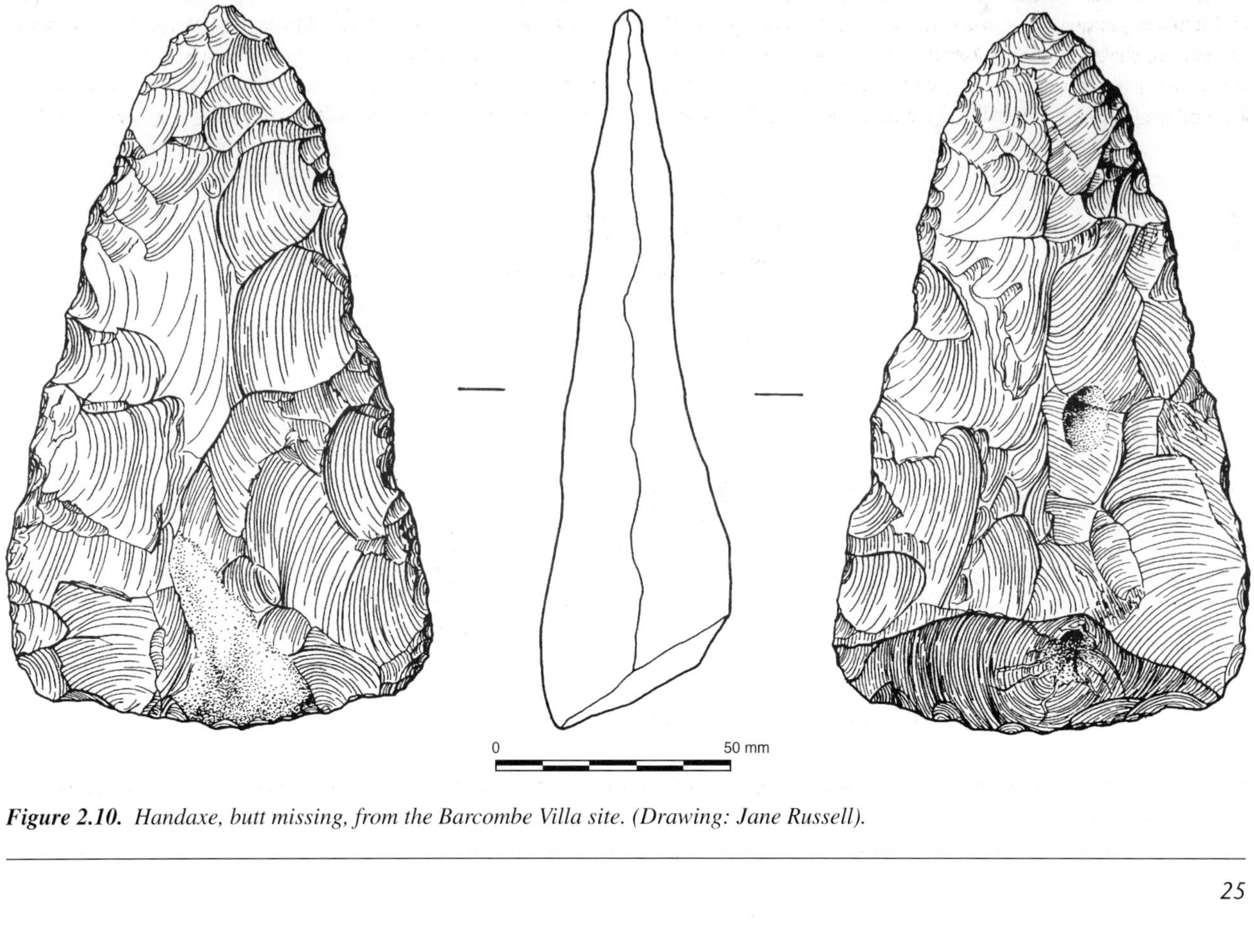

Figure 2.10. *Handaxe, butt missing, from the Barcombe Villa site. (Drawing: Jane Russell).*

6. Worthing (TQ 1120 2800)

A handaxe was recovered from a residence in Mulberry Lane, Goring-by-Sea. No further details are known about the context of this find. The artefact is a finely flaked, flat-butted and cordate biface manufactured on olive/beige flint with grey inclusions. One face retains some cortex and has a limited surface patina. The artefact appears to be unrolled and in a reasonably fresh condition.

7. Walberton (SU 958 065)

This handaxe was found by Mr Stockdale of Walberton in the bed of a stream which flows through his rear garden. Dr Paul Graves, as curator of Littlehampton Museum, reported the artefact in detail. The handaxe appears to derive from the Aldingbourne raised beach, the gravels of which make up part of the stream bed. Owing to its fresh condition, Dr Graves considers the artefact to have been *in-situ;* some weathering, perhaps due to water, is apparent. The biface retains cortex on its butt, is pointed in shape and it is described as a ficron. This find should not be confused with the handaxe recovered from the stream bed at 'The Willows' nearby earlier in the 20th century.

This brief account of recent Palaeolithic archaeology in Sussex would not be complete without some consideration of future research. Given the importance of the Sussex Coastal Plain it is reasonable to assume that it will continue to be the focus for archaeological and geological investigation well into the 21st century. With continued development and gravel extraction on the Coastal Plain, it is important that the unique geological heritage of the area is actively managed. During the next few decades we will inevitably see many hectares of Pleistocene sediments lost to quarry operations, yet implementing an adequate sampling programme over such extensive areas would be prohibitive in terms of the cost and labour required. The legislation currently in place was drafted with more conventional archaeological sites in mind and is largely inadequate when it comes to management of the Palaeolithic record, dispersed as it is at low densities through extensive areas of Pleistocene sediments (Wenban-Smith 1994). Without standard procedures in place, the management of the archaeological record of the Coastal Plain will provide a challenge that can only be met by co-operation between the planning authorities, English Heritage, developers and archaeological researchers. Recent attempts to address these issues have been highly successful in West Sussex. Through close liaison between researchers and the County planning authorities, threats to the Quaternary resource in the area have been flagged up well in advance of development and effective rescue/sampling strategies implemented. As a result of improved provision for Quaternary research in the county, a hitherto unprecedented number of site investigations are being undertaken each year within the county. In addition to the widening base of data provided by commercial archaeology, a new research programme, funded by English Heritage, is currently under way. The Raised Beach Mapping Project, run by Boxgrove Projects of University College London is a three-year mapping programme aimed at documenting the extent and nature of Pleistocene deposits on the Upper Coastal Plain. In the summer of 2001, this work commenced with a series of borehole and test pit investigations across the Coastal Plain. In due course, the project aims to increase both our understanding of the paleoenvironment of the Boxgrove Hominids and to provide a valuable tool for the future management and research of this unique geological resource. While the Coastal Plain will continue to dominate Palaeolithic research in Sussex, it is important that other possible avenues of investigation are not forgotten, even if they are not immediately addressed. The two most obvious areas for future research are the Palaeolithic records of the Sussex river valleys and the Downland plateaus they disect. Woodcock (1981) suggested the need for detailed investigation in these contexts almost twenty years ago and as yet no attempt has been made to systematically undertake this work. Yet now, given the increase in our understanding of the geology and archaeology of the Coastal Plain, the possibility exists for the results of this research to be applied to terrace deposits of the Sussex river valleys. In both the Arun and Adur valleys it should be possible to begin correlating river terraces with marine deposits preserved on the Coastal Plain. In addition, the new finds from the Ouse gravels (*see* above) indicate the possibility of rich sites within this valley and the need for geoarchaeological investigation. The development of a programme aimed at examining the potential for such work would be a worthwhile direction for Palaeolithic research in the county.

The Downs provide another possible area for future Palaeolithic research which, to date, has been somewhat neglected. Andrew Woodcock drew attention to the preservation of Palaeolithic material recovered from Downland sites such as Folkington and suggested that the Clay-with-flints deposits may contain relatively undisturbed material (Woodcock 1981; 1986). Recent excavations in Kent by Scott-Jackson have recovered apparently intact scatters of artefacts from Clay-with-flints deposits. The association of Palaeoliths with similar sediments in Sussex is therefore of potential interest and warrants some further research (Scott-Jackson 1996). Similarly, solution structures in chalk may well preserve remnants of Pleistocene landsurface and other fine-grained deposits worthy of investigation. While the detailed study of these contexts may be some time off, limited field walking and test pits surveys would provide two sensible and relatively undemanding approaches to potentially sensitive Downland areas.

Given the developments of recent research, it is easy to think that we have already seen the zenith of Palaeolithic archaeology in Sussex. Yet the results of this work have proved the existence within the county of many square kilometres of undisturbed Pleistocene sediments preserving archaeological and faunal remains. It is not unreasonable to claim that, in terms of extent and quality of archaeological preservation, the Upper Coastal Plain represents an internationally important area for the study of Middle Pleistocene hominid behaviour and palaeoecology. Perhaps the greatest challenge facing Lower Palaeolithic studies in Sussex is to fully recognise this fact and to tackle the management, research and interpretation of these deposits as part of a long-term curation strategy. In order to achieve this, a framework of management is required that approaches the Quaternary record in Sussex as tracts of preserved landscape and not as a series of isolated 'sites'. In the same way that it is possible to talk of African localities like Koobi Fora or

Olduvai as coherent archaeological entities, we need to approach the record of the Upper Coastal Plain as a preserved Middle Pleistocene palaeolandscape instead of as a series of individual sites. The archaeological record of this palaeolandscape is comparable in terms of preservation to that of Pompeii, but is amongst the oldest in Northern Europe and minutely records the daily lives of a species different to our own. It therefore provides both vast potential for future research and also for the vivid interpretation of Middle Pleistocene studies. Fully realising this potential, to a degree comparable with the management of other internationally important Palaeolithic localities, will require political will and imagination to achieve.

Acknowledgements

I am grateful to my colleagues at the Boxgrove Project, Mark Roberts, Simon Parfitt and Dimitri De Loecker for their assistance with this paper. I would also like to acknowledge the information and help provided by the following: Andrew Woodcock, John Mills, the late Con Ainsworth, Chris Butler, Caroline Wells, Sally White, Alex Holmes and Keith Watson. I would like to dedicate this paper to Con Ainsworth in recognition of his contribution to Sussex Pleistocene studies and for his continuing inspiration.

Glossary

Ficron: Handaxe with a thick butt and a slender point, often with concave edges.

Hominid: A member of the *hominidae* (human family). This includes all *Austalopithicine* and *Homo* species.

Oxygen Isotope Stage (OIS): The Pleistocene has been divided into stages based on the ratio of stable oxygen isotopes recovered from sediments at various depths in the ocean floor. OIS stages with odd numbers represent warm periods of global climate, whilst those with even numbers represent cold periods. For an introduction to how the Boxgrove sediments relate to the Boxgrove deposits refer to Pitts and Roberts 1998 (pages 125 and 138).

Palaeolithic: The Old Stone Age. Stone tools technology began in Africa in excess of 2.5 million years ago with the Oldowan Industry. The Palaeolithic ended around 10,000 years ago. The Palaeolithic is further subdivided into Lower, Middle and Upper periods.

Periglacial: Cold climatic conditions characterised by permafrost and tundra, found to the front of the main ice-sheet during glacial periods.

Pleistocene: Epoch that ran from 1.5 million to 10,000 years ago. Characterized by climatic fluctuations resulting in glacial and interglacial periods.

References

ApSimon, A.M., Gamble, C.S. and Shackley, M.L. 1977. Pleistocene raised beaches on Portsdown, Hampshire, *Proc. Hants Fld. Club and Archaeol. Soc.* **33**, 17-32.

Bates, M.R., Parfitt, S.A. and Roberts, M.B. 1997. The chronology, palaeoecology and archaeological significance of the marine Quaternary record of the West Sussex Coastal Plain, Southern England, UK, *Quaternary Science Reviews* **16**, 1227-1252.

Bates, M.R., Gibbard, P.L., Macphail, R.I., Owen, F.J., Parfitt, S.A., Preece, R.C., Roberts, M.B., Robinson, J.E.,Whittaker, J.E. and Wilkinson, K.N. In press. Late Middle Pleistocene deposits at Norton Farm on the West Sussex Coastal Plain, Southern England, *J. of Quaternary Science.*

Bergman, C.A., Roberts, M.B., Collcutt, S.N. and Barlow, P. 1990. Refitting and spatial analysis of artefacts from Quarry 2 at the Middle Pleistocene Acheulian site of Boxgrove, West Sussex, England, in E. Cziesla, S. Eickhoff, N. Arts and D. Winter (eds), *The Big Puzzle,* Bonn: Holos, 265-282.

Bowen, D.Q. 1992. Aminostratigraphy of non-marine Pleistocene mollusca in Southern Britain, *Sveriges Geologiska Undersökning* **81**, 65-67.

Bowen, D.Q. and Sykes, G.A. 1994. How old is "Boxgrove Man"?, *Nature* **371**, 751.

Calkin, J.B. 1934. Implements from the Higher Raised Beaches of Sussex, *Proc. Prehist. Soc. E. Anglia* **7**, 333-347.

Fowler, J. 1929. Palaeoliths Found at Slindon, *SAC* **70**, 197-200.

Fowler, J. 1932. The 'One Hundred Foot' Raised Beach between Arundel and Chichester, Sussex, *Quarterly J. Geol. Soc.* **88**, 84-99.

Garraway-Rice, R. 1905. Some Palaeolithic Implements from the terrace gravels of the River Arun and the Western Rother, *Proc. Soc. of Antiq.* **20**, 197-207.

Garraway-Rice, R. 1911. Report to the local Secretary for Sussex, the Palaeolithic Period, *Proc. Soc. of Antiq.* **23**, 371-373.

Garraway-Rice, R. 1920. Note on a Palaeoliths from West Chiltington, near Pulborough, Sussex, *Proc. Soc. of Antiq.* **32**, 79-82.

Grinsell, L.V. 1929. The Lower and Middle Palaeolithic Periods in Sussex, *SAC* **70**, 172-182.

Palmer, L.S. and Cooke, J.H. 1923. The Pleistocene Deposits of the Portsmouth District and their Relation to Man, *Proc. Geol. Assoc.* **34**, 253-282.

Parks, D.A. and Rendell, H.M. 1992. Thermoluminescence dating and geochemistry of loessic deposits in southeast England, *J. Quaternary Sci.* **7**, 99-107.

Pitts, M. and Roberts, M.B. 1998. *Fairweather Eden: Life in Britain half a million years ago as revealed by the excavations at Boxgrove,* London: Arrow Books.

Pope, M. 2000. Lower Palaeolithic surface finds from northern scarp slope of the Downs at Kithurst Hill, near Storrington, West Sussex, *SAC* **138**, 221-222.

Prestwich, J. 1892. The Raised Beaches and 'Head' or Rubble Drift of the South of England; their Relation to the Valley Drifts and to the Glacial Period; and on Late Post-Glacial Submergence, *Quarterly J. of the Geol. Soc.* **48**, 263-343.

Reid, C. 1892. The Pleistocene Deposits of the Sussex Coast and their Equivalent in other Districts, *Quarterly J. Geol. Soc.* **48**, 344-361.

Roberts, M.B. 1986. Excavation of a Lower Palaeolithic site at Amey's Eartham Pit, Boxgrove, West Sussex: A preliminary report, *Proc. Prehist. Soc.* **52**, 215-245.

Roberts, M.B. 1992. Boxgrove: The Lower Palaeolithic site in Amey's Eartham Pit (SU 924 085), in S. Woodward (ed), *The Archaeology of Chichester and District 1992,* Chichester: Chichester District Council, 21-24.

Roberts, M. 1999. Boxgrove, in K. Leslie and B. Short (eds), *An Historical Atlas of Sussex,* Chichester: Phillimore, 12-13.

Roberts, M.B., Stringer, C.B. and Parfitt, S.A. 1994. A hominid tibia from Middle Pleistocene sediments at Boxgrove, UK, *Nature* **369**, 311-313.

Roberts, M.B., Gamble, C.S. and Bridgland, D.R. 1995. The earliest occupation of Europe: The British Isles, in W. Roebroeks and T. van Kolfschoten (eds), *The Earliest Occupation of Europe,* Leiden: University of Leiden, 165-92.

Roberts, M.B. and Parfitt, S.A. 1999. *A Middle Pleistocene Hominid Site at Earthen Quarry, Boxgrove, West Sussex, UK.* London: English Heritage Archaeological Report **17**.

Roberts, M.B., Parfitt, S.A., Pope, M.I. and Wenban Smith, F.F. 1997. Boxgrove, West Sussex: Rescue excavations of a Lower Palaeolithic landsurface (Boxgrove Project B 1989-1991), *Proc. Prehist. Soc.* **63**, 303-358.

Roe, D.A. 1968. *A Gazeteer of British Lower and Middle Palaeolithic Sites*, CBA Res. Rep. **8**.

Roebroeks, W and Kolfschoten, T. van. 1995. A reappraisal of the evidence, in W. Roebroeks and T. van Kolfschoten (eds), *The Earliest Occupation of Europe,* Leiden: University of Leiden, 297-316.

Rudling, D. and Butler, C. 2001. Roundhouse to Villa, *Sussex Past and Present* **95**, 6-7.

Scott-Jackson, J. 1996. Lower Palaeolithic finds at Wood Hill, East Kent: A geological and geomorphological approach to an archaeological problem, *Lithics* **16**, 10-15.

Shephard-Thorn, E.R., Berry, F.G. and Wyatt, R.J. 1982. *Geological notes and local details for 1:10 000 sheets SU80NW, NE, SW and SE, SU90 NW, NE, SW and SE, TQ00NW, SW. West Sussex Coastal Plain between Chichester and Littlehampton.* Keyworth: Institute of Geological Sciences.

Sutcliffe, A.J. 1995. Insularity and Quaternary vertebrate faunas in Britain and Ireland, in R.C.Preece (ed), *Island Britain : A quaternary perspective,* Geological Society Special publication **96**, 111-126.

Wenban-Smith, F.F. 1994. Managing the Palaeolothic heritage: Looking backwards, looking forwards, in N. Ashton and A. David (eds.), *Stories in stone,* Lithic studies society occasional paper **4**, 104-114.

West, R.G. and Sparks, B.W. 1960. Coastal interglacial deposits of the English Channel, *Phil. Trans. Roy. Soc. London* B **243**, 95-133.

Woodcock, A.G. 1978. The Palaeolithic in Sussex, in P.L. Drewett (ed), *Archaeology in Sussex to A.D. 1500*, CBA Res.Rep. **29**, 8-14.

Woodcock, A.G. 1981. *The Lower and Middle Palaeolithic Periods in Sussex,* Oxford: BAR Brit. Ser. **94**.

Woodcock, A.G. 1986. The Lower and Middle Palaeolithic in Sussex: A Summary of Current Knowledge, Present Research and Future Objectives, in S.N. Collcutt (ed), *The Palaeolithic of Britain and its nearest neighbours: Recent trends,* Dept. of Archaeology and Prehistory, University of Sheffield, 31-35.

Wymer, J.J. 1994. The Sussex Raised Beaches and the Bristol Avon, *The Southern Rivers Palaeolithic Project: Report No. 3, 1993-1994.* Salisbury: Wessex Archaeology.

Young, B. and Lake, R.D. 1988. Geology of the country around Brighton and Worthing. Memoir of the BGS. Sheets 318/333 (England and Wales). Keyworth: British Geological Survey.

LATE GLACIAL AND POST-GLACIAL HUNTER-GATHERERS IN SUSSEX

Robin Holgate

Abstract

Fieldwork and research in Sussex has contributed significantly to late glacial and, in particular, post-glacial hunter-gatherer studies in Britain. In the late 19th and early 20th centuries Sussex, particularly the Weald, became one of the main counties where Mesolithic flints were collected. The study of this material by Grahame Clark in the 1930s and Roger Jacobi in the 1970s is discussed initially. The results of palaeoenvironmental work undertaken in recent years on alluvial, colluvial and peat deposits in the Sussex Weald are outlined, and an account is given of the archaeological investigation of the dozen or so Upper Palaeolithic and Mesolithic sites that has taken place since the mid-1970s. Finally, this information is used to present an overview of late glacial and post-glacial hunter-gatherers in Sussex, making reference to relevant fieldwork and research undertaken recently elsewhere in southern Britain.

Background research

Fieldwork and research in Sussex, particularly in the Weald, has contributed significantly to Upper Palaeolithic and Mesolithic studies in Britain. Thomas Honeywood's collection in the 1870s of microliths from St Leonard's Forest, near Horsham, published illustrations of which appeared in 1877, is among the earliest of its kind to be recorded in Britain (Clark 1934a, 52). Between the 1890s and the 1930s, Sussex then became one of the main counties where Mesolithic flints, then known as 'pygmy flints', were collected, mainly through the work of Garroway Rice, Calkin, Attree, Piffard and Toms. Toms, based at Brighton Museum and the first professional archaeologist working in Sussex, did much to generate interest in flint collecting; in a talk to the Brighton and Hove Natural History and Philosophical Society on May 16th 1907, he said that "compared with the other finds in England, Sussex has . . . proved very rich in this interesting group of diminutive flint tools" (Toms 1907, 6).

There is a small group of distinguished prehistorians whose fieldwork in Sussex or studies of Sussex material influenced their formative development as archaeologists: Pitt Rivers, Herbert Toms, Cecil Curwen, Grahame Clark, Stuart Piggott and Christopher Hawkes. Herbert Toms' contribution in supporting the work of collectors of Mesolithic flints has been touched upon, but the first person to begin making sense of this flintwork was Grahame Clark.

Clark (1932) undertook a systematic study of Mesolithic material not only in Sussex but also in Britain, producing a discussion of the main Mesolithic flint assemblages then known; most of this material derived from the surface of disturbed ground and was thus unstratified. He also published a note on his discovery of a later Mesolithic site at Seaford (Clark 1930) and an account of the flint assemblages collected in the Horsham area (Clark 1934a), which also included a detailed classification of microlithic forms. He observed that "there is a substantial uniformity as between the microlithic inventories of the different sites, and it seems legitimate to consider them as belonging to a homogeneous culture, the Horsham (culture)" (Clark 1934a, 62-3). His excavations on the edge of a sand pit at Selmeston located an oval-shaped feature in association with Mesolithic flints which, in line with contemporary thinking, he interpreted as a pit-dwelling (Clark 1934b, 136). In a later report on mesolithic material from Farnham and other sites on sand deposits in the Weald, he stated that:

"we have from Farnham, Selmeston, Hassocks, Horsham and the other sites a group of industries differing in detail but having in common features not found in combination elsewhere, industries moreover which occupy a well-defined geographical area and tend to occur on analogous geological formations. The conclusion is, surely, that these industries belong to a rather narrowly distributed, but self-standing, culture. In deciding on a label it seems to me that Horsham has a strong claim on grounds of its priority - the earliest published account goes back to 1877, while the detailed description, including the classification adopted here, antedates the excavations at Selmeston and Farnham, the only other claimants; it has further the advantage of being central to the area of distribution of the culture" (Clark 1939, 95-6). Sites belonging to this culture mostly centred on permanent springs and well-drained sandy soils which, with their lighter vegetation cover and good drainage qualities, offered considerable benefits for both hunting game and settlement purposes. This early work, whilst also considering the significant quantity of later Mesolithic flints collected by Calkin from the sandy soils at Peacehaven, very much focussed on Mesolithic flint assemblages recovered from the Weald.

After the Second World War, Palaeolithic and Mesolithic archaeology in Sussex received scant attention. Curwen and members of both the Worthing and the Brighton and Hove Archaeological Societies were actively involved in surveying and excavating prehistoric earthworks on the Downs. When Curwen's second edition of *The Archaeology of Sussex* was published in 1954, his discussion of the Palaeolithic and Mesolithic periods was largely a description of flint assemblages dating to these periods without further elaboration, undoubtedly due to the fact that both he and his parents were "Evangelicals of the strictest sort" who believed implicitly in Archbishop Ussher's view, based on a literal interpretation of the Bible, that the world was created in 4004 BC (Phillips 1987, 31). He summed up the Mesolithic period as follows. "We find man still a savage, without agriculture, without domesticated animals, and without pottery, living by hunting, fishing and gathering such edible fruits as nature provided" (Curwen 1954, 56-7).

Following the pre- and post-War focus of archaeological fieldwork in Sussex on the Downs, a series of projects took place in the High Weald between the mid 1950s and 1970s which resulted in the discovery of further Mesolithic sites. Mrs. S. Standing surveyed an area of Weald Clay to the south of Horsham, discovering fourteen sites (Holgate 1987), whilst Tebbutt explored the Ashdown Forest and located a series of both open and rock shelter sites (Tebbutt 1975); he went on to excavate one of these sites, the Hermitage, in the mid-1970s (Jacobi and Tebbutt 1981). Money's excavations of the rock shelters at High Rocks (Money 1960) were highly significant; charcoal recovered from shelter F in association with Mesolithic flints produced the first radiocarbon dates for a Mesolithic site in the region (*see* Table 3.1).

During the 1970s Jacobi produced a fresh review of the evidence for Mesolithic settlement in Britain (1975) and Sussex (1978). He catalogued the microliths from all Mesolithic assemblages and subjected them to statistical analysis, demonstrating that the Sussex assemblages could be divided into three main groups. The first group included assemblages with a microlithic component characterized by mainly obliquely-blunted points with only rarer triangles, bitruncated microliths and convex-backed 'lanceolate' points; amongst the non-microlithic material, convex-edged scrapers are always the most significant (Jacobi 1978, 16-17; 1981, 10). These assemblages occur mainly, but not exclusively, on the Lower Greensand and are analogous to the early Mesolithic or Maglemosian sites from the North European Plain, dating to the 10th and 9th millennia BP. The second group contains a microlithic technology consisting of a combination of obliquely-blunted points, predominantly isosceles triangles, bitruncated rhombic microliths and concave basally-retouched points, otherwise known as 'Horsham' points (Jacobi 1978, 20; 1981, 11-12). These assemblages, whose main distribution is tightly concentrated in the Weald, appear to date to the 9th millennium BP. The third group of assemblages contains mainly geometric microliths predominated by scalene triangles and narrow straight-backed bladelets, or rods (Jacobi 1978, 19; 1981,13). They occur not only throughout the Weald, but also on the Downs and the Coastal Plain, dating from the 8th to early 6th millennia BP. In addition, he reassessed the Mesolithic flint assemblages that had been recovered before the 1970s and outlined two main subjects for future work: fieldwork in the Weald to locate further undisturbed sites; and the excavation of rock shelter sites in the hope of recording stratigraphic sequences with associated organic remains which can be submitted for radiocarbon dating, creating a more detailed absolute chronology for Sussex Mesolithic assemblages.

Up to the mid 1970s, Mesolithic studies in Sussex fitted in with prevailing archaeological theory and practice. After a period of unsystematic data collection up to the 1920s, Clark's studies emulated the method advocated by Childe of grouping archaeological material into 'cultures'. Clark's later work, and Jacobi's initial approach, followed the economic paradigm that Clark himself developed out of his work with the Fenland Committee (Smith 1997). Jacobi was also concerned, in response to the refinement of radiocarbon dating following the compilation of tree-ring calibration curves in the early 1970s, with a critical review of the evidence for Mesolithic settlement and with building up a detailed chronological sequence.

Since the mid 1970s, three main developments have taken place. First, the investigation of valley deposits and the palaeoenvironmental information they contain. Second, the recovery of *in situ* Mesolithic material from a number of sites, including both open sites and rock shelters. Third, research undertaken on Upper Palaeolithic and Mesolithic sites elsewhere in southern Britain and northern Europe which, influenced in part by the theoretical perspectives offered by processual archaeology, has changed archaeologists' perceptions of the nature of late glacial and post-glacial hunter-gatherers.

Palaeoenvironmental work

A number of studies of the alluvial, colluvial and peat deposits in Wealden valleys has taken place in the last two decades. The results, particularly of fine-grained palynological studies, give an indication of the vegetational history and impact of human activity on woodland cover in the Upper Palaeolithic and Mesolithic periods. There is growing evidence, not only from the Weald in Sussex but also from other parts of southern and eastern England, for deliberate forest clearance at this time both for pasture and to increase the productivity of plant resources (Zvelebil 1994).

Site	Date (uncal. yr. BP) & lab. no.	Sample	Context
Westhampnett Area 1	9,120 ± 90 (OxA-4168)	charred hazelnuts	gully fill
Westhampnett Area 4	8,880 ± 100 (OxA-4170) 8,300 ± 90 (OxA-4171)	charred hazelnuts charcoal	pit fill pit fill
West Heath	9,040 ± 90 (HAR-7037) 8,770 ± 80 (HAR-7036) 8,100 ± 70 (HAR-645)	charcoal charcoal charcoal	pit fill pit fill pit fill below barrow I
Hermitage	7,105 ± 70 (Q-1562) 6,920 ± 110 (Q-1312) 6,800 ± 100 (Q-1311)	charcoal charcoal charcoal	hearth layer layer
High Rocks shelter F	5,730 ± 150 (BM-91) 5,650 ± 150 (BM-40)	charcoal charcoal	layer layer

Table 3.1. *Radiocarbon dates from Mesolithic sites in Sussex.*

Sedimentological, palynological and pedological analyses have been carried out on alluvial deposits on the West Sussex Coastal Plain (Fitzpatrick *et al.* forthcoming) and in the Ouse and Cuckmere valleys (Scaife and Burrin 1983; 1985). Excavations in 1992 on the Westhampnett Bypass encountered late glacial and early post-glacial deposits which included a buried soil dating to the Allerød phase of the late glacial period. The soil was a humic ranker soil which had formed on a pocket of loess during the late transitional part of the Interglacial interstadial. Pine and birch charcoal recovered from the soil produced radiocarbon dates of 10,880 ± 100 BP (OxA-4166), 10,870 ± 80 BP (AA-11769) and 10,840 ± 100 BP (OxA-4167): the time when temperatures were cooling before the onset of the severe colder conditions of the Loch Lomond glacial re-advance. The charcoal recovered represents heathland species, namely birch, pine and heathers. Palynological, molluscan and soil micromorphological analyses were undertaken, indicating that the environment locally was a swamp marsh with lush open vegetation including purple moor grass and heathers, with woodland including pine and birch growing in the vicinity. There is potential evidence for human activity in the form of a flint flake and the charcoal, which could result from human fires. There was also evidence for physical mixing of the soil, probably by trampling, indicating the presence of large herbivores (?reindeer) or other mammals in the locality.

In the Ouse valley over 6m of alluvial deposits were encountered, 2m of which represented sediments that accumulated after the removal of vegetation cover in the upper stretches of the Ouse valley in the Mesolithic period. On the Lower Greensand at West Heath, palynological analysis of palaeosols preserved underneath the barrows in the Early Bronze Age barrow cemetery suggests that heather spread locally in the Mesolithic period in the wake of burning and general opening up of the forest canopy (Scaife 1985). Soil disturbance and sand blowing occurred at other sites in the Weald as a result of Mesolithic occupation, for example at Iping Common, Oakhanger in East Hampshire and High Rocks (Scaife 1988, 17). However, not all soils on the Lower Greensand which were exploited by Mesolithic communities suffered to such an extent as the soils at West Heath and Iping Common: pedological analysis of the prehistoric soil horizons at Selmeston, which were relatively loamy and base-rich, showed that they did not deteriorate significantly as a result of Mesolithic activity (Macphail 1985). Looking in greater detail at the vegetational sequence at West Heath, the woodland cover in the early Mesolithic period was dominated by pine and hazel. By the 9th millennium BP the environment was one of heathland dominated by heather with post-clearance hazel scrub and lime (Scaife 1988, 21). High frequencies of ivy pollen were also present, probably indicating the widespread growth of ivy in areas of dead decaying trees resulting from Mesolithic forest clearance (Scaife 1988, 21-2). However, not all areas of the Lower Greensand were exploited: for example, at Rackham the initial clearance of the forest cover did not occur until the later Neolithic period (Dimbleby and Bradley 1975). There is thus evidence for localized forest clearance in parts of the Weald in the 9th-8th millennia BP.

Palynological analysis of peat deposits dating back to the early Holocene period has taken place in the Arun valley (Waton 1982), in the Brede and Pannel valleys (Waller *et al.* 1988; Waller 1993), in the lower Rother valley (Long *et al.* 1998a) and in the Ouse valley (Waller & Hamilton 1998). Pett Level, with peat deposits dating back to the start of the Mesolithic period which have been analyzed and radiocarbon-dated (Waller 1993), provides the most complete Holocene sequence so far obtained from south-eastern England. Alder occurred on the valley floor soon after 10,000 BP. In dry areas, pine and birch became established, with the expansion of hazel at *c.*9,500 BP, oak and elm between *c.*9,100 and *c.*8,400 BP, and lime after *c.*7,000 BP (Waller 1993, 365-66). There is no palynological evidence that Mesolithic communities had a major influence on vegetational development in the valley, although Mesolithic activity may have been responsible for the persistence of openings in the dryland canopy after the arrival of deciduous trees. The occurrence, albeit at low frequencies and irregularly, of pollen from what were probably dryland herbs would appear to be consistent with the archaeological evidence in the Pannel valley for a series of short-stay camps (Waller 1993, 366; Holgate and Woodcock 1989). However, other processes could have been influential in creating such openings, for example fires started by natural means and the grazing of indigenous herbivores (Waller 1993, 366). Earlier palynological analysis of deposits in the Vale of Brooks (Thorley 1971) produced some evidence for localized clearance episodes in the Mesolithic period prior to 5,700 BP. The replacement of pine and birch woodland by mixed deciduous woodland in the 9th-8th millennia BP with lime becoming the dominant tree species is evident from all sites in the Brede, Pannel, Ouse and Rother valleys investigated in recent years. This similarity in woodland cover and succession during the Mesolithic period suggests that the soils of south-east England at this time were very different to those present today, with a cover of loess probably providing uniformity (*cf.* Waller and Hamilton 1998, 120). By 5,300 BP, peat was forming and alder-dominated fen carr developing in the valleys adjoining the Walland Marsh, initially in the protected valleys of the Brede and the Pannel and on Pett Level, and then gradually spreading along the northern edge of Romney Marsh (Long *et al.* 1998b, 60-1). Radiocarbon-dating of the submerged forest on the foreshore of Pett Level suggests that this area was also inundated by the sea in the 6th millennium BP (Welin *et al.* 1972).

There is limited information for the pre-Neolithic environment on the Downs. Molluscan analysis of both dry valley colluvial deposits (Bell 1993; Ellis 1986) and the ditch fills of earlier Neolithic monuments (Thomas 1982), combined with palynological analysis of bog sediments in the Arun valley at Amberley Wild Brooks (Waton 1982) and of the Ouse and Glynde valley sediments in the vicinity of the Vale of the Brooks (Waller and Hamilton 1998), indicate that much of the Downs was under forest cover throughout the Mesolithic period. However, at Itford Bottom post-Mesolithic colluvial deposits sealed eight subsoil features, at least one of which was a tree hole created by a tree fall. Pine charcoal was recovered from the base of this feature, which produced a radiocarbon date of 8,770 ± 85 BP (BM-1544). The tree fall was followed almost immediately by burning. The associated molluscan assemblage suggests that the effects of this fire were very localized and short-lived, and the result of either a lightning strike or human activity (Bell 1993, 132-42).

Results of recent fieldwork

Over a dozen relatively undisturbed sites have been investigated during the last 20 years. Three of these sites produced material suitable for radiocarbon dating and, as a whole, the results of these excavations have provided considerable information on the location, extent and nature of Mesolithic activity throughout Sussex.

Investigations of rock shelters have taken place at Uckfield and Withyham, whilst the excavations undertaken by Tebbutt in 1974-75 at the Hermitage were published in the early 1980s (Jacobi and Tebbutt 1981). Sample excavations at the Rocks, Uckfield, in 1979-80 recovered an estimated 10,000 flints, mainly debitage. The tool assemblage was dominated by microliths, predominantly obliquely-blunted forms, with few other formal tools; no axes or axe-thinning flakes were identified. Surface collection survey in the vicinity of the excavated area produced further flintwork. All the material recovered, including the excavated material, was interpreted as representing a single period of occupation in the earlier Mesolithic period (Hemingway 1980; 1981). At the Rocks Wood rock shelters, Withyham, excavations in 1982 produced a later Mesolithic flint assemblage, mainly from disturbed contexts. Microliths predominated amongst the implements recovered, followed by cutting blades and scrapers (Harding and Ostoja-Zagorski 1987, 29). The flint mainly derived from the Chalk and Clay-with-Flints deposits of either the North or the South Downs, with some more local river gravel flints which may have come from the Medway valley 2.5km to the north of the rock shelters.

Excavations at the Hermitage sampled relatively undisturbed Mesolithic deposits. A hearth was located, charcoal from which gave a radiocarbon date, whilst two other radiocarbon dates were obtained on charcoal recovered from horizons above the hearth (*see* Table 3.1). In association with the hearth was a flint assemblage of over 4,000 pieces which included debitage, geometric microliths, burins, truncated pieces and notched pieces. The site was interpreted tentatively as a spring hunting camp. Earlier Mesolithic forms, including a Horsham point, were retrieved from lower levels.

Elsewhere in the Weald, a series of open-air sites has been investigated, one of which produced tentative structural evidence. Surface collection survey in 1986 at Moon's Farm, Piltdown recovered a group of over 300 earlier Mesolithic flints on the river terrace adjacent to the River Ouse, including debitage, scrapers, piercers, a microdenticulate, microliths, axe-thinning flakes, tranchet axe-sharpening flakes and a tranchet axe. The flint had been obtained either locally or from the Downs to the south of the site (Butler 2001). Excavations at Pannel Bridge, Pett Level in 1986 located a small cluster of over 100 later Mesolithic flints, including debitage, scrapers, a cutting blade and geometric microliths, representing the remains of a short-stay camp (Holgate and Woodcock 1989). Most of the flint derived from beach deposits.

Fieldwork has taken place at several sites on the Lower Greendsand. At West Heath, excavations in 1973-75 and 1980 of an Early Bronze Age barrow cemetery recovered nearly 2,000 flints, including debitage, obliquely-blunted microliths, microburins and scrapers, from the old ground surface underneath the barrows or from contexts associated with the barrows (Drewett 1976; 1985). A small pit sealed below barrow I produced burnt red sand, minutely shattered flint fragments and charcoal which produced a radiocarbon date (Drewett 1989: *see* Table 3.1), whilst a small hearth sealed underneath barrow IV which comprised fire-fractured flint and charcoal of ivy, ash, birch, oak and pine might also date to the Mesolithic period (Drewett 1976, 129 and 134). A pit found in 1984 when a trench was excavated to sample the colluvial deposits in the adjacent valley contained seven flints and birch, heather, hazel, ash and pine charcoal which gave two radiocarbon dates (*see* Table 3.1). Two well-defined *in situ* clusters of nearly 1,000 earlier Mesolithic flints were excavated at Rackham in 1979 adjacent to a hearth of fire-fractured flints; they contained debitage and three obliquely-blunted microliths, representing the remains of a short-stay hunting camp (Garton 1981). Surface collection at Graffham Common in 1978-85 located another earlier Mesolithic site, producing debitage, scrapers, a fabricator, microburins, obliquely-blunted microliths, a Horsham point, axe-thinning flakes and a tranchet axe-sharpening flake (Holgate *et al.* 1986).

A large cluster of flints, which included Horsham points and a range of microliths, was excavated at Rock Common, Washington in 1997 (John Lewis and Phil Harding pers. comm.). Further east, excavation at Selmeston in 1963-82 recovered nearly 2,500 flints, a significant proportion of which were debitage, scrapers and microliths of Mesolithic date (Cartwright 1985), complementing the Mesolithic assemblage recovered in 1933 (Clark 1934b). Clark's excavations uncovered three pits containing over 8,000 Mesolithic flints, fire-fractured flint, charcoal and fragmentary hazelnut shells. The flints consisted of debitage, over 100 microliths, microburins, burins, scrapers, microdenticulates and axe-sharpening flakes. More than half of the microliths were obliquely-blunted and other large earlier Mesolithic forms, whilst a small proportion were Horsham points and geometric microliths. The raw material for the assemblage was flint from the sea shore. At Streat, fieldwork in 1996 adjacent to the Lower Greensand located a large spread of fire-fractured flint and Mesolithic flints (Butler 1998). Excavations in 1996-97 revealed a shallow pit and two smaller pits. Initially, the pits were probably dug to locate and exploit a natural deposit of flint nodules for flaking. Flint was then being heated up and presumably used for cooking as huge quantities of fire-fractured flint had been dumped into the upper fills of the pits. Adjacent to the largest pit was an area of unburnt flint nodules arranged in a circle nearly 3m in diameter, with a single post-hole in the centre of this area. This could represent the remains of a temporary shelter, perhaps a tent-like structure, in which flint nodules were used to retain the sides of the tent. Large quantities of later Mesolithic flintwork were recovered, including debitage and microliths. An initial interpretation of this site suggests that it is a temporary hunting camp, repeatedly visited over a long period of time.

Until recently, little was known about Mesolithic activity on the Coastal Plain (*cf.* Jacobi 1978, 15). Pitts (1980) mapped sites where Mesolithic flintwork had been recovered before the late 1970s, indicating that almost invariably these sites overlooked water courses. Only one of these sites, Apuldram, could be dated by flint typology: here, a small group of nearly

100 flints comprised debitage and a large obliquely-blunted microlith (Pitts 1980, 159). Since then, further Mesolithic sites have been discovered near water courses and at the base of the Downs on the West Sussex Coastal Plain. Excavations at Knapp Farm, Bosham, in 1984-85 produced about 100 later Mesolithic flints, including debitage, cutting blades, a microdenticulate, truncated bladelets and a geometric microlith (Holgate 1997). A cluster of Mesolithic flints, mainly debitage, microliths and other implements, was recovered in 1985-1986 on the Fishbourne Bypass (Goodburn 1996). These sites were probably short-stay camps.

Two earlier Mesolithic clusters of flintwork were excavated in advance of the Westhampnett Bypass in 1992, both of which were located alongside the former Waterbeach-Tangmere stream course (Fitzpatrick *et al.* forthcoming). Area I, which produced over 4,500 flints, was situated on the eastern edge of a small knoll overlooking a smaller tributary of the stream course, whilst Area 4, which produced over 6,000 flints, was located on the lower slopes of a knoll overlooking the stream course. Most of the flint derives from Coombe Deposit sources within 1km of the site, whilst a small quantity came from local river gravel and Reading Beds sources, with a few pieces from non-local sources. The flints from both areas included debitage, hammerstones, backed pieces, scrapers, piercers, burins, microdenticulates, denticulates, notched pieces, microliths, microburins, a burin spall, tranchet axe-sharpening flakes and axe fragments. A shallow gully was the only subsoil feature of Mesolithic date in Area 1, charred hazelnuts from which produced a radiocarbon date (*see* Table 3.1). Area 4 revealed two groups of nine subsoil features, most of which produced Mesolithic flints, fire-fractured flint and charcoal. Charcoal, mainly oak, hazel and ash, and charred hazelnuts from one of these features produced two radiocarbon dates (*see* Table 3.1). The quantity and multiplicity of implement-types recovered, together with the location of the sites adjacent to an intermittent water course, suggest that both sites functioned as long-stay camps where a range of activities took place, including tool manufacture and preparation, food procurement and processing, and the modification of wood, bone, leather and skins. Fieldwork in 1991-92 south of Angmering Decoy at the base of the Downs in a position similar to Westhampnett recovered over 200 later Mesolithic flints, including debitage, scrapers, burins, microburins, microliths and a tranchet axe (Graves and Hammond 1993).

Recent investigations at two later Mesolithic sites on the Downs provide significant information on the nature of downland activity during this period. Excavations at Redhill in advance of the construction of the Brighton Bypass in 1989, along with surface collection in the 1920s and 1930s by Toms, produced nearly 1,000 Mesolithic flints. The excavations also revealed pits, ditches and hearths, some of which could conceivably date to the Mesolithic period but are more likely to be of later date. The site is situated on a south-facing Clay-with-Flints capped spur overlooking the coast. The flints, manufactured on nodules derived from the Clay-with-Flints, included debitage, scrapers, piercers, cutting blades, microdenticulates, notched pieces, burins, fabricators, geometric microliths, microburins, axe-thinning flakes, tranchet axe-sharpening flakes and tranchet axes (Butler and Holgate 2002). Surface collection survey of a 1km^2 area in 1985-87 and subsequent excavation in 1990 at West Hill, Pyecombe, located and defined a concentration of Mesolithic humanly-struck flint on the Clay-with-Flints capping near the scarp of the Downs. Over 1,200 flints were recovered, including debitage, scrapers, geometric microliths, tranchet axe-sharpening flakes, a tranchet axe and other axes, adzes and axe roughouts (Butler 1985). The axe-manufacturing debris indicates that flint was extracted from the Clay-with-Flints deposits on the site and then flaked into axes and other implements.

The site at West Hill links in with research undertaken in the late 1970s on the production and distribution of Mesolithic axes (Care 1979). The main areas where Mesolithic axes have been recovered in southern England are the areas where suitable flint supplies for axe manufacture were readily available. Those axes which have been recovered from the Weald are generally small in size, having been progressively reduced in size by resharpening (Care 1979, 94). By far the largest proportion of flint from Wealden assemblages, for example at the Hermitage and Rocks Wood, was obtained from the Downs. Some Wealden assemblages also contain flint from beach deposits, for example Selmeston and Pannel Bridge. It is likely that flint was obtained by communities who exploited downland and coastal resources at some stage in the year and occupied a territory taking in both the Downs and the Weald. This example of obtaining a specific resource during the annual round of food procurement is a classic instance of embedded procurement (*cf.* Binford 1979). The information gleaned from the results of recent fieldwork enables a fresh review to be undertaken of late glacial and post-glacial hunter-gatherers in Sussex.

Upper Palaeolithic settlement

The evidence for Upper Palaeolithic settlement in Sussex outlined by Woodcock (1978) has not increased substantially in the 1980s and 1990s (*see* Fig. 3.1). This period, corresponding broadly with the Devensian Glaciation, can be divided into two periods: the earlier Upper Palaeolithic, dating between 38,000 and 27,000 BP and the later Upper Palaeolithic, dating between 13,000 and 10,500 BP (Jacobi 1980, 15; Barton 1992, 177-80). The two periods are separated by the time when the maximum extent of ice occurred in Britain during the Devensian Glaciation, and evidence to date suggests that Britain was unoccupied at this time. Re-analysis of the earlier Upper Palaeolithic assemblage of over 2,000 flints from The Beedings, near Pulborough, indicates that many flints apparently discarded had been reworked, or recycled, to produce hunting equipment (Jacobi 1986). This suggests that the site was used as a field observation site by a hunting band, as the site is a good vantage point and the information gained from studying the flints suggests it was revisited on numerous occasions. A second site tentatively dated to this period on environmental evidence is the assemblage of 156 *in situ* flints from Newhaven, although the implements recovered do not fit easily into presently-known Upper Palaeolithic tool inventories (Bell 1976). A faunal deposit of reindeer and bison recovered in the early 20th-century from river gravels interbedded with organic material at Upper Beeding is also likely to date to this period (Matthew Pope pers. comm: material in the Booth Museum).

The later Upper Palaeolithic period is represented in Sussex by the possible evidence for human activity at Westhampnett

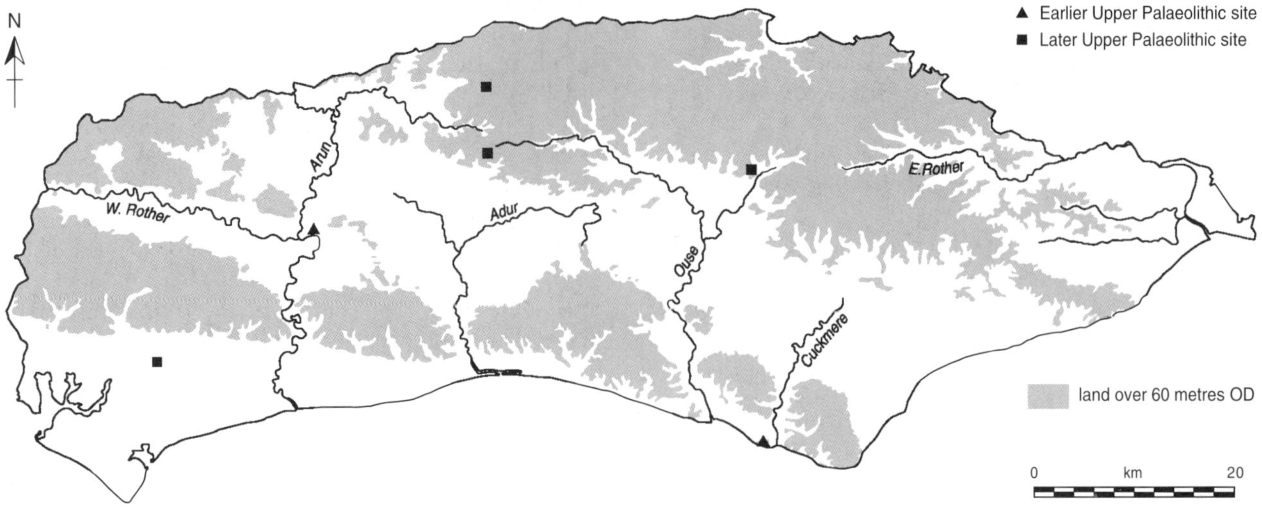

Figure 3.1. Location of Upper Palaeolithic sites in Sussex.

on the Coastal Plain (Fitzpatrick *et al.* forthcoming) and by three isolated projectile points from the Weald, namely shouldered points from Old Faygate and Hawkin's Bridge Pond, Lower Beeding, and a large tanged point from Newhouse Farm, High Hurstwood (Woodcock 1978; Jacobi 1980; Barton 1992, 187-8; *see* Fig. 3.1). The later Upper Palaeolithic period coincides with the late glacial Interstadial, when there was still a land bridge between Britain and the European mainland. Initially, tall herb communities and dwarf shrub heath colonized south-eastern England, supporting animals typical of open habitats, for example horse, reindeer and arctic fox. As the climate ameliorated, birch woodland developed in much of southern Britain; the earliest re-settlement of England is dated to this period. At least two flint technologies occurred at this time: the 'angle-backed Creswellian' assemblages found in caves and rock shelters in the limestone areas of England and Wales and the 'straight-backed blade' assemblages recovered from open-air localities in southern England, for example Hengistbury Head, Dorset and Brockhill, Surrey (Barton 1992, 187). The open-air sites have similarities with contemporary sites in northern Europe which can be interpreted as sites occupied seasonally, rather than on a permanent basis, by large hunting groups during the autumn and spring migrations of horse and reindeer (Barton 1992, 187-200). In all, there are at least 30 find-spots from this period in England, including the three Sussex examples and Stonewall Park in Kent from the Weald. Sussex, in common with other parts of southern England and northern Europe, was undoubtedly exploited by hunter-gatherers occupying a series of seasonally-occupied camps.

Earlier Mesolithic period

The post-glacial period dates from around *c.*10,300 BP. At first, the environment was relatively open, supporting horse and reindeer. Temperate conditions returned by *c.*9,700 BP, with the colonization of juniper, birch and pine in southern England, especially on sandier soils (Scaife 1988). Hazel spreads eastwards, reaching southern England by *c.*9,100 BP. With the expansion in woodland came the introduction of woodland animals, mainly elk, roe deer, pig and beaver. By *c.*9,800 BP, the earliest post-glacial flint assemblages occur, containing microliths indicative of bow and arrow hunting by hunter-gatherers living in a forested environment.

In the earlier Mesolithic period, the microlithic component of flint assemblages is dominated by obliquely-blunted points. Three major typological groupings have been identified amongst the earlier Mesolithic flint assemblages in Britain, named after the sites at Star Carr, Deepcar and Horsham (Jacobi 1975; Reynier 1997, 529). There appears to be a chronological division between these assemblage-types, with 'Deepcar' assemblages occurring slightly later than 'Star Carr' assemblages and appearing before 'Horsham' assemblages (Reynier 1997, 538-9). The earliest Sussex Mesolithic assemblages are 'Deepcar'-type assemblages (*see* Fig. 3.2): most of these, which occur both in the Weald and on the Coastal Plain, are predominantly in valley-based locations, as is the case for the majority of 'Deepcar' assemblages throughout England and Wales (Reynier 1998, 181). Such localities offer the advantages, in a wooded environment, of being near the forest margin and water where a range of terrestrial mammals, fowl and edible plant resources could be procurred. Barton (1992, 254-9), in discussing the excavated earlier Mesolithic flints from Hengistbury Head in Dorset, undertook a detailed analysis of five other earlier Mesolithic open-air sites within a 100 km radius of Hengistbury, including Iping Common in West Sussex. The assemblages could be divided into three groups on the composition of the toolkit. The first group, including both Hengistbury and Iping Common, are situated on high ground and sandy geological substrates; their toolkits mainly comprise microliths, end scrapers and microdenticulates, representing the activities of a temporary hunting camp, namely skinning, hide processing, and the repair and maintenance of hunting equipment. The second group, Downton and Thatcham, have river-edge locations and contain a variety of flint tool types, notably axes or adzes, burins and drill bits, as well as microliths, end scrapers and microdenticulates. A broad range of activities took place here, from hunting, food processing, bone and antler working, woodworking and other maintenance activities. The third group is the site on Clay-with-Flints which, besides microliths, yielded large numbers of tranchet axes and axe-sharpening flakes; this is interpreted as a temporary hunting camp where flint was obtained for axe production. Barton suggested (*pace* Binford 1983) that all these sites could lie within a projected life-time's round of a single hunter-gatherer group.

The Sussex sites (*see* Fig. 3.2) vary considerably in nature. Some sites, for example West Heath, Hassocks, Selmeston and Westhampnett, produced considerable quantities of flintwork, charcoal and pits. The pits could have been used for storing plant foods over the winter months, for example hazelnuts, charred remains of which were found at Selmeston and Westhampnett. Others, as exemplified by Rackham, yielded smaller, tightly-clustered scatters of flintwork. The Sussex Wealden sites, by analogy with Hengistbury Head and Iping Common, could be interpreted as task-specific sites. The Westhampnett sites could be considered as a form of river-edge camps where a broad range of activities took place, and other similar sites may remain to be discovered in the lower reaches of both rivers and former watercourses in Sussex. The overall pattern of settlement is that of the traditional nomadic way of life for hunter-gatherers, with the seasonal exploitation of resources taking place over a large area from a sequence of temporary residence locations occupied on more than one occasion (Jacobi 1987, 165).

The group of 'Horsham' assemblages characterized by the presence of hollow-based or Horsham points, attributed by Jacobi (1981, 11-12) to the 9th millennium BP on the basis of radiocarbon dates from the Hermitage and sites in Hampshire, are concentrated almost exclusively in south-east England (Reynier 1997, 539; 1998, 182). In Sussex, as in neighbouring counties, these assemblages occur on a broader range of geological substrates and in more varied localities than the 'Deepcar' assemblages. Reynier (1997, 539; 1998, 182) suggests that this could represent infilling of areas away from the coast, possibly corresponding with the onset of more open mixed forest which could have permitted relatively easy access for both humans and woodland mammals.

Later Mesolithic period

During the later Mesolithic period, dating from *c*.8,500 - *c*.5,500 BP, mixed deciduous woodland prevailed and sea level rose to the extent that Britain became a series of islands. Over 70 flint assemblages displaying a considerable variety of toolkits have been recovered from all parts of the Sussex landscape (*see* Fig. 3.3). The microlith component in these assemblages consists of a range of geometric forms. Ellaby (1987, 65) has suggested that the development of new microlith forms reflects a change in the way arrowheads were tipped. The more robust projectile points used in the earlier Mesolithic period would have been appropriate for strike or encounter hunting over relatively great distances, whilst the later Mesolithic emphasis on tipping arrows with barbed microliths that would puncture animal hides and then cause severe internal bleeding would be appropriate for tactical or intercept hunting at relatively close range, being far better suited to hunting in the wooded environment.

A new pattern of settlement and resource exploitation appears to have developed in the later Mesolithic period, possibly as an extension of the shift in settlement associated with the emergence of 'Horsham' assemblages. The apparent increase in the number of later Mesolithic sites, particularly in the southern half of Sussex, compared with the known number of earlier Mesolithic sites could be in response to increasing insularity and the closing in of the lime-dominated woodland canopy (*cf.* Jacobi 1987, 166). Mesolithic studies elsewhere in northern Europe have demonstrated that coastal and estuarine areas, with their abundance of edible resources, could have supported a sedentary pattern of settlement, where hunter-fisher-gatherers reside in one location from which they make forays to undertake selected activities at task-specific sites, as opposed to moving from one location to another on a seasonal cycle (Zvelebil and Rowley-Conwy 1986; Jacobi 1987, 165). This relies on exploiting successively migratory species, for example fresh- and salt-water fish, birds and sea mammals, and seasonally-available species as exemplified by shell-fish, alongside local resources with year-round availability. Short-stay temporary hunting camps represented

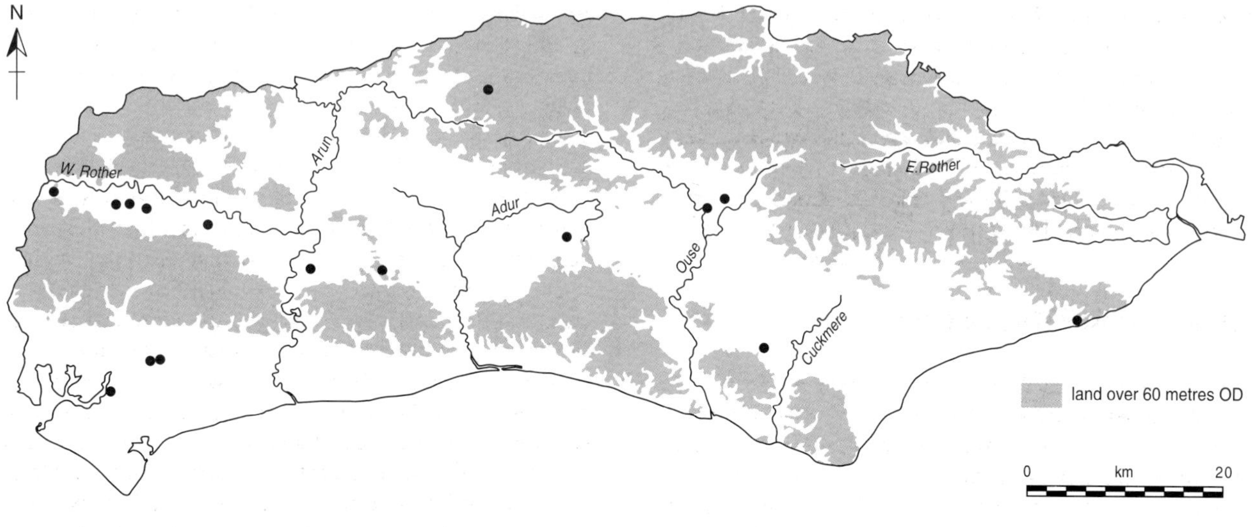

Figure 3.2. *Location of earlier Mesolithic sites in Sussex (after Holgate et al. 1986, fig. 1A with additions).*

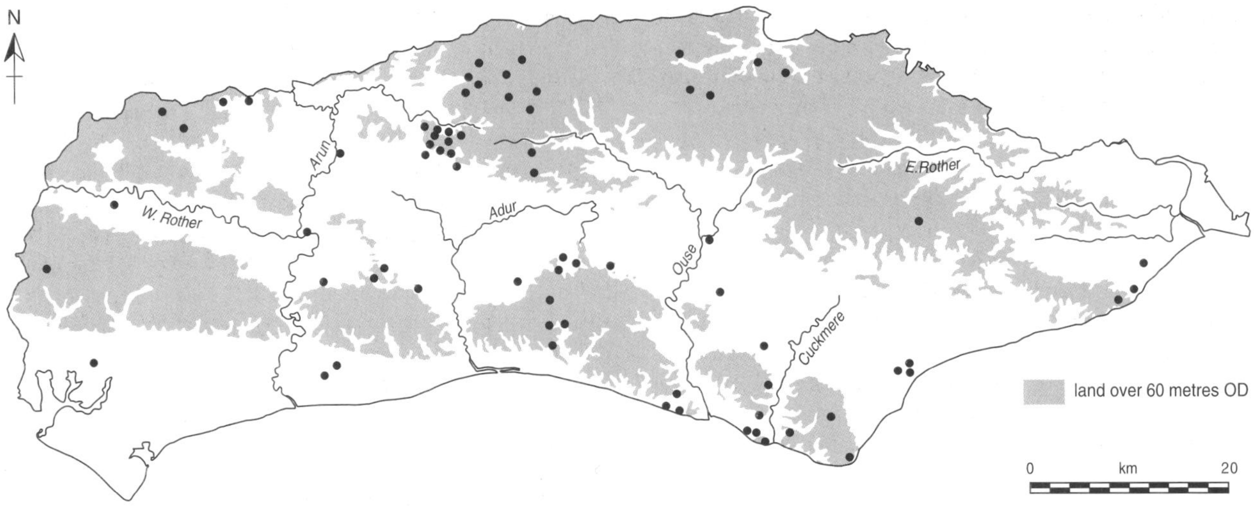

Figure 3.3. *Location of Late Mesolithic sites in Sussex (after Gardiner 1984, fig. 3.1 with additions).*

by assemblages with a limited quantity and range of implement-types occur at rock shelters and open-air locations, mainly in the High Weald. Open-air camps, some occupied on more than one occasion, are located in the Low Weald, on the Coastal Plain and on downland ridges capped with Clay-with-Flints. The shell midden, containing mainly oysters but some limpets, at Seaford (Clark 1930) indicates that exploitation of coastal and estuarine resources undoubtedly took place at the long-since vanished Mesolithic coastline, as does the flaking of flint obtained from beach deposits at some of the Mesolithic inland sites, e.g. Pannel Bridge (Holgate and Woodcock 1989, 4). Further information on coastal exploitation has been lost to coastal erosion and convincing evidence for 'base camps' remains elusive; however, the existence of inland task-specific, seasonally-occupied sites suggests that a sedentary pattern of settlement cannot be ruled out. Some of the sites away from stretches of water, and thus the forest margin, could have been occupied in the winter months for hunting woodland mammals at a time when travel through woodland was less impeded by foliage. Glades may have been created to provide browse for mammals and to increase plant diversity, possibly assisted by beaver activity alongside rivers (*cf.* Coles 1992).

Why did farming come to replace the hunter-fisher-gatherer existence? By the 6th millennium BP many of the valleys draining into the Walland and Romney Marshes were inundated by the sea, leading to the development of alder-dominated fen carr (Long *et al.* 1998b, 60-1), possibly as a result of the changing pattern of shingle barriers along the coast in response to eustatic rise. Although analysis of deposits in the lower stretches of the major valleys draining into the English Channel has not been undertaken, a study of the Combe Haven valley, west of Hastings, is instructive. Here, sediments consisting mainly of interbedded peat and clay began to form between 6,020 $\pm$ 70 BP (SRR-2683) and 5,900 $\pm$ 50 BP (SRR-2685). Pollen analysis indicates that alder was dominant on the valley bottom, with a close canopy of predominantly lime, along with oak, elm, and hazel on the valley sides (Smyth and Jennings 1988, 7). Soon after, silty clay deposits formed and the woodland was replaced by grasses and sedges, suggesting the establishment of a salt marsh community and estuarine conditions following flooding of the valley by the sea (Smyth and Jennings 1988, 10). There is little evidence of human intervention on the vegetation at this stage although later, after the mixed deciduous woodland began to become re-established, there is evidence for several temporary clearances, including the 'elm decline', at an estimated date of *c.*5,000 BP. With the gradual rise in sea level, possibly exacerbated by storm action, the configuration of certain estuaries, with their rich edible resources, changed dramatically. Thus environmental change in the early 6th millennium BP may have contributed to the development of animal husbandry and horticulture amongst indigenous communities. It culminated in the creation of woodland clearings on the loess-based downland soils and elsewhere for animal grazing and cereal plots by the time when the elm decline phenomenon was taking effect (Holgate 1988, 132; Jacobi 1987, 166; Scaife 1988).

Priorities for future work

Archaeological fieldwork and palaeoenvironmental studies in the 1980s and 1990s have resulted in the recovery of Upper Palaeolithic and Mesolithic material from a number of localities, providing considerable information on late glacial and early post-glacial settlement and economy. There is a need to search for and excavate *in situ* sites throughout Sussex, notably those where environmental, faunal and botanical remains are likely to be preserved. Stratified sites which could reveal improved chronological sequences, for example rock shelter sites and sites on the Coastal Plain and in the Weald comparable with Westhampnett (Fitzpatrick *et al.* forthcoming) and Streat (Butler 1998) respectively, are worthy of attention. Although prospection is difficult, areas under or adjacent to alluvium in the lower stretches of river valleys should also be targeted for investigation (*cf.* Evans 1992). Furthermore, raw material procurement studies, including further fieldwork to recover representative samples from flint assemblages on the Downs to assess the range of activities practised at these sites, would be productive. If work along these lines can be incorporated into regional research frameworks for south-east England and carried out, the gain in information for Upper Palaeolithic and Mesolithic studies would be considerable.

Acknowledgements

I am indebted to Andrew Fitzpatrick, Chris Butler, John Lewis, Phil Harding and David Rudling for their generosity in providing access to unpublished accounts of fieldwork undertaken in the last decade, and to Matthew Pope, Peter Drewett and Andrew Woodcock who kindly supplied information which enhanced my knowledge of recent palaeoenvironmental studies.

Note

In accordance with international convention, all radiocarbon dates are expressed in uncalibrated years before the present (BP), with the present set at AD 1950. Calibrated dates have not been referred to as the fluctuations and compressions in the calibration curve make it difficult to produce an absolute chronology, particularly for the earlier Mesolithic period.

References

Barton, R.N.E. 1992. *Hengistbury Head, Dorset. Volume 2: the Late Upper Palaeolithic and Early Mesolithic sites.* Oxford: O.U.C.A. Monograph 34.

Bell, M. 1976. The excavation of an early Romano-British site and pleistocene landforms at Newhaven, Sussex, *SAC* **114,** 218-305.

Bell, M. 1993. Valley sediments as evidence of prehistoric land-use on the South Downs, *Proc. Prehist. Soc.* **49,** 119-50.

Binford, L.R. 1979. Organisation and formation processes: looking at curated technologies, *J. Anthrop. Res.* **35**, 255-73.

Binford, L.R. 1983. *In Pursuit of the Past: decoding the archaeological record.* London: Thames & Hudson.

Butler, C. 1995. Mesolithic and Neolithic activity on the South Downs at Pyecombe, West Sussex, *Lithics* **14,** 21-3.

Butler, C. 1998. Mesolithic Streat. Ancient hunters: cooking, knapping and camping, *Sussex Past and Present* **84,6.** Lewes: Sussex Arch. Soc.

Butler, C. 2001. Mesolithic and later flintwork from Moon's Farm, Piltdown, East Sussex, *SAC* **133,** 222-224.

Butler, C. and Holgate, R. 2002. The flintwork [Excavations at Redhill], in D. Rudling (ed), *Downland settlement and land use: the archaeology of the Brighton By-Pass.* University College London Field Archaeology Unit Monograph 1.

Care, V. 1979. The production and distribution of Mesolithic axes in southern England, *Proc. Prehist. Soc.* **45,** 93-102.

Cartwright, C. 1985. The flintwork, in D. Rudling, Recent archaeological research at Selmeston, East Sussex, *SAC* **123**, 10-13.

Clark, J.G.D. 1930. A new pigmy site in Sussex, *MAN* **1-2,** 2-3.

Clark, J.G.D. 1932. *The Mesolithic Age of Britain.* Cambridge: Univ. Press.

Clark, J.G.D. 1934a. The classification of a microlithic culture: the Tardenoisian of Horsham, *Arch. J.* **90**, 52-77.

Clark, J.G.D. 1934b. A late Mesolithic settlement site at Selmeston, Sussex, *Antiq. J.* **14**, 134-58.

Clark, J.G.D. 1939. The affinities of the Farnham industry: the Horsham culture, in J.G.D. Clark and W.F. Rankine, Excavations at Farnham, Surrey (1937-38): the Horsham culture and the question of Mesolithic dwellings, *Proc. Prehist. Soc.* **5**, 91-8.

Coles, B. 1992. Further thoughts on the impact of beaver on temperate landscapes, in S. Needham and M.G. Macklin (eds), *Alluvial Archaeology in Britain.* Oxford: Oxbow Monograph **27**, 93-9.

Curwen, E.C. 1954. *The Archaeology of Sussex.* London: Methuen, 2nd edition.

Drewett, P. 1976. The excavation of four round barrows of the second millennium B.C. at West Heath, Harting, 1973-75, *SAC* **114**, 126-50.

Drewett, P. 1985. The excavation of barrows V-IX at West Heath, Harting, 1980, *SAC* **123**, 35-60.

Drewett, P. 1989. Anthropogenic soil erosion in prehistoric Sussex: excavations at West Heath and Ferring, 1984, *SAC* **127**, 11-29.

Dimbleby, G.W. and Bradley, R.J. 1975. Evidence of pedogenesis from a Neolithic site at Rackham, Sussex, *J. Arch. Sci.* **2**, 179-86.

Ellaby, R. 1987. The Upper Palaeolithic and Mesolithic in Surrey, in J. Bird and D.G. Bird. (eds), *The Archaeology of Surrey to 1540,* Surrey Archaeological Society, 53-69.

Ellis, C. 1986. The postglacial molluscan succession of the South Downs dry valleys, in G. de G. Sieveking and M.B. Hart, *The scientific study of flint and chert,* 175-84. Cambridge: Univ. Press.

Evans, J.G. 1992. River valley bottoms and archaeology in the Holocene, in B. Coles (ed), *The Wetland Revolution in Prehistory.* Exeter: WARP Occ. Pap. **6**/The Prehistoric Society.

Fitzpatrick, A.P., Allen, M.J. and Powell, A.B. forthcoming. *Archaeological excavations on the A27 Westhampnett Bypass, West Sussex, 1992: Volume 1: the prehistoric, Romano-British and Anglo-Saxon landscapes.* Salisbury: Wessex Archaeology Report.

Gardiner, J.P. 1984. Lithic distributions and Neolithic settlement patterns in central southern England, in R. Bradley and J. Gardiner (eds), *Neolithic Studies: a review of some current research,* BAR **133**, 15-40.

Garton, D. 1981. An early Mesolithic site at Rackham, West Sussex, *SAC* **118**, 145-52.

Goodburn, D. 1996. Report on the worked flint scatter and residual flintwork from the 1985-6 excavations, in B. Cunliffe, A. Down and D. Rudkin, *Chichester Excavations IX, Excavations at Fishbourne 1969-1988,* Chichester: Chichester District Council, 63-8.

Graves, P. and Hammond, P. 1993. A Mesolithic site at Angermering Decoy, West Sussex, *SAC* **131,** 195-8.

Harding, A.F. and Ostoja-Zagórski, J. 1987. Excavations in Rocks Wood, Withyham, 1982, *SAC* **125**, 11-32.

Hemingway, M.F. 1980. Preliminary explorations at the Rocks, Uckfield, East Sussex, *Sussex Archaeol. Soc. Newsletter* **31**, 209-10.

Hemingway, M.F. 1981 Further explorations at the Rocks early Mesolithic site, Uckfield, East Sussex, *Sussex Archaeol. Soc. Newsletter* **34**, 243.

Holgate, R. 1987. Excavations at Halt Mesolithic site, near Horsham, West Sussex, 1985, *SAC* **125**, 33-9.

Holgate, R. 1988. *Neolithic Settlement of the Thames Basin,* BAR Brit Ser. **194**.

Holgate, R. 1997. The flint, in M. Gardiner and S. Hamilton, Knapp Farm, Bosham: a significant find of Bronze Age pottery, *SAC* **135**, 87.

Holgate, R.D.C., Holden, E.W. and Holden, H.G. 1986. An early Mesolithic site and prehistoric flintwork from Graffham Common and neighbouring areas on the Lower Greensand, West Sussex, *SAC* **124**, 1-8.

Holgate, R. and Woodcock, A. 1989. A later Mesolithic site at Pannel Bridge, near Pett Level, East Sussex, *SAC* **127**, 1-10. 1987.

Jacobi, R.M. 1975. Aspects of the post-glacial archaeology of England and Wales. PhD thesis: University of Cambridge (unpublished).

Jacobi, R.M. 1978. The Mesolithic in Sussex, in P.L. Drewett (ed), *Archaeology in Sussex to AD 1500,* CBA Res. Rep. **29,** 15-22.

Jacobi, R.M. 1980. The Upper Palaeolithic in Britain, with special reference to Wales, in J.A. Taylor (ed), *Culture and Environment in Prehistoric Wales,* BAR **76**, 15-99.

Jacobi, R.M. 1981. The last hunters in Hampshire, in S.J. Shennan and R.T. Schadla Hall.(eds), *The Archaeology of Hampshire: from the Palaeolithic to the Industrial Revolution*, Hampshire Field Club and Archaeol. Soc. Monograph **1**, 10-25.

Jacobi, R.M. 1986. The contents of Dr. Harley's show case, in S.N. Collcutt (ed.), *The Palaeolithic of Britain and its Nearest Neighbours: recent trends*, Sheffield: Dept. of Archaeol. and Prehist., Univ of Sheffield, 62-8.

Jacobi, R.M. 1987. Misanthropic miscellany: musings on British early Flandrian archaeology and other flights of fancy, in P. Rowley-Conwy, M. Zvelebil and H.P. Blankholm (eds), *Mesolithic Northwest Europe: recent trends,* Sheffield: Dept. of Archaeol. and Prehist., Univ of Sheffield, 163-8.

Jacobi, R.M. and Tebbutt, C.F. 1981. The excavation of a Mesolithic rock shelter at Hermitage Rocks, *SAC* **124**, 119-36.

Long, D., Waller, M. and McCarty, P. 1998a. The vegetation history of the lower Rother valley: stratigraphy and pollen data for the Shirley Moor region, in J. Eddison, M. Gardiner and A. Long (eds), *Romney Marsh: Environmental Change and Human Occupation in a Coastal lowland,* O.U.C.A. Monograph **46**, 31-44.

Long, A., Waller, M., Hughes, P. and Spencer, C. 1998b. The Holocene depositional history of Romney Marsh proper, in J. Eddison, M. Gardiner and A. Long (eds), *Romney Marsh: Environmental Change and Human Occupation in a Coastal lowland,* O.U.C.A. Monograph **46**, 45-63.

Macphail, R. 1985. Soil report, in D. Rudling, Recent archaeological research at Selmeston, East Sussex. *SAC* **123**, 2-3.

Money, J.H. 1960. Excavations at High Rocks, Tunbridge Wells, 1954-56, *SAC* **98**, 173-221.

Phillips, C.W. 1987. *My Life in Archaeology*. Gloucester: Alan Sutton.

Pitts, M. 1980. A Gazetteer of Mesolithic finds on the West Sussex Coastal Plain, *SAC* **118**, 153-162

Reynier, M.J. 1997. Radiocarbon dating of early Mesolithic stone technologies from Great Britain, in J.P. and A. Thevenin (eds), *Le tardiglaciaire en Europe du Nord-Ouest*. Paris: Editions du CTHS, 529-42.

Reynier, M.J. 1998. Early Mesolithic settlement in England and Wales: some preliminary observations, in N. Ashton, F. Healy and P. Pettit, P. (eds), *Stone Age Archaeology. Essays in honour of John Wymer*. Oxford: Oxbow Monograph **102/**Lithic Studies Society Occ. Pap. **6**, 174-84.

Scaife, R.G. 1985. Palynological analysis of West Heath barrows V, VIII IX, in P. Drewett, The excavation of barrows V-IX at West Heath, Harting, 1980, *SAC* **123**, 51-9.

Scaife, R.G. 1988. The elm decline in the pollen record of South East England and its relationship to early agriculture, in M. Jones (ed.), *Archaeology and the flora of the British Isles.* Oxford: O.U.C.A. Monograph **14**, 21-33.

Scaife, R.G. and Burrin, P.J. 1983. Floodplain development in and the vegetational history of the Sussex High Weald and some archaeological implications, *SAC* **121**, 1-10.

Scaife, R.G. and Burrin, P.J. 1985. The environmental impact of prehistoric man as recorded in the upper Cuckmere valley at Steam Farm, Chiddingly, *SAC* **123**, 27-34.

Smith, P.J. 1997. Grahame Clark's new archaeology: the Fenland Research Committee and Cambridge prehistory in the 1930s, *Antiquity* **71**, 11-30.

Smyth, C. and Jennings, S. 1988. Mid- to late-Holocene forest composition and the effects of clearance in the Combe Haven valley, East Sussex, *SAC* **126**, 1-20.

Tebbutt, C.F. 1975. The prehistoric occupation of the Ashdown Forest area of the Weald, *SAC* **112**, 34-43.

Thomas, K.D. 1982. Neolithic enclosures and woodland habitats on the South Downs in Sussex, England, in S. Limbrey and M. Bell (eds), *Archaeological Aspects of Woodland Ecology*, BAR Int. Ser. **146**, 147-70.

Thorley, A. 1971. Pollen analytical evidence relating to the vegetation history of the Chalk, *J. Biogeography* **8**, 93-106.

Toms, H.S. 1907. *Pigmy flint implements found near Brighton.* Extract of a paper read before the Brighton and Hove Natural History and Philosophical Society, Thursday, May 16th, 1907.

Waller, M.P. 1993. Flandrian vegetational history of south-eastern England. Pollen data from Pannel Bridge, East Sussex, *New Phytologist* **124**, 345-69.

Waller, M., Burrin, P.J. and Marlow, A. 1988. Flandrian sedimentation and palaeoenvironments in Pett Level, the Brede and Lower Rother Valleys and Walland Marsh, in J. Eddison and C. Green (eds), *Romney Marsh. Evolution, Occupation, Reclamation,* O.U.C.A. Monograph **24**, 3-30.

Waller, M.P. & Hamilton, S.D. 1998. The vegetational history of the South Downs: Mount Caburn, in J.B. Murton, C.A. Whiteman, M.R. Bates, D.R. Bridgland, A.J. Long, M.B. Roberts, and M.P. Waller (eds), *The Quaternary of Kent and Sussex: Field Guide.* London: Quaternary Research Association, 115-20.

Waton, P.V. 1982. Man's impact on the chalklands: some new pollen evidence, in S. Limbrey and M. Bell (eds), *Archaeological Aspects of Woodland Ecology*, BAR Int. Ser. **146**, 75-91.

Welin, E., Engstrand, L. and Vaczy, S. 1972. Institute of Geological Sciences radiocarbon dates III, *Radiocarbon* **14**, 331-5.

Woodcock, A. 1978. The Palaeolithic in Sussex, in P.L. Drewett (ed.), *Archaeology in Sussex to AD 1500*, CBA Res Rep **29**, 8-14.

Zvelebil, M. 1994. Plant use in the Mesolithic and its role in the transition to farming, *Proc. Prehist. Soc.* **60**, 35-74.

Zvelebil, M. and Rowley-Conwy, P. 1986. Foragers and farmers in Atlantic Europe, in M. Zvelebil (ed.), *Hunters in Transition,* Cambridge: Univ. Press, 67-94.

TAMING THE WILD: THE FIRST FARMING COMMUNITIES IN SUSSEX

Peter Drewett

Abstract

This paper outlines developments in our knowledge about Neolithic Sussex since the 1977 Conference on Sussex Archaeology published by the Council for British Archaeology. It mentions newly discovered enclosures, long barrows and pit groups and considers the nature of settlement, economy and territorial organization in the light of current knowledge and theoretical perspectives.

Introduction

In the introduction to my paper on Neolithic Sussex at the 1977 Conference on Sussex Archaeology published by the C.B.A. I wrote: "The few radiocarbon dates from Sussex would suggest the presence of Neolithic elements by *c.* 4300 BC and that they survived until about *c.* 2500 BC. There is strong evidence that during this period there existed in Sussex socially coherent and autonomous groups occupying discrete territories" (Drewett 1978). The use of the phrase "the presence of Neolithic elements" was both cautious and deliberate, for the accepted view at the time was that "the earliest agricultural communities crossed from the continental land mass to settle in the British Isles in the middle of the 4th Millennium bc" (Megaw and Simpson 1979). It is now widely accepted that there was no major immigration of agricultural peoples into Britain and that certain Neolithic 'elements' were adopted by indigenous Mesolithic peoples more readily than others, including, perhaps, the full adoption of agriculture based on the central European model. In addition to changing theoretical perspectives about the 'Neolithic' as such, Sussex has revealed much new information over the last 20 years, new enclosures, new long barrows, flint scatters and pit clusters (Fig. 4.1). A major axe study has been published (Woodcock and Woolley 1986), environmental work continues apace (e.g. Scaife and Burrin 1983; Waller and Hamilton 1998) and a major resurvey of Neolithic enclosures and flint-mines has been undertaken by the Royal Commission on Historical Monuments for England. It is therefore clearly time to present a fresh account of Neolithic Sussex. I propose to do this in three main sections. Firstly, I shall consider briefly the environmental background. Secondly, I will consider monuments and thirdly, an outline of settlement, economy and possible territorial organization. Running through all these areas we have elements of ritual, indeed, ritual is now often seen as more of a defining factor than economy in our understanding of the Neolithic.

Environmental background

Indications are that loess was more widely spread over Sussex in the Mesolithic than was thought some 20 years ago. (e.g. Burrin 1981, Scaife and Burrin 1985). If this was the case vegetation prior to clearance may have been similar over much of Sussex. This 'Wildwood' was essentially mixed oak, with oak being the dominant species together with elm, ash, alder and lime, with hazel as the main underwood species (Sheldon 1978). Human interference with this forest cover is now thought to date back into the later Mesolithic, but more extensive forest clearance in the Early Neolithic probably resulted in extensive erosion of cover loams. This in turn resulted both in soil deterioration and in the choking of Sussex rivers causing floodplain development (Scaife and Burrin 1983). Although the broad picture of forest cover, clearance and massive soil erosion still holds true during the period *c.* 5000-3000 BC, work over the last 20 years is refining the picture.

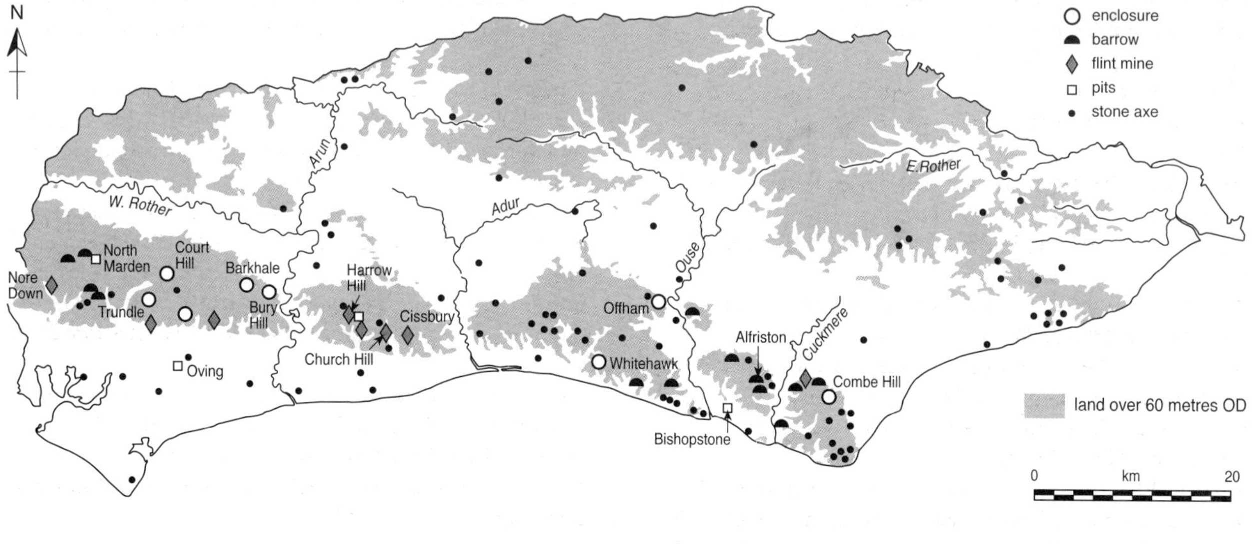

Figure 4.1. *Neolithic Sussex.*

Molluscan work by Thomas, Bell and Ellis among others has indicated a mosaic of downland clearance from the Neolithic onwards (e.g. Thomas 1977; Bell 1981; Ellis 1986). This is particularly striking in relation to the molluscan sequences from six enclosures constructed prior to 3000 BC. Four of the enclosures, Offham, Combe Hill, Bury Hill and Barkhale still had close woodland when constructed, while the Trundle and Whitehawk were constructed in areas extensively cleared (Thomas 1977).

Pollen analysis is refining this general picture of clearance with detailed insights into specific localities. Recently work by Martyn Waller, for example, around the Caburn block has shown that the steep slopes around Caburn remained wooded throughout the Neolithic. Concentrations of juniper and yew pollen from auger holes at the foot of Caburn perhaps indicate animal husbandry in a formerly cleared area as juniper is a browse-resistant species (Waller and Hamilton 1998). Although the classic pollen sequence from the Brooks does not show a dramatic change in the percentage of arboreal to non-arboreal pollen until the late 2nd millennium BC (Thorley 1971), a pollen sequence from Wellingham, north of Lewes, indicated a clearance phase in the mid-4th Millennium BC. This was associated with an increase in frequency of grass and cereal pollen (Wing 1980).

By the 5th Millennium BC Sussex was perhaps quite densely occupied by peoples who collected a variety of plant products including tubers and wild grains, fished, collected shell-fish and hunted the forests for deer, wild cattle, pigs and birds. Home bases at sites like Selmeston and Hassocks allowed easy seasonal access both south to the coast and north into the Weald. The Wealden rock shelters show ample evidence for temporary camp sites of hunting parties. The resources in Sussex were good and varied, so it has always been difficult to understand why this life style should have been given up for the toil of forest clearance, breaking the soil, sowing, weeding and harvesting crops. The earliest certain evidence for cereals in Sussex does not really appear until some 800 years into the Neolithic at sites like Whitehawk and Bishopstone. Earlier dates will clearly be found, but how much earlier remains an interesting question.

Monuments

Causewayed enclosures

Since the 1977 conference a further three enclosures have been identified as almost certainly Early Neolithic, bringing the total to eight. The additional three sites, Bury Hill, Halnaker Hill and Court Hill had escaped notice by the early pioneers of Neolithic Sussex studies, like the Curwens, because the linking of the pit-dug, ditches made them look Iron Age. These can be added to the well-known sites of the Trundle, Whitehawk, Barkhale, Offham and Combe Hill. We now have at least some carbon-14 dates from all enclosures except Barkhale, although the single date from Halnaker Hill of 900±90 bc (I-12,322) was considered by the excavator to be a 'rogue' date (Bedwin 1992). The earliest dates come from the primary silts in ditch 2 (all ditches numbered from the inner circuit outwards) at the Trundle and Court Hill. The Trundle dates of 3290+140 bc (I-11615) and 3090±170 bc (I-11616) if calibrated could well push the origin of the Trundle into the late 5th millennium BC. These dates are close to the single date from the nearby enclosure on Court Hill where a date of 3470±180 bc (I-12,893) was obtained from the primary silts. Unfortunately, suitable material was not available from the inner circuits at Whitehawk when I was obtaining dates for the enclosures in the early 1980s, so we only have dates for the outer ditches 3 and 4. Ditch 3 primary silt produced a date of 2750±130 bc (I-11846), while the primary silt in ditch 4 produced a date of 2695±95 bc (I-11847). These are remarkably close to the primary silt dates from Bury Hill of 2730±80 bc (Har-3596) and 2620±80 bc (Har-3595). The only date from the primary silts at Offham, ditch 2, is also close to this group being 2975±80 bc (BM-1414). The secondary silts in the same ditch had a date of 2790±60 bc (BM-1415). Finally, Combe Hill has a single date from the primary ditch silt of ditch 2 of 2640±110 bc (I-11613). As a group these dates clearly confirm the Early Neolithic date for all the enclosures other than Halnaker Hill and Barkhale, but structural and artefactual evidence from these sites is sufficient for Barkhale to be certainly, and Halnaker Hill to be probably, included in this group of enclosures.

It was becoming clear in the 1970s that causewayed enclosures should not be considered as single one-off constructions. Phasing can rarely be determined from artefacts or even carbon-14 dates as neither are precise enough. At Offham however the molluscan sequences within the inner and outer ditches were sufficiently different for me to be able to write in 1977 that "the inner ditch was probably dug first in a clearing made in woodland. At a slightly later date the outer bank and ditch was added" (Drewett 1977)(Fig. 4.2). I developed this theme when publishing Veronica Seton William's 1962 Combe Hill excavations. I stated that "a case could be made that all enclosures in Sussex started as small...enclosures... . The inner circles at the Trundle, Whitehawk, Offham and Combe Hill are all about the same size as the single-ditched enclosure at Bury Hill, that is some 100m in diameter. Barkhale is a little larger" (Drewett 1994). Court Hill and Halnaker Hill are also larger (Bedwin 1992). This theme of long-term use and development of the multi-circuit enclosures in Sussex has been greatly enhanced by the remarkably detailed re-surveys of all the Sussex enclosures by the Royal Commission on Historical Monuments for England (Oswald 2001). The so-called spiral ditch at the Trundle, for example, has been demonstrated to represent several superimposed enclosures rather than one single phase of construction. We are probably therefore dealing with re-construction and use over most of the Early Neolithic, a period of over 1000 years. The likelihood that the meaning of causewayed enclosures remained the same over such a long period is remote. We may perhaps be safest remaining with the RCHME conclusion that: "The form and nature of activities occurring in individual sites may, however, have been many and varied, particularly given the lengthy time-scale over which some enclosures were used and re-used." (Oswald 2001).

Figure 4.2. Offham, causewayed enclosure. Excavations 1976.

Long Barrows

As with enclosures, several new long and oval barrows have been located since I published the plans of the twelve known ones after the 1977 conference (Drewett 1978). We also have radio-carbon dates for three sites. The problems with the dating of the Alfriston oval barrow (Drewett 1975a) were noted at the 1977 conference. Essentially the oval, causewayed, ditched enclosure is probably Early Neolithic. Primary silts contained Early Neolithic pottery and waste flakes together with an antler pick dated to 2360±110 bc (Har-940). The central crouched burial and at least some of the mound may, however, be much later. The burial now has two carbon-14 dates of 640±90 bc (Har-942) and 1240±80 bc (Har-1811), while the antler pick on the buried land surface some 2.5m north of the burial pit has a date of 590±70 bc (Har 941). Substantial remodelling of the site may therefore have taken place in the Later Bronze Age. A slightly earlier date was obtained from the primary silts at the North Marden oval barrow in West Sussex (Drewett 1986) (Fig. 4.3). Here Early Neolithic pottery and lithics were associated with a date of 2760±110 bc (Har-5544), but there was evidence of continued use of the site well into the Beaker period with beaker sherds associated in secondary silts with organic material which have been used to obtain radiocarbon dates of 1600±80 bc (Har-5542) and 1640±80 bc (Har-5543). The only other carbon-14 date I was able to obtain from a long barrow came from hazel and hawthorn charcoal found in a burnt layer just above the primary silt in the ditch at Bevis's Thumb. This produced a date of 2596±95 bc (I-11,843).

Flint-mines

Flint-mines have produced some of the earliest carbon-14 dates for monuments in Sussex, but clearly the date of their use overlaps with that of the causewayed enclosures and long barrows. Church Hill, Findon, has a date of 3390±150 bc (BM-181), while Blackpatch, Worthing, has a date of 3140_±130 bc (BM-290). Cissbury has a run of three dates of 2780±150 bc (BM-185), 2770±150 bc (BM-183) and 2700±150 bc (BM-184). Harrow Hill, however, has the best run of dates with six dates now added to the original one of 2980±150 bc (BM-182). The new dates followed the British Museum's 1982 and 1984 excavations (McNabb *et al.* 1996). These were 2950±120 bc (BM-2071R), 3070±110 bc (BM-2075R), 3190±150 bc (BM-2097R), 3400±150 bc (BM-2098R), 3090±120 bc (BM-2099R) and 3110±90 bc (BM-2124R).

Prior to the 1977 conference most work on flint-mines in Sussex had concentrated on the excavation of shafts, although some work on the surfaces between shafts had been undertaken by J.H. Pull (Pye 1968). Two field projects during the 1980s,

Figure 4.3. *North Marden oval barrow ditch silts, 1982. Scale: 2m.*

however, extended our knowledge of the process of flint-working at these sites and to this must now be added the re-survey of the sites carried out by the Royal Commission on Historical Monuments for England (Barber *et al.* 1999). The British Museum's project at Harrow Hill involved the excavation both of shaft 13 and of areas to the north. It was concluded that initial open-cast quarrying was followed by the excavation of shafts. Although there was knapping on site, most of the flint appears to have been taken away for knapping elsewhere. The on-site knapping suggested a very flexible approach to knapping with no formal methodology. A 'path of least resistance' had been apparently adopted (McNabb *et al* 1996). In 1986 Robin Holgate sampled the ploughed area to the south of the main cluster of shafts on Harrow Hill. He dug 69 test-pits by hand, dry-sieving the soil through 5mm mesh sieves. This located a substantial flint-working area together with more evidence of open-cast quarrying. Dr. Holgate also revealed working areas at Long Down and Church Hill, Findon (Holgate 1991 and 1995) (Fig. 4.4).

Settlement, Economy and Territorial Organization

When considering settlement at the 1977 conference I concluded that: "The evidence for Neolithic settlement in Sussex is still very scanty, consisting of two sites where pits have been found during the excavation of sites of a later date, a series of surface flint concentrations, thought to indicate plough-spread occupation levels and some evidence of sporadic occupation of the Wealden rock shelters" (Drewett 1978). The basic problem was that we were really still looking for a Neolithic modelled on the earlier central European Linearbandkeramic. The Neolithic in 1977 needed permanent houses, possibly long-houses set in hamlets. The inhabitants should have lived by cultivating crops and domesticating animals. The Mesolithic was gone. In order to side-step the issue slightly I started looking at territories where groups of people had undertaken various activities, rather than search for specific settlement sites which could not be found. I concluded that it did appear possible in Sussex "to define socially coherent groups occupying discrete territories" (Drewett 1978). The scene was clearly set for a radical rethink of what it meant to be 'Neolithic' in Sussex, and indeed the whole of Britain. This rethink was eloquently put on paper by Julian Thomas: "Only later, with the further expansion into the North European Plain, Scandinavia and the British Isles did a fundamental change in the nature of Neolithic life styles take place. From this time on, many of the characteristic type-fossils are either absent, rare, or restricted to a very specialized set of contexts. Cereals may not have played a very large part in the subsistence practices of Neolithic Britain, while pottery may have only been used for a restricted set of practices. Large, timber-framed houses are rare in north-west Europe from the Rossen period onwards, and in Britain those few which exist are of uniformly early date. Aggregated settlements are still rarer. So, while we might concede that the Neolithic of the LBK was one which manifested itself in a highly 'economic' guise, by the time Britain entered the Neolithic community, it was a Neolithic which existed largely in the realm of ideas. Nevertheless .... it was this transformation which allowed it to be transmitted by acculturation rather than by colonisation" (Thomas 1991, 13-14).

There is little doubt that Neolithic ideas arrived in Sussex by acculturation rather than colonization. As mentioned above, later Mesolithic Sussex may have been fairly densely populated and certainly had a good resource base of plants and animals (see Holgate, this volume). In strictly economic terms why should these people have changed their economy? One possibility is that they did not until well into the Early Neolithic, another possibility is that we simply have not found the evidence yet. Perhaps the earliest evidence of crop cultivation in Sussex comes from the seed impression of naked barley *(Hordeum* sp.) from pottery at Whitehawk. This can only be given a fairly broad 4th Millennium date. More closely dated are the carbonized remains of emmer wheat (*Triticum dicoccum*) and six-row barley *(Hordeum vulgare)* from Bishopstone, associated with a date of 2510±70 bc (Har-1662). Domesticated cattle, pigs and sheep, however, come from several sites including the Trundle, Whitehawk, Bury Hill, Offham, as well as Bishopstone. Virtually all other foodstuffs found on Early Neolithic sites in Sussex are exactly the same as we would expect on later Mesolithic sites. Wild red and roe deer were still hunted, hazel nuts were collected and marine mollusca including winkle *(Littorina littorea),* cockle *(Cardium edule),* mussel (*Mytilus edulis)* and oyster *(Ostrea edulis)* were collected from the seashore and marine estuaries.

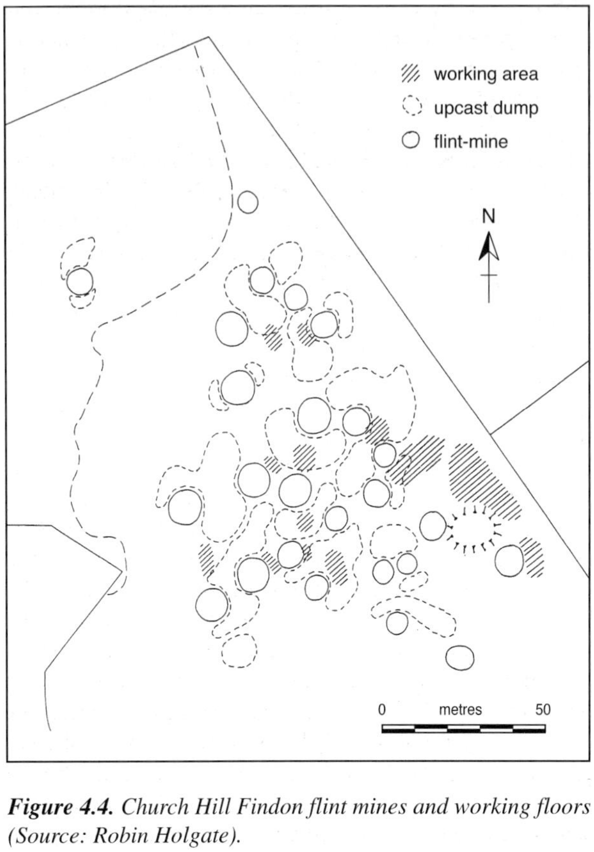

Figure 4.4. *Church Hill Findon flint mines and working floors (Source: Robin Holgate).*

Pits containing pottery and other remains of apparently 'domestic' material culture were formerly thought of as an indicator of settlement (Field *et al.* 1964). This now appears not always to be the case. The pits and their contents may represent a wider use of the landscape rather than specific settlement at the particular spot where the pit was dug. Indeed, the digging and deposition of objects in pits closely parallels the deposition of objects in other contexts such as causewayed enclosure and long barrow ditches. Pit deposits may have more of a symbolic than economic role, a way of 'fixing' domesticity in a landscape being tamed (Thomas 1991, 76). It may be worth re-examining the few pits from Sussex in this light.

Dug into the bottom of the outer ditch at Offham was a small, roughly circular pit some 600mm in diameter and 400mm deep. The pit contained sherds from a single large round-based pot with a rim diameter of about 300mm. Only part of the pot had been buried and what was deposited went into the pit as sherds. Buried with the pot was a leaf-shaped arrowhead, waste flakes and what appears to have been a careful selection of animal remains, especially teeth of both domestic and wild species. The assemblage included six red deer teeth, a cattle tooth, four roe deer teeth and, particularly rare, the tooth of a beaver (Drewett 1977). Whitehawk and the Trundle also contain pits. A line of five pits were found near the North Marden oval barrow in 1987 (Down and Welch 1990, 221). All were roughly circular with diameters of under 1m and less than 400mm deep. They contained 408 sherds representing a minimum of 30 Early Neolithic vessels, together with flintwork and animal bone. A single pit was also located during the excavation of the Copse Farm Iron Age settlement at Oving on the West Sussex coastal plain. The pit contained ten rim sherds from a single round-based pot with a rim diameter of some 250mm (Bedwin and Holgate 1985, 220).

The two pits excavated by Dr Curwen in the 1930s on New Barn Down contained fragments of grinding stones in addition to pottery, animal bones and flint tools which included part of a polished axe, a scraper and a backed knife. At Selmeston, East Sussex, a nearly complete Ebbsfleet pot was found in a small pit (Drewett 1975b) close to where sherds of Ebbsfleet ware were found deposited in the top of hollows left by Mesolithic pit diggers (Clark 1934, 134). Perhaps the most interesting group of pits, however, was that excavated by Martin Bell on Rookery Hill, Bishopstone (Bell 1977, 7-44). This is generally assumed to be a Neolithic settlement site but, in the light of the reconsideration of pits in the Neolithic, this should perhaps not remain a foregone conclusion. The somewhat curious distribution of the Neolithic features on Rookery Hill was noted by Martin Bell. The excavated area was on the slight slope to the south of the top of Rookery Hill, a location not dissimilar to that of the enclosures like Bury Hill, Barkhale and Offham. Bell comments "In fact the Neolithic features seem to be round the periphery of the excavations .... and just possibly therefore forming a rough circle of diameter about 115m" (Bell 1977, 5). The content and method of backfilling of pit 357 is of particular interest. The roughly circular pit was about 2m in diameter and some 0.85m deep. Before much weathering took place it was backfilled with some 500mm of chalk rubble containing 2437 mussel (*Mytilus edulis)* shells. Following a short weathering period three small hollows were scooped in the unconsolidated sediment. The central scoop was used for burning while the other two had no obvious function. The pit was then filled in with chalk lumps and dark brown earth containing flint artefacts, pottery and a saddle quern. The pit also contained remains of emmer wheat *(Triticum dicoccum)*, spelt wheat *(Triticum spelta)* and six-row barley *(Hordeum vulare)* together with fat hen, common orache, black bindweed, common knotgrass and chickweed (Bell 1977, 273-275). Could these careful deposits in pits arranged roughly in a 115m diameter circle have something in common with deposition of objects in roughly circular series of pits generally known as causewayed enclosures? If pits so far found in Sussex have more to do with symbolism than directly economic activities on settlement sites, where are the settlement sites?

The mostly likely explanation is that we have looked for the wrong type of evidence perhaps largely in the wrong places. On the Downs some flint scatters are assumed to represent settlement sites or at least areas of settlement. Off the Downs, and particularly in the river valleys, the location of monuments may offer the best hint as to where settlements may have been located. I will consider the flint scatters first. Neolithic flint scatters are found over much of Sussex, but with a clear concentration on the chalk Downs. This is perhaps not surprising given that the chalk is the primary source of flint and the Downs had some of the lightest and most easily workable soils in Sussex. Typochronology applied to Sussex lithic collections by Julie Gardiner (1984) separated them into 'earlier' and 'later' assemblages, but in both phases there was activity both on and off the Downs. Robin Holgate in his work in the Thames Valley suggested that settlement sites, being areas where a variety of activities took place, would be represented by a wider range of tool types than sites where specific activities only took place. In his study he suggested that lithic spreads with five or more types of tool may represent settlement sites. In 1988 I published work (Drewett *et al.* 1988) undertaken in the late 1970s (Drewett 1985) suggesting that lithic scatters on the Downs sometimes represented surface/natural exposure flint-working sites, while those in the Weald sometimes represent woodland hunting sites, and those on the coastal plain include strand and salt marsh resource utilization camps. The main concentrations of lithics currently recorded with five or more tool types are on the South Downs, but this may be an artefact of preservation and location rather than representing the earliest phases of Neolithic settlement in Sussex. One suspects that the river valleys may have been the focus of earliest Neolithic activity with regular settlement on the Downs taking place slightly later. This would be consistent with models elsewhere suggesting the importance of domestic livestock in the earliest Neolithic with a later shift away from rivers and onto the lighter drier soils following the introduction of plough cultivation agriculture (Sherratt 1981, 293).

I think it is a fair assumption that monuments built of white chalk on hills were designed to be seen, and presumably to be seen by the people for whom they were important. They would be a daily reminder of 'place'. My study of the location of long and oval barrows undertaken in the late 1970s -early 1980s suggested a clear river-valley orientation for the long, and possibly earliest, barrows, with a shift to Downland orientation for the oval barrows (Drewett 1985 and Drewett 1986). This can be well illustrated in the Cuckmere Valley in East Sussex. It is also possible to suggest that the earliest Neolithic activity is derived directly from the final Mesolithic activity patterns in the valley (Fig. 4.5). Indeed they were probably the same people doing more or less the same things but with some new 'Neolithic' ideas, ideas which left such dramatic imprints in the landscape that we formerly saw the Early Neolithic as a period of dramatic change rather than actually fairly limited change on a day by day basis.

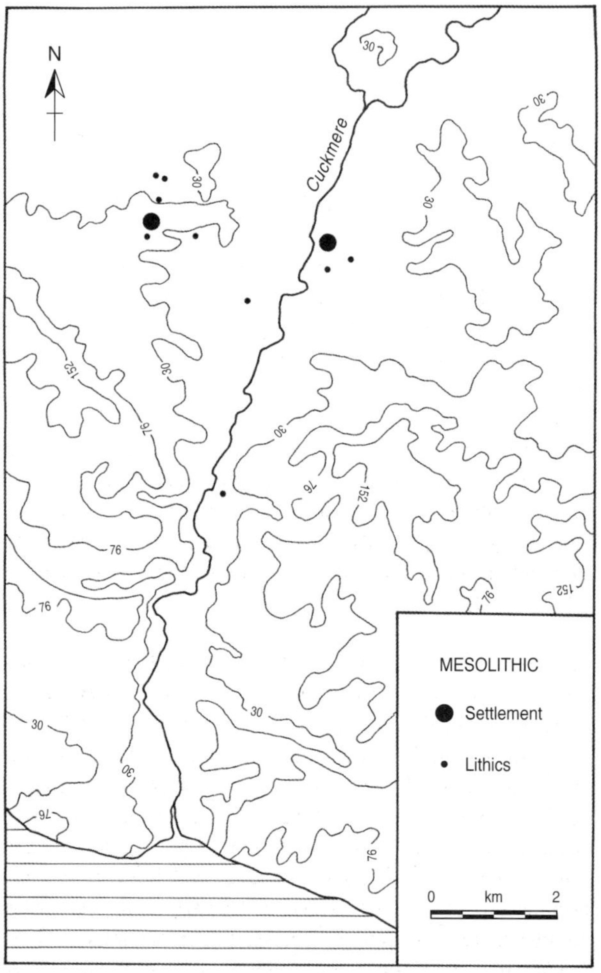

Figure 4.5. *Cuckmere Valley: Final Mesolithic settlement.*

The River Cuckmere rises on the Ashdown Sand and cuts through the Wadhurst Clay, Tunbridge Wells Sand, Wealden Clay, Lower Greensand, Gault Clay and the Chalk now entering the sea at Cuckmere Haven. In the Later Mesolithic the valley would have provided a wide range of resources including nuts and berries, roots and tubers together with fish, shellfish and wild animals like deer and pig. The river would have been tidal for many kilometres up its length and would have flooded regularly. The Mesolithic base-camps were therefore situated above the floodplain on the Greensand at Selmeston (Clark 1934, 134-158) and Endelwick Farm (Garwood 1984, 63). Small scatters of lithics around these base camps and up into the Weald suggest task groups hunting and foraging. The two base camps were dominated to the south by Windover and Alfriston Hills. These hills are visible from well into the Weald and could have been used as home

markers by returning hunting parties. They would certainly have had special meaning to the Later Mesolithic occupants of Selmeston and Endelwick Farm. It is therefore perhaps not surprising that these hills were used for the location of two large long barrows, Long Burgh to the west and the Windover Hill Barrow to the east (Fig. 4.6). A third long barrow intervisible with the two Mesolithic sites, Hunter's Burgh, was constructed on Folkington Hill. All three are false-crested with long views across the Cuckmere Valley and in the case of Windover, both up and down the length of the valley, but with very short views into the Downs. This shows deliberate orientation into the valley and away from the Downs suggesting that it was the well-watered valley that was the centre of activity. This would support the idea that in the earliest Neolithic domesticated cattle requiring water-meadow were of prime importance rather than the more easily cultivatable Downland soils.

If the oval barrows are later in the Early Neolithic than the long barrows proper, then we see a reorientation onto the Downs with the construction of barrows like those at Firle Beacon and Littlington that have long Downland views. The oval barrow on Firle Beacon, for example, is false-crested south of the hill which effectively blocks all Cuckmere and Wealden views. With extensive grazing of cattle, followed by arable on the edge soils and then the Downs, the Cuckmere rapidly became silted up, creating wide floodplains. At Stream Farm in the Cuckmere Valley, for example, boreholes have located some 6.6m of homogeneous fine sandy and clayey silts thought to represent anthropogenic erosion resulting from overgrazing and clearance for agriculture (Scaife and Burrin 1985, 27-43).

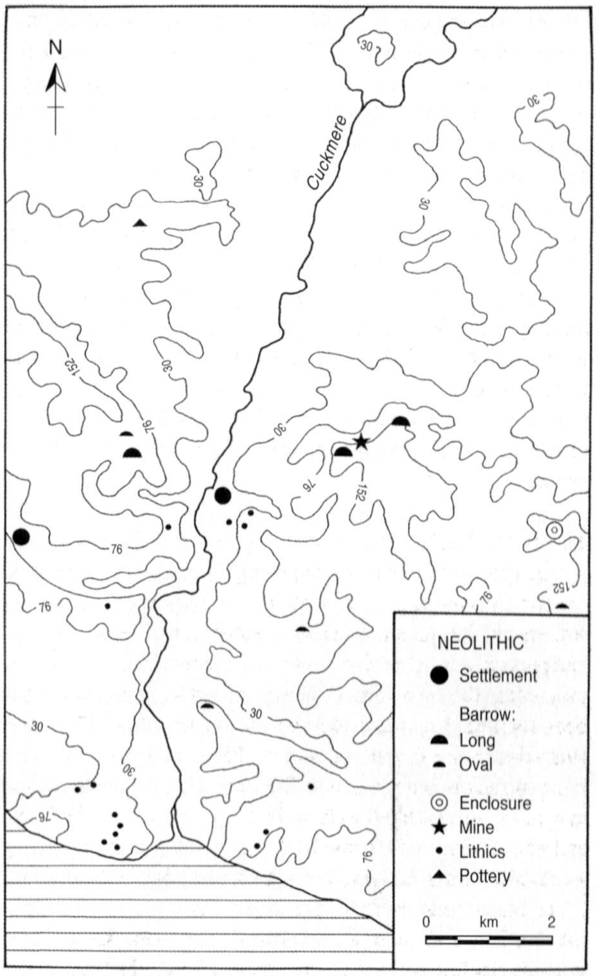

Figure 4.6. *Cuckmere Valley: Neolithic settlement.*

So where do developments in the study of Early Neolithic Sussex since the 1977 conference leave our understanding of Early Neolithic territorial organization? In the 1970s we were still attempting to impose purely hypothetical models of territorial organization based loosely on geographical models (e.g. Drewett 1978, Fig. 9). This approach was being criticized by the late 1970s. Territories should be derived from "the known or explicitly hypothesised behaviour of a population" (Harris 1978, 187). Clearly in a prehistoric context there is no 'known' behaviour so we must rely on 'explicitly hypothesised' behaviour. This led to the construction of the simple territorial models I published in The South-East to AD 1000 (Drewett *et al.* 1988, Fig. 2.9). These attempted to relate different types of sites into one territorial model. The detail of this type of model can be modified, but as a way of stressing possible relationships between different types of Early Neolithic site, I believe they still have some use. In refining a territorial model we must accept that many sites have not yet been found and that many, for a variety of reasons, never will be found. However, I think we can safely assume certain things. Firstly enclosures and long barrows represent work by groups of people probably related, perhaps by kinship. The basic territorial unit is therefore likely to involve the construction of either a long barrow or an enclosure or both within a discrete territory. Rivers and their valleys in Sussex were a major resource and means of transport and as such, may well have been *within* territories rather than functioning as boundaries *between* territories. Pottery from western Sussex as exemplified by the Trundle is different to that from central Sussex, as exemplified by Whitehawk, and both of these areas are totally different to the area east of the Ouse represented by the Combe Hill assemblage. If the use of particular decorations on the pottery were intended to display ethnic affiliation (DeBoer 1984, 550), then one could suggest three larger territories in Sussex (Drewett 1994, Fig. 1) incorporating smaller kin groups.

In conclusion it is clear that our understanding of Neolithic Sussex has increased considerably since the 1977 conference. More monumental sites, including enclosures and long barrows, have been recognized together with new flint-mines as at Nore Down (Aldsworth 1983). Old collections of lithics have been re-studied and new assemblages located. Pits both individual and in groups have been discovered generally by accident when excavating sites of later periods. Clearly many more sites, particularly at the sub-monumental level, remain to be located. It is likely, however, that more ploughed-out long barrows and even enclosures will be found. Perhaps the most important development in the last 20 years however, has been at the theoretical level. The big-bang Neolithic is gone and we now have many different Neolithics. The Trundle Neolithic may well have been different to the Combe Hill Neolithic and both may well have looked much more similar to the Later Mesolithic than to the ensuing fully agricultural Later Bronze Age.

Submitted for publication in April 1998.

References

Aldsworth, F.A. 1983. Prehistoric flint-mines on Nore Down, West Marden. *SAC* **121**, 187-189.

Barber, M., Field, D. and Topping, P. 1999. *The Neolithic Flint-mines in England.* London: English Heritage.

Bedwin, O.R. 1992. Prehistoric Earthworks on Halnaker Hill, West Sussex: Excavations 1981-1983, *SAC* **130**, 1-12.

Bedwin, O.R. and Holgate, R. 1985. Excavations at Copse Farm, Oving, West Sussex, *Proc. Prehist. Soc.* **51**, 215-245.

Bell, M. 1977. Excavations at Bishopstone, *SAC* **115**, 1-299.

Bell, M. 1981. *Valley Sediments as Evidence of Prehistoric Land-use: A study based on dry valleys in South East England.* Ph.D. Thesis, University of London (unpublished).

Burrin, P.J. 1981. Loess in the Weald, *Proc. Geol. Assoc.* **92**, 87-92.

Clark, J.G.D. 1934. A Late Mesolithic site at Selmeston, Sussex, *Ant. J.* **14**, 134-158.

DeBoer, W. 1984. The last pottery show: system and sense in ceramic studies, in S. van der Leeuw and A.C. Pritchard (eds) *The Many Dimensions of Pottery,* 527-568. Amsterdam: University of Amsterdam.

Drewett, P.L. 1975a. The excavation of an oval burial mound of the third millennium B.C. at Alfriston, East Sussex, 1974, *Proc. Prehist. Soc.* **41**, 119-152.

Drewett, P.L. 1975b. A Neolithic pot from Selmeston, East Sussex, *SAC* **113**, 193-194.

Drewett, P.L. 1977. The Excavation of a Neolithic Causewayed Enclosure on Offham Hill, East Sussex, 1976. *Proc. Prehist. Soc.* **43**, 201-41.

Drewett, P.L. 1978. Neolithic Sussex, in P.L. Drewett (ed) *Archaeology in Sussex to A.D. 1500,* C.B.A. Res. Rep. **23-29**.

Drewett, P.L. 1985. *Settlement, economy, ceremony and territorial organization in Sussex, 4th-2nd Millennium BC.* Ph.D Thesis, University of London (unpublished).

Drewett, P.L. 1986. The excavation of a Neolithic Oval Barrow at North Marden, West Sussex, 1982, *Proc. Prehist. Soc.* **52**, 31-52.

Drewett, P.L. 1994. Dr. V. Seton Williams' excavations at Combe Hill, 1962, and the role of Neolithic causewayed enclosures in Sussex, *SAC* **132**, 7-24.

Drewett, P.L., Rudling, D.R. and Gardiner, M. 1988. *The South-East to AD 1000.* London: Longman.

Down, A. and Welch, M. 1990. *Chichester Excavations 7: Apple Down and the Mardens.* Chichester: Chichester District Council.

Ellis, C. 1986. The post-glacial molluscan succession of the South Downs dry valleys. in G. de C. Sieveking and M.B. Hart (eds), *The Scientific Study of Flint and Chalk,* 175-184. Cambridge: University Press.

Field, N., Matthews, C. and Smith, I.F. 1964. New Neolithic sites in Dorset and Bedfordshire, with a note on the distribution of Neolithic storage pits in Britain, *Proc. Prehist. Soc.* **30**, 352-381.

Gardiner, J.P. 1984. Lithic distributions and settlement patterns in central southern England, in R.J. Bradley and J.P. Gardiner (eds), *Neolithic Studies,* Oxford: British Archaeological Reports **113,** 15-40.

Garwood, P. 1984. The Cuckmere Valley Project fieldwalking programme, 1982-83, *Bull. Inst. Arch.* **21**, 49-68.

Harris, D.R. 1978. Group territories or territorial groups? Comments on interdisciplinary problems in cultural ecology, in D. Green, C. Haselgrove and M. Spriggs (eds), *Social Organization and Settlement.* Oxford: BAR, Supplementary Series **47 (1)**, 187-196.

Holgate, R. 1991. *Prehistoric Flint Mines.* Princes Risborough: Shire.

Holgate, R. 1995. Neolithic flint mining in Britain, *Archaeologia Polona* **33**, 133-161.

Megaw, J.V.S. and Simpson, D.D.A. 1979. *Introduction to British Prehistory.* Leicester: University Press.

McNabb, J. Felder, P.J. Kinnes, I. and Sieveking, G. 1996. An archive report on recent excavations at Harrow Hill, Sussex, *SAC* **134**, 21-37.

Oswald, A., Dyer, C. and Barber, M. 2001. *The creation of Monuments: Neolithic Causewayed Enclosures in the British Isles*. London: English Heritage.

Pye, E. 1968. *The flint mines at Blackpatch, Church Hill and Cissbury: a report on the late J.H.Pull's excavations, 1922-55.* MA. Dissertation, University of Edinburgh (unpublished).

Scaife, R.G. and Burrin, P.J. 1983. Floodplain development and the vegetational history of the Sussex High Weald and some archaeological implications, *SAC* **121**, 1 - 10.

Scaife, R.G. and Burrin, P.J. 1985. The environmental impact of prehistoric man as recorded in the upper Cuckmere valley at Stream Farm, Chiddingly, *SAC* **123**, 27-34.

Sheldon, J. 1978. The environmental background, in P.L.Drewett (ed), *Archaeology in Sussex to AD 1500,* CBA Res. Rep. **29**, 3-7.

Sherratt, A. 1981. Plough and pastoralism: aspects of the secondary products revolution. in I.H. Hodder, N. Hammond and G. Isaaes (eds), *Patterns* of *the Past,* Cambridge: University Press, 261-306.

Thomas, J. 1991. *Rethinking the Neolithic.* Cambridge: University Press.

Thomas, K. 1977. The land mollusca from the enclosure on Offham Hill, in P.L. Drewett, The excavation of a Neolithic causewayed enclosure on Offham Hill, East Sussex, 1976, *Proc. Prehist. Soc.* **43**, 234-239.

Thorley, A. 1971. Vegetational History of the Vale of the Brooks, in R. Williams (ed), *A Guide to Sussex Excursions,* Inst. of Brit.Geogr. Conf. Part **5**, 47-50.

Waller, M.P. and Hamilton, S. 1998. The Vegetational History of the South Downs: Mount Caburn, in J. Moiton, C. Whiteman and M. Waller (eds), Quaternary: Research Association Field Guide, South East England, Cambridge: QAR.

Wing, A.S. 1980. *An analysis of the pollen fallout at Wellington peat bog near Lewes, East Sussex and a consideration of some of its climatic and historical implications.* B.Sc project, University of Sussex (unpublished).

Woodcock, A.G. and Woolley, A.R. 1986. Prehistoric stone implements from Sussex and their petrological indentification, *SAC* **124**, 9-23.

ROUND BARROWS AND FUNERARY TRADITIONS IN LATE NEOLITHIC AND BRONZE AGE SUSSEX

Paul Garwood

Abstract

The round barrows of Sussex provide us with exceptional insights into the 'manner of life' of Late Neolithic and Bronze Age communities. The evidence is diverse, richly-detailed and well-documented, and is comparable in many respects to the evidence from better-known regions of Wessex. The first half of this paper reviews the results of round barrow investigations in Sussex since 1763, identifies patterns of uneven preservation, and evaluates current knowledge of mound distributions, types, constructional forms and sequences, chronology, and funerary traditions. The second half considers the landscape settings of these monuments. The identification of supposed ceremonial enclosures ('henges') as part of the Early Bronze Age landscape is rejected, while significant spatial patterns in the organisation of funerary practices and mound-building are recognised at several different scales The striking evidence from the Chichester Downs area, in particular, suggests the creation of a complex cosmographic scheme in the Early Bronze Age that articulated and integrated a symbolic ordering of people, practices, historical narratives and celestial cycles.

Introduction

This paper is concerned with round barrow monuments and associated funerary traditions in Sussex in the Late Neolithic and Early and Middle Bronze Age (*c.*2500-1000 BC). The evidence from round barrows in Sussex, and in Britain as a whole, is extraordinarily diverse, richly detailed, and substantial in comparison with rare, poorly preserved settlement evidence: our understanding of these monuments remains central to general interpretations of social life in this period (*cf.* Ashbee 1960; Bradley 1984; Garwood 1991; Barrett 1994). The research significance of the British evidence is also exceptional at a European scale: the sheer quantity and quality of the evidence (after three centuries of fieldwork), and the presence of several well-preserved segments of prehistoric landscapes in Britain, are paralleled in few regions elsewhere. In this context, Sussex is not 'impoverished' in comparison with areas such as Wessex, but has a real contribution to make to an understanding of the extinct, unique cultural worlds that existed in north-west Europe in the 3rd and 2nd millennia BC.

It is apparent, however, that interpretative ambiguities have been recognized in the funerary evidence since the earliest attempts at synthesis and explanation. This resulted in a high degree of interpretative pessimism in studies of round barrows in Sussex: Horsfield (1824, 50) concluded that "Such are the produce of the tumuli ... How little do we learn from them of the people by whom they were raised"; this differs little from Curwen's view, 130 years later, that "with a few notable exceptions...the barrows of Sussex have contributed little to our knowledge of the Bronze Age. We are forced to admit that while we know something of their funeral customs, we know very little .. of their manner of life" (Curwen 1954, 145; 163). This judgement, however, is misplaced: to "know something of their funeral customs" is the very strength of British Early Bronze Age studies and a direct means of gaining insights into "their manner of life", if not quite in the way that Curwen imagined.

The difficulties encountered in arriving at a social understanding of round barrows, in Sussex and elsewhere, is often ascribed to a lack of empirical knowledge, but this is a poor excuse; the available evidence, in reality, is considerable and well-documented. The problem instead lies at the level of interpretation, and in misunderstandings about the nature of the evidence. Fortunately, new approaches to the analysis and interpretation of round barrow sites are beginning to revitalize the entire field of study. These include new appreciations of ritual practices (eg. Garwood 1991; Barrett 1994, 70-85; Brück 1999) and monumentalism (eg. Barrett 1990; Bradley 1993, 1998), the application of symbolist and structurationist material culture theories to funerary evidence (eg. Thomas 1991; Mizoguchi 1993; Barrett 1994, 109-31), symbolic-structural and phenomenological studies of ancient landscapes (eg. Tilley 1994; 1999, 177-238; Parker Pearson and Ramilisinona 1998), and increasingly sophisticated chronological and forensic analyses (eg. Ambers *et al.* 1999; Garwood 1999a; McKinley 1997).

The nature, condition and recovery of the evidence

An important concern, in this context, must be to evaluate the nature of the evidence from round barrow sites, and examine the extent to which our present knowledge reflects the relative occurrence and formal characteristics of the monuments built - and funerary rituals performed - in the past. These questions point to the need for two broad interlinked areas of analysis: first, to determine whether there have been systematic processes of preservation and/or destruction of round barrows; and, second, to determine whether previous fieldwork, artefact collection, and/or site-recording strategies have given rise to material biases or uneven spatial coverage of sites in the region.

Patterns of preservation and destruction in the round barrow evidence

Patterns of systematic destruction and/or obscuration of round barrow sites due to particular kinds of land-use or other practices have never been addressed seriously in Sussex, and very rarely elsewhere (*cf.* Peters 1999), although incidental observations are fairly common (eg. Grinsell 1940, 213; who notes the relationship between woodland areas and lower densities of round barrow sites). This subject really requires a major programme of research in its own right and it is only possible here to point to some areas of interest especially relevant to the Sussex evidence.

The impact of woodlands and plantations on monument survival is little understood. It is possible, for example, that the apparent rarity of small round barrows in the western half of the county is due to greater woodland coverage, with dense vegetation that has obscured the presence of low field monuments. Surviving barrows may still await discovery in these areas, potentially with well-preserved burial deposits given the lack of antiquarian attention. In this context, the presence of medieval deer parks may also prove to have been important in protecting prehistoric monuments from the destructive effects of medieval and post-medieval farming (Peters 1999). There were a large number of deer parks on the Chichester Downs, very few on the chalklands further east (Brandon and Short 1990, fig.2.5). However, the creation of woodland plantations in the 19th and 20th centuries, which must have resulted in widespread damage to prehistoric sites, was *also* most common on the West Sussex downlands. Further research is clearly required to resolve these issues.

The most striking process of monument destruction would appear at first sight to have been caused by the expansion and intensification of large-scale arable farming on the Sussex Downs since the Second World War, which has resulted in the truncation or severe erosion of most of the standing barrows recorded by Grinsell in the 1930s (*compare* Grinsell 1934, 1940; with more recent site descriptions in the East and West Sussex County Sites and Monuments Records). Earlier patterns of agricultural activity, however, may have been just as damaging, particularly in areas such as the coastal plain where continuous intensive horticulture and arable farming since the early Middle Ages may have truncated entire prehistoric landscapes long before there was any interest in the recording of ancient monuments (*cf.* Peters 1999). It is unlikely that the ring ditches excavated recently at Westhampnett were isolated examples (Fitzpatrick 1997, 10-12; A. Fitzpatrick pers. comm.; J. Kenny pers. comm.).

The impact of urban development on monument survival is also difficult to assess. In the case of Brighton and Hove, the very small number of round barrows on site distribution maps may be a reflection of rare prehistoric activity, but is more likely to be a consequence of 18th-and 19th-century destruction as these towns expanded rapidly into their rural hinterlands. There is enough circumstantial evidence from places in the Brighton conurbation such as Church Hill, Whitehawk, Hollingbury and the Ditchling Road (eg. Grinsell 1940, 210-11; Holleyman and Yeates 1960), to suggest that the latter explanation is most convincing. While there may still be opportunities to improve our understanding of monuments in the pre-urban landscapes of Sussex, as the ring ditches observed during salvage excavations in back gardens of town houses in Rottingdean (Bell 1974) and Lewes (Allen 1986) demonstrate (with implications for the identification of possible prehistoric sites in planning contexts), we have to recognize that we are faced with a permanent bias in the evidence.

In this context the fate of flint cairns in Sussex is especially instructive. As Reverend Henry Smith noted in 1870, barrows with flint-built mounds had already suffered significant and disproportionate damage: "for a length of time ... resorted to by builders and road makers and repairers" (Smith 1870, 62). A repetitive refrain in early accounts is the discovery of urns by labourers 'digging for flint' (eg. Anon. 1854a, Cooper 1879, Anon. 1888). The removal of just half of the Looe's Barn tumulus at Saltdean provided 150 tons of flint for road-building (Holgate 1987a). This activity occurred on the fringes of built-up areas of all scales, Alfriston as well as Brighton, though mostly concentrated around major towns and along roads that cross the Downs. It is evident, therefore, that one round barrow category, once very common, was selectively targeted for demolition as a source of building material and thus widely eradicated as far as modern study is concerned. The few cairn sites that have been investigated using modern methods (at Steyning Round Hill, Ditchling Field, Looe's Barn, Black Patch Down 4, and Crowlink) suggest that most were free-standing structures built of surface flint, ditches being rare, and that funerary deposits were often placed on the old land surface or within the cairn fabric. By removing the cairn, flint diggers will often have destroyed *all* trace of such monuments.

The impact of antiquarian and early archaeological activity also deserves consideration. Recognizable patterns of destruction are again elusive, but there is enough to suggest that it has been both extensive and in some areas persistent and extremely damaging. On Firle Downs, Reverend Smith (1870, 66) observed that: "Even in modern days, to say nothing of the rifling they may have received in times long gone bye, I can trace the work of several parties of explorers... Hence many barrows have been dug through, and all that can be now learned of the result of such diggings is that several urns were found of a rude character". This was a common complaint among archaeologists in the 19th century, and similar comments are found repeatedly in more recent excavation reports (e.g. Butler 1995). It may well be the case that the best-preserved burials will now be found at sites truncated or otherwise obscured before 1800, and in areas that have attracted little fieldwork.

The archaeological investigation of round barrows in Sussex

It is possible to describe the spatial coverage of patterns of fieldwork and site recording, and methods of site investigation and data collection, with a higher degree of confidence. This is based on a review of all published round barrow excavations in Sussex (since the earliest recorded example in 1763), evaluation of the research aims and field recording methodologies, and mapping of the sites investigated (*see* Appendix 1; and Figure 1). This allows, at the very least, for an assessment of potential biases in our knowledge of general material distributions and particular site categories. These aspects are discussed in more detail in the following section.

There is a general impression that the number of round barrows investigated in Sussex is small and that we know relatively little about them. This is misleading: in fact, there is information of varying quality from more than 130 sites. Of these, some 46 have been excavated to a modern standard, of which about 30 were totally or substantially excavated to reveal site plans and/or major structural features (the

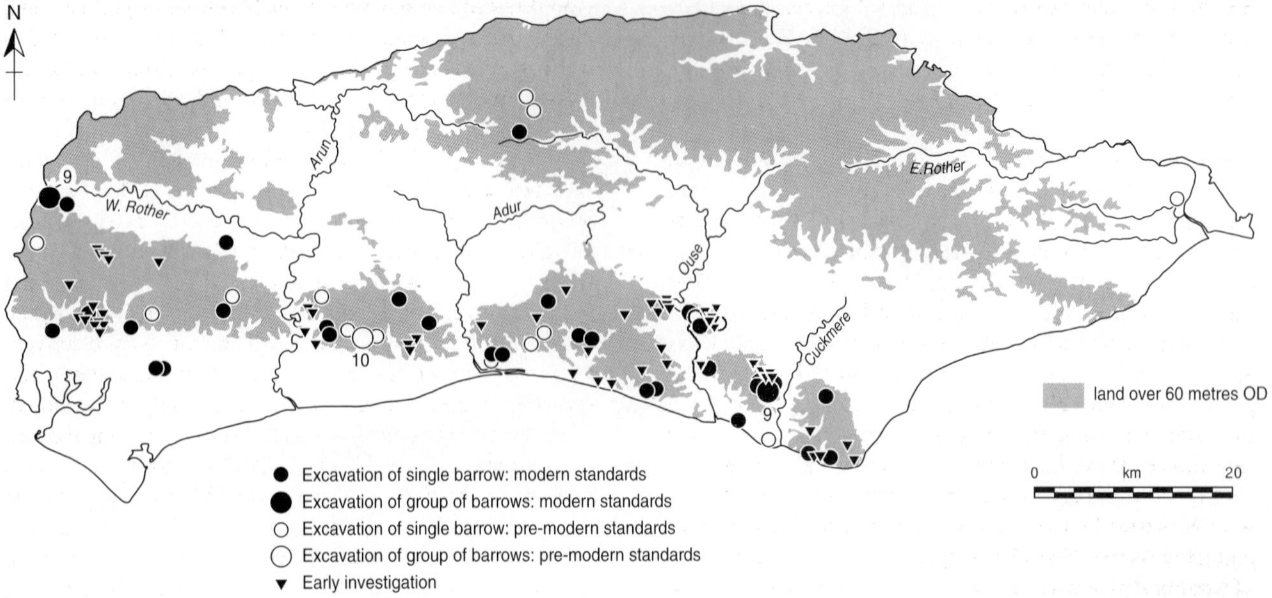

Figure 5.1. *Distribution of round barrow investigations in Sussex, 1763-2000.*

remainder attracted less than 10% sampling or evaluation). A further 25 sites have been excavated to 'pre-modern standards' (ie. with some attempt at systematic description, many with plans and/or section drawings, but limited context recording and simplistic stratigraphic analysis), of which about half were totally or largely excavated. The quality of recording and analysis of these sites varies from the very good, such as Colonel Lane Fox's excavation of Black Burgh in 1872 (Lane Fox 1877a) (which put most subsequent excavations to shame until the 1960s), through the moderately well-recorded such as Pull's excavations at Black Patch Hill in the 1920s, to poorly excavated and barely understood examples such as the site excavated by Spokes in 1930 on Cliffe Hill at Lewes (Spokes 1932). There are also records for a further 60 to 70 sites that can be accurately located (at least to the nearest 100 metres), derived from antiquarian investigations or from salvage excavations where recording was severely constrained or simply poor. Although these sites were usually trenched or haphazardly ransacked, surviving records often provide clear descriptions of artefact recovery, burial contexts and/or structural details.

The most striking feature of this history of investigation, as a glance at the distribution map of excavated sites shows (Fig. 5.1), is the consistent fieldwork emphasis on the central and east Sussex chalk downlands. There has been one major excavation project on the West Sussex Greensand at West Heath (Drewett 1976, 1985, 1989), but only one barrow site has been extensively excavated in the Chichester downland region to the west of the Arun (at Lavant), only four investigated (to any standard) in the whole of the High Weald (Money Mound, Shepherdsfield, Black Hill and Playden), and only two excavated on the coastal plain (at Westhampnett). This pattern of past fieldwork clearly restricts any attempt to interpret the spatial organization of Late Neolithic and Bronze Age society based *only* on distributions of excavated sites and artefacts. This must have a bearing on our overall appreciation of monumentalism, ritual practices and focal areas of socio-political organization in Sussex in this period.

The prehistoric round barrows of Sussex: a review of the evidence

Although there have been several interpretative syntheses of the evidence from round barrows in Sussex (eg. Curwen 1954; Ellison 1978; Drewett *et al.* 1988, 79-85; Field 1998), there has been no recent review of the evidence itself. In many respects this will inevitably still be based on the pioneering work of Leslie Grinsell, whose extraordinarily diligent efforts in recording barrow sites in the field and collating all available data from previous studies, resulted in a series of papers that remain our primary source of information (Grinsell 1934, 1940, 1941). These were later supplemented by a useful review of the ceramic evidence by Musson (1954). Site discoveries and excavations since 1940 have not been evaluated in a detailed manner, though site information is available in summary form in the East and West Sussex County Sites and Monuments Records.

Round barrow numbers and overall spatial distribution

There are about 1000 prehistoric round barrows and ring ditches recorded in Sussex. What proportion of the original number of barrows this figure represents is unknown, but many sites have certainly been destroyed and there may be hundreds more awaiting discovery. The spatial densities of known barrows (*see* Fig. 5.2) suggest that each of the downland blocks have roughly similar concentrations (though this need not imply parallel sequences in the frequency of barrow construction over time). It is important to note that the distribution of sites in Sussex shown in Figure 5.2 is based on current Sites and Monuments Records information, while the barrow densities shown for Dorset and Wiltshire, based on Grinsell's lists compiled in the 1940s - 60s and mapped by Fleming (1971), do not include recent additions and therefore show relatively lower concentrations than they should. Even so, it is very clear that prehistoric round barrow concentrations in Sussex, at this scale and measure of density,

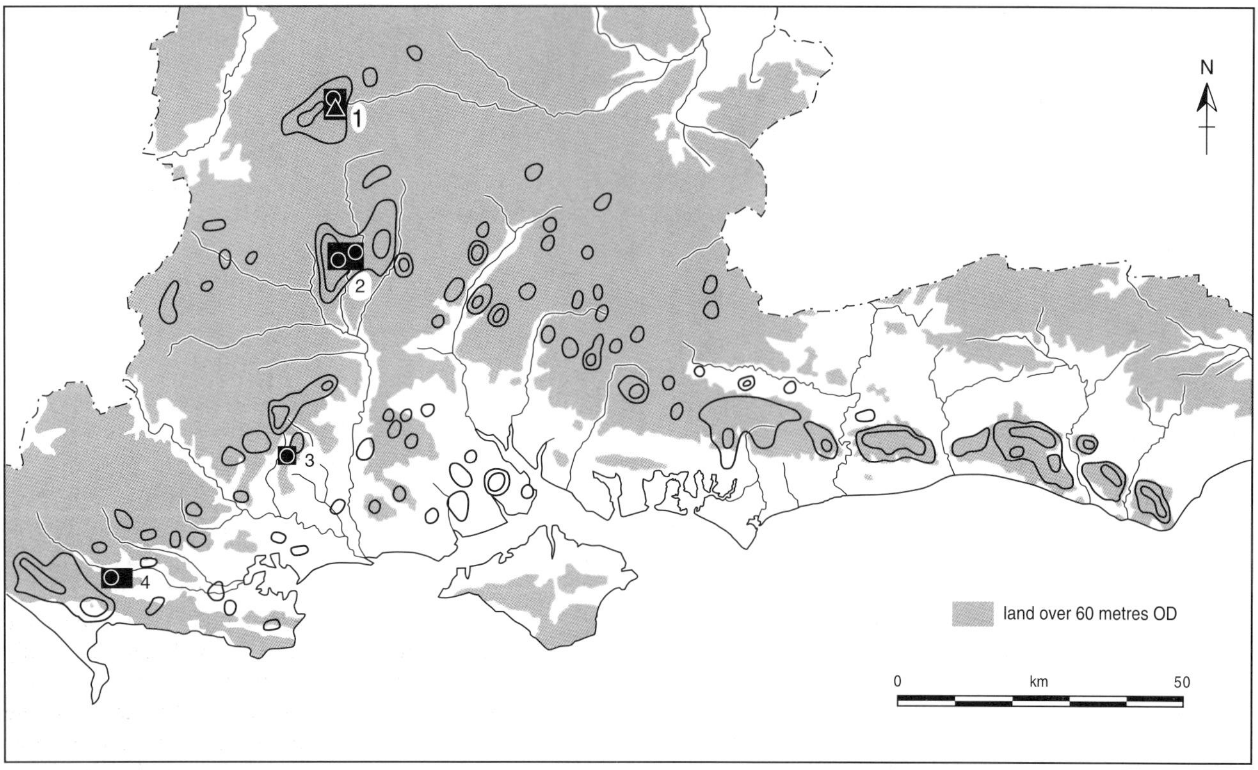

Figure 5.2. Densities of prehistoric round barrows in Sussex (after Grinsell 1940, Map III; and data from East and West Sussex Sites and Monuments Records), and Dorset, Wiltshire and Hampshire (after Fleming 1971, figs.1, 2; Cunliffe 1993, fig. 3.13). Contours at 2 and 5 barrows per km². Late Neolithic ceremonial centres in Wessex are numbered 1-4 and shown as black rectangles: 1. Avebury; 2. Stonehenge/ Durrington Walls; 3. Knowlton; 4. Mount Pleasant/Dorchester.

are similar to those in core areas of funerary monumentalism (and presumed centres of political power) in Wessex in the same period.

Grinsell estimated that over 90% of barrows were constructed on the chalklands (1934, 217; 1940, Map III), a figure which still applies. Many of these are concentrated along the top of the downland escarpment: "all along the ridgeway, at intervals of never more than a few hundred yards, are an enormous number of barrows" (Grinsell 1931, 33). In comparison, round barrows in the Weald are very rare except for clusters along the western Greensand ridge, and there are almost none on the coastal plain (Grinsell 1934, 217-18; 1940, 213-14). Future discoveries on the Greensand (*cf.* Johnson, in prep), on the coastal plain (*cf.* Bedwin 1983; Kenny 1989a; Fitzpatrick 1997, 10-13) and perhaps in the High Weald (*cf.* Tebbut 1974, Jones 1980) may demand some amendment of this pattern, but in general terms it is likely to remain substantially unchanged.

Round barrow types, construction, and chronology

Grinsell is also the key authority with regard to the identification of 'barrow types' based on mound form, especially as he was able to record the appearance of a number of barrows before they were destroyed by ploughing. He suggested that over 90% of Sussex sites were bowl barrows (Grinsell 1934, 221; 1940, 212), though many of these were already so eroded that this simple categorization may be questioned. The remainder consist of twelve bell barrows in West Sussex, about 30 flat-topped platform barrows, and fifteen ring barrows and pond barrows but no certain examples of disc barrows (Grinsell 1934, 224-27). Plough-eroded sites and ring-ditches cannot be categorized using these terms (which may in any case be unrelated to the monument classifications used by the mound-builders). The absolute dating of structural features and burials in Sussex is extremely poor (*see* Appendix 2 for a full list of radiocarbon dates).

Surprisingly, given the number of sites investigated in Sussex, detailed information concerning mound structures is limited and extremely diverse. While virtually the full range of mound and ditch forms, building methods, materials and structural features that are known in Wessex are also present in Sussex, there is no measure of their relative occurrence. Small single-phase mounds, for example, have a variety of constructional forms and clearly belong to several different funerary traditions at different times in the Late Neolithic and Bronze Age. The distinctive penannular-ditched site with an early Beaker inhumation burial at Pyecombe (Butler 1991) has little in common with the simple turf-stack mound at Minsted (Drewett 1975b), or the chalk-built barrow with a central cremation and urn burial at Duncton Down (Patchett 1938). On the other hand, several large single-phase mounds were probably designed to have the same dome-shaped appearance and berm between mound and ditch (eg. the Devil's Jumps at Treyford), with similarly elaborate architectural features such as chalk envelopes (eg. Bow Hill 2; Grinsell 1941, 115-21). These grandiose edifices, all in West Sussex, would appear to be classic Wessex-style 'bell-barrows' of the 19th - 16th centuries BC.

The diverse kinds of flint cairn construction recorded in Sussex highlight the problems in using building materials as criteria for monument classification. Flint cairns are found in a range of forms and sizes, and it is clearly not justifiable to categorize the Loasden platform cairn (Curwen and Curwen 1922), the large Looe's Barn tumulus (Holgate 1987a), and the tiny Ditchling Field cairn (Holleyman and Yeates 1960, 133-6), as the same monument 'type' simply because they were all built of flint - their social significance and ritual use were probably very different.

Turf-stack construction is especially well-represented in Sussex as a result of Peter Drewett's excavation of nine turf barrows: West Heath I-VI, VIII and IX (Drewett 1976, 1985), and Minsted (Drewett 1975b). In most cases these seem to have had simple dome-shaped turf mounds, in some cases with a ditch providing a yellow sand capping. The exception is West Heath III (phase 1) which consisted of a wood-revetted, drum-shaped turf platform rather than a domed mound as its surface appearance suggested (Drewett 1976, 132-4, pl.Va). This example again shows how eroded mound forms and building materials are not in themselves a basis for classification. Indeed, West Heath III, and other eroded mounds on the Greensand and on the Downs that once had flat tops, should be seen as the same monument type as 'platform barrows' (Grinsell 1934, 225-27; *cf.* Curwen and Curwen 1922): all designed to accommodate similar kinds of ritual practices on an elevated stage, and/or embody similar symbolic schemes or meanings (*cf.* Lynch 1993, 113-16).

Ring barrows would also appear to define a kind of bounded arena. These sites may be seen as one variant of a wider category of British Early Bronze Age ritual/funerary monuments consisting of low, circular, earth, flint or stone banks with no trace of central mounds, some with hollowed interior spaces or pavements. These are commonly described separately as pond barrows, ring barrows, and ring cairns. The evidence from Blackpatch Hill barrow 9 (Pull 1932, 80-2) and from Church Hill (Russell 1996, 29-30) is consistent with some of the evidence from pond barrow and ring cairn sites elsewhere in the country (*cf.* Barrett *et al.* 1991, 136-38; Lynch, 1993, 134-43), though formal human burials are absent. Classification of the anomalous site at Ladies Mile (Holleyman and Yeates 1960, 136-43), is especially problematic, but appears to have some features similar to those of platform mounds and ring/pond barrows, including a number of cremation and inhumation burials located in an arc around the western and southern edges of the 'bank' (*cf.* Winterbourne Steepleton in Dorset, Atkinson *et al.* 1951; and Radley Barrow Hills 4866 in Oxfordshire; Barclay and Halpin 1999, 115-28).

There is also some evidence in Sussex for 'cemetery barrows' of the 23rd-20th centuries BC. These were mounds which acted as foci for continuing funerary practices resulting in multiple burials, in some cases with free-standing timber structures and episodes of rebuilding or enlargement. Possible examples in Sussex include a mound excavated in the 19th century at Alfriston (Ade 1849; Smith 1870, 67-75), the Burgh barrow on Burpham Down (Curwen and Curwen 1922), and Black Patch Down 3 (Drewett 1982b, 352-3). These sites have features which can be compared with those of cemetery barrows in Wessex such as Amesbury 71 (Christie 1967), and in the East Midlands such as Barnack (Donaldson 1977). Timber structures at barrow sites in Sussex are exceptionally rare. Those recorded at Pyecombe, Itford Hill and Steyning Round Hill are different in character and date, and there are no examples of the concentric stake-or post-rings widely associated with cemetery barrows and other Early Bronze Age funerary monuments (eg. Britnell 1982; Donaldson 1977; Lynch 1993).

Cemetery barrows should not be confused with other multi-phase monuments which lack multiple burials, and where funerary events and associated episodes of mound-building or enlargement were widely separated in time, indicating monument re-use, appropriation or enhancement rather than continuous ritual activity. Again, there are very few well-recorded multi-phase monuments of this kind in Sussex, though examples include West Heath III and possibly West Heath VII (Drewett 1976, 132-34; 1985, 42-3), and Lavant ring ditch (D. Turner 1997; J. Kenny pers. comm.). Descriptions by early investigators suggest that they had sometimes encountered multi-phase monuments without any real understanding of the evidence (eg. at Belle Tout; Giddy 1814). Finally, there is plenty of evidence for secondary funerary activity at round barrow sites without recognizable structural additions to the existing monuments, in many cases probably centuries after the original mounds were built. Examples include the secondary urn burials at West Harting Down (West Sussex SMR 0147), at Heyshott Down barrow 10 (Lewis 1960, 15), and the cremation urn cemetery at Steyning Round Hill (Burstow 1958).

Round barrow groups

At a larger scale of analysis, West Heath is an extremely rare instance in Britain of the almost total recent excavation of a large round barrow group (Drewett 1976, 1985; Drewett *et al.* 1988, 80-3), comparable only with Snail Down (Thomas and Thomas 1955) and Shrewton in Wiltshire (Green and Rollo-Smith 1984), and Radley Barrow Hills in Oxfordshire (Barclay and Halpin 1999). Unfortunately, the chronology of the development of the West Heath monument complex remains uncertain: most of the mounds were robbed, and/or extensively disturbed by animals, artefacts were rare, only two barrows have datable funerary contexts (Barrows VI and VII), and the radiocarbon dates are imprecise. Another extensively excavated barrow group in Sussex, at Blackpatch Hill, is very difficult to reassess as the dating evidence is again limited and the contextual recording sometimes poor. Moreover, the excavator, J.H.Pull, left no scale plans of the barrow group; the two sketch maps available indicate slightly different relative locations (Pull 1932, pl.3; Pull unpubl. ms.; Martyn Barber pers. comm.) and neither conform to the distances between barrows noted in the published text.

Linear groups of large round barrows, which are especially characteristic of Early Bronze Age funerary monument complexes of Wiltshire and Dorset, are not common in Sussex, though three impressive groups can still be seen: at Heyshott and Treyford on the top of the downland escarpment to the west of the river Arun (with ten and seven mounds respectively, mostly unexcavated); and on Duncton Common on the Greensand to the north (with ten mounds, all unexcavated).

Burial contexts, grave assemblages and chronology

The widely-held perception that Late Neolithic and Bronze Age burial assemblages in Sussex were impoverished in comparison with those of Wessex is open to question. Although the evidence is certainly poor in terms of the quality of contextual information and occurrence of valuable or rare artefacts, this does not necessarily mean that the material culture of prehistoric societies in Sussex was also impoverished: it may be a reflection of antiquarian looting and recent patterns of fieldwork. Alternatively, it is possible that the rarity of fine grave goods was due to practices in the Sussex region which - in the context of particular social ideals, value systems and networks of prestige goods exchange - favoured circulation and/or re-cycling of fine objects as a symbolic strategy rather than funerary deposition (*cf.* Needham 1993), leaving little for the archaeologist to recover.

In terms of general distributions, it is possible to describe the funerary evidence according to a tripartite chronological ordering of grave assemblages and artefact types.

2500-2100 BC (Fig. 5.3). A number of early Beaker inhumation graves have been found on the fringes of the central Sussex chalklands around Brighton: at Pyecombe, Devil's Dyke, Heathy Brow, Slonk Hill and Shoreham; with two more at Cissbury, one at Burpham and possibly one at Selsey. This suggests an early concentration of Beaker burials, though future discoveries may affect this distribution.

2150-1750 BC (Fig. 5.3). The spatial emphasis on central Sussex is also evident in distributions of later Beaker, Food Vessel, Biconical Urn and Early Bronze Age complex burials. This pattern was noted by Curwen (1954, 148) with regard to Beakers: "It is a curious thing that all the known specimens come from the area between the Arun and Ouse", and was re-emphasized more recently in Drewett's identification of a concentration of Bronze Age rich graves in this area (Drewett *et al.* 1988, 84, fig.3.7).

1800-1200 BC (Fig. 5.4). In the latter part of the Early Bronze Age and in the Middle Bronze Age wider, if variable, distributions of Collared Urns and other burial types (including complex burials) are evident. Examples of Middle Bronze Age 'Deverel-Rimbury' and other cremation urns are rare: a few single burials and two definite cemeteries, at Steyning Round Hill and Itford Hill.

Unfortunately, the contextual information that should accompany this large-scale distribution is poor, especially for earlier funerary traditions. Figure 5.5 shows plans of all seven early inhumation graves in Sussex with datable assemblages and known layout and orientation: at Pyecombe (Butler 1991), Heathy Brow (Curwen 1932a), Shoreham (Witten 1978), Ditchling Road (Anon 1922), Racton Park Farm (Kenny 1989b), Black Burgh (Lane Fox 1877a), and Chanctonbury Hill (Ratcliffe-Densham 1968). The illustrations are organised chronologically from top left (earlier) to bottom right (later), spanning the period *c.*2500 to 1500 BC. It should be noted that nos 2 to 4 are schematic reconstructions based solely on textual information. There is little room here for a comparative analysis of burial practices.

The Pyecombe burial has a classic early Beaker grave assemblage datable to the period *c.*2500-2200 BC and consists of a Wessex/Middle Rhine beaker (*contra* Butler 1991, who describes the Beaker as an East Anglian type), a wristguard and a copper dagger with a bone pommel.

The Heathy Brow, Shoreham and Ditchling Road reconstructed examples are all Beaker graves, all with relatively early Wessex-Middle Rhine/ East Anglian style Beakers. The Racton Park Farm burial, which is not yet fully published, consists of an inhumation with a probable early

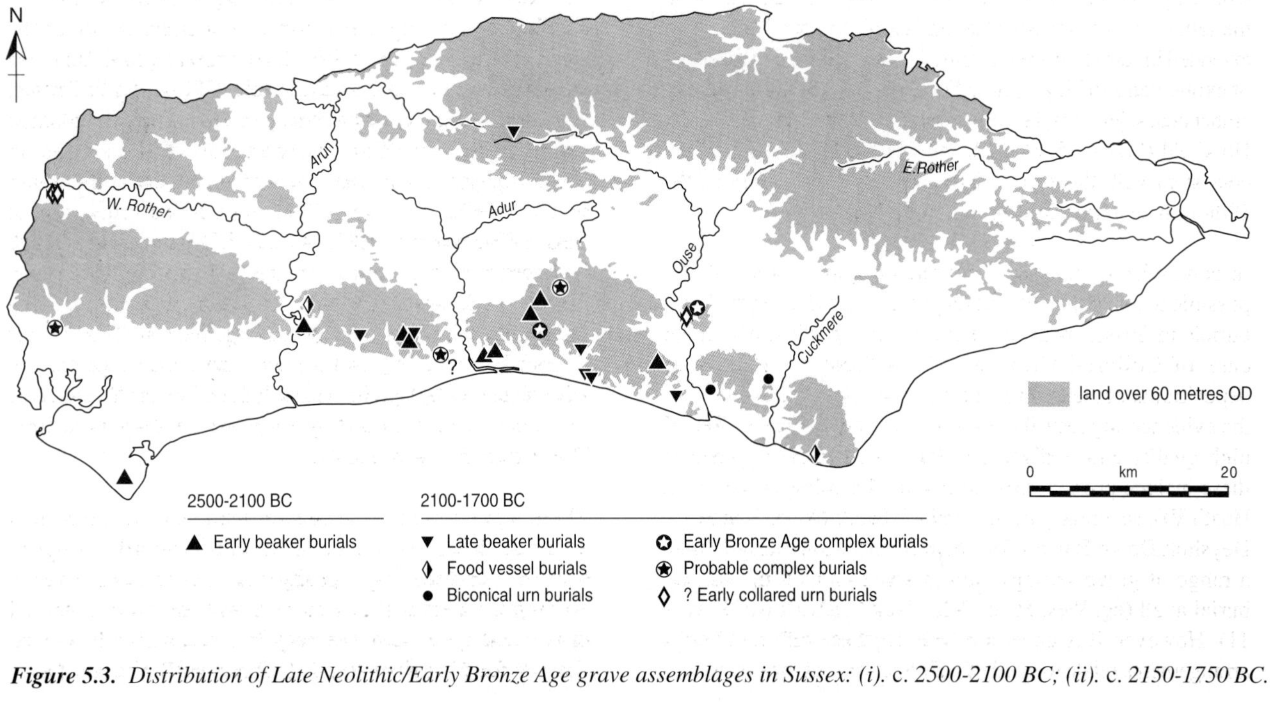

***Figure 5.3.** Distribution of Late Neolithic/Early Bronze Age grave assemblages in Sussex: (i).* c. *2500-2100 BC; (ii).* c. *2150-1750 BC.*

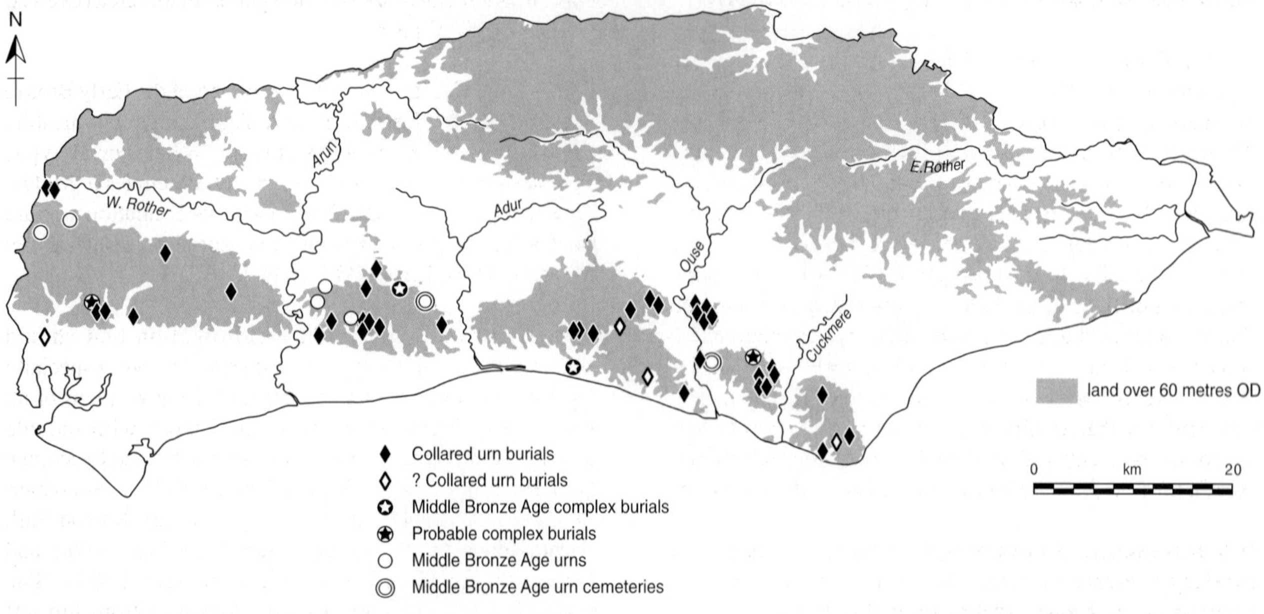

Figure 5.4. *Distribution of later Early Bronze Age and Middle Bronze Age grave assemblages in Sussex,* c. *1800-1000 BC.*

rivetted dagger, the precise depositional context of which is uncertain but certainly close to the chest. The last two graves can be reconstructed from good textual descriptions and general site plans which show the burial deposits. The Black Burgh assemblage, excavated by Colonel Lane Fox (later General Pitt Rivers), consists of a flat riveted knife dagger, a miniature vessel, a bronze awl and some 50 disc-shaped jet or shale beads, datable to the period c.2000-1800 BC. The Chanctonbury burial consists of an inhumation with a mid- to late Wessex Snowshill dagger datable to the period *c.*1800-1500 BC.

Reconstructions of the Oxteddle Down rich grave, which was excavated in 1819, are far less certain. Horsfield's drawing shows two inverted Collared Urns over cremations, between which lay an extended inhumation. Although it is possible that the latter was an intrusive Saxon burial, the combination of extended inhumation, cremations, Collared Urns, and the range of exotic items in Urn 2 (including a conical jet button, jet and amber beads, jet rings, bronze finger ring and a faience pendant: Horsfield 1824, 47-8, pl.V.22; Curwen 1954, 157-8, fig.42), is consistent with the early Wessex rich grave tradition of the 19th-18th centuries BC (*cf.* Needham 1996, 130-2).

In comparison with early inhumation graves, it should be possible to investigate the ritual practices associated with urn burials in Sussex with more confidence, particularly in the case of Collared Urns for which there are details of depositional contexts in some 50 cases. An initial review of the evidence suggests that the contextual evidence is often of high quality and is diverse in terms of funerary practices: these include primary urn burials (eg. Ditchling Road; West Heath VI), secondary burials (Black Patch Down Barrow 7; Heyshott Down Barrow 10), both inverted and upright urns, a range of grave settings, and in some cases urns with no burial at all (eg. West Heath VI; Black Patch Down Barrow 11). However, it is uncertain whether these different burial arrangements relate to symbolic distinctions (eg. age or gender categories) or to change over time. The analysis of cremated bone deposits is too patchy to identify specific bio-social or status distinctions, and the dating evidence is too limited and unreliable to attempt a chronological analysis for Sussex alone.

The last burial to consider, found during demolition of the Hove barrow in 1857, is difficult to interpret because of its unique character and the poor quality of surviving records. This consisted of a probable inhumation in a timber coffin accompanied by the finest grave assemblage found in Sussex: an amber cup, Scandinavian stone battle axe, perforated whetstone pendant, and bronze dagger (Phillips 1857; Curwen and Curwen 1924; D V Clarke *et al.* 1985, 277, illus. 4.45). The radiocarbon date, artefact types and grave form are all consistent with a Middle Bronze Age date in the late 16th or 15th centuries BC, but the social significance of the site remains elusive, especially given the unusual nature of the grave assemblage, the coffin, huge mound (published size estimates are inconsistent: *cf.* Grinsell 1941, 43, fig.2; Curwen 1954, 153), and lack of knowledge concerning its landscape setting. The prevailing interpretation of the site as an especially significant elite funerary monument at the centre of a Middle Bronze Age polity that extended across central Sussex (Drewett *et al.* 1988, 84-6, fig.3.7) is appealing, though it is worth noting that other rich graves of this period certainly existed in Sussex, including a burial with a bulb-headed bronze pin and miniature cup in a large barrow at Firle Point (Horsfield 1824, 48), and a grave containing a perforated whetstone pendant (an item usually found in late Wessex rich grave contexts) disturbed by early barrow diggers in Bow Hill barrow 3 (Anon. 1854a).

This brief review of key aspects of the Sussex round barrow evidence shows that we are faced with extremely complex, diverse, sometimes high quality material evidence. Even at an empirical level it is apparent that the wide range of monument types and funerary traditions should not be characterized in unitary terms. As Reverend Smith noted over

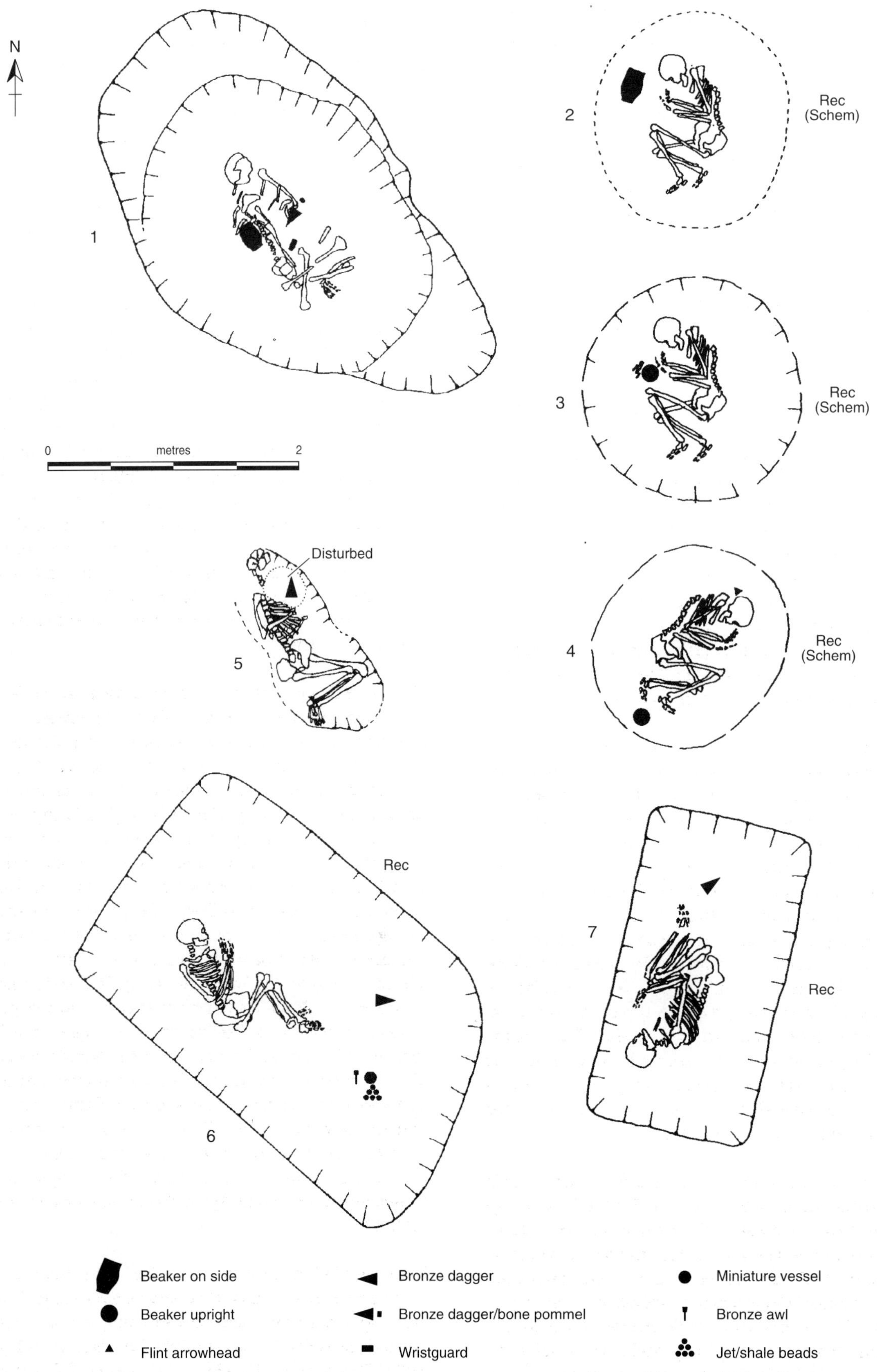

Figure 5.5. *Plans of inhumation graves in Sussex with datable artefact assemblages of the period* c. *2500-1500 BC: 1. Pyecombe; 2. Heathy Brow; 3. Shoreham; 4. Ditchling Road; 5. Racton Park Farm; 6. Black Burgh; 7. Chanctonbury Hill.*

a century ago: 'It is very remarkable that in opening barrows hardly any two are found to correspond in their contents, or in the apparent purpose of their formation' (Smith 1870, 59-60). Rather than trying to deny this variation by assuming that round barrows represent a simple burial function undifferentiated in space or time, except for some superficial cultural 'gloss', we should recognize that many different kinds of funerary monumentalism and practice existed, which changed over time and which were subject to changing interpretations *in the past* as the socio-religious, aesthetic, and political contexts of mound-building and funerary ritual also changed (Garwood 1991).

Themes and representations in round barrow studies in the 19th and 20th centuries

General interpretations of the Bronze Age in Sussex have changed markedly since the early 19th century as prevailing explanatory models have been successively replaced, each having very different aims, methodologies and interpretations. An evaluation of past interpretative approaches is directly relevant to current round barrow studies because the 'facts' that we have inherited, and still use, cannot be separated from the intellectual conditions in which they were produced, or the particular agendas of past workers. However, to examine this knowledge-base critically is no easy matter: we are faced with a kind of intellectual stratigraphy which has undergone much reworking and re-deposition, leaving an interwoven accumulation of evidence and interpretations.

To some extent, the paradigm shifts that have taken place in archaeology in the last two centuries have embodied an oscillation between Romanticism and Rationalism in the way that the search for the past was conducted, interpretations arrived at, and sentiments attached to the past worlds thus produced (*cf.* Sherratt 1997). The romantic and rather melancholic images of ancient heroes, long dead ancestors and ruinous tumuli found in Horsfield's *History of Lewes* (1824), are typical of the elite aesthetics and cultural historicism of the early 19th-century. This contrasts with the rationalism and objectivism of British archaeology in the late 19th-century, which encouraged a style of precise observation and cautious empirical interpretation. Colonel Lane Fox is an exemplary figure: eagerly pursuing his quasi-scientific investigations at Black Burgh (1877a), fully conversant with the aims and agendas of the scientific 'revolution', social Darwinism and the Three Age system.

From the 1920s there was a strong revival of Romanticism in general evocations of prehistoric *zeitgeist*: the Bronze Age as 'a realm of kings and warriors' (for example: Ashbee 1960, 172), and in narratives of 'folk' diffusions and invasions that drew upon richly detailed material culture descriptions and (extremely dubious) characterizations of ethno-racial 'types'. Curwen's (1954) interpretation of the Bronze Age in Sussex typifies this 'culture history' approach: he explains the appearance of Beaker burials, for example, in terms of an intrusive folk migration, and appeals to ethno-racial stereotypes in the way Beakers are seen to provide "a respectable antiquity for the *Teutonic* habit of beer drinking" (Curwen 1954, 150: my emphasis). This is characteristic of culture historical imagery; it was not just an invasion of Beaker people, but an invasion of 'German' Beaker people (a view of Beakers which has long since been discredited: *cf.* Lanting and van der Waals 1972; Burgess 1980, 62-8).

The rejection of culture history by exponents of 'processual archaeology' in the 1960s brought about a revolution in British archaeology. Processual archaeology involved a new 'scientific' approach to fieldwork and analysis in the form of systematic recording systems, sampling strategies, and hypothetico-deductive reasoning. This was accompanied by new interpretative models rooted in neo-evolutionary theories of cultural adaptation and systemic explanations of social behaviour in particular environmental settings (discussed in more detail below). This profoundly influenced fieldwork on prehistoric sites in Sussex, first marked by the excellent quality of excavation and recording undertaken by the Sussex Archaeological Field Unit (eg. Drewett 1975a, 1975b, 1976), and later by detailed landscape studies (eg. Drewett 1982a, 1982b). It is evident, however, that culture history ideas persisted in general interpretations: Ellison's (1978, 30-6) discussion of the Early Bronze Age still used a migration argument to explain the appearance of Beakers, and relied on limited artefactual evidence to 'describe' the period while monuments were barely considered - implying that barrows with little in them had very little 'to say'. This contrasts with the far more lengthy treatment of the Later Bronze Age settlement evidence.

The most striking contribution of processual archaeology to interpretations of Late Neolithic and Early Bronze Age society in Sussex is Drewett's model of prehistoric social systems in south-east England (Drewett *et al.* 1988, fig. 3.8). This provides an abstract view of cultural life as an integrated functioning system (Fig. 5.6). Although this approach is theoretically and analytically coherent as a means of explanation, it marginalizes human agency; people acting in knowledgeable ways are invisible, lost in the workings of the model (*cf.* Shanks and Tilley 1987, 51-4). This style of description also tends to be ahistorical and chronologically imprecise, in this case compressing 1500 years of cultural life into one systemic form. This image is at odds with the evidence for cultural diversity and change now recognized in round barrow sites. The model is also questionable in representational terms. Most of the symbols and lines on the diagram, apart from those denoting round barrows, represent things for which there is almost no direct evidence, but which are necessary to the model given *a priori* assumptions about the nature of social life in the period (such as non-existent ceremonial enclosures; Wolstonbury, for example, is now known to be Late Bronze Age in date; Hamilton and Manley 1997, 95-7).

Since the 1980s there has been another shift in interpretative paradigms, evident in post-Processual interests in prehistoric mentalities, material culture and meaning, social structures and their reproduction, and so forth (*see*: Shanks and Tilley 1987; Tilley 1994; Hodder *et al.* 1995). Of particular significance for understanding Late Neolithic and Bronze Age funerary monuments in Sussex are new approaches to the study of prehistoric cultural landscapes.

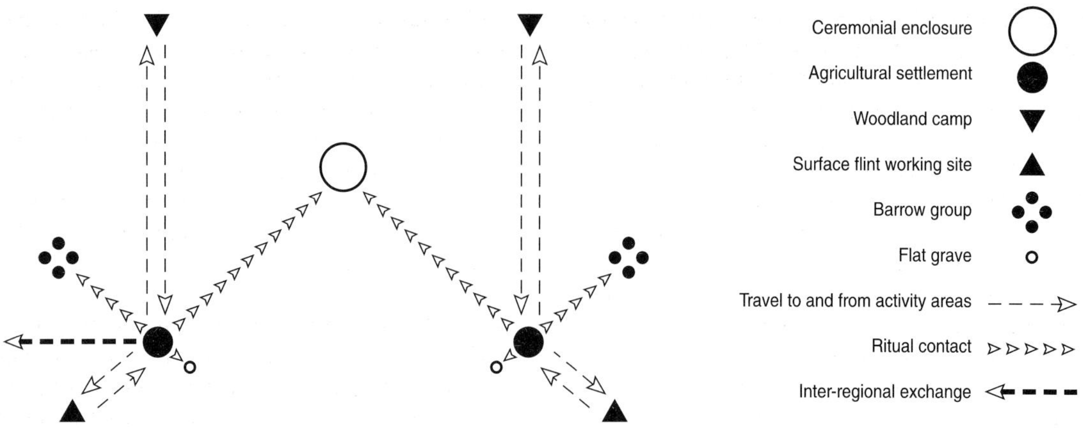

Figure 5.6. Systemic model of Late Neolithic/Early Bronze Age society in southern England proposed by Drewett for the period c. *3000-1500 BC (after Drewett* et al. *1988, fig.3.8).*

Round barrows in the cultural landscapes of the Bronze Age

Interpretations of ancient landscapes in processual archaeology assume that the functioning of social systems is adapted to particular geographical settings and organised *spatially* in ways which structurally integrate economic strategies, settlement patterns and socio-political and religious practices. Landscape is envisaged as a kind of two-dimensional canvas on which the workings of past societies were painted, leaving layered residues to be disentangled and reconstructed in terms of patterns of behaviour and social organization. Influential examples of this approach in British Late Neolithic and Bronze Age studies, by Fleming (1971) and Renfrew (1973), define forms of social organization (segmentary tribes and chiefdoms respectively) based largely on the character and spatial distribution of ceremonial centres, round barrow concentrations, and rich graves. These material categories and interpretative themes are clearly central to Drewett's model of a rich grave concentration and chiefly polity in the central downland area of Sussex (Drewett *et al.* 1988, 84, fig.3.7).

Although symbolic-structural studies of ancient landscapes (eg. Darvill 1997, Field 1998) have very different interpretative assumptions and objectives (ie. to explore the meanings invested in cultural landscapes), they share the same methodological concern with spatial patterns in the material evidence. Whether a processual or post-processual framework for study is adopted, it is necessary to delineate the spatial articulation and practical/symbolic relationships of different site categories and kinds of social behaviour, and to demonstrate the temporal coherence of the patterns that are recognized.

Ceremonial monuments and cultural landscapes: the question of 'henges'

In this context, the identification of several henges or 'ceremonial enclosures' in Sussex by Russell (1996, 1997), deserves particular critical evaluation. This is important to round barrow studies in Sussex for two reasons: first, Russell argues that at least some if not all the proposed henges were being used - and possibly built - in what would otherwise be called the Early Bronze Age, and were thus part of the contemporary cultural landscape dominated by round barrows; second, even if these sites were not in contemporary use, their presence alone would still be significant because of the way that round barrows are increasingly understood in the context of particular landscape settings in which monuments already ancient, such as long barrows, causewayed enclosures and henges, were a visible and meaningful element (Garwood 1991).

While it is easy to agree with the spirit of enquiry, the interpretations on offer and the analytical premises involved are questionable. In many respects Russell's argument draws upon Clare's (1986, 1987) extension of Late Neolithic henge categories to encompass a wider range of 'ceremonial sites' within one classificatory scheme and framework of interpretation, including distinctive Early Bronze Age structures such as stake rings at round barrow sites. The systematic integration and comparison of such diverse site types, which have little in common in formal or depositional terms and which may be unrelated chronologically, is clearly flawed and was sharply criticized by Barclay (1989), but set a precedent for the critical evaluation of received categories and the creation of more 'open' monument typologies. Unfortunately, although the redefinition of Neolithic and Bronze Age site classifications is entirely valid in principle, it can all too easily become a polemical exercise involving a highly selective reading of the evidence to support a preferred *a priori* interpretation.

The six proposed Late Neolithic/Early Bronze Age ceremonial sites identified in Sussex (Russell 1997, 74-6), at Black Patch Hill barrow 9, Church Hill, Itford Hill, Wolstonbury, Cockhill, and Mile Oak, are in fact questionable in every case, and there is nothing to support the contention that, together, they formed a distinct component of the ceremonial landscape on the central Sussex downlands in this period.

At Black Patch Hill barrow 9 (Pull 1932, 80-2; Russell 1996, 28-9) the disarticulated skeletal remains and artefact assemblage, the absence of central burials, and the small circular enclosure, invite comparisons with Early Bronze Age pond barrows such as Winterbourne Steepleton and Down Farm rather than henges (Barrett *et al.* 1991, 136-38). The similar scale and form of the Church Hill site (Russell 1996, 29-30, Illus.13; the caption incorrectly refers to Black Patch Hill barrow 9), and the circular post settings, suggest a comparison with Snail Down pond barrow (Annable 1958). At Itford Hill (Holden 1972; Russell 1996), the weathered Beaker sherds in the shallow 'construction trench' and a post-hole provide a *terminus post quem* for activity at the site, but do not resolve the temporal relationship between the post circle and the Middle Bronze Age cemetery. This chronological ambiguity, the absence of structured deposits and the insubstantial form of the post circle must cast doubt on its interpretation as a Late Neolithic/Early Bronze Age 'ceremonial' site.

At Wolstonbury (Curwen 1930; Russell 1996, 34-5; Russell 1997, 74; Hamilton and Manley 1997, 95-7), radiocarbon dates and ceramic evidence now confirm that this is a *Late* Bronze Age hilltop enclosure. There appears to be nothing to indicate an earlier phase: a single Collared Urn sherd does not make this a 'henge'. At Cock Hill (Ratcliffe-Densham and Ratcliffe-Densham 1961; Russell 1996, 31), a large Middle Bronze Age pottery assemblage in the upper ditch fills, internal round houses, and the irregular enclosure shape, are all consistent with the original interpretation of the site as a Middle Bronze Age settlement. There is no evidence for an earlier ceremonial function. Finally, at Mile Oak (Russell 1997, 74; Russell 2000; D. Rudling pers. comm.), there is no evidence for Neolithic or Early Bronze Age artefact deposition, the ceramic assemblage is Middle Bronze Age in date, and radiocarbon dates from the primary ditch silts provide a *terminus post quem* for the silting of the enclosure ditch in the mid-2nd millennium BC: Mile Oak is a multi-phase Middle Bronze Age settlement site.

It is apparent that these sites, represented as a related group of Late Neolithic/Early Bronze Age ceremonial enclosures, in fact consist of two Early Bronze Age 'pond' or 'ring' barrows, a small timber structure of uncertain character and date, a Late Bronze Age 'hillfort', and two Middle Bronze Age settlements. Neither the identification of these sites as 'ceremonial enclosures', nor the spatial pattern proposed, stand up to scrutiny.

Lands of the living, domains of the dead: the large-scale organisation of the Bronze Age landscape

Another recent attempt to establish a large-scale spatial framework for understanding the round barrow evidence in Sussex is a symbolic-structural study by David Field (1998). This explains the chalkland distribution of funerary monuments in terms of the creation of a vast sacred landscape extending from Beachy Head to the Meon valley, in which activities were deliberately kept separate from areas of settlement and resource procurement on the coastal plain and in intervening river valleys (ie. well-watered, fertile and sheltered areas). Rather than a landscape of continuous settlement and associated clusters of round barrows, the downland escarpment is seen as a marginal and sacred domain forming a physical and spiritual boundary, but also a mediatory zone of transition, between the worlds of everyday social activity to the south, and the natural, 'wild' expanse of the Weald to the north (Field 1998, 314-21). The large separate clusters of round barrows on the Greensand to the north of the downs in West Sussex, in this context, are seen as more localized examples of the same kind of symbolic-structural zonation of sacred and profane practices; "we might imagine... a number of separate ritual landscapes set around the Greensand..., together with one long linear ritual landscape along the South Downs escarpment" (Field 1998, 321; *cf.* Tilley 1999, 177-238).

This interpretation of the structuring of the Late Neolithic and Early Bronze Age landscape has much to recommend it. The spatial and qualitative distinctions between geographical zones in Sussex in material culture terms are well-established, and the particular model suggested by Field is both plausible and well-supported by a wider review of the evidence from southern England. The discussion of archaeological and anthropological studies of sacred geographies also provides a strong theoretical and comparative basis for interpretation (Field 1998, 319-23). In addition, the argument follows a long-established tradition of study in British Neolithic and Bronze Age studies, having close similarities, for example, with Fleming's (1971) idea of Early Bronze Age ritual landscapes in upland areas of Wessex, central to the territories of transhumant pastoralists. The definition of symbolic oppositions and boundaries (rather than centrality in socio-religious organization) obviously draws upon more recent post-Processual theoretical perspectives (eg. Tilley 1994), and can be compared with other examples of the genre (eg. Richards 1996, Darvill 1997, Parker Pearson and Ramilisinona 1998).

It is apparent, however, that models of ancient sacred geographies run the risk of imposing static, synchronic schemes of reference on what may have been relatively dynamic and changing forms of social practice and cosmological representation (*cf.* Barth 1987; Garwood 1991). In addition, one sacred model need not represent the full range of beliefs and practices mapped out across the cultural landscapes of the period: far more complex, cross-cutting frames of social organization and traditions of ritual practice should be envisaged, as innumerable ethnographic studies demonstrate (eg. Parkin 1991). While this does not necessarily invalidate Field's model, it should raise questions about other sacralized spatial principles that may have been just as significant but very different in meaning and purpose. The striking arrays of funerary monuments on the top of the downland ridges, for example, may have been encountered in a directional lineal sequence *along* the escarpment, in the course of processions or pilgrimages, and approached as discrete ceremonial centres for particular ritual events. These forms of practice are not mutually-exclusive (though they may be separated socially and temporally).

Another issue to consider is the relationship between cultural process and meaning, and the constitution of ritual and monument-building traditions. The round barrows of the Sussex chalklands did not come into being overnight, but in the course of a thousand years of mound construction and changing funerary practices. The landscape of monuments interpreted in 2000 BC would not have been interpreted in the same way in 1700 BC, as the material and intellectual contexts of social engagement and cultural reference would have changed. There is no reason to believe that one model can be applied to the whole period in question, and every reason to explore how and when coherent sacred landscapes did come into being. To define the precise chronology and spatial articulation of the built structures in the landscape thus becomes especially important as a means of recognizing widely-shared architectural designs and practices that were consistent with some general cosmographic scheme.

These themes cannot, however, be addressed entirely at a large spatial scale. People visualize and experience landscape 'on the ground', in particular places which are endowed with specific meanings in specific social situations (Tilley 1994). While mapping can reveal material patterns, it provides no way of investigating how these patterns came to exist in the course of social practices, or as realizations of the beliefs which informed and motivated such practices. This suggests that symbolic-stuctural analysis should focus on the architectural settings from which landscapes were meant to be appreciated in specific ways, like round barrow monument complexes, and interpretations extended from these places to the landscape beyond.

Finally, as Field observes, there is a wider context in which sacred geographies make sense. They cannot be disengaged from the landscapes of routine everyday life and the demands of production, exchange and consumption; not only because they are spatially organized in relation to one another, but also because the religious and moral principles embodied in funerary monuments and ritual practices will have informed the values and beliefs of people in ordinary social situations. However, the contextualization of sacred landscapes should not be limited to economic activity (Field 1998); it should also take account of the structuring of power relations, which may have a direct bearing on the spatial organization and character of ritual practices and forms of monumentalism. The rich grave concentration identified in the area from the Adur valley to the Firle Downs, interpreted as the core area of an elite group, (Drewett *et al.* 1988, fig.3.7; *cf.* Figures 5.3, 5.4) implies a framework of spatial perception that transcended or manipulated the kinds of principles *ideally* built into sacred landscapes.

The socio-political organization of the cultural landscapes of the Late Neolithic and Bronze Age clearly deserves further evaluation. Besides the distribution of rich burials, it is also possible to map the distribution of round barrows according to mound sizes (based on Grinsell's measurements, calibrated using occasional re-measurements noted in Sites and Monuments Records). On this basis it is possible to identify the distribution of especially massive round barrows (greater than 200 and 500 cubic metres). The spatial distribution of these sites (Fig. 5.7) is instructive: even if the groups of large mounds along the western Greensand ridge - where light turf construction would be a relatively easy task - are excluded, the concentration of especially large monuments on the Chichester Downs is unmistakable. This distribution, of course, is not necessarily fully representative (the former presence of large cairns or mounds - now destroyed - in the vicinity of Brighton should be borne in mind), but there is no reason to doubt the absence of large monuments between the Arun and Adur, where prehistoric sites were reasonably well-preserved in Grinsell's day.

The identification of core areas of social and political organization in Sussex in the Early and Middle Bronze Age thus requires some revision. The rich grave concentration to the east of the Adur, and the concentration of large funerary monuments to the west of the Arun, with central foci some 40 kilometres apart (*see* Fig. 5.2), can be seen as different but equally impressive expressions of social power and cultural identity. This spatial pattern parallels the distribution of Late Neolithic ceremonial centres and Early Bronze Age barrow concentrations in Wessex, often interpreted as the

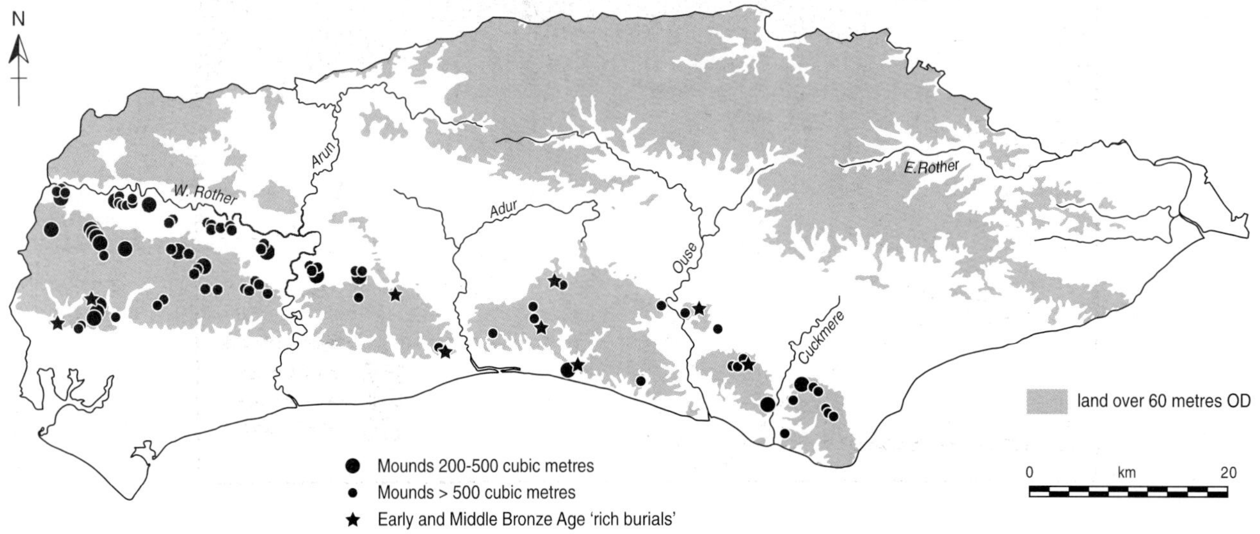

Figure 5.7. *Distribution of large round barrows in Sussex with mound volumes of more than 200 cubic metres and more than 500 cubic metres.*

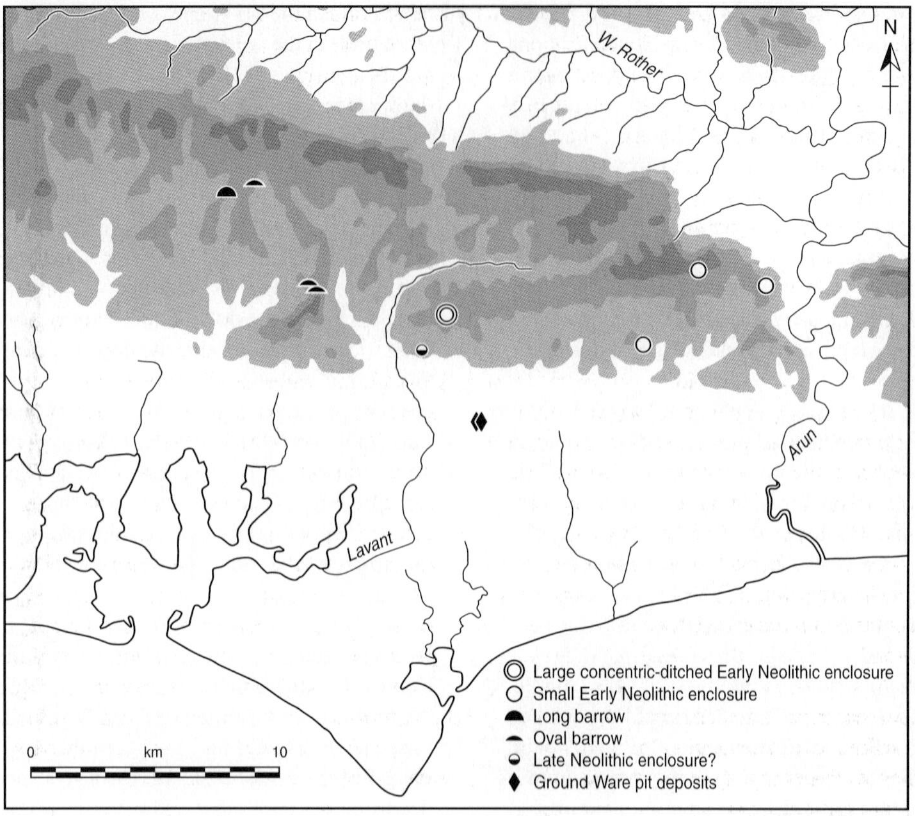

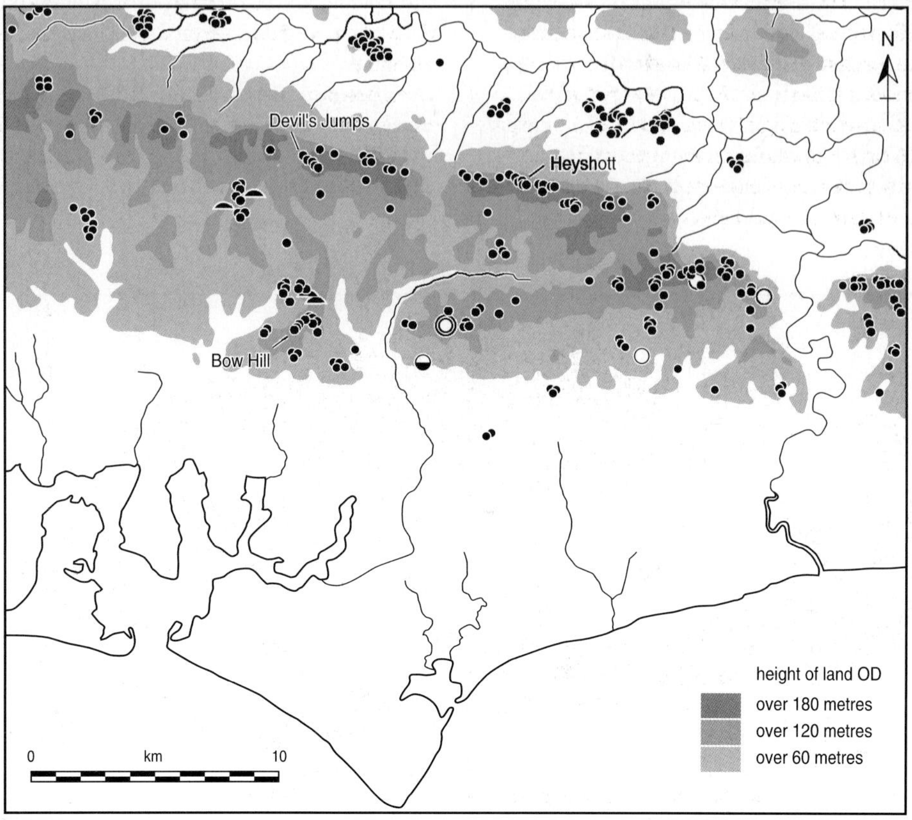

Figure 5.8 *(top). Distribution of Neolithic enclosures, funerary monuments and pit deposits in the Chichester region,* c. *4000-2500 BC.*
Figure 5.9 *(bottom). Distribution of Late Neolithic and Early and Middle Bronze Age round barrows in the Chichester region,* c. *2500-1000 BC.*

centres of chiefly polities (Renfrew 1973; *cf.* Cunliffe 1993, figs. 3.3, 3.13). It is also evident that, like the concentrations of monuments in Wessex, those in Sussex developed over a very long period of time from the early 4th millennium BC. The distribution of Early Neolithic enclosures and long mounds in Sussex indicates the existence of two regional groups of monuments centred on large multi-ditched enclosures, The Trundle and Whitehawk (Drewett, this volume). If this is compared with later concentrations of rich graves and large round barrows it would appear that this spatial pattern had very long-term significance, continuing through the Late Neolithic, Early Bronze Age, and into the Middle Bronze Age.

In this context, the development of the cultural landscape on the Chichester Downs and the coastal plain to the south is especially interesting. In the Early Neolithic (Fig. 5.8) there is a broad spatial division between small enclosures to the east of the Lavant, and long and oval mounds to the west, suggesting different zones of practice. The Trundle enclosure is situated between these zones in a high central location overlooking the Lavant valley and the coastal plain. It was precisely in this area, just to the south-west of The Trundle, that a probable Late Neolithic enclosure with a continuous beaded ditch was later built, with deer antlers arrayed around the base of the ditch (D. Turner 1997; J. Kenny pers. comm.). Further south, two Grooved Ware deposits in pits at Westhampnett Area 4 (A. Fitzpatrick pers. comm.) suggest ritual activity on the coastal plain. Although this evidence is limited, it may be no coincidence that the first good evidence for Late Neolithic monument-building and ritual practices in Sussex has been found close to the centre of one of the Early Neolithic monument concentrations.

The distribution of Early Bronze Age monuments (Fig. 5.9) confirms this spatial focus and again suggests very large-scale structuring of the landscape. Most of the largest round barrows were built to the west and north of the Lavant (*cf.* Fig. 5.7), and all are situated in elevated topographical locations around the fringes of a landscape zone centred on The Trundle, with which they are all intervisible (Fig. 5.9). Furthermore, the spatial forms and experiential qualities of the two major linear barrow groups in this region, the Devil's Jumps and the Heyshott barrows, 8 kilometres apart, share certain features in common (Fig. 5.10). They have similar landscape settings in prominent positions on south or south-west facing slopes near the top of the downland escarpment; in both cases, as one proceeds uphill beside the line of mounds, views towards the north are obscured by the rising ground until - near the end of the monument alignments - there are especially impressive long-distance views towards prominent eminences on the downland ridge and across the Weald to the north-west. Finally, and most striking of all, both barrow alignments are oriented in exactly the same direction: towards a point on the horizon where the sun sets on Midsummer's day (Figs 10, 11).

It is apparent that these funerary monument complexes embodied design features that reified an elaborate cosmological scheme, invoking relationships among monuments old and new, between the past and the present, along lines of dynastic succession or sequences of the eminent dead, and between these and natural cycles that transcended the social domain. Cosmological order was implicated in social order, and *vice versa*, realized in terms of visual inter-referencing and the spatial organization of ritual practices. The ordered nature of this world was not just appreciated abstractly, but was seen and felt to be so in the course of ritual performances. How much more directly could the 'truth' of a cosmological scheme be revealed than through personal experience of its reality (eg. in *seeing* the Midsummer sun set in the place ordained), and through bodily conformity with

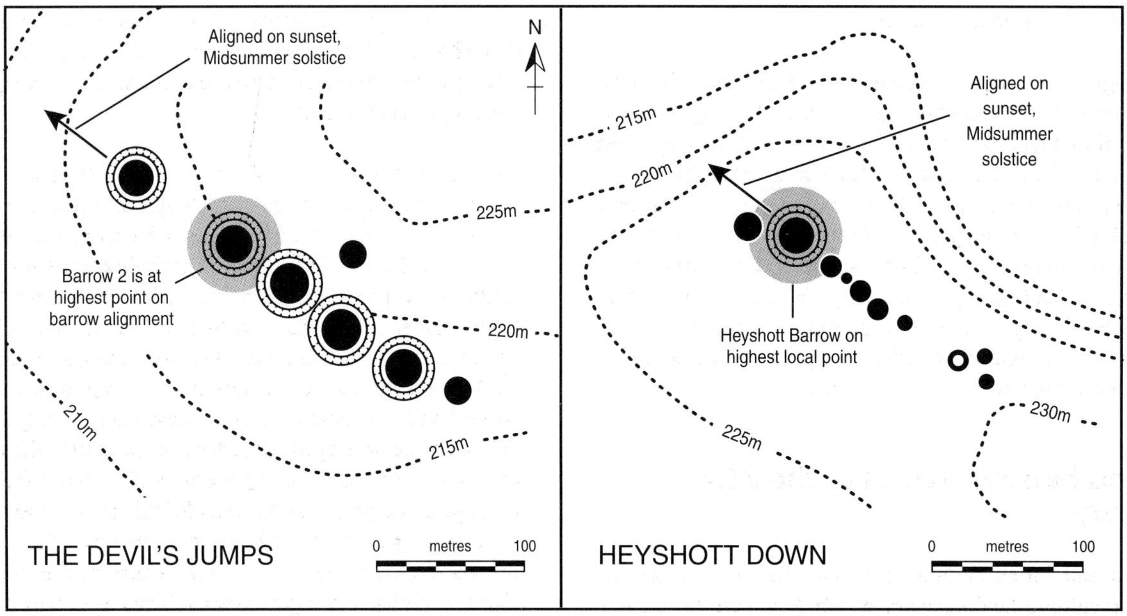

Figure 5.10. *The spatial organization and landscape settings of the Devil's Jumps and Heyshott linear round barrow groups, West Sussex (plans of barrow groups from West Sussex County Council SMR).*

Figure 5.11. *The Devil's Jumps: view along the line of mounds towards the point on the horizon where the sun sets on Midsummer Day.*

structures that symbolized its fundamental tenets (eg. by walking in procession beside a line of mounds oriented in such a way that the status of the elite descent group was directly implicated in eternal solar cycles) ? The round barrow evidence does indeed allow us insights into 'their manner of life': through an appreciation of landscape aesthetics and the construction of cosmographies that described a symbolic ordering of people, practices, historical narratives and celestial cycles in relation to one another.

Although direct dating evidence is limited, the historical specificity of linear round barrow group development, the dating of mound types (i.e. bell barrows), and the whetstone pendant from Bow Hill barrow 3 (a characteristic late Wessex funerary item), suggest that these arrays of monuments came into being in the period *c.* 1900-1600 BC. In this world, round barrow groups were not simply the dull cemeteries of the illustrious dead, but progressively elaborated monument complexes incorporating linear processional ways and open arenas (*cf.* Garwood 1999b); the principal foci for ceremonial practices in the landscapes of the time.

Round barrow studies in the 21st century

Present and future studies of round barrow sites and the striking cultural landscapes of which they were a part, will be conditioned by specific research agendas and theoretical perspectives, but it is important - whatever approach is taken - to recognize the complexities of the evidence, and to abandon simplistic assumptions about the funerary traditions of the Late Neolithic and Bronze Age. Future studies should aim to exploit the real strengths of the Sussex evidence (*cf.* Drewett *et al.* 1988, 63-86): the artefact assemblages from grave contexts, the patterned clusters of round barrow groups, the non-funerary function of some of these monuments (recalling Reverend Smith's identification of 'cenotaphs' in 1870) and the spatial distribution of round barrow and funerary categories. Above all, it is necessary to assume diversity and change in monument forms, their landscape settings, their ritual purpose, and the largely unexplored meanings attached to these.

In this context, the condition of sites that are being progressively destroyed by ploughing should be reassessed. Some 70% of the standing Sussex barrows recorded by Grinsell (1934, 1940) have been entirely destroyed or virtually flattened by ploughing, and this process of destruction is continuing as mound remnants (where these survive), old land surfaces, upper ditch deposits, and even deep grave contexts are being truncated. Considering the exceptional research interest and diverse character of these sites, simply to map the locales of destroyed round barrows, and treat them as an unvarying site category, represents a significant failure of heritage conservation and research. This is one situation in which high quality data collection for its own sake is called for. Moreover, to be able to make sense of the changing character and spatial organization of ritual practices at round barrow sites, the aim should be total excavation however unrewarding this may seem to be. As Lane Fox (1877a, 286) argued in his Black Burgh excavation report: "It must be remembered that comparatively few of these barrows are now left to be explored, and upon those who dig into them devolves the duty of recording carefully all that they find. In our present state of ignorance concerning them we cannot tell upon what points of detail theories in after ages may be made to turn".

It is also apparent that present dating methods are insufficient to meet the needs of fine-grained cultural interpretation; if a temporal scale of centuries is required, it is futile to rely *only* on radiocarbon age ranges that are most accurate at a scale of half millennia. This should encourage the revival of typo-chronological analysis as a research tool, and the careful integration of typo-chronological frameworks with radiocarbon date assemblages derived from secure depositional contexts. The excavation and high precision radiocarbon dating of as many well-preserved burials as possible should be a research priority. This also requires a new respect for the evidence from burial contexts (*cf.* Thomas 1991). Funerary ritual involves deliberate acts by a specific grouping of people, who self-consciously construct ideal images of the dead person in both material and non-material terms, made comprehensible in the bounded, socially contingent settings of the funeral ceremony and act of deposition. Evidence surviving from such events provides a direct means of exploring systems of social classification, stereotypical representations, aesthetics of ritual expression and the symbolic schemes of past cultures.

To make sense of this evidence requires a contextual understanding of wider social practices, contemporary political discourses, symbolic codes and metaphors worked into material forms, and the technologies and materials of social and economic life. If this sounds complicated, and dependent on extremely sensitive material analysis and elaborate interpretative argument, then so it should. It is difficult enough to explain the workings and form of our own society in the present, why should it be easier to describe a cultural world that is foreign to us and which no longer exists?

It may have appeared at one time that an understanding of the Late Neolithic and earlier Bronze Age of Sussex, despite 200 years of recording 'facts', was poor and fragmented. But really we have barely started; the interpretative disappointments that marked many previous attempts to make sense of the evidence are explicable once it is realized that the wrong questions were being asked, based on false or arguable premises. We are only now beginning to appreciate the nature of past practices embedded in the material remains of round barrows, and just starting to ask appropriate questions about them. In this light, the Sussex evidence - in both its present form, and in terms of its (unpredictable, but promising) future - is as rich and as interesting as we wish to make it.

Acknowledgements

I am grateful to Mark Taylor and John Mills, West Sussex County Council, and to Andrew Woodcock and Martin Brown, East Sussex County Council, for providing Sites and Monuments Records data and other information. Andrew Fitzpatrick, Chris Greatorex, Casper Johnson, and James Kenny were most helpful in allowing access to site information prior to publication. My thanks also to Lis Dyson for commenting on the text, and to Harry Burglass for transforming my drawings into clear illustrations. I am especially grateful to David Rudling for inviting me to present this paper at The *Archaeology of Sussex to AD 2000* conference and for his patience in waiting for the final text.

Appendix 1. Round barrow sites investigated in Sussex, 1763-2000

The following lists of round barrow investigations in Sussex (*see* text for details of site investigation categories) are drawn mainly from the following sources: Horsfield 1824; Grinsell 1934, 1940, 1941; Musson 1954; Curwen 1954; recent excavation reports; and County Sites and Monuments Records. Sites are listed from west to east. Single finds of Late Neolithic and Bronze Age artefacts and/or burials are not included unless they were definitely associated with round barrows.

A. *Excavations to modern standards.*

West Heath I.	Total exc.	Drewett 1976.
West Heath II.	Total exc.	Drewett 1976.
West Heath III.	Total exc.	Drewett 1976.
West Heath IV.	Total exc.	Drewett 1976.
West Heath V.	Total exc.	Drewett 1985.
West Heath VI.	Total exc.	Drewett 1985.
West Heath VII.	Total exc.	Drewett 1985.
West Heath VIII.	Total exc.	Drewett 1985.
West Heath IX.	Total exc.	Drewett 1985.
Minsted.	Total exc.	Drewett 1975b.
Racton Park Farm.	Partial exc.	Kenny 1989.
Bow Hill (Devil's Humps) 2.	Sample.	Grinsell 1941.
Lavant.	Total exc.	Turner, D. 1997.
Westhampnett, Area 2.	Sample.	Fitzpatrick 1997.
Westhampnett, Area 3.	Total exc.	Fitzpatrick, in press.
Duncton Quarry	Total exc.	Johnson, in prep.
Slindon.	Sample.	Drewett 1978.
Barpham 1.	Total exc.	Barr-Hamilton 1980.
Barpham 2.	Total exc.	Barr-Hamilton 1980.
Chanctonbury Hill.	Partial exc.	Ratcliffe-Densham 1968.
Steyning Round Hill.	Total exc.	Burstow 1958.
Slonk Hill 1.	Total exc.	Hartridge 1978.
Slonk Hill 2.	Total exc.	Hartridge 1978.
Money Mound.	Total exc.	Beckensall 1967.
Pyecombe.	Total exc.	Butler 1991.
Ditchling Field.	Total exc.	Holleyman & Yeates, 1960.
Ladies Mile.	Total exc.	Holleyman & Yeates, 1960.
Looe's Barn, Saltdean.	Sample.	Holgate 1987a.
Rottingdean.	Sample.	Bell 1974.
Lewes.	Sample.	Allen 1986.
Round the Down, Lewes.	Total exc.	Butler 1995.
Itford Hill.	Total exc.	Holden 1972; Russell 1996.
Rookery Hill, Bishopstone.	Total exc.	Bell 1977, 45, 193
Black Patch Down 1.	Sample.	Drewett 1982b.
Black Patch Down 2.	Sample.	Drewett 1982b.
Black Patch Down 3.	Sample.	Drewett 1982b.
Black Patch Down 4.	Sample.	Drewett 1982b.
Black Patch Down 5.	Sample.	Drewett 1982b.
Black Patch Down 6.	Sample.	Drewett 1982b.
Black Patch Down 7.	Burial only.	Holgate 1987b.
Black Patch Down 10.	Sample.	Drewett 1982b.
Black Patch Down 11.	Sample.	Drewett 1982b.
Alfriston.	Total exc.	O'Connor 1976.
Folkington Hill.	Uncertain.	Margary 1960.
Crowlink cairn.	Total exc.	Greatorex, in press.
Cornish Farm.	Total exc.	Drewett 1993.

B. *Excavations to pre-modern standards.*

West Harting Down.	Urns only.	Unpubl.; W. Sussex SMR 0147.
Apple Down.	Urn only.	Down and Welch 1990.
Goodwood.	Sample.	Curwen and Curwen 1933.
Duncton Down.	Sample.	Winbolt 1932; Patchett1938.
Rackham.	Sample.	Curwen 1932b.
Blackpatch Hill 1.	Total exc. ?	Pull 1932; NMR.

Blackpatch Hill 3.	Total exc. ?	Pull 1932; NMR.
Blackpatch Hill 4.	Total exc. ?	Pull 1932; NMR.
Blackpatch Hill 5.	Total exc. ?	Pull 1932; NMR.
Blackpatch Hill 6.	Total exc. ?	Pull 1932; NMR.
Blackpatch Hill 7.	Uncertain.	Pull 1932; NMR.
Blackpatch Hill 8.	Uncertain.	Pull 1932; NMR.
Blackpatch Hill 9.	Total exc. ?	Pull 1932; Russell 1996, 28-9.
Blackpatch Hill 11.	Uncertain.	Pull 1932; NMR.
Blackpatch Hill 12.	Total exc. ?	Pull 1932; NMR.
Church Hill, Findon	Total exc. ?	Unpubl.; Russell 1996, 29-30.
Cock Hill barrow 1.	Sample.	Ratcliffe-Densham, H & M. 1961, 93.
Shepherdsfield, Lower Beeding.	Total exc.	Green 1976; W.Sussex SMR 4395.
Black Hill.	Uncertain.	Green 1976.
Shoreham.	Burial only.	Witten 1978.
Black Burgh tumulus.	Partial exc.	Lane Fox 1877a.
Chalk Pit, Lewes	Total exc.	Spokes 1932.
Glynde Hill.	Partial exc.	Currey and Curwens, 1923.
Seaford Head.	Partial exc.	Lane Fox 1877b.
Playden.	Total exc.	Cheney 1935; Cleal 1982.

C. *Early investigations, and poorly-recorded sites.*

Bow Hill (Devil's Humps) barrow 3.	Anon. 1854a.
Bow Hill (Devil's Humps) ?	Anon. 1792; Anon. 1854a.
Bow Hill, west spur (two Bronze Age barrows ?).	Smith 1870, 59-60.
Bow Hill, east spur (four barrows investigated).	Smith 1870, 63-5.
Devil's Jumps (four barrows investigated).	Anon. 1854a.
Heyshott Down Barrow 10.	Lewis 1960, 15.
Burpham Downs, the Burgh.	Curwen & Curwen 1922, 8-10.
Burpham Downs, round barrow.	Curwen & Curwen 1922, 13-14.
Loasden.	Curwen & Curwen 1922, 16-20.
Burpham, Arundel road.	Lewis 1960, 15.
Cissbury (two barrows ?).	Grinsell 1931, 39.
Storrington.	Dixon 1848.
Sullington Warren.	Cartwright 1830, 127-8.
Beeding Hill.	Horsfield 1824, 44.
Devil's Dyke, Brighton.	Grinsell 1931, 39.
Clayton Windmill.	Horsfield 1824, 43-4.
Hove tumulus.	Phillips 1857; Curwen, E & E C, 1924.
Ditchling Road, Brighton.	Anon. 1922, 55-6.
Church Hill and other areas, Brighton (several barrows).	Grinsell 1934, 232; 1940, 210-11.
Whitehawk, Brighton.	Horsfield 1824, 43.
Bostle Hill, Brighton (several barrows).	Burstow and Norris, 1951.
Telscombe Tye.	Grinsell 1931, 37, 66.
Heathy Brow, Rodmell.	Curwen 1932a.
Falmer Hill ?	Horsfield 1824, 48.
Balmer Farm, Falmer.	Anon. 1956.
Boxholt Bottom, Lewes.	Turner, Rev. E. 1870, 192-4.
Mount Harry, Lewes.	Anon. 1854b, 64-5.
Cuckoo Bottom, Lewes.	Anon. 1888.
Offham Hill, Lewes (five barrows).	Horsfield 1824, 44-5.
Ox-settle Down, Lewes.	Horsfield 1824, 47-8, pl.V.
Ox-settle Bottom, Lewes.	Horsfield 1824, 48.
Mount Caburn, Lewes (several barrows).	Horsfield 1824, 46-7.
Beddingham.	Cooper 1879.
Firle Point.	Horsfield 1824, 48.
Alfriston.	Vine 1763; Horsfield 1824, 43.
Alfriston.	Horsfield 1824, 43.
Alfriston.	Anon. 1890.
Alfriston.	Ade 1849; Smith 1870, 67-75.
Alfriston (two further barrows investigated).	Smith 1870, 66-7, 76-6.
Belle Tout, Birling (two barrows).	Giddy 1814.
Crowlink Barrow, East Dean.	Figg 1852.
Crapham Down, Eastbourne (two barrows).	Budgen and Grey 1933.
Beachy Head, Eastbourne (three barrows).	Turner, Rev. E. 1870.

Appendix 2. Radiocarbon dates from round barrow sites in Sussex

The radiocarbon dates listed below are calibrated using the high precision decadal calibration curve for the period AD 1950-6000 BC (Stuiver and Becker 1993). Calibrated age ranges are quoted to the nearest ten years. Dates from Pyecombe (GU-2574: 7520+/-140 bp) and West Heath IV (HAR-1647: 1150+/-100 bp) are unrelated to Late Neolithic and Bronze Age activity and are not included. In four cases age estimates are extremely imprecise (> +/- 110 years) and have little value for dating purposes. Two of the dates for West Heath VI are probably on old wood and unrelated to the use of Collared Urns and mound-building (HAR-5285, 5325). The error estimate originally quoted for the date from Hove Barrow is undoubtedly too small: wider age ranges to encompass the age of the sample material should be considered at both levels of probability.

Conventional date bp.	Calibrated age ranges (cal BC)	
	c.1s (68%)	c.2s (95%)
Black Patch Down barrow 3. Human bone, from child burial in pit (10). HAR-3976 3830+/-80 bp	2450-2190	2480-2030
Crowlink cairn. 1. Onion couch tuber, in fill (41) of cut (40) containing burnt human bone. OxA-8979 2990+/-40 bp	1260-1110	1380-1050
2. Onion couch tuber, in fill (41) of cut (40) containing burnt human bone. OxA-8980 3145+/-40 bp	1440-1390	1500-1310
3. Charcoal, in fill (39) of cut (32) containing burnt human bone. OxA-8981 3820+/-45 bp	2330-2140	2460-2130
4. Charcoal, in fill (39) of cut (32) containing burnt human bone. OxA-8982 4015+/-45 bp	2570-2460	2830-2400
Hove Barrow. Piece of wood from oak coffin. BM-682 3190+/-35 bp	1490-1410	1500-1390
Playden. Charcoal from oak timbers. BM-450 3690+/-115 bp	2210-1880	2460-1740
West Heath II. Charcoal, OLS. HAR-646 3110+/-160 bp	1530-1110	1710-900
West Heath III. 1. Charcoal, OLS. HAR-647 3630+/-100 bp	2140-1860	2230-1690
2. Charcoal, top fill phase 1 ditch. HAR-648 3220+/-180 bp	1690-1260	1920-1010
West Heath VI. 1. Oak and hazel charcoal, from Collared Urn, top of burial pit (8). HAR-5285 4340+/-70 bp	3030-2890	3100-2870
2. Oak charcoal, from Collared urn on OLS (context 20). HAR-5323 4240+/-120 bp	2920-2630	3100-2470
3. Charcoal, fill (17) of burial pit (8). HAR-5322 3650+/-100 bp	2140-1880	2290-1740
4. Oak and hazel charcoal, from Collared Urn (21), top fill (13) of burial pit (8). HAR-5321 3560+/-100 bp	1980-1740	2140-1620
5. Oak charcoal, turf mound. HAR-5281 3400+/-70 bp	1750-1600	1840-1500
6. Charcoal, fill of pit (7). HAR-5282 3330+/-70 bp	1690-1500	1750-1440
7. Oak charcoal, from Collared Urn (15) set in turf stack. HAR-5283 3310+/-70 bp	1640-1490	1740-1410
West Heath VII. Oak charcoal, from fill of central burial pit. HAR-5320 3620+/-100 bp	2050-1780	2230-1680

References

Anon. 1792. King's Graves. *The Gentleman's Magazine* Vol **II**, July-December, 593.

Anon. 1854a. Appendix: proceedings at the annual meeting of the Archaeological Institute, *SAC* **7**, 51-3.

Anon. 1854b. Proceedings, meeting of the Archaeological Institute, 6th Jan. 1854, *Arch. J.* **11**, 62-73.

Anon. 1888. Archaeological discovery at 'Cuckoo Bottom', Lewes, *SAC* **36**, 238-56.

Anon. 1890. Discovery of cinerary urns at Alfriston, *SAC* **37**, 193-4.

Anon. 1922. Discoveries at Brighton, *Ant. J.* **2**, 53-67.

Anon. 1956. Research Committee, *SNQ.* **14** (9/10), 172-73.

Ade, C. 1849. On some urns lately found in a tumulus at Alfriston, *SAC* **2**, 270-1.

Allen, M. 1986. A possible barrow at Lewes, *SAC* **124**, 252-4.

Ambers, J., S. Bowman., P. Garwood., R. Hedges., and R. Housley. 1999. Appendix 1: Radiocarbon dating, in A. Barclay and C. Halpin, *Excavations at Barrow Hills, Radley, Oxfordshire. Vol I: The Neolithic and Bronze Age monument complex*, Oxford: Oxford Archaeological Unit. Thames Valley Landscapes Monograph **1**, 330-337.

Annable, F.K. 1958. Excavation and fieldwork in Wiltshire, 1957, *Wilts. Arch. Nat. Hist. Mag.* **52**: 2-17.

Ashbee, P. 1960. *The Bronze Age Round Barrow in Britain.* London: Phoenix House.

Atkinson, R.J.C. Brailsford, J. and Wakefield, H. 1951. A pond barrow at Winterbourne Steepleton, Dorset, *Arch. J*, **108**, 1-24.

Barclay, A. and Halpin, C. 1999. *Excavations at Barrow Hills, Radley, Oxfordshire. Vol I: The Neolithic and Bronze Age monument complex.* Oxford: Oxford Archaeological Unit.; Thames Valley Landscapes Monographs Vol. **1**.

Barclay, G. 1989. Henge monuments: reappraisal or reductionism?, *Proc. Prehist. Soc.* **55**, 260-62.

Barrett, J. 1990. The monumentality of death: the character of Early Bronze Age mortuary mounds in southern England, *World Archaeol.* **22**, 179-89.

Barrett, J, 1994 *Fragments from Antiquity. An archaeology of social life in Britain, 2900-1200* BC. Oxford: Blackwell.

Barrett, J., Bradley, R., and Green, C. 1991. *Landscape, Monuments and Society. The prehistory of Cranborne Chase.* Cambridge: University Press.

Barr-Hamilton, A. 1980. The excavation of two Bronze Age barrows at Friday's Church, Barpham Hill, *SAC* **118**, 171-82.

Barth, F. 1987. *Cosmologies in the Making.* Cambridge: University Press.

Beckensall, S.G. 1967. The excavation of Money Mound, *SAC* **105**, 13-30.

Bedwin, O. 1983. The development of prehistoric settlement on the West Sussex coastal plain, *SAC* **121**, 31-44.

Bell, M. 1974. A suspected barrow at Rottingdean, *SAC* **112**, 156-7.

Bell, M. 1977. Excavations at Bishopstone, Sussex, *SAC* **115**.

Bradley, R. 1984. *The Social Foundations of Prehistoric Britain.* London: Longman.

Bradley, R. 1993. *Altering the Earth. The origins of monuments in Britain and continental Europe.* Edinburgh: Soc. Ant. Scotland.

Bradley, R. 1998. *The Significance of Monuments.* London: Routledge.

Brandon, P., and Short, B. 1990. *The South East from AD 1000.* London: Longman.

Britnell, W.J. 1982. The excavation of two round barrows at Trelystan, Powys, *Proc. Prehist. Soc.* **48**, 133-201.

Brück, J. 1999. Ritual and rationality: some problems of interpretation in European archaeology, *European J. Archaeol.* **2**(3), 313-44.

Budgen, Revd. W. and Grey, Lt. Col. J.V. 1933. Eastbourne, *SAC* **74**, 246.

Burgess, C. 1980. *The Age of Stonehenge.* London: Dent.

Burstow, G.P. 1958. A Late Bronze Age urnfield on Steyning Round Hill, Sussex, *Proc. Prehist. Soc.*, **24**, 158-64.

Burstow, G.P. and Norris, N.E.S. 1951. Excavations of barrows on the Bostle, Balsdean, *SNQ.* **13**(6), 129-31.

Butler, C. 1991. The excavation of a Beaker bowl barrow at Pyecombe, West Sussex, *SAC* **129**, 1-28.

Butler, C. 1995. The excavation of a Bronze Age round barrow at Round-the-Down near Lewes, East Sussex, *SAC* **133**, 7-18.

Cartwright, E. 1830. *The History of Western Sussex. Vol 2, Pt.2: The parochial topography of the Rape of Bramber.* London: Nichols and Son.

Cheney, H.J. 1935. An Aneolithic occupation site at Playden near Rye, *Ant. J.* **15**, 152-64.

Christie, P.M. 1967. A barrow-cemetery of the second millennium BC in Wiltshire, England, *Proc. Prehist. Soc.* **33**, 336-66.

Clare, T. 1986. Towards a reappraisal of henge monuments, *Proc. Prehist. Soc.* **52**, 281-316.

Clare, T. 1987. Towards a reappraisal of henge monuments: origins, evolution and hierarchy, *Proc. Prehist. Soc.* **53**, 457-77.

Clarke, D.L, 1970 *Beaker Pottery of Great Britain and Ireland.* Cambridge: University Press.

Clarke, D.V., Cowie, T. and Foxon, A. 1985. *Symbols of Power at the Time of Stonehenge.* Edinburgh: National Museum of Antiquities of Scotland.

Cleal, R.M.J. 1982. A re-analysis of the ring-ditch site at Playden, East Sussex, *SAC* **120,** 1-17.

Cooper, J. 1879. On some recently discovered ancient British urns, *SAC* **29**, 238-39.

Cunliffe, B. 1993. *Wessex to AD 1000.* London: Longman.

Currey, B., Curwen, E., and Curwen, E.C. 1923. Notes on the examination of a barrow on Glynde Hill, *SAC* **64**, 189-90.

Curwen, E.C. 1930. Wolstonbury, *SAC* **71**, 237-45.

Curwen, E.C. 1932a. On three barrows in the parishes of Iford and Rodmell, *SNQ.* **4** (3) 70-1.

Curwen, E.C. 1932b. Rackham Bank and earthwork, *SAC* **77**, 168-86.

Curwen, E.C. 1954. *The Archaeology of Sussex.* 2nd edition, London: Methuen.

Curwen, E. and Curwen, E.C. 1922. Notes on the archaeology of Burpham and the neighbouring Downs, *SAC* **63**, 1-53.

Curwen, E. and Curwen, E.C. 1924. The Hove tumulus, *Brighton & Hove Archaeologist* **2**, 20-8.

Curwen, E. and Curwen, E.C. 1933. A Beaker skeleton from Goodwood, *SNQ.* **4** (7), 195-7.

Darvill, T. 1997. Ever increasing circles: the sacred geographies of Stonehenge in its landscape, in B. Cunliffe and C. Renfrew (eds), *Science and Stonehenge* London: Proc. Brit. Acad. **92**, 167-202.

Dixon, F. 1848. On a British sepulchral urn and brass pin found on Storrington Downs, *SAC* **1**, 55-7.

Donaldson, P. 1977. The excavation of a multiple round barrow at Barnack, Cambridgeshire 1974-76, *Ant. J.* **57**, 197-231.

Down, A. and Welch, M. 1990. *Chichester Excavations. Vol 7: Apple Down and the Mardens*. Chichester: Chichester District Council.

Drewett, P. 1975a. The excavation of an oval burial mound of the third millenium BC at Alfriston, East Sussex, 1974, *Proc. Prehist. Soc.* **41**, 119-152.

Drewett, P. 1975b. The excavation of a turf barrow at Minsted, West Sussex, 1973, *SAC* **113**, 54-65.

Drewett, P. 1976. The excavation of four round barrows of the second millennium BC at West Heath, Harting, 1973-75, *SAC* **114**, 126-50.

Drewett, P. 1978. The excavation of an oval mound and a round barrow at Slindon, West Sussex, 1976, *SAC* **116**, 257-60.

Drewett, P. 1982a. *The Archaeology of Bullock Down, Eastbourne, East Sussex: the development of a landscape*. Lewes: Sussex Arch Soc Monograph **1**.

Drewett, P. 1982b. Later Bronze Age downland economy and excavations at Black Patch, East Sussex, *Proc. Prehist. Soc.* **48**, 321-400.

Drewett, P. 1985. The excavation of barrows V-IX at West Heath, Harting, 1980, *SAC* **123**, 35-60.

Drewett, P. 1989. Anthropogenic soil erosion in prehistoric Sussex: excavations at West Heath and Ferring, 1984, *SAC* **127**, 11-29.

Drewett, P. 1993. The excavation of Bronze Age round barrow (site 15), Cornish Farm, Eastbourne, *SAC* **130**, 235-8.

Drewett, P., Rudling, D. and Gardiner, M. 1988. *The South-East to AD 1000*. London: Longman.

Ellison, A. 1978. The Bronze Age of Sussex, in P. Drewett (ed), *Archaeology in Sussex to AD 1500,* CBA Res. Rep. **29**, 30-7.

Ellison, A. 1980. The Bronze Age, in D.J. Freke (ed), The Archaeology of Sussex Pottery, *SAC* **118**, 1-136 (31-42).

Field, D. 1998. Round barrows and the harmonious landscape: placing Early Bronze Age burial monuments in south-east England, *Oxford J. Archaeol.* **17**, 309-26.

Figg, W. 1852. On the opening of a barrow at Crowlink, in Friston, *SAC* **5**, 207-12.

Fitzpatrick, A.P. 1997. *Archaeological Excavations on the Route of the A27 Westhampnett Bypass, West Sussex, 1992. Vol.2: the Late Iron Age, Romano-British and Anglo-Saxon cemeteries*, Wessex Archaeol. Rep. **12**.

Fitzpatrick, in press. *Archaeological Excavations on the Route of the A27 Westhampnett Bypass, West Sussex, 1992. Vol.1: the settlement.*

Fleming, A. 1971. Territorial patterns in Bronze Age Wessex, *Proc. Prehist. Soc.* **37**, 352-81.

Garwood, P. 1991. Ritual tradition and the reconstitution of society, in P. Garwood, D. Jennings, R. Skeates and J. Toms (eds), *Sacred and Profane. Archaeology, ritual and religion*. Oxford: O.U.C.A. Monograph **32**, 10-32.

Garwood, P. 1999a. The chronology of depositional contexts and monuments (with contributions by A. Barclay), in A. Barclay and C. Halpin, *Excavations at Barrow Hills, Radley, Oxfordshire. Vol I: The Neolithic and Bronze Age monument complex,* Oxford Archaeological Unit: Thames Valley Landscapes Monograph Vol **1**, 275-93.

Garwood, P. 1999b. Radiocarbon dating and the chronology of the monument complex, in A. Barclay and C. Halpin, *Excavations at Barrow Hills, Radley, Oxfordshire. Vol I: The Neolithic and Bronze Age monument complex.* Oxford Archaeological Unit: Thames Valley Landscapes Monograph Vol **1**, 293-309.

Giddy, D. 1814. Letter, 24th June 1813. Opening of barrow at Birling, *Archaeologia* **17**, 321-39.

Greatorex, C. in press. Further evidence of Sussex Prehistoric Ritual Traditions: The Archaeological investigations of a Bronze Age funerary monument situated on Baily's Hill, near Crowlink, Eastbourne. *SAC* **139**.

Green, T.K. 1976. The work of the Mid-Sussex Archaeological Society, 1961-65, *SAC* **114**, 324-5.

Green, C. and Rollo-Smith, S. 1984. The excavation of eighteen round barrows near Shrewton, Wiltshire, *Proc. Prehist. Soc.* **50**, 255-318.

Grinsell, L.V, 1931. Sussex in the Bronze Age, *SAC* **72**, 30-68.

Grinsell, L.V. 1934. Sussex barrows, *SAC* **75**, 217-75.

Grinsell, L.V. 1940. Sussex barrows: supplementary paper, *SAC* **81**, 210-14.

Grinsell, L.V. 1941. Sussex barrows: supplement no.II, *SAC* **82**, 115-23.

Hamilton, S. and Manley, J. 1997. Points of view. Prominent enclosures in 1st millennium BC Sussex, *SAC* **135**, 93-112.

Hartridge, R. 1978. Excavations at the prehistoric and Romano-British site on Slonk Hill, Shoreham, Sussex, *SAC* **116**, 69-141.

Hodder, I., Shanks, M., Alexandri, A., Buchli, V., Carman, J., Last, J. and Lucas, G. (eds). 1995. *Interpreting Archaeology.* London: Routledge.

Holden, E. 1972. A Bronze Age cemetery-barrow on Itford Hill, Beddingham, Sussex, *SAC* **110**, 70-117.

Holgate, R. 1987a. The Looe's Barn tumulus, Saltdean, East Sussex, *SAC* **125**, 230-2.

Holgate, R. 1987b. An inurned cremation from Black Patch Barrow 7, East Sussex, *SAC* **125**, 232-4.

Holleyman, G. and Yeates, C. 1960. Excavations in the Ditchling Road area north of Brighton, 1950-57, *SAC* **98**, 131-49.

Horsfield, T.W. 1824. *The History and Antiquities of Lewes and its Vicinity.* Lewes: Baxter.

Johnson, C. in prep. Excavation of a ring ditch at Heath End, Duncton, West Sussex.

Jones, G. 1980. An early Bronze Age barrow in Ewhurst parish, *SAC* **118**, 367.

Kenny, J. 1989a. A possible Bronze Age barrow on the West Sussex coastal plain, *SAC* **127**, 235.

Kenny, J. 1989b. Westbourne: Racton Park Farm, *The Archaeology of Chichester and District, 1989,* 42-43.

Lane Fox, Col. A. 1877a. Opening of the Dyke Road, or Black Burgh Tumulus, near Brighton, in 1872, *J. Roy. Anthrop. Inst.* **6,** 280-87, Pl. XIII, XIV.

Lane Fox, Col. A. 1877b. Excavations in the camp and tumulus at Seaford, Sussex, *J. Roy. Anthrop. Inst.* **6**, 87-97, Pl. XV.

Lanting, J. & van der Waals, J. 1972. British Beakers as seen from the continent, *Helinium* **12**, 20-46.

Lewis, G. 1960. Some recent discoveries in West Sussex, *SAC* **98**, 12-28.

Lynch, F. 1993. *Excavations in the Brenig Valley: a Mesolithic and Bronze Age landscape in north Wales.* Bangor: Cambrian Archaeological Monograph **5**.

McKinley, J. 1997. Bronze Age 'barrows' and funerary rites and rituals of cremation, *Proc. Prehist. Soc.* **63**, 129-45.

Margary, I.D. 1960. Sussex Archaeological Society Autumn Meeting: research committee, *SNQ.* **15** (7), 249-50.

Mizoguchi, K. 1993. Time in the reproduction of mortuary practices, *World Archaeol.* **25,** 223-35.

Musson, R.C. 1954. *An illustrated catalogue of Sussex Beaker and Bronze Age pottery, SAC* **92**, 106-24.

Needham, S. 1993. Displacement and exchange in archaeological methodology, in C. Scarre and F. Healy (eds), *Trade and Exchange in Prehistoric Europe* Oxford: Oxbow Monograph **33**, 161-69.

Needham, S. 1996. Chronology and periodisation in the British Bronze Age, in K. Randsborg (ed), Absolute Chronology: Archaeological Europe 2500-500 BC, *Acta Archaeologica* **67**, Copenhagen, 121-40.

O'Connor, T.P. 1976. The excavation of a round barrow and a cross-ridge dyke at Alfriston, East Sussex, 1975, *SAC* **114**, 151-63.

Parker Pearson, M. and Ramilisinona, 1998. Stonehenge for the ancestors: the stones pass on the message, *Antiquity* **72**, 308-26.

Parkin, D. 1991. *Sacred Void. Spatial images of work and ritual among the Giriama of Kenya.* Cambridge: University Press.

Patchett, F.M. 1938. Bronze Age cinerary urn from Duncton Hill, *SNQ.* **7**, 52-4.

Peters, F. 1999. Bronze Age barrows: factors influencing their survival and destruction, *Oxford J. Archaeol.* **18**, 255-64.

Phillips, B. 1857. Discovery of a tumulus at Hove, near Brighton, *SAC* **9**, 119-24.

Pull, J.H. 1932. *The Flint Miners of Black Patch.* London: Williams and Norgate.

Ratcliffe-Densham, H. 1968. A woman of Wessex Culture, *SAC* **106**, 38-48.

Ratcliffe-Densham, H. and Ratcliffe-Densham, M. 1961. An anomalous earthwork of the Late Bronze Age, on Cock Hill, Sussex, *SAC* **99**, 78-101.

Renfrew, C. 1973. Monuments, mobilisation and social organisation in Neolithic Wessex, in C. Renfrew (ed), *The Explanation of Culture* Change, London: Duckworth, 539-58.

Richards, C. 1996. Monuments as landscape: creating the centre of the world in late Neolithic Orkney, *World Archaeol.* **28**(2), 190-208.

Russell, M. 1996. *A Reassessment of the Bronze Age Cemetery-barrow on Itford Hill, East Sussex.* Bournemouth University, School of Conservation Sciences Res. Rep. **2**.

Russell, M. 1997. Neo-'Realism': an alternative look at the Neolithic chalkland database of Sussex, in P. Topping (ed), *Neolithic Landscapes.* Oxford: Oxbow Monograph **86**, 69-76.

Russell, M. 2002. Excavations at Mile Oak, in D. Rudling (ed), *Downland Settlement and Landuse: The Archaeology of the Brighton By-pass,* UCL Field Archaeology Unit Monograph **1**.

Shanks, M. and Tilley, C. 1987. *Social Theory and Archaeology.* Cambridge: Polity Press.

Sherratt, A. 1997. Introduction. Changing perspectives on European prehistory, in *Economy and Society in Prehistoric Europe.* Edinburgh: University Press, 1-34.

Spokes, S. 1932. A Bronze Age barrow, *Sussex County Magazine* **6**, 651-6.

Smith, Revd. H. 1870. Notes on prehistoric burial in Sussex, *SAC* **22**, 57-76.

Stuiver, M. and Becker, B. 1993. High-precision decadal calibration of the radiocarbon time scale, AD 1950 - 6000 BC, *Radiocarbon* **35**, 35-65.

Tebbutt, C.F. 1974. The prehistoric occupation of the Ashdown Forest area of the Weald, *SAC* **112**, 34-43.

Thomas, J. 1991. Reading the body: Beaker funerary practice in Britain, in P. Garwood, D. Jennings, R. Skeates and J. Toms (eds), *Sacred and Profane. Archaeology, ritual and religion.* Oxford: O.U.C.A. Monograph **32**, 33-42.

Thomas, N. and Thomas, C. 1955. Excavations at Snail Down, Everleigh 1953 and 1955: an interim report, *Wilts. Arch. Nat. Hist. Mag.* **56**, 127-48.

Tilley, C. 1994. *A Phenomenology of Landscape.* Oxford: Berg.

Tilley, C. 1999. *Metaphor and Material Culture.* Oxford: Blackwell.

Turner, D. 1997. Pipelines from Lavant, *The Archaeology of Chichester and District, 1997,* 19-24.

Turner, Revd. E. 1870. Miscellanies, *SAC* **22**, 185-200.

Vine, S. 1763. Letter, 15th August 1763, *The Gentleman's Magazine*, 396.

Winbolt, S.E. 1932. A Bronze Age burial on Duncton Down, *SNQ.* **4**, 218.

Witten, F. 1978. A Bronze Age burial from Shoreham-by-Sea, *SAC* **116**, 398.

SUSSEX NOT WESSEX: A REGIONAL PERSPECTIVE ON SOUTHERN BRITAIN C. 1200-200 BC

Sue Hamilton

Abstract

This paper focuses on the later Bronze and Early and Middle Iron Ages of Sussex. It considers the implications of recent finds, and addresses these and the pre-existing databases in the context of the significant re-orientations in our theorizing of later prehistoric Britain over the past two decades. The paper presents the Sussex data as significantly differing from the traditional Wessex-based (Dorset, Wiltshire and Hampshire) framework within which the 1st millennium BC archaeology of southern Lowland Britain is typically characterized.

Introduction

The last major surveys of Sussex's Iron Age archaeology were published approximately two decades ago (Bedwin 1978a, 1984). In 1978 the idea of an Iron Age seemed un-problematic. Since then Barrett's (1980) work in isolating the later Bronze Age pottery of southern England has resulted in the re-dating of a significant amount of material and sites previously thought to be Early Iron Age. In particular, the origins of a classic icon of the Iron Age, namely hillforts, are now seen to lie in the Late Bronze Age. The current data suggest that major changes occurred between the Middle and Late Bronze Ages, rather than at the Late Bronze Age-Iron Age transition. This article focuses on the 1st millennium BC, and particularly the Late Bronze, Early and Middle Iron Ages of Sussex. By the Late Iron Age it is difficult to consider Sussex as a unified whole owing to the very different socio-economic trajectories which are evidenced in East and West Sussex. The Late Iron Age of West Sussex is the subject of a separate paper (Davenport this volume).

Using the long view provided by a millennium, I have chosen to isolate major interpretative themes and archaeological patterns rather than detail individual sites and finds. My Sussex review takes place within the regional context of south-central Britain. In doing so, I counteract the isolation which county-based studies inevitably generate, and highlight the fact that Sussex has much to contribute to our understanding of 1st millennium BC societies in south-central Britain as a whole.

Since the last Sussex 1st millennium BC reviews there has been a 30% growth in 1st millennium BC site numbers, and a significant increase in well-stratified finds and the number of radiocarbon dates (Appendix 2). Additionally, detailed work on Sussex 1st millennium BC Sussex pottery now allows for a refined sequencing of sites (Hamilton 1993; Hamilton and Manley 1997; Hamilton and Manley 2001). Six hillforts have received further excavation (Belle Tout, Caburn, Ditchling Beacon, Highdown, Thundersbarrow Hill, and Wolstonbury: Appendix 1), and the Late Bronze Age settlement and trackways associated with Shinewater and the Willingdon levels have added a major new category of landscape occupation: marshland, (Greatorex this volume). Recent work has also included reassessments of old databases in the light of current research issues (Hamilton 1998; Hamilton and Gregory 2001; Russell 1996a).

Wessex not Sussex

Since the late-19th-century excavations of Pitt Rivers, Wessex (Dorset, Hampshire, and Wiltshire) has been the seedbed of interpretations of the later prehistory of the chalklands, and has provided the framework within which adjacent downland regions such as Sussex have been interpreted. Indeed, Sussex and Wessex have long had notable excavators and researchers in common (Cunliffe, Ellison, Hawkes, Pitt Rivers). This has increased the tendency to subsume Sussex into a Wessex whole. In most text books 1st millennium BC Sussex has been considered as being something like, but a poorer version of, the classic Bronze and Iron Age traditions of Wessex. In turn, Wessex's later prehistory with its roundhouses, enclosed farmsteads, and hillforts has been taken as the stereotype for Lowland Britain (Collis 1994; ix; Fitzpatrick 1997a).

The earlier 20th-century history of Sussex fieldwork has further worked to give it Wessex-like credentials. During the 1930s some 44% of Sussex's hillforts were excavated. No other British county had so many hillfort excavations in a decade. Hillforts then being considered to be the major monument of the Iron Age, Sussex became fixed as a 'typical' Iron Age county of Lowland Britain. The pottery from these Sussex hillfort excavations was central in the creation of Iron Age regional distributions and chronologies (Curwen 1939; Hawkes 1959, 1939; Kenyon 1952). Hodson's (1962 and 1964) seminal reanalyses of the British Iron Age again utilized Sussex pottery and metalwork (from Green Street (Eastbourne), Park Brow, and Findon Park: Appendix 1) to rethink the then current perceptions of the Iron Age as the product of sequential Continental invasions. Instead, he isolated the existence of a strong indigenous tradition based on roundhouses, standard artefact types (such as weaving combs and ring-headed pins), and regional pottery styles, and termed it the 'Little Woodbury culture' after the type-site in Dorset. The juxtaposition of Sussex examples with a Wessex-centric terminology further reinforced the idea of Sussex as a normative, Wessex-like county. This has subsequently remained unchallenged and is here highlighted as a hindrance to our proper understanding of regional variation in 1st millennium BC Southern Britain.

Sussex environment

The manner in which Sussex fronts continental Europe is certainly different to that of Wessex. Its coast affords access to *both* Atlantic Europe (Brittany) and North-East Europe (Eastern France to Belgium), and contrasts with the Atlantic orientation of Wessex. Additionally, Sussex is particularly distinguished by a series of closely juxtaposing resource zones, which are the outcome of the varied topography, geology and vegetation of the Downs and Wealden strata. No site outside the central Weald is more than 7km from a major resource change. This makes the strategic use of the landscape both scenically and economically more likely (Hamilton and Manley 2001), and reduces the need for economic centralization, which has been a prevalent theme of the Wessex 1st millennium BC studies (Fitzpatrick and Morris 1994).

The Middle Bronze Age background: 15th to 12th/11th centuries cal BC

Introduction:

A brief outline of the Sussex Middle Bronze Age here serves to emphasize the extent to which the Late Bronze Age develops from, and breaks with, preceding traditions. More detailed summaries of the Sussex Middle Bronze Age (Deverel-Rimbury) pottery, settlement and cemetery material, and their chronology can be found in Bruck (1995), Ellison (1978; 1980), Drewett (1982a) and Needham (1996, Period 5).

Middle Bronze Age chronology:

Sussex Deverel-Rimbury traditions have a considerable chronological depth. Several sites (such as Mile Oak, Downsview and Varley Halls) have produced 16th-century cal BC and earlier radiocarbon dates, while Itford Hill has a radiocarbon dating of 13th-11th century cal BC (Appendix 2). Individual sites also exhibit some time depth, as is exemplified by the Itford Hill plan, which has been interpreted as a series of sequential operational units (Ellison 1978, fig. 16). Similarly, the range of radiocarbon dates for individual houses at Black Patch (spanning more than 200 years) suggests long-lived traditions of settlement location and the use of individual buildings (Needham 1996).

Middle Bronze Age settlements and cemeteries:

During the Middle Bronze Age, for the first time, settlements come to the forefront of archaeological visibility in Lowland Britain. They comprise small groups of roundhouses with or without enclosing embankments or palisades. Sussex now has over 20 settlements dating to this period (Table 6:1). The settlements are located in 'invisible' topographies, on south-facing slopes of the South Downs rather than on hilltops (Greig 1997, 7; Parker Pearson and Richards 1997, 49). Of particular note is the repeated presence of operational units comprising a main house and one or two ancillary houses/ buildings (Ellison 1978, 36; Drewett 1982a). Recent excavations of the newly discovered sites affirm and consolidate this view (Varley Halls: Greig 1997; Patcham Fawcett: Greatorex 2002; Downsview: Rudling 2002b; Mile Oak: Russell 2002), and have afforded more detail for discussion of contemporary issues such as settlement lifecycles (Bruck 1999; Russell 1996a). Sussex Middle Bronze Age roundhouses appear to have been regularly replaced by new buildings on adjacent new plots, rather than continuously repaired *in situ* (e.g. Varley Halls: Greig 1997, 9). This perhaps signifies single generation occupation and a non-parental *habitus* tradition for the adult offspring.

Table 6.1. *Sussex Middle Bronze Age settlements and enclosures (see Appendix 1 for references). Sites in bold are newly discovered and/or have had excavations since Bedwin 1978. Starred sites are on the Coastal Plain.*

South Downs/Coastal Plain:					Weald
W. of Arun	**Arun/Adur**	**Adur/Ouse**	**Ouse/Cuckmere**	**E. of Cuckmere**	
Settlements: Kingley Vale *Selsey E.B.[1]	Amberley Mount Blackpatch Cock Hill **Highdown** New Barn Down Park Brow **Potlands[3]**	Castle Hill Ditchling Beacon **Downsview** Kingston Buci* **Mile Oak** **Patcham Fawcett** Plumpton Plain A **Varley Halls** W. Blatchington*	Bishopstone Black Patch Charleston Brow Denton Hill Itford Hill	None known	**Henfield[2]**
Enclosures: None known	None known	**Highdown?** **Thundersbarrow**	Hollingbury?	None known	None known

[1] Selsey East Beach (Kenny 1989): Middle Bronze Age pottery, but these may relate to cremations.
[2] Henfield: Archaeology South-East assessment produced part of a Middle Bronze Age lugged urn. It may relate to a cremation or a settlement.
[3] Burnt mound.

Settlement use and deposition patterns:

Deverel-Rimbury houses are relatively rich in artefact finds. Drewett's (1982a, 342) analysis of Black Patch has been highly influential in spawning considerations of the uses of the main and ancillary houses and the implications of these for social organization. In the case of Black Patch a division in labour and residence between men and women has been suggested on the basis of specific artefact and feature finds within individual houses. For the Sussex sites, such observations have in turn generated debate as to the actual derivation of artefacts in excavated Deverel-Rimbury houses. These have been variously isolated as: i) *in-situ* pots; and either ii) *in situ* rubbish (Drewett 1982a) and votive depositions (Barrett and Needham 1988); and/or iii) secondary rubbish deposited in the houses on their abandonment (Seager Thomas 1999). In some cases it is clear that the artefacts came from colluvium which has filled the abandoned house platforms (Greig 1997, 15, 17, 21).

A small number of settlement features suggest communal activities and resources. These include the recurrent presence of ponds. The burnt mound, clay-lined trough, and hearth from Potlands Farm (the site has Middle and Late Bronze Age pottery and a Late Bronze Age radiocarbon date, S. Stevens 1997), a 'burnt-stone mound' from New Barn Down (Curwen 1934), and a small structure containing large quantities of ironstone from Downsview (Rudling 2002b) are variously interpreted as communal facilities for hot-water production, or sauna bathing, or cooking.

Cemeteries:

The Middle Bronze Age burial tradition comprised clusters of individual cremations, often spreading out as a flat cemetery from a central focus formed bya low barrow (Drewett 1982a; Holden 1972). These cemeteries can be directly related to the inhabitants of the individual settlement close by, on account of their adjacent location, the number of burials, and the use of the same pottery for the in-urned cremations as occurs on the proximate settlement (Ellison 1978). This database has remained conspicuously unchanged over the last two decades.

Late Bronze Age (12th to 8th centuries cal BC) and Early Iron Age (750 to 450 cal BC)

Introduction:

The Sussex Late Bronze Age (Needham 1996: Period 6, 1150-950 cal BC, and Needham 1996, Period 7: 950-750 cal BC) and Early Iron Age (750-450 cal BC, Hill 1995) evidence craft innovation, socio-economic change, and continental contact.

Pottery:

Sussex has a substantial number of Late Bronze Age post-Deverel-Rimbury pottery assemblages (Fig. 6:1). These new ceramics add to the increasing size range of vessels already isolated for preceding Deverel-Rimbury traditions (Ellison 1978; Woodward 1995) and comprise bowls and jars in various sizes, together with small cups (Fig. 6:2). Not only does this indicate that pottery containers had become central to the storage, preparation *and* consumption of food and drink, it suggests an increased emphasis on socializing centred on eating, drinking, and feasting (Barrett 1980). Given that pottery is now a staple, craft specialization would have been more viable. Experimentation with new technological tricks (e.g. slab building, finger-pinched bases, angular shoulders, and new ways of fixing rims), together with even-coloured firings and the use of refined clays all point to craft specialization in Sussex pottery production (Hamilton 1980, 203; Hamilton 1987, 58; Hamilton 2002a).

Several of the Sussex Late Bronze Age assemblages were previously not recognized (e.g. Kingston Buci, Charleston Brow: Barrett 1980). Additionally, many of these assemblages are 'new' finds of the 1980s and 1990s (e.g. Ford, Selsey East and West Beach, Testers, and Yapton: Appendix 1). In particular, Sussex has a good number of earliest post-Deverel-Rimbury plain ware assemblages. There are currently fewer later, decorated assemblages. The latter are dated to the latest Bronze Age/earliest Iron Age and are decorated with finger-impressed and incised decoration on the rims and shoulders. Notable decorated assemblages are those from Harting Beacon (Hamilton 1979; S. Morris 1978), Chanctonbury Ring (Hamilton 1980, 2002b), Stoke Clump (Cunliffe 1966), Hollingbury (Hamilton 1984), and the Caburn (Drewett and Hamilton 1999; Hawkes 1939). Collectively these early 1st millennium BC Sussex pottery assemblages have enough stratigraphic security to provide an important regional sequence for south-east/south-central Britain (Hamilton 1993; Drewett and Hamilton 1999). This long sequence is not matched in Wessex where 'plain ware traditions' are uncommon, possibly owing to the longer survival of Deverel-Rimbury traditions (Needham 1996).

Metalwork:

The pattern of deposition of Sussex early 1st millennium BC metalwork is ripe for rethinking in the light of Bradley's (1990) work on deliberate deposition of prehistoric metalwork. The concentration of Late Bronze Age hoards and single finds of metalwork on the West Sussex Coastal Plain has been recognized for some time (Bedwin 1983; Ellison 1978, 34, fig. 14; Taylor 1980, appendix 1, map 5). Recent finds have added to this pattern (Rudling 1987). This, together with the now prevalent, coeval settlement evidence (*see* below) suggests that this area was an important socio-economic zone in the Late Bronze Age.

Alongside the latter distribution, a pattern of prestige metalwork deposition near distinctive coastline promontories and topographies is evident. This distribution includes the three expanded-terminal (Covesea-type) gold bracelets from Selsey (Curwen 1937, fig 65; Taylor 1980, appendix 1); the Cuckmere Haven small gold penannular hoop ('ring-money') (Curwen 1937, 212; Kendrick and Hawkes 1932, 128); the Beachy Head hoard of four gold Covesea bracelets, a Carps Tongue sword, and socketed and winged axes (Drewett 1982b, 71); three Covesea gold bracelets from Eastbourne (Taylor

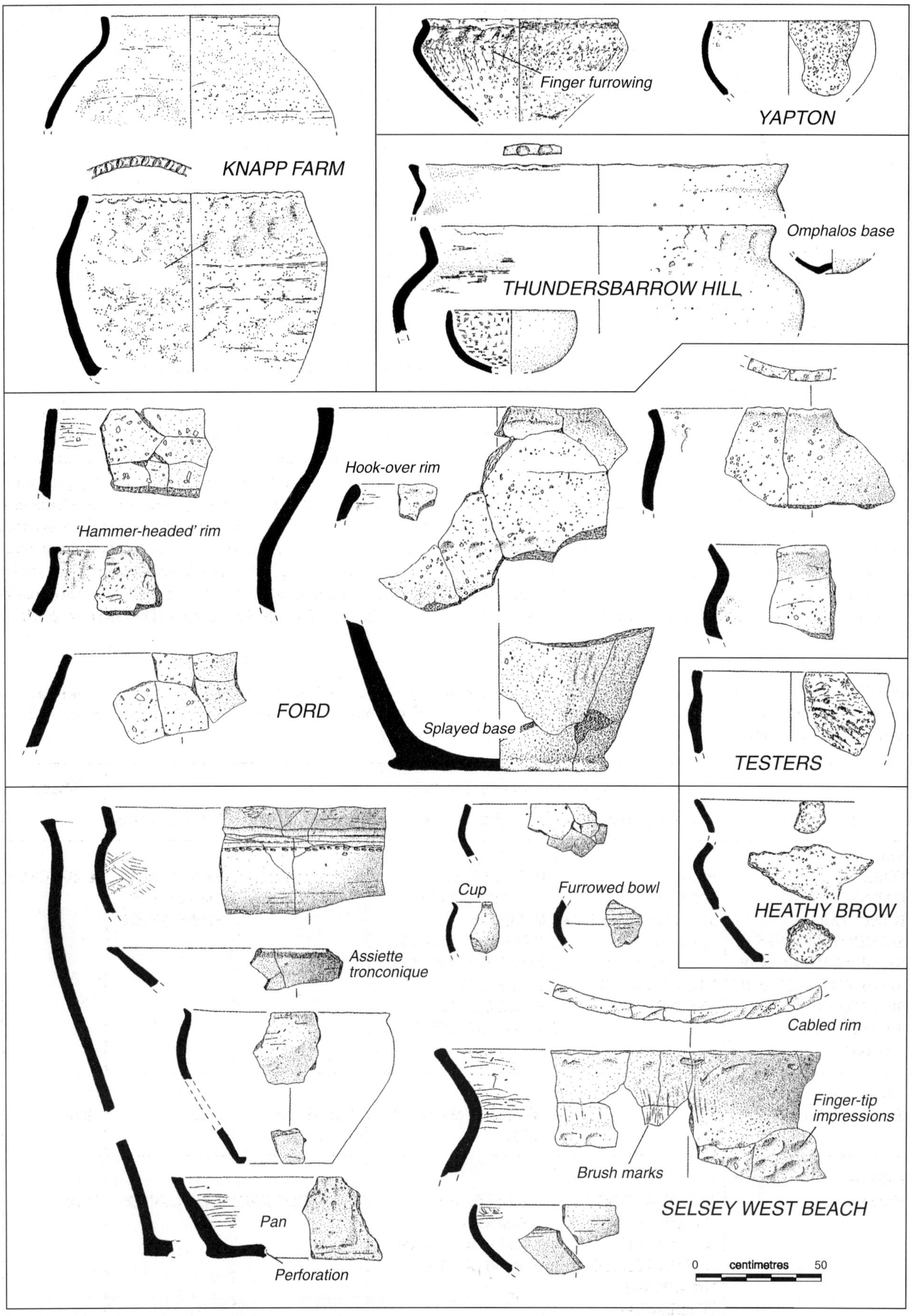

Figure 6.1. *Sussex earlier 1st millennium BC pottery. Sources: Knapp Farm (Gardiner and Hamilton 1997); Yapton (Hamilton 1987); Thundersbarrow Hill (Hamilton 1993); Heath Brow (Hamilton 1982); Testers (Hamilton 1988); Ford: Drawings by M. Seager Thomas (unpublished excavation by RPS Consultants,* see *Appendix 6.1: 2000-02); Selsey West Beach (Seager Thomas 2001).*

1980, appendix 1); and the Newhaven Head 'carpenter's hoard' (Curwen 1937, 208) (Fig. 6:3). This pattern may be a variant on the later Bronze Age tradition of votive deposition in watery places already isolated for south-eastern and eastern Lowland Britain (Bradley 1990). It suggests high status Sussex early 1st millennium BC coastal communities, amongst which acts of competitive wealth disposal may have taken place. Two hillforts (Harting Beacon and Highdown Hill), and one hill top (Hollingbury hill prior to hillfort enclosure) also have deliberate depositions of exotic metalwork, suggesting that prominent hill locations may also have had a role in such disposal (Table 6:2).

Settlement density:

A 'Wessex view' of the Bronze and Iron Ages as being defined by their downland economies would be an over-simplification of the Sussex data. The once observed absence of settlement sites west of the Adur (Bedwin 1983, 34) is no longer the case (Table 6:2). During the past decades an increasing number of settlement sites and pottery findspots have been located on the West Sussex Coastal Plain (e.g. Ford: Appendix 6:1; Rustington: Rudling 1990; Selsey West Beach: Seager Thomas 1998; Yapton: Rudling 1987). East of the Adur, the number of Late Bronze Age sites becomes markedly less, and contrasts with the substantially higher density of early 1st millennium BC Wessex sites (Bedwin 1984:46; Cunliffe 1991, 228). The East Sussex situation might now be seen as resulting from the concentrating of population and activity *off* the Downs at Shinewater and the Willingdon levels (Greatorex 97/98 and this volume). Towards the end of the Late Bronze Age the climate became colder and wetter. This is specifically evidenced for Sussex post *c.* 700 BC by the environmental sequence from Little Cheyne Court, Romney Marsh (Waller *et al.* 1999). This may explain the relatively short-lived later Bronze Age occupation of the Willingdon Levels (Shinewater). During the later Bronze Age, there are also indications of a low-level spread of settlement on to the Weald (e.g. Ashington, America Wood: Priestley-Bell 1994, Table 2). The location of some Late Bronze Age hillforts on the northern edge of the Downs (proximate to the Weald: Hamilton and Manley 1997; Hamilton and Manley 2001), and the use of Wealden resources on downland hillforts and settlements, suggest that the Weald was of some importance to early 1st millennium BC communities.

Settlement layout and architecture:

Evidence of early 1st millennium BC Sussex domestic architecture is quite rare. There is a substantive loss of the Deverel-Rimbury settlement formula and of the roundhouse tradition. Late Bronze Age pottery finds suggest some continued use of Middle Bronze Age settlement site locations. However, the pottery is associated with less substantial roundhouses, with more erratically placed structural posts (Varley Halls: Greig 1997, 28-9), and scattered post-holes (Mile Oak: Russell 2002). It also occurs in colluvial deposits within Middle Bronze Age houses (Downsview: Rudling

Table 6.2. *Sussex Late Bronze Age (capitals), Early Iron Age (denoted by +) and late Early Iron Age (denoted by ++) settlements, enclosures and hillforts. Sites in bold have been discovered or excavated since Bedwin 1978. Starred sites are on the Coastal Plain. See Appendix 1 for sources.*

South Downs/Coastal Plain:					**Weald**
E. of Adur	**Arun/Adur**	**Adur/Ouse**	**Ouse/Cuckmere**	**E. of Cuckmere**	
Settlements: **FORD*** **CARNE'S SEAT** **KNAPP FARM*** SELSEY GOLF LINKS* **SELSEY EAST BEACH*** **SELSEY WEST BEACH*** Stoke Clump+ TRUNDLE **YAPTON**	Bow Hill **LAVANT** MUNTHAM COURT++ Park Brow I++ Rustington A++* **RUSTINGTON B*** **TESTERS**	**DOWNSVIEW** KINGSTON BUCI* **MILE OAK** PLUMPTON PLAIN B **PATCHAM FAWCETT** SLONK HILL **VARLEY HALLS** WEST BLATCHINGTON*	Bishopstone++	HEATHY BROW Green Street++ **SHINEWATER**	**ASHINGTON**
Enclosures: **Rummages Barn?**[2]	None known	**THUNDERSBARROW HILL**	BISHOPSTONE GLYNDE	None	None
Hillforts: None known	*CHANCTONBURY* Goosehill++ HARROW HILL HARTING BEACON **HIGHDOWN** TORBERRY++[1]	Ditchling Beacon+ Hollingbury+ **Thundersbarrow Hill+** **WOLSTONBURY**	**SEAFORD HEAD**	**BELLE TOUT**	None

[1] First phase: promontory fort

[2] Enclosure ditch with Early Iron Age pottery, Kenny 1985, fig. 4.

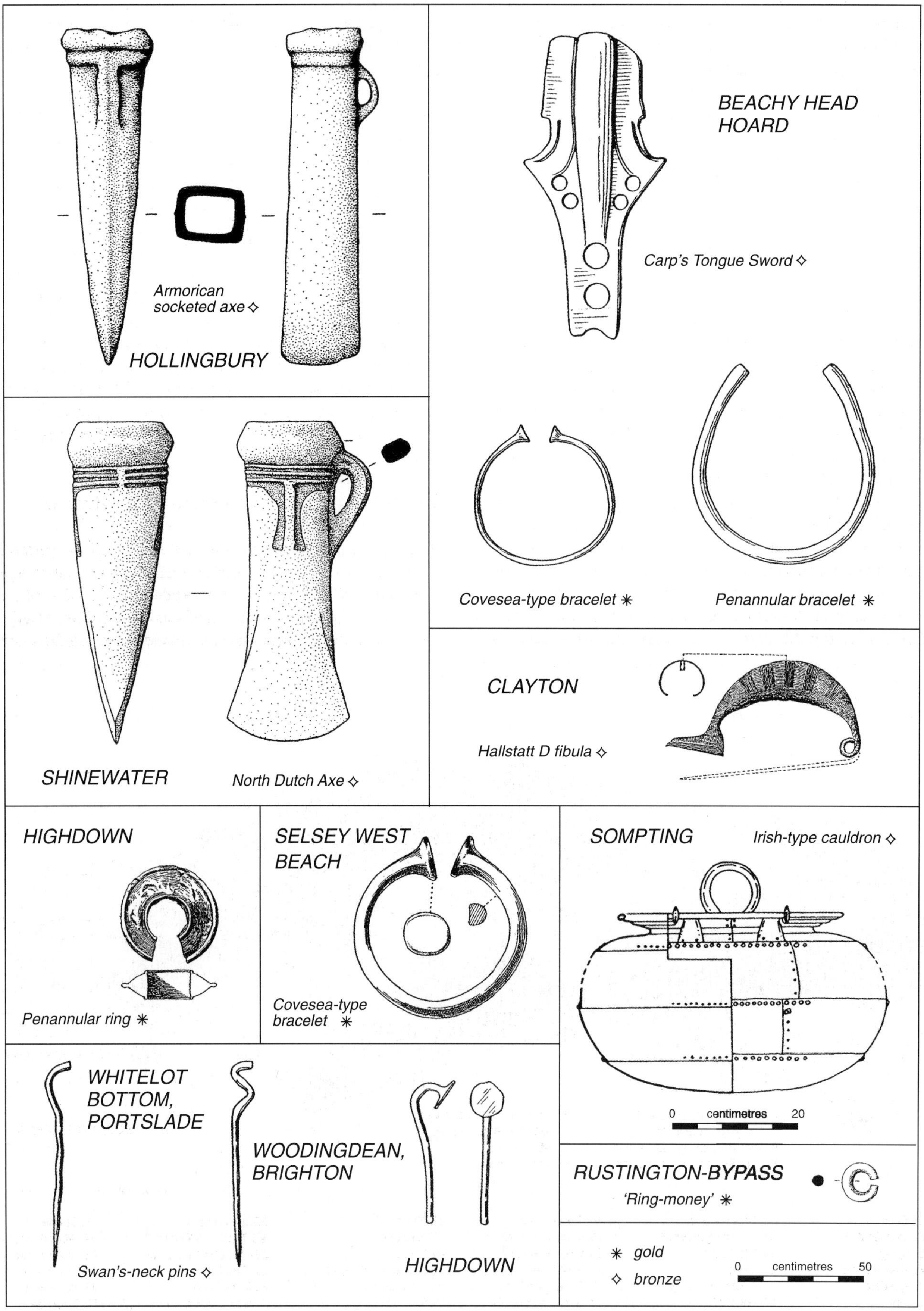

Figure 6.2. *Examples of Sussex earlier 1st millennium BC metalwork 'exotica'. Unless otherwise stated, redrawn by J. Russell from the following sources: Hollingbury: R. Thomas 1983; Beachy Head hoard, Clayton, Highdown and Selsey West Beach Curwen 1937; Rustington Bypass: Rudling and Gilkes 2001; Sompting, Whitelot Bottom, Portslade and Woodingdean, Brighton: Cunliffe 1991; Highdown: drawn from the original by J. Russell, unpublished excavation by M. Gardiner.*

2002b). Two early 1st millennium BC sites do, however, have clusters of roundhouses (Lavant: unenclosed Late Bronze Age/Early Iron Age settlement, and Hollingbury: Early Iron Age hillfort). At these sites house diameters range from 5.5m to 13m (Kenny 1994; Bedwin 1984; Holmes 1984). At Hollingbury only the shallow penannular ring gullies (wall-bedding trenches, or for the eaves drips?) remained. The Lavant houses comprised single-post ring structures with porches. These Sussex roundhouses markedly contrast with the larger, more sturdily constructed Wessex Iron Age roundhouses of *c.* 15m-20m diameter, which have double-ring post circles and a central setting of four timbers (Bersu 1940; Harding and Blake 1963; Wainwright 1979).

The substantial Wessex roundhouses, together with their ditch-enclosed farmyard compound, typify the idealized Iron Age farm of southern Britain (Fitzpatrick 1997a, 75). In Sussex earlier 1st millennium BC *non*-hillfort houses are not thus enclosed. The only evidence of anything mirroring either the Middle Bronze Age 'operational units' or the Wessex Iron Age farmyard format remains the Heathy Brow complex of two houses, a "working hollow", a field system, and double lynchet trackways noted by Bedwin (1982). In contrast to Wessex, new shapes of houses occur. Heathy Brow has one oval, and one rectangular, house. At Charleston Brow and Park Brow rectangular depressions with domestic debris indicate the possible presence of rectangular houses. Additionally, at Park Brow two parallel rows of post-holes defining an area 10m by 3m, and similar configurations at Muntham Court and Bishopstone, also suggest rectangular structures (Bell 1977; Burstow and Holleyman 1957a, 101; Hawley 1927; Holleyman and Burstow 1955, fig. 3; Smith 1927).

The possible symbolic implications of Bronze and Iron Age roundhouse architecture have been a major theme in recent publications. Fitzpatrick (1997a, 77) has highlighted the potential for counting the passage of time around a roundhouse in relation to cardinal solar directions. British Iron Age roundhouse entrances are predominantly orientated to the east. The cosmological referent of this to sunrise is notable (Oswald 1997, fig 10.4; Parker Pearson and Richards 1997). By contrast, Sussex Middle Bronze Age house entrances have a southerly orientation (Oswald 1997, fig. 10.7), and a subsequent 1st millennium BC uniformity in entrance orientation is lacking (e.g. house entrances point both east and west at Lavant: Kenny 1994). The Sussex rectangular buildings suggest a radical reorganization and reconceptualization of domestic space, which clearly deviates from a Wessex cosmology.

Deposition patterns and settlement abandonment:

Recent excavation work provides a good range of comparative contexts to suggest that Late Bronze Age and Early Iron Age settlement decommissioning/abandonment, and rubbish disposal, were more formalized than preceding Middle Bronze Age traditions. In the Late Bronze Age artefacts and

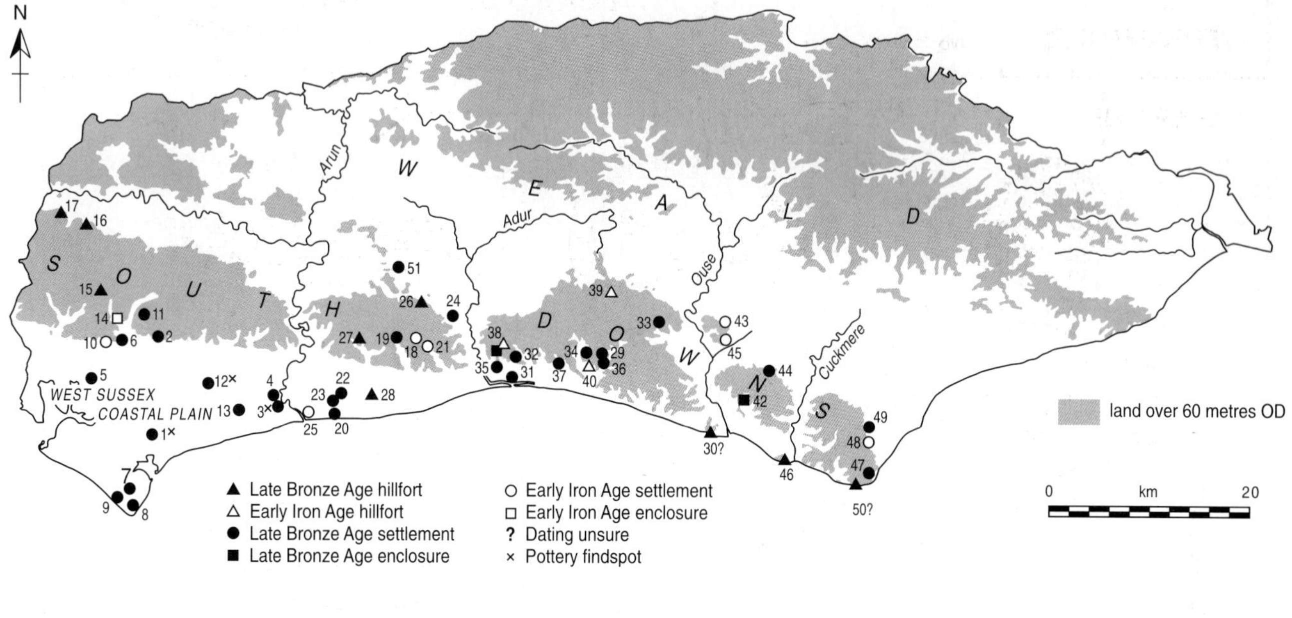

1. Birdham
2. Carne's Seat
3. Climping
4. Ford Aerodrome
5. Knapp Farm
6. Lavant
7. Selsey Golf Links
8. Selsey East Beach
9. Selsey West Beach
10. Stoke Clump
11. Trundle (pre-hillfort)
12. Westergate
13. Yapton
14. Rummages Barn
15. Goosehill
16. Harting Beacon
17. Torberry (first phase promontory fort)
18. Findon Park
19. Muntham Court
20. Littlehampton
21. Park Brow
22. Rustington Site A
23. Rustington Site B
24. Testers
25. Wickbourne
26. Chanctonbury
27. Harrow Hill
28. Highdown
29. Downsview
30. Castle Hill, Newhaven
31. Kingston Buci
32. Mile Oak
33. Plumpton Plain B
34. Patcham Fawcett
35. Slonk Hill
36. Varley Halls
37. West Blatchington
38. Thundersbarrow Hill
39. Ditchling Beacon
40. Hollingbury
41. Wolstonbury
42. Bishopstone
43. Caburn (pre-hillfort)
44. Charleston Brow
45. Glynde
46. Seaford Head
47. Heathy Brow
48. Green Street
49. Shinewater
50. Belle Tout
51. America Wood

Figure 6.3. *Distribution map of Sussex Late Bronze Age/Early Iron Age sites.*

rubbish were systematically removed from house interiors and variously placed in: i) dug-out scoops (Yapton: Hamilton 1987; Knapp Farm: Gardiner and Hamilton 1997); ii) wells (Selsey West Beach: Seager Thomas 1998 and pers. comm. for feature 55); and iii) on middens (Caburn pre-hillfort settlement: Drewett and Hamilton 1999). Such clearance would have either taken place while the houses were in use, and/or prior to abandonment. While these early 1st millennium BC traditions of house clearance make it difficult to ascertain the activities associated with specific structures, a wide range of tasks including pottery production, metalworking, spinning and weaving, and cereal processing are evidenced on these settlements (Hamilton 1993; Seager Thomas 1998, 12-13).

Burial:

Monumentality associated with funerary rites largely disappears in the British Late Bronze Age (Bruck 1995). For Sussex, there are indications that burial and other rituals increasingly took place *within* the settlement context. Examples include; i) the votive placement of objects (bronzes under the Shinewater platform, Greatorex 1998, 15); and ii) human burial within the settlement area. The latter evidence comprises single examples of inhumations from Shinewater (Greatorex this volume), Varley Halls (with a Middle/Late Bronze Age radiocarbon date: Greig 1997, 27), Mile Oak (with a Late Bronze Age radiocarbon date: Russell 2002) and a cremation under a low barrow associated with the Caburn pre-hillfort settlement (Wilson 1939, 206).

Hillforts:

The number of Sussex Late Bronze Age and Early Iron Age hillforts is impressive (Fig. 6.1). The phase is associated with 36% of all Sussex hillforts (11 examples: Table 2; Hamilton and Manley 1997). It has long been recognized that morphologically these hillforts are a highly disparate group (Bedwin 1978a; 1984), but they do have common characteristics of location, which distinguish them from the Middle Iron Age hillforts (Hamilton and Manley 1997; Hamilton and Manley 2001). The earliest hillforts are generally on the *edges* of the South Downs. Those along the northern escarpment of the South Downs have far-ranging views into the Weald, and are proximate to Wealden geologies and resources. These hillforts are inter-visible, suggesting that they connect places, resources and landscapes (Hamilton and Manley 2001). With the exceptions of Highdown and Hollingbury, evidence of actual habitation remains minimal and their traditional interpretation as pastoral enclosures remains apposite (Bedwin 1984; Bradley 1971). The growing number of settlement sites and pottery finds spots recognized over the past two decades off the Downs serves to further emphasize the liminal locations of these hillforts.

Table 6.3. *Sussex early first millennium BC metalwork 'exotica'.*

Site	Central European types	Atlantic types	Other	References
Beachy Head	hilt of Carp's Tongue sword	Covesea-type bracelets	Bracelet*	Curwen 1937, plate XVII:3.
Bracklesham Beach	None	None	Ring-money*	Taylor 1980, appendix 1.
Brighton	1 swan-necked pin+	1 Armorican axe+	Ring-money*	Curwen 1937, plate XX R. Thomas 1983.
Clayton	1 Hallstatt D fibula+	None	None	Curwen 1937, fig. 63.
Cuckmere Haven	None	None	Ring-money*	Curwen 1937, 211; Kendrick and Hawkes 1932, 128
Eastbourne Beach	None	4 Covesea-type bracelets*	None	Curwen 1937, 211.
Harting Beacon	None	None	2 pennannular rings*	Keef 1953.
Highdown Hill	1 swan necked pin+ 1 Hallstatt D sunflower pin+	None	1 penannular ring*	Gardiner 1984 unpublished excavations.
Hollingbury	None	1 Armorican axe+	None	R. Thomas 1983.
Patcham	None	3 Covesea-type bracelets*	None	Taylor 1980, appendix 1.
Portslade	2 swan-necked pins 1 bulb-headed pin+	None	None	Curwen 1937, plate XX.
Rustington	None	None	Ring-money*	Taylor 1980, appendix 1; Rudling 2001.
Selsey W. Beach	None	3 Covesea-type bracelets*	Ring-money*	Curwen 1937, fig. 65.
Shinewater	1 north-Dutch axe+	None	None	Greatorex 1997/98
Sompting	phalera+	7th century BC Irish-type cauldron+	None	Curwen 1948.
Westbourne	None	None	Ring money*	Rudling 2001.

* = gold; + = bronze; NB one of the Patcham Covesea-type bracelets is gold-plated bronze. One of the Rustington examples and the Westbourne example of ring-money are formed of alternate transverse layers of gold and silver.

Substantial land boundaries:

Sussex has an exceptionally large number of linear bank and ditch (variously single, double, or multiple) land boundaries known as cross-ridge dykes. At least 80 cross-ridge dykes are known for Sussex. There is considerable variation in their siting and morphology. Many *are* built across downland ridges. Some are in the vicinity of settlements, and others are associated with hillforts. The majority are undated, but based on the excavated examples, a Late Bronze Age and Early Iron Age dating is presumed (Bedwin 1979a). These major boundaries indicate a formalization and possible reorganization of land divisions at the beginning of the 1st millennium BC. Bradley (1971) has associated this with a growth of pastoralism in the Late Bronze Age, and the Sussex hillfort evidence concurs with this (*see* above). Given the number and variety of Sussex cross-ridge dykes, they clearly require further study and detailed survey mapping (Hamilton, work in progress).

Resource territories, and cultural/exchange networks:

The existence of regional networks during the Sussex early 1st millennium BC is indicated by the recurrent presence of Wealden stone on downland and Coastal Plain sites (e.g. Lodsworth-type Lower Greensand used for querns, Peacock 1987). This trend is pre-established, having already been observed for Middle Bronze Age Deverel-Rimbury sites (Drewett 1982a; Seager Thomas 1999). In East Sussex, the use of iron oxide-rich clays in earlier 1st millennium BC pottery production further evidences contacts with the Weald (Hamilton 1980 and 1993). Finds of Kimmeridge (Dorset) shale bracelets (Appendix 3) point to wider inter-regional contacts, as do the style traits of Sussex Late Bronze Age pottery, which share technological and stylistic similarities with the contemporary assemblages of the Thames Valley (Gardiner and Hamilton 1997, 81).

Particularly distinctive of the Sussex Late Bronze Age and Early Iron Age is the presence of Continental imports and types. Again, in this respect Sussex shares more in common with the Thames valley and Kent, than with Wessex. The pottery assemblages of Plumpton Plain B, Selsey West Beach, and Shinewater include a small number of Continental forms derived from Eastern France and the Low Countries. These include Ellison's (1978, 32) Type 16 pottery form, and 'assiettes tronçoniques' - wide plates (Shinewater pottery assemblage, unpub. and Selsey West Beach: Seager Thomas 2001).

The most overt evidence of Continental contact is the presence of a range of metalwork 'exotica' particularly relating to the beginning of the 1st millennium BC (Fig. 6:2, Table 6:2). The finds have a coast-orientated distribution, the most recent find being the North Dutch/North German zone axe found at Shinewater. The majority of Continental metalwork in Sussex has long been known. Its striking combination of both north and central European Hallstatt C (7th/6th centuries BC) and Hallstatt D (7th/6th centuries BC) metalwork (Dunning 1934), *and* finds of Atlantic type or origin, however, merits comment. The Hallstatt D finds include a single sunflower pin from Highdown Hill (Fig. 6.2; Gardiner 1984 unpubl. excavations), with most British finds of this type coming from Scotland (Cunliffe 1991, 424). The Atlantic-type metalwork includes a notable concentration of Covesea-type gold bracelets (*see* above and Table 6:2). The latter are found predominantly in north-east Scotland and are related to Late Bronze Age types in north-western Europe. The Sompting hoard singularly combines this duality of connections with its class B2 Irish (?) cauldron and a Hallstatt phalera (Curwen 1948).

Middle Iron Age (c. 450 to 50 cal BC)

Introduction:

Evidence for the Sussex Middle Iron Age is distinctive in its: i) uneven distribution, and for East Sussex its low-density of settlements and findspots (Fig. 6:4); and ii) the scant evidence for the occupation of hillfort interiors.

Pottery and metalwork:

A lack of closely datable metalwork finds, together with a negligible number of radiocarbon dates, means that the sequencing of the Sussex Middle Iron Age mostly relies on pottery chronologies. Wessex radiocarbon chronology suggests that the saucepan pottery, which characterizes the Middle Iron Age, may span a period as long as three centuries from the 4th to the 1st centuries BC (Cunliffe 1984, 242; Hamilton 2002a). Much of the Sussex saucepan pottery falls within the stylistic group termed 'Caburn-Cissbury style' (Cunliffe 1991, 80) characterized by curvilinear tooled designs, but West Sussex has saucepan vessels decorated in Cunliffe's 'St Catherine's Hill-Worthy Down style' with decoration characterized by bands of impressed dots (Hamilton 1985, 225). In comparison to Wessex, the distribution extent of the style zones of these saucepan decorative types is small (Hamilton and Manley 1999, 21: fig. 2, and discussed further below). This suggests a relatively low level of craft specialization or inter-community contact.

Settlement density:

During the Middle Iron Age the greater concentration of settlement in West Sussex continues (Table 6:4, Fig. 6:4). Some 44% of all Sussex Middle Iron Age settlements lie west of the Arun. Over the last two decades aerial photography and excavation have greatly expanded our previously limited knowledge of the Middle and Late Iron Age occupation of the West Sussex Coastal Plain. Extensive networks of drainage ditches characterize this occupation. These ditches form the boundaries of rectangular fields, which are often linked by double lynchet trackways (Aldsworth 1976; Bedwin 1984). Excavations of ditched complexes at North Bersted (Bedwin and Pitts 1978), Old Place Farm Westhampnett (Bedwin 1984, 49-50), and Oving (Bedwin and Holgate 1985) have produced both saucepan pottery and later Iron Age pottery, suggesting a continuity of land management through the later Iron Age. Morphologically these ditch systems suggest a co-ordinated layout involving a great deal of construction effort, possibly at a community level. At North Bersted the network extends for at least 5 hectares. Irrespective of their possible community level of construction, excavated evidence suggests that once established they were exploited from individual farmsteads, with single houses being identified at both Copse Farm and North Bersted (*see* below). It is possible that these sites were used on a seasonal basis, given that during the winter months much of the Lower Coastal Plain was under standing water (Bedwin and Holgate 1985, 235). Conversely, it can be argued that the drainage ditches may have been the necessary investment for full-time occupation. The area would have provided good grazing land and cattle bones predominate at North Bersted and at Copse Farm, Oving. The relationship between the sites of the West Sussex Coastal Plain and the contemporary Trundle hillfort on the adjacent Downs is an interesting, unresolved issue.

Aerial photography of the southern edge of the West Sussex Downs has additionally revealed examples of Wessex-type banjo-shaped enclosures (Carne's Seat, Denge Bottom and Selhurst Park). These are absent elsewhere in Sussex (Holgate 1986a), but first appear elsewhere in the Middle Iron Age. Of these only Carne's Seat has been excavated, with its ditch fills being associated with saucepan pottery (Hamilton 1986).

These new settlement and enclosure forms suggest a re-organization of the West Sussex landscape during the Middle Iron Age. By contrast there is a distinct lack of Middle Iron Age settlement sites and findspots in East Sussex (Table 6:4). The major settlements of this period remain the downland sites of Bishopstone (Bell 1977) and Slonk Hill (Hartridge 1978). Both of these sites have earlier 1st millennium BC occupation (*see* above), and the collective, albeit negligible, settlement evidence for the East Sussex Middle Iron Age suggests continuity, but population decline and a dire lack of dynamism. Recent trial excavations at Norton (in the Ouse valley, proximate to Bishopstone) suggest another possibility, namely that Middle Iron Age activity in East Sussex may be masked by substantial colluvial deposits (G. Thomas 2001). If so, there may have been a shift of occupation off the Downs during the Middle Iron Age, which has effectively rendered the archaeology invisible.

Settlement architecture:

Examples of Middle Iron Age house types are negligible. At North Bersted a small roundhouse was evidence by a penannular gully some 6m across with a 1.23 m-wide entrance gap associated with a single posthole. The gully is interpreted as the bedding trench for the house walls (Bedwin and Pitts 1978). At Oving a single house was likewise evidenced by a penannular ring gully of 7m diameter, with some post-holes associated with the gully and entrance break (Bedwin and Holgate 1985). Oving also had a circular depression interpreted as a working area associated with pits, post-holes and metalworking debris (iron slag and an unfinished bronze brooch: Oldham 1985, 229). These sites lack the storage pits typical of the chalkland Middle Iron Age sites. This is obviously a reflection of their Coastal Plain siting and consequent proximity to the water table, which would result in the waterlogging of deep pits.

Settlement abandonment:

Bedwin and Pitts (1978, 301) suggest the lack of post-holes associated with the North Bersted house may be the result of the stakes or posts being withdrawn from the ground and not allowed to rot *in situ*. This could suggest a deliberate act of dismantling on the closing down of a site. The dispersed distribution of unabraded conjoining sherds at Oving also suggests a single act of site levelling and abandonment, rather than the gradual infill of negative features such as the ditches (Hamilton 1985). Given that neither structure produced any artefact finds, the continuance of earlier 1st millennium BC traditions of ongoing, and final, site clearance seems likely.

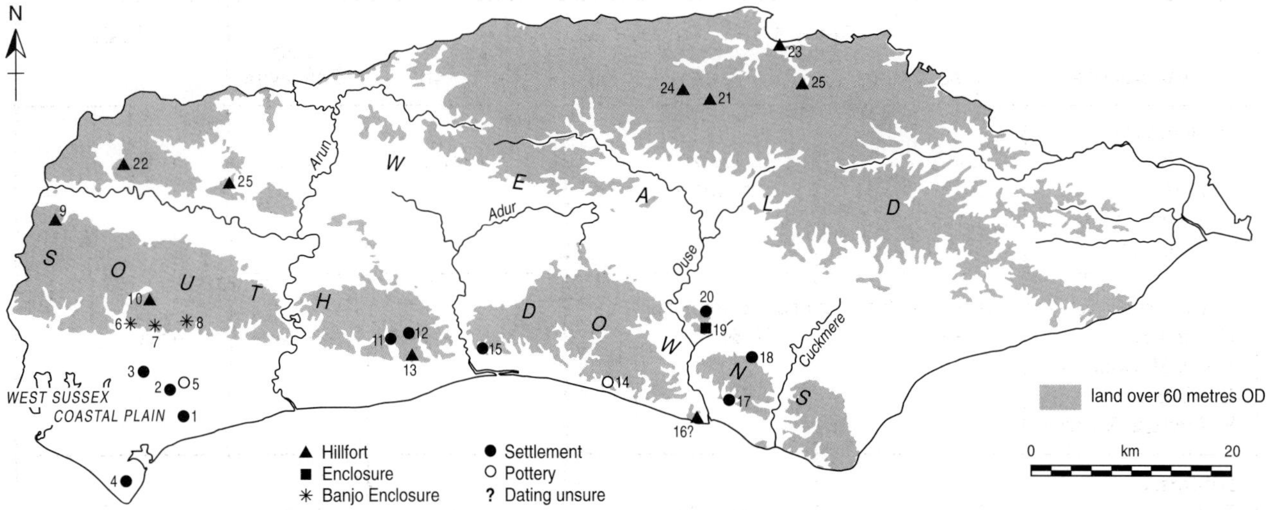

1. North Bersted
2. Oving (Copse Farm)
3. Oldplace Farm
4. Selsey Golf Links Lane
5. Tote Copse
6. Carne's Sea
7. Denge Bottom
8. Selhurst Park Farm
9. Torberry
10. Trundle
11. Findon Park
12. Park Brow
13. Cissbury
14. Elm Grove
15. Slonk Hill
16. Castle Hill
17. Bishopstone
18. Charleston Brow
19. Glynde
20. Caburn
21. Garden Hill
22. Hammer Wood
23. High Rocks
24. Philpots
25. Piper's Close
26. Saxonbury

Figure 6.4. *Distribution map of Sussex Middle Iron Age sites.*

Deposition patterns, burial and ritual:

The lack of formal funerary remains, which characterizes the earlier 1st millennium BC, continued in the Sussex Middle Iron Age. There are a small number of articulated human burials in storage pits (Bishopstone: burial 2: Bell 1977, 81-83; Slonk Hill: Hartridge 1978, 80). The low-level presence of disarticulated human remains on settlements (suggesting that excarnation was practised), and the structured nature of certain types of settlement deposits, point to an increased focusing of ritual practices within secular contexts. Sussex examples of disarticulated human remains in Middle Iron Age non-funerary contexts include the jaw, skull, femur and ulna fragments from separate pit and gate post-hole contexts at the Trundle hillfort and three human jaw bones from the base of separate pits at the Caburn hillfort (Hamilton 1998). Ditch contexts at both Copse Farm Oving and North Bersted collectively included a small number of human leg bones and skull fragments (Bedwin and Holgate 1985, 232; Bedwin and Pitts 1978, 339; Fitzpatrick 1997b, table 20). Given that the latter two sites have produced both Middle and Late Iron Age pottery, the human remains cannot be precisely dated within this time range.

The Sussex Middle Iron Age 'domestic' activity on the Downs is characterized by the presence of storage pits. In recent years there has been a rethinking of the meaning of, and processes associated with, Iron Age deposition in pits and ditches (Hill 1995b). This work has primarily centred on Wessex sites. Reanalysis of past excavations suggests that the structured patterns of deposition in redundant storage pits recognized for Wessex also occurred in Sussex. The best database is the 140 pits from the Caburn, but Middle Iron Age pits from other hillforts (e.g. the Trundle) and settlements (e.g. Bishopstone) exhibit a communality of patterning. The latter includes the specific deposition of quern stones, weaponry (seemingly deliberately broken), wild animal bones (wild fowl, fox and badger), and occasional human remains at the base of pits (Hamilton 1998). These recurrent and exclusive combinations lack the characteristics of random rubbish disposal or site abandonment and suggest that they are governed by overarching beliefs or customs relating to the deposition of specific artefacts, and human and animal remains.

Hillforts:

Sussex's most visually dramatic hillforts date to the Middle Iron Age (Hamilton and Manley 2001). In common with Wessex the number of active hillforts is substantially less than in the preceding period. Three of the Sussex Middle Iron Age hillforts are new establishments (the Caburn, Cissbury, and the Trundle, although the former two have pre-hillfort occupation). Of the remaining two Torberry was substantially enlarged and reconfigurated, and Castlehill Newhaven, which has a substantial collection of Middle Iron Age saucepan pottery, may have already been enclosed by the Late Bronze Age or Early Iron Age (Hamilton and Manley 1997). The major downland hillforts are positioned centrally on individual, chalkland blocks, which has traditionally led to them being interpreted as central places, as has been suggested for Wessex hillforts (Cunliffe 1991, 354, figs. 14.27). These Sussex hillforts, however, lack evidence for being major centres of production exchange or occupation (Hamilton and Manley 2001). Limited finds of Middle Iron Age pottery suggest that hillforts were being constructed for the first time in the Weald, although their main period of use dates to the Late Iron Age (Hamilton and Manley 1997; Hamilton and Manley 2001).

Table 6.4. *Middle Iron Age settlement sites in Sussex. Sites in bold have been discovered or excavated since Bedwin 1978. Starred sites are on the Coastal Plain.* (See *Appendix 1 for sources)*

South Downs/Coastal Plain:					Weald
West of Arun	**Arun/Adur**	**Adur/Ouse**	**Ouse/ Cuckmere**	**E. of Cuckmere**	
Settlements: North Bersted* **Oving*** **Oldplace Farm** Tote Copse*	Elm Grove[1] Findon Park Park Brow II	Slonk Hill Charleston Brow	Bishopstone	None	None
Enclosure complexes (possibly with associated settlement):					
Carne's Seat **Denge Bottom** **Lordington** **Selhurstpark Farm**	None	None	None	None	None
Hillforts: Torberry Trundle	Cissbury	Castle Hill?	**Caburn**	None	Garden Hill Hammer Wood High Rocks Piper's Copse Saxonbury

[1]pottery finds, see Curwen 1939, finds date unknown

Since the 1980s, the supposed defensive role of hillforts has been called into question (Bowden and McOmish 1987; 1989.) In spite of their highly visual ramparts, it is difficult to understand the Sussex Middle Iron Age hillforts as simply acting in these terms (Drewett and Hamilton 1999). There is an elaboration of entrances (e.g. entrance corridors at the Caburn, the Trundle and Torberry, and heightening of the ramparts near the entrances at Cissbury), but this seems to have been as much about architectural drama and prestige as defence. The extensive multivallation associated with the classic Wessex hillforts is absent (Cunliffe 1991, 322). The consistent downslope location of the Sussex ramparts monumentalizes, rather than defensively obscures, hillfort interiors (Hamilton 1998; Hamilton and Drewett 1999). The concentration of Middle Iron Age sites around Cissbury and the Trundle suggests that the landscapes around hillforts, rather than the hillforts themselves, were the loci for settlement (Bedwin and Holgate 1985, fig. 14). Indeed the distances over which settlement tasks (or indeed defence activities) could have been co-ordinated within any Sussex Middle Iron Age hillfort are limited (Figure 6:5). This is due to the topography of these hillforts which causes restricted intra-site visibility. The hillforts themselves are not inter-visible but, within the downland block associated with each Middle Iron Age hillfort, coeval extra-mural settlements are inter-visible with the hillfort of that block (Hamilton and

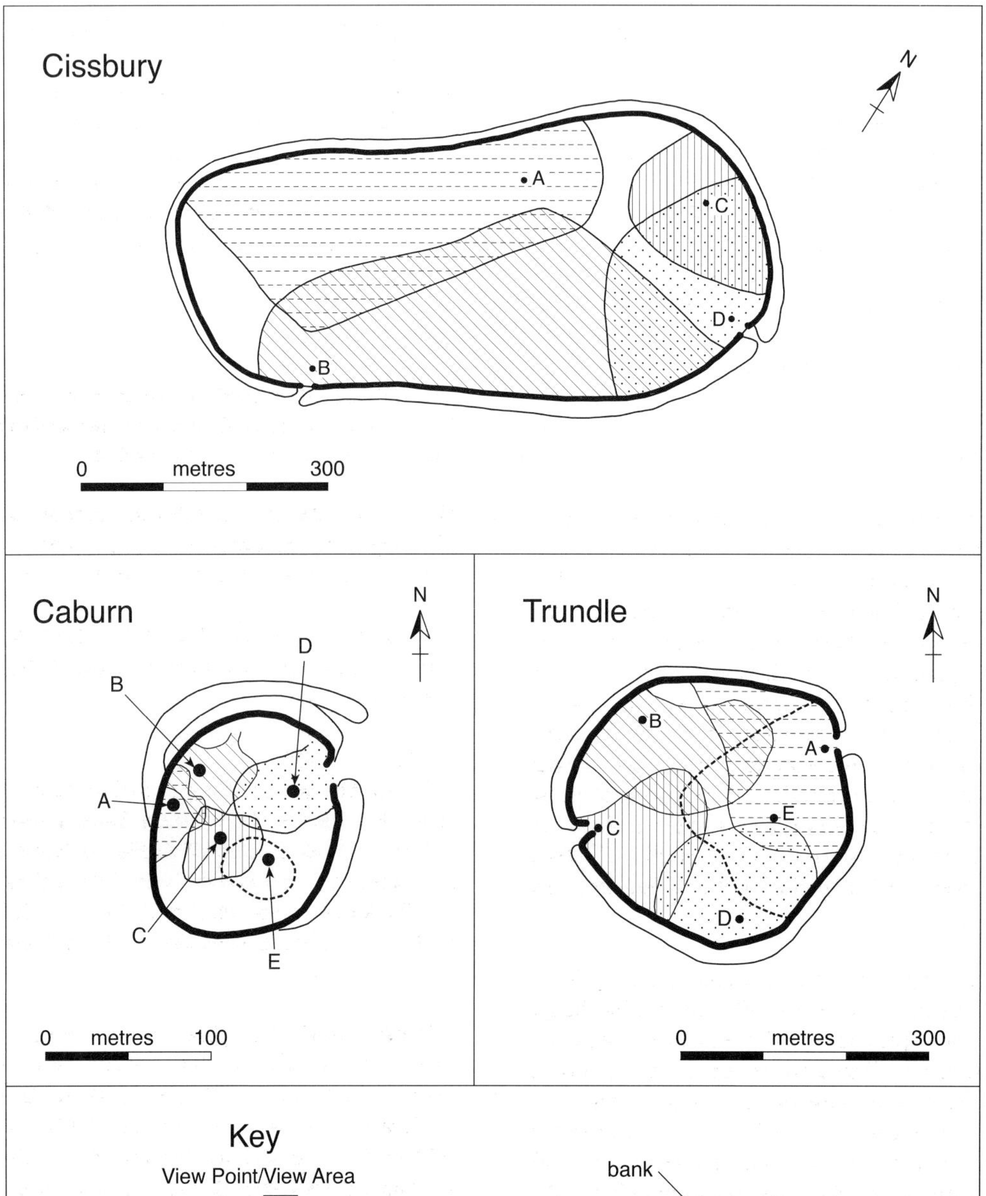

Figure 6.5. *Intra-site visibility maps of three Sussex Middle Iron Age hillforts. View points of maximal visibility were selected for mapping.*

Manley 1997; Holgate 1986a, 48). The hillforts therefore seem to have acted as central monuments and focal points to dispersed communities outside the hillforts. These hillforts clearly functioned differently (in terms of their locations and monumentality) to the earlier 1st millennium BC hillforts and perhaps replaced the role of cross-ridge dykes in marking territories, albeit in a rather different way.

Resource territories, and cultural/exchange networks

The excavated evidence from Middle Iron Age farmsteads suggests small-scale industrial activity involving both bronze metalworking and iron forging, together with textile production (Bedwin and Holgate 1985). Continued accessing of the resources of the Weald is evidenced in the presence of Wealden sandstone (for querns) and iron slag (Bedwin and Holgate 1985) on settlements.

The Wessex Middle Iron Age is associated with a marked increase in distinctive types of pottery being made at centralized production locations, together with inter-regional and regional distributions extending up to 80km, and 30km, from source respectively (E. Morris 1994, 377). By contrast, Sussex saucepan traditions suggest small-scale centralization, with style and fabric-type distribution zones being less than 12km across, suggesting a very different scale of centralization and longer distant contacts for Wessex.

Conclusion

The time frame within which the latest prehistory of Sussex must now be perceived is the 1st millennium BC rather than the Iron Age (Hamilton and Gregory 2001). Sussex has produced a substantial number of 1st millennium BC finds over the last two decades. In addition, there are wholly new emphases and approaches to 1st millennium BC studies which this paper has been structured around. I have addressed the latter both in terms of reconsidering older databases, as well as using more recently discovered material. Some themes are markedly absent from my review. The most problematic is the lack of a discussion of subsistence strategies. What can be said is already fully summarized (Bedwin 1978a; 1984), and this is one area in which major additional data have not been recovered.

Future periodic reappraisals of Sussex later prehistory in the light of new finds and approaches will undoubtedly change the narrative. For the present, it can be suggested that Sussex is notable for having a striking Late Bronze Age development. This is particularly evidenced by: i) long-distance connections; ii) an *orientation* (e.g. in hillfort placement) to non-downland locales; iii) a major re-configuration of domestic and craft organization; and iv) an imbuing of the topographic landscape with symbolic meaning through the votive deposition of prestige metalwork. Many of these changes seem best paralleled in the Thames Valley rather than Wessex. Our detailed understanding of the Sussex Middle Iron Age, by contrast, is worryingly obscure. The period is particularly associated with the establishment of new, highly visual hillforts and an intensification of evidence for structured deposition. The apparent depopulation of Central and East Sussex, together with the appearance of new types of ditched settlements in West Sussex are the pre-eminent settlement features of this period.

1st millennium BC Sussex is uniquely different to Wessex. The known settlement densities, particularly in East Sussex are different to those of Wessex, and enclosed farmstead sites with highly visual houses are absent. Additionally, the scale of regional centralization, be it in the roles of hillforts, or in pottery style zones and production, is significantly smaller for Sussex. By the Late Iron Age, Sussex is not a coherent whole, with increased population in West Sussex alongside centralized production (e.g. of pottery: Hamilton 1985) and new rituals (e.g. the Westhampnett cemetery, Fitzpatrick 1997b).

During the later 2nd millennium BC and the 1st millennium BC, Sussex is important because it is *different*. It has internal diversity possibly at a scale greater than at any other point in its prehistory. It is not just a marginal version of the Wessex Iron Age. In offering a fragmentary world that cannot be typified by single-region models, it significantly contributes to our awareness and understanding of diversity in 1st millennium BC Lowland Britain.

Appendices

Appendix 6.1. *Published discoveries and excavations of Sussex Middle and Late Bronze Age sites and Iron Age sites by decade (of publication) since the 1920s.*

Within each decade the sites are ordered alphabetically. Compiled from Hamilton 1993, with subsequent additions. Also *see* Hamilton and Gregory 2001 for further discussion.

Abbreviations: E= Early; M= Middle; L= Late; BA= Bronze Age; IA= Iron Age; * excavated sites published in more than one decade.

1920s
*Caburn (EIA pre-hillfort palisaded settlement/MIA hillfort, E. and E.C. Curwen 1927); Green Street, Eastbourne (pit with EIA pottery finds, Budgen 1922); Findon Park (LBA/EIA/MIA/LIA settlement, Fox and Wolseley 1928); Park Brow (LBA/EIA/MIA/LIA settlement, Hawley 1927; Smith 1927); Trundle (LBA pre-hillfort settlement/MIA hillfort, Curwen 1929).

1930s
*Caburn (LBA/EIA pre-hillfort settlement, and MIA hillfort, Wilson 1939); Castle Hill, Newhaven (LBA/MIA/LIA hillfort, Field 1939); Charleston Brow (LBA/MIA/LIA settlement, Parsons and Curwen 1933); Cissbury (MIA hillfort, Curwen and Williamson 1931); Crowhurst Park (Romano-British iron-working site with some LIA activity/pottery, Piggott 1938); Devil's Dyke (hillfort, LIA?, Burstow and Wilson 1936); *Ditchling Beacon (LBA/EIA hillfort, Crow 1930); Harrow Hill (LBA hillfort, Holleyman 1937); Highdole Hill (predominantly Romano-British, but includes unstratified finds of LIA pottery, Holleyman 1936 and dating discussed in Hamilton 1993); *Hollingbury (LBA pre-hillfort enclosure; EIA hillfort, Curwen 1932); Horsted Keynes (LIA pottery finds in a ditch, settlement?, Hardy and Curwen 1937); Kingston Buci (LBA/MIA/LIA settlement, E. Curwen *et al.*

1931); New Barn Down (MBA settlement, Curwen 1934); Philpots (LIA promontory fort, Hannah 1932); Pipers Copse (MIA/LIA hillfort, Winbolt 1930); Plumpton Plain A and B (MBA/LBA settlements, Holleyman and Curwen 1935); *Saxonbury (LIA hillfort, Winbolt 1930); Selsey, Golf Links Lane (LBA, MIA and LIA pottery, settlements?, White 1934); *Thundersbarrow (MBA and LBA pre-hillfort enclosure/MIA hillfort, Curwen 1933); Trundle (LBA pre-hillfort settlement; MIA hillfort, Curwen 1931); *Wolstonbury (LBA/EIA hillfort, 1930).

1940s
*Highdown (pre-hillfort MBA settlement, LBA/EIA hillfort, Wilson 1940; Portfield gravel pit, Chichester (Romano-British site with some LIA pottery finds, Curwen and Frere 1947); Sedlescombe (LIA pottery finds - settlement?, Chown 1947).

1950s
Blackpatch (MBA settlement, Ratcliffe-Densham 1953); Goosehill Camp (EIA hillfort/enclosure, Boyden 1956); Harting Beacon (LBA hillfort, Keef 1953); Hammer Wood (MIA/LIA hillfort, Boyden 1958); *Highdown (MBA pre-hillfort settlement/LBA/EIA hillfort, Wilson 1950); High Rocks (MIA/LIA hillfort, 1950s/60s excavation, see below); Itford Hill (MBA settlement, Burstow and Holleyman 1957b); Muntham Court (LBA/EIA settlement, Burstow and Holleyman 1957a; Holleyman and Burstow 1955); Steyning (MBA barrow, Burstow 1958); West Blatchington (EIA pottery - settlement?, Norris and Burstow 1950; 1952).

1960s
Glynde, Balcombe quarry (EIA/MIA enclosure and settlement?, Burstow and Norris 1958-62); Cock Hill (MBA settlement, Ratcliffe-Densham 1961); High Rocks (MIA/LIA hillfort, Money 1968); Stoke Clump (EIA pottery - settlement?, Cunliffe 1966).

1970s
*Belle Tout (LBA hillfort?, Bradley 1971b, Drewett 1975); Bishopstone (LBA, EIA, MIA, LIA settlement, Bell 1977); Broadfields-Goffs Park (LIA/Roman-British iron-working sites, Gibson-Hill 1975; 1976; Cartwright 1992: full-write-up of 1970s excavations); Garden Hill (MIA/LIA hillfort, Money 1977; 1980); Harting Bedwin (LBA hillfort, Bedwin 1978b); Itford Hill (MBA cemetery, Holden 1972); Littlehampton (LBA/EIA pottery-settlement?), Bedwin 1979c; North Bersted (MIA/LIA settlement and enclosures, Bedwin and Pitts 1978); Slonk Hill (LBA/MIA settlement, Hartridge 1978); Torberry (EIA/MIA hillfort Cunliffe 1976); Tote Copse, Aldingbourne (MIA and LIA pottery finds, Pitts 1979).

1980s
Black Patch (MBA settlement, Drewett 1982a); Carne's Seat (MIA/LIA banjo enclosure, LBA pottery also recovered (residual?), Holgate 1986a); Chelwood Gate (LIA pottery and associated kiln debris, Wickenden 1986); *Chanctonbury Ring (LBA hillfort, Bedwin 1980); Devil's Ditch, Boxgrove (Chichester Dykes: LIA territorial enclosure, Bedwin and Orton 1984; Bedwin and Place 1995); *Ditchling (LBA/EIA hillfort, Rudling 1985); Heathy Brow (LBA settlement, Bedwin 1982); *Highdown (MBA pre-hillfort settlement/ LBA/EIA hillfort, Gardiner, unpublished excavation); *Hollingbury (EIA hillfort, Hamilton 1984, Holmes 1984, NB excavated in 1967-9); Lancing Down (LIA shrine, Bedwin 1981); Lordington (possible LIA enclosure, Holgate 1986b); Oving (MIA/LIA settlement and enclosures, Bedwin and Holgate 1985); Ounces Barn, Boxgrove, Enclosure 1 (LIA enclosure with moulds for the production of coin blanks in its ditch, Bedwin and Place 1995); Rummages Barn (EIA enclosure ditch with pottery, Kenny 1985); St Anne's Road, Eastbourne (L. Stevens 1987); Seaford Head (LBA hillfort, Bedwin 1986); Selsey East Beach (EIA pottery, settlement? Kenny 1989); Testers (LBA/LIA pottery, settlements? Gardiner 1988); *Thundersbarrow (MBA/LBA pre-hillfort enclosure/EIA hillfort, Rudling unpublished excavation; Hamilton 1993); Yapton (LBA settlement, Aldsworth 1983; Rudling 1987).

1990s
America Wood, Ashington (LBA settlement features and pottery, Priestley-Bell 1994); *Belle Tout (LBA hillfort?, Russell 1996b); *Caburn (LBA/EIA pre-hillfort palisaded settlement/MIA hillfort, Drewett and Hamilton 1999); Denge Bottom (MIA enclosures, Holgate 1986a); Downsview (MBA/LBA settlement, Rudling 2002); Halnaker Hill (LBA/ EIA field system, excavated 1981-83, Bedwin 1992); Lavant (LBA/EIA settlement, Kenny 1993); Mile Oak (MBA/LBA settlement, Russell 2002b); Knapp Farm (LBA settlement, Gardiner and Hamilton 1997); Littlehampton (Gosden Road and Wickbourne Estate (LBA/EIA, MIA, and LIA pottery finds, Gilkes 1993, NB write-up of Cutler and Blick's late 1940's and 1950's excavations); Patcham Fawcett (MBA settlement, Greatorex 2002); Potlands Farm (MBA? burnt mound, some MBA and LBA pottery, LBA radiocarbon date, Stevens 1997); Rustington (Site B: LBA pottery, Site A EIA/ MIA and LIA pottery - multi-period settlement activity?, Rudling 1990, NB finds 1986-88); Selsey West Beach (LBA settlements, Seager Thomas 1998 and 2001); Shinewater (LBA settlement, Greatorex 1998 and this volume); Varley Halls (MBA/LBA settlement, Greig 1997); Westhampnett (LIA cemetery, Fitzpatrick 1997b); *Wolstonbury (LBA/EIA hillfort, Russell 1996c).

2000-02 (*NB mostly currently unpublished sites*). UCL= University College London; MOLAS = Museum of London Archaeological Services.
Angmering MBA and LBA pottery and settlement features (Oxford Archaeological Unit and UCL Field Archaeological Unit: TQ 079034, Angmering By-pass; TQ 072037: Roundstone Lane); Birdham (SU 824000) LBA pottery finds (UCL Field Archaeology Unit); Climping (SU 999022) LBA pottery finds (UCL Field Archaeology Unit); *Chanctonbury Ring (LBA hillfort, Rudling 2002c); Ford Aerodrome (SU 994033) LBA/EIA ditch and pit complex (RPS Consultants), Shopwyke (SU 888052) MIA and LIA pottery and settlement features (MOLAS); Westergate (SU 940054) LBA pottery finds (UCL Field Archaeology Unit).

Appendix 6.2. Summary of Sussex radiocarbon dates for Middle Bronze Age to Late Iron Age (calibrated using the CALIB programme of Stuiver and Reimer 1998)

Period/Site	Lab Number	Radiocarbon result BP	Calibrate date range (2 sigma)
MIDDLE BRONZE AGE			
Black Patch			
Grain from hut platform 4, pit 5	HAR-2939	2780 ± 80	1206-800 cal BC
Grain from hut platform 4, pit 3	HAR-2940	3020 ± 70	1430-1020 cal BC
Grain from hut platform 4, pit 4	HAR-2941	2790 ± 70	1187-805 cal BC
Grain from hut platform 1, pit	HAR-3735	2970 ± 80	11410-935 cal BC
As above	HAR-3736	3080 ± 70	1504-1128 cal BC
As above	HAR-3737	2850 ± 70	1258-832 cal BC
Downsview			
Charcoal from fire-pit 2146 on hut terrace 2046	UB-3783	3201 ± 28	1521-1422 cal BC
As above	UB-3784	3175 ± 25	1517-1406 cal BC
As above	UB-3785	3199 ± 27	1521-1411 cal BC
As above	UB-3786	3220 ± 27	1524-1428 cal BC
Charcoal from posthole 2391 on hut terrace 2262	GU-5429	3140 ± 80	1600-1134 cal BC
Charcoal from posthole 2802 on hut terrace 2262	GU-5430	3170 ± 70	1603-1263 cal BC
Charcoal from posthole 4073 on hut terrace 4065	GU-5432	2980 ± 70	1408-999 cal BC
As above	GU-5433	3020 ± 60	1413-1049 cal BC
Charcoal from fire-pit 4029	OxA-4809	3270 ± 40	1680-1439 cal BC
Charcoal from posthole 2406 on hut terrace 2262	OxA-4811	3110 ± 60	1517-1135 cal BC
Itford Hill			
Burnt barley on floor of storage pit, hut E	GrN-6167	2950 ± 35	1292-1018 cal BC
Mile Oak			
Ungulate tibia, primary silt, ditch 243	OxA-5106	3250 ± 60	1684-1408 cal BC
Cattle radius from posthole 1579, hut 1	OxA-5107	3260 ± 65	1688-1408 cal BC
Cattle tooth, base of pond 1504	OxA-5108	2975 ± 50	1382-1015 cal BC
Cattle mandible, posthole 1522	OxA-5109	2975 ± 50	1382-1015 cal BC
Deer femur, primary silt, ditch 1557	OxA-3153	3480 ± 80	2024-1605 cal BC
Deer bone, posthole 386	OxA-3154	3050 ± 80	1495-1046 cal BC
Animal bone, posthole 4108, hut B	OxA-3155	2950 ± 100	1427-898 cal BC
Thundersbarrow Hill pre-hillfort enclosure			
Antler, floor of enclosure ditch	HAR-8182	3220 ± 70	1682-1320 cal BC
Varley Halls			
Cattle ulna, palisade ditch	BM-2917	3050 ± 50	1428-1129 cal BC
Human humerus and cranium	BM-2919	2890 ± 60	1287-903 cal BC
Charcoal associated with daub, hut 3	BM-2936	3130 ± 50	1517-1263 cal BC
LATE BRONZE AGE			
Bishopstone			
Thermoluminesent date on two pottery sherds	Source: Bell 1977, 290	Average TL date: 950 ± 300 BC)	Probable limits: 1550-350 cal BC
Climping			
Mixed charcoal, upper fill (context 81) of large pit	BETA-152860	2610 ± 70	900-540 cal BC

Appendix 6.2. (continued).

Ford			
Charcoal?, context 1085, deposit, above context 1113 (see below)	BETA-144445	2820 ± 60	1206-830 cal BC
Charcoal?, context 1113, pit fill	BETA-144446	2800 ± 60	11186-826 cal BC
Charcoal?, Context 1264, pit fill	BETA-144447	2580 ± 40	817-560 cal BC
Ditchling Beacon			
Bone, base of rampart ditch	HAR-5935	2560 ± 100	902-401 cal BC
Mile Oak			
Cattle bone from make-up of mound KII	OxA-511	2820 ± 50	1186-833 cal BC
Potlands Farm, Patching			
Twigs from large waterlogged pit	Q-3259	2690 ± 30	901-801 cal BC
Selsey West Beach			
Alder charcoal, context 40, base of upper context of well	AA-40932 (GU-9225)	2695 ± 45	966-798 cal BC
Immature oak, context 53, base of well fill	AA-40933 (GU-9225)	2520 ± 40	798-414 cal BC
Shinewater			
Young structural timber	BM-2990	2630 ± 70	915-547 cal BC
As above	BM-3002	2690 ± 35	904-800 cal BC
Wooden handle (maple) of socketed sickle	OxA-6176	2655 ± 50	902-787 cal BC
Varley Halls			
Cattle humerus, burial	BM-2917	2790 ± 50	1048-827 cal BC
Wolstonbury			
Lower ditch fills of main enclosure	BETA-949592	2730 ± 80	1048-791 cal BC
Yapton			
Charcoal, pit 2, middle layer	HAR-7038	2600 ± 70	897-522 cal BC
EARLY IRON AGE			
Chanctonbury Ring			
Animal bone from pit	HAR-2703	2320 ± 80	759-181 cal BC
Harting Beacon			
Human skull, upper fill of south ditch terminal	HAR-2411	2220 ± 80	404-49 cal BC
Wolstonbury			
Middle ditch fills, main enclosure	BETA-949581	2410 ± 80	792-262 cal BC
MIDDLE/LATE IRON AGE			
Bishopstone			
Charcoal, pit 11	HAR-1086	2220 ± 80	404-49 cal BC
North Bersted			
Charcoal, ditch 1, upper fill	HAR-2276	2020 ± 70	199 cal BC - cal AD 128
As above	HAR-2277	2050 ± 70	348 cal BC - cal AD 117
Oving			
Charcoal from wooden plank, pit 60	HAR-4252	2180 ± 70	396-4 cal BC
LATE IRON AGE			
Broadfields			
Charcoal, site 2, furnace 2	HAR-979	2010 ± 60	171 cal BC - cal AD 126
Charcoal, site 2, furnace 5	HAR-971	2140 ± 80	391 cal BC - cal AD 47

Appendix 6.3. *Sussex finds of Late Bronze Age/Early Iron Age Kimmeridge shale bracelets.*

Caburn (1):from hut B, Wilson 1939,fig. X:44; Charleston Brow (1): pit 3, dating not secure, Parsons and Curwen 1933, 176; Heathy Brow (1): in posthole 29, Bedwin 1982, 79, fig. 35:72; Slonk Hill (1): in grave 2 associated with Middle Iron Age involute brooch, Hartridge 1978, 80; Torberry (1):associated with Middle Iron Age saucepan pottery, Cunliffe 1976: 14, 16, fig. 14:5; Trundle (2): in pits 1 and 9, Curwen 1928, 64; 1931, 146; Selsey East Beach (1): Kenny 1989; Shinewater Park (1): associated with an inhumation, Greatorex this volume.

References

Aldsworth, F.G. 1976. Settlement site at Oving (SU 8950 0600), *SAC* **114**, 328.

Aldsworth, F.G. 1983. A Bronze Age hoard and settlement at Yapton, *SAC* **121**, 196-198.

Barrett, J. 1980. The pottery of the later Bronze Age in lowland England, *Proc. Prehist. Soc.* **46**, 297-320.

Barrett, J. and Needham, S. 1988. Production, circulation and exchange: problems in the intrepretation of Bronze Age metalwork in Britian, in J. Barrett and I. Kinnes (eds), *The Archaeology of Context in Neolithic and Bronze Age Britain - Recent Trends*. Sheffield: University of Sheffield, 127-140.

Bedwin, O. 1978a. Iron Age Sussex: the Downs and coastal plain, in P.L. Drewett (ed) *Archaeology of Sussex to AD 1500*. CBA Res. Rep. **29**, 44-51.

Bedwin, O. 1978b. Excavations inside Harting Beacon Hillfort, 1976. *SAC* **116**, 225-240.

Bedwin, O. 1979a. The excavation of a cross-dyke at Old Erringham Farm Upper Beeding, West Sussex 1976, *SAC* **117**, 11-19.

Bedwin, O. 1979b. Excavations at Harting Beacon, West Sussex; second season 1977, *SAC* **117**, 21-36.

Bedwin, O. 1979c. Early Iron Age pottery from Littlehampton, *SAC* **117**, 255-256.

Bedwin, O. 1980. Excavations at Chanctonbury Ring, Wiston, West Sussex 1977, *Britannia* **11**, 21-36.

Bedwin, O. 1981. *Excavations at Lancing Down, West Sussex* 1980, *SAC* **119**, 37-55.

Bedwin, O. 1982. The pre-Roman Iron Age on Heathy Brow, in P. Drewett, *The Archaeology of Bullock Down, Eastbourne, East Sussex: The Development of a Landscape*. Sussex Archaeological Society Monograph **1**, 74-96.

Bedwin, O. 1983. The development of prehistoric settlement on the West Sussex coastal plain, in *SAC* **121**, 31-44.

Bedwin, O. 1984. Aspects of Iron Age settlement in Sussex, in B. Cunliffe and D. Miles (eds), *Aspects of the Iron Age in Central; Southern Britain*, Oxford: Univ. Comm. Archaeol. Monogr. **2**, 46-51.

Bedwin, O. 1986. Excavations at Seaford Head Camp, East Sussex, 1983, *SAC* **124**, 25-33.

Bedwin, O. 1992. Prehistoric earthworks on Halnaker Hill, West Sussex: Excavations 1981-1983, *SAC* **130**, 1-12.

Bedwin, O. and Holgate, R. 1985. Excavations at Copse Farm, Oving, West Sussex, *Proc. Prehist. Soc.* **51**, 215-45.

Bedwin, O. and C. Orton, 1984. The excavation of the eastern terminal of the Devil's Ditch (Chichester Dykes), Boxgrove, West Sussex 1975-76, *SAC* **122**, 63-74.

Bedwin, O. and Pitts, M. 1978. Excavation of an Iron Age settlement at North Bersted, Bognor Regis, West Sussex, 1975-76, in *SAC* **116**, 293-346.

Bedwin, O. and Place, C. 1995. Late Iron Age and Romano-British occupation at Ounces Barn, Boxgrove, West Sussex; excavations 1982-83, *SAC* **133**, 45-101.

Bell, M. 1977. Excavations at Bishopstone, in *SAC* **115**, 1-299.

Bersu, G. 1940. Excavations at Little Woodbury, Wiltshire, part I, *Proc. Prehist. Soc.* **6**, 30-111.

Bowden, M. and D. McOmish, 1987. The required barrier, *Scott. Archaeol. Rev.* **4**: 76-84.Bowden, M. and D. McOmish, 1989. Little boxes: more about hillforts, *Scott. Archaeol. Rev.* **6**: 12-15.

Boyden, J.R. 1956. Excavations at Goosehill Camp, *SAC* **94**, 70-99.

Boyden, J.R. 1958. Excavations at Hammer Wood, Iping, *SAC* **96**, 149-64.

Bradley, R. 1971. Stock raising and the origins of hillforts on the South Downs, *Antiq. J.* **51**, 8-29.

Bradley, R. 1971b. An Iron Age promontory fort at Belle Tout, *SAC* **109**, 8-19.

Bradley, R. 1990. *The Passage of Arms*. Cambridge: Univ. Press.

Bruck J. 1995. A place for the dead: the role of human remains in Late Bronze Age Britain. *Proc. Prehist. Soc.* **61**: 191-245.

Bruck, J. 1999. Houses, lifecycles and deposition on Middle Bronze Age settlements in southern England, *Proc. Prehist. Soc.* **65**, 145-66.

Budgen, W. 1922. Hallstatt pottery from Eastbourne, *Antiq. J.* **2**, 354-60.

Burstow, G.P. 1958.A Late Bronze Age urnfield on Steyning Round Hill, Sussex, *Proc. Prehist. Soc.* **24**, 158-64.

Burstow, G.P. and G.A. Holleyman, 1957a. Excavations at Muntham Court, Findon, Sussex, *The Archaeological Magazine* **6**(4), 101-02.

Burstow, G.P. and G.A. Holleyman 1957b. Late Bronze Age settlement on Itford Hill, Sussex, *Proc. Prehist. Soc.* **23**, 167-212.

Burstow, G.P. and N. Norris, 1958-62. Excavations at Balcombe quarry, Glynde, *SNQ* **15**, 307-9.

Burstow, G.P. and A.E. Wilson, 1936. Excavation of a celtic village on the ladies golf course, the Dyke, Brighton, *SAC* **77**, 195-201.

Cartwright, C. 1992. The excavation of a Romano-British iron working site at Broadfield, Crawley, West Sussex, *SAC* **130**, 22-59.

Chown, E. 1947. Painted Iron Age pottery from Sedlescombe, *SNQ* **11**, 148-51.

Collis, J. 1994. Foreward, ix, in A. Fitzpatrick and E. Morris (eds), *The Iron Age in Wessex: Recent Work*. Salisbury: Trust for Wessex Archaeology.

Crow, D.A. 1930. Excavations at Ditchling Beacon, *SAC* **71**, 259-261.

Cunliffe, B. 1966. Stoke Clump, Hollingbury and the Early pre-Roman Iron Age in Sussex, *SAC* **104**, 109-20.

Cunliffe, B. 1976. The pre-Roman Iron Age hillfort at Torberry, Sussex, in B. Cunliffe (ed), *Iron Age Sites in Central Southern England*, CBA Res. Rep. **16**, 1-29.

Cunliffe, B. 1984 *Danebury: An Iron Age Hillfort in Hampshire*, CBA Res. Rep. **52**.

Cunliffe, B. 1991. *Iron Age Communities in Britain* (3rd edition), London and New York: Routledge.

Curwen, E.C. 1929. Excavations in the Trundle, Goodwood 1928, *SAC* **70**, 33-85.
Curwen, E.C. 1930. Wolstonbury, *SAC* **71**, 237-45.
Curwen, E.C. 1931. Excavations in the Trundle, second season, 1930, *SAC* **72**, 100-50.
Curwen, E.C. 1932. Excavations at Hollingbury Camp, Sussex, *Antiq. J.* **12**, 1-16.
Curwen, E.C. 1934. A Bronze Age farm and neolithic pit-dwelling on New Barn Down, Clapham, near Worthing, *SAC* **75**, 137-170.
Curwen, E.C. 1937. *The Archaeology of Sussex*. London: Methuen.
Curwen, E.C. 1939. The Iron Age in Sussex, *SAC* **80**, 214-16.
Curwen, E.C. 1948. A bronze cauldron from Sompting, Sussex, *Antiq. J.* **28**, 157-63.
Curwen, E. and E.C. Curwen, 1927. Excavations at the Caburn near Lewes, *SAC* **68**, 1-56.
Curwen, E., E.C. Curwen, and C.F.C. Hawkes, 1931. Prehistoric remains from Kingston Buci, *SAC* **72**, 185-217.
Curwen, E.C. and Frere, S. 1947. A Romano-British occupation site at Portfield gravel pit, Chichester, *SAC* **86**, 137-40.
Curwen, E.C. and R.P.R. Williamson, 1931. The date of Cissbury Camp, *Antiq. J.* **11**, 14-36.
Drewett, P. 1975. A section through the Iron Age promontory fort at Belle Tout, *SAC* **113**, 184-6.
Drewett, P. 1982a. Later Bronze Age downland economy and excavations at Black Patch, East Sussex, *Proc. Prehist. Soc.* **48**, 321-400.
Drewett, P. 1982b. *The Archaeology of Bullock Down, Eastbourne, East Sussex: The Development of a Landscape*. Sussex Archaeological Society Monograph **1**.
Drewett, P. and S. Hamilton, 1999. Making space and marking time; excavations and landscape studies at the Caburn hillfort, East Sussex, 1996-98, in *SAC* **137**, 7-36.
Dunning, G.C. 1934. The swan's neck and ring-headed pin of the Early Iron Age in Britain, *Archaeol. J.* **91**, 269-95.
Ellison, A. 1978. The Bronze Age in Sussex, in P. Drewett (ed), *Archaeology of Sussex to AD 1500*. CBA Res. Rep. **29**, 130-137.
Ellison, A. 1980. The Bronze Age, 31-42, in D. Freke (ed), The Archaeology of Sussex pottery, *SAC* **118**, 1-405.
Field, L. 1939. Castle Hill, Newhaven, *SAC* **80**, 263-68.
Fitzpatrick, A. 1997a. Everyday life in Iron Age Wessex, in A. Gwilt and C. Haselgrove (eds), *Reconstructing Iron Age Societies*, Oxford: Oxbow Monograph **71**, 73-86.
Fitzpatrick, A. 1997b. *Archaeological Excavations on the Route of the A27 Westhampnett Bypass, West Sussex, 1992. Volume 2: the cemeteries*. Salisbury: Trust for Wessex Archaeology.
Fitzpatrick, A.P. and Morris, E.L. (eds), 1994. *The Iron Age in Wessex: Recent Work*. Salisbury: Trust for Wessex Archaeology/Association Française de l'Etude de l'Age du Fer.
Fox, C.F. and G.R. Wolseley, 1928. The Early Iron Age site at Findon Park, Findon, Sussex, *Antiq. J.* **8**, 449-60.
Frere, S.S. 1940. A survey of archaeology near Lancing, *SAC* **81**, 138-72.
Gardiner, M. 1988. Excavations at Tester's, White Horse Square, Steyning, 1985, *SAC* **126**, 53-76.
Gardiner, M. and S. Hamilton, 1997. Knapp Farm, Bosham: a significant find of Bronze Age pottery, *SAC* **135**, 71-91.
Gibson-Hill, J. 1975. The excavation of a Romano-British iron-working site at Broadfields, Crawley, West Sussex, in P.L. Drewett (ed), Rescue archaeology in Sussex 1974, *Univ. London Inst. Archaeol. Bull.* **12**, 35-42.
Gilkes, O. 1993. Iron Age and Roman Littlehampton, *SAC* **131**, 1-20.
Gibson-Hill, J. 1976. Further excavations at the Romano-British iron-working site at Broadfields, Crawley, West Sussex, in P.L. Drewett (ed) Rescue archaeology in Sussex, 1975, *Univ. London Inst. Archaeol. Bull.* **13**, 247-63.
Greatorex, C. 2002. Appendix 3: Excavations at Patcham Fawcett: A Summary, 271-275, in D. Rudling 2002a.
Greatorex, C. 1998. Late Bronze Age waterlogged remains at Willingdon Levels, Sussex, *Archaeology International 1997/98*, 14-15.
Greig, I. 1997. Excavation of a Bronze Age settlement at Varley Halls, Coldean Lane, Brighton, East Sussex, *SAC* **135**, 7-58.
Hamilton, S. 1979. The Iron Age pottery, 27-30, in O. Bedwin, Excavations at Harting Beacon, West Sussex; a second season 1977, *SAC* **117**, 21-36.
Hamilton, S. 1980. The Iron Age pottery, 196-203, in O. Bedwin, Excavations at Chanctonbury Ring, Wiston, West Sussex 1977, *Britannia* **11**, 173-222.
Hamilton, S. 1982. The Iron Age pottery, 81-88, in O. Bedwin 1982.
Hamilton, S. 1984. Earlier first millennium BC pottery from the excavations at Hollingbury Camp, Sussex, 1967-9, *SAC* **122**, 55-62.
Hamilton, S. 1985, Iron Age pottery, 220-228, in O. Bedwin and R. Holgate, Excavations at Copse Farm, Oving, West Sussex, *Proc. Prehist. Soc.* **51**, 215-245.
Hamilton, S. 1986. Late Bronze Age and Iron Age pottery, 43-44, in R. Holgate, Excavations at the late prehistoric and Romano-British enclosure complex at Carne's Seat, Goodwood, West Sussex, 1984, *SAC* **124**, 35-50.
Hamilton, S. 1987. Late Bronze Age pottery, 53-63, in D. Rudling, 1987.
Hamilton, S. 1988. Latest Bronze Age and latest Pre-Conquest pottery, 61-7, in M. Gardiner 1988.
Hamilton, S. 1990. Bronze Age pottery, 8, in D. Rudling, 1990.
Hamilton, S. 1993. First Millennium BC Pottery Traditions in Southern Britain. Unpubl. Ph.D. thesis, University of London.
Hamilton, S. 1998. Using elderly data bases, *SAC* **136**, 23-39.
Hamilton, S. 2002a. Between ritual and routine: prehistoric ceramic production and exchange, in A. Woodward and J.D. Hill (eds), *Prehistoric Britain: the Ceramic Basis*. Oxford: Oxbow Books, 38-53.
Hamilton, S. 2002b. A review of the early 1st millennium BC pottery from Chanctonbury Ring: a contribution to the study of Sussex hillforts of the Late Bronze Age/Early Iron Age transition, in D. Rudling 2002c.
Hamilton, S. and Manley, J. 1997. Points of view: prominent enclosures in 1st millennium BC Sussex, *SAC* **135**, 93-112.
Hamilton, S. and J. Manley, 1999. Regional traditions *c.* 1000-100 BC, in K. Leslie and B. Short (eds), *An Historical Atlas of Sussex*, 20-21. Chichester: Phillimore.
Hamilton, S. and Gregory, K. 2001. Updating the Sussex Iron Age, *SAC* **138**, 57-74.
Hamilton, S. and J. Manley, 2001. Hillforts, monumentality, and place: a chronological and topographic review of first

millennium BC hillforts of south-east England, *J. of European Archaeology,* 7-42.

Hannah, I. 1932. Philpots Camp, West Hoathly, *SAC* **73**, 157-67.

Harding, D.W. and I.M. Blake, 1963. An Early Iron Age settlement in Dorset, *Antiquity* **37**, 63-4.

Hardy, H.R. and E.C. Curwen, 1937. An Iron Age pottery site near Horsted Keynes, *SAC* **78**, 252-65.

Hartridge, R.. 1978. Excavations at the prehistoric site and Roman-British site on Slonk Hill, Shoreham, Sussex, *SAC* **116**, 69-141.

Hawkes, C.F.C. 1939. The Caburn pottery and its implications, *SAC* **80**, 217-62.

Hawkes, C.F.C. 1959. The ABC of the British Iron Age, *Antiquity* **33**, 170-82.

Hawley, W. 1927. Further excavations at Park Brow, *Archaeologia* **76**, 30-40.

Hill, J.D. 1995a. The pre-Roman Iron Age in Britain and Ireland, (*c.* 800 BC-AD 100): an overview, *J. of World Prehistory* **9**, 47-98.

Hill, J.D. 1995b. *Ritual and Rubbish in the Iron Age of Wessex*, BAR Brit. Ser. **242**.

Hodson, F.R. 1962. Some pottery from Eastbourne, the 'Marnians' and the pre-Roman Iron Age in southern England, in *Proc. Prehist. Soc.* **28**, 140-155

Hodson, F. R. 1964. Cultural groupings within the British pre-Roman Iron Age, *Proc. Prehist. Soc.* **30**, 99-110.

Holden, E. 1972. A Bronze Age cemetery-barrow on Itford Hill, Beddingham, *SAC* **110**, 70-117.

Holgate, R. 1986a. Excavations at the late prehistoric and Romano-British enclosure complex at Carne's Seat, Goodwood, West Sussex, 1984, *SAC* **124**, 35-50.

Holgate, R. 1986b. Excavations at Lordington, Stoughton, West Sussex 1984, *SAC* **186**, 244-51.

Holleyman, G.A. 1936. An early British agricultural village site on Highdole Hill, near Telscombe, *SAC* **77**, 202-21.

Holleyman, G.A. 1937. Harrow Hill excavations 1936, *SAC* **78**, 230-52.

Holleyman, G. A. and Burstow, G. P. 1955. Excavations at Muntham Court, Findon, Sussex, *The Archaeological Newsletter* **5** (10), 204-05.

Holleyman, G.A. and E.C. Curwen, 1935. Late Bronze Age lynchet-settlements on Plumptom Plain, Sussex, *Proc. Prehist. Soc.* **1**, 16-38.

Holmes, J. 1984. Excavations at Hollingbury Camp, Sussex, 1967-9, *SAC* **122**, 29-52.

Keef, P. 1953. Two gold penannular ornaments from Harting Beacon Sussex, *Antiq. J.* **33**, 204-6.

Kendrick, T.D. and Hawkes, C.F.C. 1932. *Archaeology in England and Wales 1914-1931*. London: Methuen.

Kenny, J. 1985. Excavations at Rummages Barn, Binderton, West Sussex, *SAC* **123**, 61-72.

Kenny, J. 1989. *Selsey Bill (SZ 859924),The Archaeology of the Chichester District 1988,* 32-36. Portsmouth: Chichester District Council.

Kenny, J. 1994. Lavant: the reservoir site at Chalkpit Lane (SU 868 095), in *The Archaeology of the Chichester District 1993,* 26-29. Portsmouth: Chichester District Council.

Kenyon, K.M. 1952. A survey of the evidence concerning the chronology and origins of Iron Age A in Southern and Midland Britain, *London Institute of Archaeology Annual Report* **8**, 29-78.

Money, J.H. 1968. Excavations in the Iron Age hill-fort at High Rocks, near Tunbridge Wells, 1957-61, *SAC* **106**, 158-205.

Money, J.H. 1977. The Iron Age hill-fort and Romano-British iron-working settlement at Garden Hill, Sussex: an interim report on excavations 1968-76, *Britannia* **8**, 339-50.

Money, J.H. 1980. Garden Hill, *Britannia* **11**, 398-400.

Morris, E. 1994. Production and distribution of pottery and salt in Iron Age Britain: a review, *Proc. Prehist. Soc.* **60**, 371-393.

Morris, S. 1978. The pottery, 231-39, in O. Bedwin, Excavations inside Harting Beacon hill-fort, West Sussex, 1976, *SAC* **116**, 225-40.

Needham, S. 1996. Chronology and periodisation in the British Bronze Age, *Acta Archaeologica* **67**, 121-40.

Norris, N.E.S. and G.P. Burstow. 1950. A prehistoric site at West Blatchington Hove, *SAC* **89**, 1-56.

Norris, N.E.S. and G.P. Burstow, 1952. A prehistoric site and Roman-British site at West Blatchington, Hove, part 2; the finds, *SAC* **90**, 221-40.

Oldham, B. 1985. Metalwork, 229, in O. Bedwin and R. Holgate, Excavations at Copse farm Oving, West Sussex, *Proc. Prehist. Soc.* **51**, 215-45.

Oswald, A. 1997. A doorway on the past: practical and mystic concerns in the orientation of roundhouse doorways, in A. Gwilt and C. Haselgrove (eds), *Reconstructing Iron Age Societies*, Oxford: Oxbow Monograph **71**, 87-95.

Parker Pearson, M. and C. Richards, 1997. Architecture and order: spatial representation and archaeology, 38-72, in M. Parker Pearson and C. Richards (eds), *Architecture and Order: Approaches to Social Space*. London: Routledge.

Parsons, W.J. and E.C. Curwen, 1933. An agricultural settlement on Charleston Brow, near Firle Beacon, *SAC* **74**, 164-180.

Peacock, D.P.S. 1987. Iron Age and Roman quern production at Lodsworth, West Sussex, *Antiq. J.* **67**, 61-85.

Pitts, M. 1979. Some recent finds of Iron Age pottery on the West Sussex coastal plain, *SAC* **117**, 259-60.

Piggott, C.M. 1938. The non-Roman pottery from Crowhurst Park, 229-332, in E. Straker and B.H. Lucas, A Romano-British bloomery in East Sussex, Sussex, *SAC* **79**, 224-232.

Priestley-Bell, G. 1994. Archaeological excavations at America Wood, Ashington, West Sussex, *SAC* **132**, 33-52.

Ratcliffe-Densham, H.B.A. and M.M. 1953. A Celtic farm on Blackpatch, *SAC* **91**, 69.

Ratcliffe-Densham, H.B.A. and M.M. 1961. An anomalous earthwork of the Late Bronze Age on Cock Hill, Sussex, *SAC* **99**, 78-101.

Rudling, D. 1985. Trial excavations at Ditchling Beacon, East Sussex 1983, *SAC* **123**, 251-4.

Rudling, D. 1987. The excavation of a Late Bronze Age site at Yapton, West Sussex, 1984, *SAC* **125**, 51-67.

Rudling, D. 1990, Archaeological finds at Rustington, West Sussex, 1986-88, *SAC* **128**, 1-20.

Rudling, D. (ed), 2002a. *Downland Settlement and Land-use: The Archaeology of the Brighton By-pass.* London: Archtype.

Rudling, D. 2002b. Excavations adjacent to Coldean Lane, 141-201, in D. Rudling (ed) 2002a.

Rudling, D. 2002c. Chanctonbury Ring revisited: the excavations of 1988-1991, *SAC* **139**, 75-121.

Rudling, D. and Gilkes, G. 2001. Important discoveries made during the construction of the A259 Rustington Bypass, 1990. *SAC* **138**, 15-28.

Russell, M. 1996a. Problems of phasing: a reconsideration of the Black Patch Middle Bronze Age 'nucleated village'. *Oxford J. Archaeol.* **15** (1), 156-65.

Russell, M. 1996b. *Archaeological Excavation at Belle Tout, Eastbourne, East Sussex: Interim Statement.* Bournemouth: Bournemouth University.

Russell, M. 1996c. *Archaeological Excavation at Wolstonbury Hill, Pyecombe, West Sussex: Interim Statement.* Bournemouth: Bournemouth University.

Russell, M. 2002. Excavations at Mileoak Farm 1989-90, 5-81. in D. Rudling (ed) 2002a.

Seager Thomas, M. 1998. New evidence for a Late Bronze Age occupation of Selsey Bill, *SAC* **136**, 7-22.

Seager Thomas, M. 1999. Stone finds in context: a contribution to the study of later prehistoric artefact assemblages, *SAC* **138**.

Seager Thomas, M. 2001. Two early first millennium BC wells at Selsey, West Sussex and their wider significance, *Antiq. J.* **81**, 15-50.

Smith, R.A. 1927. Park Brow, the finds and foreign parallels, *Archaeologia* **76**, 14-29.

Stevens, L. 1987. A Late Iron Age site at St Anne's Road, Eastbourne, *SAC* **125**, 75-80.

Stevens, S. 1997. Excavations at Potlands Farm, Patching, West Sussex, *SAC* **135**, 59-70.

Stuiver, M and Reimer, P.J. 1998. *CALIB User's Guide Rev. 4*. University of Washington, Quaternary Isotope Laboratory.

Taylor J. 1980. *Bronze Age Goldwork of the British Isles.* Cambridge: Univ. Press.

Thomas, G. 2001. Norton, Tales of the unexpected, *Sussex Past and Present* **95**, 4-5.

Thomas, R. 1983. An Armorican socketed axe from Hollingbury Hill, *SAC* **121**, 198-199.

Wainwright, G.J. 1979. *Gussage All Saints: An Iron Age Settlement in Dorset.* London: Department of the Environment Archaeological Report **10**.

Waller, M.P., A.J. Long; D. Long, and J.B. Innes, 1999. Patterns and processes in the development of coastal mire vegetation: Multi-site investigations from Walland Marsh, Southeast England, *Quat. Sci. Rev.* **18**, 1419-1444.

White, G.M. 1934. Prehistoric remains from Selsey Bill, *Antiq. J.* **14**, 40-52.

Wickenden, N. 1986. Excavations at Chelwood gate: interim report, *Sussex Archaeological Society Newsletter* **4**, 6-7.

Wilson, A.E. 1938. Excavations in the ramparts and gateway of the Caburn, August-October 1937, *SAC* **79**, 169-94.

Wimbolt, S. 1930. Excavations at Saxonbury Camp, Sussex, *SAC* **71**, 222-236.

Wilson, A.E. 1939. Excavation at the Caburn 1938, *SAC* **80**, 193-213.

Wilson, A. 1940. Report on the excavations on Highdown Hill, Sussex, August 1939, *SAC* **81**, 173-203.

Wilson, A. 1950. Excavations on Highdown Hill, 1947, *SAC* **89**, 163-78.

Wolseley G.R., R.A. Smith, and W. Hawley, 1927. Prehistoric and Roman remains on Park Brow, *Archaeologia* **76**, 1-40.

Woodward, A. 1995. Vessel size and social identity in the Bronze Age of southern Britain, in I. Kinnes and G. Varndell (eds), *Unbaked Urns of Rudley Shape: Essays of British and Irish Pottery for Ian Longworth*, Oxford: Oxbow monograph **5**, 195-202.

LIVING ON THE MARGINS? THE LATE BRONZE AGE LANDSCAPE OF THE WILLINGDON LEVELS

Christopher Greatorex

Abstract

Outstanding Bronze Age structural remains preserved by waterlogging have recently been discovered on the Willingdon Levels near Eastbourne. The principal prehistoric complex comprises a rare wooden occupation platform and associated track. Two discrete timber alignments have also been recorded. At present the platform site has only been subject to a limited programme of evaluation. Nevertheless, this paper will demonstrate the considerable potential of the Levels' archaeological and palaeoenvironmental deposits to illuminate many fundamental aspects of Bronze Age society in South-East England.

Introduction

During the prehistoric period, the wetlands of the British Isles were often plentiful habitats offering a wide range of natural resources. However, the majority of these unique landscapes have since been destroyed, while few that survive have escaped 20th-century development or drainage. This is regrettable as wetlands can conceal a remarkable archaeological and environmental record, rich in vivid detail about past human existence. One such area is the Willingdon Levels, an expanse of marshland situated between Polegate and Eastbourne, East Sussex (Fig. 7.1).

The Levels formation of clays, silts and a thin peat horizon at *circa* + 1.0m O.D. has yielded some of the most important prehistoric archaeology in the country. An overlying layer of clay alluvium with an average thickness of 0.65m has protected the evidence physically, while helping to trap moisture and maintain a high ground-water content. The anaerobic character of the resultant waterlogged deposits has delayed bacterial and fungal decay and hence preserved a wide range of organic materials that would have perished on dry land.

In 1995 the Levels became subject to considerable change, owing to the construction of a landscaped park, the A22 road improvement and a school. At this time nothing was known of the extensive prehistoric utilization and settlement of the area; the marsh was in effect an archaeological void. However, in August of that year, numerous *in-situ* timbers were revealed during groundworks on that part of the Levels known as Shinewater Marsh. The University College London Field Archaeology Unit was consequently commissioned to evaluate and record the archaeological potential of these superbly preserved remains. A largely undamaged raft of dense timber, currently thought to cover a safeguarded area of approximately 2,000m^2, was quickly identified (NGR TQ 6155 0295) (Fig. 7.2). This remarkable Late Bronze Age occupation platform was connected to the western edge of the marsh by a broad wooden track. In the absence of detailed investigation, the recorded data is difficult to interpret. However, the platform is the first monument of its type to be found in South-East England and is clearly of national, if not international, importance (Greatorex 1996).

The Shinewater Platform

A section with a length of *c.* 50m had been cut across the platform site by the landscaping contractors. Particular attention was paid to this exposure, as it can be assumed that the revealed deposits demonstrate the basic character and condition of the surviving buried structure (Fig. 7.3).

The platform was built of large oak posts, found below the alluvium and driven vertically into the underlying freshwater peat and lower marine clay. These piles had a maximum recorded length of 2.6m and were associated with horizontal timbers of varied sizes placed on the original peat surface to form a firm base. This supported a finer layer incorporating slender wooden rods, intermittent patches of sandy gravel and areas of reed or rush matting. The majority of the horizontal timbers were identified as oak during the on-site evaluation. Even so, one particular segment of the platform substructure was removed from the exposed section, for post-excavation species identification and analysis (Fig.7.4). This study, undertaken at the Institute of Archaeology, University College London, has indicated a definite level of choice in the types of wood used. The lower 'foundation' element of the platform fragment was indeed constructed from oak. However, the upper layer was comprised almost exclusively of short hazel rods set at right-angles to the larger material below. These specimens all had extended first year's growth consistent with having come from a cut stump or coppice stool, perhaps as a managed woodland product (Hather 1996). Three *in-situ* hearths, characterized by charcoal lenses raised above the platform on deposits of clay, were also recorded in section. Although the nature of any associated standing buildings has not been determined, the high quality of timber preservation does suggest that important structural information may be retrieved on excavation.

A distinctive 0.2m thick layer of accumulated cultural debris, including large quantities of pottery and bone, plus worked and burnt geological material, was located on the platform surface. The full range of activities undertaken at the site has still to be ascertained. However, these finds are clearly indicative of Late Bronze Age occupation dating to the period *c.* 900-800 BC.

A number of rarer, higher status items were also found during the evaluation (Fig. 7.5). These highlight the exceptional potential of the complex to inform many social and economic facets of Late Bronze Age life. The peat from the platform area has in particular yielded some finely crafted bronze

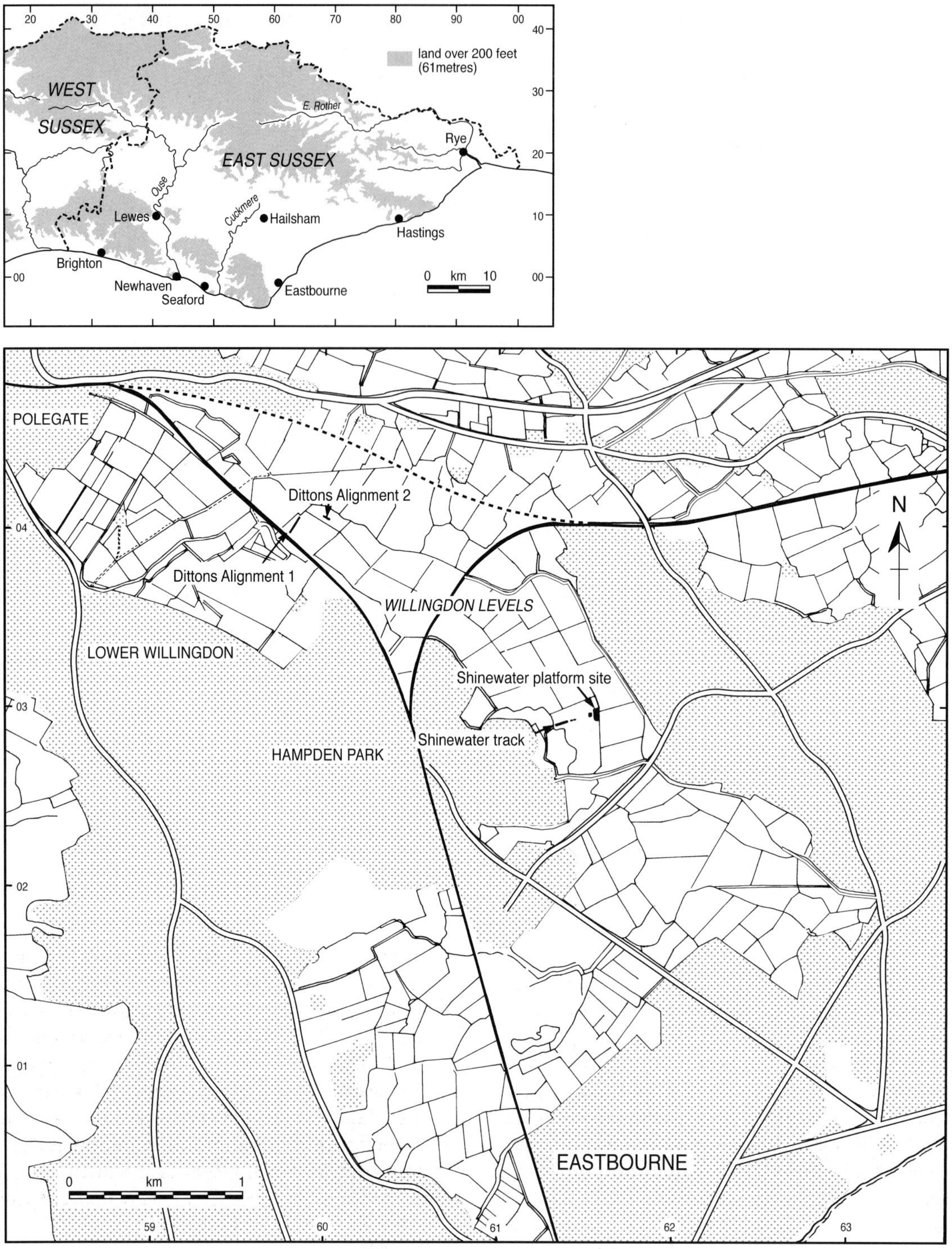

Figure 7.1. *Location of the sites at Shinewater and Dittons.*

artefacts, including three socketed and one end-winged axe, a chisel and a bracelet. Yet the most spectacular discovery was identified originally as a bronze sickle complete with intact wooden handle (Fig. 7.6). On the basis of recent ethnographic records of farmers still using traditional technologies and tools, Gordon Hillman of the Institute of Archaeology has suggested that this unique recovery is in fact a reed hook. The short blade was designed to facilitate efficient cutting, while the crooked end of the haft would have helped prevent the implement from slipping or pulling from the grasp of the user (Hillman pers. comm.). The handle itself is made from especially selected field maple and has been dated by Accelerator Mass Spectrometry to 2655 ± 50 BP (OxA-6176). This result accords closely with a standard radiocarbon date of 2678 ± 31 BP (BM-2990 and BM-3002) produced for a horizontal platform timber exposed in section. The utilization of the site during the 9th century BC has thus been confirmed.

Other notable finds retrieved from the evaluation include a rare Class I, single-peg antler bridle piece, four amber beads, two lead 'purse' pendants and a fragment of shale bracelet. Indeed, the limited investigation undertaken so far has recovered an extraordinary assemblage.

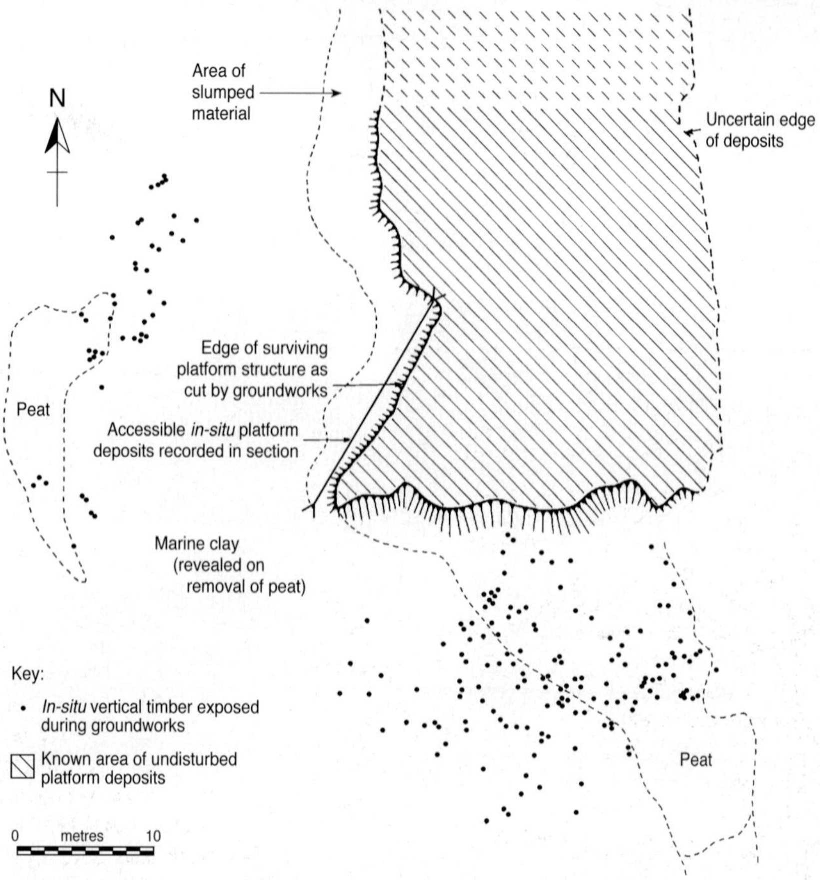

Figure 7.2. *Plan of the Shinewater platform site.*

European prehistory is characterized by contact and trade. The exchange of ideas, artefacts, materials and food was essential if ancient societies were to survive and prosper. Any excavation of the platform thus promises to reveal a wide range of interactions with the outside world. Of course, most of the resources utilized at the site would have been garnered from the local environment. However, solid evidence for inter-regional connections has been recorded. For example, the shale bracelet was in all probability manufactured out of Kimmeridge Shale from Dorset. A distinctive pottery bowl may also indicate coastal links with the Thames Valley.

During the Late Bronze Age, the British Isles were situated on the edge of a great European communication system. Indeed, it is apparent from discoveries such as the Dover Boat, that people were crossing the English Channel on a regular basis. Unfortunately, the organization of this traffic is only poorly understood. However, it does seem logical to suggest that seaborne vessels would have sailed directly between sites placed strategically along either side of the Channel. The location of the Shinewater platform, just behind the contemporary coastline presents a rare opportunity to investigate this theory through excavation.

In fact, the fieldwork undertaken on the Levels has already yielded a number of possibly continental artefacts. These draw attention to the advantageous setting of the site for socio-economic interchange. Certainly, most of the amber used in prehistoric Europe originated from the Baltic, while some of the finest pottery found at the platform may have also been traded from abroad. One of the recovered socketed axes is of specific interest as the style matches that of a group clustered in northern Holland and north-west Germany (Fig. 6.2). This is only the second artefact of its type discovered in Britain. It can therefore be seen that the detailed archaeological contexts preserved at Shinewater have the potential to increase our understanding of Bronze Age trade/exchange patterns and continental contacts in the South-East.

The hafted reed hook could provide important information concerning functional aspects of use. Indeed, wear analyses may help to ascertain the reasons for deposition of many of the metal objects. This topic is one of particular significance, for some of the bronze artefacts were retrieved from below the stratigraphic level of the platform. The location and apparently pristine condition of these specific items may thus indicate that they were deliberately dug into the peat from above, rather than simply abandoned. It is perhaps even valid to conclude that at least some of the higher status artefacts found at the site represent ritual deposits. Such activity is well-evidenced throughout prehistory, across both mainland Europe and the British Isles. For example, the waterlogged Bronze Age site at Flag Fen near Peterborough, Cambridgeshire, has yielded many artefacts which were apparently ritually deposited (Pryor *et al.* 1992).

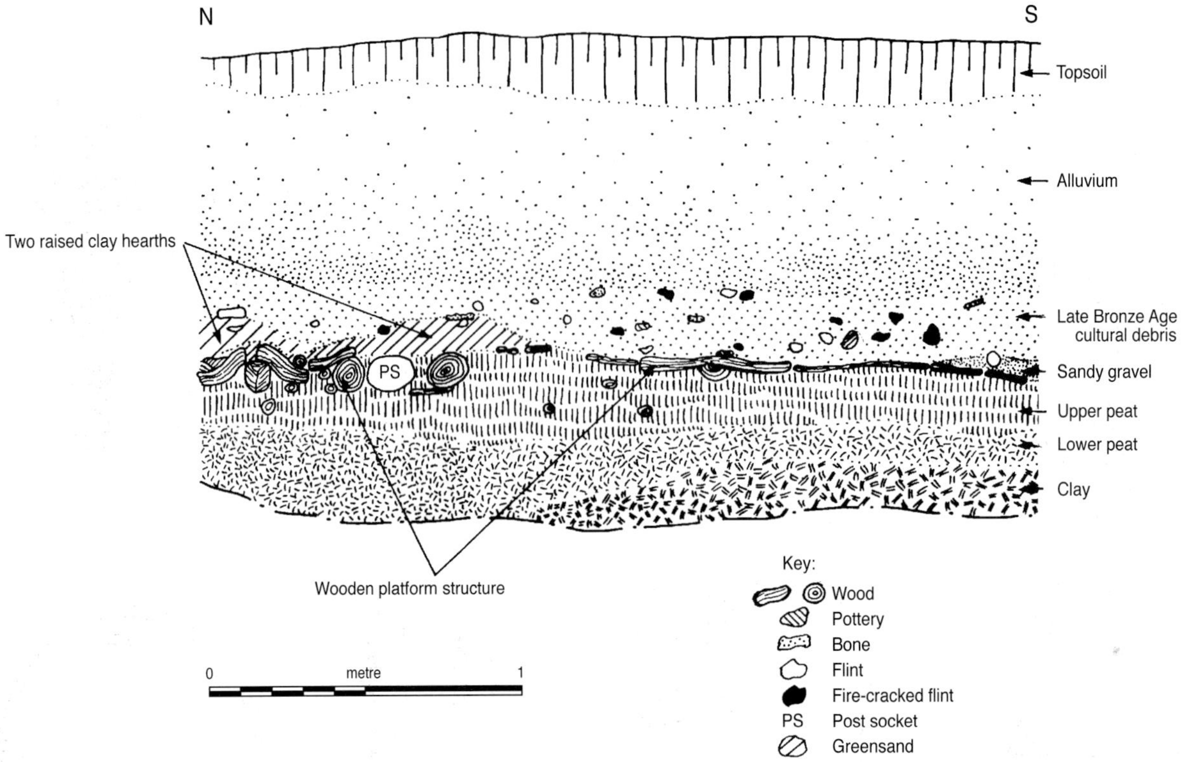

Figure 7.3. *Section of the Shinewater platform.*

At least 50 human bones have also been recovered from the area of the platform. These include 17 skull fragments, a burnt clavicle and the disarticulated remains of a child aged between 10 and 12 years old. It is possible to interpret this assemblage as an example of a wider phenomenon in which skeletal elements were deposited in chosen locations across many settlements of the period. Increasingly, it is becoming clear that bones symbolized a variety of socio-political concerns central to Late Bronze Age communities (e.g. Brück 1995). Perhaps the deliberate placing of human material within occupation sites was a way of renewing or strengthening links between the inhabitants and their predecessors. This could have reinforced community identity and given meaning to different parts of a settlement. The power and status of those related to, or associated with, the bones may also have been reinforced by such endeavours. Ritual/ceremonial deposition of both human remains and metalwork could have even formed a coherent programme of appeasement to nature and the 'afterlife'. Certainly, it appears that during the Late Bronze Age, the dead were a resource that could be utilized to illustrate ideas and legitimize power. A consideration of the human bone from Shinewater may therefore illuminate some profound issues addressed by the platform occupants on a daily basis.

The discoveries outlined above suggest that the levels were perhaps significant within the Bronze Age landscape for reasons additional to subsistence, trade and exchange. This suggestion should not, however, detract from the examination and interpretation of the substantial evidence for settlement. At this point it is perhaps also worth observing that the inevitable limitations of the archaeological rescue work undertaken at Shinewater, have almost certainly led to recovery bias in the finds collection. Only a full-scale excavation of the platform will yield a representative artefact assemblage and database suitable for detailed study and meaningful resolution.

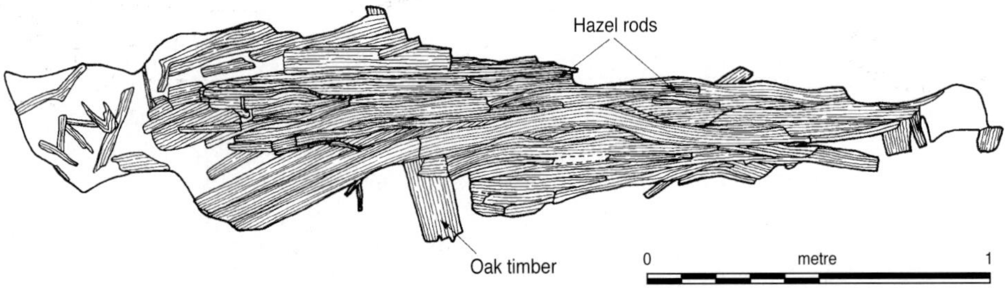

Figure 7.4. *Detail of part of the Shinewater platform substructure.*

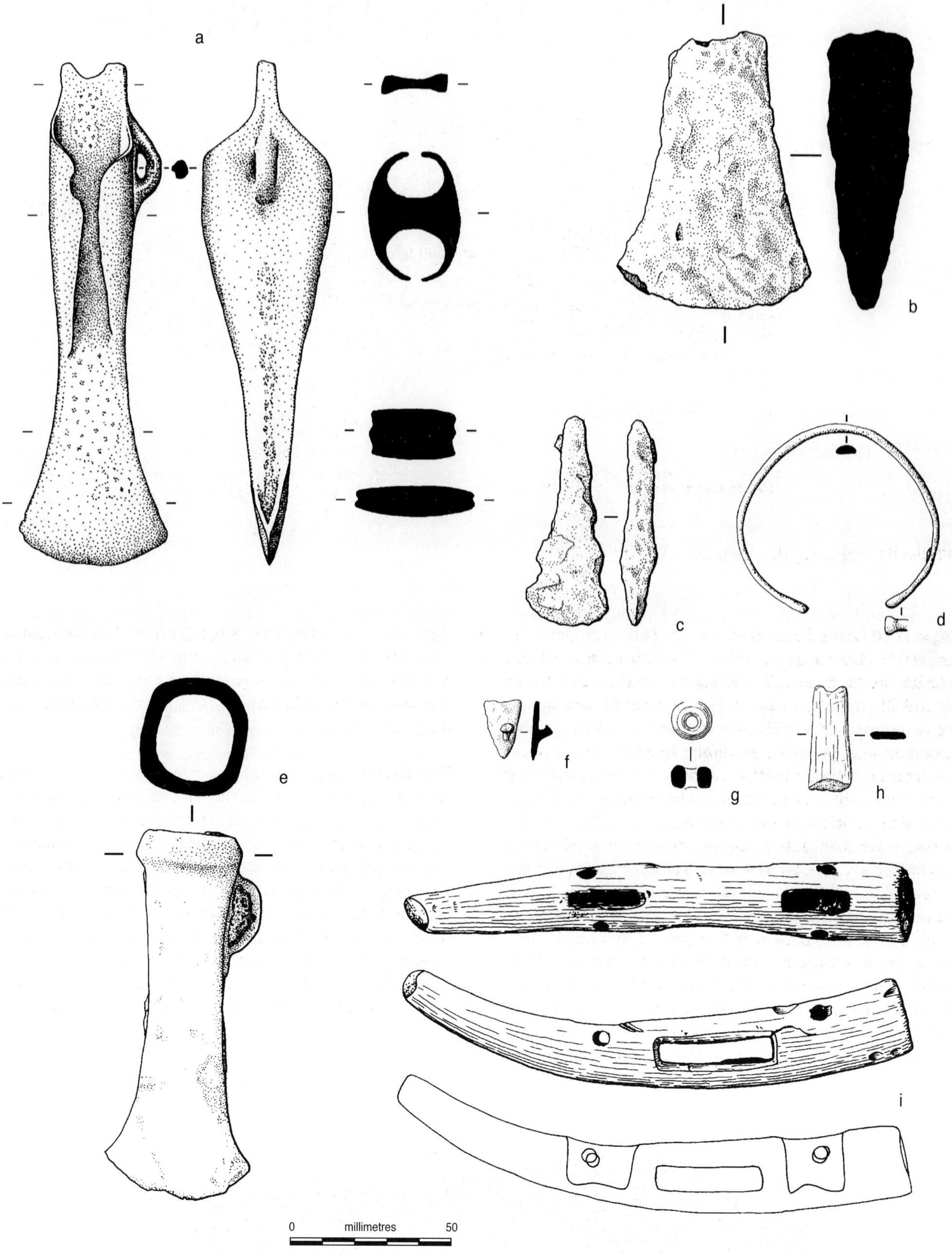

Figure 7.5. A selection of the higher status finds from the Shinewater platform site. A: end-winged axe; B and E: copper alloy socketed axes; C: copper alloy chisel; D: copper alloy bracelet; F: misc. lead item; G: amber bead; H: polished antler plaque; I: antler bridle piece.

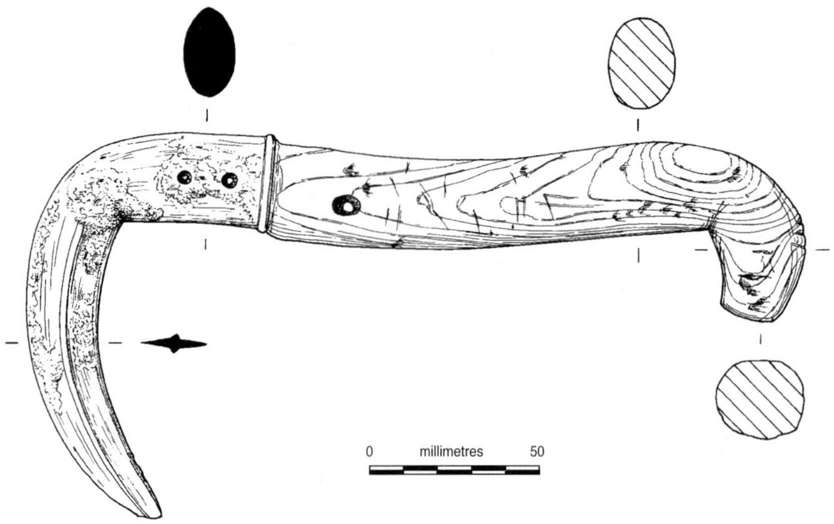

Figure 7.6. *Reed hook with copper alloy blade and maple wood handle.*

The Shinewater Track

The platform structure was connected to higher dry land approximately 250m to the south-west, by a substantial timber track or causeway (Fig. 7.1). A 60-metre length of this alignment was excavated by the Field Archaeology Unit, in advance of groundworks associated with the A22 improvement scheme (NGR TQ 614 029) (Greatorex 1998).

The surviving track comprised a series of horizontal beams and rails 6m-wide, located within the top 50mm of the Willingdon Peat (Fig. 7.7). Some of the smaller wooden elements were set within localized deposits of imported sand, which would have provided support over uneven or wetter patches of the marsh. The structure was secured by three parallel rows of *in-situ* vertical oak posts, which may also have marked the route during periods of flooding. Thirty of these piles were sampled for dendrochronological analysis in conjunction with 16 timbers retained from the original platform evaluation. This study, undertaken at the University of Sheffield Dendrochronology Laboratory, resulted in the production of a floating 75 year tree-ring sequence. Although calendar years cannot as yet be assigned to this chronology, the precise relative dating achieved has provided valuable information concerning the construction and development of the Late Bronze Age complex (Hillam forthcoming).

Initial interpretation of the dendrochronological data indicates that building activity at the trackway site was restricted to one or two years. However, the evidence for assembly and repair across the platform spans a broader period of at least a decade. The earliest recorded timbers were those sampled from the south-west sector of the trackway excavation. These specimens were cut down in the summer of ring 65 in the current chronology and may have been stockpiled until the winter of the following year, when the remaining causeway posts were felled. It can thus be suggested that construction on Shinewater Marsh began at the westernmost end of the track and continued out into the Levels, towards the eventual occupation site. Certainly, the preliminary results of the study do intimate that the track was built before work commenced on the platform. Relatively good cross-matching between the identified ring sequences also implies that a single area of woodland was being exploited for the structural oak. All analyzed samples were found to be under 70 years-old at the time of felling. Additionally, the dendrochronolgy links together a number of the radiocarbon measurements. This has enabled the application of Baysian analysis and the production of a refined 830-800 cal BC date for the timbers of both the track and platform.

Part of a shale bracelet, a bronze blade tip and an extremely unusual bronze skinning knife (Fig. 7.8) were retrieved from the track. Pottery, animal bone and worked flint were also recovered.

The Shinewater Track clearly provided a safe and direct route across the boggy and perhaps seasonally flooded Levels. However, it is wider than most recorded Bronze Age trackways and more substantial than would be expected for a simple walkway or drove-road. The alignment may therefore have had an additional role or significance within the contemporary landscape. From *c.* 1700 BC large areas of Sussex downland were brought under the management of organized farmsteads, set amongst discrete plots and territories defined by linear boundaries. Some of these land divisions may still have been respected and utilized during the Late Bronze Age. Although little is known about linear demarcations in low-lying areas, it is possible that the platform track functioned as a physical and perhaps symbolic barrier or boundary. Certainly, many of the prehistoric roads and trackways located on dry land served as property markers. Later prehistoric societies asserted and reinforced their identity at territorial margins, a process which often found its expression in both the scale of monuments and ceremonial/ritual acts. Indeed, there is increasing evidence for the deposition of metal artefacts on boundaries, especially during times of tension. The marine inundation that occurred across the Willingdon Levels at the end of the Bronze Age (*see* below) would in all probability have led to heightened social stress within the resident community. It may be these particular tensions that are evinced by the signs of ritual activity at the platform site.

The suggestions proffered above are of course currently matters of conjecture. However, it *is* clear that the establishment and maintenance of favourable conditions for the more functional demands of transport, trade and communication was a priority for the local Late Bronze Age population. The importance attached to access over the Willingdon Levels during prehistory has been emphasized by the discovery of a further two smaller timber trackways dating to the Bronze Age. Both of these alignments were found during a watching brief undertaken on a part of the marsh known locally as Dittons, which is situated to the north-west of the main Shinewater complex (Fig. 7.1).

The Dittons Alignments

The first alignment investigated at Dittons comprised two parallel rows of paired posts running from the south-west to north-east and set approximately 0.5m apart. (NGR TQ 598 040). No horizontal structural elements were recorded across the 100m-long exposure. The excavated piles varied in length from 0.4m to 1.5m and included radially and tangentially split oak, ash and alder. They had all been driven through the Willingdon Peat and into the underlying clay. Radiocarbon dating has assigned this possible raised walkway to the period 1440-1310 cal BC (BM-3060; 3100 ± 50BP).

A 46m-long stretch of the second Dittons alignment was identified within the top of the Levels peat (NGR TQ 600 041). The remains were characterized by a single meandering line of pointed oak, alder and wild cherry pegs sunk into the lower clay. These stakes marked and secured a 1.40m wide series of small horizontal rods and occasional larger timbers which would have almost certainly constituted the original track surface (Fig. 7.10). This structure headed in an approximate south-east to north-west direction and has been radiocarbon dated to 2460-2205 cal BC (Beta-106608; 3870 ± 70BP).

Additional fieldwork is required to ascertain the full length and ultimate destination of both Bronze Age alignments found in this area.

The evidence of tracks, trade and exchange recorded on the Levels, demonstrates that the platform formed part of a complex network of prehistoric settlements and communication channels. Obviously, the site should not be studied in isolation, but instead considered as an integral and indeed dynamic element of the wider landscape. Such an approach would yield greater insights into how the contemporary population perceived their surroundings and the significance they attached to the distinctive location of the platform. For example, the site may have been chosen for reasons of defence, or perhaps more likely, the exploitation of natural wetland resources. Certainly, the position of the platform and track on the margin of several discrete environments must have been of particular importance.

Figure 7.7. *Plan of part of the Shinewater track.*

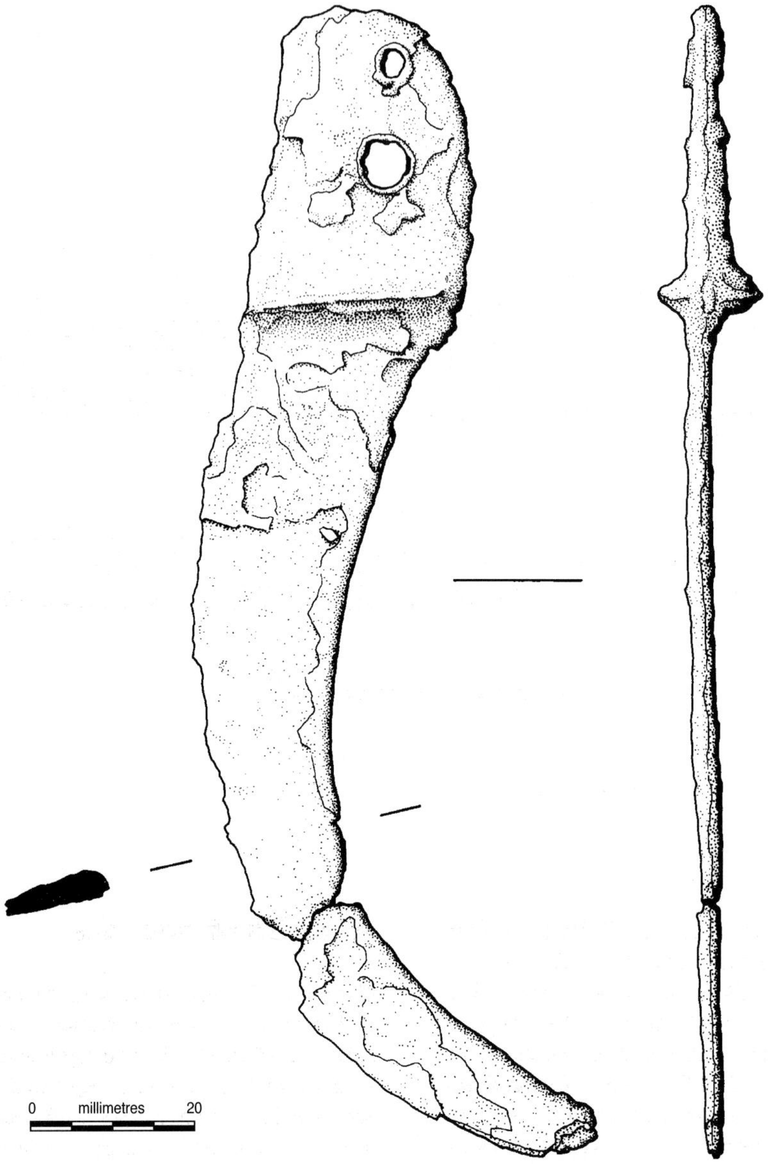

Figure 7.8. *Copper alloy skinning knife from the Shinewater track.*

The environmental setting of Shinewater platform and track

Palaeoenvironmental data relating to the development of the Willingdon Levels has previously been presented by Burrin (e.g. 1982; 1983) and Jennings and Smyth (e.g. 1985; 1987a; 1987b; 1990). However, a more detailed examination of the local sedimentary sequence is currently being conducted by Dr Simon Jennings of North London University. The results of this work in progress are summarized below.

Approximately 9,000 years ago, the Levels occupied a former small valley which was steadily silting with a blue-grey clay as the English Channel encroached. However, by the Bronze Age the sea had retreated from the resulting estuary or inlet. This marine regression was induced by the accumulation of thick mud under salt marsh conditions and probably aided by the formation of a sand or gravel beach across the bay entrance. Consequent peat growth in the less saline water conditions led to a further raising of the Levels and established the surface upon which the Shinewater complex was constructed.

During the Bronze Age, the platform was situated towards the southern edge of the contemporary fen. This location would have provided a brackish to freshwater environment, just north of an expanse of salt marsh and mudflats. It should also be noted that the bog was dissected by a number of brackish channels that fed into the estuary covering the lower part of the Levels. Indeed, one large palaeochannel is known to have existed immediately to the east of the platform (Fig. 7.12).

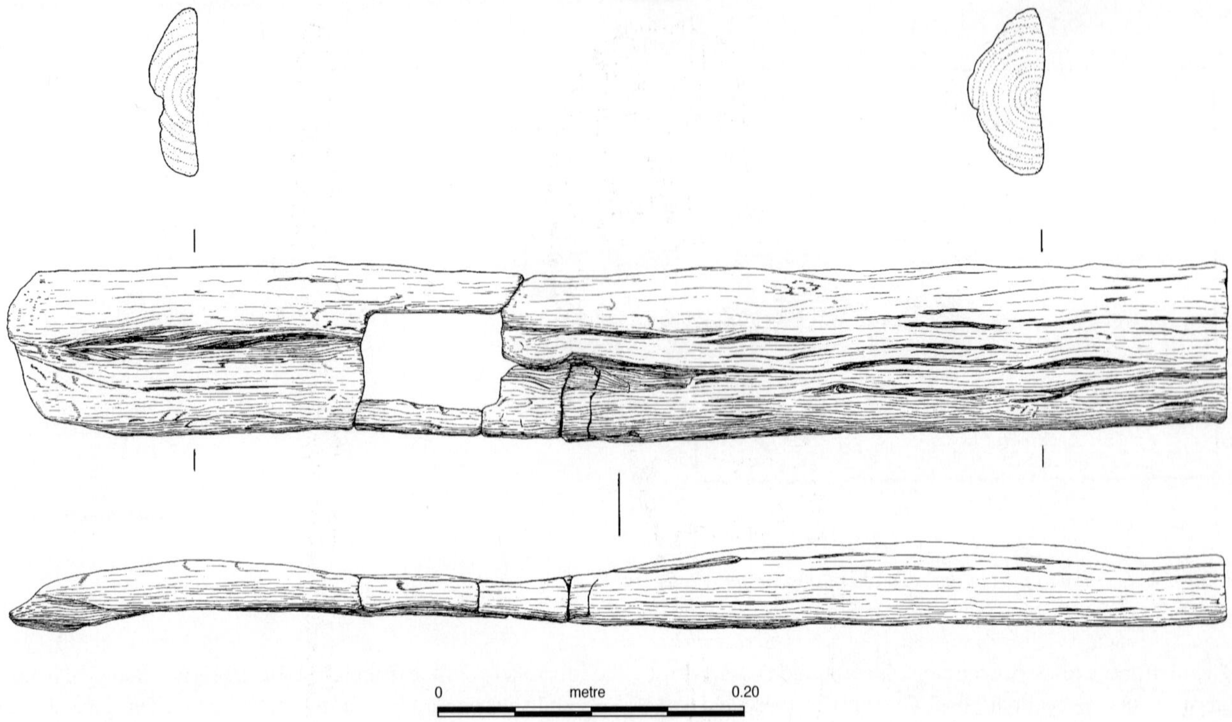

Figure 7.9. *Worked oak recovered from the Shinewater track.*

At the time of the site occupation, the Willingdon peat supported grasses, reeds and sedges. Scattered alder, willow and oak was also growing on the fen or along its boundaries. However, the area was essentially open, so that anyone standing on the adjacent chalk hills could have had a clear view of the timber structures below. Certainly, pollen analysis suggests that during the Late Bronze Age, crops were being grown on the surrounding downland slopes, while the Levels were more suitable for grazing. Fossil evidence has confirmed that platform construction corresponded with the driest conditions since fen development.

Nevertheless, by the Early Iron Age (*c.* 800 BC) settlement on Shinewater marsh had become untenable owing to flooding from the sea. This marine transgression has been observed at a number of coastal sites in South-East England, although its cause is not fully understood. The episode is clearly demonstrated in the Levels formation by a thick layer of alluvial clay, which immediately overlies the cultural deposits of both platform and track.

Of course, questions concerning final disuse of the site are of great importance. Any future research will therefore aim to verify why towards the end of the Bronze Age, the platform was apparently abandoned over a relatively short period, perhaps under catastrophic circumstances. The present evidence indicates persuasively that this abandonment of the Levels resulted directly from the marine inundation of the coastal region. Yet the increasing use of iron, the development of fortified centres and the associated shift in socio-economic organization at this time, may have all contributed to the discontinuation of the site.

A wealth of evidence

The Sussex Downs have been the focus of exhaustive scrutiny and excavation for many decades. Indeed, the bulk of the attested evidence for Bronze Age Sussex relates to those areas of downland where upstanding remains have survived until recently. Other regions in the South-East lack basic fieldwork and research and certainly no intensive combined archaeological and palaeoenvironmental wetland projects have been undertaken. This is surprising as in counties such as Cambridgeshire and Somerset, the Late Bronze Age is known as a period of increasing wetland exploitation. The variable pattern of excavation and relative dearth of lowland surveys, has perhaps resulted in an unbalanced picture of Late Bronze Age settlement and activity distribution.

One region that has been subject to detailed study is the Thames Valley. Here extensive ditch systems and a high concentration of Late Bronze Age casual finds indicate the presence of pastoral farmsteads. The density of occupation recorded in the Thames Valley is surely mirrored across other lowland regions of southern England. However, actual settlements have proved elusive, as sites in river valleys are often buried under alluvial and colluvial deposits, while much of the coastal plain has been exposed to damaging agricultural activity. The Willingdon Levels is therefore important as an example of a low-lying area devoid of upstanding monuments, producing evidence of significant Late Bronze Age exploitation and occupation. Clearly a regional reassessment of lowland, and in particular, wetland utilization during this period is required.

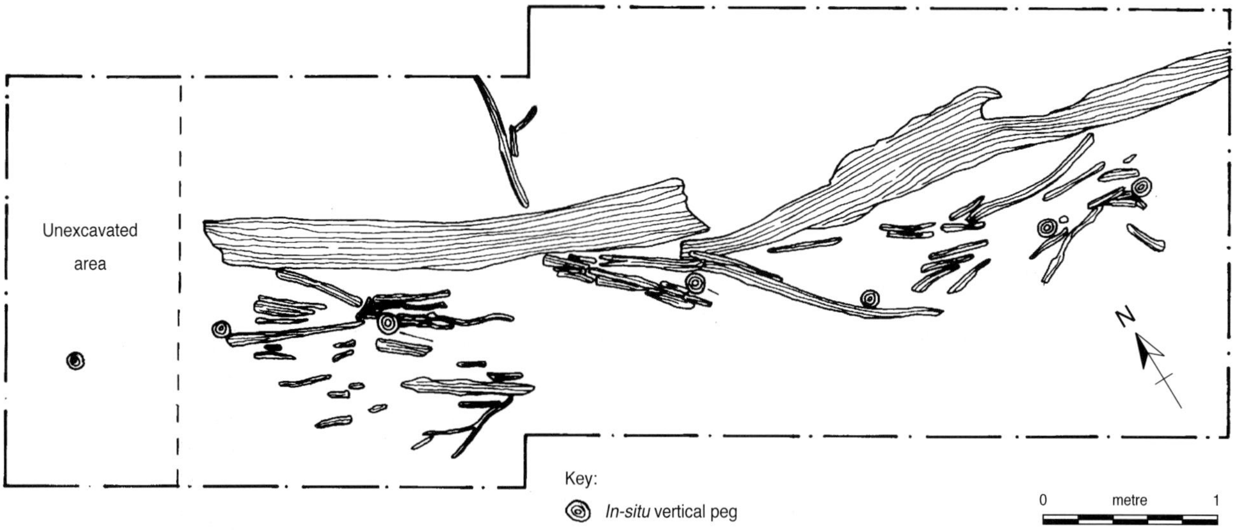

Figure 7.10. *Plan of part of the second Dittons timber alignment.*

The platform and associated track incorporate thousands of pieces of *in-situ* structural wood. The superbly preserved posts perhaps represent the most visually dramatic of the discoveries made so far. As prehistoric timber only survives in exceptional circumstances, a study of this material would provide valuable information on Late Bronze Age resources, species selection and woodland management. It should also enhance our appreciation of ancient woodworking techniques and tools.

A preliminary examination of the dished facets found on all excavated piles has already confirmed that these timbers were shaped into points using bronze axes or adzes (Fig. 7.11). At least one mortise hole exhibiting a knowledge of joinery has also been recorded (Fig. 7.9). Furthermore, the recovery of structural wood offers the prospect of a full dendro-chronological and radiocarbon dating programme. As already demonstrated, dendrochronology in particular could contribute significant data when attempting to establish phases of prehistoric construction. It is unfortunate that there are currently relatively few tree-ring chronologies covering the Late Bronze Age in the South-East. Nevertheless it may eventually prove possible to assign exceptionally precise dendrochronological dates to any large individual timbers uncovered at Shinewater.

The many artefacts recovered from the platform are all in excellent condition and must represent only a fraction of those that await excavation. Certainly, the discovery of the hafted reed hook suggests that other whole items with wooden handles may be found. This is especially important, as prehistoric articles with preserved organic elements are extremely rare. It is even feasible that objects made entirely of wood or other perishable materials, such as leather or textiles, have survived.

The initial evaluation of the platform yielded a large pottery assemblage, subsequently assessed by Sue Hamilton at the Institute of Archaeology. This work has indicated that much of the cultural material at the site is located in approximately the same position as when left or abandoned 2,800 years ago.

It is also possible that prehistoric debris was amassed in fairly undisturbed middens or 'protected areas'. The excavation of such features could provide evidence of the economy, diet and size of the Shinewater community and may even help to resolve the crucial question of whether the platform was occupied all year round or seasonally. The presence of at least three *in-situ* hearths is further verification that the extant archaeological contexts comprise a comprehensible stratified ensemble. This contrasts with the much-discussed Bronze Age settlements of the South Downs, which have nearly all suffered from severe erosion or plough damage.

The precise nature of human activity at the platform has yet to be ascertained. However, the extraordinary preservation of the remains promises many detailed insights into the daily routine of the occupants and the associated social organization of the site. For example, future investigation may reveal further evidence for the integration of ritual into prehistoric life. In fact, it can already be suggested that the probable deliberate deposition of some of the located bronze artefacts represents a display of prestige by an elite class. The discovery of these rarer items certainly indicates a prosperous community of high regional status. The presence of imported objects and general range and quality of the materials, demonstrates that, whatever its function, the platform held a position of importance within the local settlement hierarchy and beyond. The political standing of the Shinewater site, its relationship with other contemporary activity centres and role in the passage of continental goods are thus all topics fundamental to our perception of the Sussex Bronze Age.

Of course, an archaeological site can only be genuinely understood if account is taken of the surrounding landscape, with its constituent natural resources. Fortunately, the Willingdon Levels offers a major potential for palaeoenvironmental analysis: identified plant macrofossils comprise seeds and leaves as well as wood, while areas of reed or rush matting have been recorded at the platform. The recovered animal remains include the fragile parts of birds and small mammals. This rich floral and faunal evidence should establish in spectacular detail the local economies and

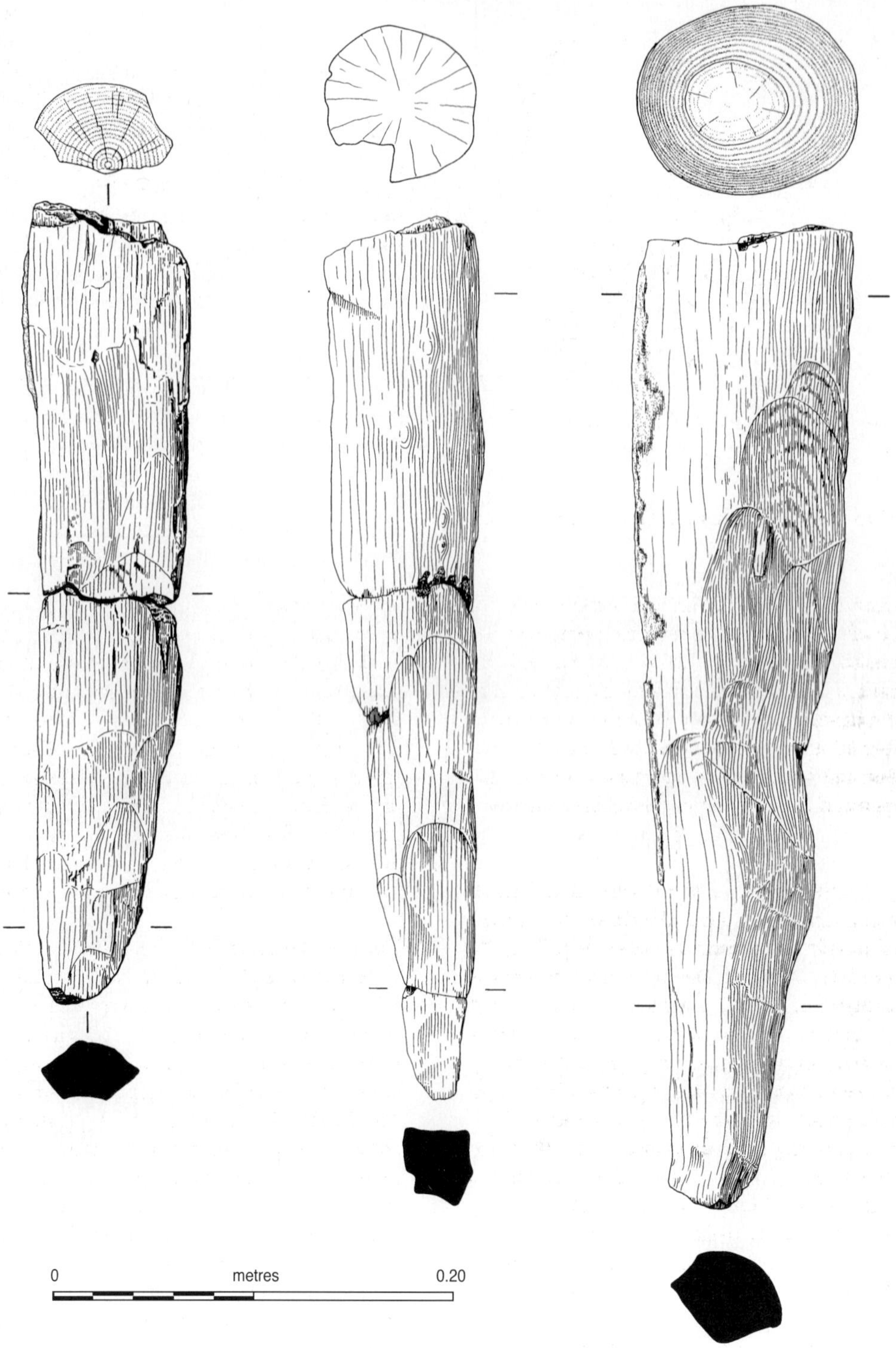

Figure 7.11. Vertical pegs from the second Dittons alignment.

range of available food sources. The environmental history of the Levels may also be refined through a study of any preserved pollen, charcoal, insects, beetles, mollusca, soils and microfossils. Clearly Shinewater Marsh has the potential to contribute extremely valuable data concerning the relationship of a Late Bronze Age community with its surroundings and the impact of that society on the environment.

Preservation measures

In the absence of any funded programme of further excavation, various measures have been taken to protect the platform from future damage and decay. Under the instruction of Dr Andrew Woodcock (the East Sussex County Archaeologist) a vertical plastic membrane was first inserted around three sides of the undisturbed part of the site. This

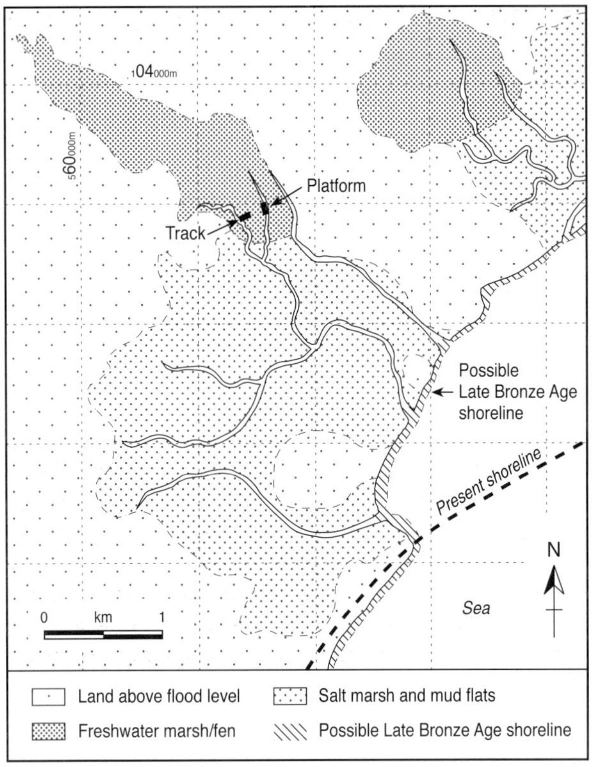

Figure 7.12. *The possible Late Bronze Age setting of the Shinewater platform and track. (Courtesy of Dr Simon Jennings, North London University).*

was designed to reduce drainage away from the archaeological layers and halt the entry of oxygen and micro-organisms. A substantial embankment was then built up against the exposed face of the platform structure, both to hold the membrane in place and prevent slumping.

English Heritage has also funded the installation of nine monitoring stations on and around the site, to record the level and quality of water within the critical horizons. Assessment of the results of this work by the Royal Holloway Institute for Environmental Research and the Ancient Monuments Laboratory (English Heritage) has shown a basic stabilization in the condition of the Bronze Age deposits since discovery.

However, it should not be forgotten that the measures described above represent merely a short-term solution. Permanent *in-situ* preservation of the platform under present circumstances remains only a remote possibility.

Conclusion

An intensive excavation and analysis of the waterlogged structures located on the marsh, within their contemporary environment, would enable the comprehensive interpretation of a previously unrecorded prehistoric landscape. The extraordinary archaeological wealth of these important discoveries would provide a graphic account of the people whose remains have been so vividly preserved for almost three millennia. Perhaps even more importantly, this is a unique opportunity to extend our understanding of the social, economic and ideological factors that underpinned wider Bronze Age society in the South East.

Acknowledgements

All fieldwork undertaken across the Levels has been funded by East Sussex County Council, Eastbourne Borough Council and the British Museum. The Field Archaeology Unit would like to acknowledge the expertise of Dr Andrew Woodcock (East Sussex County Archaeologist), Dr Simon Jennings of North London University and Stuart Needham of the British Museum. Dr Needham has conducted an assessment of the special finds assemblage and is chairman of an academic advisory panel for the project. Radiocarbon dates have been supplied by the British Museum, Oxford University Radiocarbon Accelerator Unit and Beta Analytic Inc.

The author would like to express his personal thanks to all those who have assisted the project, sometimes in appalling field conditions. Mike Seager-Thomas acted as site supervisor throughout the platform evaluation and Chris Derham discovered the two Dittons alignments during many long winter months engaged in a watching brief on the marsh. Except where noted, the illustrations were prepared by Jane Russell and Rob Goller. Karen Hughes of the British Museum drew the end-winged axe. The project is managed for the Field Archaeology Unit by David Rudling.

References

Brück, J. 1995. A place for the dead: the role of human remains in Late Bronze Age Britain, *Proc. Prehist. Soc.* **61,** 245-77.

Burrin, P.J. 1982. The coastal deposits of the Southern Weald, *Quat. Newsletter* **38,** 16-24.

Burrin, P.J. 1983. On the coastal deposits of East Sussex, A further comment, *Quat. Newsletter* **39**, 29-31.

Greatorex, C. 1996. *An archaeological evaluation at Shinewater Park, Eastbourne,* University College London Field Archaeology Unit Report No. 358.

Greatorex, C. 1998. *The Shinewater Track: an excavation of a Late Bronze Age waterlogged structure on the Willingdon Levels, near Eastbourne, East Sussex,* University College London Field Archaeology Unit Report No. 408.

Hather, J. 1996. Wood sampled from Shinewater, in Greatorex 1996.

Hillam, J. Forthcoming. Tree-ring analysis of oak timbers from Shinewater Park and Willingdon Drove, Eastbourne, East Sussex.

Jennings, S. and Smyth, C. 1985. The origin and development of Langney point: a study of coastal and sea level change, *Quat. Newsletter* **45,** 12-22.

Jennings, S. and Smyth, C. 1987a. Coastal erosion and planning at Eastbourne, East Sussex, *Quat. Newsletter* **53,** 10-16.

Jennings, S. and Smyth, C. 1987b. Coastal sedimentation in East Sussex during the Holocene, *Progr. Oceanogr.* **18**, 205-41.

Jennings, S. and Smyth, C. 1990. Holocene evolution of the gravel coastline of East Sussex, *Proc. Geol. Ass.* **101 (3),** 213-24.

Pryor, F. *et al.* 1992. Current research at Flag Fen, Peterborough, *Antiquity* **66**, 439-531.

THE LATE PRE-ROMAN IRON AGE OF THE WEST SUSSEX COASTAL PLAIN: CONTINUITY OR CHANGE?

Chris Davenport

Abstract

The 150 years prior to the Roman Invasion saw major changes in the archaeological record of the West Sussex coastal plain. With its geographical position well suited to cross-channel trade, Chichester Harbour was a gateway for both imported materials and new ideas from Gaul, as it became increasingly embedded in the Roman Empire. Although neither the detailed chronology nor the exact processes are clear, external influences seem to have fused with local traditions changing such diverse areas as ritual practice and site location, coinage was introduced and there were new fashions in eating and drinking. It can be inferred that, as in the Thames Valley, new elite social structures were developing, although no centre for the oppidum has been identified and there is no parallel to the rich graves found north of the Thames. However, the early development of Hayling Island and its close archaeological links to Fishbourne and Chichester all suggest that this area of Sussex was becoming romanised well before the invasion changed the political links with Rome.

Introduction

The aim of this review is to consider the archaeological evidence for change and development on the West Sussex coastal plain (Fig. 8.1) in the Late Pre-Roman Iron Age which is defined as the period starting when Mediterranean imports are first recognizable in British contexts, from about the end of 2nd century BC, until the Roman conquest in AD 43. The historical and geographical contexts will be considered first, before grouping the evidence within the five main themes of coinage, settlement and production sites, ritual sites, contact and trade and finally elite development. These issues will then be considered against our theoretical understanding of this period, and finally it is hoped to draw some tentative conclusions and to highlight further work that needs to be carried out.

Historical Context

Although archaeological evidence will be the primary source used in this discussion, the Late Pre-Roman Iron Age is the period when British prehistory first becomes British proto-history with Mediterranean writers such as Caesar and Strabo referring to Britain and its peoples (Cunliffe 1992). It is therefore instructive to consider Britain in the wider context of European history. However, care should be taken to recognize the problems with the textual evidence, since much of the early material was based on 'travellers tales' and even Caesar's texts had political rather than historical aims. We know, from these sources, that the Roman province of Transalpina was established in southern Gaul soon after 124 BC (Cunliffe 1984a). From the middle of the 1st century BC the Roman empire expanded to the channel so that for nearly 100 years, until the invasion in AD 43, Sussex and its coastal neighbours were on the frontier. During this period, as Gaul became increasingly romanized, traditional cross-channel links will have changed both in structure and content, with the consequence that the culture of southern Britain was potentially open to new ideas, to the exchange and trade of cross-channel goods, and to political manipulation.

Geographical Context

It is also helpful to consider the geography of the West Sussex coastal plain at this time. There is some evidence that sea levels differed significantly during the period: the excavation of the Iron Age site of North Bersted (Bedwin and Pitts 1978), yielded evidence indicating that Aldingbourne Rife was then tidal, signifying higher sea levels than today. In spite of these changes, prehistoric tidal regimes were probably very similar to those of today, eroding the Selsey peninsula (Cunliffe 1973) which would have extended considerably further south than now.

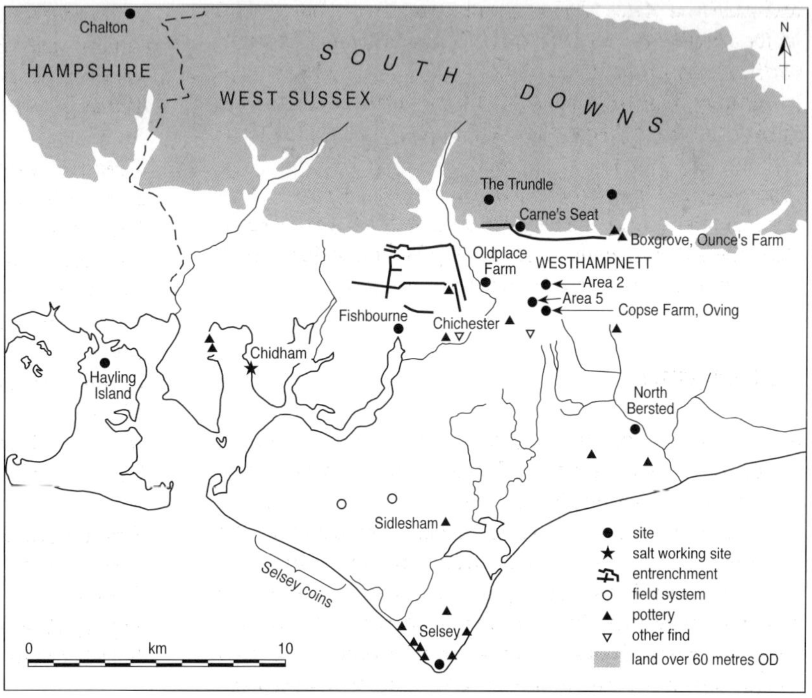

Figure 8.1. Iron Age sites on the West Sussex coastal plain (Source: Fitzpatrick 1997, 8; with permission).

The River Lavant, which now flows out to Fishbourne Harbour, was possibly diverted in the Roman period (Cunliffe 1973), or maybe later in the 1st millennium AD (Magilton 1996). In the Late Pre-Roman Iron Age, the Lavant would have been an important route inland and probably ran further east to meet the sea at Pagham harbour. The Solent, with the protection of the Isle of Wight, has relatively calm seas, which would have fostered the development of local marine contacts.

McGrail (1987) showed that the route from the Seine to the Solent would have been an important cross-channel link during the period (Fig. 8.2, Route 7) and Chichester and Pagham Harbours are some of the most suitable locations for cross-channel shipping to await satisfactory conditions of wind and tide before setting sail for France. Because of the distance and difficulties of sailing along the coast around the extended Selsey Bill, overland portage routes would have been important, crossing the top of Selsey Bill between Chichester Harbour and the eastern coastal plain. Thus the harbours of West Sussex are geographically well placed to develop both cross-channel links and coastal trading, particularly to the west through the Solent.

Coinage

Although there is still much debate about the function and chronological development of coinage in the period under consideration (Nash 1987; Haselgrove 1996), the plotting of find-spots can demonstrate interregional contact (Van Arsdell 1989). There are over 550 coins in the Celtic Coin Index for the Chichester region, a collection which is particularly remarkable for the variety of the origins of the coins, which include imports from Northern France, Normandy and Brittany (De Jersey 1997). Most of these coins are thought to date to the middle of the lst century BC. De Jersey also notes that the only comparable assemblage in Britain is from the Hayling Island (Hampshire) 'cult' site suggesting that both of these areas, which are physically linked by Chichester Harbour, were used by the same group of people. For this reason I have stretched the definition of West Sussex to include the Hayling Island excavation.

Further evidence for even longer-range contacts is argued by Creighton (2000) who shows that the iconography of many of the coins issued in the Late Pre-Roman Iron Age in central southern Britain, follows the visual imagery of coins,

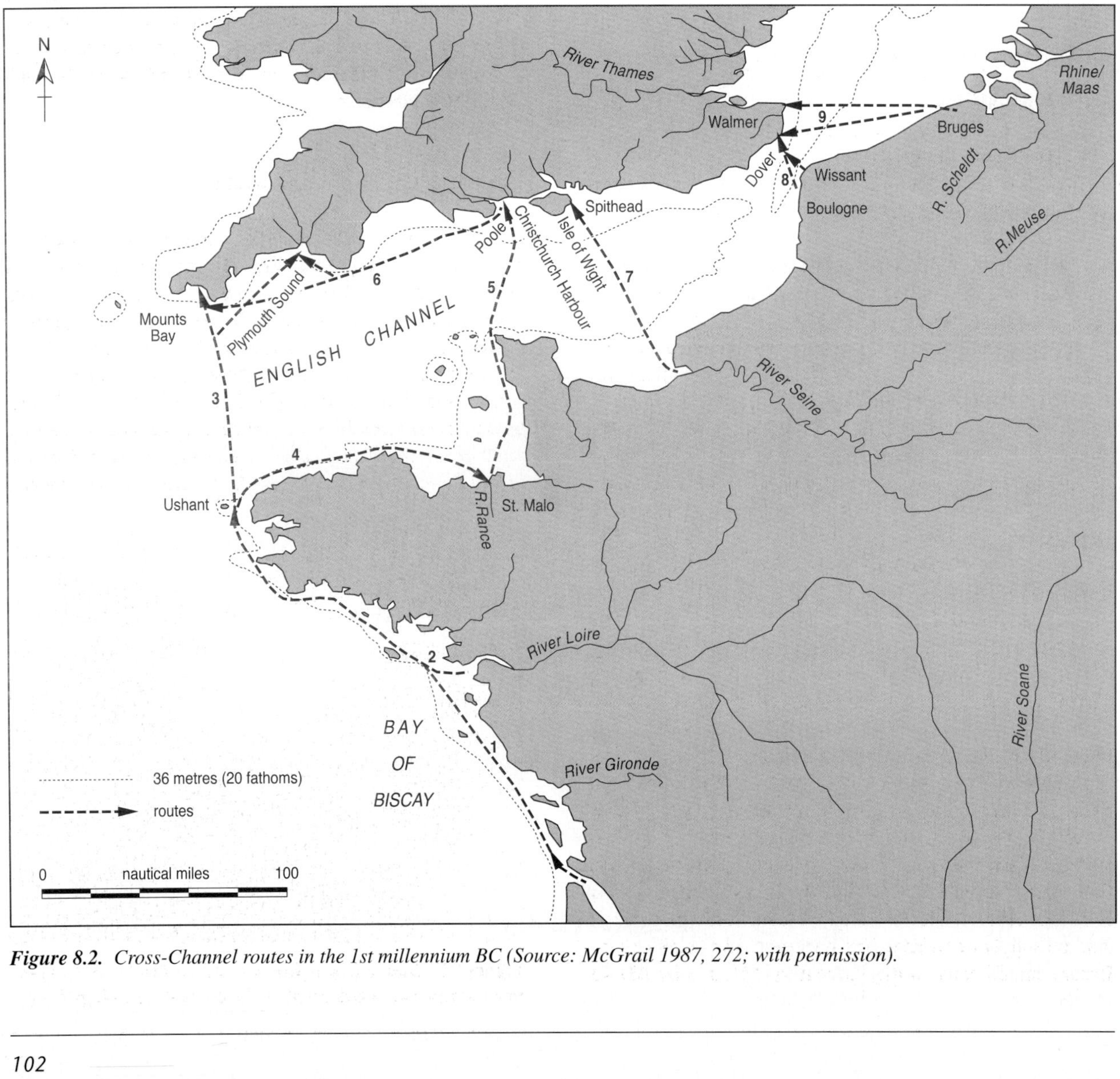

Figure 8.2. *Cross-Channel routes in the 1st millennium BC (Source: McGrail 1987, 272; with permission).*

sculpture and wall paintings from Rome itself, as Octavian, later Augustus, sought to establish his position following the assassination of Caesar in 44 BC. Since these images are not paralleled in Gallic coin issues, he suggests that there were direct contacts with Rome during the second half of the first century BC. These contacts, he argues, were mediated by institutionalized relationships between the Roman *Princeps* and 'friendly kings' from both southern Britain and other kingdoms around the periphery of the Roman world.

Continental and Inter-Regional Trade and Contact

Although imported artefacts are very visible in the archaeological record and have a high profile because of their potential for linking British contexts to European historical dates, they were often not the prime material exchanged nor was the trade route necessarily newly established in order to exchange these exotic materials. Thus tin is thought to have been supplied to the Mediterranean from Cornwall via Western Gaul and the Carcassonne gap (Hawkes 1977; Cunliffe 1984b) long before the first Italian wines in amphorae began to follow the same route in the 2nd century BC. It is, however, the presence of small assemblages of Dressel 1A amphorae together with other Armorican pottery that demonstrates, archaeologically, the northern nodes of this European trade route (Cunliffe and de Jersey 1997). Dressel 1A amphorae have been found at several points along the south coast of Britain, such as Mount Batten, Plymouth, Devon (Cunliffe 1988) and Hengistbury Head, Dorset (Cunliffe 1987), at Knighton, Isle of Wight (Fitzpatrick 1985), at Hayling Island, Hampshire (Downey *et al.* 1979) and on the Arun at Pulborough, Sussex (Cunliffe *et al.* 1996).

As the Empire's influence spread and the frontier moved north, the network of routes across Gaul became more complex, the importance of the Rhone valley as a trade corridor increased and routes to the channel down the Seine, Somme and Rhine developed (Cunliffe 1984a). At the same time the origin and range of traded products and their archaeologically visible amphorae becomes more diverse. From about 70 BC new containers such as the Italian Dressel 1B superseded the older types for existing products and from about 20 BC the Dressel 1-Pascual 1 began to transport new products such as Spanish wine (Fitzpatrick 1985). The number of find-sites in the West Sussex area of Dressel 1B amphorae: Fishbourne (Cunliffe 1971); Chichester (Down 1989); Copse Farm (Bedwin and Holgate 1985) and Ounces Barn (Bedwin and Place 1995; Cunliffe *et al.* 1996) confirm an increasing tempo of contact with France and suggest a wider dissemination of at least some classes of imported material.

In the first half of the first century AD, prior to the invasion of Britain, we can recognize other imported fine wares from romanized Europe, such as Arretine and the early Gallo-Belgic wares: *Terra Rubra* and *Terra Nigra*. These are more restricted in their distribution, but were found at Fishbourne and Chichester (Cunliffe *et al.* 1996) and Ounces Barn (Bedwin and Place 1995). More generally, Williams (1995) has shown that the supply of Dressel 20 amphorae to the south-east of Britain started early in the 1st century AD, and by AD 43 supplies of Spanish olive oil were arriving in southern Britain as though it were already part of the Empire.

From Copse Farm (Bedwin and Holgate 1985) there is evidence of the movement of goods both along the coast (e.g. Kimmeridge shale from Dorset) and inland (e.g. quernstone fragments from the Weald). It is also likely that the coastal region was sending salt inland during the Late Pre-Roman Iron Age, since there is evidence of salt production around Chichester harbour, at sites such as Chidham (Bedwin 1980), in both the 1st millennium BC (Bradley 1975) and in the Roman period (Bradley 1991).

At Hayling Island (Downey *et al.* 1979), as De Jersey noted (1997), cross-channel contact is highlighted by Augustinian coins from Belgic and Central Gaul. The remainder of the British coins emphasize links with Hampshire and Dorset rather than the Thames Valley, as do the Kimmeridge shale bracelets and the swords which are paralleled at Owselbury, near Winchester, Hampshire (Collis 1968). Iron (possibly Wealden) currency bars at Hayling Island and coin moulds (Fig. 8.3) at Ounces Barn (Bedwin and Place 1995) remind us that all of the raw materials for metalworking would have been imported from outside the West Sussex region.

The coin and trade evidence combine to suggest that during the Late Pre-Roman Iron Age the area around Chichester was an important Solent landfall for cross-channel contacts which were combined with extensive links both inland and through the Solent to the west.

Trade and Local Contact

It is inherently difficult to recognize archaeologically the local movement of most goods, since they are rarely intrusive in their new location. There is, however, some evidence that the communities of the coastal plain were economically linked in the late 1st century BC. Hamilton (1993) isolated wheel-thrown pottery at Copse Farm (Bedwin and Holgate 1985) which used quartz sand temper from the Greensand Ridge, to the north of the Downs. She then proceeded to identify another 13 find-spots spread across the coastal plain, demonstrating not only trade in these basic products over an

Figure 8.3. *Iron Age coin flan mould from Ditch 1 at Ounces Barn, Boxgrove. (Photograph: UCL Field Archaeology Unit).*

area 8-10 kilometres across, but also centralized and probably specialized manufacturing of these ceramics. So far as we know this centralization of production was a new development for West Sussex in the Late Pre-Roman Iron Age, since the pottery from the Westhampnett cemetery, which is dated to the period between 90 BC and 50 BC, is virtually all of handmade fabrics that do not suggest centralized production (Fitzpatrick 1997).

Ritual

It is a modern western belief that one can neatly separate ritual from other activities. In contrast ethnographic evidence suggests that within prehistoric societies most activities were carried out within a ritual framework. For example, the preferred orientation of Iron Age round-house entrances to the east and south-east is clearly not accidental, but arises from a belief about the 'right' way to construct this type of structure (Fitzpatrick 1995, Fig. 8.7). In spite of the problem of identifying sites with ritual significance in the past, I have selected three sites as seeming to have particular importance: firstly, the Trundle, secondly the Westhampnett cemetery, and lastly Hayling Island.

Although the role of hillforts is not well understood, their importance as ritual centres is being increasingly recognized, firstly because of the presence of rectangular "shrines" within sites such as Danebury, Hampshire (Cunliffe 1984b), and secondly because the contents of many of their pits are now being interpreted as deliberate depositions within a presumed ritual context (Hill 1995; Hamilton 1997).

There is no evidence for continued structural development of Sussex hill-forts in the Late Pre-Roman Iron Age (Hamilton and Manley 1997), and the Trundle was thought by Curwen (1937) to have been abandoned early in the 1st century BC. Whether the Trundle was actually abandoned or whether less archaeologically visible practices continued, its presence and visibility from the coastal plain would have continued to impact on subsequent developments, since an area normally develops in a way that relates both to the physical and to the social landscapes that already exist.

Below the Trundle, on a low ridge to the east of the River Lavant, a cemetery was established soon after the beginning of the 1st century BC at Westhampnett (Fitzpatrick 1997). Evidence from the accompanying fibulae suggest that the site continued to be used until about 50 BC. This religious site comprised 161 cremation burials, at least two rectangular 'shrines' and a range of pyre sites and related features which makes it one of the largest Late Pre-Roman Iron Age cremation cemeteries so far excavated in Britain. A distribution map of Late Iron Age cremation burials and selected shrines in southern England has been produced by Fitzpatrick (1997, fig 115). One of the cemetery structures is similar to a pre-Roman structure from the site of the Lancing Down Roman temple which Bedwin (1981) interpreted as an Late Pre-Roman Iron Age shrine. In spite of its size, Westhampnett was not the exclusive repository on the coastal plain for human remains, since human bone deposits have also been recovered at Copse Farm, North Bersted (Bedwin and Pitts 1978), and Hayling Island (Fitzpatrick 1997, 220).

The Westhampnett cemetery was probably used by the Copse Farm community, the latter lived about 1 kilometre to the south, but given the cemetery's large size and the short duration of its use, it is also probable that the cemetery was serving other local communities, thereby acting as a focal centre for corporate ritual activity of a larger group. Many of the ceramic vessels are of turned, grog-tempered pottery, and share the same forms as similar pottery in the Thames Valley (Thompson 1982). Other vessel forms in the cemetery, such as the pedestalled bowls, also confirm links to Dorset and the west (Fitzpatrick 1997, 131).

West of Chichester Harbour on Hayling Island (Hampshire) is the site of a 'cult centre' (Downey *et al.* 1979; King and Soffe 1994). Although this has not been fully published, the excavators distinguished both Iron Age and Roman phases. Its earliest phases, dated to the middle of 1st century BC, consisted of a series of gullies surrounding a circular area containing pits and post-holes, many of which contained "votive" offerings. As we have already noted, the coin profile links the temple's usage to the Chichester area, and both were linked to northern France.

The second phase consisted of the rebuilding in stone of a substantial circular structure, possibly a tower, with a surrounding rectangular wall. Unfortunately, these changes appear to have truncated much of the stratigraphy from the early 1st century AD. However, coin evidence again suggests that the rebuilding was linked to similar 'improvements' at Fishbourne and Chichester, both dated to after AD 43. The quality of this second phase continues to confirm Hayling Island as an important centre in the mid-1st century AD, when the site still had direct links to the Fishbourne/Chichester area.

To summarize the evidence from these three sites. The Trundle was an existing centre from the Middle Iron Age and was probably abandoned early in the Late Pre-Roman Iron Age. Generally the disposal of the dead in the earlier Iron Age is archaeologically invisible apart from occasional burials comprising individuals or small groups (Whimster 1981). However, soon after the beginning of the 1st century BC the Westhampnett cemetery was established, incorporating new ideas, probably from Belgic Gaul, about how and where the rituals for the dead should take place (Fitzpatrick 1997). It is tempting to see the presence of the rectangular shrines at Westhampnett, as refocusing some of the traditional practices from the hillfort in the new ritual space thereby leading to changes in practice or the total abandonment of the Trundle itself. The establishment of the Hayling Island site, probably early in the 1st century BC, may reflect a new or parallel developments in ritual and cult practice, but there is no clear link to Westhampnett, and no specific evidence suggesting Hayling Island as a continuing centre for mortuary rites.

Settlement and Production

Bedwin (1983) suggested that the Late Pre-Roman Iron Age saw an increase in the number of farming settlements on the West Sussex coastal plain. There are several sites to the east of the River Lavant such as Copse Farm, Old Place Farm, North Bersted and Carnes Seat, of which only Copse Farm and North Bersted have been excavated to modern standards.

However, both of these have an interrupted stratigraphy late in the 1st century BC or early in the 1st century AD, and we can also now add the Westhampnett cemetery as showing a similar discontinuity at around the middle of the 1st century BC.

Below and to the east of the Trundle, and intervisible with it, is the site of Carnes Seat (Holgate 1986). This site, which was based on a "banjo" enclosure, has apparent occupation debris in the upper fills of the ditches, which from excavations at similar sites in Hampshire (Perry 1969; 1972; Fasham 1987) probably implies mixed farming. The unstratified pottery was consistent with occupation from the 2nd century BC (ie 'saucepan' wares), through the 1st century BC (Aylesford-Swarling type wares) and into the Roman period (including Alice Holt wares).

Nearer the sea, to the east of Aldingbourne Rife, another farming site has been excavated at North Bersted (Bedwin and Pitts 1978). This comprised a roundhouse, with domestic debris, in an area of at least 12 acres networked by drainage ditches, which formed the boundaries to irregular rectangular fields. Middle Iron Age saucepan wares were succeeded by Aylesford Swarling type wares, which are Late Iron Age wheel-thrown wares. There is, finally, evidence of destruction and deliberate site clearance in the excavated area, suggesting abandonment of the roundhouse probably late in the 1st century BC, since there is no Gallic-Belgic component to this assembly. However observation of Romano-British pottery in the upper fills of the surrounding ditches suggests continuing use of the fields and a ceramic progression from the Late Iron Age into the Roman period is soon to be published from these contexts (M. Lyne pers. comm.). Indications of very high temperatures in at least one of the pits suggests the possibility of ironworking on the site.

Closer to modern Chichester to the east of the River Lavant, the sites of Copse Farm (Bedwin and Holgate 1985) and Oldplace Farm (Bedwin 1983) were additional farmsteads with ditched enclosures. Excavation at Copse Farm produced large quantities of butchered bone and smaller quantities of amphora sherds, metalwork, slag, fired clay and worked bone in contexts which contained no Romano-British pottery and could therefore be regarded as a sealed Late Iron Age stratigraphic sequence. The principal focus of the industrial activities was a shallow depression about 7 m in diameter within a ditched enclosure, the entrance to which led to the entrance of an adjacent roundhouse. As at North Bersted, saucepan pottery was succeeded by Aylesford Swarling type pottery, but there were no Gallo-Belgic wares which suggests that the site was abandoned early in the 1st century AD. The crop component of the Copse Farm assemblage lacks chaff. This suggests that the cereals were being processed elsewhere before being imported to the site, possibly in exchange for the worked output from the site.

Further east, below Halnaker Hill, is the site of Ounces Barn which lies at the eastern terminal of the Chichester entrenchments. Here a series of cross-cutting ditches create enclosures, and although the stratigraphy is complicated (Bedwin and Orton 1984; Bedwin and Place 1995) it appears that at least one of the enclosures was integrated to the entrenchment terminal. The lack of a roundhouse or obvious domestic debris, and the presence of coin moulds (Fig. 8.3) in the ditch fills, may indicate an industrial site, specifically for working metals and producing coins.

To the south of Chichester the various finds in excavations around the tip of Selsey Bill can be grouped together, because this is the land closest to the proposed site of the eroded "Selsey oppidum", the "missing" urban core for the coastal plain (Cunliffe 1991). Together these finds could constitute evidence for such a settlement. A gazetteer of Iron Age sites (Bedwin and Pitts 1978) records that there is evidence of "extensive" field systems towards the western side of the peninsula, and it is probable that dispersed farming settlements covered the higher dry land from Chichester to the coast. However, marine flooding would have occurred regularly, limiting both the establishment of settlements and the use of the lower-lying areas.

Because the peninsula is still an area of continuing erosion, much of the archaeological material has been found unstratified within the inter-tidal zone, in situations which are now well offshore. To the east of the Bill two Late Pre-Roman Iron Age gold coins, of Commius and Verica, were found in 1935 (Kenny 1989, 22), and Heron-Allen (1911, 54 and 74) reported an "Iron Age floor eroding into the sea" and Iron Age pottery in the low cliff which runs along the foreshore. There is a similar report of four Iron Age hut sites being washed away in 1954 (Desham 1954). Unfortunately, neither Heron-Allen's, nor Desham's, report can be ascribed safely to the Late Pre-Roman Iron Age. More recently at Broadreeds, close to the present shore line, the terminal of a ditch 7 m wide was excavated which contained large sherds of Late Pre-Roman Iron Age pottery (Kenny 1989). To the west of the Bill there have been various finds of pieces of gold and gold objects, some of which were thought to have come from minting activity. However, Brown (1979) reviewed all of this material and came to the conclusion that it originated from an Anglo-Saxon hoard, possibly that of a goldsmith. This had been mixed by the sea, with the scattered remains of three Iron Age coin hoards (Allen 1960; Aldsworth 1987).

Inland at Selsey there have been various excavations of Late Iron Age material at Green Lawns (Kenny 1990) and below the Sidlesham Roman Villa (Wilson 1955). The excavation at Golf Links Lane (White 1934) produced 'Class D' pottery identified by Hamilton (1993) as the Copse Farm Late Pre-Roman Iron Age wheel-thrown fabric. Dannell also refers to early Samian pottery found at Selsey (Down 1993, 149). The Copse Farm fabric links Selsey and Chichester during the second half of the 1st century BC, and the presence of early Samian suggests that these links continued into the 1st century AD.

The Oppidum and Elite Development

The Chichester entrenchments are a complex of 15 linear earthworks with a total identified length of 27 kilometres. Surviving sections still have banks 3 m high and ditches 6-9 m wide. Further east, nearer to the River Arun, there are other surviving dykes which may originally have been linked to the Chichester complex, but research is needed to establish this relationship.

Dyke systems like the Chichester Entrenchments are found elsewhere in Britain. Examples are the Lexden Dykes at Colchester, Essex (Hawkes and Hull 1947) and Grimms Dyke, Oxfordshire (Bradley 1968). They have generally been classified by Cunliffe (1991) as defining a territorial oppidum (Collis 1984). Oppidum is the term applied by Caesar to the strongholds of "Celtic" power that he encountered in France and Britain.

Dating discontinuous earthworks is always difficult, however, Bradley (1971) completed both a field survey of all of the surviving elements, and a review of documentary references to them. Pottery found by Murray (1956) suggested a date in the middle of the 1st century BC and Bradley's own finds of sealed Late Pre-Roman Iron Age sherds supported this dating.

Some doubts regarding the dates for the Halnaker section were raised by Bedwin's (1982) finding medieval pottery within the ditch fill, however, excavations further east at Ounces Barn (Bedwin and Orton 1984; Bedwin and Place 1995) support Bradley's earlier dating.

From a detailed examination of the earthwork intersections Bradley proposed a three-phase development. The most northerly contour-following dykes are considered by Bradley to be the earliest phase, enclosing an area of about 160 sq. hectares (60 sq. miles). Subsequent additions were straighter and reinforced natural boundaries, such as the River Lavant. Bradley's phased development suggests that the function of the entrenchment complex changed over time. Perhaps the earliest structures acted only as boundary markers, whereas the later developments, which encompassed less territory, would have been more defendable and appear to group around the head of Chichester Harbour, which may indicate an increasing focus of activity to the west of the Selsey peninsula.

We have seen that soon after the middle of the 1st century BC Westhampnett ceased to be used, and that subsequently several of the settlement sites, to the east of the former course of the River Lavant, were abandoned. This could reinforce the possibility raised by the development of the entrenchments of a change of focus from the east to the west of Selsey Bill. If this was a real shift, one possible factor might have been a change in the preferred trading access from the River Lavant to Chichester Harbour, which offered better access to the west. Alternatively the continued presence of the Hayling Island ritual centre could have made Fishbourne harbour a more significant location.

It has been argued that there should be a nucleated core somewhere within the oppidum on the coastal plain. The lack of firm evidence from Chichester itself has led to the proposal of a "Selsey oppidum" lost to archaeology because it was on land since eroded by the sea (Cunliffe 1991). Bedwin (1983) reviewed all of the finds from Selsey and came to the conclusion that the provenance of much of the pre-Roman Iron Age material was suspect, a view endorsed by Aldsworth (1987, 49) who refers to the "minimal finds from Selsey". Thus in practice the evidence for a nucleated centre on eroded Selsey is less than satisfactory.

There is, in fact, a wide variation in the characteristics which made up an oppidum (Woolf 1993). Dispersed activities were common and an urban or nucleated core was not always present. However, over 220 sherds of pre-conquest imported fine wares have now been found in Fishbourne and Chichester (Cunliffe *et al.* 1996), reinforcing the view suggested for Hayling Island that the elite activities which started in the middle of the 1st century BC continued through to AD 43 and beyond.

Chichester has been excavated and published as a continuing program, but it poses a set of problems which are additional to those experienced at other sites on the coastal plain (Down and Rule 1971), (Down 1974; 1978; 1981; 1989; 1993), (Cunliffe *et al.* 1996). Firstly, because it is a modern city, excavation is dictated by redevelopment and is therefore arbitrary with very little in the south-west quadrant which contains the Cathedral. Secondly, the size of the city means that, in spite of the substantial work carried out, only a very limited proportion has been excavated. Thirdly, two millennia of urban occupation have resulted in a great deal of mixing of stratigraphy so that the earliest layers are much disturbed, fragmentary and difficult to interpret with closed contexts virtually non-existent.

Over time there has been a growing dichotomy between the lack of evidence for Iron Age occupation, apart from three roundhouses found at the Cattle Market site (Down 1989, 151), and accumulating artefactual evidence of first century AD Iron Age presence in the form of amphorae, late Augustan Arretine pottery, early Gaulish Samian pottery and early Gallo-Belgic wares. It is now known from Silchester (Fulford 1987), and Colchester (Rodwell 1977) that both rectangular houses and a gridded street plan can predate the invasion. It is therefore possible, and not inconsistent with the published evidence, that in Chichester the pre-conquest period should have included some of the rectangular structures presently assumed to have been established after 43 AD.

There is increasing evidence for imports in the Fishbourne/Chichester area. This suggests a local elite presence, but apart from the limited and early settlement at the Cattle Market, there are no definite pre-conquest structures. Perhaps the elite continued to live in roundhouses, which further excavation may reveal, or maybe in increasingly romanized, rectangular homes which we have not yet recognized. These issues can only be resolved by further research including re-evaluation of the present evidence.

Theoretical Model

Considering how prehistoric societies and their elites may have exercised power, Rowlands (1980) put forward a model for the Bronze Age based on the exchange of prestigious gifts between elites and on the subsequent control and restriction of their local distribution. Frankenstein and Rowlands (1978) elaborate this model for the Early Iron Age of south-western Germany, postulating a hierarchy both of settlement sites, and of their rich associated burials. In the Late Pre-Roman Iron Age of Britain, Haselgrove (1982) used a similar dynamic to create a model which explains the interaction between an increasingly romanized Gaul and the tribal society of Britain, based upon the importance of prestige imports in British society. The model envisages elites competing to acquire

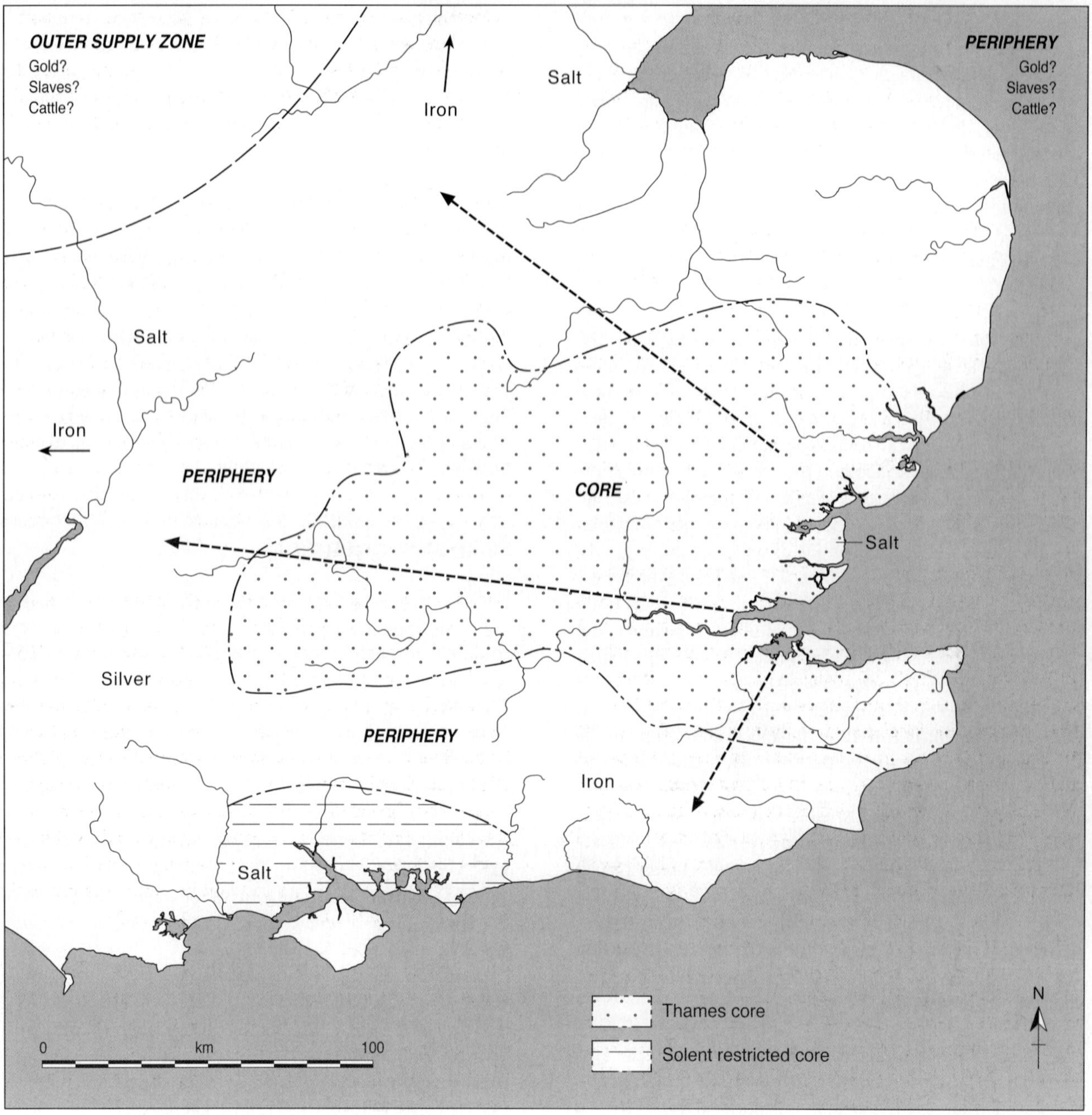

Figure 8.4. The exchange of prestige goods during the Late Pre-Roman Iron Age (after *Bradley 1984, 155 and Haselgrove 1982).*

prestige traded goods with which they can reward their supporters. This system involved 'positive feedback' with successful elites able to influence increasing areas of territory and thereby controlling even more trade, resulting in a widening differential of wealth and power both within societies, and between areas. Because certain areas had better access to the continental imports, this geographical advantage helped them develop more strongly than others. This model predicts the formation of core areas in direct contact with continental trade and a periphery comprising areas where contact is indirect, via the core areas. Haselgrove applied this model to the Thames Valley where it appears to work well. However communities in the Solent region, like Chichester, were in a geographically circumscribed position since they could encourage direct trade with the continent, which would have allowed them to develop core attributes, but their hinterland was restricted by the presence of the Thames Valley itself (Fig. 8.4). Thus within the predicted model they remain 'restricted cores' with a limited supporting periphery. As a result, they have a different development trajectory from that of areas further north. Limited in its expansion, and perhaps always in competition with the Thames area, Chichester may have needed cross-channel contacts and support to maintain its independence, and therefore may have been particularly open to Roman influence. There is increasing acceptance that the cross-channel links were so well developed prior to AD 43 that Chichester harbour may itself have been one of the beachheads for the Claudian invasion (Hind 1989; Cunliffe 1998).

Conclusions

Attempting to synthesize the evidence, even from an area which has had as much archaeological attention as West Sussex, is an impossible aim because of the varied quality of the evidence, the different nature of the sites being considered and the imprecision of the chronological indicators, particularly when compared with the historical background. We should expect discontinuities, rather than data being compressed into a seamless whole, since it is the discontinuities which can direct the attention towards future research.

In southern Britain generally the Late Pre-Roman Iron Age is characterized by particularly rapid change. We have evidence for the spread of new ideas such as coinage, new technology incorporating the fast potters wheel, new approaches to eating and drinking, (particularly of wine) and new mortuary rituals incorporating cremations with grave goods. In West Sussex we have evidence for all of these, but there is no evidence for the development of elite cremation burials with significant quantities of imported grave goods, such as occur to the north of the Thames, and which may indirectly reflect increasing differentiation of wealth and power in that region. On the coastal plain it is simply not clear where disposal of the dead continued after Westhampnett ceased to be used, nor what new rites developed. Since we lack both funeral and habitation evidence, the trajectory of elite development during the Late Pre-Roman Iron Age is difficult to gauge. However, the speed with which the area developed after AD 43 suggests Chichester as a centre with well-established social structures rather than a new foundation, in spite of its Roman name *Noviomagus*, i.e.: New Market. Wider political developments in south-eastern Britain catalysed by cross-channel contact were also creating a new environment of competition between regions. Chichester was able to trade directly with the continent, but its expansion was restricted, and it may therefore have been forced to intensify its own output.

The coin and other artefactual evidence shows that the area had contacts and was trading goods both along the coast to the west and across the channel to Armorica, Normandy and the Seine Valley. However, the relative importance of these relationships is not clear, nor do we know what other materials were being imported or exported, although foodstuffs such as grain, salted meat and fish could all have been available for export from the West Sussex coastal plain. The evidence for abandonment of the eastern settlement areas, but continuity at Hayling Island and development of the entrenchments further west, all tend to suggest the increasing importance of Chichester harbour and the Fishbourne/ Chichester area. This is a view supported by the subsequent development of the military granaries and Roman palace at Fishbourne. Unfortunately, we still lack the firm evidence to judge the extent of developments immediately prior to the conquest or the amount to which these pre-conquest developments were romanized in their form. Clearly, there needs to be further research of, and a finer chronology for, the period immediately prior to AD 43.

The aim of this review has been to consider the archaeological evidence from West Sussex for developments during the Late Pre-Roman Iron Age. There were major changes during the period, some of which were stimulated by ideas imported across the channel, which then fused with local tradition to initiate and create new practices as, for example, the new burial rite with the traditional rectangular shrines at Westhampnett. The impact of these material changes on the political, religious and social structures which comprised West Sussex Iron Age society is less clear. This area's geographical position made it a 'restricted core' and gave it a unique development profile, but there are still many significant gaps in our understanding of these developments. The question is thus not "Continuity or Change?' since we see evidence for both. We need further research to understand how the balance between change and continuity was evolving before the impact of the Roman conquest ended the pre-Roman Iron Age and created a new dynamic for the coastal plain of West Sussex.

Acknowledgements

I wish to thank the following for permissions to use/modify their published illustrations:
Andrew Fitzpatrick (Fig. 8.1); Sean McGrail and Pearson Education Ltd. (Fig. 8.2); and Richard Bradley and Pearson Education Ltd. (Fig. 8.4).

References

Aldsworth, F.G. 1987. Prehistoric and Roman Selsey, *SAC* **125**, 41-50.
Allen, D. 1960. The Origination of Coinage in Britain in S. Frere (ed), *The Problems of The Iron Age in Southern Britain.* London: Institute of Archaeology.
Bedwin, O.R. 1980. Neolithic and Iron Age Material from a Coastal Site at Chidham, West Sussex, *SAC* **118**, 163-170.
Bedwin, O.R. 1981. Excavations at Lancing Down, West Sussex, 1980, *SAC* **119**, 37-56.
Bedwin, O.R. 1982. Excavations at the Devil's Ditch, Boxgrove West Sussex 1981, *SAC* **120**, 37-43.
Bedwin, O. R. 1983. The Development of Prehistoric Settlement on the West Sussex Coastal Plain, *SAC* **121**, 31-44.
Bedwin, O. R. and Holgate, R. 1985. Excavations at Copse Farm, Oving, West Sussex, *Proc. Prehist. Soc.* **51**, 215-245.
Bedwin, O. R. and Orton, C. 1984. The Excavation of the Eastern Terminal of the Devil's Ditch (Chichester Dykes), Boxgrove, West Sussex, 1982, *SAC* **122**, 63-74.
Bedwin, O.R. and Pitts, M.W. 1978. The Excavation of an Iron Age Settlement at North Bersted, Bognor Regis, West Sussex 1975-76, *SAC* **116,** 293-346.
Bedwin, O. and Place, C. 1995. Late Iron Age and Romano-British occupation at Ounces Barn, Boxgrove, West Sussex; excavations 1982-83, *SAC* **133**, 45-101.
Bradley, R. 1968. The South Oxfordshire Grimm's Dyke and its Significance, *Oxoniensia* **33**, 1-13.
Bradley, R. 1969. The Chichester Dykes-A Dissenting Judgement, *SAC* **107**, 137-140.
Bradley, R. 1971. A Field survey of the Chichester Entrenchments in B. Cunliffe (ed), 17-36.

Bradley, R. 1975. Salt and Settlement in the Hampshire Sussex Borderland, in K. De Brisay and K. Evans (eds), *Salt: The Study of an Ancient Industry,* Colchester: Colchester Archaeological Group, 20-25.
Bradley, R. 1984. *The Social Foundations of Prehistoric Britain.* London: Longman.
Bradley, R 1991. Roman Salt Production in Chichester Harbour: Rescue Excavations at Chidham, West Sussex, *Britannia* **23**, 27-44.
Brown, J. 1979. *The Gold Finds from Selsey Bill, Sussex,* Undergraduate Thesis, Institute of Archaeology, University of London (Unpublished).
Collis, J. 1968. Excavations at Owselbury, Hants. : An Interim Report, *Ant. J.* **48**, 18-31.
Collis, J. 1984. *Oppida : Earliest Towns North of the-Alps.* University of Sheffield.
Creighton, J. 2000. *Coins and Power in Late Iron Age Britain.* Cambridge: University Press.
Cunliffe, B. 1971. *Excavations at Fishbourne 1961-69,* London: Soc. Antiq. Res. Rep. **26** and **27**.
Cunliffe, B. 1973. *The Regni,* London: Duckworth.
Cunliffe, B. 1984a. Relations Between Britain and Gaul in the First Century B.C. and Early First Century A.D., in S. Macready and F. H. Thompson (eds), *Cross-Channel Trade Between Gaul And Britain In The Pre-Roman Iron Age,* London: Soc. Antiq. Occas. Pap. (New Series) **IV**, 3-24.
Cunliffe, B. 1984b. *Danebury An Iron Age Hill Fort in Hampshire Volume 1 The Excavations 1969-78 : The Site Volume 2: The Excavations 1969-78: The Finds. CBA Res. Rep.* **52**, London.
Cunliffe, B. 1987. *Hengistbury Head, Dorset,* Oxford: O.U.C.A.
Cunliffe, B. 1988. *Mount Batten, Plymouth,* Oxford: O.U.C.A.
Cunliffe, B. 1991 *Iron Age Communities In Britain,* 3rd ed. London: Routledge.
Cunliffe, B. 1992. *The Celtic World,* London: Constable and Co. Ltd.
Cunliffe, B. 1998. *Fishbourne Roman Palace.* Stroud: Tempus Publishing Ltd.
Cunliffe, B. and de Jersey, P. 1997. *Armorica and Britain.* Oxford: O.U.C.A.
Cunliffe, B., Down, A. and Rudkin, D. 1996. *Chichester Excavation IX.* Chichester: Chichester District Council.
Curwen, 1937. *The Archaeology of Sussex.* London: Methuen.
De Jersey, 1997. Counting the Coinage, *Sussex Past and Present* **81**, 6.
Desham, H. 1954. *Selsey, Sussex Notes and Queries* **XIV**, 69.
Down, A. 1974. *Chichester Excavations 2,* Chichester: Phillimore.
Down, A. 1978. *Chichester Excavations 3,* Chichester: Phillimore.
Down, A. 1981. *Chichester Excavations 5,* Chichester: Phillimore.
Down, A. 1989. *Chichester Excavations 6,* Chichester: Phillimore.
Down, A. 1993. *Chichester Excavations 8,* Chichester: Chichester District Council.
Down, A. and Rule, M. 1971. *Chichester Excavations 1.* Chichester: Phillimore.
Downey, R., King, A. and Soffe, G. 1979. The *Hayling Island Temple.* London: Downey.
Fasham, P. 1987. *A Banjo Enclosure in Micheldever Wood, Hampshire.* Hampshire Field Club Monograph **5**.
Fitzpatrick, A. 1985. The Distribution of Dressel 1 Amphorae in North-West Europe, *Oxford Journal of Archaeology* **4(3)**, 305-340.
Fitzpatrick, A. 1997. *Archaeological Excavation on the Route of the A27 Westhampnett Bypass, West Sussex 1992 Volume 2: the Cemeteries,* Wessex Archaeology Report **12**, Salisbury.
Frankenstein, S. and Rowlands, M.J. 1978. The Internal Structure and Regional Context of Early Iron Age Society in South West Germany, Univ. London Inst. Archaeol. **15**, 73-112.
Fulford, M. 1987. Calleva Atrebatum : An Interim Report on the Oppidum 1980-86, *Proc. Prehist. Soc.* **53**, 271-278.
Hamilton, S. 1993. *1st Millennium BC Pottery Traditions in Southern Britain.* Ph.D. Thesis, University of London (Unpublished).
Hamilton, S. 1997. Replacing the Caburn and its finds, *Sussex Past and Present* **83**, 9.
Hamilton, S. and Manley, J. 1997. Points of View : Prominent Enclosures in 1st millennium Sussex, *SAC* **135**, 93-112.
Haselgrove, C. 1982. Wealth Prestige and Power: The Dynamics of Political Centralisation in South-East England, in C. Renfrew, and S. Shennan (eds), *Ranking, Resource and Exchange,* Cambridge: University Press.
Haselgrove, C. 1991 The Later Iron Age in Southern Britain and Beyond, in M. Todd (ed), *Research on Roman Britain 1960-89.* Britannia Monograph Series **11**, 1- 18.
Haselgrove, C. 1996. Iron Age Coinage: Recent Work in T. Champion, and J. Collis (eds), *The Iron Age in Britain and Ireland Recent Trends.* University of Sheffield: J. R. Collis Publications.
Hawkes, C.F.C. 1977. *Pytheus : Europe and the Greek Explorers.* Oxford.
Hawkes, C.F.C. and Hull, M.R. 1947. *Camulodunum, First Report on the Excavations at Colchester, 1930-1939,* Oxford: Soc. Antiq. Res. Rep. **14**.
Heron-Allen, E. 1911. *Selsey: Bill Historic and Prehistoric.* London: Duckworth.
Hill, J.D. 1995. *Ritual and Rubbish in the Iron Age of Wessex,* BAR Brit. Ser. **242**.
Hind, J. 1989. The Invasion of Britain in AD43-an alternative strategy for Aulus Plautius, *Britannia* **20**, 1-22.
Holgate, R. 1986. Excavations at the Late Prehistoric and Romano-British Enclosure Complex at Carne's Seat, Goodwood, West Sussex, 1984, *SAC* **124**, 35-50.
Kenny, J. 1989. *Excavations at Selsey 1988.* Chichester: Chichester Archaeological Unit.
Kenny, J. 1990. Selsey: Green Lawns Caravan Park, *Archaeology of Chichester and District 1990.* Chichester: Chichester District Council, 40.
King, A. and Soffe, G. 1994. The Iron Age and Roman Temple on Hayling Island, Hampshire in A. Fitzpatrick, and E. Morris (eds), *The Iron Age In Wessex: Recent Work.* Salisbury: Trust for Wessex Archaeology.
McGrail, S. 1987. *Ancient Boats in North West Europe.* London: Longman.
Magilton, J. 1996. Chichester, The Burghal Hidage and the diversion of the River Lavant, in S. Woodward (ed), *The Archaeology of Chichester and District 1996.* Chichester: Chichester District Council.
Murray, K.M.E. 1956. The Chichester Earthworks, in A.E. Wilson, The Beginnings of Roman Chichester, *SAC* **94**, 139-143.
Nash, D. 1987. *Coinage in the Celtic World.* London: Seaby.
Perry, B. 1969. Iron Age Enclosures and Settlements on the Hampshire Chalklands, *Arch. J.* **129**, 29-43.

Perry, B. 1972. Excavation at Bramdean, Hampshire 1965 and 1966 and a discussion of similar sites in Southern England, *Rec. Hants Field Club and Archaeological Society* **29**, 41-78.

Rodwell, W. 1977. Buildings and Settlements in South East Britain in the Late Iron Age, in B. Cunliffe and T. Rowley (eds), *Lowland Iron Age Communities In Europe*. Oxford: 25-39.

Rowlands M. 1980. Kinship, alliance and exchange in the European Bronze Age, in J. Barrett, and R. Bradley (eds), *Settlement and Society in the British Later Bronze Age*, B.A.R. **83**, 15-55.

Thompson, I. 1982. *Grog-tempered 'Belgic' Pottery of South-eastern England,* BAR Brit. Ser. **108**.

Van Arsdell, R. 1989. *Celtic Coinage of Britain.* London: Spink.

Whimster, R. 1981. *Burial Practices In Iron Age Britain: a Discussion and Gazetteer of the Evidence c. 700 BC-AD 43,* BAR Brit. Ser. **90**.

White, G.M. 1934. Prehistoric Remains from Selsey Bill, *Ant. J.* **14**, 40-52.

Williams, D. 1995. The Impact of the Roman Amphora Trade in Pre-Roman Britain, in T.C. Champion (ed), *Centre and Periphery.* London: Routledge.

Wilson, A. 1955. Sussex on the Eve of the Roman Conquest, *SAC* **93**, 59-77.

Woolf, G. 1993. Rethinking the Oppida, *Oxford J. Archaeol.* **12(2)**, 223-233.

ROMAN RURAL SETTLEMENT IN SUSSEX: CONTINUITY AND CHANGE

David Rudling

Abstract

The Roman invasion of Britain in AD 43 had a dramatic impact on this island. Social, economic and technological developments resulted in the establishment in Sussex of various new settlements/sites. They also caused major changes at some indigenous sites and more minor changes at others, both during and after the period of the client kingdom of Togidubnus. In the 1st century the favourable economic and political climates of the client kingdom led to the construction of both a town at Chichester and a number of elaborate early villas in the countryside. By the 2nd century the owners of these early villas faced growing competition from a large number of other rural settlements, and at some of these farms there are increasing signs of romanization. During the later 3rd and 4th centuries the development of villas began to decline in some areas, especially on the coastal plain, but elsewhere such establishments continued to develop and some may have remained in occupation until the late 4th or early 5th century. Many of the downland 'peasant' farms also continued to be occupied until the end of the Roman period (c.AD 410), a fate which may not have been shared by many of the other rural industrial sites following the collapse of the former monetary economy.

Introduction

The Roman invasion of Britain in AD 43 resulted in dramatic alterations to this island's social and economic environments. The results of these changes, together with other major developments in technology, make the period of Roman occupation one of the most dynamic and distinctive episodes in the history of South-East England (Drewett *et al.* 1988, 178-180).

In this paper, which is an updated version of that presented at the Archaeology of Sussex Conference of 1998, I examine the nature of Roman rural settlement in Sussex and consider some of the evidence for this with regard to both continuity and change. These observations are designed to complement those aspects of Roman settlement in Sussex which were reviewed in two papers presented at the 1977 Conference: 'Chichester and the Chilgrove Valley' (Down 1978) and 'Roman Sussex – the Weald' (Cleere 1978). In turn this paper is complemented in this volume by two papers concerned with specific aspects of Roman Sussex: a detailed consideration by John Manley of the layout of the palace at Fishbourne, and a synthesis by Malcolm Lyne of the pottery supply within our study area. The reader's attention is also drawn to a number of general reviews of Roman Sussex: those by Winbolt (1935), Cunliffe (1973), Rudling (1979, 1982a, 1998, 1999) and www.romansinsussex.co.uk. Discussion of Chichester (*Noviomagus Regnensium*), the only Roman town of any size in Sussex, is outside the scope of this paper and the reader is referred to a book on this subject by Down (1988) and a summary note by Magilton and Rudkin (1999). Similarly, the iron industry of the Weald is beyond its scope and those interested in this important subject should consult Cleere (1978), Cleere and Crossley (1995) and Hodgkinson (1999).

The 'Roman Invasion' of AD 43

A major topic of debate during the last few years has concerned the initial stages of the Roman conquest of Britain which began in AD 43. Of particular concern has been the location/s where the Roman forces landed: the 'traditional view' preferred Richborough in Kent, whilst others since 1989 have been re-advocating locations in the Chichester/Solent area (Hind 1989). In the absence of conclusive evidence the verdict remains open, but various arguments support the postulated Sussex/Hampshire landings, including:

- the Roman desire to restore King Verica to his Atrebatic kingdom located in parts of the modern counties of Sussex, Surrey, Hampshire and Berkshire;
- the presence along this part of the south coast of safe harbours;
- the advantages from the Roman point of view of starting their campaign in friendly territory where they could perhaps rely on safe disembarkment and local support. These and other related issues form the basis of a book by John Manley (2002).

Martin Henig (1998, 2002) has even queried the use of words such as 'conquest' with regard to parts of southern Britain. He has referred instead to 'Roman liberation'. Thus, as stated by the Roman writer Dio Cassius, the official reason for the 'invasion' was the expulsion of whoever had invaded King Verica's territory. Henig also suggests that Britain's romanized southern rulers may have welcomed the arrival of the Romans and profited from it afterwards. Such circumstances may help to explain the apparent absence of Claudian forts in Sussex, Hampshire, Surrey, Berkshire and adjacent areas: they may have been unnecessary in a situation of liberation/Roman intervention.

Whether the initial landings took place in Sussex or not, there is some evidence from both Chichester (Down 1988) and Fishbourne (Cunliffe 1971) that has been interpreted as indicating an early Roman military presence at these locations (Fig. 9.1). The evidence from Fishbourne 1961-1969, together with discoveries made since, includes a large ditch which, from its primary silts, has yielded pieces of Arretine pottery dating to the AD 30s and part of an ?Augustan military sword scabbard (Rudkin 2002). Other very early features at Fishbourne include those of Cunliffe's (1971) Period 1A: two rectangular timber storage buildings and various gravel roads. Whilst all or some of such finds may belong to a period of pre-conquest indigenous occupation of the site, they *might* relate to a *Roman* establishment prior to AD 43 (Creighton 2001, 9-11). Such a Roman military site *may* have been associated with the formation/protection of a client kingdom, or perhaps with preparations for the planned, but aborted, invasion of Britain by the emperor Caligula. This type of

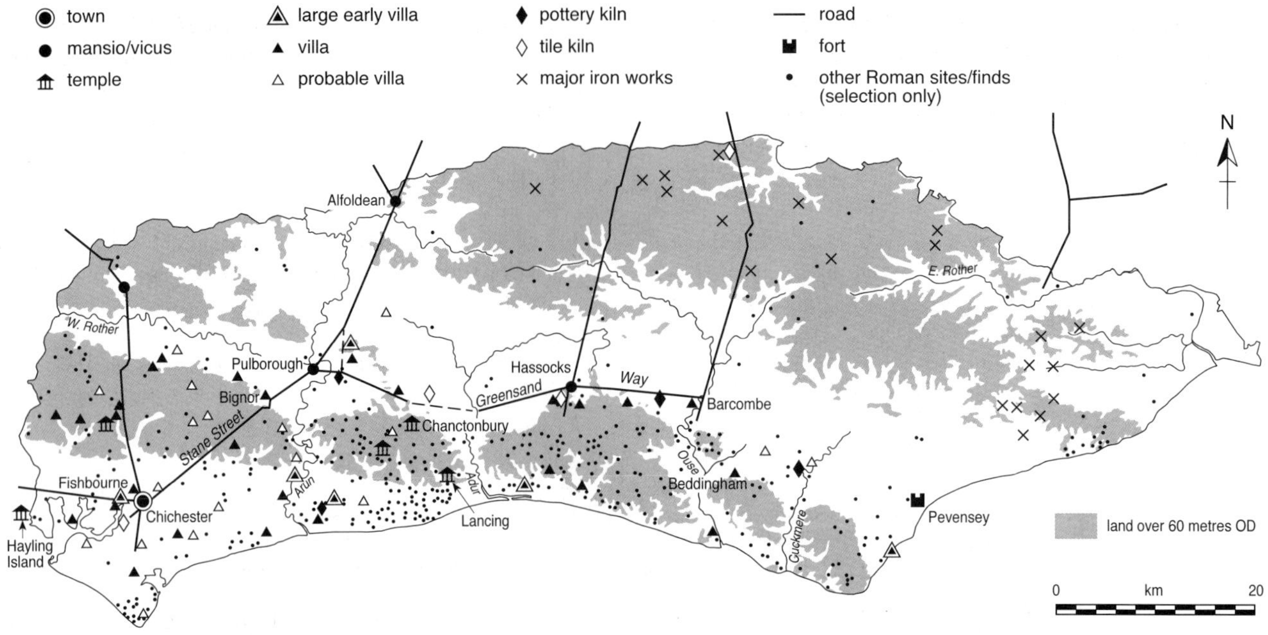

Figure 9.1. *Distribution map of various Roman sites in Sussex.*

radical hypothesizing, the various discoveries of pre-conquest examples of imported Roman material culture, the local coinage with its Latin legends and Roman iconography, and the flight to Rome of tribal leaders such as Verica in AD 40, indicate the probable complexities of the social, political and economic environments in Sussex during the last few decades prior to AD 43. Thus by the time of the 'conquest', at least some of the inhabitants of Sussex, especially those in the Chichester area, were already familiar with various aspects of a romanized way of life (Henig 1998; Hamilton and Manley 1999; Davenport this volume).

Of the 'invasion' of AD 43 there is no definite archaeological evidence from Sussex. Whilst at Fishbourne the various Period 1A features from the Palace site (i.e. the storage buildings and gravel roads referred to above) were originally thought to be Claudian and parts of an early military supply base, these features *could* pre-date AD 43 (*see* above). Similarly, the various examples of Claudian coinage found at Fishbourne between 1961 and 1999 need not necessarily relate to events in AD 43 – they might belong to a later phase of Claudian construction at the site, perhaps the building of the putative principia revealed by John Manley and David Rudkin between 1995 and 1999 (Manley 2000; Manley this volume; Fig. 10.9; Rudling forthcoming). At Chichester, the relative proportions of coin finds of the emperors Caligula and Claudius (44.19% : 55.81%) have been used to suggest an early (40s) date for the postulated military presence (Sauer 2000, 49). Finally, an early Roman military feature in Sussex which may date from *c.*AD 43 is the southernmost alignment (and ?original stretch) of Stane Street between Chichester Harbour and a crossing of the river Arun at Pulborough (Fig. 9.1; Magilton 1996). The importance of the Pulborough area in both the Late Iron Age and early Roman periods is well established by such discoveries as Dressel 1A and 1B wine amphorae and the large villa at Borough Farm respectively. At Pulborough, Stane Street changes direction to follow a more direct route towards London. The other major Roman roads in Sussex (Fig. 9.1) were also presumably built by the military, but probably later during the period of consolidation of the province after AD 43.

The Client Kingdom of Togidubnus

Soon after the invasion of AD 43, the Romans established or re-established in southern England a client kingdom consisting of part of Sussex and probably also other areas to the north and west. We have no evidence that Verica returned to rule this kingdom, and the only historical information about a client kingdom in this area concerns one Tiberius Claudius Togidubnus (Barrett 1979; Bogaers 1979; Tomlin 1997, 129). Barrett's work suggests that Togidubnus (or Cogidubnus as he was previously known) became king between AD 43 and AD 52 and that he was dead or had retired *before* AD 78 (i.e. the excavator's suggested dating for the construction of the Period 2 Palace at Fishbourne: Cunliffe 1971), and probably before the end of Nero's reign in AD 68. According to the classical writer Tacitus (*Agricola* 14), the king remained loyal to the Romans for a long time. It is also clear from the archaeological evidence from Sussex that during his reign Togidubnus was fairly successful in introducing elements of Roman culture into his kingdom – the famous temple dedication stone (*RIB* 91) found in Chichester is an impressive example. In addition to the generally widespread acceptance and distribution of products of Roman manufacture, such as pottery and coins, various other archaeological discoveries in Sussex also shed light on the processes of romanization during the period of the client kingdom, especially so in Chichester, which was clearly developing as a romanized centre/town. The undated dedication inscription referred to above is evidence that there was a temple to the classical divinities Neptune and Minerva, that this structure was built with the permission of King Togidubnus, and that it was paid for by a guild of smiths. Another dedicatory inscription (*RIB* 92) can be dated to AD 58. In the north-west part of the town Claudian military-type timber buildings were superseded by new timber-framed structures and extensive areas of industrial activity (Down 1988, 18). This concentration of craft work may indicate a developing civilian market.

Romanization during the client kingdom was also occurring in the countryside. Sussex has a relatively large number of early villas (Cunliffe 1973, 79; Black 1987; Rudling 1998) and at least some of these may date to the reign of Togidubnus. Borough Farm, Pulborough (Fig. 9.2) and Westhampnett Church, and possibly also The Shepherd's Garden, Arundel, and a site at Newhaven, have all yielded half-box tiles – the earliest type of wall-jacketing found in Britain. Such tiles probably predate *c.*AD 75-80 (Black 1987, 12). Subsequently, in the late 1st/early 2nd century, new types of wall jacketing were introduced. Finds of the new type of box tiles at over 15 sites demonstrate both a considerable expansion of villa construction (as at Compton, Fishbourne, Lavant, Bignor, Tortington, Arundel, Angmering (x 2), Southwick, Beddingham and Eastbourne) and alterations to earlier buildings.

Who were the owners of these establishments, and what were the economic conditions which financed such building

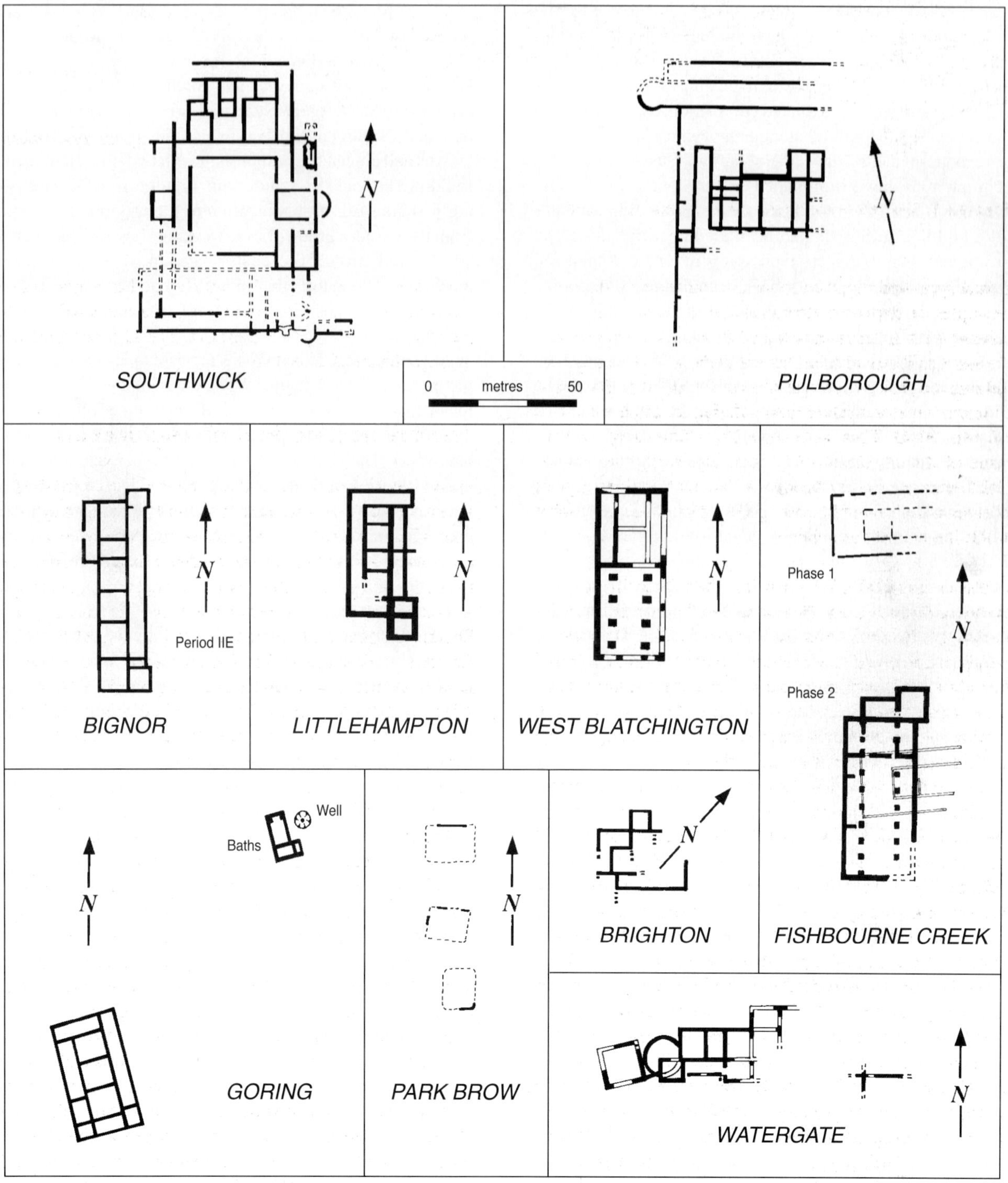

***Figure 9.2.** Plans of various Sussex villas and a group of three buildings (collectively a possible 'house') at Park Brow.*

projects? It is possible that these villas were owned by the native aristocracy, which was left in peace to develop in the strongly philo-Roman atmosphere created by the client kingdom of Togidubnus (Cunliffe 1973, 79). The wide distribution of the large early villas may be very significant: each was located on a distinct block of land which may "represent the territory over which the land-owning aristocracy held control" (Cunliffe 1973, 79; Fig. 9.1). This pattern might be due to one distribution of the tribal sub-units, the *pagi*, about which very little is known (Ernest Black pers. comm.). In most cases the main source of wealth for the tribal elite would have been the sale of agricultural surpluses from the villa estates and tenant farms. In some cases these sales may have included valuable military supply contracts (Black 1987, 17). Other sources of finance for the villa-building projects may have included the profits from various industries, or recourse to Roman moneylenders. Some of the early villa developments may have been over-ambitious and later necessitated contraction, especially since the favourable economic advantages which are thought to have benefited the tribal aristocracy of Sussex in the 1st century, may have diminished in the course of the 2nd century (Black 1987, 34). Possibly the motivation for early villa building in Sussex had been a competitive desire by prominent men to display their status in a new, romanized way. If so, these villas must have been displayed to people who mattered, governors or procurators, or *legati iuridici* (Ernest Black pers. comm.).

The Palace at Fishbourne (*see* paper by Manley) may be an example of such an over-ambitious project, but parts of it at least continued in use until the late 3rd century. The precise functions, dating and ownership of both the 'Proto-Palace' and Palace at Fishbourne remain uncertain. Originally Professor Cunliffe suggested that the owner of both phases of buildings might have been King Togidubnus (Cunliffe 1971, 75 and 153). Other possibilities, however, include the descendants of Togidubnus, other members of the local aristocracy; foreign businessmen (*negotiatores*), or high-ranking Roman administrators, perhaps after the death or retirement of Togidubnus. The whole 'Proto-Palace' complex has been interpreted as a bath building (Black 1993, 236), and may have been part of a military base, perhaps incorporating the newly revealed Building 3/'?principia' referred to above (*see* also Fig. 10.4).

Integration into the Roman Province

Following the death or retirement of King Togidubnus (perhaps before AD 68 – *see* above), his extensive kingdom was integrated into the Roman province of *Britannia* and probably divided into three regional tribal units or *civitates*, to which various administrative functions were delegated. This pattern would have followed the well-tried Roman system of local self-government based upon cities. Much of Sussex, especially the areas to the south of the Weald and part of south-eastern Hampshire formed the *civitas* of the *Regni*, with a capital at Chichester (Cunliffe 1973; Fig. 9.1). Other parts of Sussex, especially large areas of the Weald where there were major 1st- and 2nd-century iron-workings, some associated with the *Classis Britannica* (the Roman fleet), may have been separately administered as an Imperial Estate (Cleere and Crossley 1985, 66-69). If this was the case, it may help to explain the apparent absence of both agricultural and urban settlements to the north and east of Eastbourne.

Communications

Perhaps the main traces of early military activity in Sussex are the major roads (*see* above; Fig. 9.1). The whole subject of Roman roads in Britain, and especially those in the south-east, formed the basis of a lifetime of research by the late Ivan Margary, who was a prominent member of the Sussex Archaeological Society. Although the reader is referred to the published results of Margary's work (Margary 1965, 1967), it should be noted that not all of Margary's roads and routes have been confirmed by excavation. Roads linked Chichester to London via a crossing of the river Arun at Pulborough; to Winchester and Silchester (ie other *civitas* capitals); to Selsey and Chichester Harbour. Other major roads included the Greensand Way which lies to the north of the Downs and connected Pulborough with two important roads: London-Hassocks-Brighton and London-Lewes. The two north-south roads probably provided transportation routes to/from the western group of iron-working sites. Another north-south road linked the eastern group of iron-works to Rochester. The many other minor Roman roads are likely to have served a wide variety of rural farms and industries.

Whilst some of the Roman roads in Sussex may have followed the routes of Iron Age trackways, the building of at least the major highways probably had in Roman times, as now with modern roads, a massive impact on both the social and economic landscapes. Their construction required the confiscation of land and the division of fields, landholdings and local trackways on one hand, but brought increased communications and improved access to markets on the other. Some of these roads are still prominent features in the landscape, either as earthworks or as the routes of modern highways.

Other important communications would have been affected by boat, by sea and river. Although little evidence is available about maritime routes, the association of the *Classis Britannica* with the eastern iron-works is attested by the discovery at some sites of tiles stamped *CL BR*. The main exportation of iron from this area was presumably by sea via the estuaries of the rivers Rother and Brede. Elsewhere the importance of river transport is probably indicated by the location of villa settlements close to the rivers Arun, Ouse and Cuckmere. The Arun is one of the few rivers in Britain for which we know its Roman name: *Trisantona* (Rivet and Smith 1979, 45).

Minor Urban Settlements

At least two of the major Roman roads in Sussex had associated posting stations (*mansiones*): those at Hardham, near Pulborough (Winbolt 1927), Alfoldean (Winbolt 1923, 1924) and Iping (Margary 1953, 1-4, 7). These three sites, which all have rectangular earthworks, were part of the imperial communications system and provided not only accommodation for official travellers, but perhaps also some 'local policing' and administrative functions. Alfoldean, the most recently re-considered of the Sussex posting stations, had a sequence of occupation which started with a *mansio* complex constructed at the end of the 1st century (Luke and Wells 2000). During the second half of the 2nd century this primary complex was enclosed by a substantial bank and ditches which did not follow the original site layout. Investigations outside the earthwork enclosure have revealed extensive traces (up to 9 ha) of occupation to the south of the posting station. This extra-mural settlement, which was divided into plots defined by ditches laid out perpendicular to Stane Street, continued at least into the early 4th century. It would have served both as a resting-place for travellers and as a market for the surrounding countryside.

The development of roadside settlement into quite large local centres – *vicus* settlements/small towns – can be expected at other locations in Sussex, particularly at river crossings and crossroads. One such site is at Hassocks where the Greensand Way and the London-Brighton road intersected. The archaeological evidence at Hassocks has included extensive traces of occupation and a large cemetery (Lyne 1994).

Rural Farms

In his book *The Regni,* Professor Cunliffe (1973, 74) selects two things to characterize the pattern of rural settlement in Roman Sussex: "a strong element of continuity, many sites originating well back into the preceding Iron Age or even earlier, and a very marked discrepancy in wealth which appears dramatically within thirty years of the Roman invasion and remains a feature of the social scene until the early decades of the 5th century". He further states that "the relative distribution of rich and poor settlement is not random. The poorer establishments, the peasant farms and villages, are fairly evenly scattered over the chalk Downs and the coastal plain, but the richer farms – the villas – tend to select various locations where the soil is more productive". Such locations are identified as being concentrated in three zones: the coastal plain, the southern fringes of the Downs and the Upper Greensand ridge which lies just to the north of the Downs. Whilst the majority of these Roman rural sites were associated with farming, others were either fully or partly involved in industry.

The Roman economy depended primarily on farming to produce sufficient surpluses to support the more sophisticated aspects of Roman life: the towns, the luxurious country and seaside houses of the rich, large-scale manufacturing industries (such as the production of iron and pottery) and the army. Given the importance of farming, it is surprising that there has been relatively little detailed study of this aspect of the Roman countryside, especially land-use and settlement patterns, field systems, methods of drainage, the crops and domesticated animals, and farm tools and buildings. In contrast, considerable effort and resources have been expended to investigate one particular aspect of the rural landscape: the 'villas'. However, before resuming the review of some of the extensive evidence for the development of villas in Sussex, we will begin by examining some of the more humble and less sophisticated rural farms, which made up by far the large majority of rural settlements in our area.

Native farmsteads

Traces of large numbers of native/'peasant' Romano-British farmsteads have been found in Sussex, especially on the coastal plain and on the Downs (Fig. 9.1). Many of these sites originated in the Late Iron Age or earlier, and some continued into the 5th century. Bishopstone is a good example of such continuity, and is a site which has been excavated on a large scale using modern methods (Bell 1977). A rectangular enclosure (0.35 ha) was laid out early in the Roman period. This was sited in the north-east corner of an Early Iron Age enclosed settlement, which in turn had been located on the site of Neolithic occupation as represented by a series of pits. Although occupation at Bishopstone in the Iron Age could be assigned to three broad phases: a primary unenclosed settlement, followed by an enclosure (both Early Iron Age), and finally a period of unenclosed settlement (later Iron Age), it was not possible to tell whether the change in settlement location between the earlier and later phases reflects a hiatus or continuous development (Bell 1977, 134). The Roman enclosure was divided into two by a cross-ditch, the northern part being approximately twice as large as the area to the south. The enclosed ditch had become silted up by the late 2nd century and the excavator suggests that there may have been a reduced level of activity on the site during the 3rd century, followed by a more intensive period of occupation in the 4th century, when a 'corn-drying oven' was in operation. The function of so-called 'corn-drying ovens' has been the subject of much debate and it is possible that such ovens were used for various purposes including the drying of grain prior to storage, malting, and the preparing of grain prior to milling (*see* Drewett *et. al.* 1988, 208). Other features included pits and post-holes, some of the latter being in groups suggestive of structures, but nothing which could be definitely interpreted as a domestic building. Finds of animal bones and charred seeds from the excavations indicate that the settlement's economy was based on mixed farming. Romano-British occupation at Bishopstone may have lasted into the 5th century, before being replaced by a Saxon settlement. There is, however, no definite proof to suggest direct continuity between the two settlements. A field system outside the Iron Age and Romano-British enclosures yielded evidence for intermittent cultivation from the Neolithic to Roman periods.

On Bullock Down, Beachy Head, an intensive multi-period settlement project located two Romano-British sites and extensive traces of associated fields and trackways (Rudling 1982b; Fig. 9.3). During the Roman period these field systems and trackways, which had been established in the Late Bronze Age-Early Iron Age, continued in use and were considerably developed and expanded. The two Romano-British settlement sites are located on, or adjacent to, a double lynchet trackway which may have linked an Early Iron Age settlement site at the eastern boundary of Bullock Down to the large earthwork enclosure at Belle Tout to the west. Many of the prehistoric/Roman fields on Bullock Down were laid out perpendicular to this trackway.

Neither of the Romano-British settlement sites on Bullock Down can be shown with certainty to have been occupied before the conquest in AD 43, the later Iron Age being only poorly represented in the results generally of this landscape project. (There may have been a reduction in activity on this part of the Downs after the abandonment of the Early Iron

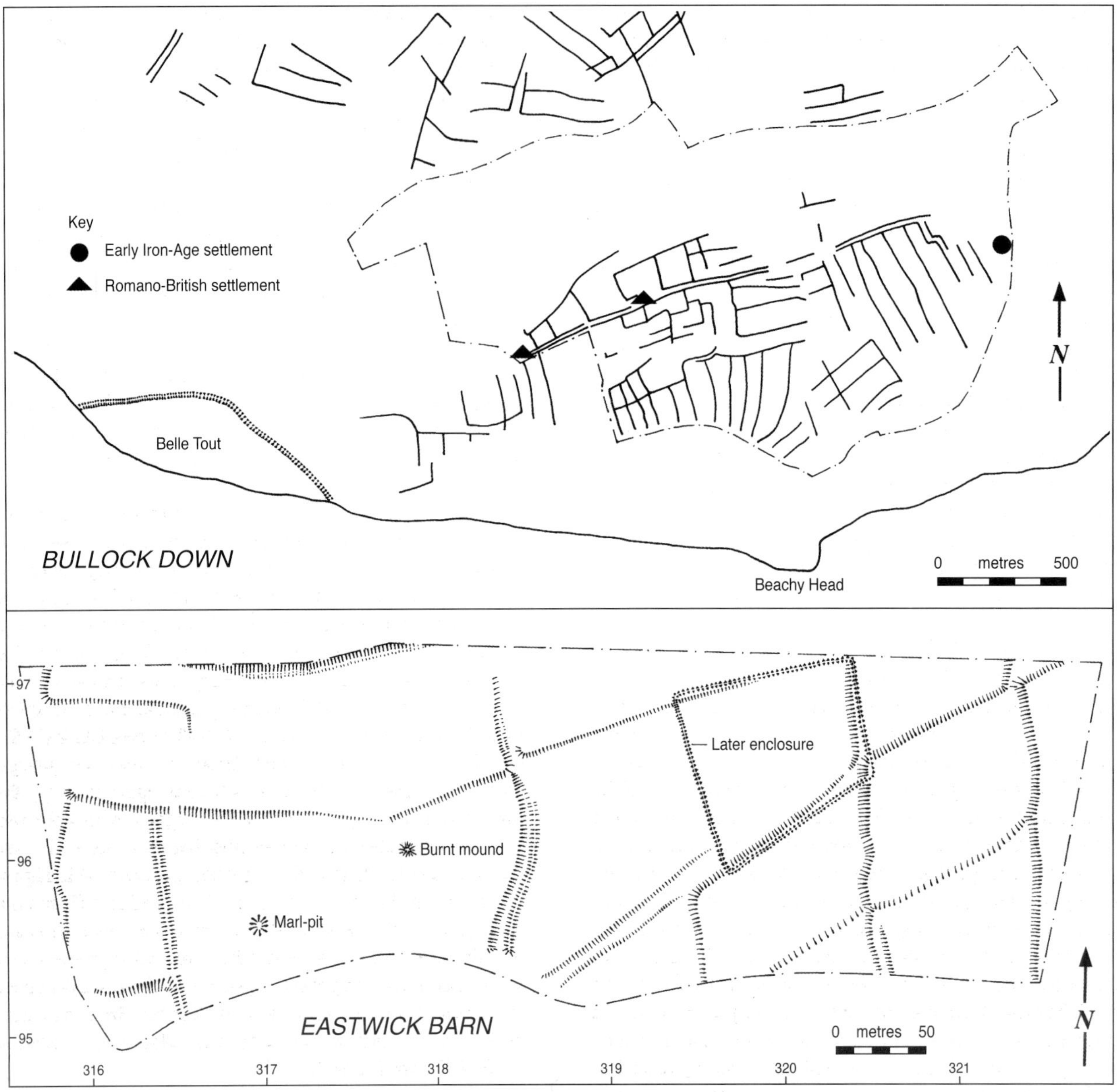

Figure 9.3. *Plans of field systems, trackways and settlement sites at Bullock Down, (Beachy Head) and Eastwick Barn (Brighton).*

Age settlement referred to above). However, some of the finds at both Romano-British settlement sites date from the 1st century AD and could perhaps have spanned the Late Iron Age/early Romano-British periods. At one of the Roman settlements, 'Site 16', survey work revealed nine possible 'house platforms' arranged in three pairs and a probable fourth pair (or perhaps a group of three). The total excavation of one of the platforms revealed a definite terrace with a possible fence line, several pits, a number of isolated post-holes, but no obvious structural evidence for any building. The large quantities of domestic pottery found, however, suggest that there might have been a dwelling. If so, it must have been of a type which did not leave any trace in the archaeological record, or if it did, one which has subsequently been destroyed by ploughing. Possible explanations for such elusive evidence might include forms of timber framing and the use of either cob or turf walls. It is therefore possible that at Site 16 there had once been four groupings of at least two buildings each. Such groupings may have formed separate 'houses' (*see* Park Brow below). It is likely that such houses were contemporary since their platforms are spaced out fairly evenly within an area set back from the double lynchet trackway. If this theory is correct, the settlement might have been of the 'hamlet' type or the residence of an extended family. Occupation spanned the 1st to 3rd centuries, and finds included several 3rd-century coin hoards and a number of exotic metal objects.

Excavations at the other Romano-British site on Bullock Down, 'Site 44', focused on a possible farmyard area adjacent to a ditched enclosure which is thought to have contained the settlement area. Features associated with the postulated farmyard included two corn-drying ovens, a possible threshing floor, fence lines, and various pits and isolated post-holes. The date range for Site 44 extends from the early 1st to the late 4th century *or later*. As is often usual elsewhere in Roman Britain, the bronze coinage sequence ends *c.*370-380. There were, however, reasonable quantities of late-4th-century pottery types, including the locally produced

Pevensey Ware. One sherd of handmade grit- and grog-tempered ware with 'wyrm' stamps of Germanic character could date to the early 5th century (Rudling 1982b, Fig. 52: no. 150; Lyne this volume).

The Romano-British economy on Bullock Down was, as at Bishopstone, mixed farming. Evidence for arable agriculture includes the associated field systems and marl-pits, the threshing floor and corn-dryers at Site 44, carbonized seeds, and possible grain-storage pits in the settlement area at Site 44. Animal husbandry is attested mainly by animal bones, but also by pottery cheesepresses, spindle whorls (for processing sheeps' wool) and possible animal pens at Site 44. The faunal remains indicate a predominance of sheep, which may have been kept for their wool and butchered on site for meat. The relative quantities of sheep and cattle bones contrast sharply with the evidence obtained from the villa at Newhaven (Bell 1976). As Martin Bell has stated, it is likely that such differences reflect the fact that the waterless Downs are better suited to sheep, whereas a villa located in a river valley would have been able to support a bigger head of cattle.

Another large-scale modern investigation of a Romano-British field system in Sussex was undertaken near Eastwick Barn in advance of the construction of the Brighton Bypass (Barber *et al.* 2002; Fig. 9.3). Although the excavations did not reveal any settlement evidence, the extensive trenching yielded information about the development and layout of the fields and an associated double-lynchet trackway. The earliest part of the field system lay in the eastern area and dated to the earlier Iron Age. These fields were flanked on the western side by a contemporary double-lynchet trackway. Finds of pottery to the west of the trackway indicate, however, that some cultivation also took place in this area during the earlier Iron Age, but perhaps on a less intensive scale than to the east. The lack of Middle and Late Iron Age pottery from the site generally is interesting, and possible explanations include a change in cultivation practices without manuring (and thus the deposition of refuse including pieces of pottery); a switch of land-use from arable to pasture; or the abandonment of the fields during this period. The Romano-British period saw a resumption of intense cultivation/manuring, possibly with some pastoral phases interspaced. All areas of the earlier Iron Age field system were re-cultivated on both sides of the trackway, and modifications in both areas, including the creation of new field boundaries, were made to the existing field layouts. It was during this period that the area to the west of the trackway was more intensively used than it had been, and this involved the subdivision of some earlier fields. Other modifications/improvements to this part of the field system included the digging of a marl-pit and the creation of a mound of burnt stone, especially sarsen sandstone. It is possible that this mound represents attempts to break up for removal large sarsen boulders which occur locally as erratics and would have been obstructions to cultivation. Such actions may indicate increasing pressures on land for agricultural purposes, and perhaps more able and organized farmers.

Since tangible evidence for domestic buildings at Bishopstone, Bullock Down (with the exception of the 'house-platforms' at Site 16) or other recently excavated downland sites does not exist, we must turn to an early-20th-century excavation in order to shed light on their nature. The site in question is Park Brow, to the north of Cissbury, where survey and excavations revealed a sequence of three separate settlement sites: Late Bronze Age, earlier Iron Age, and Late Iron Age/Romano-British, all linked by trackways and field systems (Wolseley *et al.* 1927). The Late Iron Age/Romano-British settlement consisted of five rectangular 'house sites', various pits, and three possibly successive boundary ditches. One of the houses was totally excavated and proved to have had walls constructed of vertical timbers with wattle and daub infilling, which was internally decorated by the application of red painted plaster. The discovery of clay roofing tiles, window glass and a door key are other indications of the level of sophistication and 'romanization' of this building. Further evidence for Roman influence and contacts at this downland site includes finds such as Samian ware and amphorae.

Without good dating evidence it is difficult to interpret the five rectangular buildings/huts, since it is not known how many were in use at any one time. They may represent successive single 'hut houses'. Alternatively, if some of the huts were contemporary individual houses, they may have formed a "hamlet of cottages" (Cunliffe 1973, 98). It is also possible, however, that contemporary 'huts' may have been used by one family for different purposes and that collectively these formed a 'house' (Rivet 1964, 108). Ernest Black (1987) theorized that the huts at Park Brow fall into two groups, each with a principal building which is approximately the same size in each group. He further suggested that the two groups were not contemporary and that they "look like two discrete houses". One of these groups is illustrated in Figure 9.2 alongside the plans of various villas, and it is clear from these plans, which are drawn to the same scale, that the house postulated at Park Brow would have provided ground-floor accommodation comparable in size with the main domestic buildings at small villas such as Goring. Such pairings/groupings of single room 'huts' may also have existed at Bullock Down Site 16 (*see* above).

To summarize, the material culture of the downland 'native' settlements discussed above shows both continuity from the past (including the well-established field systems and sometimes the settlement sites themselves), and various signs of romanization, especially in the case of the relatively elaborate rectangular 'hut' at Park Brow, the acceptance of the coinage system, the acquisition of various manufactured goods, and the construction of such features as 'corn-drying ovens' and marl-pits. There was also a very noticeable increase in the use of iron, especially as nails. It is clear that some of these settlements were occupied for long periods, with possible continuity into the 5th century. Fewer settlements have been recorded off the Downs, although this situation is likely to change as a result of the last decade of rescue excavations on the coastal plain brought about by the implementation since November 1990 of Planning Policy Guidance Note 16 (PPG 16). Examples of published settlement sites on the coastal plain include Boxgrove (Bedwin and Place 1995) and Middleton-on-Sea (Barber 1994). The site at Boxgrove, which includes the eastern terminal of the Chichester Dykes system, shows continuity from the Late Iron Age.

Villas

Although less common than 'peasant' farmsteads in Roman Sussex, rural villas have attracted the most investigation. The term 'villa' is often used to refer to a domestic house or complex which significantly reflects the Roman style of rural life. In terms of archaeological evidence this assessment is usually determined by the discovery of one or more of such features as: masonry footings, multiple rooms, clay tiles, mosaic or tessellated floors, painted wall plaster, window glass, hypocaust (underfloor) heating systems and bath-suites. Most of these sites are assumed to have been the centres of farm-estates, although other functions are also possible, such as involvement in rural industries, such as iron-making (eg at Garden Hill, Hartfield – Money 1977).

The villa buildings of Sussex have been reviewed in several surveys (Cunliffe 1973; Down 1979; Rudling 1982a; Black 1987; Rudling 1988; Scott 1993; Rudling 1998). The earliest, and amongst the largest and most elaborate of the Sussex villas are the 'Early Villas' discussed above in the section on the client kingdom and which date to the 1st century. These villas include Fishbourne (Cunliffe 1971; Cunliffe *et al.* 1996; Manley this volume); Pulborough (Praetorius 1911); Arundel (Rudling 1984); Angmering (Scott 1938; 1939; Wilson 1947; Gilkes 1999); Southwick (Winbolt 1932; Rudling 1985); and Eastbourne (Sutton 1952; Stevens and Gilbert 1973), and possibly other sites at Newhaven (Bell 1976), Brighton (Dudley 1981) and near Westhampnett Church. Some of these villas, such as Fishbourne (which is more a palace than a villa; Fig. 10.1), Southwick and Pulborough (Fig. 9.2), are exceptional and are clearly derived from Mediterranean rather than North Gallic-type villas. The buildings at these sites share similarities in elements of design, construction and decoration, and some probably involved the same architects and craftsmen. Since there is a general lack of evidence from these sites for any significant pre-conquest occupation, some or most of these villas may have been built on new sites. They are thought to reflect the presumed favourable political and economic climates of the client kingdom. Only the site at Fishbourne has been investigated on any scale under modern conditions and it is interesting that here the post-1969 excavations to the east of the Palace have now revealed evidence for a possible pre-conquest usage of the site.

In contrast to many of the large 'Early Villas' discussed above and which may have been imposed 'fully fledged' on to the Late Iron Age settlement pattern, most Sussex villas 'grew organically' out of native farms, a pattern which is normal for many areas of Britain (Applebaum 1966, 99). Such growth usually involved gradual development, often with a change from a rectangular house built of timber (a 'proto-villa'), followed by a building made of stone (or with masonry footings) of much the same size, to which luxuries such as simple mosaics, baths and perhaps hypocaust heating might be added. The two phases of aisled buildings at Fishbourne Creek (Rudkin 1986; Fig. 9.2 – note also the change of orientation for the second building) and the late 2nd- to 3rd-century villa at Bignor (Frere 1982; Fig. 9.2) are good examples. These sites also represent the two main types of villa house found in Sussex and elsewhere in Britain: the 'aisled villa' and the 'winged corridor villa' respectively. Whilst the aisled villa at Fishbourne does not exhibit continuity from the Late Iron Age, that at Bignor may have done so, and such a sequence of occupation seems to have occurred at the site of a winged corridor villa at Littlehampton (Gilkes 1993; Fig. 9.2). At two sites in Sussex, at Beddingham (Rudling 1997, 1998, 52-59) and Barcombe (Rudling and Butler 2002; Butler and Rudling 2002), the sequence of building development extends back (although not necessarily to pre-AD 43) to timber, circular structures/houses of indigenous type (Fig. 9.4).

At Beddingham, where evidence for earlier prehistoric occupation of the site included Late Bronze Age/Early Iron Age finds and several pits, there was only a little evidence (including two coins) for possible settlement during the Late Iron Age. Dated to the early 1st century, although this date does not necessarily include the period before the conquest, is a two-phase, timber circular structure – perhaps a domestic 'house', or possibly a shrine (Rudling 1997) or estate office (Black 1997). The location of this structure was apparently respected long after it had gone out of use, and encroachment (presumably unintentional) only occurred during the eighth and last building phase of the villa. This very long period of respect for or memory of the location of the circular structure is an extremely important and rare indication of continuity of ownership. Phase I of the adjacent Roman masonry house, which does not encroach upon the circle of post-holes, is thus thought to have been constructed alongside it. This phase of building is dated to the Flavian period, and therefore indicates that the timber, circular structure was either also of this period, or earlier. It is also possible that the Phase I house replaced a timber 'proto-villa' building at the same location.

The main period of occupation at Beddingham villa dates from the late 1st to the mid-4th centuries, and included a large domestic building with masonry foundations, a stone-lined well, a shrine, a detached bath-house, a building made of timber and two phases of enclosure ditch (Figs. 9.4, 9.5). Later modifications to the simple Phase I strip-villa included the addition of baths (Phases II-IV) at the northern end of the building, which later went out of use, perhaps when new baths were built in the north-east corner of the enclosure. Another major development (Phase V – probably Antonine) involved the addition of a corridor/range to the west face and a corridor and two wing rooms to the eastern side of the main range of rooms, thus creating a 'winged corridor villa'. Other additions included a passageway, a range (Phase VI) above the former baths and a verandah (Phase VIII), which incorporates an irregular curved section along the eastern half of its south wall (Fig. 9.4). The eastern end of the verandah overlies the northern part of the timber circular 'house' described above, and it is assumed that the shape of the irregular section of verandah wall was designed to respect the location of the now invisible circular structure. Continuity of native ownership at Beddingham is also suggested by the large number of 'ritual' deposits, including those of carefully placed objects, such as pottery vessels, articulated animal remains, or human infants (Waldron *et al.* 1999). Such deposits, perhaps foundation deposits or rituals of commencement or termination, may have links with Late Iron Age practices. Occupation, perhaps not continuous, may also have continued after the abandonment of the main house, probably *c.* AD

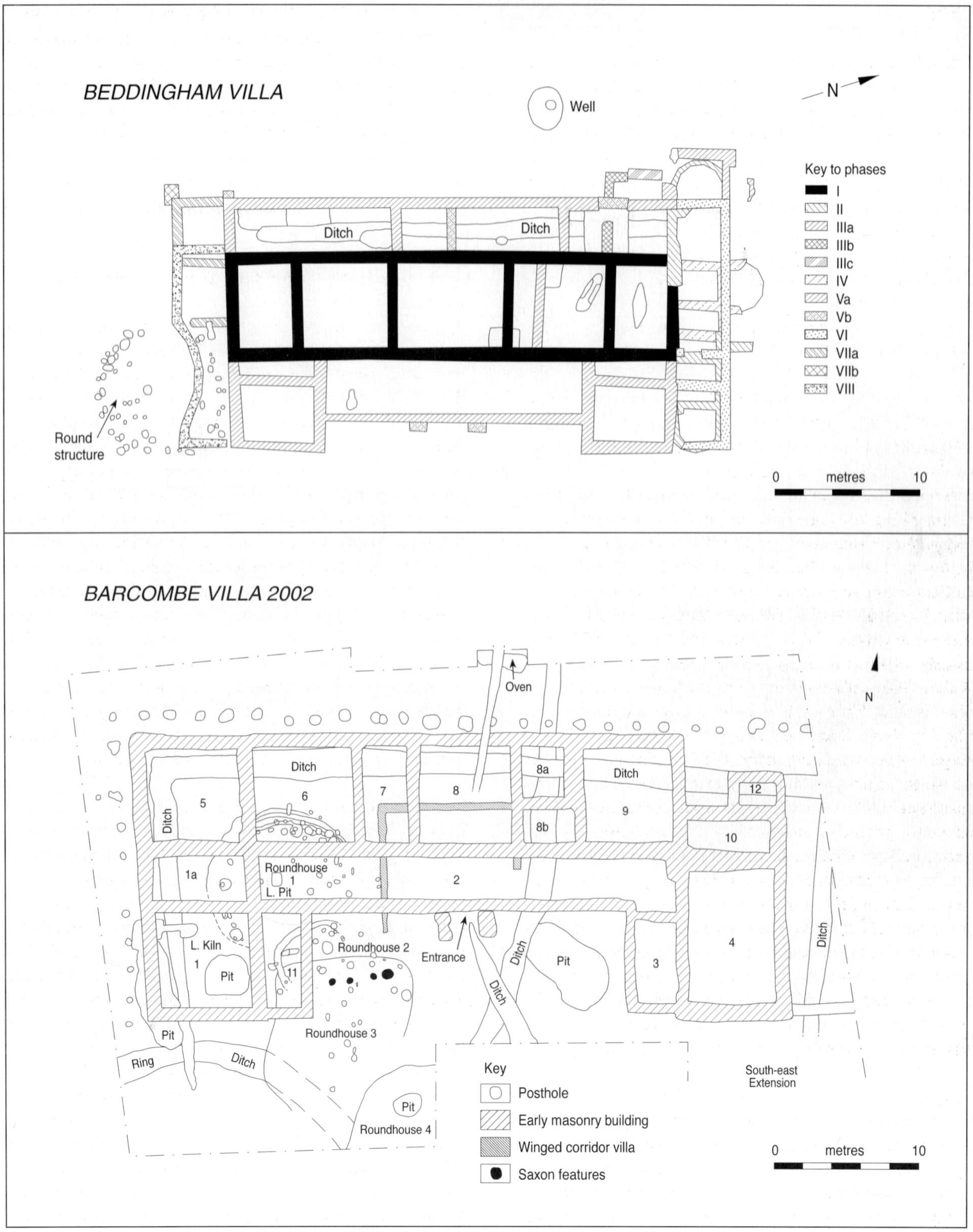

Figure 9.4. *Plans of the main Romano-British houses at Beddingham and Barcombe, together with other significant discoveries in the vicinities of these buildings.*

330. Evidence for this idea concerns the recovery from deposits in the abandoned, masonry Roman shrine (Fig. 9.5) of sherds of both early Saxon and late Romano-British pottery (Malcolm Lyne pers. comm.). Thus by the end of the 4th century or early in the 5th century, part of the villa complex, but apparently not the former main house, was occupied or perhaps occasionally used by people (Romano-British and/or Saxons) using Saxon pottery. Finally, another important aspect of both continuity and change at Beddingham relates to the two phases of ditched enclosure (Fig. 9.5). The earlier and smaller circuit of enclosure ditches was replaced during the mid-2nd century by a considerably

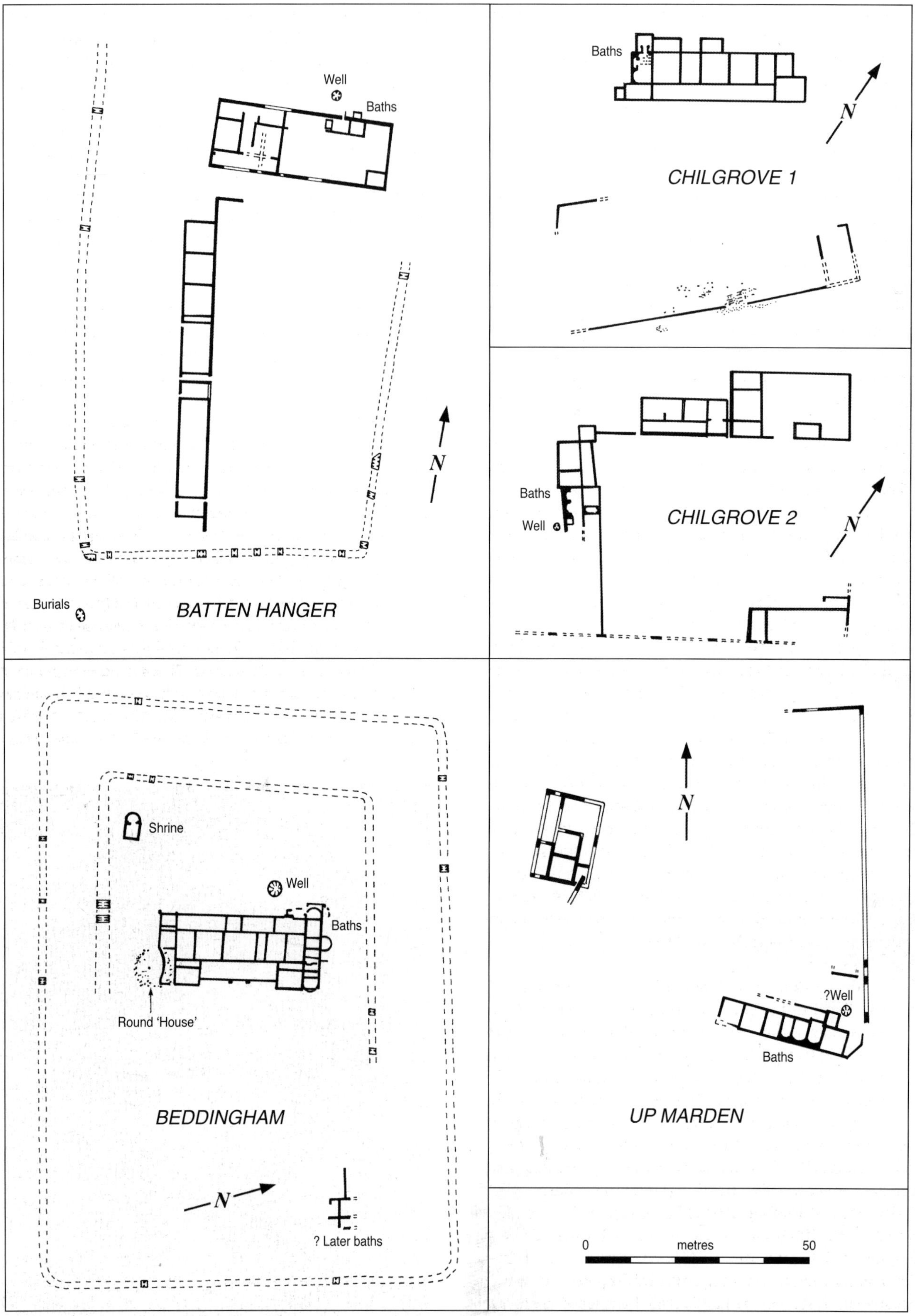

Figure 9.5. Plans of various Sussex villas.

larger version, and this change presumably indicates an increase in prosperity at the site. This and the other developments outlined above demonstrate that at sites like Beddingham things were far from static throughout the Roman period, and that we should expect to discover evidence for both continuity and change.

The first two seasons (2001-2002) of a major new research project at the Barcombe villa site concentrated upon the excavation of another winged corridor villa building. Again the site has yielded evidence for use during prehistoric times, including a ring ditch from a probable Bronze Age burial mound. The first major phase of intense settlement evidence, however, involves a number of timber roundhouses (Fig. 9.4), three of which partly underlie the later villa building. Roundhouse 3, which is approximately 9m in diameter and comprises an outer wall made of wattle and daub, may be the oldest, and possibly of Late Iron Age or very early Roman date. Roundhouse 1, which is almost entirely located beneath the masonry villa, was found beneath two stratified deposits of flints and burnt clay respectively. The burnt clay deposit has been dated by archaeomagnetic dating to *c.* AD 140-200 at the 95% confidence level and thus provides a *terminus-ante-quem* for the disuse of Roundhouse 1. This roundhouse was later replaced by a simple rectangular building with narrow flint footings (Fig. 9.4), suggestive of a timber-framed structure. Various features may be contemporary with this phase of the villa, especially the ditched enclosure whose western, northern and eastern ditches are parallel to the corresponding walls of the building. In the next phase, perhaps in the 3rd century, the building with narrow masonry foundations was demolished and replaced by a much larger structure: a winged corridor villa. The discovery of small mosaic cubes and larger tile tesserae, as also at the Beddingham villa, indicate the former presence of at least one mosaic (in Room 8 at Barcombe) and probably various tessellated floors. After the abandonment of the villa, currently thought to have occurred *c.* AD 300, there is no evidence for activity until the later Saxon period. The relatively early dates for the abandonments of the main domestic buildings at Barcombe and Beddingham, *c.* AD 300 and 330 respectively, may have been due to the vulnerability of these sites to coastal raiding (*see* below) via the river Ouse.

Our third case study is the site at Bignor, one of the largest villas in Britain. It is situated on the southern slope of the Upper Greensand, just north of the chalk Downs. Although extensive excavations at this site have failed to reveal any evidence for either roundhouses or indisputable occupation in the Late Iron Age, the developmental history of this villa is of exceptional interest since it includes significant changes: from timber 'proto-villa' (from *c.* AD 180) to simple masonry villa (from *c.* AD 250), to an exceptionally large and luxurious courtyard villa (*c.* AD 300-350) (Frere 1982; Black 1983; Aldsworth and Rudling 1995; Figs 9.6 and 9.7). The most recent (1991-2000) programme of research excavations at Bignor, which were directed by the writer, was partly designed, however, to investigate the earlier phases of Roman occupation at the site, which included a ditched enclosure and masonry foundations on a slightly different alignment to the later winged corridor villa/west wing of the courtyard villa (Fig. 9.7). These quite extensive but still poorly understood stone footings had first been discovered by the antiquarian Samuel Lysons (1817, 1819, 1821), and were later further investigated by Frere (1982) and Aldsworth (Aldsworth and Rudling 1995). The ditched enclosure has yielded late 1st- to 2nd-century pottery from its lower fills and large quantities of late-2nd- and early-3rd-century pottery from the upper fills. At some stage the northern boundary of the enclosure was probably established to the south of its final position. The southern border was also apparently of two phases: the excavations revealed two ditches just to the north of, and roughly parallel with, the southern masonry perimeter wall of the 4th-century villa. The two ditches and wall demonstrate the continuity of this boundary from the 1st to 4th centuries.

It is, however, the exceptional developments at Bignor *c.* AD 300 which are of even greater interest to our review of rural continuity and change. Whilst the sequence and nature of such developments have been outlined in theory and supported by excavation data (Frere 1982; Black 1983; Aldsworth and Rudling 1995), the reasons for such sudden expansion and wealth are less clear. Suggestions have included a change of ownership (perhaps to someone from overseas or elsewhere in Britain, including the coastal plain and river valleys of Sussex, which may have become increasingly insecure as a result of coastal raiding); the coming together of several families (probably related) for economies of scale and/or greater protection; or other social and economic developments at this villa, probably at the cost of other nearby rural farms which may have been taken over by the Bignor estate. Bignor Villa is probably an example of a wider phenomenon in 4th-century Britain: the emergence of a small number of super-rich landlords who lived in luxurious villas surrounded by larger households. This was the 'Golden Age' of Roman Britain (de la Bédoyère 1999), although the

Figure 9.6. *Part of a mosaic at Bignor Villa. Head of 'Venus'. (Photo: Trustees of Bignor Roman Villa).*

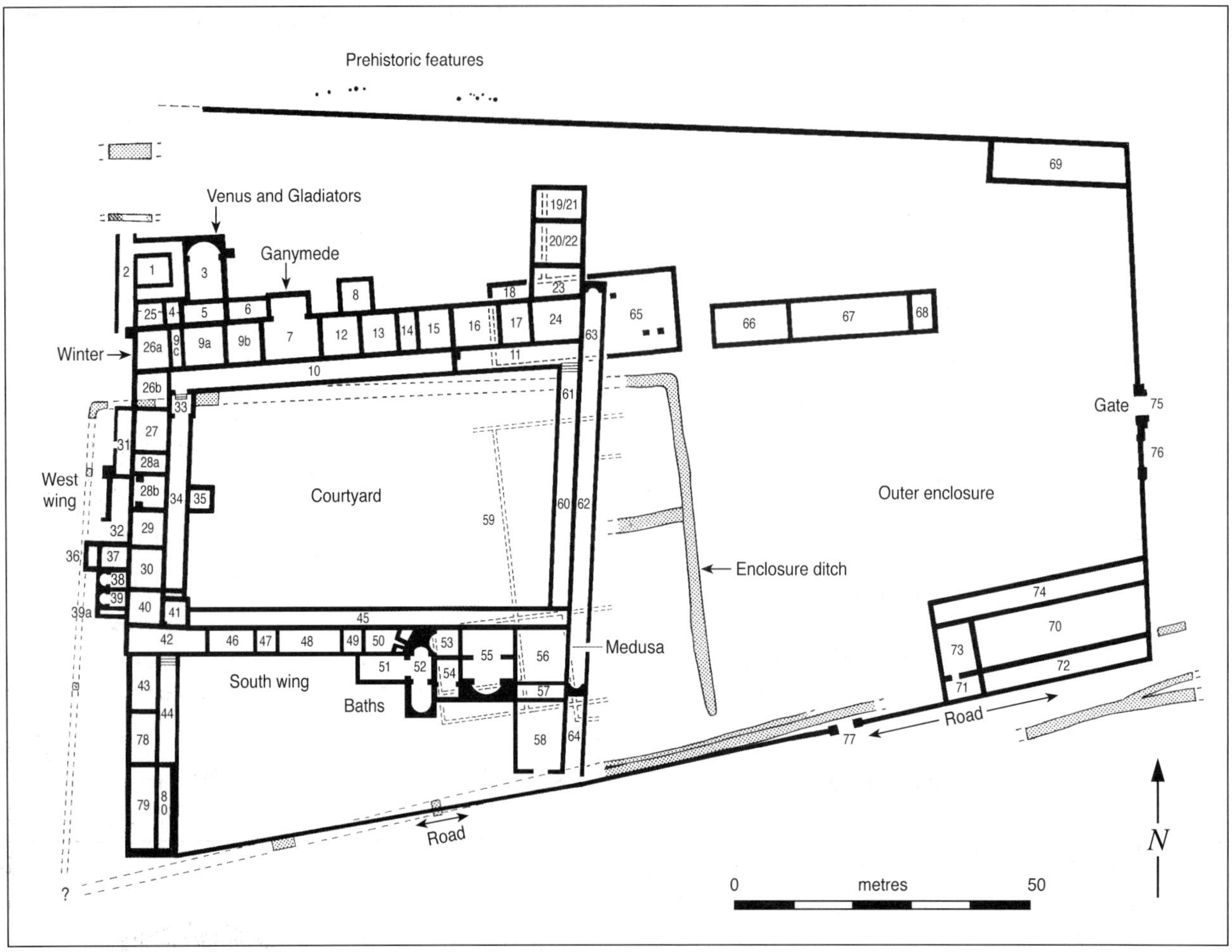

Figure 9.7. Multi-phased plan of Bignor Roman Villa. Room numbers 1-77 are based on Lysons (1819) and Frere (1982), numbers 78-80 have been added by Aldsworth and Rudling (1995).

extreme wealth of such an elite may have been much resented by those lower down the social order (Faulkner 2000). Unfortunately, the final stages of occupation at Bignor Villa are still poorly understood, but the intensity of activity as evidenced by finds of pottery and coins seem to have been much reduced in the second half of the 4th century. Did this site suffer a period of decline (perhaps with an absentee owner and a resident bailiff), and when, why and how was it abandoned or destroyed?

Religious Sites

Another important feature of the Romano-British countryside were religious sites. Whilst some shrines/temples are known from Iron Age Britain including an important example on Hayling Island near the Sussex border (Woodward 1992, 17-30), most of the religious sites in existence prior to AD 43 will have left few obvious traces in the archaeological record, many being apparently associated with sacred groves, trees and watery places. It has recently been suggested, however, that ritual significance can be attributed to the 'structured deposition' of material in pits at Mount Caburn, near Lewes, an Iron Age 'hillfort' site (Hamilton 1998). Here a shaft 3.3m deep at the base of a large depression inside the enclosure contained some Roman pottery and might thus indicate continuity of ritual use after the conquest. At Findon, a Roman well/ritual shaft *c*.267 feet deep yielded a wide range of interesting deposits and is another example of structured deposition (unpublished excavations). Finds from this shaft included mid-3rd to early-4th century coins and pottery (Malcolm Lyne pers. comm.). Such shafts may have been common in Roman times, but will now be difficult to locate. Other structured deposition occurred at Muntham Court, Findon, where a circular timber structure (Fig. 9.8) enclosed three pits, each with an ox skull resting on other bones, various bronze objects and a miniature baked clay model of a human leg. From a mound in front of this 'shrine' came many finds, including the well-known bronze boar plaque (Burstow and Holleyman 1956, 1957).

At Slonk Hill, Shoreham, two Bronze Age burial mounds were surrounded in the Roman period by a rectangular ditched enclosure, the northern boundary of which lay immediately to the north of an Iron Age gully. In the 4th century both ditches were filled in and a square structure of wooden posts was built around the eastern mound. Roman ritual deposits at the site include leg bones from lambs and piglets in a hollow cut into the upper filling of the western barrow ditch, and a group of twelve 4th-century coins from a nearby 'post-hole'/pit. Other Bronze Age barrows in Sussex were also places where offerings of Roman coins were made. These include the Money Mound, Lower Beeding, where various Roman artefacts and 156 coins (spanning the period AD 69-388) were

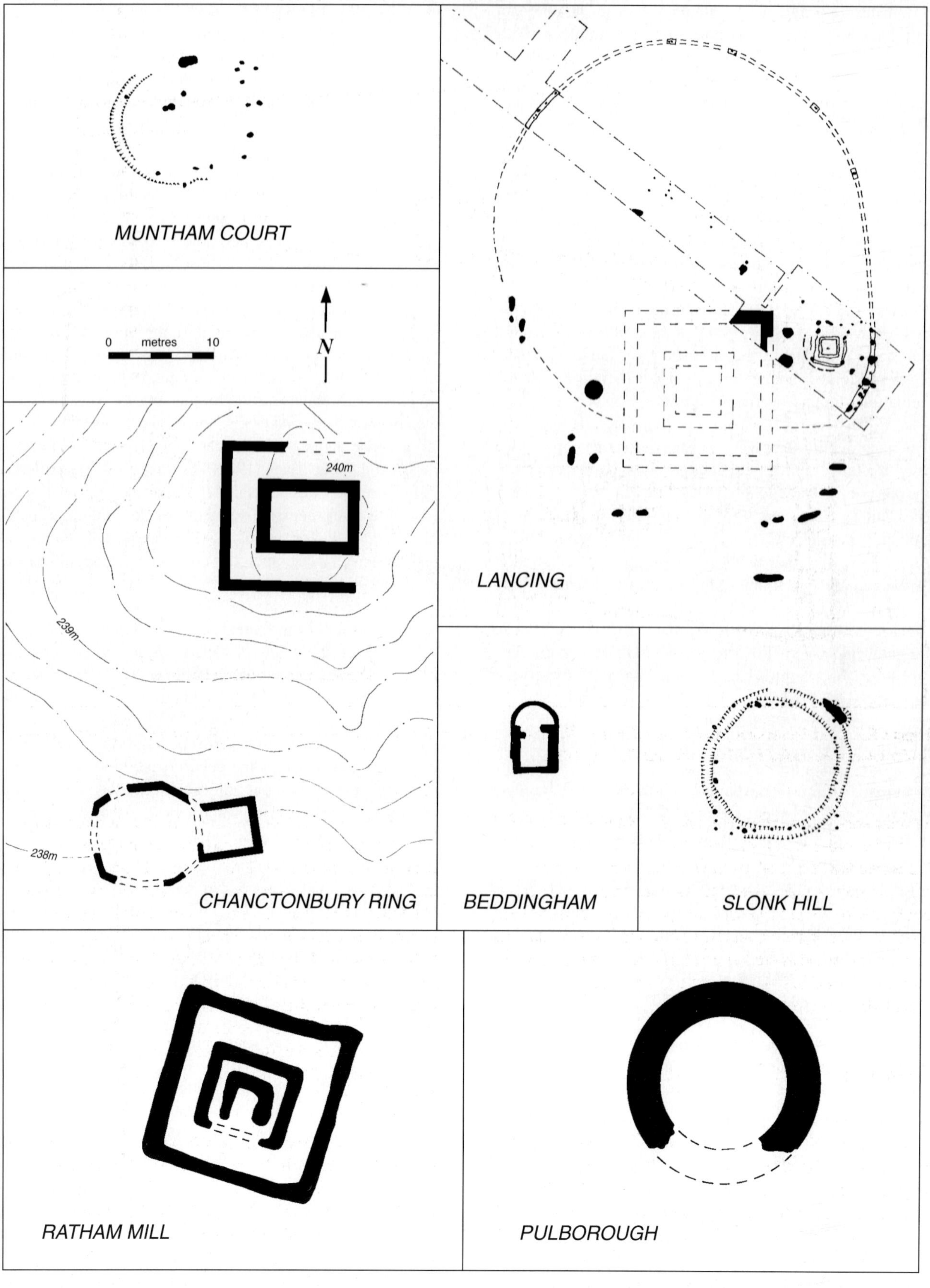

Figure 9.8. *Plans of Romano-British temples and shrines in Sussex.*

apparently buried as votive offerings (Beckensall 1967, 20). Such sites indicate Romano-British respect for, and re-use of (as shrines), ancient burial mounds.

Fortunately, some religious sites in rural Sussex were constructed in masonry and their remains have thus proved easier to detect (Fig. 9.8). These sites, which include temples of Romano-Celtic type at Chanctonbury, Lancing and Ratham Mill, have been the subject of three reviews (Cunliffe 1973, 107-109; Bedwin 1980; Rudling 2001/2002).

At Lancing Down the Roman temple was sited in an area of pits containing cremated remains and offerings, the earliest find being a Bronze Age cremation. Most of the finds of pre-conquest date belong to the Late Iron Age and include silver coins. Some of the cremations are Roman and thus show considerable continuity of this practice at the site. Excavations in 1980 re-located part of the temple, and nearby were discovered traces of a small timber square-within-a-square structure and part of a temenos gully (Bedwin 1981; Fig. 9.8). The 'shrine' is dated on limited ceramic evidence to the very end of the Iron Age. Its ground plan and proximity to the later masonry temple indicate religious significance, although some association with the cremation burials is also a possibility.

At Chanctonbury Ring various excavations have provided us with a fairly detailed knowledge of this Romano-British temple complex (Mitchell 1910; Bedwin 1980; Rudling 2001/2002). Here there were two masonry temples, one of typical Romano-Celtic form with a *cella* surrounded by an ambulatory, the other being polygonal with a rectangular entrance chamber. Although both temples are located within a Late Bronze Age enclosure or 'hillfort', and in the vicinity of various Bronze Age barrows, there is little evidence to suggest any use of the site in the Late Iron Age. The discovery of examples of Romano-British 'structured deposition' of animal bones in the hillfort ditch, and the finding of parts from at least 84 pigs' skulls at the polygonal temple, indicate, however, similarities of cult practices with those of pre-conquest Sussex. The selection of the abandoned hillfort would have provided the temple builders with a convenient temenos enclosure, and the high elevation of the site would have ensured prominent visibility of at least the Romano-Celtic rectangular temple.

Rural Industries

In addition to agriculture and iron-making, various other industries developed in Roman rural Sussex (Cunliffe 1973, 114-125; Williams 1971). These included: the making of pottery (*see* Lyne this volume) and tiles, the extraction of salt and stone, and forestry. The origins of some of these industries, such as East Sussex Ware pottery, salt extraction at Chidham (Bradley 1992) and the production of querns at Lodsworth (Peacock 1987) can be traced back to the Iron Age. Others, such as the making of tiles as at Hartfield (Rudling 1986), were completely new enterprises and were needed to meet the demands of Roman material culture, including the construction industry. Other changes in technology, such as milling at Rustington (Rudling and Gilkes 2000), led to the emergence of new industries related to agriculture. The Roman road network played an important role in the distribution of various products, one example being some of the tiles manufactured at Hartfield (Middleton *et al.* 1992; Middleton 1997). In the late 4th century, the end of the supply of bronze coinage to Britain must soon have caused major new problems to both rural and urban industries.

A Military Frontier

During the 3rd century the south coast became increasingly threatened by Saxon and pirate raiding. This problem may have been one of the reasons for the sudden end of the eastern group of large iron-working sites in Sussex (Cleere and Crossley 1995, 84-85) and the destruction and abandonment of some of the Sussex coastal villas, including perhaps the Palace at Fishbourne, which was destroyed by fire in the late 3rd century. The Roman response to such raiding was the gradual establishment of a system of coastal fortifications: the 'Saxon Shore Forts' (Johnson 1976; Johnson 1977; Maxfield 1989; Pearson 2002). Some of these forts, including that at Pevensey (*Anderita*) - the only Sussex example, and perhaps also nearby Portchester in Hampshire, may, however, have been constructed by the usurpers Carausius and Allectus in order to defend Britain from invasion by the central empire (White 1961). Whatever the reasons for the construction of the Pevensey fort *c.* AD 293 (Fulford and Tyres 1995, 1012), its presence may have had a detrimental effect upon nearby rural settlements. Black (1987, 42) has argued that whilst the military market was beneficial for villas located at a distance from the army centres, agricultural communities in the hinterland of the forts would have been especially vulnerable to the requisition (as opposed to contract purchase) of supplies by the military.

The seriousness of the threat of coastal raiding is probably also reflected in the late-3rd- or early-4th-century modifications, including the addition of D-shaped bastions, to the defences of Chichester. Although there is as yet only limited evidence from Chichester for the construction at this time of masonry houses comparable to those being constructed as villas in the countryside, the town's strong defences may have become an increasingly desirable attraction to wealthy landowners on the coastal plain and up the river valleys of Sussex.

Conclusions

Roman rural settlement in Sussex involved both continuity of locations and functions, many farms indeed "originating well back into the preceding Iron Age or even earlier" (Cunliffe 1973, 74), but also change, both in terms of the development of new locations and new types of site, and also both minor and major alterations to long-established settlements, technologies and material culture. There are thus many examples of continuity from the Late Iron Age *with* change, but also many examples of both continuity and change during the Romano-British period. Whilst some aspects of romanization were quickly and widely adopted by the natives of Sussex, especially with regard to material things, other aspects of Roman culture, such as religious beliefs and rituals did not gain such general acceptance and often failed to replace traditional practices. It would be true to say, however, that some aspects of Roman life that were adopted were continued by the sub-Roman society that lived on in Sussex during the 5th century.

References

Aldsworth, F.G. and Rudling, D.R. 1995. Excavations at Bignor Roman Villa, 1985-1990, *SAC* **133**, 103-188.

Applebaum, S. 1966. Peasant economy and types of agriculture, pages 99-107 in C. Thomas (ed), *Rural Settlement in Roman Britain*. London: Council for British Archaeology.

Barber, L. 1994. The excavation of a Romano-British site at Moraunt Drive, Middleton-on-Sea, West Sussex, 1992, *SAC* **132**, 87-100.

Barber, L., Gardiner, M. and Rudling, D. 2002. Excavations at Eastwick Barn, pages 107-140, in D. Rudling (ed), *Downland Settlement and Land-use, The Archaeology of the Brighton Bypass,* UCL Field Archaeology Unit Monograph No. **1**. London: Archetype Publications.

Barrett, A.A. 1979. The career of Tiberius Claudius Cogidubnus, *Britannia* **10**, 227-242.

Beckensall, S.G. 1967. The excavation of Money Mound, *SAC* **105**, 13-30.

Bédoyère, de la, G. 1999. *The Golden Age of Roman Britain.* Stroud: Tempus.

Bedwin, O. 1980. Excavations at Chanctonbury Ring, Wiston, West Sussex 1977, *Britannia* **11**, 173-222.

Bedwin, O. 1981. Excavations at Lancing Down, West Sussex 1980, *SAC* **119**, 37-56.

Bedwin, O. and Place, C. 1995. Late Iron Age and Romano-British occupation at Ounces Barn, Boxgrove, West Sussex; excavations 1982-1983, *SAC* **133**, 45-101.

Bell, M. 1976. The Excavation of an early Romano-British site and Pleistocene Land Forms at Newhaven, Sussex, *SAC* **114**, 218-305.

Bell, M.G. 1977. *Excavations at Bishopstone. SAC* **115**.

Black, E.W. 1983. The Roman Villa at Bignor in the Fourth Century, *Oxford J. Archaeol.* **2**, (**1**), 93-107.

Black, E.W. 1987. *The Roman Villas of South-East England,* BAR Brit. Ser. **171**.

Black, E.W. 1993. The Period 1C bath-building at Fishbourne and the problem of the Proto-palace, *J. Roman Archaeol.* **6**, 233-237.

Black, E.W. 1997. Afterthoughts, in R.M. & D.E. Friendship-Taylor (eds), *From Round 'house' to Villa,* Fascicle 3 of the Upper Nene Archaeological Society, 59-61.

Bogaers, J.E. 1979. King Cogidubnus in Chichester: another reading of *RIB 91, Britannia* **10**, 243-254.

Bradley, R. 1992. Roman Salt Production in Chichester Harbour: Rescue Excavations at Chidham, West Sussex, *Britannia* **23**, 27-44.

Burstow, G.P. and Holleyman, G.A. 1956. Excavations at Muntham Court, Findon, interim report 1954-1955, *SNQ* **14**, 196-198.

Burstow, G.P. and Holleyman, G.A. 1957. Excavations at Muntham Court, Findon, Sussex, *The Archaeological News Letter* **6** (**4**), 101-102.

Butler, C. and Rudling, D. 2002. Working through the ages, *Sussex Past & Present* **98**, 10-11.

Cleere, H. 1978. Roman Sussex – the Weald, in P.L. Drewett (ed), *Archaeology in Sussex to AD 1500,* CBA Res. Rep. **29**, 59-63.

Cleere, H.F. and Crossley, D.W. 1995. *The Iron Industry of the Weald.* 2nd edition (ed. J. Hodgkinson). Cardiff: Merton Priory Press.

Creighton, J. 2001. The Iron Age-Roman Transition, in S. James and M. Millett (eds), *Britons and Romans: advancing an archaeological agenda,* CBA Res. Rep. **125**, 4-11.

Cunliffe, B.W. 1971. *Excavations at Fishbourne 1961-1969, Vol. I: The Site; Vol. II: The Finds.* Society of Antiquaries of London Res. Reps **26** and **27**.

Cunliffe, B.W. 1973. *The Regni.* London: Duckworth.

Cunliffe, B.W., Down, A. and Rudkin, D. 1996. *Chichester Excavations 9, Excavations at Fishbourne 1969-1988,* Chichester: District Council.

Down, A. 1978. Roman Sussex – Chichester and the Chilgrove Valley, in P.L. Drewett (ed), *Archaeology in Sussex to AD 1500,* CBA Res. Rep. **29**, 52-58.

Down, A. 1979. *Chichester Excavations 4, The Roman Villas at Chilgrove and Up Marden.* Chichester: District Council.

Down, A. 1988. *Roman Chichester.* Chichester: Phillimore.

Dudley, C. 1981. A re-appraisal of the evidence for a Roman villa in Springfield Road, Brighton, following further discoveries on the site, pages 68-88, in E. Kelly and C. Dudley, Two Romano-British Burials, *SAC* **119**; 65-88.

Faulkner, N. 2000. *The Decline and Fall of Roman Britain.* Stroud: Tempus.

Frere, S. 1982. The Bignor Villa, *Britannia* **13**, 135-195.

Fulford, M. and Tyres, I. 1995. The date of Pevensey and the defence of an *Imperial Britanniarum, Antiquity* **69**, 1009-1014.

Gilkes, O.J. 1993. Iron Age and Roman Littlehampton, *SAC* **131**, 1-20.

Gilkes, O.J. 1999. The bathhouse of Angmering Roman villa, *SAC* **137**, 59-69.

Hamilton, S. 1998. Using elderly databases: Iron Age pit deposits at the Caburn, East Sussex and related sites, *SAC* **136**, 23-39.

Hamilton, S. and Manley, J. 1999. The End of Prehistory *c.*100 BC-AD 43, in K. Leslie and B. Short (eds), *An Historical Atlas of Sussex.* Chichester: Phillimore.

Hartridge, R. 1978. Excavations at the Prehistoric and Romano-British site on Slonk Hill, Shoreham, Sussex, *SAC* **116**, 69-141.

Henig, M. 1998. Togidubnus and the Roman Liberation, *British Archaeology* **37**, 8-9.

Henig, M. 2002. *The Heirs of King Verica, Culture & Politics in Roman Britain.* Stroud:Tempus.

Hind, J.G.F. 1989. The invasion of Britain in AD 43 – An Alternative Strategy for Aulus Plautius, *Britannia* **20**, 1-21.

Hodgkinson, J. 1999. Romano-British iron production in the Sussex and Kent Weald: a review of current data, *J. Hist. Metallurgy Soc.* **33**, (**2**), 68-72.

Johnson, S. 1976. *The Roman Forts of the Saxon Shore.* London: Paul Elek.

Johnston, D.E. (ed) 1977. *The Saxon Shore,* CBA Res. Rep. **18**.

Luke, M. and Wells, J. 2000. New evidence for the origins, development and internal morphology of the Roman roadside settlement at Alfoldean, *SAC* **138**, 75-101.

Lyne, M.A.B. 1994. The Hassocks Cemetery, *SAC* **132**, 53-85.

Lysons, S. 1817. An Account of the Remains of a Roman Villa, discovered in Bignor, in Sussex, *Archaeologia* **18**, 203-221.

Lysons, S. 1819. *Reliquiae Britannico-Romanae Vol. III, Remains of a Roman Villa Discovered in Bignor in Sussex.*

Lysons, S. 1821. An Account of Further Discoveries of the Remains of a Roman Villa at Bignor in Sussex, *Archaeologia* **19**, 176-177.

Magilton, J. 1996. Roman Roads in the Manhood Peninsula, *The Archaeology of Chichester and District 1995,* 31-34.

Magilton, J. and Rudkin, D. 1999. Roman Chichester and Fishbourne, pages 26-27 and 145, in K. Leslie and B. Short (eds), *An Historical Atlas of Sussex.* Chichester: Phillimore.

Manley, J. 2000 (2001). Measurement and metaphor: The design and meaning of Building 3 at Fishbourne Roman Palace, *SAC* **138**, 103-113.

Manley, J. 2002. *AD 43 – The Roman Invasion of Britain: a reassessment.* Stroud: Tempus.

Margary, I.D. 1953. Recent discoveries by the Ordnance Survey of Roman roads in Sussex, *SAC* **91**, 1-19.

Margary, I.D. 1965. *Roman Ways in the Weald.* 3rd (revised) edition. London: Phoenix House.

Margary, I.D. 1967. *Roman Roads in Britain.* 2nd (revised) edition. London: John Baker.

Maxfield, V.A. (ed) 1989. *The Saxon Shore: A Handbook.* Exeter: University Press.

Middleton, A.P., Cowell, M.R. and Black, E.W. 1992. Romano-British relief-patterned flue tiles: a study of provenance using petrography and neutron activation analysis, in S. Mery (ed), *Earth Sciences and Archaeological Ceramics, Experimentations, Applications, Documents et Travaux, IGAL, Cergy,* No. **16**, 49-59.

Middleton, A. 1997. Tiles in Roman Britain, pages 158-163, in I. Freestone and D. Gaimster (eds), *Pottery in the making.* London: British Museum Press.

Mitchell, G.S. 1910. Excavations at Chantonbury Ring, 1909, *SAC* **53**, 131-137.

Money, J.H. 1977. The Iron Age hillfort and Romano-British iron-working settlement at Garden Hill, Sussex: interim report on excavations, 1968-1976, *Britannia* **8**, 339-350.

Peacock, D. 1987. Iron Age and Roman Quern Production at Lodsworth, West Sussex, *Antiq. J.* **67**, 61-85.

Pearson, A. 2002. *The Roman Shore Forts.* Stroud: Tempus.

Praetorius, C.J. 1911. Report on the villa at Borough Farm, Pulborough, *Proc. Soc. Antiq. of London* **23**, 121-129.

Rivet, A.L.F. 1964. *Town and Country in Roman Britain.* 2nd edition. London: Hutchinson.

Rivet, A.L.F. and Smith, C. 1979. *The Place-Names of Roman Britain.* London: Batsford.

Rudkin, D.J. 1986. The excavation of a Romano-British site by Chichester Harbour, *SAC* **124**, 51-77.

Rudkin, D. 2002. Military forces, *Sussex Past & Present* **98**, 9.

Rudling, D.R. 1979. Invasion and Response: Downland Settlement in East Sussex, (pages 339-356), in B.C. Barnham and H.B. Johnson (eds), *Invasion and Response: The Case of Roman Britain,* BAR Brit. Ser. **73**.

Rudling, D.R. 1982a. Rural Settlement in Late Iron Age and Roman Sussex, (pages 269-288), in D. Miles (ed), *The Romano-British Countryside, Studies in Rural Settlement and Economy,* BAR Brit. Ser. **103**.

Rudling, D.R. 1982b. The Romano-British Farm on Bullock Down, Chapter 6 (pages 97-142), in P. Drewett, *The Archaeology of Bullock Down, Eastbourne, East Sussex: The Development of a Landscape,* Sussex Archaeological Society Monograph **1**.

Rudling, D.R. 1984. Excavations in Tarrant Street, Arundel, West Sussex, *Univ. London Inst. Archaeol. Bull.* **21**, 45-47.

Rudling, D.R. 1985. Excavations on the site of the Southwick Roman Villa, 1965 and 1981, *SAC* **123**, 73-84.

Rudling, D.R. 1986. The Excavation of a Roman Tilery on Great Cansiron Farm, Hartfield, East Sussex, *Britannia* **17**, 191-230.

Rudling, D.R. 1988. A Colony of Rome, AD 43-410, Chapter 6 (pages 178-245), in P. Drewett, D. Rudling, and M. Gardiner, *The South East to AD 1000.* London: Longman.

Rudling, D.R. 1997. Round 'house' to Villa: The Beddingham and Watergate Villas, in R.M. and D.E. Friendship-Taylor (series eds), *From Round 'house' to Villa,* Fascicle 3 of the Upper Nene Archaeological Society.

Rudling, D.R. 1998. The development of Roman villas in Sussex, *SAC* **136**, 41-65.

Rudling, D.R. 1999. Roman Sussex, pages 24-25 and 144-145, in K. Leslie and B. Short (eds), *An Historical Atlas of Sussex.* Chichester: Phillimore.

Rudling, D. 2001 (2002). Chanctonbury Ring revisited, The excavations of 1988-1991, *SAC* **139**, 75-121.

Rudling, D.R. Forthcoming. The coin finds from Fishbourne, 1961-1999, in J. Manley and D. Rudkin (eds), Excavations at Fishbourne Roman Palace 1995-1999.

Rudling, D. and Butler, C. 2002. Barcombe Roman Villa, *Current Archaeology* **179**, 486-489.

Rudling, D. and Gilkes, O. 2000. Important archaeological discoveries made during the construction of the A259 Rustington Bypass 1990, *SAC* **138**, 15-28.

Sauer, E.W. 2000. Alchester, a Claudian 'Vexillation Fortress' near the Western Boundary of the Catuvellauni: New Light on the Roman Invasion of Britain, *Archaeol. J.* **157**, 1-78.

Scott, E. 1993. *A Gazetteer of Roman Villas in Britain,* Leicester Archaeology Monographs No. **1**.

Scott, L. 1938. The Roman Villa at Angmering, *SAC* **79**, 3-44.

Scott, L. 1939. Angmering Roman Villa, *SAC* **80**, 89-92.

Stevens, L. and Gilbert, R. 1973. *The Eastbourne Roman Villa.* Eastbourne: Crain Services.

Sutton, T. 1952. The Eastbourne Roman Villa, *SAC* **90**, 1-12.

Tomlin, R.S.O. 1997. Reading a 1st-century Roman gold signet ring from Fishbourne, *SAC* **135**, 127-130.

Waldron, T., Taylor, G.M. and Rudling, D. 1999. Sexing of Romano-British baby burials from the Beddingham and Bignor villas, *SAC* **137**, 71-79.

White, D.A. 1961. *Litus Saxonicum: the British Saxon Shore in Scholarship and History.* Madison (WI): Department of History, University of Wisconsia.

Wilson, A.E. 1947. Angmering Roman villa, *SAC* **86**, 1-21.

Winbolt, S.E. 1923. Alfoldean Roman Station: first report, 1922, *SAC* **64**, 81-104.

Winbolt, S.E. 1924. Alfoldean Roman station: second report (on 1923), *SAC* **65**, 122-127.

Winbolt, S.E. 1927. Excavations at Hardham Camp, Pulborough, *SAC* **68**, 122-127.

Winbolt, S.E. 1932. Roman villa at Southwick, *SAC* **73**, 13-32.

Winbolt, S.E. 1935. Romano-British Sussex, in L.F. Salzman (ed), *The Victoria History of the Counties of England, A History of Sussex,* Volume **3**, 1-70.

Wolseley, G.R., Smith, R.A. and Hawley, W. 1927. Prehistoric and Roman Settlement on Park Brow, *Archaeologia* **76**, 1-40.

Woodward, A. 1992. *Shrines and Sacrifice.* London: Routledge.

INSIDE/OUTSIDE: ARCHITECTURE AND THE INDIVIDUAL AT FISHBOURNE ROMAN PALACE

John Manley

Abstract

This paper attempts to understand the layout of Fishbourne Roman Palace, and particularly the effect of the architecture on the individuals who lived in, used and visited the building. One theme that is explored is the way the building functioned from both the inside and the outside. The idea that the Palace was approached through semi-formal gardens is questioned. The discovery of a large masonry building close to the principal eastern front of the Palace suggests a much more inward-looking building than had previously been imagined.

Introduction

> "The approach to the Palace must have been spectacular, the drive passing through an open grassy field flanked to the north by the rich gardens producing fruit and vegetables and to the south by the stream flowing in a shallow valley to the harbour, and there in front, looming magnificent, the low mass of the great building dominated by its huge and inspiring entrance hall."
> Barry Cunliffe, *Fishbourne Roman Palace* (1997)

The discovery of Fishbourne Roman Palace in the 1960s and its gradual excavation over a number of summer seasons by Barry Cunliffe, brought to light the ground plan of a building which is unique in the architecture of Roman Britain (Figs. 10.1-10.3). The plan of the complex is well-known: four ranges, each over 120 metres in length, surrounded a formal internal garden some 100 metres north-south, by 75 metres east-west. The building was assumed to be one storey in height and to have a principal entrance from the east. The original excavator sought parallels for the building in Rome itself – specifically the Palace of Domitian on the Palatine Hill. The uniqueness of the building and its affinities with Roman Italy are emphasized today by its promotional literature, in which it is described as the 'largest civilian building north of the Alps'. There are other features, of course, which separate the building from the architectural corpus of Roman Britain: the quality, number and early date of the mosaics, the variety of architectural embellishments and, not least, the evidence of the planned, internal garden.

The word 'palace' itself, has implicit connotations when applied to the building and its setting. Such connotations of grandeur, size, opulence and spaciousness are clearly in the minds of visitors when they come to the site today, so much so that the reality of the ruins (foundations of walls only) and rather ordinary approach (through a modern housing estate) can often disappoint. The word 'palace' in contemporary English suggests at least two automatic images. The first is clearly that of a very high-status building, fit for the residence of a ruler or sub-regent. A palace, by definition as a building, has a rarity value. The present-day owners of Fishbourne Roman Palace clearly realize this: a marketing cachet attaches to the word palace and it is used to differentiate their visitor attraction from the many other villas that are open to the public.

The second concerns the setting, and presupposes that a palace is usually situated in high-status surroundings where the approaches to a palace are specifically marked, usually by a mixture of gardens and 'special' roads that lead to it. The obvious English examples are buildings such as Buckingham Palace (approached from the Mall flanked by St. James' Park) and Kensington Palace (approached through Kensington Gardens). Hampton Court is exceptional in not being fronted by formal approaches over land. This is because its major access, used by the monarch, was by boat along the River Thames and therefore this counted as the principal access avenue.

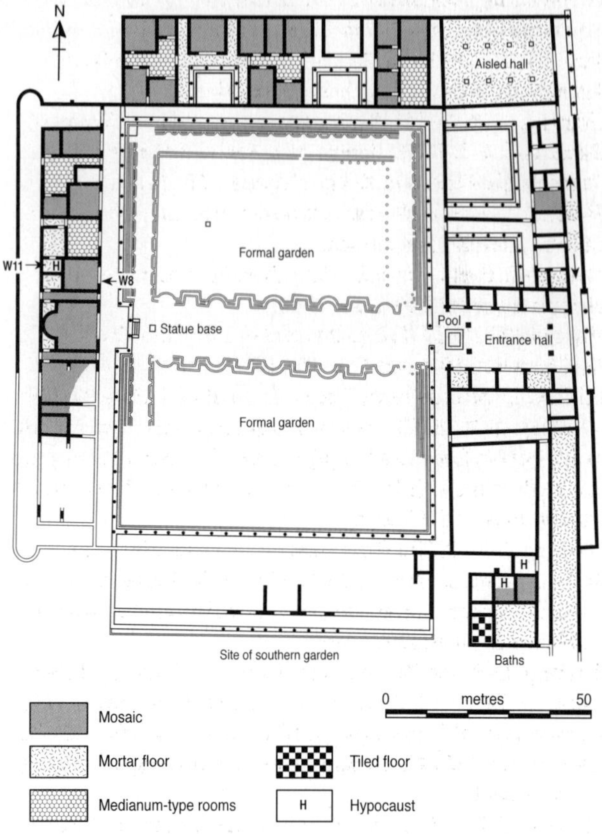

Figure 10.1. *Plan of Fishbourne Roman Palace and its formal internal garden in the Flavian period. The ground-plan shows the distribution of mosaics and mortar floors, and the possible identification of* medianum*-type rooms. Note the hypocaust in room W11. Doorways are shown where evidence survived. From a drawing supplied by Ernest Black.*

Figure 10.2. *Aerial view of the Palace from the east. Note the sweep of the modern A27 (bottom right) and the cover building over the north range of the Palace. The excavation and site of Building 3, marked by 'B', lies between the A27 and the Palace.*

Figure 10.3. *Aerial view of the location of the Palace from the south. Note the easy access provided by the easternmost arm of Chichester harbour. The site of the Palace lies at the top of the inlet.*

The template of formal approaches to palaces (and, one suspects, the more recent template of 18th-century country houses looking out on to sweeping drives set in Capability Brown landscapes) has influenced commentators on the likely setting of Fishbourne Roman Palace. In addition, the discovery of the formal *internal* gardens has heightened anticipation that there would be formal *external* gardens. Since land transport is much more familiar to us than sea or riverine transport, it has been natural for commentators to assume that the major entrance to the Palace from the east (i.e. over land) would be landscaped in some way. This template of a landscaped approach to the Palace finds most expression in the work of Down (Cunliffe *et al.* 1996), who excavated large areas to the east of the complex, particularly under the line of the A27.

At the end of the 1960s, Barry Cunliffe (1971) was confident enough to suggest that the building, constructed around AD 75, may have been built for the loyal client king Togidubnus. Subsequent research over the last 30 years has challenged, although not refuted, the tentative conclusions reached at the end of the 60s. A revised dating has been proposed (closer to AD 110) by Black (1985, 1987, 1993), but rejected by Cunliffe (1991). The 'palace' interpretation has been scrutinized and alternatives offered (Black 1987). Finally, the link with Togidubnus has been questioned, although others (Henig 1996) have gathered circumstantial evidence linking the Fishbourne site with the ruling, newly enfranchized elite of a client kingdom.

What has received relatively little discussion in print has been the functioning of the internal spaces within the complex, and the way the building was viewed by the individual, both from within and without. Such a discussion is perhaps timely, given the recent literature on the manner in which architectural spaces were designed to structure social interaction in Roman residences (eg Hingley 1990; Scott 1990; Samson 1990a, 1990b; Laurence and Wallace-Hadrill 1997; Leslie 1999). The most detailed review of the functioning of the internal spaces has been supplied by Cunliffe, Smith and Black. Smith (1997) generally follows the scheme outlined by Cunliffe, while Black differs from both on several key points. An overview is presented below.

The inside and outside

Before beginning a description of the layout of the rooms in Fishbourne Roman Palace, three points are worth making concerning our ability to 'read' the functions of the individual rooms. The first is the relatively simple one that Fishbourne was abandoned after a fire and all artefacts that could be salvaged were removed, leaving little to demonstrate what even the *last* use of the rooms had been in the late 3rd century. The second is that many rooms in Roman houses were not mono-functional (Nevett 1999, 290), their uses could change throughout the day. The third is that the spatial ideology of some large Roman houses was structured to reinforce a dominant ideology, that of the *paterfamilias*[1]. Such reinforcement succeeded by not obviously emphasizing the identities of other residents of the household with any specific rooms (Laurence 1997).

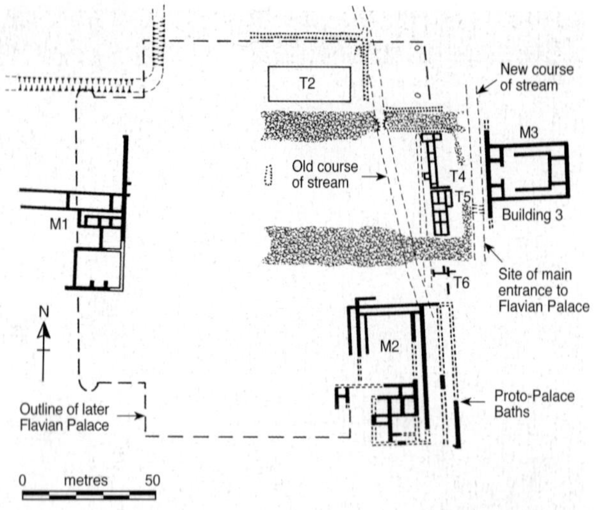

Figure 10.4. *A composite plan showing the main structures and features underlying the Flavian Palace. Not all these features are contemporary. Timber buildings are represented by T2, T4, T5 and T6. The three masonry buildings are M1, M2 (the* proto-palace *baths) and M3 (Building 3); these are likely to have been contemporary in Period 1c. M1, however, may never have been completed, M2 was incorporated into the Flavian Palace in Period 2a, and M3 (Building 3) may have lasted into the 3rd century. Superimposed on the composite plan is the outline ground-plan of the later Flavian Palace.*

The earlier baths (Fig. 10.4 - the so-called 'proto-palace' constructed around AD 60-65) in the south-east corner of the complex were incorporated into the palace's eastern range and acted as a facility serving the residents and guests in the building. Set centrally in the eastern range the monumental entrance hall (Fig. 10.5), fronted by six columns (rather like a temple), contained flanking cubicles (five on each side) where visitors to the Palace may have discussed matters with various functionaries of the owner; (the easternmost pair may have housed porters (Smith 1997, 176) – they had masonry benches along their walls).

Some of these functionaries may have resided to the north of the entrance hall in a set of two living units that were arranged along the eastern side of two courtyards (Fig.10.1). Pink mortar floors, perhaps suggestive of a lower status[2], survived in two rooms, but fragments of a destroyed mosaic were found in another room. In addition, in each suite a larger room was located in an axial position to give a view across its private courtyard. This suggests that these suites were probably high-status apartments. It is also noteworthy that while the floor accommodation is less in these eastern range apartments than in the apartments in the northern range, the courtyards of the eastern apartments are larger than those in the northern range.

In the north-east corner stood an aisled hall, fronted by a colonnade (Fig. 10.5) and entered from the east. This appears to be a space, like the entrance hall, where inside met outside, where outsiders could seek an audience with officials of the owner. The difference between the 'entrance hall' and the 'aisled hall' lies, of course, in terms of the quantitative social articulation between inside and outside. In the aisled hall the linkage was between one/several/inside and many/outside;

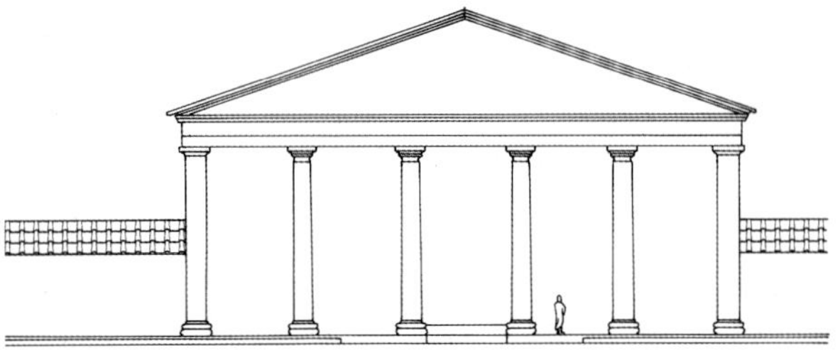

The main entrance

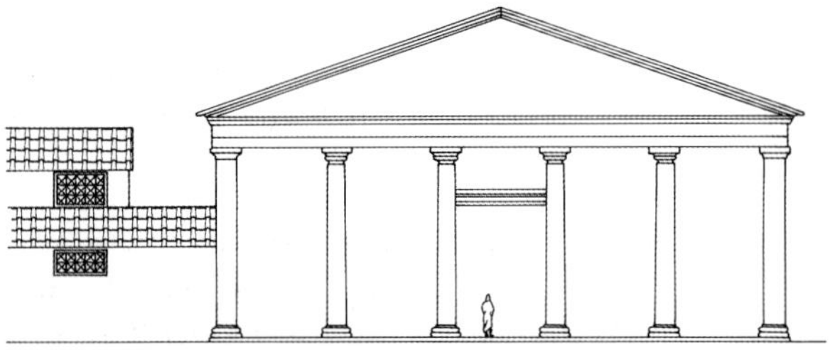

The entrance to the aisled hall

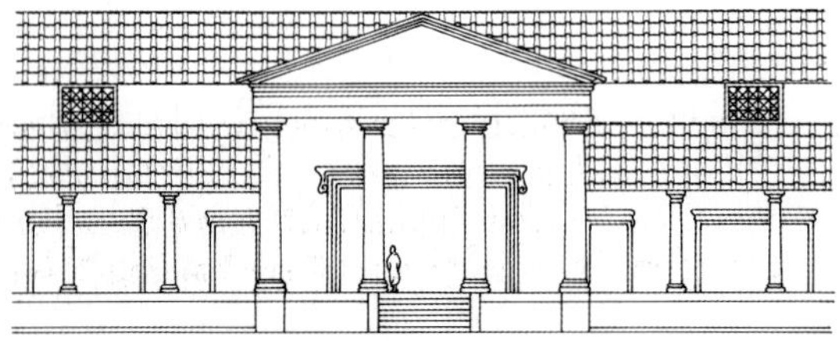

The entrance to the reception room/dining room

Figure 10.5. *Elevations of the main entrance to the Palace, the entrance to the aisled hall and the entrance to the apsed reception room/dining room (after Nigel Sunter in Cunliffe 1997).*

in the entrance hall the linkage was presumably on a more individual basis. However, in both architectural units the interchanges took place after the outsiders had passed between stone columns and these were undoubtedly architectural features that communicated messages of inequality on different levels: technical, architectural, status and authority. Columns were perennial symbols of power and had the effect of marking out spaces as prestigious (Wallace-Hadrill 1988, 68,70). There may have been other signals associated with these thresholds – both tangible (e.g. the surmounting of steps) and reverential (the alteration of dress code and body language) that emphasized the differences between inside and outside[3].

The rooms in the north range (Fig. 10.1) are grouped around two smaller courtyards, and many of these rooms contain the much-admired mosaics. The predominant style of mosaic displayed geometric patterns using largely black and white tesserae, less often red. Although the layout of the rooms is not symmetrical, there are elements of symmetry – such as the large, mosaic-floored central rooms to the north of the two courtyards. The general consensus is that these rooms may have made up separate apartments or living units, for dignitaries and their households, and there seems space for three such apartments. The rooms seem to be grouped together in an arrangement similar to the *medianum* type of house (Clarke 1991, 350ff; Ellis 2000, 73-8). Other rooms were grouped around the *medianum,* which acted as a circulation area or hallway and gave access to them. Three units of this type were being advertised for rental in insula vi.6 (the insula Arriana Polliana) at Pompeii in AD 79 (Pirson 1997,165ff), and others are found in 2nd-century Ostia. In the Palace the smaller rooms can perhaps be identified as bedrooms, and the larger ones as reception and living rooms. Some of the latter were probably dining rooms, and the two large rooms isolated by passages to the north of each courtyard seem to be the equivalent of *exedra.* (Although the scale of Fishbourne Roman Palace is unique in Britain, its plan is not. Another house, at Southwick *c.*40 kilometres to the east, resembled it closely and was presumably built at the same time or shortly afterwards[4]). At the north-west corner of the complex is the only evidence for the kitchen. Associated facilities, such as quarters for slaves[5], may have existed and it is generally assumed that these lay to the west of the north range.

The western range was constructed on a terrace formed by cutting away the ground to the east, giving it a visual elevation over the internal garden and over the path of any individual or delegation that approached the central apsidal chamber. Apses emphasized prestigious internal spaces (Wallace-Hadrill 1988, 68) and this must indicate that this was the most important room in the Palace. It was clearly the inner reception room and/or dining room of the Palace, and the setting for a semi-circular bench or range of seats was located within the apse. This may be an early example of the *stibadium*, the curving dining couch, which became popular in the later Roman period (Ellis 1995). A dining room with a *stibadium* comprised three elements - an entrance way, a middle space and the apsed dining area. The entrance was often imposing (Fig. 10.5), sometimes marked by an inscription, and used for the display of expensive food and wines. The middle space was kept free for the circulation of dancers and entertainers, while the diners sat in somewhat restricted spaces on the curved couch within the apse. The view from the *stibadium* through the entrance was meant to be one of the most dramatic in the house (Ellis 1997).

The rooms to the north of the apsidal chamber gradually decrease in size, and represent domestic accommodation. They also contain the only evidence of a hypocaust (room W11). The hypocaust was designed to heat the mosaic-floored room directly to the east (room W8), probably the bedroom, *cubiculum*, of the owner. There is a persistent pattern in large Roman houses of larger reception rooms juxtaposed to smaller rooms of suitable proportions for a bedroom (Wallace-Hadrill 1988, 93). Our sense of privacy is not a universal one and in particular was not shared by the Romans (Riggsby 1997, 47). The *cubiculum* could be a place for the more informal reception of guests and for the transaction of business (Riggsby 1997, 41; Wallace-Hadrill 1988, 94). The location of the probable *cubiculum* of the head of the household next to the reception room/dining area at Fishbourne Roman Palace is therefore consistent with this pattern. Low-status mortar floors north and south of the hypocaust suggest that these rooms might have been used by slaves. It is possible to identify two *medianum*-type apartments in the western range to the north of the apsidal chamber. These may well have constituted the domestic accommodation of the owner and his family. Another two apartments may have existed to the south of the apsidal chamber. The long north-south corridor running the entire length of the west range may have allowed the owner and his advisors the opportunity to walk and discuss matters, conceivably while a delegation was diverted to a waiting room, or walked in the garden.

What is remarkable about the architectural arrangements so far described, seen from the perspective of the occupants of the various spaces, was that all their views were directed inwards. (In this respect it was like other well-appointed houses in urban settings (*cf.* Pompeii), where views were directed inwards rather than outwards to the street). However, there are differences in these inward views. The occupants of the apartments in the eastern and northern ranges enjoyed views over their own private, peristyle-courtyards; the occupants of the western range could look out directly onto the formal garden. None of the ranges of the building so far described (i.e. the east, north and west) had lengthy external colonnades or, indeed, any external windows at a height where external views could be obtained. Most reconstruction drawings of the external walls *assume* small and high windows (Fig. 10.3) (Cunliffe 1997, 55 (fig. 17) & 86 (fig. 43)). The only views from within were those enjoyed by the outsiders who could glimpse back through the inter-columnar spaces of the entrance hall and aisled hall. All the insiders (functionaries, guests, aristocrats, etc.) looked inside; all the outsiders could only look back and outside.

It is presumed that the formal way for the individual to approach the apsidal chamber, no doubt accompanied by a functionary of the Palace, was by walking east to west along the centre line of the formal garden (Figure 10.6). Along this line the rigidity of the architectural and horticultural syntax (lots of straight lines) was broken by a number of semi-circular and right-angled recesses framed by multiple box hedges. It is tempting to imagine that these recesses held statues or certainly some features that would emphasize the status of this particular garden path and signal clearly to the approaching individual the inequalities prevalent between received and receiver. The statues themselves could have been 'authority figures', *bringing back to life* figures from the past, and would have heightened the individual's sense of being monitored.

The impact upon the visitor or delegation approaching along the garden path was further heightened by the elaborate *'trompe l'oeil'* mural that formed a vertical wall on the western side of the garden, facing the oncoming individuals. Together with the columns in front of the audience chamber, these were designed to convey messages of status and to underline the power inequalities between the grantor of the audience and the visitors.

The southern range (Fig. 10.1) has so far not been mentioned. In part this is because our evidence for the internal arrangements of this range is practically non-existent, since it lies buried beneath a modern road and housing. What is

Figure 10.6. *Interior view. It shows the approach to the apsidal reception chamber along the central path in the formal garden (courtesy of Graeme Puckett).*

remarkable about the southern range, however, is the presence of an *external* colonnade; no information is available on whether there was an internal colonnade. (Excavations in the 1960s proved the existence of the external colonnade; the area in which the remains of the internal colonnade might lie is unfortunately under the modern road).

Here the architectural syntax might have been reversed; the range and its occupants looked out, rather than looked inside. This may mean that this range housed more private apartments. Who occupied such prestigious apartments is unknown. These rooms could have formed the summer residences of the owner and his household, or more accommodation for household staff and dignitaries. It was important in a Roman household of high standing to have a multiplicity of choices in terms of reception rooms and bedrooms (Wallace-Hadrill 1988, 92). One of the particular reasons for changing the room location of activities was to adapt to seasonal changes in climate and temperature (Nevett 1999, 291). Whoever the occupants were, they could afford to gaze outside, and enjoy the luxury of being able to turn their backs on the politics of the Palace. In addition they enjoyed their only private view – that to the south. Here, over a few hundred metres, the ground shelved imperceptibly down across the southern garden towards the waters of Chichester harbour. Here too there were (faint) echoes of terraced gardens in front of the villas of southern Italy, stepping down to the Mediterranean.

The insiders and outsiders

Fishbourne Roman Palace, then, has been described and peopled in outline, with observations that the three ranges of the building (north, east, and west) were focused on the internal events taking place in the enclosed garden, and essentially ignored the exterior. The southern range, however, may have in part reversed this sequence, quite possibly because it housed private apartments of high-status individuals. Access to outsiders was carefully regulated through two monumental entrances to imposing rectangular spaces – the entrance and aisled halls. The internal garden was carefully laid out to underline power inequalities between visiting and receiving personages.

It is possible to see, in the surviving room arrangements, several different apartments or living units. However, it is important not to assume that these apartments functioned in the same way as we would understand the word apartment in its modern, western, usage. Concepts such as privacy are culturally specific, and are likely to have been very different in the Roman world from our own. We should not, therefore, assume that these apartments were necessarily private spaces, and areas like the formal garden, public spaces. Similarly, within the individual apartments, individual rooms may have been furnished in similar ways but hosted a variety of different activities. In addition, a notable absence from all the literary descriptions of a Roman house is the notion of personalized space: there is virtually nothing to suggest that individual household members had their own rooms (Nevett 1999, 297).

Fishbourne Roman Palace was clearly designed as a single architectural construction; therefore it is legitimate to seek to understand the motivations of the architect. There can be no doubt that the 'looking inwards' of the building was designed to reinforce exclusiveness and exclusion. It was designed to monitor and control people flows and events in the north, east and west ranges and in the internal garden. The latter, with its rigid classical syntax, its geometric divisions, and its control (of plants and vegetation) was a potent reminder to visitors of the control exercised by the owner, offering at the same time a clear contrast between the irregularity and disorder of the outside and the ordered regularity of the inside. In short, the building complex was a mechanism for the control of people and a metaphor for the control of nature.

For the outsiders, approaching the building was like approaching a long, blank wall, broken only by the columns of the entrance hall and the aisled hall. Perhaps the interior would be glimpsed through the columns at the rear of the entrance hall. Such a glimpse was carefully contrived by the design of the building, offering a 'visual transparency'. The vista offered allowed an outsider to see into the heart of the building down the central garden path towards the reception room/dining room, but prevented sight of residents who would have been mostly in the north, south and east ranges of the Palace (Grahame 1997, 163). On other occasions the rear of the entrance hall would have been simply closed off. Neither visual nor spatial access was granted easily, therefore, and the architecture reinforced the separateness of the interior. If granted access, the outsider crossed a threshold into a highly controlled architectural environment, where his movements were carefully predetermined by colonnaded walkways and garden paths. There were few places to walk unseen. For the indigenous outsider the building symbolized the presence of a foreign power; artificial, certainly; powerful, definitely.

The individuals in this building were both constrained by the architecture and spaces they moved in, and capable of manipulating the architectural spaces and getting around these constraints in order to provide outcomes that they desired. The controlling (and enabling) aspect embedded in the overall architectural design must therefore have been emphasized or challenged by individuals, intentionally and unintentionally, producing both desired and unforeseen results. In other words the deliberate elements of control that had been carefully designed in the building at its outset could be employed by a

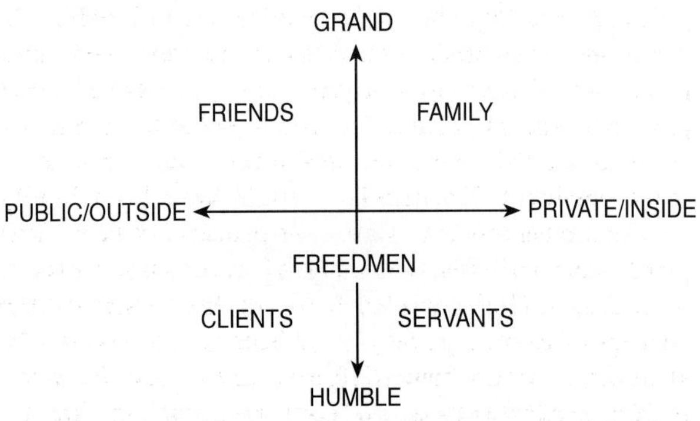

Figure 10.7. *The two principal axes that structured social relations within and without the Roman house (after Wallace-Hadrill 1988).*

variety of occupants in the Palace for their own ends. In this sense the architectural properties of the Palace are analogous to *structure* (organized as rules and resources), which both constrain and enable the situated activities of the powerful *agents*. The duality of *structure* and *agent* governs the continuity or transformation of both the architecture and the social system comprised by the agents (Giddens 1984, 25).

The people that visited (or indeed lived) in the complex regularly can be divided into various segments: the owner himself and his household; fellow nobles and aristocrats; functionaries and bureaucrats; slaves and, of course, the outsiders. The identity of the original owner has, of course, been the subject of considerable, but in the end inconclusive, debate over the years. The case for Togidubnus is likely, but cannot be proven. However, the similarity, albeit on a much larger scale, of Fishbourne Palace to other early villas in coastal Sussex, suggests it is logical to associate the Palace with one of the newly enfranchized indigenous elite in the client kingdom. Given the likely population mix of Roman Britain around AD 75, the slaves were probably drawn from an already Romanized local population, as indeed may have been the nobles and aristocrats. Functionaries and bureaucrats may have been drawn from both British (perhaps freedmen) and non-British (Gaulish or Roman) populations. The remaining category – the outsiders – one assumes were mostly Romano-British, although occasional Roman citizens and foreign embassies may have presented themselves at the Palace.

It is important at this point to elaborate on the Roman concepts of public and private (Wallace-Hadrill 1988). The Roman house was the locus of public *institutional* life as well as private, quite different from late 20th-century European concepts of the house as a largely private arena[6]. In addition, the Roman house was designed to admit, at least into certain areas, the uninvited public as well as the invited (Vitruvius - *Book VI*, chapter V, 1 - Morgan 1960,181-2). The Roman house, therefore, was designed to invite outsiders in, in effect putting the residents on show for both the invited and uninvited public. Fishbourne Roman Palace must have been a working Palace, where much economic and diplomatic business was carried out, as well as a high-status residence.

Residents as well as visitors to a large Roman house, and no doubt to Fishbourne Roman Palace, were structured according to an orthogonal matrix that opposed *grand:humble* and *public:private* (Fig. 10.7, after Wallace-Hadrill 1988, 78). According to this structure the outsiders at Fishbourne Roman Palace would have been acquaintances, clients and other aristocrats and associates. The aisled hall at the north-east corner of the Palace was the ideal place to receive some of these outsiders. The insiders would have been family members, other residents, slaves, and perhaps freedmen, from which some of the functionaries and bureaucrats would have been drawn. Grahame (1999) has further developed the concept of Roman privacy by indicating that it could be structured along two different axes, that between *resident:resident* and a second between *resident:outsider*. This emphasizes the fact that there were varying degrees of privacy and access enjoyed by *different residents* and these variations were structured by the architectural arrangement of the various rooms in the Palace.

However, the spatial details of how such structuring took place are difficult to find. A study of artefact distributions, and activities inferred therefrom, in a group of Pompeian houses indicated that the spatial distribution of activities might be much more mixed than hitherto imagined (Allison 1999). This study came up with the following conclusions:

- there was ample evidence that the front of the house was used for general domestic activities, both seemingly public and private;
- utilitarian activities were not necessarily excluded from formal garden areas, or from richly decorated rooms;
- kitchens (*culinae*) could be used for food-preparation, but formal cooking may have taken place in rooms much closer to where the food was to be consumed;
- both the forecourts (*atria*) and garden areas seem to have been open to visitors;
- formal gardens could also be the setting for domestic activities;
- there was little support for the terms 'main entrance' and 'tradesman's entrance' being applied to Pompeian houses;
- there was little support for stratification by status, gender, age (or any other category) in Pompeian houses (Allison 1999, 350-3).

For the slaves, working in the building must have added a certain status to their lives, with a standard of accommodation that was better than most of their like enjoyed. They may have perceived it as an opportunity for personal advancement through the acquisition of more sophisticated skills or as a vehicle for financial or status gain through the selling or passing of knowledge or favours to outsiders. The institution of slavery was critical to an elite Roman household and was essential for ordinary domestic tasks such as cooking, gardening, hairdressing and doorkeeping, and for more specialized administrative and commercial tasks. The abundance of slaves was an indication of the status of the master. However, even in large houses, separate slave quarters were not necessarily needed for the accommodation of all slaves[7]. Slaves sometimes slept, for instance, in the master's bedroom on a portable wooden pallet (George 1997).

For the owner the building represented status and articulated his loyalty to Rome. It symbolized absolute acceptance of the Roman value system and reinforced the owner's divorce from indigenous conditions. For the Roman rulers of Britain the Palace likewise symbolized the owner's divorce from indigenous conditions. In addition, the barren facades of the structure, and the enclosing ranges of the complex, may have functioned as much to incarcerate and monitor, as to provide accommodation for, the owner and his household.

The building and its occupants, therefore, could in one sense be viewed as a microcosm of Romanization in its most elaborate form. New forms of architecture, new channels and paths of communication, new values, customs and new clothes were displayed to an indigenous population and shared unequally between locals and immigrants. The building provided a controlled environment in which these innovations could be paraded and any resultant tensions between the various occupants could be negotiated.

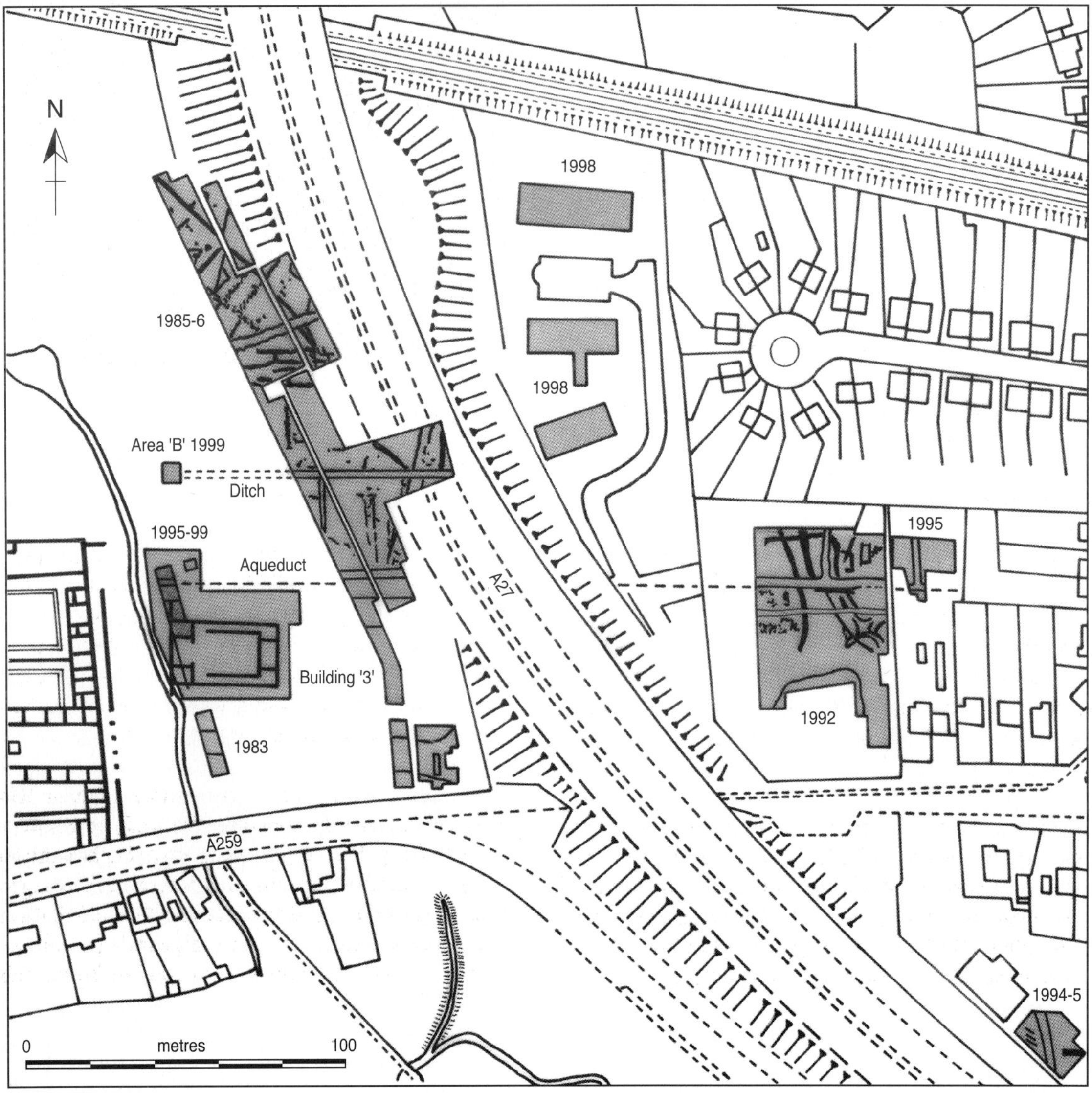

Figure 10.8. The location of all excavations east of Fishbourne Roman Palace (courtesy of Southern Archaeology and York Archaeological Trust). Dates on the map indicate the year(s) the excavations were undertaken.

The complex mixture of people in the Palace could act either collectively, or in the cause of their own particular group. Alternatively, one could act individually, with desired or unanticipated outcomes. Reality probably dictated that each individual held a variety of motivations, sometimes acting one way, sometimes another. A chronological (diurnal, monthly, calendrical) trajectory, with its formal rites and occasions, seasonal celebrations and festivities, imposed another level of control and/or enablement (as well as the architectural) on its participants. At any one time the social interactions and business of the Palace, in all its myriad forms and levels, were therefore conducted in both an ever-changing as well as a uniform environment. The Palace, therefore, became the setting for the sequenced encounters and the seriality of daily life (Giddens 1984, 73), where the routinization of daily activities, such as the morning *salutatio*, the afternoon bathing and the later *cena* (George 1999, 303), were acted out by knowledgeable participants.

Where the controlled environment could have broken down, of course, was in the one unstructured space – the bath-house. This potentially provided a noisy and confused setting where all sorts of information could be passed from individual to individual, although they could also be venues for pomp and display, such as when a master or mistress formally attended by slaves, entered the facility. Almost certainly, control in this environment was provided by temporal constraint on who used the facility. Mixed bathing was offensive to Roman sentiment and specific times must have been allocated for same-sex bathing (Wallace-Hadrill 1988, 51). By limiting the bath-house to certain individuals or groups at certain times, a degree of restraint could be imposed.

Outside the palace

Such was Alec Down's conviction that a semiformal garden lay to the east of the Palace (Fig. 10.8), that he interpreted many of the features he uncovered as elements in that garden. For instance, he located what he described as a series of bedding trenches – linear slots filled with a darker soil. He also uncovered a number of post-hole patterns, some of which

he described as belonging to 'trellis' structures in the garden. Indeed, there is some evidence for overall planning at least dictating the alignment of structures in front of the Palace. Further excavations have been carried out by the Sussex Archaeological Society and the now defunct Southern Archaeology (Kenny 1992, 1995a, 1995b, Kenny and Magilton 1995), revealing many more structures and features to the east of the Palace. These features probably range in date over all four centuries of the Roman period, and therefore it is likely that some post-date the destruction and abandonment of the Palace towards the end of the 3rd century AD. However, some obvious comments can be made at this stage. The area outside the Palace was heavily used, especially to the north of what is presumed to be the main road running westwards from Chichester to the Palace. Most of the remains in this area comprise ditches, pits, and post-holes – the standard elements of most Romano-British archaeological sites. Some of these areas and features can be tied to particular functions. For instance, there is a possible area of metal-working (Fig. 10.8) and there is a main east-west aqueduct, with feeder pipes from the north, that led water towards the Palace. There appears to have been some overall planning outside the Palace in that the major axes for a number of features are north-south and east-west. Indeed there is a timber building (Fig. 10.8) that has an east-west alignment. Some of this planning may relate to the construction of roads on east-west axes in AD 43.

The regularity of these orientations seems to break down to the north of a major east-west ditch (Fig. 10.8) where several features that run north-west – south-east can be observed. The major element of surprise is the recently revealed masonry building (Building 3 – Figs. 10.4, 10.8 and 10.9) that sits just to the east of Fishbourne Roman Palace. This is clearly, as far as we can observe at present, the largest building outside the Palace. While it must be repeated that all these features are likely to be of different dates within the Roman period, their overall layout does suggest that the presence of Fishbourne Roman Palace, and more probably the alignment of the major road leading to the Palace, governed the alignment of features outside the Palace.

Plate 10.10. *The gold signet ring found to the east of Fishbourne Roman Palace. Its mirror-image inscription identifies it as a signet ring of Tiberius Claudius Catuarus; his name indicates he was a new Roman citizen of Celtic origin.*

It is worth commenting on two further points at this stage. From the deposits filling one of the feeder pipes to the main aqueduct (Fig. 10.8; Fig. 10.10) a gold ring bearing the name Tiberius Claudius Catuarus was recovered. This ring has been fully documented by Roger Tomlin (1997). It indicates that the original wearer was an indigenous person to whom citizenship was granted by Claudius or Nero. While the

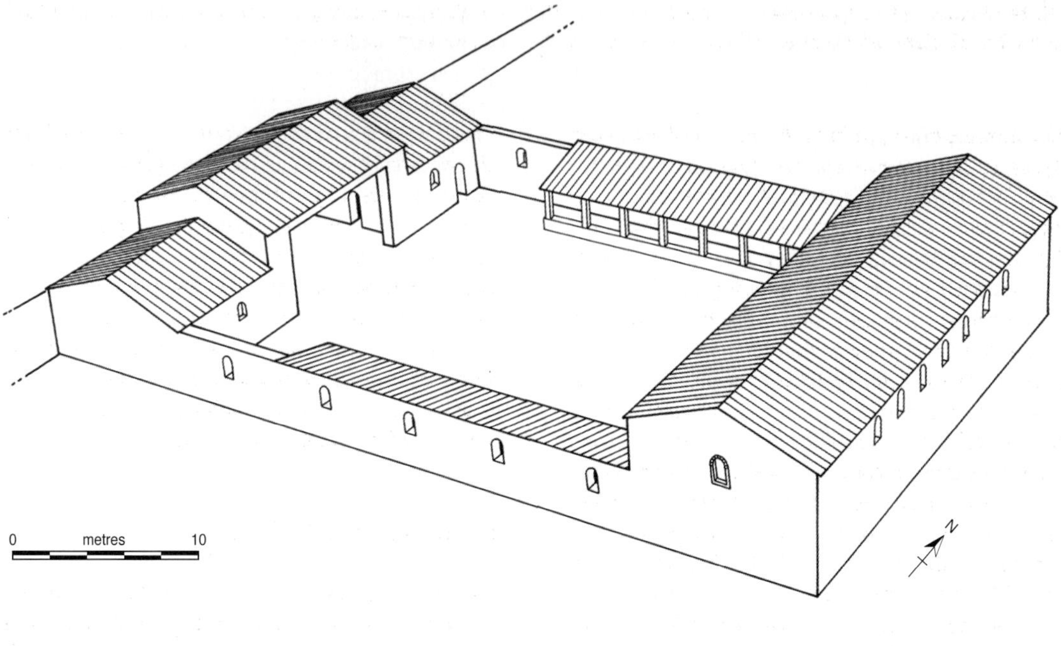

Figure 10.9. *Hypothetical reconstruction of Building 3, from the south-east. Note the 'flanking' walls that extended north and south from the presumed front of the building. These walls were demolished, probably when the stream was diverted at the start of period 1c - c.AD 60. The building, however, remained standing until early in the 3rd century.*

Figure 10.11. View, from the north, of the foundations of the west side of Building 3. The stream that separates Building 3 from the Palace is to the right.

context of discovery tells us little of where Tiberius Claudius Catuarus may have lived or worked, it is possible, as Tomlin suggests, that he may have been a blood relative of Tiberius Claudius Togidubnus. Circumstantially, the discovery of the ring adds weight to the possibility that the site of Fishbourne Roman Palace, at some stage in its development, was associated with the newly enfranchized elite of the client kingdom of the Atrebates.

The second point that should not be overlooked outside the Palace is the fact that when the 'proto-palace' was constructed in AD 60-65, the original stream (further to the west) was canalized into a new channel that ran east of the baths and east of the facade of the later major Palace. While in itself this was a fairly straightforward task for Roman civil engineers, its importance symbolically should not be forgotten. One of the significant ways in which Roman 'civilization' made an impression on indigenous communities, and indeed emphasized its partial control over nature, was through the management of water. In addition, the existence of a small stream in front and outside of the Palace would have formed a clear physical and symbolic boundary that separated the individual from the complex itself. Water had to be crossed for the individual to gain access to the Palace.

It is time to return to the area immediately outside the Palace which is now known to have contained at least one large masonry building (Figs. 10.8, 10.9; Fig. 10.11). Walls of this structure (Building 3) were first located by Down in 1983, but it was the excavations by the Sussex Archaeological Society in 1995-1997 that revealed the complete ground plan of the building. The first point to mention is that the western end (and possibly front) of this building lies within 25 metres of the front eastern facade of Fishbourne Roman Palace. Secondly, the building was laid out around a courtyard. It had ambulatories north and south and a large eastern range or hall divided into three major rooms, with symmetrically placed rooms either side of the entrance in its western wing[8]. An unusual feature of the building are the two flanking walls that ran north and south from the west side of the building. Excavation has indicated that these walls were not secondary, but of the same foundation depth as the walls of the main building. The new masonry building outside the Palace, therefore, belonged to some larger architectural complex or simple walled enclosure, the function and size of which are as yet unknown.

In his Trench C, which uncovered part of the north flanking wall, Down discovered the east-west aqueduct, which he intimated was probably constructed around AD 100 and only abandoned and filled in around AD 260. Recent excavation of a section of the aqueduct by the Sussex Archaeological Society has revealed a substantial quantity of pre-Flavian pottery in the bottom of the feature. This suggests that the aqueduct may have been built closer to the middle of the 1st century AD. Aqueducts were usually constructed to supply water to baths, rather than drinking water. An obvious context for its construction would have been to supply water to the 'proto-palace' baths. It is interesting to speculate on who constructed the aqueduct. Such constructions demanded significant surveying and engineering expertise, especially over the flattish ground such as that to the east of the site, and it is not inconceivable that the complex of main aqueduct and feeder channels was laid out by the military (Trevor Hodge 1995).

As noted above, Down (1983) also located a few post-holes that he claimed were part of 'trellises' in the semi-formal garden outside the Palace. However, according to his published plan (Fig. 10.12), one of these 'trellis' post-holes sits neatly over the filled-in aqueduct. It is therefore highly unlikely that such post-holes related to trellis or garden features and some other explanation must be sought. It is not the intention here to deconstruct Downs' work outside the Palace or to provide an interpretation of the role of the masonry building discovered by him and the Sussex Archaeological Society. The interpretation must await comprehensive publication. Nevertheless, some useful points can be noted here which will add to our understanding about the outside of the Palace and throw additional light on how the approaching individual may have viewed the complex.

The conventional phasing of the Roman site at Fishbourne was established by the Cunliffe excavations. The phase preceding the Palace (Fig. 10.4) was sub-divided into three:

1a Military supply depot *c.*AD 43 – timber buildings 1,2
1b House and Workshop *c.*AD 50 – timber buildings 4,5
1c 'Proto-palace' baths *c.*AD 60-65 – masonry building M2

The Palace phase was simply divided into two major periods:
2 Construction and initial use *c.*AD 75-100
3 Continued use, modifications, and subsequent destruction by fire *c.*AD 100-275.

Based on a preliminary assessment of the stratigraphy and distribution of finds, excavation of the large masonry building (Fig. 10.8) has shown that it would probably best fit into period 1b, was therefore constructed before AD 75, and probably before AD 60. (This assumes that the phasing established by Cunliffe for the Fishbourne site is accepted, and that there are no further phases to be added). The most telling piece of stratigraphic evidence supporting the construction date is that the re-aligned stream (re-aligned in the Roman period before the construction of the baths in AD 60) cuts across the southern flanking wall of the masonry building. In addition, the distribution of finds of Roman date indicate that whereas approximately 2000 finds were located in and over the masonry building, some 7000 were found to the north of its north wall. A cache of pottery on top of the foundations of the northern wall can be dated approximately to AD 200. Finally, a small gully cut through the southern foundations for drainage purposes after the building had been demolished. An almost complete New Forest Beaker of *c.* AD 270-320 lay in this drainage channel. Taken together, these pieces of evidence strongly suggest that the masonry building lasted through more than half of the life of the major Palace, probably being demolished around AD 200. However, one of its main walls was situated only some 25 metres from the eastern wall of the Palace. It is likely that the construction of the *proto-palace baths* began after the flanking walls of masonry building 3 were demolished, but the building itself remained intact and functioning.

The function of the flanking walls is problematic. If Building 3 predated the 'proto-palace' (and was therefore constructed in period 1b, say between AD 50 and 60), the flanking walls would have *hidden* the area occupied by the later Flavian Palace. This area in 1b period was occupied by timber buildings of presumed military and commercial functions, although it must be stated that our understanding of the layout and functions of this space is very partial. Entry to this 'special' area could have been provided by entering Building 3 from the east and passing into this area through its western end. The realignment of the stream, necessitated by the construction of the 'proto-palace' baths required the demolition of the flanking walls. It is possible that the realignment of the stream also provided a symbolic and practical barrier, *replacing* that provided by the flanking walls, separating the 'special' area west of the stream from Building 3 and other areas to the east.

Approaching the palace

What does this reveal about how the individual approached the Palace from the east? The belief that the Palace could have been approached from the east across open ground and through a semi-formal garden is interpreted by modern reconstruction drawings of the setting of the Palace currently on display at Fishbourne. The sterility and 'green-lawn-like' quality outside the edifice suggests a semi-formal garden and

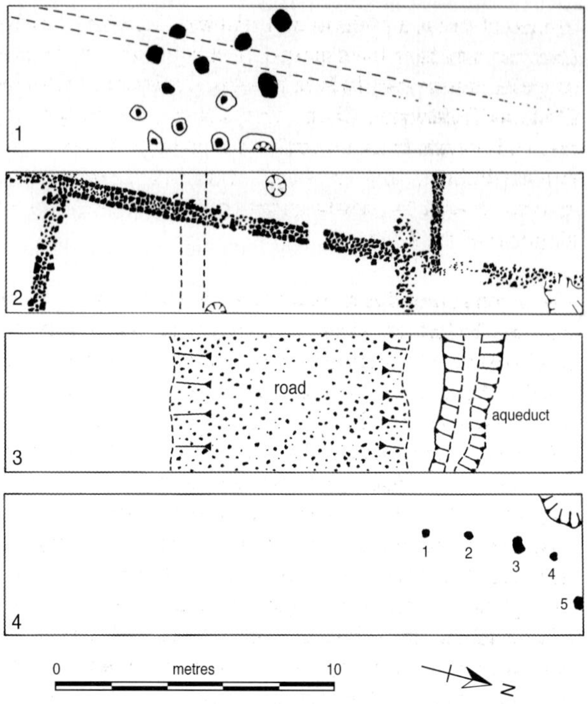

Figure 10.12. *Four phases of activity recorded by Alec Down from the same trench. Note that post-hole 2 (assumed to be part of a garden trellis), in the latest phase, lies over the top of the aqueduct from the previous phase found in the same trench.*

a Palace set in the middle of a green-field estate. The only features conjectured in front of the Palace are trees and well-tended roads and paths. Such a construction owes as much to the lack of information available about the area outside the Palace as it does to any misconceptions.

For someone approaching, say in AD 90, the reality experienced must have been very different. The long eastern facade of the building was never capable of being viewed in its entirety from any distance. Instead, the approaching individual probably looked upon relatively open ground to the south towards the Chichester harbour, but to the north at a completely built-up environment with roads, buildings, fences, aqueducts and a possible metal-working area. The area to the north of the approach road therefore contained people, movement and sound – as well as built structures.

As he got closer to the Palace, the dominant perspective would not have been that of the Palace façade, but that of the exterior of a large hall-like structure the east end of the masonry building outside the palace. The columnar facade of the entrance would have been visible, but not that of the aisled hall. The prominence in visual terms of the masonry building, and its peripheral position just outside the Palace, may also give some clue as to its potential functions. It is conceivable that the building functioned as some sort of shrine, not to the major deities (since offerings would be expected and none have been found), but to the household gods (*lares*) of the residents (Black 1999, 12). A liminal position for shrines is manifest in Roman contexts (*cf.* the temples outside the Balkerne Gate in Colchester - Isserlin 1998, 132). Such a function may have been ideologically exaggerated by the relative austerity in appearance of the masonry building compared with the elegance and architectural flamboyance of the Palace itself. No wall-plaster has been recovered in association with Building 3, suggesting that the structure both externally and internally relied on tile-courses and the interplay of flint and greensand for any decorative relief. There are difficulties with this interpretation, however. Despite completely excavating the area of Building 3, very few artefacts have come from the building, and generally they are unhelpful in suggesting definitive functions. What is clear at this stage is that there is nothing in the artefactual record that looks remotely religious[9].

A more plausible hypothesis is that Building 3 was constructed by the military. In overall size, and in plan form, the building has superficial parallels with military *principiae*. Most notable parallels are with the timber *principia* at Hod Hill and Baginton, the former Claudian, the latter Neronian (Johnson 1983, 129). There are other parallels, none of them exact, with *principiae* in Wales (Jarrett 1969, 158). (It should be noted that there are variations between *principiae*, so that most illustrate some deviation from what was the ideal). Such an interpretation would make the central room in the hall a shrine (*sacellum*) for the standards of the garrison, and the square pit in the eastern range, although not an original feature, a sunken strong room for military pay.

If *principia* is the function of Building 3, it was surely, for most if not all of its life, a headquarters building not for a campaigning army, but rather for a military presence fulfilling basic security and administrative duties. If Fishbourne was the seat, for however short a time, of a ruling client king, then the presence of presumably high-ranking Roman military officers may have been both to support and oversee the actions of a very loyal, but still foreign, supporter. Indeed Togidubnus may have had an army himself. It was common practice elsewhere in the Empire for client kings to possess their own armed forces, even modelling them on those of the militarily successful imperial power (Kennedy 1999, 82), and it might be safer to assume that Togidubnus must have had an army. If so, it must have had need of an administrative building and perhaps Building 3 should be interpreted in that context. When Togidubnus died, and that cannot have been much later than AD 100, Fishbourne Roman Palace may well have been taken back into formal control of the Roman provincial administration. It may have continued in a quasi-governmental role, and Building 3 may have acted in part as a control and security post, vetting entries and exits from the Palace proper.

Once past the masonry building, the visitor was able to cross a series of thresholds to gain admittance to the Palace. The first was the canalized stream, emphasizing the symbolic nature of the area to the west. Second was the threshold, in whatever form it took, leading to the inter-columnar spaces before the entrance and aisled hall. Finally, if the individual's importance warranted further progress, doors could be opened at the end of the entrance hall to allow access to the inside of the Palace with its formal garden. Such control must have underlined the dramatic importance of the path the individual was taking, and the significance of what and who lay within. Visually, the transformation must have been successive and, once inside the Palace, final and absolute as the geometrically constrained tranquillity inside compared with the unregulated clamour outside. In addition, for the visitor, there were transformations in other ways. Outside, he could look around, observe and monitor in all directions. Inside, he became the observed and monitored. Correspondingly his views were circumscribed by the four ranges of the Palace complex. In addition, if the visitor was allowed to reside in the Palace, he or she was immediately confronted with the mosaics of the guest ranges, and the other architectural and decorative wonders of the Palace, such as the extensive and colourful wall paintings. Here the visitor was brought face to face with objects of Roman technical superiority[10]. Geometrical patterns depicted in the mosaics underlined the ideology of control and domination. The Palace in its form between AD 75 and 100, therefore, may have functioned as much as a metaphor for the ruling ideology of 'Romanitas', as a device for both emphasizing to fellow indigenous Britons the benefits of allegiance with Rome and for underlining the loyalty of the newly-enfranchized elite towards their Roman overlords. The architecture of Fishbourne Roman Palace therefore conveyed both physical and ideological messages. For the departing visitor, retracing his steps, leaving the building may have brought some psychological relief.

In conclusion, as the supposed residence of client king Togidubnus, the Flavian building at Fishbourne was indeed a Palace. But it was a *Roman* Palace and clearly was a building that was *inward looking*. It may not have had carefully designed and landscaped approaches from the east, and the visual impact of its eastern façade was clearly obscured by the presence of a large masonry building. There could have been few greater contrasts between outside and inside in 1st-century Roman Britain than that experienced when crossing the threshold of Fishbourne Roman Palace.

Acknowledgements

I wish to thank the Director of Fishbourne Roman Palace, David Rudkin, for his helpful comments on an earlier draft of this paper. I also received considerable assistance from Barry Cunliffe, Ernest Black, Mark Grahame, Mark Hassall and Richard Jones. David Budd kindly prepared the artwork.

End Notes

1. Not all Roman houses supported this ideology, however, and different houses may have given importance to different social identities. For instance, smaller houses made it more difficult for the *paterfamilias* to remove himself spatially (and therefore socially) from his inferiors. (The author is grateful to Dr Mark Grahame for this insight).
2. A lower *relative* status for rooms with pink mortar floors might be suggested given the high number of rooms with mosaics at Fishbourne.
3. If Fishbourne Roman Palace was the residence of Togidubnus then the significances of these symbols and codes would have been known to him, and learnt, during his formative years before AD 43, some of which may have been spent in Rome. How the deeper and correct meanings of such things became known to the 'native' population is an interesting point, but one supposes that a tangible and visible signal (such as a column or a different mode of dress) was the starting point to appreciate *difference*.
4. The similarity of plan in the Southwick villa raises the obvious point about whether the same architect was involved in both buildings. Its similarity also suggests that Southwick (and other rich Early Villas in Sussex) might have been the residences of the lesser elite of the client kingdom (Rudling 1998, 44).
5. Locating quarters for slaves in Roman houses is fraught with difficulties. They may not have had separate rooms, and some may have slept in the same room as their masters (George 1999, 316).
6. Modern private houses are the settings for informal semi-public occasions such as coffee mornings or political meetings.
7. The exact status of many rooms in a villa is made problematic by Pliny's remark that some of the slave quarters in his Laurentine villa were also suitable for guests (*Letters* 2.17.9 - Radice, 1981,76).
8. It is worth pointing out that this is not the only reconstruction possible. An alternative, and equally valid reconstruction, would see a building framed by four corner towers, with lower roof heights between the towers, echoing the facades of some winged-corridor villas. In addition, it is by no means certain that the entrance to the building was from the west. Since the wall foundations showed no breaks at either eastern or western ends of the building, it is possible to argue for either or both ends as entry points.
9. This paper was submitted in May 2001 in advance of the completion of post-excavation studies for Building 3. Statements concerning the functions and associated artefacts of Building 3 are therefore provisional.
10. Superior to those versed in Roman culture but not necessarily to those new to it.

References

Allison, P. 1999. Artefact distribution and spatial function in Pompeian Houses, in B. Rawson and P. Weaver (eds), *The Roman Family in Italy*, Oxford: University Press, 321-54.

Black, E.W. 1985. The dating of relief-patterned flue-tiles, *Oxford J. Archaeol.* **4**, 353-76.

Black, E.W. 1987. *The Roman Villas of south-east England*, BAR BS **171**, Oxford.

Black, E.W. 1993. The period 1C bath-building at Fishbourne and the problem of the 'proto-palace', *J. Roman Archaeol.* **6**, 233-7.

Black, E.W. 1999. Fishbourne - New Thoughts on Society, *Practical Archaeol.* **1**, 10-12.

Clarke, J.R. 1991. *The Houses of Roman Italy 100BC – AD250. Ritual, space and decoration.* Berkeley: University of California Press.

Cunliffe, B. 1971. *Excavations at Fishbourne, 1961-1969*, Vols I & II, London: The Society of Antiquaries.

Cunliffe, B. 1991. Fishbourne revisited: the site in its context, *J. Roman Archaeol.* **4**, 160-9.

Cunliffe, B. 1997. *Fishbourne Roman Palace*, Stroud: Tempus.

Cunliffe, B.W., Down, A.G. and Rudkin, D.J. 1996. *Chichester Excavations* **9**, *Excavations at Fishbourne 1969-1988*, Chichester: Chichester District Council.

Ellis, S.P. 1995. Classical reception rooms in Romano-British houses, *Britannia* **26**, 163-78.

Ellis, S.P. 1997. Late-antique dining: architecture, furnishings and behaviour, in R. Laurence and A. Wallace-Hadrill (eds), 41-51.

Ellis, S.P. 2000. *Roman Housing*, London: Duckworth.

George, M. 1997. Servus and Domus: the slave in the Roman House, in R. Laurence and A. Wallace-Hadrill (eds), 15-24.

George, M. 1999. Repopulating the Roman House, in B. Rawson and P. Weaver (eds), *The Roman Family in Italy*, Oxford: University Press, 299-319.

Giddens, A. 1984. *The Constitution of Society*, Cambridge: Polity Press.

Grahame, M. 1997. *Public and Private in the Roman House: the Casa del Fauno*, in R. Laurence and A. Wallace-Hadrill (eds), 137-64.

Grahame, M. 1999. Reading the Roman house: the social interpretation of social order, in A. Leslie (ed), 48-74.

Henig, M. 1996. A royal portrait head from Fishbourne, West Sussex, *J. British Archaeol. Assoc.* **149**, 83-6.

Hingley, R. 1990. *Domestic Organisation and Gender Relations in Iron Age and Romano-British Households*, in R. Samson (ed), 125-47.

Isserlin, R.M.J. 1998. A spirit of improvement? Marble and the culture of Roman Britain, in R. Laurence and J. Berry (eds), *Cultural Identity in the Roman Empire*, London: Routledge, 125-55.

Jarrett, M.G. (ed) 1969. *The Roman Frontier in Wales.* Cardiff: University of Wales Press.

Johnson, A. 1983. *Roman Forts.* London: Adam and Charles Black.

Kennedy, D. 1999. Greek, Roman and Native cultures in the Roman Near East, in J.H. Humphrey (ed), *The Roman and Byzantine Near East, 2, Some Recent Archaeological Research,* Rhode Island: Portsmouth, 76-105.

Kenny, J. 1992. Fishbourne: Westward House, *The Archaeology of Chichester and District 1992*, 32-37.

Kenny, J. 1995a. Fishbourne Glebe Meadow, *The Archaeology of Chichester and District 1995,* 15-16.

Kenny, J. 1995b. 51 Fishbourne Road East, *The Archaeology of Chichester and District 1995*, 13-14.

Kenny, J. and Magilton, J. 1995. 36 Fishbourne Road East, *The Archaeology of Chichester and District 1995*, 14-15.

Laurence, R. and Wallace-Hadrill, A. (eds) 1997. Domestic Space in the Roman World: Pompeii and Beyond, *J. Roman Archaeol. Supplementary Series,* **22**.

Laurence, R. 1997. Space and text, in R. Laurence and A. Wallace-Hadrill (eds), 7-14.

Leslie, A. (ed) 1999. *Theoretical Roman Archaeology and Architecture*, Glasgow: Cruithne Press.

Morgan, M.H. 1960. (trans), *Vitruvius: the ten books on architecture*, New York: Dover Publications.

Nevett, L. 1999. Perceptions of Domestic Space in Roman Italy, in B. Rawson and P. Weaver (eds), *The Roman Family in Italy*, Oxford: University Press, 281-98.

Pirson, F. 1997. Rented accommodation at Pompeii:the evidence of the Insula Arriana Polliana VI.6, in R. Laurence and A. Wallace-Hadrill (eds), 165-81.

Radice, B. 1981. *The Letters of the Younger Pliny*, Harmondsworth: Penguin Classic.

Riggsby, A.M. 1997. 'Public' and 'Private' in Roman Culture: the case of the cubiculum, *J. Roman Archaeol.* **10**, 36-56.

Rudling, D. 1998. The development of Roman Villas in Sussex, *SAC* **136**, 41-65.

Samson, R. (ed) 1990a. *The Social Archaeology of Houses*, Edinburgh: University Press.

Samson, R. 1990b. *Comments on Eleanor Scott's 'Romano-British villas and the Social Construction of Space'*, in R. Samson (ed), 173-80.

Scott, E. 1990. *Romano-British Villas and the Social Construction of Space,* in R. Samson (ed), 149-72.

Smith, J.T. 1997. *Roman Villas – a study in social structure*, London: Routledge.

Tomlin, R.S.O. 1997. Reading a 1st-century Roman gold signet ring from Fishbourne, *SAC,* **135**, 127-30.

Trevor Hodge, A. 1995. Aqueducts, in I.M.Barton (ed), *Roman Public Buildings*, Exeter: University Press, 127-49.

Wallace-Hadrill, A. 1988. The Social Structure of the Roman House, *Papers of the British School at Rome* **56**, 43-97.

THE POTTERY SUPPLY TO ROMAN SUSSEX

Malcolm Lyne

Abstract

This paper aims to document and explain the nature of, and changes over time to, the supply of pottery within Roman Sussex. A major aspect of the pottery used in both Late Iron Age and Roman Sussex were differences in the supply of pots west and east of the River Adur. In terms of local production the wares produced east of the Adur remained firmly rooted in the Iron Age technology of hand made pottery, whilst that to the west of the Adur was much influenced by the importation of both Gallo-Belgic and Roman wares into initially the Late Iron Age oppidum defended by the Chichester Entrenchments, and subsequently into the Roman town of Chichester (and its hinterland) which replaced the oppidum. The principal reason for those differences in supply is thought to be due to the lack of any significant urban centre in East Sussex for the dissemination of Romanizing influences into the countryside around. Although those differences continued throughout the Roman occupation, they became less marked during the late Roman period, when demand led to the establishment of small wheel-turned Romanized pottery industries in East Sussex. Whilst West Sussex was aceramic by the 420s, the simpler technologies practised by the East Sussex potters enabled limited production of handmade wares to continue into the mid-5th century, coupled with the importation of small amounts of pottery from the Mediterranean world into Pevensey.

Introduction

Roman Sussex can be divided into two strikingly different ceramic zones, west and east of the River Adur respectively. These differences had their origin back in the Late Iron Age when West Sussex lay within a Southern Atrebatic ceramic zone characterized by sand-tempered, sometimes wheel-turned, wares of good quality. East Sussex lay within a somewhat more backward Eastern Atrebatic ceramic zone where handmade grog-tempered wares were predominant.

The territorial oppidum within the Chichester-Selsey area, as indicated by the Chichester Entrenchments, but with any main focus or focii of occupation as yet unlocated, attracted trade with the Continent. Ceramic imports during the early-1st-century AD included fine Roman Arretine and Gallo-Belgic Terra Rubra and Terra Nigra tablewares, the quality of which may have influenced and advanced the technology of the Southern Atrebatic potters supplying the oppidum. Excavations at Fishbourne in 1999 (Manley and Rudkin forthcoming) sectioned a ditch of military appearance containing late Augustan Arretine and Terra Rubra imports: this suggests a Roman military or quasi-military presence on the site as early as *c.* AD 20, which may have acted as a further catalyst for local ceramic development before the Conquest. Terra Rubra and other finewares were also imported into East Sussex, but the lack of any significant proto-urban centre demanding superior quality pottery all but nullified its impact on the native handmade wares of the local producers.

The foundation of the civitas capital of *Noviomagus Regnensium* at Chichester as a successor to the oppidum and initially as the capital of the client-kingdom of Togidubnus, accelerated the process of Romanizing the products of the industries supplying its population and that of its rural hinterland. The continued lack of any equivalent centre in East Sussex resulted in little technological improvement in the native grog-tempered wares of the region other than limited copying of Gallo-Belgic forms.

Early Imported Roman Pottery

Most pre-Flavian pottery imports into the kingdom of Togidubnus came from Gaul: *Terra Rubra* and *Terra Nigra* girth beakers, bowls and dishes, whiteware pitchers and butt-beakers from the Amiens region were shipped into the new town at Chichester *(Noviomagus Regnensium)* in large quantities (Rigby 1978, 190-201, 1989, 109-124). Two Neronian kilns producing Gallo-Belgic as well as local Southern Atrebatic forms were, however, excavated at Chichester in 1971 and indicate the presence of at least one Gallic potter in the town during the period AD 60-70 (Down 1978, 204-209): their imported technology must surely have played a significant role in the Romanization of local Southern Atrebatic pottery industries.

South Gaulish Samian bowls and dishes from La Graufesenque were, however, the most important 1st-century ceramic import. These and much smaller amounts of Montans Samian are found on sites across Sussex, although the greatest form variety is at Chichester and shows it to have been the main port of entry for these wares and centre for distribution (Millett 1980).

Other imports included rough-cast cups and beakers, mica-dusted and glazed vessels and lamps which were imported from Lyons and elsewhere in Central Gaul after being first transported overland to the Seine and then shipped across the Channel with other goods. Any detailed discussion of imported amphorae and their contents lies outside the scope of this paper, but suffice it to say that large quantities of globular Dressel 20s containing olive oil from southern Spain, and amphorae containing wine, fish sauce and other products from Southern Gaul, Spain and Iberia, were imported by sea during the 1st-century and later.

Local Production during the First century

The main concentration of Hardham industry kilns, whose works derived from Southern Atrebatic traditions, lies in the Arun valley, just north of the Downs. Just recently, however, another kiln has been excavated in Littlehampton: I therefore suggest that this industry should be renamed Arun Valley. The siting of the main Hardham/Wiggonholt kiln concentration at a major road junction (Fig. 11.1) led to late-1st-century marketing via Stane Street to both Chichester and London, and east along the Sussex Greensand Way as far as the Ouse valley.

There is a wide range of distinctive Arun Valley pottery forms, some of which clearly have their origins in the Late Iron Age Southern Atrebatic tradition. Whether these pre-conquest forms indicate early manufacture in the Arun Valley is uncertain, but it seems more than likely. The Romanized Iron Age forms included distinctive grey-ware girth-carinated cooking-pots and fine-ware versions (Fig. 11.2: 1, 2) and jars with stubby everted rims (Fig. 11.2: 3). Flanged bowls with deep, horizontal external rilling were a distinctive new post-conquest form (Fig. 11.2: 4) as are compass-scribed and combed Dragendorff (Dr.) 37 and 29 copies, beakers and bottles in a micaceous black-surfaced fine-ware. Fine red colour-coated wares imitating South Gaulish *Terra Sigillata* bowl forms, but with rouletted decoration were also made (Winbolt 1927, Plate 11), as were cream-ware flagons, honeypots, mortaria, funnels and other forms (Evans 1974).

The early Rowlands Castle industry (Fig. 11.1) shared the bulk of the Chichester coarseware market with the Arun Valley kilns. Some tournette-finished jars in a fabric very similar to the distinctive high-fired grey-ware characteristic of Roman Rowlands Castle products, but with more flint inclusions, came from Late Iron Age contexts at Hazel Road, North Bersted, and suggest an early origin for this industry as well.

Much smaller quantities of Northern Atrebatic grey-wares from the Alice Holt/Farnham kilns were supplied down the Silchester to Chichester road during the late-1st-century, and unusually large numbers of otherwise rare Alice Holt grey-ware lagenae fragments from Fishbourne Palace suggest that this trade may have been associated with the supply of a liquid commodity such as wine.

The continuing handmade and clamp-fired Iron Age character of most Eastern Atrebatic wares from east of the River Adur has been convincingly argued by Green (1980, 82-85) to be due to the lack of an urban centre in the area to Romanize the surrounding countryside and provide a market. The production of such wares may have taken place on coastal salt-production sites and Wealden iron-working ones: both industries ensured a regular supply of briquetage and fired clay for filler. There are indications for both early East Sussex Ware and salt production at Bishopstone and Newhaven at the mouth of the River Ouse (Bell 1977, 92, 155; Fig. 11.1).

Late 1st century assemblages from the Beddingham Roman villa further up the Ouse valley (Fig. 11.1; *see* also paper above by David Rudling) are dominated by handmade East Sussex wares, although small, but significant, quantities of superior wheel-turned Arun Valley coarse-grey and fineware products were imported, as were tiny amounts of Rowlands Castle, Alice Holt and Upchurch greywares from even further afield (Fig. 11.3).

The collapse of the South Gaulish Samian industry at the end of the 1st-century gave a boost to fine-ware production by the Arun Valley industry. It is possible that the lead-glazed vessels from the St Pancras cemetery in Chichester (Down and Rule 1971, Pl.14, 15 and 16) originated in the Arun valley. A glazed, ovoid, bead-rimmed beaker, in particular, is of a form associated with that industry.

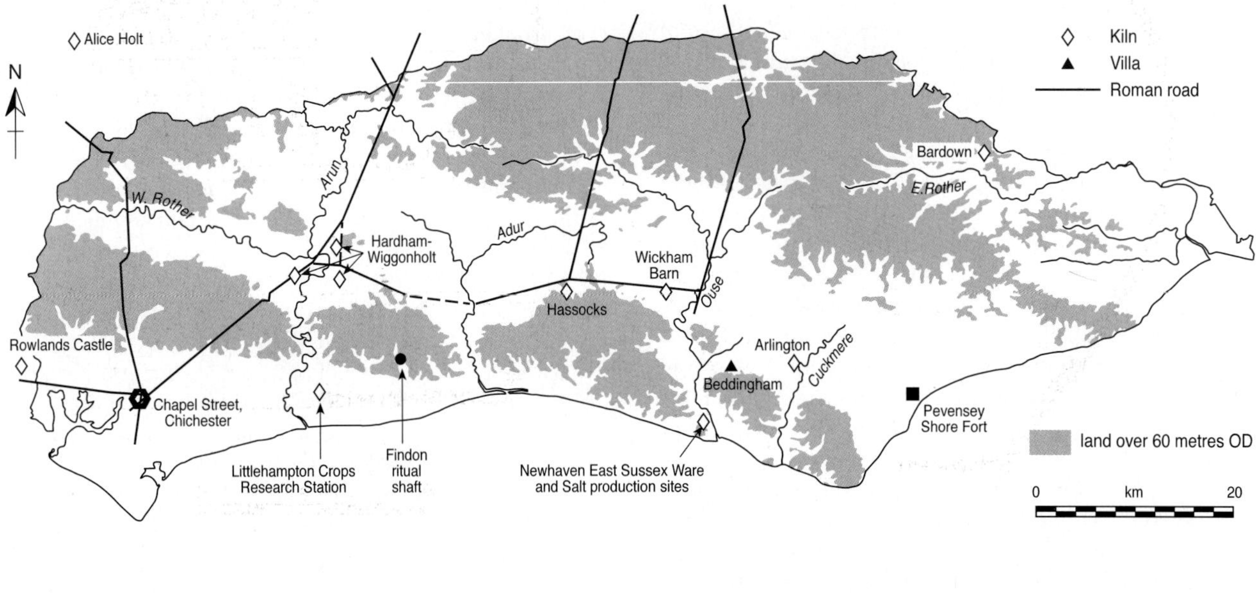

Figure 11.1. *Map to show the locations of local pottery kilns and other important sites mentioned in the text.*

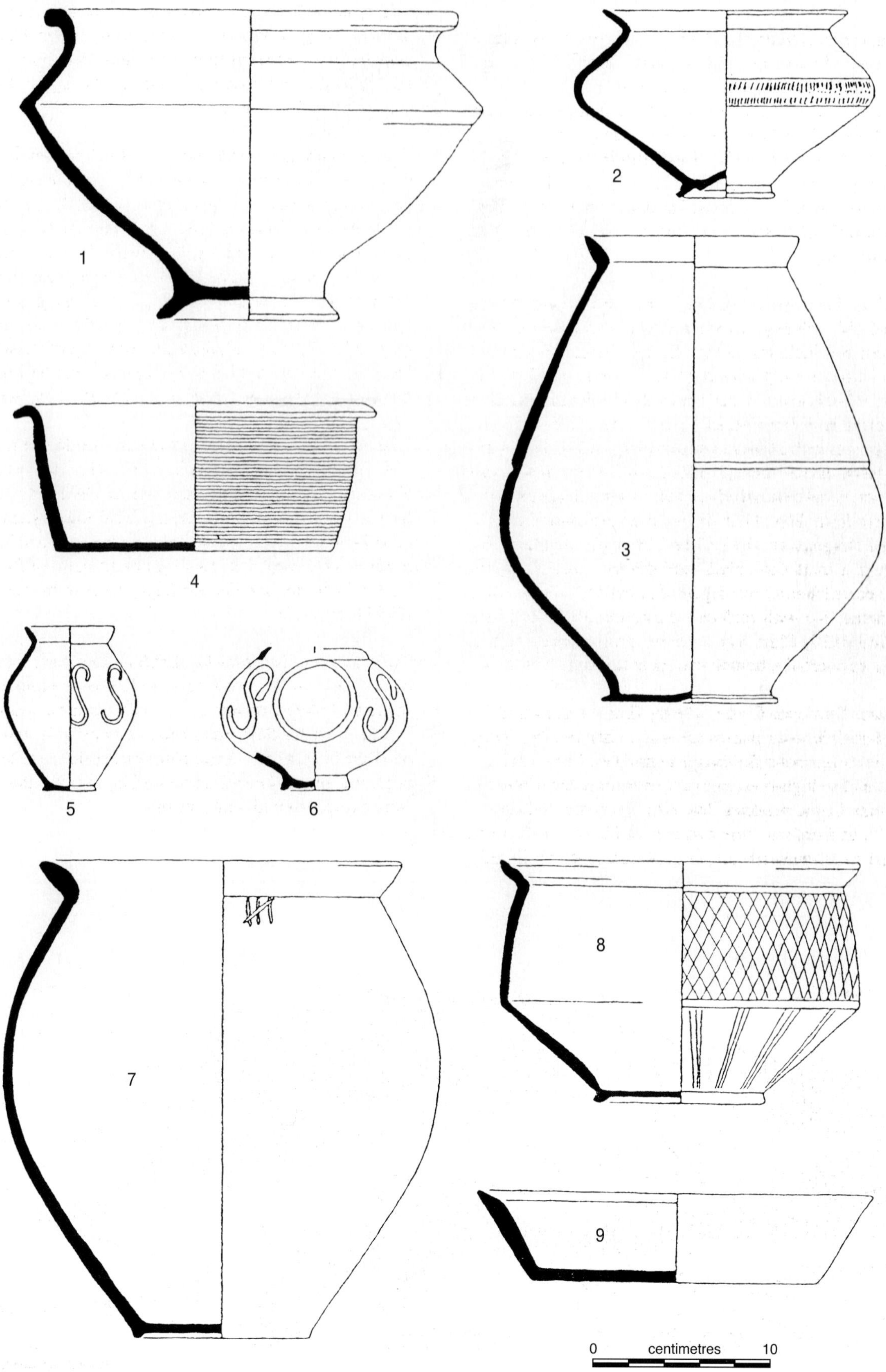

Figure 11.2. *1st – early 3rd century pottery forms.*

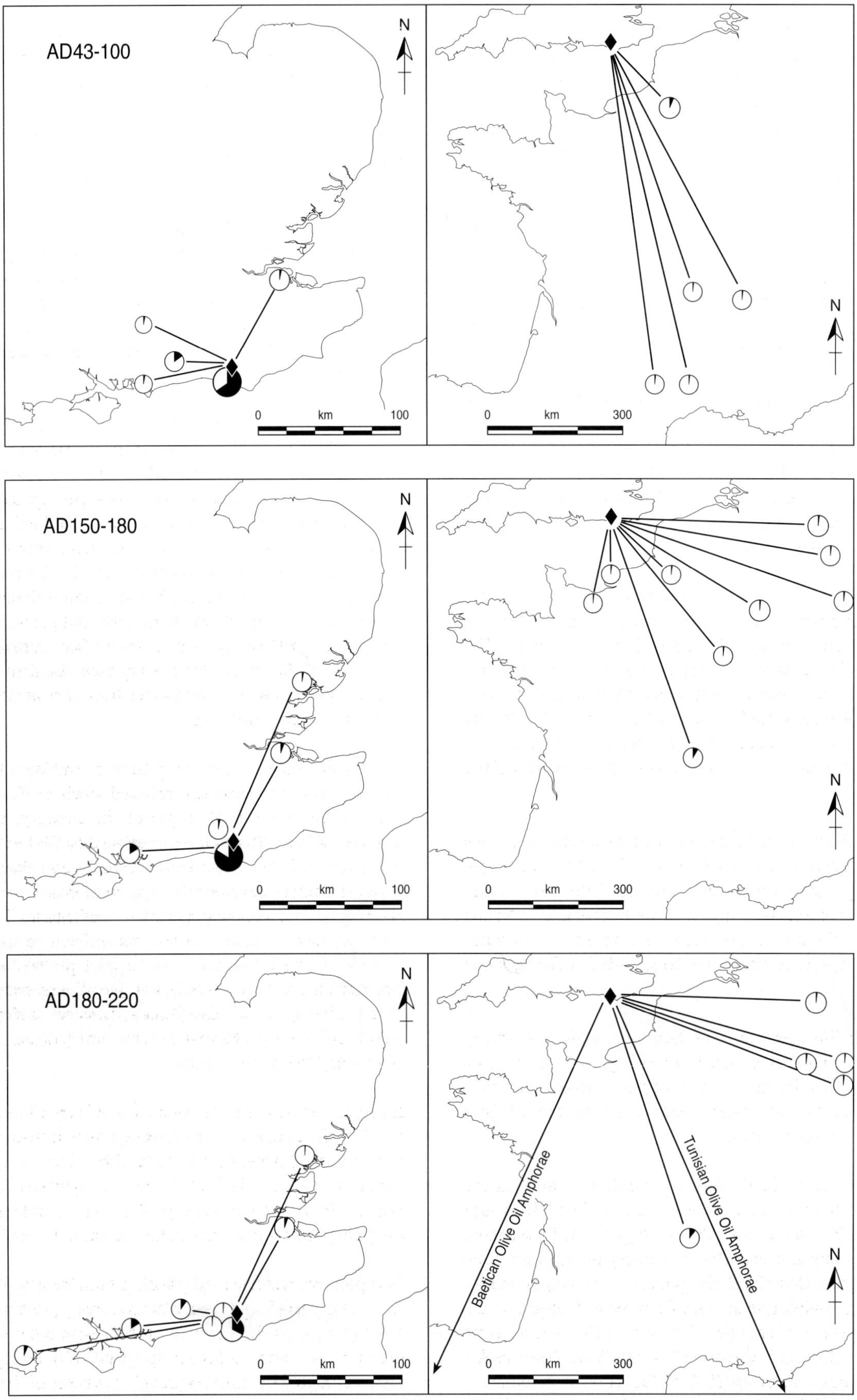

Figure 11.3. *Sources of pottery supplying the Beddingham villa during the periods AD 43-100; AD 150-180 and AD 180-220.*

Second-century Pottery

Real, but rather carelessly finished Samian ware was made at Pulborough in the Arun valley during the early 2nd century: the potter made use of old Central-Gaulish moulds, some of which were found at Borough Farm during the 19th-century (Simpson 1952). Products have been found across Sussex, at Silchester, St.Albans and in London, but their scarcity suggests that the industry was very short-lived.

Central Gaulish Samian only became significant after AD 120 and enjoyed a widespread distribution in Sussex during the later 2nd-century. Small quantities of rough-cast Argonne, Sinzig and Cologne bag-beakers and hunt-cups were also imported into Sussex during this period, as was East Gaulish Samian from Rheinzabern and Trier.

A fine-ware potter somewhere in mid-Sussex produced unusual poppy-head beakers. An example found at Wiggonholt was decorated SSSSSSS in barbotine (Fig. 11.2: 5; Evans 1974, Fig. 15-140), another from Hassocks SOSOSO (Fig. 11.2: 6; Lyne 1994a, Fig. 9-59) and yet another from the Beddingham villa, was decorated with Ss separated by diamond-shaped barbotine dot panels.

The early-3rd-century saw the collapse of the Arun Valley industry after which the Chichester coarseware market was largely taken over by Rowlands Castle products. The characteristic Rowlands Castle jars with stubby everted rims and scored batchmarks are accompanied by carinated bowls with reeded-rims, straight-sided dishes (Fig. 11.2: 7-9) and ceramic beehives, and together account for up to half of all coarse pottery present in assemblages from sites west of the Arun.

Handmade East Sussex Ware from various sources continued to dominate coarse-ware markets east of the Adur during the 2nd-century, with few typological changes. Pottery production at the Bardown iron-working site, near Ticehurst, is indicated by wasters. The wasters include wheel-turned cordoned jars of Kentish type, deep dishes, and handmade East Sussex Ware forms.

East Sussex Wealden ware was the pottery made and used by most of the iron-workers and lacks variety: Stane Street, as a trade route used by the Arun Valley and Rowlands Castle potters, formed an effective barrier to the circulation of these wares in the west of Sussex.

East Sussex Downland Ware was probably made in the Newhaven/Seaford area as a continuation of Iron Age production. It is characterized by an altogether wider and more Romanized late-2nd-to early-3rd-century range of products and dominates Downland site pottery assemblages east of the Adur. Antonine assemblages from the Beddingham villa have such wares accounting for up to 80% of the coarse pottery, but Rowlands Castle and Dorset Black Burnished 1 (ie BB1) wares make up 39% of the Severan assemblage recovered from deposits associated with the construction of a well, and appear to have partially supplanted the local native pottery by 220. This may not be the full story, however.

Third-century Pottery

Two early-3rd-century cremation pots from the Hassocks cemetery are very unusual. The first of these vessels is handmade and its profuse filler consists of angular fragments of crushed ironstone, some so large that they project from both interior and exterior surfaces of the pot (Lyne 1994a, Fig. 4-23). The second vessel is a handmade pot of much better quality, but is very fussily decorated with rudimentary lug-handles (Lyne 1994a, Fig. 2, Gp. 2: 3). It was clearly made by someone with expertise in working clay, but not in mass-producing pottery. The crushed tile filler suggests that it was produced at a tilery as a sideline. These pots and crude 'homemade' sherds from other sites seem to point to a 3rd-century shortage of pottery in East Sussex, which could not be entirely remedied even by increased importation of wares from surrounding areas.

Dorset Black-burnished Ware (BB1) has the widest distribution of all Romano-British coarse-wares. Large quantities were supplied to military establishments in the highland zone from c. AD 120 onwards, perhaps as part of a supply contract also involving grain and salt. Similarly large amounts are also present in mid-3rd-century pottery assemblages from newly-walled towns in the south-east, including Chichester, and may be associated with the transfer of northern garrisons during those unsettled years. Evidence for the seaborne supply of Black-burnished ware along the Sussex coast during the 3rd-century takes the form of large percentages of pottery assemblages from sites at the mouths of the rivers Arun and Adur.

Three successive 3rd-century pottery assemblages from the Beddingham villa show that reduced levels of East Sussex Ware were supplied throughout the century, and that Rowlands Castle Ware had been replaced by BB1 before 250. The supply of BB1 to the west of Sussex and elsewhere in lowland Britain was normally geared to bowls and dishes, but cooking-pots are predominant at Beddingham. Most 3rd-century pottery industries were rather deficient in open forms and it may be that the ability of the BB1 potters to provide large quantities of such vessels was one of the secrets of their success. Here, in rural East Sussex, however, a shortage of all types of pottery led to more varied supply demand for and supply of, BB1 pattern forms.

BB1 was partially replaced by a local imitation between 250 and 270: these copies are good enough to have been made by a migrant BB1 potter (Lyne 1994b, 256). The last quarter of the 3rd-century saw both BB1 and its copyist supplanted by pottery from a wide variety of sources, reflecting the increasing inability of local potters to meet demand.

This problem was effectively dealt with at the new Pevensey shore-fort. Local East Sussex Ware is scarcely present in early-4th-century deposits: the bulk of the coarse pottery is from greyware producing kilns set up specifically to supply the fort, although BB1 made up nearly a quarter of the pottery present.

The New Forest potteries owed their initial success to the large-scale manufacture of purple-colour-coated beakers.

These are present in virtually every mid-late 3rd-century Sussex pottery assemblage and, like BB1, were probably supplied by sea.

A deep ritual shaft at Findon near Worthing (Fig. 11.1) contained large quantities of pottery of the late-3rd to early-4th-century pottery as well as some prepared potters' clay. Wares include imitation East Gaulish Samian, an imitation Oxfordshire parchment-ware bottle, bag-beakers in a version of New Forest purple colour-coat with surface blisters, handmade BB1 imitations and coarse copies of Alice Holt grey-wares with white-slip decoration. Finally, we have Rowlands Castle style cooking-pots. We may be dealing with the products of a skilled temple potter making votive vessels which copied the various types in local circulation.

The importation of fine pottery from the German limes by sea to Sussex and elsewhere in Britain continued after the end of Central Gaulish Samian and colour-coat supply around AD 200. Rheinzabern Trier Samian and dark metallic colour-coated beakers from the Moselle region were imported into Sussex in limited quantities: the latter as drinking vessels accompanying barrels of wine. The sheer variety of German fine-ware imports at the Beddingham villa suggests that one of the ports dealing with shipping from the Rhine and Meuse at this time was at the mouth of the Ouse (Fig. 11.3). An abnormal number of Amiens region pentice-beaker fragments from the same site indicates that some ships were also trading out of the Somme to East Sussex during the late 2nd and early 3rd centuries.

This Continental trade was severely curtailed by barbarian hordes crossing the Rhine and sacking the cities where the pottery was manufactured: ceramic trade with Sussex ports nearly ended for the next 100 years, although early-4th-century imports are occasionally found on sites. This curtailment of ceramic trade with the Continent is clearly seen at the Beddingham villa, where the only import of the period AD 270-350 is a greyware jar with handle from the Pas-de-Calais or Picardy immediately across the Channel (Fig. 11.4) (*see* also the known sources of 4th century pottery to the farmstead site at Bishopstone – Green 1977, Fig. 80).

Two kilns of New Forest type were recently excavated at Wickham Barn by the Sussex Greensand Way (Fig. 11.1; Butler and Lyne 2001). The products have a wide distribution east of the Adur, but are never more than a minority component in any late-3rd-to early-4th-century assemblage. Kiln 2 is the earliest and produced mainly jars (Fig. 11.5: 1-3) and necked bowls (Fig. 11.5 :4-6) in gritty, wheel-turned fabric. Incipient-beaded-and-flanged bowls (Fig. 11.5: 7-11), dog-dishes (Fig. 11.5: 12), beakers (Fig. 11.5: 13-18) and flagons of 3rd-century types (Fig. 11.5: 19) were also produced in small quantities.

It is interesting to note that there is now evidence that pottery was produced at the three points along the Sussex Greensand Way where the north-south routes of Stane Street and Margary's Roads 150 and 14 intersect it (Fig. 11.1). The siting of pottery industries at road junctions would have greatly benefited the distribution of their outputs (the evidence from Hassocks takes the form of two obvious wasters of probable 2nd-century-date recovered during sand extraction).

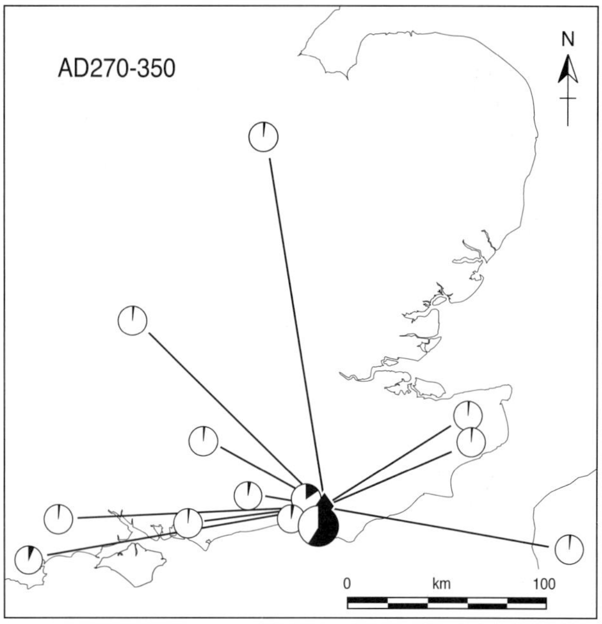

Figure 11.4. *Sources of pottery supplying the Beddingham villa during the period AD 270-350.*

Fourth- and Early-Fifth-century Pottery

The beginning of the 4th-century saw a greatly intensified marketing of Alice Holt pottery in south-east Britain. This coincided with the production of larger numbers of open forms than had previously been made, but these open forms did not normally outnumber cooking-pots. London and Chichester are two major exceptions to this rule: the earliest 4th-century assemblages there have more Alice Holt bowls and dishes than jars and may be an example of a successful manoeuvre to seize these key urban markets by adopting the marketing strategy of the BB1 potters. The success of the Alice Holt industry may have been aided by the use of some of its storage jars and flagons as packaging for local commodities, such as wine and honey (Lyne and Jefferies 1979, 57).

The Wickham Barn potters may have adopted a similar strategy: Kiln 1 is of early-4th-century date and differs from Kiln 2 in having a wider range of vessel forms associated with it. Developed beaded-and-flanged bowls and dog-dishes (Fig. 11.6: 6-12) are as significant as cooking-pots (Fig. 11.6: 1-5), and there are flagons and beakers of 4th-century types (Fig. 11.6: 15-16). Kiln 1 also seems to have been engaged in the production of mortaria, of a type identical to New Forest parchment ware Type 106, and in very similar fabric (Fig. 11.6: 17). The presence of these mortaria, of imitation purple-colour-coat beaker sherds and the kiln type, indicate connections between the Wickham Barn and New Forest potters.

During the late-3rd-century there was a switch in the production of East Sussex Ware in the Ouse valley to rural sites on the South Downs between Brighton and Shoreham. Large and extremely crude Thundersbarrow-type storage jars from this area are common after 350. There was a significant East Sussex Ware revival at Beddingham and elsewhere in East Sussex during the early years of the 4th century (Fig. 11.4). A further great increase in the importance of such wares

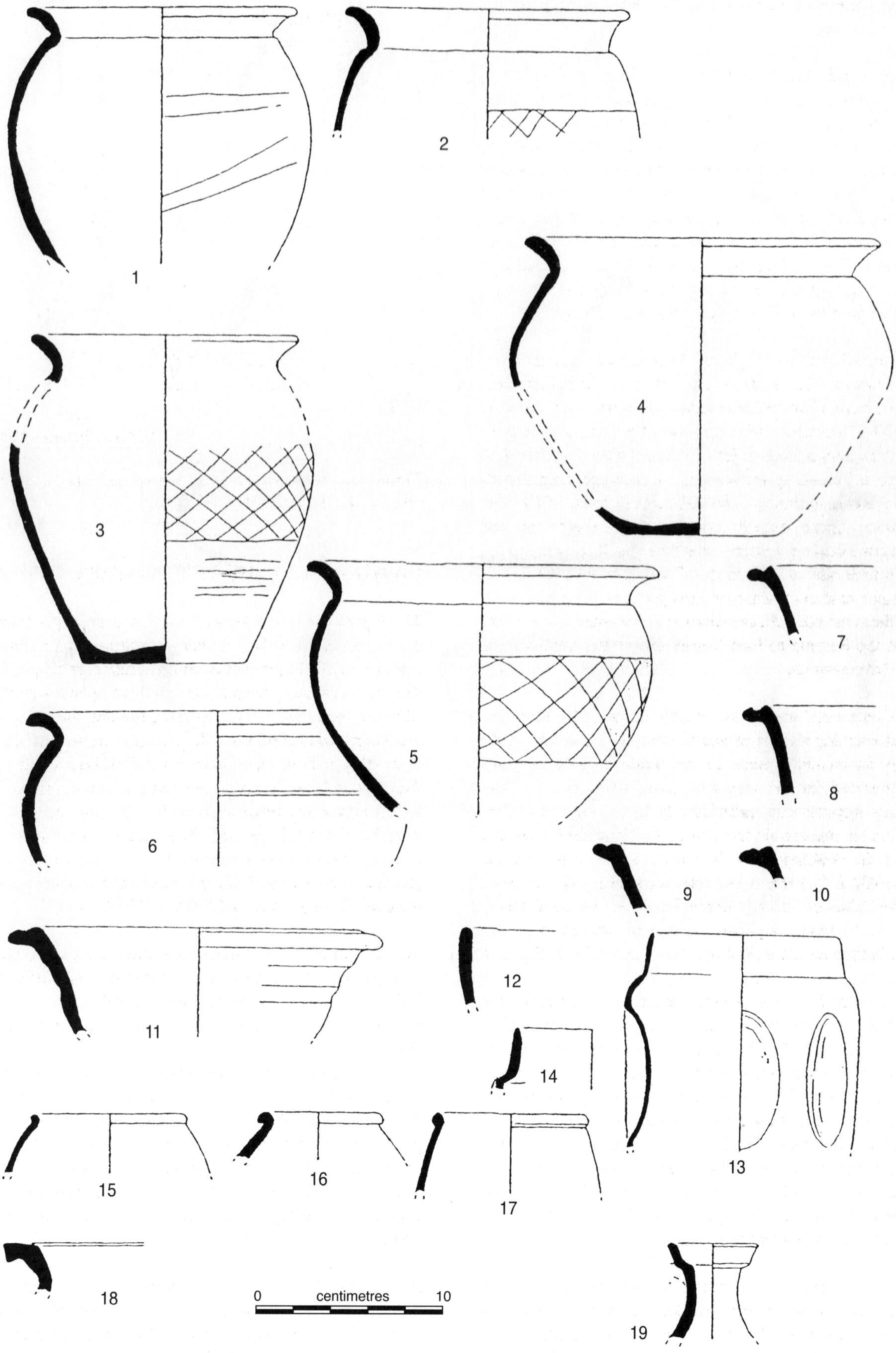

Figure 11.5. *Late 3rd century products of Kiln 2, Wickham Barn, East Sussex.*

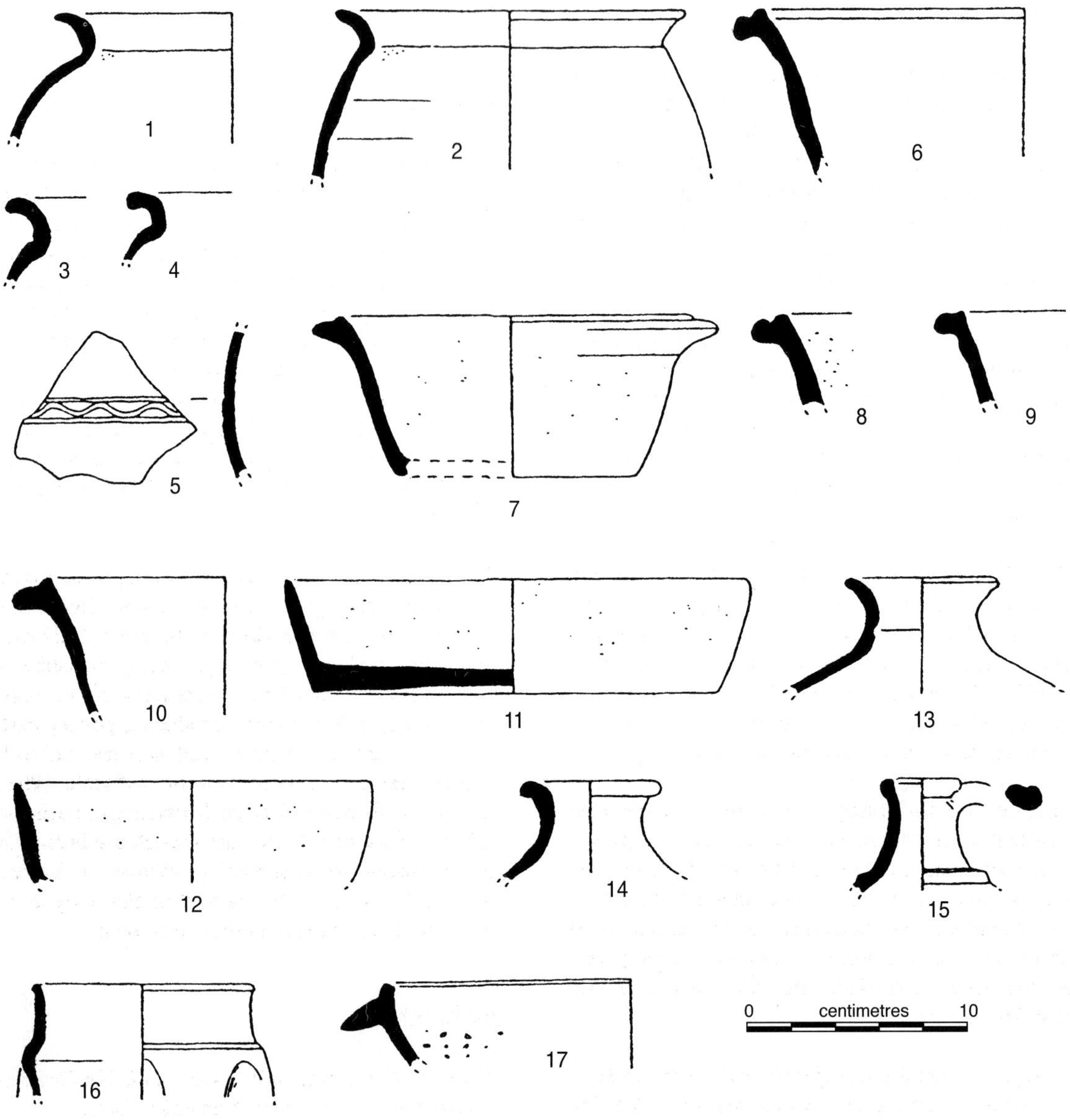

Figure 11.6. *Early 4th century products of Kiln 1, Wickham Barn, East Sussex.*

took place after 370: quantified pottery assemblages from East Sussex suggest a new production centre at, or near Pevensey, where pottery assemblages of post-370 date are very largely made up of local East Sussex Ware and Alice Holt products.

The importance of handmade grog-tempered wares also increased in Kent and the Hampshire Basin after 370. Peacock has pointed out that in recent times wares of this type were produced by part-time household industries in economically depressed areas when the main occupation was incapable of providing a living by itself (Peacock 1982, 18 and 88).

All of these industries producing grog-tempered ware were situated on or near the coast, and the economic deterioration implied by their increased importance after 370 may either reflect the ravages of Saxon pirates, the added burden placed on local populations in having to provide the shore-fort garrisons with an *annona,* or some other factor as yet undetected.

It appears that after 370, although there were fewer industries, their wares were distributed more widely than ever before. Nearly all of the wheel-turned greywares are from the Alice Holt kilns, and colour-coated finewares and mortaria are mainly Oxfordshire products.

The Alice Holt distribution area continued to expand into the earliest years of the 5th-century, yet the latest Alice Holt kiln waste dumps tend to be smaller and more scattered than earlier ones (Lyne and Jefferies 1979, Fig. 11.2). A transect made across the early 4th-century Alice Holt pottery distribution zone shows a steady reduction in percentage shares of pottery assemblages away from the kilns. Two exceptions to this steady decline are London and Chichester, where Alice Holt percentages are abnormally high and suggest supply to *negotiatores* within these towns for local marketing.

Transects through the late-4th to early-5th-century Alice Holt distribution zone suggest that the industry had ceased to supply *negotiatores* in London and Chichester and it may be that the apparent maintenance of its core distribution area masks much reduced sales of all pottery. The appearance of a wide peripheral zone where the pottery was traded much more thinly can also be seen in the post-370 marketing area of the kilns producing shell-tempered ware at Harrold in Bedfordshire (Lyne 1994b, 511). This industry's main marketing zone extended no further south than London, but most post-370 pottery assemblages from sites in Kent, Sussex and Hampshire have just one or two jars from this source. This pattern of pottery distribution is one which would fit with a situation of both falling demand and production. Such a situation could have led to pottery salesmen having to travel further to sell a smaller quantity of goods.

The fall-off in demand may not have applied to military establishments. At some time after 350 a new industry was set up at, or near, Pevensey producing copies of stamped and painted Oxfordshire red-colour-coat bowls and other forms (Fulford 1973). Pevensey itself has yielded most examples of this ware, but small amounts are found as far west as Portchester, and as far east as Ickham in Kent.

Continuing demand for pottery at Pevensey and the other shore-forts led to a revival in the importation of continental wares after 370: Argonne Samian and lid-seated Mayen ware cooking-pots from the Eifel are most common, but there are also German marbled ware flagons and other wares of as yet unknown origin. The occasional examples of late imported wares at Chichester and rural sites in Sussex may have been distributed from Pevensey.

Overwey-type horizontally-rilled jars in buff to cream fabrics appeared in Sussex during the second quarter of the 4th-century and became more common after 370. As the distribution is very random with no well-defined centre, they appear to have been made by itinerant potters. One cluster of pottery assemblages with high percentages of Overway-type jars is in East Sussex: this and the presence of unusual forms and fabric variants suggests local manufacture somewhere on the edge of the Weald, north of Brighton. Itinerant potting would have been one way of coping with a more scattered and thinner market: industries producing wares of Overwey/ Portchester D type were amongst the last to disappear and probably lasted through the first quarter of the 5th-century.

As a result of the collapse of the monetary economy, the organized manufacture of Roman pottery largely ended during the second decade of the 5th-century. There is evidence, however, of very limited production of handmade grit-and-grog-tempered wares of the poorest quality at Pevensey into the mid-5th century. Amounts are very small, but one or two sherds are known from Bullock Down (Beachy Head) as well, including a sherd with wyrm stamps of Germanic character (Rudling 1982, Fig. 52-150). Sub-Roman Pevensey also imported a few Palaeochristian wares from Southern Gaul, and the presence of a fragment from a 5th-century Macedonian grey-ware bowl (Anderson-Stojanovic 1992, 66; Lyne 1999, 284) indicates the maintenance of tenuous trading links with the far-off Aegean.

Conclusions

The ceramic distinctions between the western and eastern halves of Sussex can be seen to have persisted throughout the Roman occupation, although both wheel-turned kitchen ware and fineware pottery suppliers, such as the Alice Holt/ Farnham and Oxfordshire industries, had acquired a considerably greater share of markets east of the Adur by the Late-4th century than similar, Romanized industries during the early Roman period. This blurring of the distinctions between the two halves of the county can also be seen in West Sussex, where handmade, grog-tempered wares, this time from coastal Hampshire and the Isle of Wight, were present for the first time after *c.* AD 300, but in insignificant quantities.

It is interesting to see that there is little or no evidence for Sub-Roman pottery manufacture in West Sussex after 410-420, whereas in East Sussex the more technologically backward handmade pottery producing industries seem to have weathered the collapse of the monetary economy more successfully and continued producing pottery east of the Cuckmere and at Pevensey well into the mid-to-late 5th century, albeit on a much more limited scale. Whether the reason for this survival lay in the making of such wares as a sideline to the more important sea-salt production industry, in the simplicity of the technology involved, or is due to some other factor, such as the survival of Pevensey as a British stronghold and market, remains to be seen.

References

Anderson-Stojanovic, V.R. 1992. *Stobi, The Hellenistic and Roman Pottery*. Princeton: University Press.

Bell, M 1977. *Excavations at Bishopstone, SAC* **115**.

Butler, C. and Lyne, M. 2001. *The Roman Pottery Production Site at Wickham Barn, Chiltington, East Sussex,* BAR Brit. Ser. **323**.

Down, A. and Rule, M. 1971. *Chichester Excavations 1.* Chichester: Phillimore.

Down, A. 1978. *Chichester Excavations 3,* Chichester: Phillimore.

Evans, K.J. 1974. Excavations on a Romano-British Site, Wiggonholt,1964, *SAC* **112**, 97-151.

Fulford, M. 1973. A Fourth-Century Colour-Coated Fabric and its Types in South-East England, *SAC* **111**, 41-44.

Green, C. 1977. The Roman Pottery, in M. Bell, Excavations at Bishopstone, Sussex, *SAC* **115**, 152-178.

Green, C. 1980. Handmade Pottery and Society in Late Iron Age and Roman East Sussex, *SAC* **118**, 69-86.

Lyne, M.A.B. 1994a. The Hassocks Cemetery, *SAC* **132**, 53-85.

Lyne, M.A.B. 1994b. *Late Roman Handmade Wares in South-East Britain,* PhD thesis, University of Reading. Unpublished.

Lyne, M.A.B. 1999. The End of the Saxon Shore Fort system in Britain: new evidence from Richborough, Pevensey and Portchester, *Proc. of the 17th International Congress of Roman Frontier Studies*, Zalau, 283-292.

Lyne, M.A.B. and Jefferies, R.S. 1979. *The Alice Holt/ Farnham Roman pottery industry*, CBA Res. Rep. **30**.

Manley, J. and Rudkin D. Forthcoming. Excavations at Fishbourne, 1994-1999.

Millett, M. 1980. Aspects of Romano-British pottery in West Sussex, *SAC* **118**, 57-68.

Peacock, D.P.S. 1982. *Pottery in the Roman World*. London: Longman.

Rigby, V. 1978. The Early Roman Fine Wares, in A. Down, *Chichester Excavations* **3**. Chichester: Phillimore, 190-203.

Rigby, V. 1989. The Roman Imported Fine Wares, in A. Down, *Chichester Excavations* **6**, Chichester: Phillimore, 109-124.

Rudling, D.R. 1982. The Romano-British Farm on Bullock Down, in P. Drewett, *The Archaeology of Bullock Down, Eastbourne, East Sussex: The Development of a Landscape*, Sussex Archaeological Society Monograph **1**.

Simpson, G. 1952. The Aldgate Potter: a maker of Romano-British samian ware, *J. Roman Stud.* **42**, 68-71.

Winbolt, S.E. 1927. Excavations at Hardham Camp, Pulborough, April, 1926, *SAC* **68**, 89-132.

ECONOMY AND LANDSCAPE CHANGE IN POST-ROMAN AND EARLY MEDIEVAL SUSSEX, 450-1175

Mark Gardiner

Abstract

Between the end of the Roman period and the late 11th century, when Domesday Book was compiled, the population of England dropped considerably. The decline in population was marked by a retreat of settlement and agriculture from the slopes of the South Downs to the valleys. Fields cultivated in the Roman period reverted to pasture. Two periods of economic activity are identified. During the first from 450-900, settlements were largely self-sufficient, drawing on resources from different regions of Sussex. From 900 onwards agriculture was increasingly commercialized. Markets developed to trade agricultural and industrial goods. Sussex failed to develop one central town, but by 1100 had a multiplicity of urban centres. It is argued that this was the result of the fragmentation of power, a feature which affected Sussex throughout the whole of the period examined.

Introduction

It is conventional to divide the medieval era in England into two parts, the Anglo-Saxon period before 1066 and the later medieval period after. The Anglo-Saxon period is further subdivided into convenient 200-year blocks, Early, Middle and Late. Whatever value this periodization might have for the examination of some aspects of the past, these divisions have very little relevance to the subjects discussed in this paper. The Norman invasion had little impact upon the English economy which was already set upon a course of rapid change and the tripartite division of the Anglo-Saxon period does not relate closely to phases of economic change.

The present study seeks to outline a new view of the economy and changes in the landscape in the context of Sussex which cuts across the conventional chronology. It combines a study of the landscape and its use with an examination of the development of the economy. Two periods may be identified. The first begins after the collapse of the monetarized Roman economy at the beginning of the 5th century and extends until about 900. The second covers the first stage of the growth of the medieval commercial economy from about 900 and extends until about 1175. The latter date is chosen since the inflation of the late 12th century brought about a number of changes, including the development of demesne agriculture and was followed by a period of very rapid economic growth in the early 13th century. These two phases from 450 to 900, and 900 to 1175 are called here the Post-Roman and Early Medieval periods.

The emergence of the commercialized economy in England has been one of the major themes of historical research in the last decade (Britnell 1996; Miller and Hatcher 1995). The subject has obvious connections with the long-standing interest of archaeologists in the re-emergence of towns and the growth of trade in the Middle Ages, but in many respects the thinking of historians has leapt ahead. No longer is it necessary for excavators of individual towns to search for the particular factors which led to their growth. It is now clear that the whole economy of England was growing, and towns established in the 11th and 12th centuries were planted in a very favourable environment. The impact of commercialization was not limited to the towns. The developing trade from 900 onwards was based upon the sale of agricultural produce, often in small markets. As the urban population grew, the demand by those with no access to land for food and other goods also increased. The countryside was progressively drawn into production of agricultural goods for the market so that by the late 13th century, when it can be clearly identified in medieval accounts, lords, and probably peasants too, were growing crops not directly for their subsistence but for sale.

If the period 900 to 1175 is distinguished by the development of commercialization, then the period 450 to 900 is notable for the absence of significant levels of trade. Roman coins ceased to reach Britain in any numbers after 411 and the widespread clipping of coins in the final phase of use suggests a collapse in authority which would have otherwise prevented that problem. Clipping would have rapidly destroyed the acceptability of the coins, and by about 420 it is probable that Britain ceased to be a coin-using economy (Esmonde Cleary 1989, 139-41; Burnett 1984). Barter, tribute and gift-exchange were the most common means by which goods were transferred in the following centuries, but there is little evidence that even through these mechanisms significant quantities were exchanged (Grierson 1959). For example, most pottery found in Sussex before about 900 was probably produced by households to supply their needs and perhaps those of their neighbours. The methods of production implied by the pots themselves and the variability of fabrics suggests numerous small-scale manufacturers of pottery.

Population change

It is difficult to examine either landscape change or alterations in the economy without outlining first the very considerable changes which took place in the population in the second half of the 1st millennium. However, while it is clear that the population probably declined in the post-Roman period and was growing in the Early Medieval period, it is difficult to make more precise statements. We may compare the fairly reliable figure for England based on the figures of Domesday Book of 1.5 million in the late 11th century with the population estimate given for Roman Britain of 4 to 5 million in the first half of the fourth century (Hooke 1997, 66-7, 87). Even if we allow for the population of Wales and Scotland included in the second of the figures, it is apparent that the population declined very considerably. Furthermore, there is fairly good evidence that the population in the late 11th century was rising, suggesting that it had been lower still in the preceding centuries. The implication is that the population had fallen very dramatically in the post-Roman period.

The gap between the 4th-century and 11th-century population levels has usually been filled with plagues and catastrophe, but there is little hard information. Gildas, once a much cited source, but whose historical stock is now considered to be almost valueless, was keen to fill post-Roman Britain with numerous plagues and other disasters (Sims-Williams 1984). Bede's *Historia Ecclesiastica* is rather more specific, mentioning, for example a plague in 664 which began in southern Britain and then spread to Northumbria (*HE* 3.27) and another, evidently of the late 7th or early 8th century, which afflicted Britain, but miraculously spared the monastery at Selsey (*HE* 4.14; Thacker 1995, 108-9). But even this more detailed information does not provide the sort of material from which a population history can be constructed.

Paradoxically, the best evidence for population change may be the landscape itself. Fieldwork in many parts of England has indicated the extraordinary density of Roman settlement sites, even on some of the poorest and most intractable soils. Field-walking on the claylands of north-west Essex, for example, has identified a density of 1.3 settlements per square kilometre in the later 4th century (Williamson 1984, 228). The widespread character and the density of sites suggests that most of lowland England was under cultivation during the Roman period. Some of the corn grown may have been exported or have gone to pay the *annona* or tax, but there must have been a very considerable rural population to work such a large area of land. The numerous 'Celtic' fields on the Sussex Downs, which are found even on thin soils on steep slopes and on areas of heavy Clay-with-Flints, suggest a high population density, a view supported by the traces of Roman farmsteads found in the area (Holleyman 1935; Drewett 1978, 74-6). The slopes of the Downs had been denuded of much of their soil well before the Roman period and the flint-strewn fields cannot have been very productive for agriculture. The two complimentary techniques, the examination of lynchets on the lower sides of fields and the study of soil in the valley bottoms which had been washed off the hillslopes, provide a way of measuring the agricultural activity. Drewett (1982, 213) and others have shown through the excavation of lynchets and field survey that Bullock Down, near Eastbourne, was extensively cultivated during the Roman period. A section cut by Bell across a dry valley on Bullock Down identified a sorted flinty deposit which he suggested had been laid down during a single storm event. He indicated that such material might only have been mobilized if there was extensive arable agriculture (Bell 1983, 213, 127; Allen 1991).

Studies of the Downs have confirmed the view that there was a change in economy and land-usage in the late Roman or early Post-Roman period. Arable cultivation ceased around the end of the Roman period and did not return until around the 13th century at Bullock Down (Drewett 1982, 213). At Bishopstone the 5th- and 6th-century Anglo-Saxon settlement was constructed over former fields, which molluscan samples suggest had reverted to pasture (Bell 1977, 271). Anglo-Saxon activity, probably from the period 450 to 700 on the evidence of the pottery, was identified in a valley section at nearby Itford Bottom, but little colluvium had been deposited during that period implying that the agricultural regime was pastoral rather than arable (Bell 1983, 140). Comparable work at Chalton just over the county boundary in Hampshire suggests that intense arable cultivation did not resume there until the 11th century (Bell 1983, microfiche 36; Bell 1989, 280). Thus the Sussex evidence suggests changes in the land-use of chalkland similar to those recorded in Oxfordshire. In both areas the higher areas of the downland gradually reverted to pasture and in some places woodland developed (Hooke 1987 135-7).

The change in usage of the Downs is also marked by a withdrawal of settlement from the slopes and hilltops into the more fertile valleys. The evidence for this is less clear than it might be, since a greater number of Post-Roman sites are known from the downland slopes and hilltops than from the valley floors. However, excavations at Botolphs near Bramber showed that valley-floor sites may be buried under considerable depths of later medieval colluvium (Gardiner 1990, 241). Consequently, sites in these positions have been much more difficult to find than those on the thin soils of the top of the chalk and the presently known distribution pattern is unlikely to be representative. Chance finds of pottery in work, such as at Itford Bottom mentioned above, in the valley sections along the line of the A27 Brighton bypass (Wilkinson *et al.* 2002) and at Steyning at the foot of the Downs (Gardiner 1988, 55, 59), are indicative of wider occupation on the better soils, on the lower slopes where water might be more readily obtained. Certainly by the Early Medieval period downland settlements were almost entirely located in the valleys and the higher land was used for pasturing stock (Welch 1985, 21-2).

The Post-Roman Economy

It has already been noted that by 420 coins had gone out of circulation and there is little evidence for significant levels of trade until about 900. That conclusion is not contradicted by the recent discovery of the Patching hoard which shows that some coins were still reaching England in the mid-5th century (White *et al.* 1999), or by the gold solidus of Valentinian III dated to *c*.450 from within the walls of Chichester (Down 1974, 33). We must presume that such trade as did occur operated at the level of gift-exchange and barter. Finds from Saxon graves suggest that there was a movement of brooches within southern England and from continental Europe (Welch 1983, 163-75). The level of trade may have increased from about 700 onwards, when a number of ports were established in Kent and to the west of Sussex at *Hamwic* (Southampton). Sussex, however, lacked the close association which Kent had with the Franks and the Merovingians (Wood 1983), or the power which allowed the kings of Wessex to establish a port at *Hamwic*, lay out a boundary ditch and construct a series of roads (Yorke 1989; Andrews 1997). The only place in Sussex identified as a possible port is Pagham, where the presence of a number of sceattas (coins), together with rather slight historical evidence, might indicate a landing place (Metcalf 1984, 52; Munby 1984). The speculation that this might have been a trading centre has not yet been substantiated by a close study of excavated remains from work within the last few years at Becket's Barn and the nearby churchyard. However, the results of the 1974 excavations at Becket's Barn did not support the identification as a trading site. Evidence was found of a cobbled path which ran out

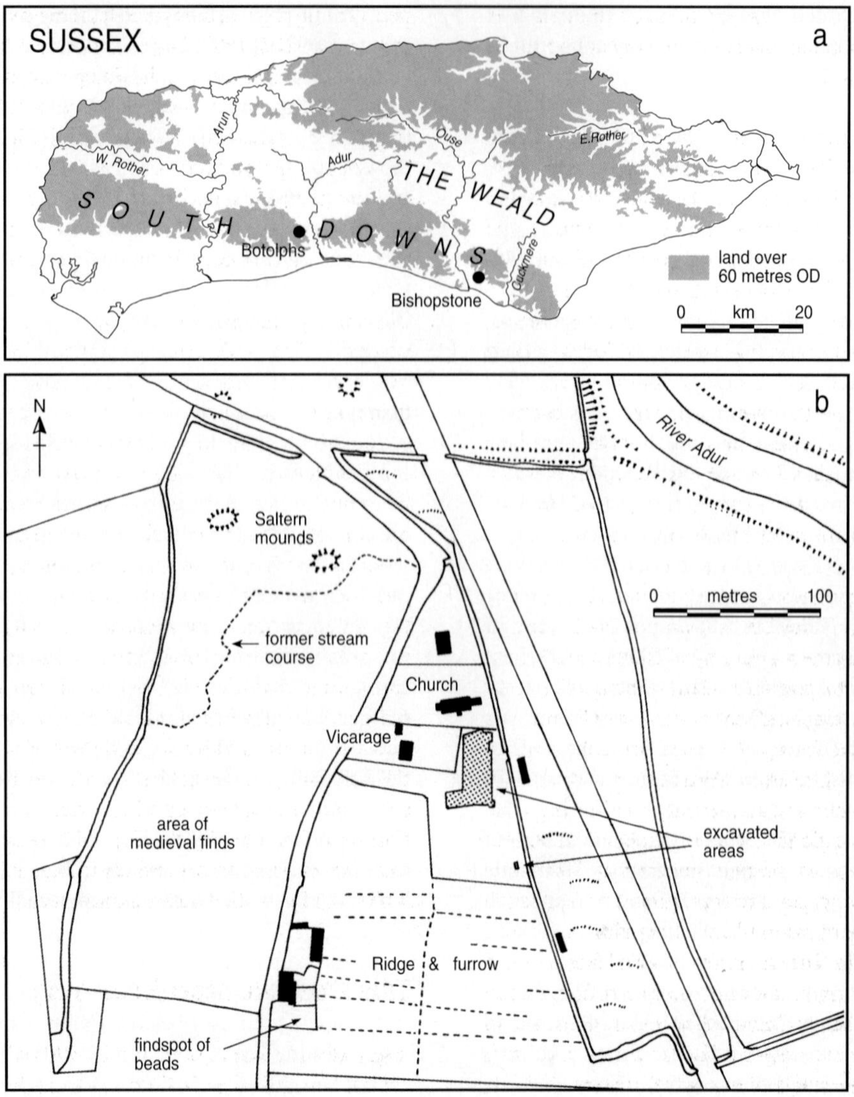

*Figure 12.1. **(a)** The location of the settlement of Bishopstone and Botolphs and **(b)** the setting of excavation within the Adur valley.*

into Pagham lagoon. The path was partially overlain by a midden containing locally-made pottery, but no imports were recognized (Gregory 1976).

More substantial conclusions may be drawn about the domestic economy of post-Roman settlements. Estates of this period normally included a variety of land-types. The better soils provided land for arable, the poorer soils were used for pasture, the wet valleys for meadow and the woodland for timber, firewood and grazing. The diversity of resources on which settlements were able to draw is evident from the archaeological record. Excavations on the sites of Bishopstone and Botolphs both indicate that these settlements were able to get access to resources over a considerable distance (Fig. 12.1a).

The settlement of Bishopstone, which dates from the 5th to 6th centuries, stood on a chalk ridge overlooking the estuary of the River Ouse. Only about one third of the area of the settlement was excavated, suggesting that it might have comprised a total of about 60 buildings. It is improbable that all of these were occupied simultaneously. Re-consideration of the finds suggests that one of the excavated houses, discovered by chance in a small trench cut to the south of the main area of excavation, probably belongs to the 7th or 8th century (Drewett *et al.* 1988, 270). Bishopstone may well be an example of a *Wandersiedlung,* or wandering settlement. The focus of many settlements of this period gradually shifted as old buildings were demolished or fell into disrepair and new ones were constructed on adjoining sites. Over a period of time the focus of the entire hamlet might change position (Hamerow 1991). The form of the Bishopstone settlement, although constructed over former Roman fields and ditches, does not seem to have been influenced by these earlier features.

The main evidence for the economy must be taken from the excavated 5th- and 6th-century buildings (Table 12.1). Impressions of barley found in the pottery suggest that that crop was grown, presumably on fields near the settlement. In addition to cattle, sheep and pigs, geese and fowl were kept. Shellfish were gathered from the coast, and conger eel and whiting were caught at sea. The presence of deer bone suggests that hunting was practised. The majority of the pottery from Bishopstone came from clay which seems to have been dug in the Weald (Bell 1977).

The evidence from the late 5th- or early 6th-century settlement at Botolphs in the Adur valley is similar (Fig. 12.2). The site lies in a valley in the Downs very close to the floodplain of the Adur which at that date was a broad estuary. The site is further from the open sea than Bishopstone, but sea shells suggest that these were gathered from the coast. A piece of whale bone is unlikely to have come from a hunted cetacean, but was probably stranded in the estuary or on the coast. Hunting is indicated by red deer bone. Clay was gathered from the Weald some miles to the north to make pottery, and stone from the same area was used for querns (Gardiner 1990).

Temporary sites were established by the home settlements, such as Bishopstone and Botolphs, in peripheral areas as part of the strategy of resource procurement. The archaeological evidence for such temporary settlements is not considerable, since they were by their nature ephemeral, but two sites may be identified which may have served this function. A single sunken hut set in the silted ditch of a prehistoric oval barrow found high on the Downs near Marden was interpreted by the excavator as a shepherd's hut (Drewett *et al.* 1986; Drewett pers. comm.). That suggestion seemed even more probable when subsequent work failed to find any further trace of activity of Saxon date in the vicinity (Down and Welch 1990, 221). The second place identified as a temporary base for resource procurement was a 9th-century iron-working site found at Millbrook on Ashdown Forest. The character of exploitation is suggested by a number of characteristics of the site. Iron was being smelted on a small scale. The slag was not tapped from the furnace but remained in the bottom until it had cooled. It would have been necessary to dismantle the furnace, at least in part, to remove the bloom. Almost all the processes of iron-working were evidently being practised in one small area: charcoal was burnt for fuel, there was a furnace for smelting and a hearth for either forging or compacting the bloom. Only the hearth necessary for roasting ore was not found. There was no evidence for an adjoining settlement. The presence of pottery tempered with water-rounded flint indicates contact with the Downs to the north or south, and indeed may have been brought by those living nearer the chalk who were seeking small quantities of iron (Tebbutt 1982).

The historical evidence from Sussex for the economy of the Post-Roman period is very poor by comparison with that from the adjoining kingdom of Kent. The charters from this period for the most part concern land lying to the south of Chichester and do not provide abundant evidence of the landscape. A grant of 692 mentions three separate estates at Lidsey and Aldingbourne, *Lenstedegate* which is possibly Westergate and Mundham, each with a value of about 10 hides (Sawyer 1968, 45). Other estates in the area were less highly valued. Nunna, the king of the South Saxons gave 4 hides at the unidentified place called *Herotunun*, 3 hides at the unknown *Tættæshamstede* and 3 hides at Sidlesham (Sawyer 1968, no. 42). One reason for the number of grants of land in the Chichester region was the proximity of these estates to Selsey, the centre of the Sussex diocese.

The historical evidence for the rest of Sussex is slight. It is, however, possible to draw some inferences from the evidence of topography, the documentary record and by analogy with the practices in the adjoining areas of Kent. It has already been noted that the resources of the Weald were integral to the economy of the settlements lying near the coast. The older view that the Weald was a trackless waste, the furthest recesses of which were only penetrated in the 10th or 11th century is not sustainable (Salzman 1931, 23-4). It seems highly improbable that settlers advanced progressively further and further into the heartland of the Weald, as Witney (1976, 74-6, fig. 7) has suggested for Kent. He concluded that the border between Sussex and Kent was drawn through the Weald along the line in the woodland at which herdsmen from the two counties met. The line of the county boundary indicates that this is very improbable. The boundary with Kent follows a series of watercourses - the Kent Water, River Medway, the Teise, the Bewl, the Kent Ditch and finally the River Rother (Fig. 12.3). It leaves these streams and rivers only briefly to cross the watersheds separating those watercourses which drain northwards into the Medway and eastwards to the Rother. The boundary between Surrey and Sussex presents an interesting contrast. It follows a line of ridges from the east of Haslemere as far as Gatwick, deviating only where it crosses the valleys of three tributaries of the River Arun.

The boundaries with Kent and Surrey, therefore, both follow well-defined natural features which would have been readily identifiable, even in an area which was not intensively used. These boundaries are unlikely to have been defined in an *ad hoc* manner on the ground by groups of pioneering wood-folk. They appear to have been agreed by the people of Sussex with, on the one hand, the kingdom of Kent, and on the other

Table 12.1. *Diversity of Resource Exploitation in 5th- and 6th-century Sussex*

	Bishopstone	**Botolphs**
Hunting	Red deer and antler from roe deer	Red deer
Fishing	Conger eel and whiting (caught from boat)	No fish, but fragment of whale bone (found on foreshore)
Sea shell	Mussels, also periwinkle and oysters	Small number of oysters and mussel
Pottery	84% of pottery made from Wealden clay source	Some pottery made on site. Three out of 12 fabrics made from Wealden sources
Stone	Beach pebbles	Wealden sandstone querns; non-local pebbles used for whetstones

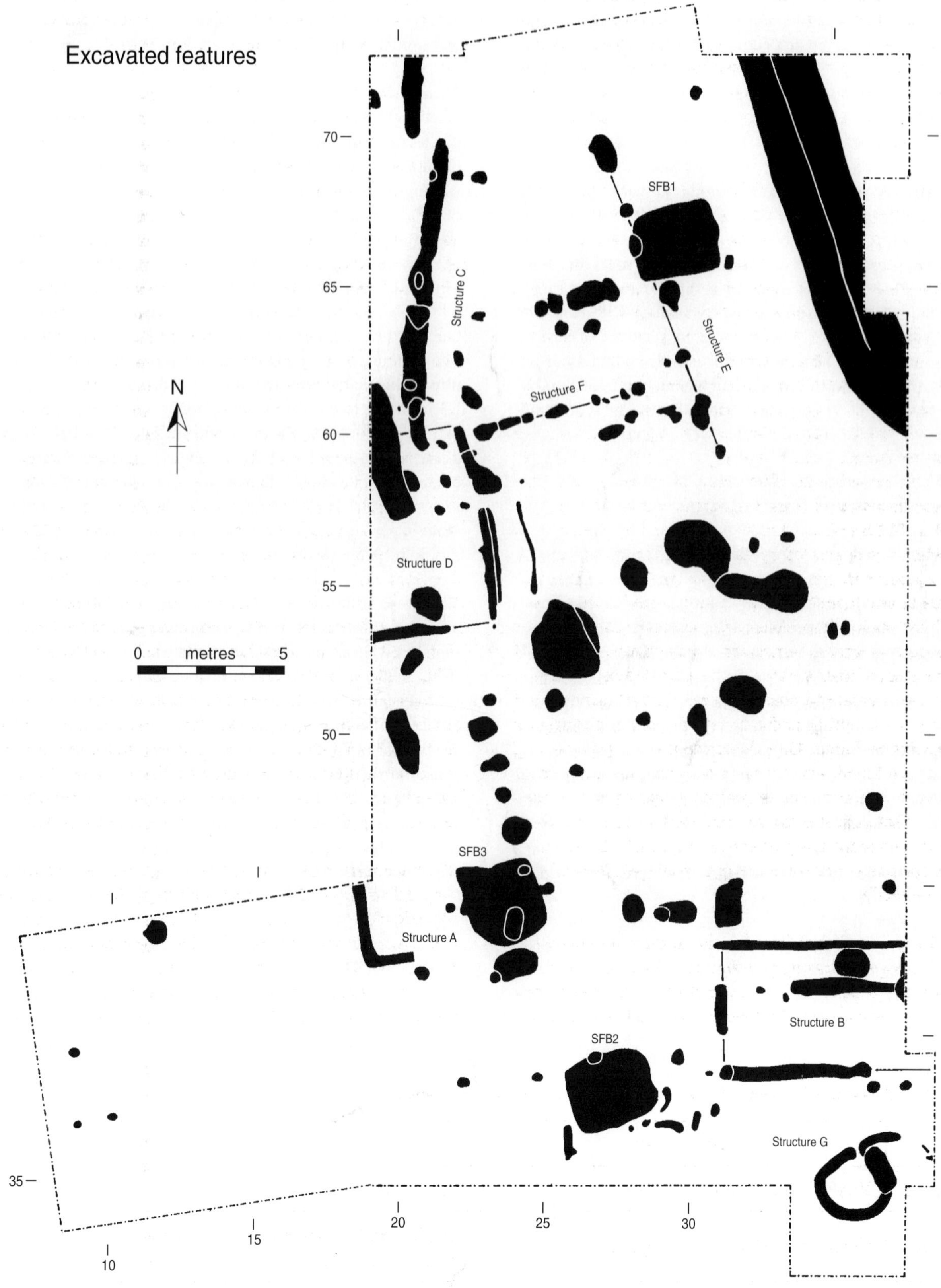

Figure 12.2. *The 5th-/6th-century and late 10th-/11th-century settlements at Botolphs, Bramber, West Sussex. The earlier phase is represented by the sunken-feature buildings (SFB 1-3) and the later by Structures A-G.*

with Surrey, the *Suthrige* or southern region of the Middle Saxons. The boundary may have been established along this line by the mid-8th century, when a charter of the estate of Stanmer records lands extending northwards as far as Burleigh in Worth. It is unfortunate that the charter only survives in a 13th-century copy and incorporates some 11th-century interpolations, including, perhaps, the reference to Burleigh (Kelly 1998, 103-6).

We may conjecture that the Weald of Sussex was divided into a series of strips in a manner similar to that of Kent, and perhaps of Surrey (Brooks 1989, 67-84: Blair 1991, 12-24). These regions may have been similar to, but were certainly not the same as, the rapes or administrative districts recorded in Domesday Book in the late 11th century. The rapes partitioned Sussex into five areas. By analogy with Kent we may suggest that the settlements in the coastal areas of Sussex had common rights of pasture in the corresponding areas on the Weald to the north. Such arrangements are indicated by some Saxon charters which mention 'dens' or woodland pastures

Early Medieval Landscape

During the course of the 10th century Sussex appears to have undergone a fairly considerable change. A rising population led to increasing division of the land, large-scale industrial production started and towns began to develop for the first time since the Roman period. The population growth was clearly an important factor, though industrial production and urban development are not necessarily precipitated merely by an increase in density of people. Hooke (1988, 128-9) has argued that the fragmentation of the estates recorded in many 10th-century charters seems to have occurred in areas of higher population and more intense settlement. Charters suggest that the land at the foot of the scarp slope to the north of the Downs and in the river valleys cut through the Downs, had been divided into narrow bands, a pattern preserved in part by the narrow strip parishes which are particularly characteristic of the downland fringes. Many of the medieval parishes originated in the tithes granted by the lord of an estate to support his proprietary or parish church and were therefore coterminous with Early Medieval lordships.

The charter of Annington (near Botolphs in the Adur valley) dated to 956 records such an estate bounded on the east by the river Adur (Sawyer 1968, no. 624). Annington was bounded to the south by the estate of Coombes and that of Bidlington to the north. On the downland to the west lay lands of the estates of Sompting and Dankton, the latter represented now by an isolated barn. The charters of South Heighton dated to 957 and 988 suggest a similar arrangement (*Liber Monasterii de Hyda* 1866, 167-70, 238-42; Sawyer 1968, nos. 648, 869). South Heighton lay on the east side of the river Ouse and the charter bounds describe an area similar to the 19th-century parish and mention a series of landmarks which hint at the character of the area (Bell 1978, 68). The charter begins at the river Ouse and mentions a 'fleet' or creek in the estuary (Coles 1997) and continues to the cliff on the chalkland at the edge of the valley. The river cliffs are still evident, in spite of recent quarrying. Other bounds mentioned are 'the white way' - a track on the chalk downs - , 'the red stone' - perhaps a notable sarsen - and *Smyewykke* - probably a farm high on the downland.

Wic sites, in the sense used in the place-name *Smyewykke*, were specialist farms. Similar farms were found on the Essex marshes where they were occupied by shepherds overseeing the large flocks and we may presume that the *wics* in Sussex served a similar purpose (Round 1903, 369-74). Earthworks at Thornwick Barn on the downland above Storrington and Eastwick Barn at Patcham near Brighton mark the site of the probable medieval settlements and enclosures for folding sheep (Curwen and Curwen 1923, 17-19; Barber *et al.* 2002). Domesday Book (i, 26a) records 10 shepherds at Patcham, near Brighton in the late 11th century, but no doubt there were others elsewhere.

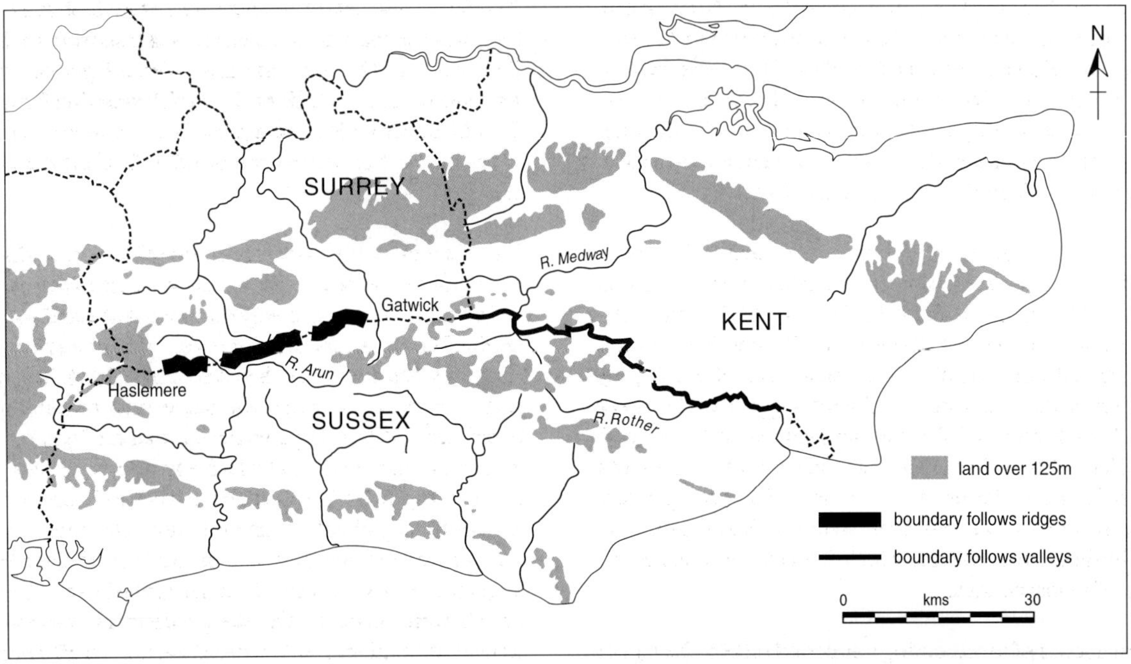

Figure 12.3. *The northern boundary of Sussex defined by ridges in the west and valleys in the east.*

The valley of the western Rother provides a further example of strip parishes. The parishes form two tiers. Those at the foot of the Downs used the fertile soils of the Lower Chalk and Upper Greensand, but also extended southwards to include pasture land on the scarp slope and downland summit, and northwards to woodland on the clay. The second tier were situated near to the River Rother and had areas of grazing and woodland on the poorer soils near to the Surrey border. The pattern had been established, at least in part, by the mid-10th century when a charter granting the estate of Ambersham to the church at Meon in Hampshire records an area similar to the later parish (Sawyer 1968, no. 718; Mawer and Stenton 1929-30, 97n-8n). The estate extended in a narrow band a little more than a quarter of a mile wide for a distance of almost nine miles. Until the 19th century Ambersham correctly was not a separate parish, but a chapelry of the Hampshire parish of Steep. This anomaly was created by the 10th-century grant, for Steep had been associated ecclesiastically with the parish of East Meon (Gardiner 1984, 81-2). The Vale of Rother was therefore divided in a rational way between a series of manors to give each a share of the better soils for arable and of the poorer soils for grazing and for woodland.

The small scale of industrial production in the Post-Roman period contrasts with the greater level of activity by the 10th century. Iron was produced at a *ferraria* in East Grinstead hundred, perhaps at Lavertye, which was of sufficient value to merit record in Domesday Book (i, 22b; Wood 1996, 10, 14). The same source mentions quarries at Stedham, Grittenham and Iping (DB i, 23a, 23b, 29b). It seems likely that all may have been producing millstones from the Lower Greensand, much as had been done in the Iron Age and Roman period in the same area (Peacock 1987, 61-85). Millstones are specifically described as the product of the quarry at Bignor (DB i, 25a). Domesday Book also records the production of salt. Sussex had a greater number of salterns than any other county in England. Until recently a large number of such mounds survived to the north of Lancing in the Adur valley (Fig. 12.1b) and other mounds have been noted in the Pevensey Marshes. Pottery of Saxo-Norman date was found on a salt mound at New Monks Farm near Lancing (Holden and Hudson 1981; Dulley 1968, 28-9). The greatest concentration of salt-making in the 11th century was on Walland Marsh near Rye, but coastal erosion and the flooding of the eastern Rother valley in the 13th century appears to have removed all evidence of the sites of salterns.

Excavation in Chapel Street, Chichester, located the site of six pottery kilns and remains of two further kilns were found nearby (Down 1978, 158-9; Down 1981, 190). An archaeomagnetic date of 860-990 at 95% confidence level was obtained from one of these, which places them slightly earlier than the excavator originally suggested (Gardiner 1990, 251). Pottery similar, but not identical to the wasters from Chapel Street, has been found on sites across the south of west Sussex as far as the River Adur. The pottery rarely occurs in Lewes, but has been found at Hastings Castle (unpublished excavations), which it evidently reached by means of seaborne trade.

The emergence of towns during this period reflects the higher level of agricultural and industrial production which produced a surplus for trade. The towns may be divided into those which began as *burhs* founded in the late 9th or early 10th century as part of a defensive scheme against Viking raids, and those which developed subsequently. The document known as the Burghal Hidage, probably compiled in *c.* 919, lists five fortified sites and allows their perimeter defences to be calculated. The first, *Eorpeburnan*, was the smallest and has not been definitely identified. Davison suggested the site of Castle Toll in Newenden, just over the county border in Kent, but Kitchen has proposed Rye as an alternative (Davison 1972; Kitchen 1984a, 1984b). The other forts of the Burghal Hidage - Hastings, Lewes, Burpham and Chichester - can be readily recognized, although unwarranted doubts have been raised about *Haestingaceastre*, usually identified as Hastings, with the suggestion that the site was in fact at Pevensey (Combes and Lyne 1995). All these, with the exception of Burpham, developed into major towns during the course of the 10th century. The defensive earthworks still survive to a considerable height at Burpham where they cut off a peninsula which projects into the marshland of the Arun valley. That fort may not have been intended as a commercial settlement, and it had been replaced by the late 11th century by Arundel, which lies a short distance downstream.

Further towns developed within the walls of the Roman fort at Pevensey and also at Steyning, Rye and Winchelsea. Many of these were evidently stimulated by trade with France which seems to have developed even before the Conquest (Gardiner 2000). There were close connections across the Channel which were strengthened when, in a series of grants in the early 11th century, the abbey of Fécamp was granted land close to these towns. It was given the manor of Brede, the port and tolls of Winchelsea and *Rammesleah*, an unidentified site which might have included part of Hastings. It may also have been granted land at Steyning before the Conquest, and certainly held land there afterwards (Haskins 1918; Matthew 1962, 19-22). In 1054 the abbey was given a church at Eastbourne and an endowment which included 12 houses at *Caestra*. The latter place was very probably Pevensey, near to which lay other lands of the endowment (Gardiner and Whittick 1990, 261). It is likely that at each of these towns there was a landing place similar to that discovered at Lewes. Excavations there identified a broad gravel spread immediately below Cliffe Bridge, which must date from before the 12th or early 13th century, and is likely to have been laid down as a hard on which ships could be beached (Gardiner *et al.* 1996, 75-8, 99).

The changes in the town and countryside during the Early Medieval period have been traced most clearly in the Adur valley. Excavations at Botolphs showed that a settlement was established in the late 10th or early 11th century close to a causeway and ford over the river (Fig. 12.1b). The church was constructed at about the same time or shortly after (Gardiner 1990). A large enclosure marked by a bank and ditch was constructed at Old Erringham on the opposite side of the valley around the same time. The enclosure contained a chapel and probably a manor house. The entrance to the interior was marked by a gap in the bank flanked by two larger post-holes between which ran a cobbled trackway. Two burials were found on the south side of the chapel in the limited excavations inside the enclosure. A small distance to the east of the enclosure lay some slight banks marking the site of an adjoining settlement (Holden 1980). These sites suggest that around AD 1000 settlement, which may have previously been scattered, coalesced around the sites of newly constructed churches or chapels.

It is likely that the same process of village formation was taking place in many parts of England. Villages emerged on the poorer soils rather later than on the more densely settled areas of better arable land. Settlement change in the Adur valley may be contrasted with the late growth of Hangleton village only a few miles to the east. Excavations at Hangleton suggested that the site of the village, high up on the Downs, was not occupied before the late 12th century (Holden 1963).

Steyning, at the head of the valley cut by the River Adur through the chalk, also developed as an urban centre during the course of the 11th century. Domesday Book (i, 17a) records Steyning at the point at which it was becoming recognizably urban, noting that the burgesses, as they then were, used to work at the lord's court like ordinary peasants. Excavations within the town and reconsideration of the documentary sources have produced a clear record of its growth (Fig. 12.4). Steyning was a religious centre, important enough to serve as the initial burial place of Æthelwulf, the father of King Alfred, and also of St Cuthman, whose grave had become a place of pilgrimage by the 10th or early 11th century (Blair 1997). It also became a commercial centre, although this is only hinted at by the archaeological record. A sunken-floored building found opposite the church is typical of urban sites elsewhere (Gardiner and Greatorex 1997, 160-61). Sherds of French imported pottery have been found in most of the excavations within the town and may be related to the port of St Cuthman, which was evidently of some significance in the mid-11th century (*Calendar of Documents... in France*, Round 1899, 37-8).

The success of Steyning seems to have prompted the foundation of a rival town at Bramber, a short distance down-river (Hudson 1980). The latter town stood either side of a causeway constructed over the marshes of the River Adur. Excavations have shown that causeway was built partly of flint pebbles and the land on which the houses stood was raised above the floodplain by dumping soil (Holden 1975, 105-6; unpublished watching brief). A port had evidently been established by 1070 when the sole surviving ship from a fleet carrying stone from Normandy landed there after a violent storm (Gem 1987). The tolls on ships taken at Bramber were the subject of contention between the abbey of Fécamp, the lord of Steyning, and William de Briouze, the lord of Bramber (*Calendar of Documents... in France*, Round 1899, 37-8).

The Adur valley, which has been particularly well served by excavation and documentary study, may stand as an example of the changes which took place in other areas of Sussex during the Early Medieval period. The development of Arundel and villages in its vicinity was, no doubt, rather similar, and the growth of the towns of Winchelsea and Rye at the east end of Sussex also mirrored the expansion of Steyning. But, by contrast, the area surrounding Winchelsea and Rye, the High Weald, remained a sparsely settled area with few villages until the 13th century (Gardiner 1997). It would be too easy to over emphasize the remoteness of that region. The monks of Battle laid out a town at the gates of the abbey and were successful in attracting immigrants from France and local people from the surrounding area of Sussex, as Clark (1980) has demonstrated. We can see in studies such as hers evidence of the formation of urban communities that archaeology alone can rarely show.

Conclusions

It is useful to conclude by standing back and considering the position of the kingdom of the South Saxons, and later the county of Sussex, in relationship to England as a whole. Sussex has a long seaboard with numerous landing-places and its position, close to continental Europe, should have made it particularly open to foreign influence and concourse. Yet, curiously, it was rarely in the forefront of developments introduced from that quarter or of European trade, unlike neighbouring Kent which played a leading role in both. It cannot be that the agricultural heartland of Sussex and its centre of wealth lay in the west of the county, too far from the Straits of Dover and the shortest crossing point to the European mainland. A position even further west did not prevent the growth of *Hamwic*, Saxon Southampton.

There may have been a series of reasons for Sussex's minor role. Sussex remained an independent, but small kingdom until its conquest by Offa of Mercia in the 760s and early 770s. It was dwarfed in importance by its powerful neighbours, Wessex to the west and Kent to the east, but was sufficiently large to retain its independence until comparatively late. Unlike Kent, it failed to develop continental alliances which might have increased its importance and its wealth. The rulers of Sussex did not play a significant role within England. They were evidently not particularly wealthy, a fact reflected in the small number of lands granted to the church at Selsey. In the 11th century Selsey remained one of the poorest of all English sees. It also had no Anglo-Saxon monastery of any importance. It may be, as Kelly (1998, lxxvi) has suggested, that political authority within Sussex was fragmented. The four or five kings recorded in the 760s may have ruled over tribal areas, though this remains very uncertain. It seems that

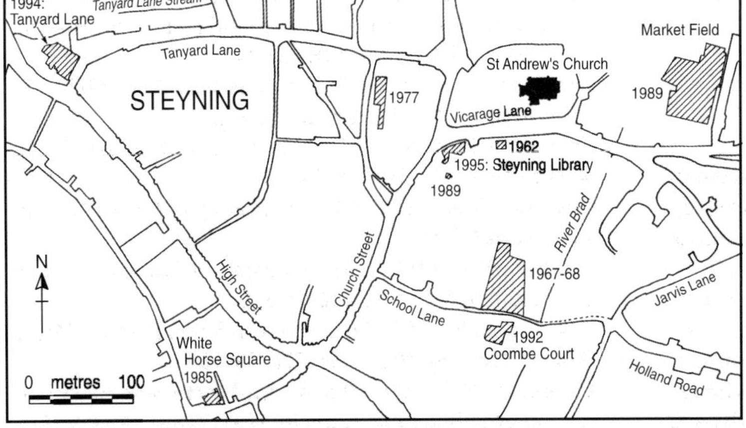

Figure 12.4. *Areas investigated by excavation in Steyning between 1962 and 1995. The work has suggested that the Early Medieval town lay around the church.*

Sussex lacked powerful lords, either religious or lay, who might act as a link to the centres of power nationally and internationally. There was no tendency towards the centralization of location within the county which might have been promoted by a strong and wealthy individual. Sussex developed no centre comparable to Canterbury or Winchester, or even to Thetford - the major pre-Conquest town in East Anglia - or Exeter.

The fragmentation of power was effectively institutionalized after the Norman settlement by the division of the county into five rapes, each of which had its own lord and, remarkably, its own sheriff (Round 1905, 352). It cannot be certainly proven, either that there were rapes before the Conquest, or that there was a sheriff in each, but the Domesday entry (i, 26a) for Lewes which implies that there had been rules common to the whole rape and therefore enforceable in a rape court, suggests that this might have been the case.

These matters are not merely of administrative or political interest, but go to the heart of the character of Sussex. The structures of power and the distribution of wealth had a profound effect on the course of the economic development of the county. The axes of communication ran north-south uniting the better soils of the coastal region with the woodland of the Weald. They did not run east-west, a direction which might have produced a unified county. Much the same point has been developed by Saul (1986, 57-61) in his discussion of 14th-century gentry. He has argued that there was not a single county community, but a series of groups with local interests and connections.

We can, therefore, pick out a fundamental feature which underlies hundreds of years of history. This enduring theme in the structure of Sussex may be explained by reference to the ideas of the *Annales* historians. The *Annalistes* would interpret these features of human society persisting over many centuries - the *longue durée* - as the result of the underlying geography, creating a geohistory which enabled and constrained activity. The *Hæstingas,* a shadowy group who occupied the east of Sussex and who were conquered by Offa in 771, the people of the Hastings district harried by the Vikings in 1011 and the communities in eastern Sussex considered by Saul were all aspects of the same fragmentation of the county (Mawer and Stenton 1929-30, xxiii-xxiv). Viewed from this perspective, we can see the changing patterns of existence in the period 450-1175 as a series of responses to the physical geography of Sussex.

References

Allen, M.J. 1991. Analysing the landscape: a geographical approach to archaeological problems, in A. J. Schofield (ed), *Interpreting Artefact Scatters: Contributions to Ploughzone Archaeology,* Oxbow Monogr. **4**, 39-57. Oxford.

Andrews, P. 1997. *Excavations at Hamwic, 2,* CBA Res. Rep. **109**.

Barber, L., Gardiner, M. and Rudling, D. 2002. Excavations at Eastwick Barn, in D. Rudling (ed), *Downland Settlement and Landuse: The Archaeology of the Brighton Bypass,* University College London Field Archaeology Unit Monogr. **1**. London: Archetype.

Bell, M.G. 1977. Excavations at Bishopstone, *SAC* **115**, 1-291.

Bell, M.G. 1978. Saxon Sussex, in P.L. Drewett (ed), *Archaeology in Sussex to AD 1500,* CBA Res. Rep. **29**, 64-9.

Bell, M.G. 1983. Valley sediments as evidence of prehistoric land-use on the South Downs, *Proc. Prehist. Soc.* **49**, 119-50.

Bell, M.G. 1989. Environmental archaeology as an index of continuity and change in the medieval landscape, in M. Aston, D. Austin and C. Dyer (eds), *The Rural Settlements of Medieval England,* 269-86. Oxford: Blackwell.

Blair, J. 1991. *Early Medieval Surrey: Landholding, Church and Settlement before 1300.* Stroud: Alan Sutton.

Blair, J. 1997. Saint Cuthman, Steyning and Bosham, *SAC* **135**, 173-92.

Britnell, R.H. 1996. *The Commercialisation of English Society 1000-1500.* Manchester: University Press.

Brooks, N.P. 1989. The creation and early structure of the kingdom of Kent, in S. Bassett (ed), *The Origins of Anglo-Saxon Kingdoms.* Leicester: University Press, 55-74.

Burnett, A. 1984. Clipped siliquae and the end of Roman Britain, *Britannia* **15**, 163-8.

Clark, C. 1979. Battle *c.*1110. An anthroponymist looks at an Anglo-Norman new town, *Proc. of the Battle Conference on Anglo-Norman Studies* **2**, 21-41.

Coles, A. 1997. fleot: Distribution and use of this OE place-name element, *J. English Place-Name Society* **29**, 79-87.

Combes, P. and Lyne, M. 1995. Hastings, Haestingaceaster and Hastingaport, *SAC* **133**, 213-24.

Curwen, E. and Curwen, E.C. 1923. Sussex lynchets and their associated field-ways, *SAC* **64**, 1-65.

Davison, B.K. 1972. The Burghal Hidage fort of Eorpeburnan: a suggested identification, *Medieval Archaeol.* **16**, 123-7.

Down, A. 1974. *Chichester Excavations 2.* Chichester: Phillimore.

Down, A. 1978. *Chichester Excavations 3.* Chichester: Phillimore.

Down, A. 1981. *Chichester Excavations 5.* Chichester: Phillimore.

Down, A. and Welch, M.G. 1990. *Chichester Excavations 7: Apple Down and the Mardens.* Chichester: Phillimore.

Drewett, P.L. 1978. Field systems and land allotment in Sussex 3rd millennium B.C. to 4th century A.D., in H.C. Bowen and P.J. Fowler (eds), *Early Land Allotment,* BAR BS **48**, 67-80.

Drewett, P.L. 1982. *The Archaeology of Bullock Down, Eastbourne, East Sussex: The Development of a Landscape,* Sussex Archaeol. Soc. Monogr. **1**. Lewes.

Drewett, P.L., Holgate, B., Foster, S. and Ellerby, H. 1986. The excavations of a Saxon sunken building at North Marden, West Sussex, 1982, *SAC* **124**, 109-18.

Drewett, P.L., Rudling, D.R. and Gardiner, M.F. 1988. *The South-East to 1000 AD.* London: Longman.

Dulley, A.J.F. 1968. The Level and Port of Pevensey in the Middle Ages, *SAC* **104**, 26-45.

Esmonde Cleary, A.S. 1989. *The Ending of Roman Britain.* London: Batsford.

Gardiner, M.F. 1984. Saxon settlement and land division in the western Weald, *SAC* **122**, 75-83.

Gardiner, M.F. 1988. Excavations at Testers, White Horse Square, Steyning, 1985, *SAC* **126**, 53-76.

Gardiner, M.F. 1990. An Anglo-Saxon and medieval settlement at Botolphs, Bramber, West Sussex, *Archaeol. J.* **147**, 216-275.

Gardiner, M.F. 1997. Trade, rural industry and the origins of villages: some evidence from south-east England, in G. De Boe and F. Verhaeghe (eds), *Rural Settlements in Medieval Europe* (papers of the 'Medieval Europe Brugge 1997' conference) **6**, 63-73. Belgium: Zellik.

Gardiner, M.F. 2000. Shipping and trade between England and the continent during the eleventh century, *Anglo-Norman Studies* **22**, 71-93.

Gardiner, M.F. and Greatorex, C. 1997. Archaeological excavations in Steyning, 1992-95: further evidence for the evolution of a late Saxon small town, *SAC* **135**, 143-71.

Gardiner, M.F., Russell, M. and Gregory, D. 1996. Excavations at Lewes Friary 1985-6 and 1988-9, *SAC* **134**, 71-123.

Gardiner, M.F. and Whittick, C.H.C. 1990. Some evidence for an intended collegiate church at Pevensey, *SAC* **128**, 261-2.

Gem, R. 1987. Canterbury and the cushion capital: A commentary on passages from Goscelin's De Mireculis Sancti Augustini, in N. Stratford (ed), *Romanesque and Gothic: Essays for George Zarnecki* **1**, Woodbridge: Boydell, 83-101.

Gregory, V.L. 1976. Excavations at Becket's Barn, Pagham, West Sussex, *SAC* **114**, 207-217.

Grierson, P. 1959. Commerce in the Dark Ages: a critique of the evidence, *Trans. Roy. Hist. Soc.* fifth ser., **9**, 123-40.

Hamerow, H. 1991. Settlement and mobility and the 'Middle Saxon Shift': rural settlement and settlement patterns in Anglo-Saxon England, *Anglo-Saxon Eng.* **20**, 1-17.

Haskins, C.H. 1918. A charter of Canute for Fécamp, *Eng. Hist. Rev.* **33**, 342-4.

Holden, E.W. 1963. Excavations at the deserted medieval village of Hangleton, part 1, *SAC* **101**, 54-181.

Holden, E.W. 1975. New evidence relating to Bramber Bridge, *SAC* **113**, 104-17.

Holden, E.W. 1980. Excavation at Old Erringham, Shoreham, West Sussex. Part II, the 'chapel' and ringwork, *SAC* **118**, 1980, 257-97.

Holden, E.W. and Hudson, T.P. 1981. Salt-making in the Adur valley, Sussex, *SAC* **119**, 117-48.

Holleyman, G.A. 1935. The Celtic field-system in South Britain, *Antiquity* **9**, 443-54.

Hooke, D. 1987. Anglo-Saxon estates in the Vale of the White Horse, *Oxoniensia* **52**, 129-43.

Hooke, D. 1988. Early forms of open-field agriculture in England, *Geografiska Annaler* **70B**, 123-31.

Hooke, D. 1997. The Anglo-Saxons in England in the seventh and eighth centuries: location in space, in J. Hines (ed), *The Anglo-Saxons from the Migration Period to the Eighth Century: An Ethnographic Perspective*, 65-99. Woodbridge: Boydell.

Hudson, T.P. 1980. The origins of Steyning and Bramber, *Southern Hist.* **2**, 9-29.

Kelly, S.E. 1998. *Charters of Selsey*. (Anglo-Saxon Charters **6**). Oxford: University Press for The British Academy.

Kitchen, F. 1984a. The *Burghal Hidage*: towards the identification of *Eorpeburnan*, *Medieval Archaeology* **28**, 175-7.

Kitchen, F. 1984b. Rye: a 9th-century foundation, *SAC* **122**, 224.

Liber Monasterii de Hyda (1866, Rolls series), ed. E. Edwards. London: HMSO.

Matthew, D. 1962. *The Norman Monasteries and the English Possessions*. Oxford: University Press.

Mawer, A. and Stenton, F.M. 1929-30. *The Place-Names of Sussex* **1**, **2** (English Place-Name Society **6**, **7**). Cambridge: University Press.

Metcalf, D.M. 1984. Monetary circulation in southern England in the first half of the eighth century, in D.H. Hill and D.M. Metcalf (eds), *Sceattas in England and on the Continent*, BAR BS **128**, 27-69.

Miller, E. and Hatcher, J. 1995. *Medieval England: Towns, Commerce and Crafts 1086-1348*. London: Longman.

Munby, J. 1984. Saxon Chichester and its predecessors, in J. Haslam (ed), *Anglo-Saxon Towns in Southern England*, Chichester: Phillimore, 315-30.

Peacock, D.P.S. 1987. Iron Age and Roman quern production at Lodsworth, West Sussex, *Antiq. J.* **67**, 61-85.

Round, J.H. 1899. *Calendar of Documents Preserved in France* **1**, London: HMSO.

Round, J.H. 1903. Introduction to the Essex Domesday, in W. Page (ed), *Victoria History of the County of Sussex* **1**, 351-85. London: Constable.

Round, J.H. 1905. Introduction to the Sussex Domesday, in H.A. Doubleday and W. Page (eds), *Victoria History of the County of Essex* **1**, 333-425. London: Constable.

Salzman, L.F. 1931. The Rapes of Sussex, *SAC* **72**, 20-9.

Saul, N. 1986. *Scenes from Provincial Life: Knightly Families in Sussex 1280-1400*. Oxford: University Press.

Sawyer, P.H. 1968. *Anglo-Saxon Charters: An Annotated List and Bibliography*. London: Royal Historical Society.

Sims-Williams, P. 1984. Gildas and the Anglo-Saxons, *Cambridge Medieval Celtic Studies* **6**, 1-30.

Tebbutt, C.F. 1982. A Middle-Saxon iron smelting site at Millbrook, Ashdown Forest, Sussex, *SAC* **120**, 19-35.

Thacker, A. 1995. *Membra Disjecta:* the division of the body and the diffusion of the cult, in C. Stancliffe and E. Cambridge (eds), *Oswald: Northumbria King to European Saint*, Stamford: Paul Watkins, 97-127.

Welch, M.G. 1983. *Early Anglo-Saxon Sussex,* BAR BS **112**. Oxford.

Welch, M.G. 1985. Rural settlement patterns in the Early and Middle Anglo-Saxon periods, *Landscape History* **7**, 13-25.

White, S., Manley, J., Jones, R., Orna-Ornstein, J., Jones, C. and Webster, L. 1999. A Mid-Fifth Century Hoard of Roman and Pseudo-Roman Material from Patching, West Sussex, *Britannia* **30**, 301-315.

Wilkinson, K., Barber, L. and Bennell, M. 2002. The examination of six dry valleys in the Brighton area: the changing environment, in D. Rudling (ed), *Downland Settlement and Landuse: The Archaeology of the Brighton Bypass,* University College London Field Archaeology Unit Monogr. **1**, London: Archetype.

Williamson, T.M. 1984. The Roman countryside: settlement and agriculture in N.W. Essex, *Britannia* **15**, 225-30.

Witney, K.P. 1976. *The Jutish Forest: A Study of the Weald of Kent from 450 to 1380 A.D.* London: Athlone Press.

Wood, I.N. 1983. *The Merovingian North Sea*. Alingsås, Sweden.

Wood, P.D. 1996. East Grinstead in the Domesday survey, *East Grinstead Society Bulletin* **58**, 3-23.

Yorke, B. 1989. The Jutes of Hampshire and Wight and the origins of Wessex, in S. Bassett (ed), *The Origins of Anglo-Saxon Kingdoms*, Leicester: University Press, 84-96.

ECCLESIASTICAL SITES IN SUSSEX

Mark Taylor

Abstract

This paper (essentially the lecture presented in 1998) outlines the establishment of monastic sites in Sussex from the end of the 7th century to their decline and extinction in the 16th century at the Dissolution. After 1066, but particularly in the 12th century, Norman endowments were responsible for a significant rise in the number of religious houses founded. As well as the church buildings themselves being constructed or rebuilt in a style showing continental influence, the institution of the Church in England and monastic life underwent reform. After the Norman Conquest Sussex monasteries frequently had links to religious houses across the Channel since, in the new Anglo-Norman kingdom, their founders had lands and interests there. These close links with the Continent ensured that as Religious Orders emerged it was not long before houses belonging to the new orders appeared in England also. The Augustinian canons were popular in Sussex, but later on the Friars are regularly found in the urban centres. By the 16th century, standards of monastic life were undeniably in decline but the official accusation of wrongdoing and moral depravity appear to have been deliberately exaggerated. The physical dismembering of the religious houses at the Dissolution destroyed what were probably the finest medieval churches in Sussex.

Monasticism in Saxon Sussex

In Saxon Sussex the creation of a diocese co-terminous with the South Saxon kingdom and today's counties of East and West Sussex can be traced back to the time of Bishop Wilfrid at the end of the 7th century. Wilfrid was not the first, however, to introduce Christianity to Sussex, for when he arrived in 681 there was a small community of Irish monks under Dicul based at Bosham (Fig. 13.1). Bede was undoubtedly biased in favour of his fellow countryman and gives the Celtic community little credit, but it is undeniable that the main impetus for the conversion of the South Saxons to Christianity began with Wilfrid. Wilfrid founded the cathedral at Selsey sometime after 681. It appears, from charter evidence, to have been originally for Benedictine monks under an abbot who was also a bishop, but it was subsequently for secular canons (Hobbs ed. 1994).

Elsewhere in Saxon Sussex there was a small religious community at South Malling, and this was probably founded before Wilfrid's departure. Aldulf, ruler of the South Saxons, is recorded granting land *c*.765 to a monastery here, apparently already established, and probably of Benedictine

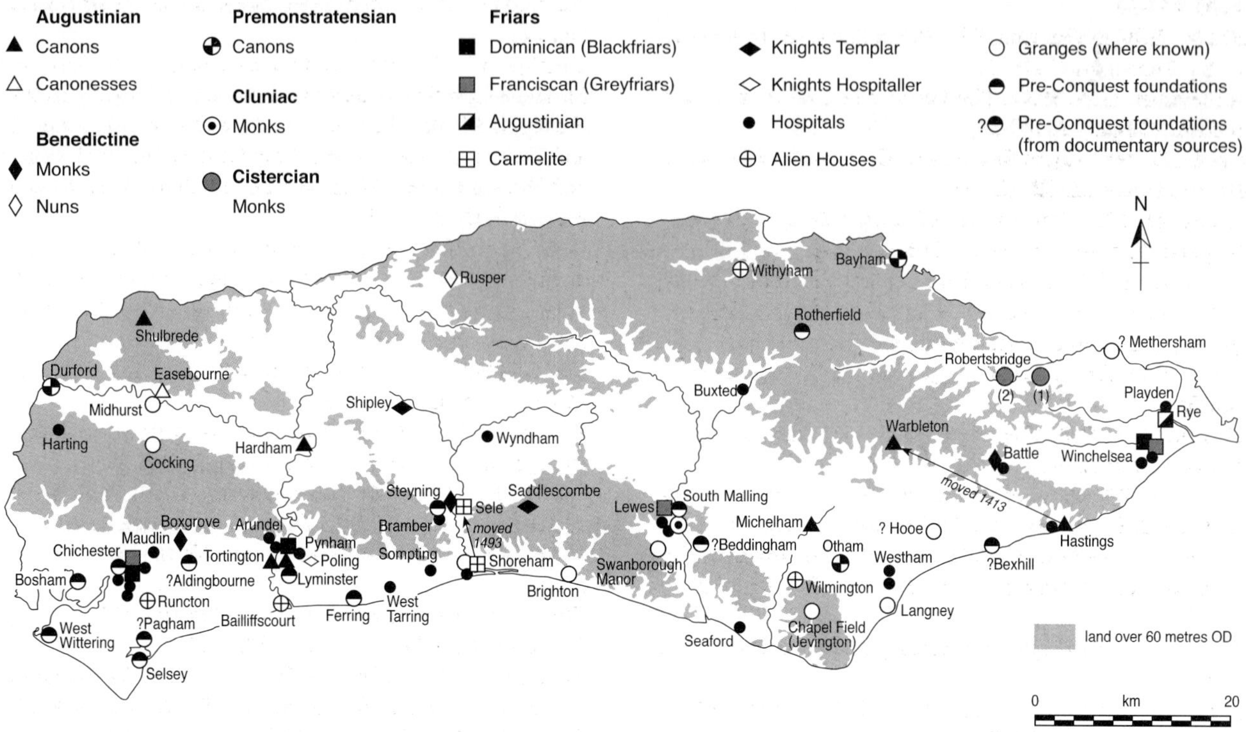

Figure 13.1. Distributions of ecclesiastical sites in Sussex.

monks, who were later replaced by secular canons (Knowles and Hadcock 1971, 418, 439 and 482). At Chichester, the Benedictine nunnery of St. Peter was displaced to accommodate the canons from Selsey when the Cathedral was moved in 1075. A monastery certainly seems to be implied by a charter in 956 of King Edwy to the brethren of Chichester, and William of Malmesbury suggests a pre-Conquest minster of St. Peter, perhaps a double monastery (Knowles and Hadcock 1971, 253, 257). At Steyning, there is some evidence for a possible minster of secular canons before 858, when Ethelwulf, father of King Alfred, was buried here. There are also hints of Saxon colleges of canons at Ferring (8th century) (Knowles and Hadcock 1971, 414, 473), and at Bexhill and Beddingham (Knowles and Hadcock 1971, 467). King Offa, in the later part of the 8th century, granted land for the service of God which may be interpreted as secular colleges. On the whole, there was a framework in place based upon missionary *'monasteria'* or minster churches, of which the cathedral was the head minster, with other minsters staffed by bodies of secular canons supporting the lesser churches and field churches, but compared with the situation in Sussex after 1066, and the development which takes off in the 12th century, the picture of monastic life in Saxon Sussex is obscure.

Developments after 1066

After the Norman Conquest the pattern of development in terms of religious reform and reconstruction and the foundation of monastic institutions provides a dramatic contrast. No radical changes were made immediately (indeed the rate at which major new abbeys were created in England in the reign of the Conqueror and his son William Rufus was slow by comparison with the surge of activity in the 12th century), but by the Conqueror's death in 1087, only one English-born bishop (Wulfstan of Worcester) and two abbots of pre-Conquest days (Ramsey and Bath) were in post. Of the 18 bishops appointed between 1070 (when Lanfranc of Bec was appointed Archbishop of Canterbury) and Lanfranc's death in 1089, 16 were of Norman birth or training.

The new Norman clergy were not just eager for spiritual reform. They also brought about a construction (and re-construction) programme of churches on a scale never seen before in England, and with style and grandeur to match. Every major church in England was rebuilt in the decades following 1066 except Westminster and Waltham (Westminster undoubtedly because it was modelled on Jumièges and was therefore already Norman in style). William of Malmesbury wrote:

> "After their coming to England they revived the rule of religion which had there grown lifeless. You might see great churches rise in every village, and, in the towns and cities, monasteries built after a style unknown before".

Under Lanfranc's reforms Canterbury asserted its supremacy over York, and the dioceses were reorganized. Where necessary the cathedral of the diocese was moved from rural areas to urban centres. (For example, the cathedral of the diocese of Chichester was moved from Selsey and rebuilt in Chichester itself *c.*1070 -75.)

New houses founded

When Duke William landed in 1066 there were about 50 Benedictine monasteries in England. By the end of the 11th century the number of monastic establishments had risen to about 130 (45 were independent abbeys, 29 were cells of parent monasteries, and 45 were alien priories) and there was a notable increase in the number of monks in England in the years after the Conquest, drawn partly from the new Norman ruling classes and their children. The first generation of Norman barons in England, however, were more preoccupied with consolidating their hold on their newly acquired land and wealth by building castles, and when benefactions were made, they tended to enrich the existing houses in France rather than endow substantial new foundations here. In Sussex, there were about ten alien priories, cells or granges linked to a mother house across the Channel.

Boxgrove, founded after 1105 and a daughter house of Lessay (declared independent 1339), provides a good example of a regular monastery, on a small scale, with church and conventual buildings modelled in plan and design upon the greater abbeys. (The 12th-century guest hall nevertheless compares favourably in size with those of larger houses.)

Although nearly all of the new foundations made by the end of the 11th century were Benedictine, there were five Cluniac houses in England and the Priory of St. Pancras at Lewes, founded by William de Warenne (*see* below), was the chief house of the Cluniac Order and one of two major religious foundations which were established in Sussex soon after the Battle of Hastings. Here, William de Warenne, seneschal of Duke William, succeeded in persuading Cluny to send monks to set up a daughter house. He had visited Cluny with his wife, Gundrada, and had been overwhelmed by the elaboration of the liturgy and generous hospitality. The Cluniac Order, however, did not establish itself extensively in England. Bermondsey (founded by a London merchant, Alwin Child, about 1087 and richly endowed by the Conqueror's successor William Rufus), was the only Cluniac priory to approach Lewes in wealth and importance.

Before the Battle of Hastings, William had taken an oath to found an abbey in thanksgiving if he were to be successful. In the event, the Conqueror's own foundation, staffed with monks from Marmoutier, was built on the high ground where the battle action had been fiercest, the high altar carefully sited on the very spot where Harold fell. The Battle Abbey Chronicle (Searle 1980) recounts some objection from the monks to the impracticality of such a hilly site, but William was insistent (Fig. 13.2). There were clearly problems associated with building on such a slope as the results of the excavations at Battle Abbey in recent years demonstrated (Hare 1985).

Figure 13.2. Battle Abbey: medieval gateway. (Photograph: Andrew Woodcock).

Emerging Religious Orders

In the 12th century, the structure of monastic life took on a more complex pattern. Other Orders emerged from the Benedictine mainstream in response to a desire to return to the early values of a simple, austere life of work and prayer. The Cistercians, so named after their founding house at Cîteaux in Burgundy, were the most significant and far-reaching influence in English monastic life. The houses of this Order are characterized by their remote settings, but although the Cistercians initially shunned the opulence of Benedictine houses like Cluny and were known for the austerity of their lifestyle and plain, unadorned churches, they were so successful in taming the wilderness and farming its resources (especially in producing wool from rearing sheep) that they collectively became very wealthy and often attracted even more wealth from benefactions.

In Sussex, Robertsbridge was the only Cistercian house. Founded by Alured de St. Martin, *c.* 1176, the initial site proved unsatisfactory due to flooding (Knowles and Hadcock 1971, 124). In the early 13th century the abbey moved to its present location to the south of the River Rother. Robertsbridge was never a large house by Cistercian standards. A recent survey of the upstanding remains has shown that the dormitory was rebuilt on a larger and more grand scale in the late 13th century (Fig. 13.3; Martin and Martin 1995).

The Canons of the Order of Prémontré were modelled on the Cistercians and followed their ideal of withdrawal from the world to remote places. Their house at Bayham Abbey on the border between Kent and East Sussex is a substantial monastery in Sussex terms, constituting probably the most complete, publicly accessible monastic precinct in the historic county. The abbey, founded between 1199 and 1208, amalgamated the communities at Brockley and Otham to create a body of about 20 canons (by 1315). Bayham was directly dependent upon the mother house of Prémontré, but held abbey status - a privilege only allowed to one other Premonstratensian foundation in England - St. Radegund's, near Dover. Far to the west, at the opposite end of Sussex and close to the border with Hampshire, was a slightly smaller and earlier Premonstratensian house at Durford. Founded by Henry Husey II before 1161, the abbey was for the usual 13 canons, increasing to 15 canons besides the abbot *c.*1327. Unhappily a series of misfortunes beset Durford: the house was robbed in 1317, and again in 1335 when some of its buildings were burnt. In 1417 the tower was struck by lightning and burnt. Plague struck in 1482 when only the abbot and 3 canons appear to have survived, but thereafter there were signs of efforts being made to increase numbers and re-establish the community, and a core of about 10 canons lasted until the Dissolution (Knowles and Hadcock 1971, 188).

Augustinian Canons

While Cluny and Cîteaux began as Benedictine houses but developed into Orders in their own right, there had existed in England, for some decades before the Conquest, in parallel with communities of Benedictine monks, a body of regular clergy known as the Canons of St. Augustine, or Austin Canons. For many years, virtually from the creation of minster churches and the introduction of Christianity into England, minsters had been served by bodies of clerks or canons who were separate from the monks under religious vows obeying the Rule of St. Benedict and from the parish priests serving churches single-handed. The canons lived a communal life sleeping in a common dormitory, and shared meals in a common refectory. Before the Norman Conquest, however, they were different from the monks under vows of celibacy, as canons might often be married men. Reform was already under way in England in the 10th century under Dunstan, but after the Conquest, the continental movement to bring bodies of canons under a rule more resembling that of monks and enforce strict observance of vows of chastity and poverty was readily adopted by the Normans. From the 12th century into the 14th century, new houses continued to be founded. By the 14th century, there were over 200 in England.

Augustinian houses are well-represented in Sussex. Houses were founded at Easebourne near Midhurst (Augustinian canonesses), Hardham near Pulborough, Hastings (which transferred to Warbleton or Rushlake in 1413, when the former priory was in danger of inundation from the sea), Michelham, Pynham near Arundel, Tortington (again near Arundel) and Shulbrede near Linchmere.

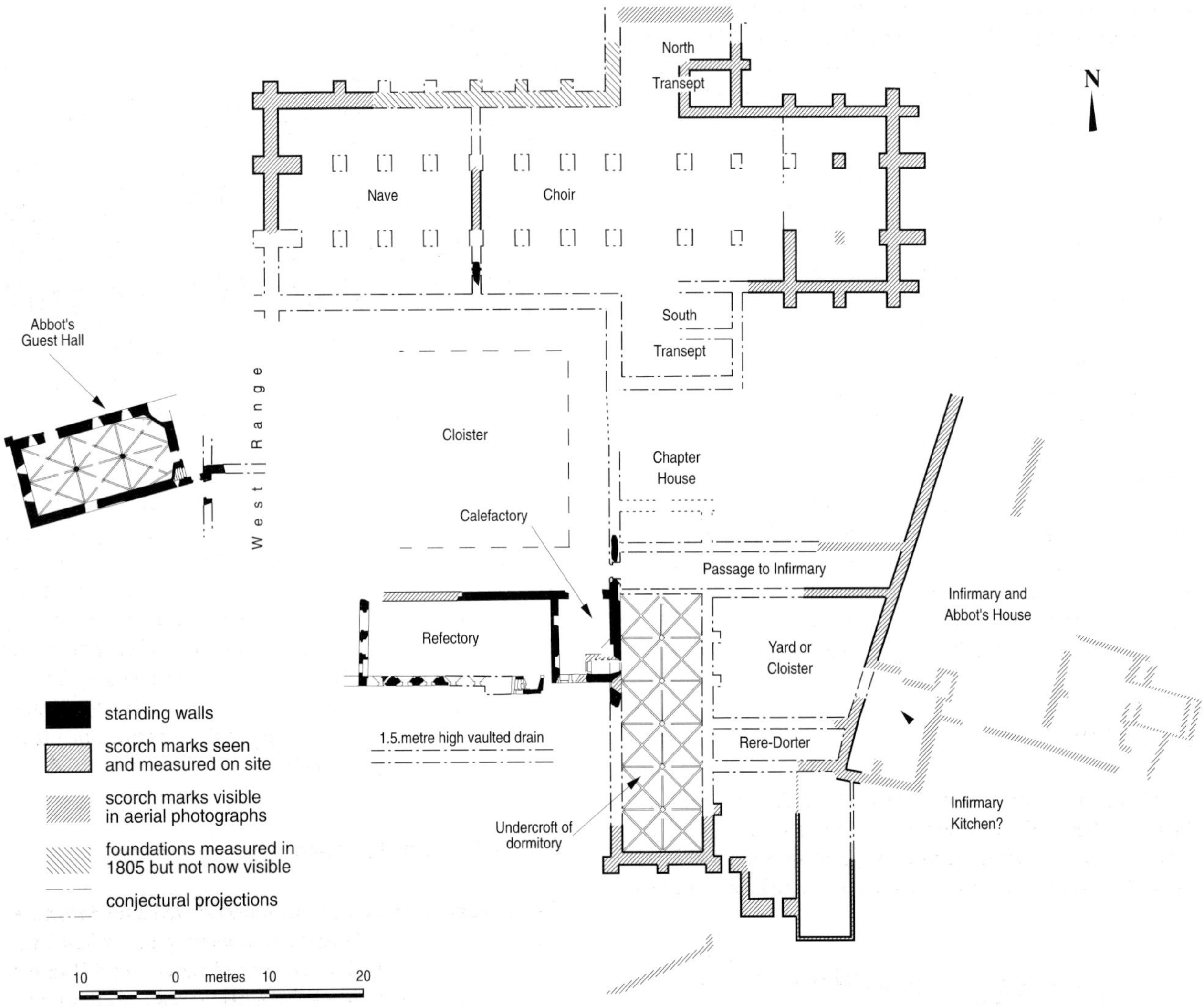

Figure 13.3. *St. Mary's Abbey, Robertsbridge: Ground floor plan (after Martin and Martin 1995).*

Although Augustinian houses tended to follow the classic conventual monastic layout of post-Conquest times, they were on a much smaller scale than great Benedictine or Cluniac houses like Battle or Lewes. Tortington is probably one of the more substantial houses, founded before the end of the 12th century (possibly by Hadwissa Corbet), but there were only eight or nine canons before the Black Death, and only about five canons thereafter until the suppression. Michelham Priory was founded by Gilbert of Laigle in 1229. It was stated in 1353 that the priory had been for 13 canons, but 8 were absent, presumably because of the Black Death (Knowles and Hadcock 1971, 166). Throughout the 15th and into the 16th century leading up to the suppression, Michelham had about 10 canons. According to Knowles and Hadcock (1971), Michelham, like Hastings, seems to have been in the Order of Arrouaise. Arrouaise was an abbey near Bapaume in France, where the Augustinian rule was adapted to include many Cistercian principles. Hardham Priory, the Priory of St. Cross, perched on a steep bank overlooking a former channel of the River Arun and founded in the mid-13th century, seems to have retained a small staff of about four or five canons throughout its history, at best the numbers rising to seven at the end of the 15th century (Knowles and Hadcock 1971, 158). Shulbrede, founded by Robert Arden just before the end of the 12th century, was much the same throughout its history with a complement of about six canons. At the more modest end of the scale, the Priory of St. Bartholomew, Pynham, founded before 1151 by Adela, second wife of Henry I, when she was countess of Arundel, was established to undertake the repair of the causeway and bridge over the Arun and to maintain a hospital or hostelry for poor travellers. There were only two or three canons, and when the priory was suppressed for the sake of Cardinal Wolsey's College at Oxford in 1524 (along with many other small houses), there was only one canon left (Knowles and Hadcock 1971, 171).

The Friars

The Friars or mendicant orders whose religious ideal, unlike that of the monks and canons, was to be of service in the secular world rather than to withdraw from it, are well-represented in the more populated medieval Sussex towns at Arundel (Blackfriars), Chichester (Blackfriars, Greyfriars,

Austin friars), Lewes (Greyfriars), Rye (Austin friars, Friars of the Sack) Shoreham (Carmelites), and Winchelsea (Greyfriars and Blackfriars). They often occupied marginal sites close to rivers, or near the sea in the case of some of the ports. At Lewes the Greyfriars site, excavated in the 1980s (Gardiner *et al.* 1996; Fig. 13.4) was on low-lying, reclaimed, marshy land on the floodplain of the River Ouse, squeezed between the town ditch to the west and the River Ouse to the east. At Arundel what remains of the Blackfriars' buildings is immediately beside the River Arun to the north of the bridge (Hudson 1993).

As a reminder that coastal change and sea level rise was just as much a problem in historic times as today, the records of the friary sites in Sussex show that at Shoreham and Winchelsea (as with the Augustinian canons at Hastings), the friars had to move to alternative locations when their establishments were in imminent danger of being washed away. Both the Blackfriars and Greyfriars of Old Winchelsea were granted sites in Edward I's new planned town (Fig. 13.5; and *see* David Martin's article on Winchelsea in this volume), and the Carmelite friars of Shoreham moved to the former Benedictine priory of Sele (Upper Beeding) in 1493.

Hospitals

Also based in or close to the towns were numbers of hospitals. Medieval hospitals were not exclusively for the care of the sick, the term covered a broad range of institutions. Some might be founded to serve the poor and aged, to provide a hostel for travellers, or to provide a combination of all these facilities. They were staffed by a chaplain and clergy assisted by brethren and sisters who in most cases followed a strict life and observed a rule which was effectively monastic. Hospitals were usually based in the midst of the community they served, or close to key routes/crossing points for travellers and pilgrims. Leper hosptials were naturally located at a distance from the town (*see* Maudlin; St James, Chichester; Bidlington by Bramber; St. Leonards, Seaford - destroyed by the sea in 1368).

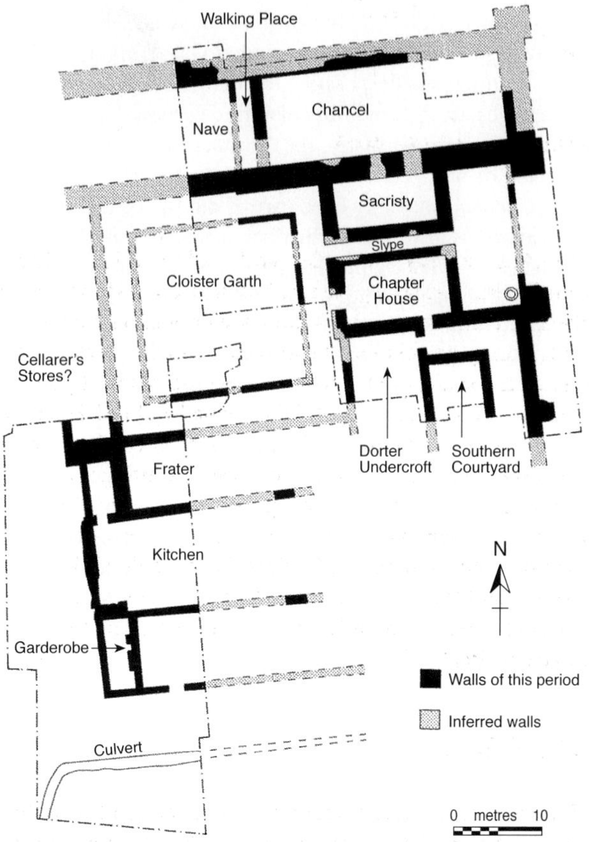

Figure 13.4. *Lewes Friary: Period 4 (?late 13th/early 14th century) plan. After Gardiner et al. 1996.*

Figure 13.5. *Chancel of the Greyfriars Church, Winchelsea: viewed from the south. (Photograph: David Rudling).*

The Military Orders

The military orders can also be found in medieval Sussex. At Poling the Knights Hospitallers were granted land and property in the early 14th century (Knowles and Hadcock 1971, 305). At Shipley, the Knights Templar were granted the manor and church by Philip de Harcourt *c.*1125 and at Saddlescombe the Templars were granted a manor by Geoffrey de Say (Knowles and Hadcock 1971, 295).

The monastic 'household'

The numbers of monks or canons in monastic establishments may often appear small compared with the potential accommodation in the complex of conventual buildings attached to the church. In practice the monastic household comprised more than the core of monks or canons alone and would include a number of servants and other staff with administrative duties. For every monk at Norwich there were more than two servants, and for every canon at Nostell Priory there were three (Butler and Given-Wilson 1979). There were also a number of 'hangers-on'. There might be guests, paying or not - using the monastery in effect as a hotel, and this could account for a sixth of the numbers. Retired abbots or priors would often be given a pension as well as rooms, clothing and a food allowance. The most numerous lodgers were corrodians, often bringing their wives and families with them, who had given money or land to the house in the past as an annuity in return for being looked after in old age. Bayham sold a corrody to a man and his disabled son and guaranteed to provide for his daughters, teach his younger sons a trade, pay all his debts and send an annual fee to his lawyer (Butler and Given-Wilson, 1979, 76).

Decline

By the early 16th century it was clear that monasticism in England was in decline. The numbers of religious men or women in individual houses were falling; in many cases the houses were in financial difficulties and the buildings themselves were in a poor state of repair. The process of closing down religious houses had already started at the end of the 15th century in order that the buildings, land and other resources could be put to new uses. The Bishop of Ely closed down a nunnery in Cambridge in 1497 so that its buildings and endowments could be used for his newly founded Jesus College. Similarly a few years later the Bishop of Rochester applied the property and revenue of two small nunneries to his new college of St. John's. In the 1520s Cardinal Wolsey embarked on a more ambitious project in which 29 religious houses were suppressed to provide endowments for a grammar school in Ipswich, his birthplace, and a new college in Oxford - i.e. Christchurch (Bayham, in 1525, and Pynham, also in 1525, were Sussex examples amongst these.)

Dissolution

When the Act for the Suppression of the Lesser Monasteries was introduced in 1536, it was proposed as a measure for reform rather than profiteering from lands and income. The process by which the spiritual wellbeing of the monasteries (or lack of it) was assessed involved rapid visitations carried out by a small team of officials. They covered nearly every monastery and nunnery in the country in the six months preceding the introduction of the Act of Suppression. But once the reports of the royal appointees' findings came back to Henry VIII's minister, Thomas Cromwell, his policy shifted rapidly towards total suppression, and damaging accusations of wrongdoing and moral laxity were seen as compelling means of achieving this. The letters to Cromwell from Richard Layton, the royal appointee who visited houses in Sussex, contain some memorable, if not scurrilous claims, but their reliability is questionable. Layton was scathing about the Abbot of Battle, and no less so about the monks and the abbey itself: "so beggary a house I never see, nor so filthy stuff....the stuff is like the persons" (Knowles 1955 III, 284). In similar vein on Durford Abbey, Layton remarked that it had better be called "Dirtford". Of Boxgrove, Layton remarked that the prior had only two mistresses, and his monks were of the same pattern. After he visited Shulbrede, Layton wrote that the prior had seven mistresses and his monks four or five each (Knowles 1955 III, 482). (Earlier visitations by the bishop, in the 1520s, and shortly beforehand in 1536, had not identified any irregularity at either house.)

As soon as the suppression of a monastery had been ratified, the process of turning their buildings and contents into cash began. It was the 16th-century equivalent of a car boot sale, but on a national scale. All the plate and jewels that had not already been appropriated for the Crown were sent up to the royal treasury, and all the portable items were put up for auction on the spot (whether church furniture, vestments and fittings, or building materials and equipment which could be recycled, such as brick, tile, paving stones, glass, ladders, etc.)

No object was inappropriate, no offer too small. As for the buildings, the official instructions were that the commissioners should 'pull down to the ground all the walls of the churches, steeples, cloisters, fraters, dormitories, chapter houses' and the rest (Knowles 1955). At Lewes, the demolition was speedily performed by Giovanni Portinari and his team of 25 Italian workmen. The great church of St. Pancras with its high steeple and its vault 93ft over the high altar (i.e. nearly half as high again as the nave of Chichester Cathedral) was soon 'pulled down to the ground'. Lewes Priory had been granted to Thomas Cromwell on 16th February 1638, and was given by him to his son Gregory as a residence. The pace of the destruction is breathtaking. Portinari had begun work shortly before 20th March, and by April 11th Gregory was able to write to his father that Mrs. Cromwell 'found the place so commodious that she thinketh herself to be here right well settled'.

The function of the monasteries

It would be wrong to assume that by this time monasteries had become irrelevant to lay people. They had always been popular throughout the Middle Ages and had an important social function to perform. The monasteries did not simply exist for the sake of the monks within the cloister; the founders and benefactors of monasteries saw monks performing an essential function by praying for their souls and acting as substitutes to undertake on their behalf penances which otherwise they themselves would have been unable to perform. For example, in 923, the Frankish bishops imposed on everyone who had fought at the Battle of Soissons a three-year penance which involved fasting on bread, salt and water for three periods of 40 days in each year. This might just have been physically possible to endure, but it would have put a large part of the nobility of northern France out of action for some time. Similarly, the Norman bishops imposed a penance of one year for each man killed at Hastings. Had such a penance actually been carried out by the members of the victorious army, the further conquest and subjugation of England would have ground to a halt. The monasteries, staffed by monks bound by religious vows, offered the surest way of fulfilling a supernatural debt by being endowed with the resources to take on the penance on another's behalf. The monasteries also often helped to provide a career outlet and an honourable position in society for the younger sons and daughters of the nobility who could not expect to inherit.

Archaeological Investigations: Recent and Future Work

Turning to archaeological evidence, what contribution has been made to our understanding of the subject by archaeological fieldwork and structural survey? In the years since the Sussex Archaeological Society was first brought into existence by cutting the route of the London Brighton and South Coast Railway through the site of Lewes Priory in 1846, there has been relatively little investigation in the ensuing 150 years or more with notable exceptions (*see* below). Most of the smaller monastic sites (such as the Augustinian houses converted to farmhouses, etc.) are in private ownership and protected by a combination of

scheduling or listing (or both). Given the present legislative control and planning policy, the prospects of research excavation seem remote and such sites are unlikely to be the subject of the kind of development proposals which would require trial excavation and recording under the terms of Government Planning Guidance on Archaeology and Planning (PPG16). In consequence, there are sites where the upstanding remains are no better understood now than they were over a century ago.

However, a rare opportunity recently presented itself as part of the scheduled monument consent application to English Heritage and planning application to Arun District Council, for conversion of farm buildings to create a single-storey dwelling at Tortington Priory. The initial evaluation was carried out by Archaeology South-East in 1997 (Stevens 1997) and further recording by this organization took place in 1998 and 2001 (Johnson 1999; Griffin 2001). The 1998 recording was undertaken in advance of, and during, groundworks for rafted foundations for the new residential accommodation, and for new drains and services. The preliminary evaluation of 1997 demonstrated that the base of the foundation for the south aisle wall of the priory church could be identified at a depth of more than a metre below the ground level of the former farm yard. Although the plan of the foundations of the east end of the priory church is readily visible as a series of soil-covered banks, it was unclear what evidence of the other conventual buildings might survive.

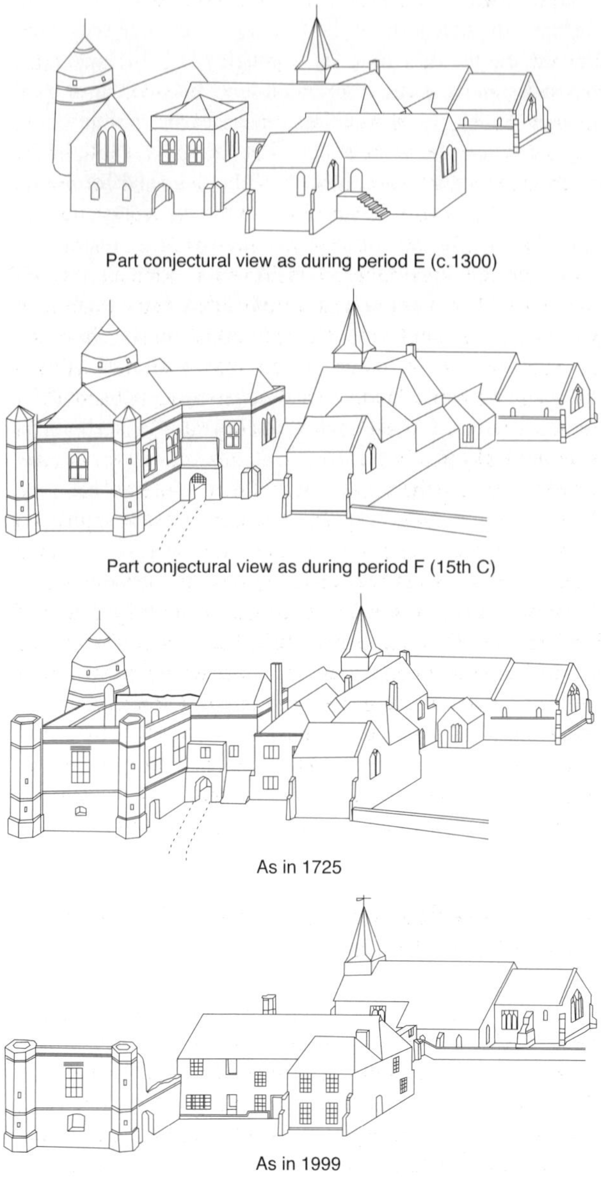

Figure 13.6. *Wilmington Priory: Bird's eye views of the house from the south-east (after Martin and Johnson 2000, Drawing 3).*

In 1909 fieldwork was undertaken by P. M. Johnston, but he never completed a proper report on the excavation beyond a set of brief notes, and any plans of the excavations alluded to in the notes appear to have been lost. A summary of the findings of those notes was published by L.F. Salzman (1946). The notes can be seen with other P.M. Johnston material on Sussex churches at WSRO Acc 10,352 (file 39). Of the key points cited by Salzman, it can be concluded that the plan of the monastic church and precinct was recoverable over an extensive area. A layout typical of a large cruciform aisled and vaulted church with central tower is described, but the early excavators were in some doubt whether the south aisle of the nave and the south transept were ever built, as all traces of their foundations had apparently disappeared. As an afterthought the notes intriguingly suggest that "To the south of the church, foundations of numerous buildings, including a gate-house (partly of timber) and various halls and chambers were also uncovered and planned out". Clearly the early excavators had not gone deep enough to find the traces of the south aisle wall foundation, the wall itself presumably having been completely robbed out as part of the destruction following the Dissolution.

The recording undertaken in 1998 in advance of the construction of the new dwelling produced further significant discoveries corroborating Johnston's observations on the potential extent of the site. It established that the west wall of the priory church survives for its entire length and in some places is up to a metre or more in height. Furthermore, remains of a central doorway in the west wall, with steps down into the nave, were discovered, as were traces of the bases supporting the attached shafts of the aisle arcades. This information, taken in conjunction with the location of the shafts supporting the springing of the north aisle vaulting enables the position of the bases of the piers of the nave aisles to be pinpointed accurately (Fig. 13.7). Equally exciting was the discovery of a very small patch of tiled nave flooring attached to the north aisle arcade shaft base on the east-facing elevation of the surviving west wall. The floor had been finished in a striking diagonal pattern of black and pale creamy yellow tiles. The nave flooring was presumably stripped out at the Dissolution, together with other reusable materials. Adjacent to the southern end of the west wall was an area of tiled flooring which is thought to have been part of the cloister walk. Although the south nave aisle wall had been extensively robbed, it was discovered, while monitoring a drain run in the location of the south transept, that both the west and east walls lie *in situ* not more than 300mm or so below the present ground surface. Clearly the potential for the foundations of other elements of the conventual plan to survive below ground is considerable and suggests that Johnston's 1909 account of an extensive monastic complex is valid.

The evaluation and further recording action has in itself established key evidence. The location of the south nave aisle wall and the south transept has been fixed, and it would appear that the entire ground plan of the priory church, though suffering from a badly robbed or damaged length of south aisle wall, is *in situ* and traceable, and that the position of the nave aisle piers can be established. The level of the nave floor, and by implication the choir floor, can be fixed from a surviving *in situ* fragment, and the striking contrast of black and cream tiles can be pictured. The location of the central west doorway has been established and the presence of the steps leading down from the external ground level (and the presence of a plinth course reflecting the higher external ground level abutting the west-facing elevation of the west wall) show that the layout of the church and claustral buildings had to take account of the gentle slope of the ground from west to east towards the River Arun, and were 'terraced in'. This was presumably because the chancel, as was often the case, would have been constructed and dedicated first of all, and the builders then worked from east to west, constructing the central crossing and the nave until the west wall had to be partly built into the slope. Internal details such as the position of shaft bases of the aisle arcades enable the site of column bases to be plotted with accuracy. During July 2001 a watching brief to monitor groundworks involved the recording of a substantial chalk rubble wall which is suspected to be the foundations of the southern cloister wall. In addition, a well-made lintel drain and the edge of a second wall, both forming part of the services and structure for the eastern range of buildings within the precinct, were also located. Thus as a result of the various recent archaeological works much more detail is now known about this Augustinian Priory (Fig. 13.8).

There will be an opportunity for further recording when the barn roof is repaired and re-thatched, and structural details of the external elevations of the north aisle wall can be examined more closely. The barn was built post-Dissolution (probably in the 17th century) using the upstanding remains of two walls of the former church that had not been completely levelled: namely the north aisle wall and the west wall of the north transept. In effect the external walls of the church have become the internal walls of the barn and *vice versa,* giving the effect that the structure appears to have been turned inside out.

At Hardham Priory near Pulborough, an Augustinian site overlooking a former tributary of the Arun, a resistivity survey was carried out in 1996 by Stratascan on behalf of the owner and West Sussex County Council. Although the survey, which is unpublished, did not reveal evidence of the foundations of the former church, it did show other foundations. The plotted data indicate possible buried foundations or foundation trenches of former buildings in the lawns and grassy areas around the remains of the south range and Chapter House. They also suggest that the south range may have been double the width, perhaps as a result of a later phase of construction, but at the undercroft level, the columns of the south elevation appear to be 'in the round' and embedded in the walling as if they were once free-standing and originally part of a larger undercroft area. There are a number of possible explanations; there could have been partial destruction of the south range at the Dissolution, but it is also possible that this part of the south range experienced structural problems early on and was being undermined by the river channel which it overlooked. The resistivity survey indicated that the western range of claustral buildings is likely to survive as foundations or foundation trenches below ground level. The site of the reredorter and what might be a stone-lined monastic drain may also appear in the resistivity survey plots, but until such anomalies can be tested by excavation, this must remain largely speculative.

Pynham by Arundel, referred to earlier, is another Augustinian site that merits further research. The nature of the present building, a square tower-like block with later additions serving as outshuts to the north and south of the main part of the former farmhouse, is not well understood. There are buttresses to the rear (west elevation) of this main block and apparently evidence of window splays internally which indicate that the central, main block was clearly free-standing. Viewed from the east, the elevation of the farmhouse that one sees when descending the A27 towards Arundel is largely made up of re-used stone and the impression is given that the original medieval fabric was truncated. In an early volume of the *Sussex Archaeological Collections,* G.M. Hills (1866, 54-59) referred to Pynham in the context of Hardham and Tortington, and considered that the surviving building represented the remains of the common room (below the dormitory). Although this is possible in terms of the orientation of the building, the site at Pynham is so restricted that there is no likelihood that there was a conventual layout based around a cloister. Much could be discovered from a detailed study of the standing fabric, and a resistivity survey might establish the presence of footings below the lawn to the north of the central block.

During the last three decades there has been a significant increase in both excavation and survey work, examples of such projects including: Lewes Friary (Gardiner *et al.* 1996, Fig. 13.4); Lewes Priory (Lyne 1997); St. Nicholas Hospital, Lewes (Gardiner 1994, Barber and Sibun forthcoming); Bayham Abbey (Streeten 1983); Battle Abbey (Hare 1985); Boxgrove Priory (Priestley-Bell and Gardiner 1996); Robertsbridge Abbey (Martin and Martin 1995, Fig. 13.3); Hastings Priory (Martin 1973); Warbleton Priory (Martin and Martin 1976a and b); Wilmington Priory (Martin and Johnson 2000; Fig. 13.6) and Michelham Priory (Barton and Holden 1967; Stevens and Stevens 1991; Martin and Martin 1999) and survey work on the Greyfriars and Blackfriars sites at Winchelsea (Martin and Martin 2001). Overall there is still considerable scope for further research, particularly on Augustinian priory sites in Sussex.

Conclusions

The Norman Conquest made a significant impact upon monastic life in England and introduced far-reaching reform of the Church which overtook the process of reform already under way from Dunstan's time. The Norman nobility, already enthusiastic for endowing monastic establishments in their homeland, before long focused that enthusiasm on the English side of the Channel. The construction and reconstruction of

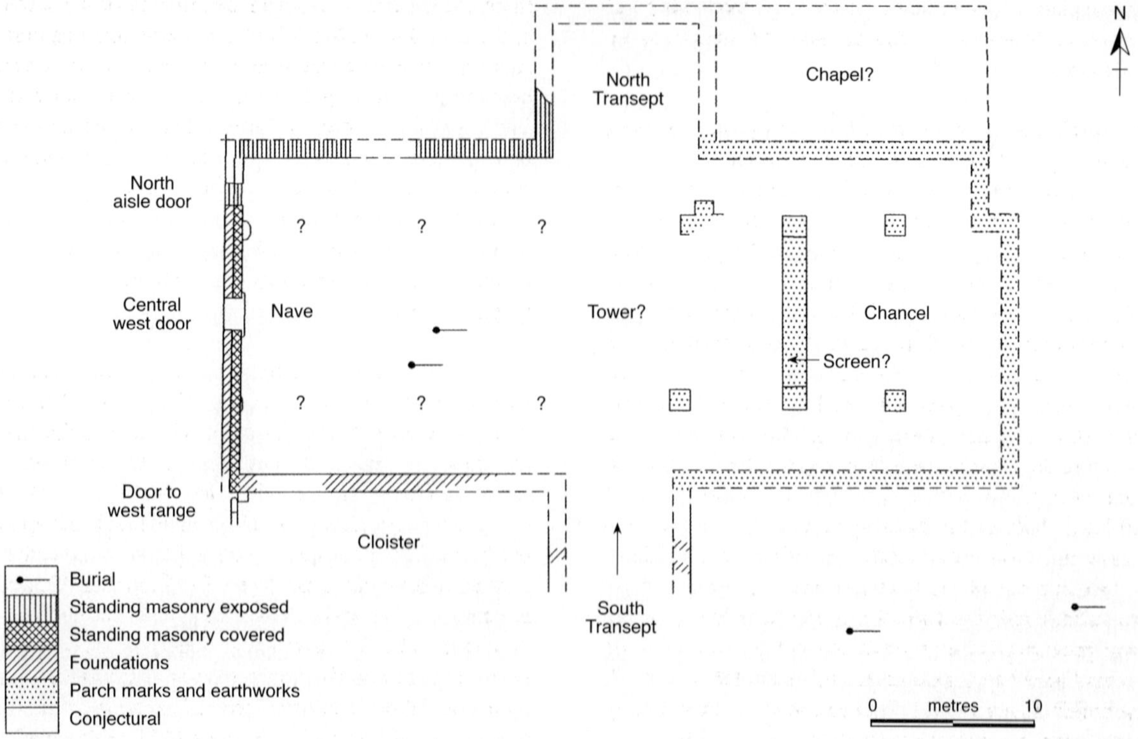

Figure 13.7. *Tortington Priory Barn: Postulated plan of Tortington Priory Church (after Johnson 1999, Fig. 7).*

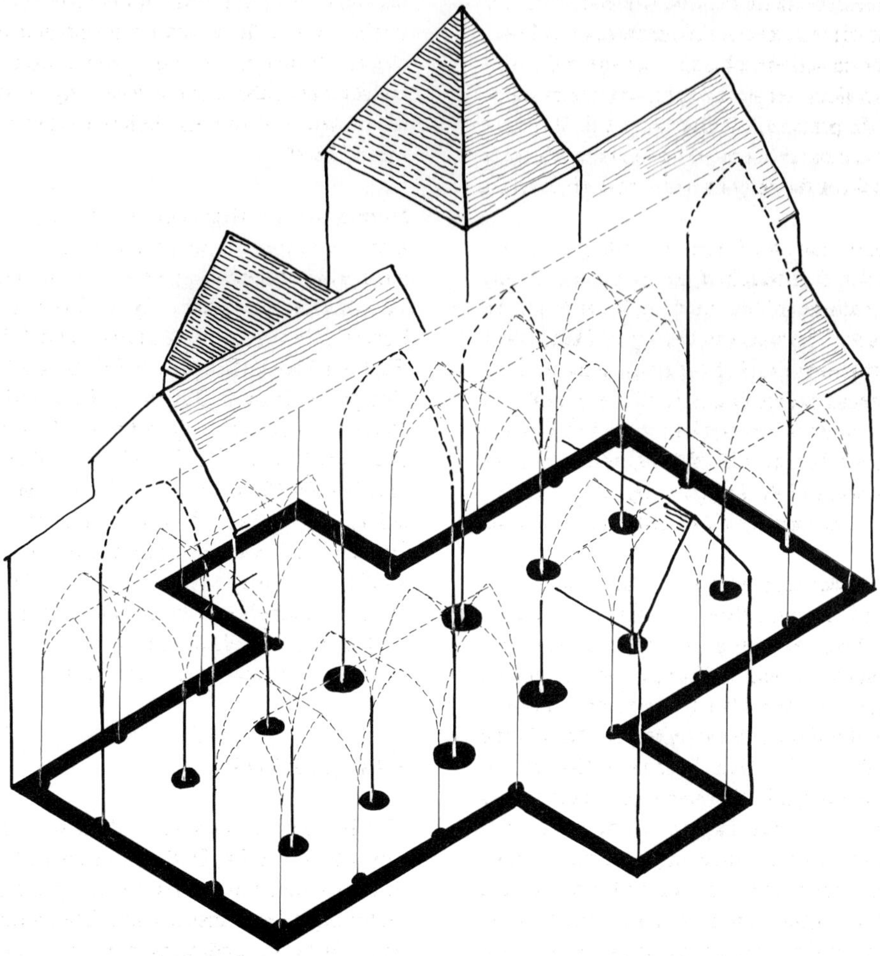

Figure 13.8. *Tortington Priory. Sketch drawing of how the church and vaulting might have worked. Viewed from the south-west.*

so many major churches following the Conquest represents an architectural revolution in England. The precinct of buildings belonging to monastic establishments developed a regular plan and layout which was common to the majority of Orders (except in specific cases such as Carthusian houses), whereas beforehand the communities had lived in an informal collection of structures. R.A. Brown (1969) summing up their influence, felt that the impetus given to the development of church building in England by the Normans, in time made its own contribution to the 12th century renaissance in the West, and anticipated the achievement of Gothic architecture seen by many as the triumph of the High Middle Ages. The paradox of the Dissolution is that while the devastation and iconoclasm deprived Sussex of what, in the great priory church of St. Pancras at Lewes was probably the finest and most elaborate church in the diocese, the effect elsewhere in Britain was to preserve, albeit as ruins, the appearance of the medieval design. Had monasteries been allowed to survive and had continued to be sustained by noble patronage, it is possible that the pressure for change and the influence of architectural innovation may have seen the destruction, in any event, of some of the fine medieval churches as Romanesque and Gothic gave way to the Baroque.

Appendix

In Sussex, Atherington (i.e. Bailiffscourt, Climping) founded before 1102, was an alien grange of Séez; Cocking appears to have been a cell of Séez; Boxgrove Priory, founded after 1105, was an alien priory of Lessay; Hooe, founded 1106, was an alien grange of Bec-Hellouin; Lyminster nunnery, founded c. 1082, was an alien priory of Almenèches; Rotherfield, founded pre-Conquest possibly as early as 790, was an alien priory of St. Denis; Runcton, founded before 1086, was an alien cell of Troarn; Sele, founded before 1126,was an alien priory of St. Florent-de-Saumur; Steyning church and manor were granted to Fécamp by Edward the Confessor, seized from them by Harold Godwinson, and returned to Fécamp by William I; Warminghurst, founded *c.*1085, was an alien grange of Fécamp; and Wilmington, founded before 1086 as an alien grange of Grestain became an alien grange to Grestain sometime before 1243.

References

Barber, L. and Sibun, L. Forthcoming. The excavation of the Medieval Hospital of St. Nicholas at Lewes.

Barton, K.J. and Holden, E.W. 1967. Excavations at Michelham Priory, *SAC* **105**, 1-12.

Brown, R.A. 1969. *The Normans and the Norman Conquest.* London: Constable.

Butler, L. and Given-Wilson, C. 1979. *Medieval Monasteries of Great Britain.* (1987 second impression). London: Michael Joseph.

Gardiner, M. 1994. 100 bodies at Medieval hospital, *Sussex Past & Present* **73**, 9.

Gardiner, M., Russell, M. and Gregory, D. 1996. Excavations at Lewes Friary 1985-6 and 1988-9, *SAC* **134**, 71-123.

Griffin, F. 2001. *An Archaeological Watching Brief at Priory Farm, Tortington, Arundel, West Sussex,* Archaeology South-East Project 1404. Unpublished.

Hare, J.N. 1985. *Battle Abbey, The Eastern Range and the Excavations of 1978-80,* London: Historic Buildings & Monuments Commission for England, Archaeological Report **2**.

Hills, G.M. 1866. Hardham Priory of Canons of St. Augustine, *SAC* **18**, 54-59.

Hobbs, M. (ed). 1994. *Chichester Cathedral: An Historical Survey.* Chichester: Phillimore.

Hudson, T.P. 1993. Arundel's Blackfriars Located, *SAC* **131**, 114-118.

Johnson, C. 1999. *Archaeological monitoring and recording at Tortington Priory Barn, Arundel, West Sussex.* Archaeology South-East Project 984. Unpublished.

Knowles, D. 1955. *The Religious Orders in England.* Cambridge: University Press.

Knowles, D. and Hadock, R.N. 1971. *Medieval Religious Houses in England and Wales.* London: Longman.

Lyne, M. 1997. *Lewes Priory Excavations by Richard Lewis, 1969-82.* Lewes: Lewes Priory Trust.

Martin, D. 1973. *Hastings Augustinian Priory – an excavation report.* Hastings Area Archaeological Papers.

Martin, D. and Martin, B. 1976a. *Warbleton- The Priory.* Revised report of 1967. Rape of Hastings Architectural Survey. Unpublished. ESRO HBR 1/0604.

Martin, D. and Martin, B. 1976b. *Warbleton – Remains of the Claustral Buildings.* Rape of Hastings Architectural Survey. Unpublished. ESRO HBR 1/0141.

Martin, D. and Martin, B. 1995. *Salehurst – Robertsbridge Abbey.* Revised report for the Rape of Hastings Architectural Survey. Unpublished. ESRO HBR 1/0604.

Martin, D. and Martin, B. 1999. *An Archaeological Interpretative Survey of Michelham Priory, Arlington, East Sussex, including selective archaeological recording of the roofs.* Archaeology South-East Project 987. Unpublished. ESRO HBR 1/1056.

Martin, D. and Johnson C. 2000. *An Interpretative Survey of Wilmington Priory, Wilmington, East Sussex, incorporating a report on Archaeological Investigations, 1998-2000.* Archaeology South-East Project 895. Unpublished. ESRO HBR 1/1046.

Martin, D. and Martin, B. 2001. *A Quarter by Quarter Analysis of the Town of Winchelsea, East Sussex.* Unpublished. Copy in the East Sussex Record Office.

Priestley-Bell, G. and Gardiner, M. 1996. Boxgrove Priory: Recording and Trial Excavation, *The Archaeology of Chichester and District 1995*, 16-17.

Salzman, L.F. 1946. Tortington Priory Excavations, *SNQ* **11**, No. 2, 45-46.

Searle, E. 1980. *The Chronicle of Battle Abbey.* Oxford: Clarendon Press.

Stevens, L. and Stevens, P. 1991. Excavations on the South Lawn, Michelham Priory, Sussex 1971-1976, *SAC* **129**, 45-79.

Stevens, S. 1997. *An Archaeological Evaluation at Tortington Priory Barn, Arundel,* Archaeology South-East Project 762. Unpublished.

Streeten, A. 1983. *Bayham Abbey, Recent research, including a report on excavations (1973-76) directed by the late Helen Sutermeister,* Sussex Archaeological Society Monograph **2**.

HASTINGS TO HERSTMONCEUX: THE CASTLES OF SUSSEX

Richard Jones

Abstract

This paper seeks to identify current weaknesses in the study of the castles of Sussex and to identify areas for future research. Despite a number of individual castle excavations, little attempt has been made to understand the development of the network of fortifications built across the county between 1066 and 1500. This paper attempts to begin that task, but does not purport to follow this to its final conclusion.

Introduction

To treat castles in isolation, as was first intended here, is at one and the same time to exaggerate their military importance (it was from castles and nowhere else that Sussex was defended), and to reduce their potency (how could Sussex be defended from so few strongholds?). In reality, the defence of Sussex, and ultimately the defence of the realm, relied on a network of defensive works which included not only castles *per se*, but also fortified churches, abbeys, and priories, moated sites, crenellated manors and walled towns. To ignore the role that these other sites played is dangerous, if not fatally flawed, so while the castle must be treated as a unique medieval phenomenon, other defensive measures must be considered alongside.

First, we must define what we mean by a castle. To help us we have the dictionary definition: castle: *n.* a fortified house or fortress: the residence of a prince or nobleman, or a large country mansion generally… [O.E. – *castel* – L. *castellum*, dim. of *castrum*, a fortified place]. It should immediately be clear that the castle is difficult to classify: is it simply a defensive structure or is it also a residence? The answer, of course, is both, and a lot more besides.

As already noted, castles are just one of a number of types of medieval fortification. They are unique to the period, which we may define in England as 1066 - *c.*1500, being almost entirely non-existent in the Pre-Conquest period and superfluous to need by the end of the Middle Ages. They were a product of their time and of the society in which they were built. Unlike the defended town, whose origins can be traced back first through the Anglo-Saxon period, to the Iron Age and earlier prehistoric periods, the castle has little or no history in England prior to 1066. While similar functions, primarily that of defence, were shared, it is as well to identify the fundamental differences between the castle and all other fortification types. Prehistoric enclosures, Roman walled towns, Anglo-Saxon burhs and the medieval defended towns were designed to defend large areas and extended communities against a common threat, albeit driven by a social élite more interested in defending its own interests. In the castle, the pretence of defence for all was lost altogether. It is of interest here to note that in the Latin, *castellum* is the diminutive form of *castrum*, in itself suggesting smaller scales of operation. The castle was the categorical statement of the powerful and wealthy few that they were prepared to invest time, money and effort, in securing their own individual futures. In this regard the castle has no precursors, no pedigree.

Castles, however, were more than defensive redoubts. They acted as garrison centres and supply bases from which offensive actions could be mounted. They acted as administrative centres for public authorities, as well as for private lordship, where fealty was rendered and services performed. They provided spacious, and sometimes luxurious, accommodation for their owners, and they were used as the physical symbols or badges of social, political, and economic standing. Given all these factors, therefore, it is perhaps unsurprising that the castle adopted so many shapes and forms.

So to the castles of Sussex, a county that can boast the first historically (note not archaeologically) recorded castles in England: at Pevensey which was used on landing (William of Jumièges: *Gesta Normannorum Ducum*), and soon after at Hastings, and one of the last at Herstmonceux. In a break with tradition in Sussex, where the efforts of both historians and archaeologists have tended to be concentrated on individual sites, this paper will look at the broader picture. How many castles were built in Sussex? When were they constructed, or for what reason? Is their distribution significant? And what form did they take? (see Fig.14.1)

Numbers and dates

Taking the loosest definition of a castle, incorporating the roles of defence and/or residence, nearly 300 sites with defensive capabilities can be identified. By far the largest number of these are the moated sites, which predominate on the Wealden clay and on the coastal plain. Over 230 have so far been recorded (Brandon 1974, 136; Aldsworth 1980, *passim*). In addition to these, four ecclesiastical houses fortified during the period can be added (Battle Abbey, Lewes Priory, Michelham Priory, Wilmington Priory), to say nothing of the parish churches which may have been used for local defence, as they were in Normandy (Jones 1994, 39-42). Our definition also allows us to recognize the existence of a fourth category of site, the crenellated manor, of which Sussex possesses 12 (Blaauw 1861), and a fifth, hunting lodges, of which there are three (Verdley, Knepp and Sedgewick).

Eighteen 'true' castle sites, defined as those whose primary function was defence, have been identified in Sussex. These include major royal and baronial foundations and lesser defences too. They range today from significant masonry remains, to earthworks, to soil marks identified from aerial photographs. In toto, the defences of Sussex did not exist contemporaneously. To produce a distribution map of these sites, as has been the tradition, therefore leads to the erroneous

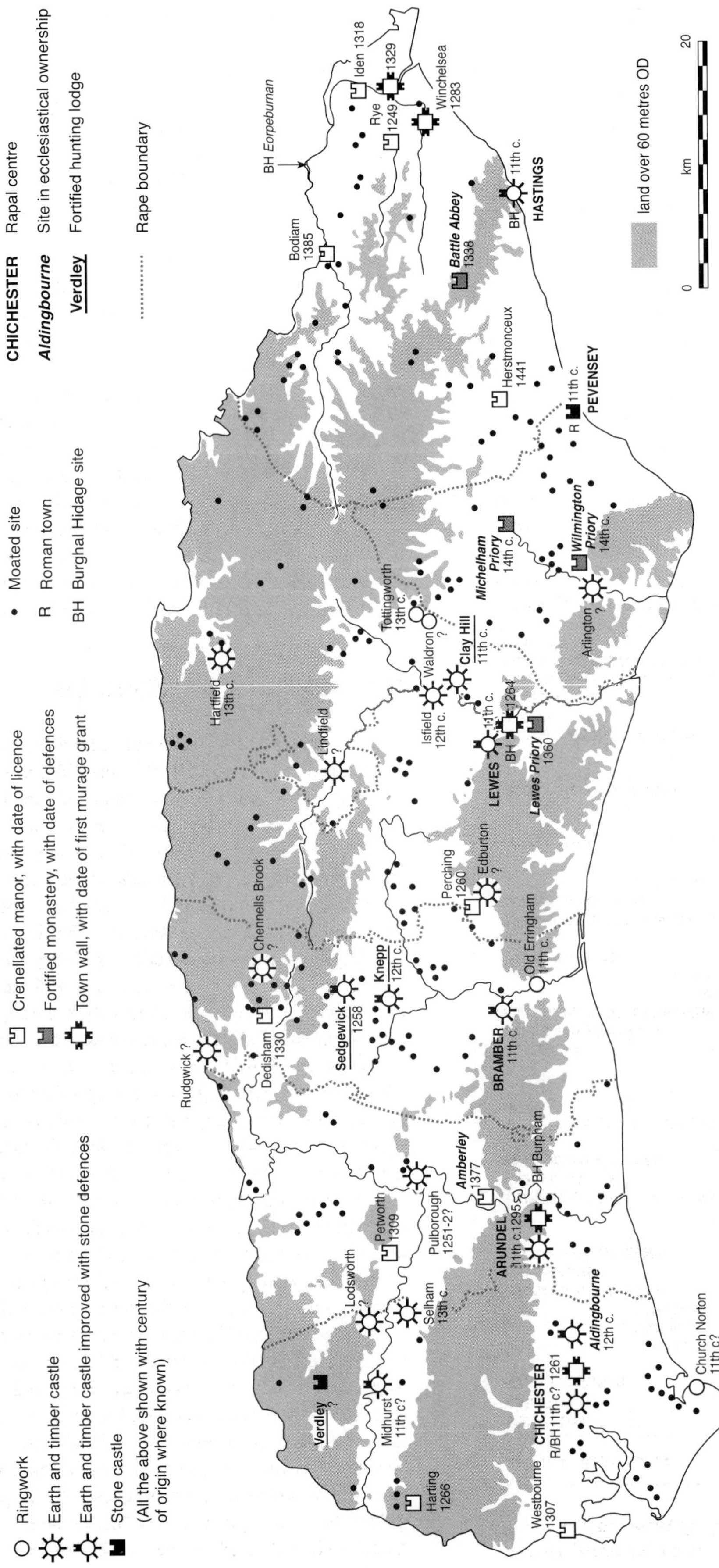

Figure 14.1 The castles and other defensive sites of Sussex: some attempt has been made here to represent chronology as well as distribution. (Jones 1999)

conclusion that Sussex was well-served by fortifications at any one time. In fact, the network of fortifications was slow to evolve and never linear. As some castles were constructed others were abandoned or demolished (Fig. 14.2). Chichester castle, for example, was ordered to be destroyed in 1217 and the site was vacant by 1222 (Magilton 1995). It is therefore essential that each site be considered within its chronological brackets if meaningful relationships are to be produced.

This necessitates the marriage of both historical and archaeological sources. Not all defended sites in Sussex appear in the written record, and likewise not all sites have been scientifically excavated. Put together, however, the following pattern of evolution emerges. By 1100, after the initial military phase of the Norman Conquest, 11 fortified sites had been established. These included the six rapal castles of Chichester, Arundel, Bramber, Lewes, Pevensey, and Hastings, the pivotal centres of medieval Sussex. By 1150 the number of castles *and other fortified sites (but excluding moated sites)* had risen to 22, and increased to 26 by the end of the 12th century. This increase follows national trends and can be attributed to two factors: first the anarchy during the reign of King Stephen (1135-53), which saw the proliferation of adulterine or unlicensed castles; and second, with the establishment of political power, the spread of castle builders, from the King and the major magnates to the lesser infeudates who copied their overlords. The 13th century saw a drop in the number of fortified sites relating to a period of greater stability and reduced threat from overseas. Renewed conflict with France from the first half of the 14th century however was mirrored by an increase from 16 strongholds in 1250 to 26 fortified sites in 1400. This rise is largely accounted for by the construction of town walls at Arundel, Lewes, Winchelsea and Rye, together with the fortification of ecclesiastical sites such as the priories of Lewes, Michelham and Wilmington, the abbey of Battle and the Bishop of Chichester's manor of Amberley. The general process of fortification and refortification can therefore be related to other social, political and military factors, in line with other areas of the country. The overall picture is unlikely to alter radically with more research but the actual figures should be expected to change slightly with further work. But the importance of the identification of these sites cannot be measured simply in numbers. The importance lies in their distribution. This in turn can be seen in three ways – networks and relationships, actual location, and spheres of influence.

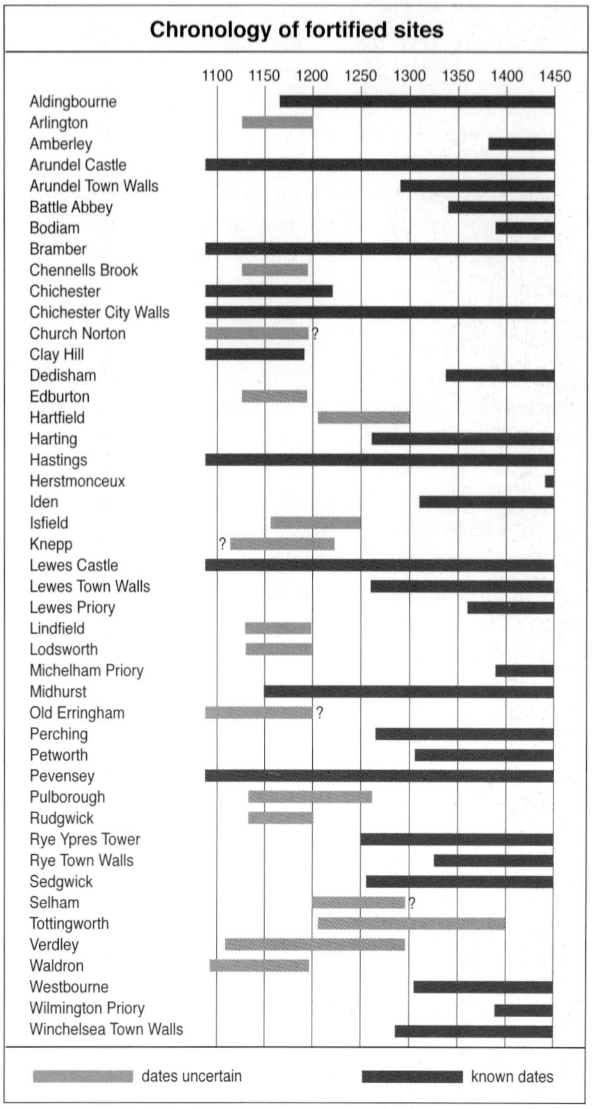

Figure 14.2. *Tentative chronology of Sussex castles and other fortifications, based on documentary and archaeological evidence.*

Networks and Relationships

The basis of the early medieval defensive system was the Rape, a Norman innovation (Mason 1964, *passim*). Sussex was originally split into four major administrative units, stretching north from the coast over the South Downs and the Weald to the northern border of the county (each controlled from an important castle). These were the Rapes of Hastings, Pevensey, Lewes and Arundel, granted to a major magnate with close links and proven loyalty to William I. By 1086, a fifth Rape was in the process of being added, that of Bramber, carved from the western half of Lewes and the eastern part of Arundel. A sixth was ultimately created, centred on Chichester, originally the western part of the enormous Rape of Arundel. While these rapes were in large part administrative, breaking up old Anglo-Saxon landholding patterns and producing more consolidated estates, they functioned on a military level too. Not only did this division help to strengthen the defence of the south coast, they also guaranteed communication between the two Norman powerbases: the Duchy of Normandy and their new capital of London. A major concern of the Conqueror was rebellion. Had Sussex been granted to a single magnate (as was the case in Kent, although here the magnate was Odo of Bayeux who had strong familial links with the Conqueror), and had that magnate turned against the King, access to and from Normandy would have been cut. The rapal system was organized as a series of communication corridors. If one or more was lost, then others would still allow movement between the centres of power. It was far less likely that six magnates would rebel at one moment. The Rapes therefore reflect the unique position that Sussex held – a front line 'state', to be defended and held at all cost, but also the vital link in the chain between England and the Continent.

From these major centres, secondary fortifications were established throughout the individual rapes. It is rare, however, for these links to be made explicit. Knepp (a fortified hunting lodge) from Bramber (a castle) is an exception. The historical sources show the hierarchical relationship between the two. In a letter dated 18th May 1214, King John ordered Roeland Bloet, his agent at Knepp,

> '...without delay, to transfer all the stores which you have at Knapp, or elsewhere, and which you may be able to gather, to Bremble; and that you fortify that house in the best possible manner you can, while resident in that castle; that you destroy altogether the houses at Knapp...' (Burrell 1850, 8).

Here the supremacy of Bramber over Knepp is clear: the latter would be sacrificed for the former in times of trouble. More often, however, the links between castles can only be inferred. That two sites are located within the same Rape implies some sort of relationship through lordship. This scenario has been argued for the foundation of Midhurst by Roger of Montgommery from the rapal castle of Arundel (Thompson 1996, 49).

Relationships between castles were not restricted to rapal boundaries. Over time, castles designed to act independently became linked through ownership. In the Treaty of Winchester (November 1153) William of Blois, the son of King Stephen and husband of Isabel, who was the daughter of William, third Earl of Warenne, was given all the holdings pertaining to the Warennes (Lewes Rape in Sussex), and the castle and other holdings belonging to the honour of Pevensey. This arrangement produced a powerful block in central Sussex under single lordship (Douglas and Greenaway 1953, 405). That the castles of Sussex were designed to act in unison, and not independently, for the defence of the realm, also emerges from the later documentary evidence. In 1233-4 Henry III ordered Peter of Rivaux to deliver up the castles of Bramber, Knepp and Pevensey, to Robert de Sauvage, on account of the danger of war with France, those castles being on the seacoast and the truce then existing being about to expire (Burrell 1852, 144). Further work is required to understand fully these relationships. How were these castles garrisoned? How were the garrisons financed? The inter-relationship between sites was complex and fluid, yet this aspect of castle studies holds many of the keys to unlock the chronological and topographical development of the defence of Sussex.

Location

To understand further how these castles operated together one must look at their location. Location and function are interlinked. One can explain the other. Commentators have been quick to point out that the six rapal castles are all located to the south of their administrative area, apparently looking to defend the coast rather than the interior. Indeed, the conclusion that the rapes were designed to ensure royal passage back and forth from London to Normandy is now well-established. Beyond these simple observations, however, little has been written concerning the location of the lesser fortifications.

Several castles were located to dominate river valleys and their bridging points. The western Rother, for example, was protected by castles at Midhurst, at Selham (Lodsworth Mill), and at Lodsworth itself, while the confluence of the Rother with the Arun was dominated by the castle at Pulborough. The fortification at Arlington was located at the narrowest point of the Cuckmere valley as it passes through the South Downs, while away from the river, the elevated location of Lewes castle allowed a major stretch of the river Ouse to be surveyed. Arundel and Bramber make interesting cases. In both instances the Normans ignored the Anglo-Saxon centres and created new ones of their own. This must have been done for a reason. For Arundel the reasons appear twofold: first the castle dominated a lower bridging point than Burpham, its predecessor; and second from the new site the mouth of the Arun could be seen. This may explain the two mottes at Lewes. From the lesser of the two, Brack Mount, considered by some as the earlier, the town is dominated but views to the coast are restricted. From the top of the keep on the greater of the two the sea can be seen. The castle of Bramber, ignoring Steyning, was also moved closer to the river Adur and the bridging point. Below Bramber was the site of Old Erringham, while above it was the fortified hunting lodge of Knepp. By the mid-1100s, therefore, all the major rivers running to the coast had their own fortifications.

Inspection of castle location suggests that surviving Roman infrastructure profoundly affected the medieval defensive system. This historic factor is rarely brought to the fore when explaining the medieval military networks. It is therefore worth looking at the Sussex evidence here since it may have implications for other areas of the country. Two sites have obvious links. At Chichester and at Pevensey the medieval castles were constructed within Roman fortifications. Less evident is the influence of the Roman road system. Three fortified sites were positioned along the Lewes-London Roman road – Lewes, Isfield and Hartfield. While not strictly a castle, it is interesting to note that the fortification at Isfield is located at the confluence of the rivers Uck and Ouse, using both in its defensive works, at the very place where the Lewes-London Roman road crosses the river. There is also a Mote Field at Holtye, again on the line of the road, which may suggest an as yet unidentified fourth castle site. Along Stane Street are found Chichester itself, with Pulborough and the fortified manor of Dedisham no more than half a kilometre from its line. The Greensand Way running north of the scarp of the Downs was dominated by Edburton and Perching, and if its line is projected beyond Barcombe it runs very close to Clay Hill, north of Ringmer. Clearly, therefore, just as the rivers were defended, effort was made to defend the major road arteries run through the county. It was well understood that to defend large areas one must restrict an enemy's movements.

Spheres of Influence

Castles could protect large hinterlands. In 1111 King Louis VI of France warned his captains that they should not go within eight or ten miles of Le Puiset, then in enemy hands, for fear of ambush (Jones 1999b). This provides some idea of the kind of area that each site in Sussex may have dominated. Whilst accepting that theoretical exercises like

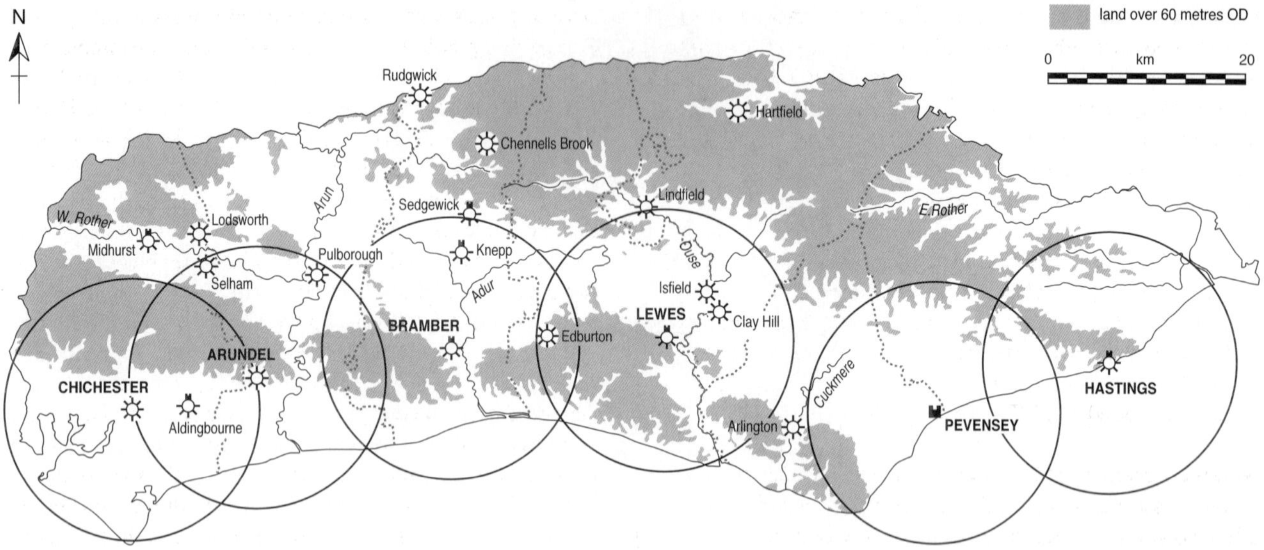

Figure 14.3. Spheres of influence c.1150-1200: the rapal castles based on an 8 mile radius. The map clearly shows the weak link in the system at the Cuckmere valley. Note where the arcs from Arundel, Bramber and Lewes meet on the coast, showing efficient coverage. Note also the proximity of many secondary sites to these arcs – Selham, Pulborough, Sedgwick, Edburton, Tottingworth, Arlington etc. (after Jones 1999).

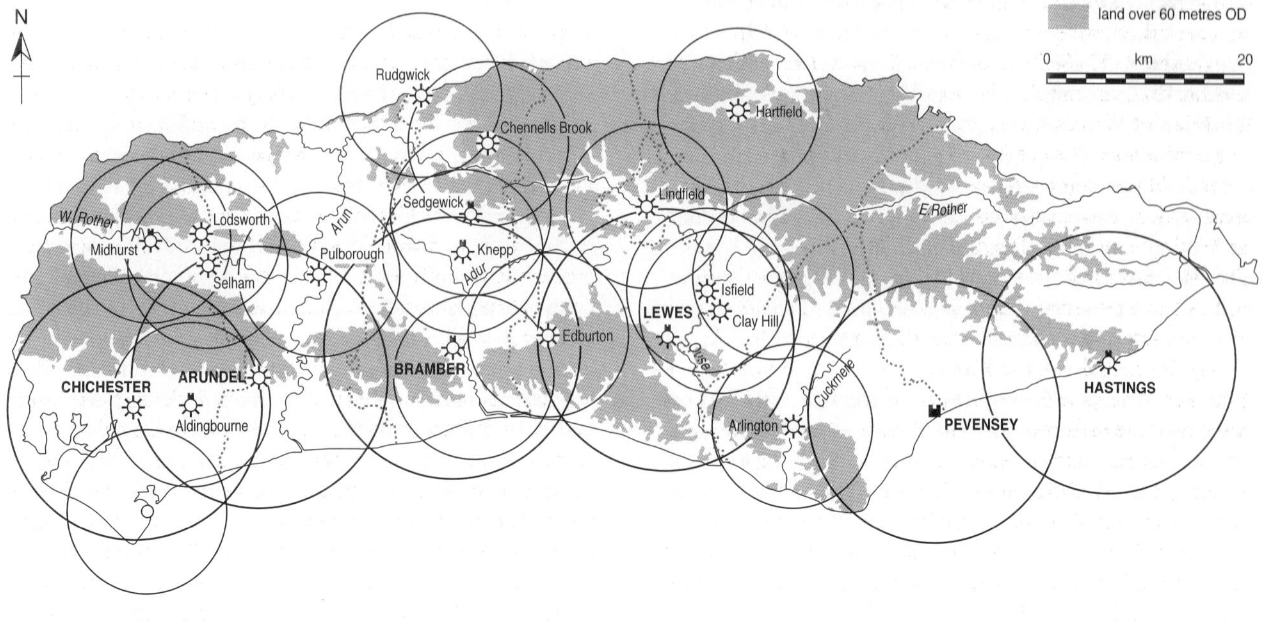

Figure 14.4. Spheres of influence c.1150-1200: the evolved system, based on an 8-mile radius for rapal castles and a 5-mile radius for secondary sites (after Jones 1999).

this carry with them huge dangers, it is interesting to plot out nominal spheres of influence for the known sites (Fig. 14.3). The pattern that emerges is interesting. It is possible to see immediately how the distribution of sites allows good coverage south of the South Downs. Similarly, it can readily be seen that the major routes through the Downs, the rivers, are well-protected. Indeed, if there is a question mark over the interpretation of The Rookery at Arlington as a true castle site, the need for a fortification here, to close the gap, might add credence to the interpretation (Fig. 14.4). The castle site at Edburton, too, has been the subject of much debate. It is unique in being located on the Downs themselves. Again, however, it is possible to see that Edburton links the spheres of influence between Bramber and Lewes. It is perhaps unsurprising to note that the Weald appears more poorly covered than the areas to the south. Gaps in the coverage might suggest that these areas were simply impenetrable during the period under review. Alternatively, the gaps might suggest areas where further archaeological investigation could reveal 'lost' medieval fortifications (Fig. 14.5). Or should we, in fact, give greater military status to the many moated sites in the Weald? Perhaps we have been too quick to dismiss their military potential and their military role.

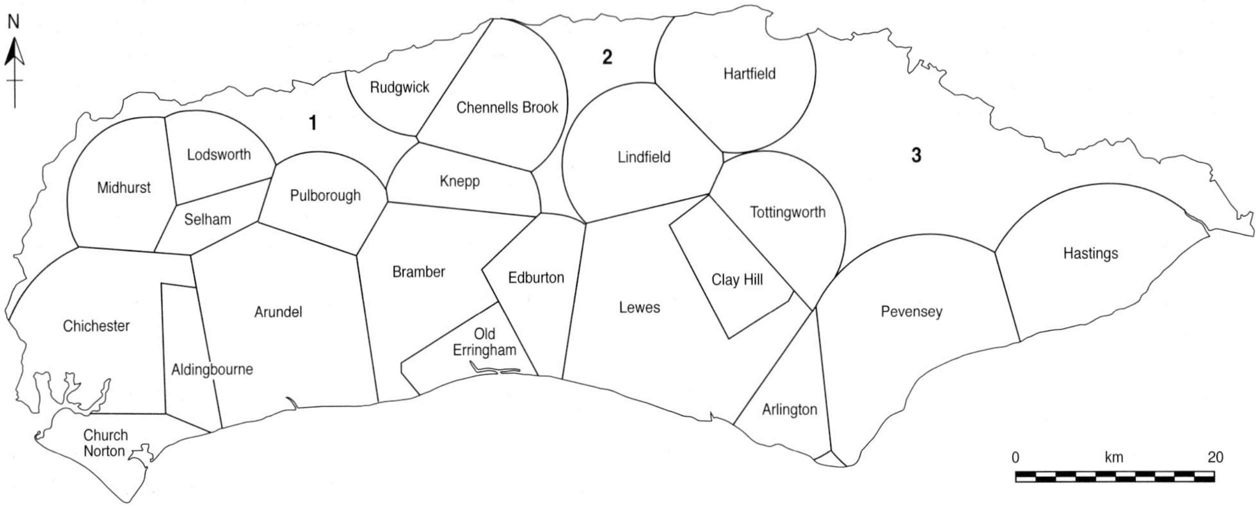

Figure 14.5. Spheres of influence c.1150-1200: based on an 8-mile radius for rapal castles and a 5-mile radius for secondary castles. Rapal castle influence has been allowed to take precedence over secondary castle in instances where there are multiple overlaps. The map clearly shows how the majority of the coast was covered, but also shows significant gaps in the system (nos. 1, 2 and 3) where further fortifications might be predicted.

The Reasons for Construction

Why were fortifications built and against what threat? To answer this question, dating the construction of castles, as we have seen, is critical. With a date or a date range, construction can be put into an historical context, and the social, political, economic and military factors which might have encouraged construction established (*see* Numbers and Dates *supra*). For the later period, at least, historical sources survive which might potentially solve this problem. Licences to crenellate help, but they ultimately fail to reveal the story fully. They are of limited use in two respects: first they relate to the latter half of the period only (in Sussex, the first licence dates to 1258 and the last to 1479); second, their prosaic, legalistic and formulaic nature tends to ignore the reasons behind the licence in favour of what could be undertaken. For the majority, such as Harting, Perching, Petworth and Sedgewick, the documents are silent about the reasons behind crenellation. For instance, at Sedgewick:

> '...that he [John Maunsel, Treasurer of York] may enclose and fortify his house of Seggewick in the County of Sussex, with fosses and a wall of stone and lime, and crenellate and fortify it, as may seem to him and his most expedient, without contradiction or impediment from us or our heirs...' (Blaauw 1861, 106).

It should perhaps be assumed that crenellation of this type was undertaken for social rather than military reasons. The licence for Bodiam, however, is more specific:

> '...that he [Edward Dallingridge] may, with a wall of stone and lime, fortify and crenellate the manse of his manor of Bodiam, near the sea, in the County of Sussex, and may construct and make thereby a castle for the defence of the adjacent country for resistance against our enemies...' (Blaauw 1861, 114).

Here the reasons for crenellation are explicity stated as military, a counter to the threat posed by French raiders along the south coast. Echoes of this licence are found in the later licence for Winchelsea (town not castle):

> 'they [the Mayor and burghers of Winchelsea] may enclose, crenellate, entower, and embattle, the said wall, and may enclose with the said foss, the said town so fortified, entowered, crenellated, and embattled, we are earnestly desirous that those places which are adapted for fortification should be made strong for the security and defence of the people subject to us, and for the terror and repulse of our enemies, and considering how the said town lies situated on the coast of the sea, and on the frontier of our enemies, and is to all and singular our lieges, and our friends passing at sea by there, as it were, the key, refuge and guard of those parts against the tempestuousness of the sea, and the insults of our said enemies...' (Blaauw 1861, 116).

It is archaeology, and the close dating of the foundations of the castles of Sussex, which potentially hold the clues to the reasons behind fortification, particularly in the early stages of fortification (1066-1258). These two factors are clearly interlinked, one cannot be understood without the other, and yet we remain uncertain about the specific chronology of castle building in Sussex, and appear happy to accept the general trends identified elsewhere in the country.

Castle Plans and Design

No two castle designs are the same. While subsets of castle types can be identified – motte-and-bailey, square keep, concentric, courtyard, etc. – every castle plan varies as a result of an infinite number of factors, predominant amongst which are date of construction, topography, financial resources, and function. Even sites constructed at the same period vary greatly. The six rapal castles in Sussex demonstrate this well: Hastings constructed within a prehistoric enclosure, Pevensey and Chichester within Roman fortifications, and Lewes within Anglo-Saxon defences. Arundel and Bramber were constructed on virgin sites. Of these, five adopted the classic motte-and-bailey form, but all were different. Lewes possessed two mottes and a single bailey, while Arundel possessed a single motte with two baileys. At Chichester and Hastings the mottes appear to have been raised at one end of the bailey, the 'normal' position, but at Bramber the motte was central to a large elliptical bailey. Pevensey never appears to have had a motte.

It is interesting to speculate about what the Sussex evidence can say about the evolution of the castle on a European scale. Does the variation of the early castle designs suggest an established tradition of castle building where the builders were fully cognisant of the required elements and were adapting them for their own purposes? Or, conversely, does it suggest that castle building was still in its infancy, that no perfect model had been formed, and that experimentation was taking place? Certainly, it is now the view that the classic motte-and-bailey castle cannot be said to have been imported into this country by the Normans. Few such sites have been identified in Pre-Conquest Normandy (Davison 1969, *passim*). It would appear that military expediency and the coming together of people from different parts of Europe – Normans, Flemings, Bretons, Saxons – provided the seedbed for technical innovation. Indeed, some have argued that the mature motte-and-bailey form was then introduced onto the continent from England in the aftermath of the Conquest (Davison 1969, *passim*). It therefore seems that the Sussex examples should play a greater role in our understanding of this type of work than they presently do.

Variations in plans also occur amongst the lesser castles sites. Some, such as Selham (Holden 1967), have a motte without surrounding bailey, while others, such as Pulborough (Murray 1960), Lodsworth (Anon. 1996), and Chennelsbrook near Horsham (Braun 1936), follow the typical pattern of a motte raised at one end of a single bailey. In Sussex it can also be shown that mottes and ringworks, such as Church Norton (Aldsworth 1979; 1981) and Old Erringham (Holden 1980), were used contemporaneously. This is in line with current theories concerning the two site types. Once the ringwork was seen as the simple precursor to the motte-and-bailey castle, now they are considered to be coeval defensive solutions (Higham and Barker 1992).

Variation continued once the timber defences were replaced by masonry walls. At Lewes and Arundel, the motte was capped with a shell-keep. At Bramber the motte appears to have been abandoned in favour of a powerful gate-keep (Barton and Holden 1977), and at Pevensey by an imposing rectangular keep (Renn 1971). To this two apsidal projections were added, probably at the end of the 12th century, for the same defensive reasons that octagonal towers were added to the shell-keep at Lewes in the 13th century. Variation can be found in the lesser fortified sites too. At Aldingbourne the keep was constructed before the motte (Brewster and Brewster 1969), while at Knepp the process was reversed following the expected pattern. Innovation and change were to continue right down to the end of the period. The building of Bodiam in the 1380s saw a radical change from what had gone before. The central defences were reduced in size, to enable a smaller garrison to man the defence efficiently, while much was made of water obstacles, and crude attempts were made to incorporate new gunpowder weaponry in defence, with the addition of gunports in the gatehouse. Sixty years later, the building of Herstmonceux brought a further innovation with the change from stone to brick construction. Herstmonceux, a true transitional edifice, being in large part residential rather than defensive, neatly defines the end of the traditional medieval castle building, not only in Sussex, but nationwide.

Archaeology and Sussex Castles

The archaeological investigation of the castles of Sussex has generally led to a better understanding of origins and evolution rather than of function. This stems in part from reliance on specific site excavation and the failure to set conclusions against the evidence from other sites. Nevertheless, important (mainly chronological) discoveries have been made. Thus at Church Norton, for example, excavation has proved the site to be of medieval rather than post-medieval date (Aldsworth 1979; 1981). Other examples include Aldingbourne where it was shown that the motte was constructed around the keep and not *vice versa* (Brewster and Brewster 1969). Discovery of Anglo-Saxon coins beneath the ringwork at Old Erringham suggests an early date for construction (Holden 1980). At Sedgwick it has been proved that an early site was fortified more strongly in the 13th century in line with the date for the licence to crenellate (Winbolt 1925). The sites of Tottingworth (Gardiner 1993) and Isfield (Montgomerie 1934; Gardiner 1992) also provided dating evidence allowing the sites to be set within their chronological framework. In two instances, however, excavation has also allowed sites to be radically reinterpreted and consequently added to the list of fortifications. At Hartfield, earlier suggestions that the site was not a castle have been refuted by evidence of a large ditch surrounding the mound and of the probable levelling of the mound summit (Salzman 1914; Tebbutt 1980), while at Rudgwick, a site previously thought to be a tumulus has been shown to be a Post-Conquest construction (Winbolt 1929). The sum of this evidence is this. First, it is clear that further investigation will alter our dating of sites. Dating by means of typology of upstanding earthworks and masonry is fraught with danger. Castle forms were long-lived. A design that might be considered militarily obsolete could be adopted at a later date for reasons other than purely defence. For instance, while most motte-and-bailey castles can be dated to the immediate Post-Conquest period, there are examples dating to the 13th century, as at Selham (Holden 1967) and Hartfield (Tebbitt 1980), which may suggest a spreading of castle building through the social echelons. Secondly, close inspection of earthworks has demonstrated that some sites have been incorrectly classified in the past. In Sussex the omnipresence of *bona fide* prehistoric burial mounds, an obsession for 19th century antiquarians, might have 'robbed' the landscape of medieval earthworks, as at Rudgwick. Certainly, at present, Sussex appears to be poorly provided with medieval castle sites, in particular by comparison with the regions of Normandy facing England. It is probable, not simply possible, that future excavation of so-called tumuli, will add further castle sites to the current list.

The journey from Hastings to Herstmonceux appears at facevalue to be a simple one, well signposted along the way. But as so often happens, when the traveller sets out, even with a map, things look very different on the ground. It is surely time for a new edition of the Sussex castles map, one that not only takes account of evidence from specific excavations, but which also incorporates these findings into the countywide picture.

References

Aldsworth, F.G. 1979. The Mound at Church Norton, Selsey, and the site of St. Wilfrid's Church, *SAC* **117**, 103-8.

Aldsworth, F.G. 1980. *Some Medieval Sites in West Sussex – an archaeological survey*. West Sussex County Council. Unpublished.

Aldsworth, F.G. 1981. Excavations on 'The Mound' at Church Norton, Selsey, in 1911 and 1965, *SAC* **119**, 217-20.

Anon. 1996. Lodsworth, *The Archaeology of Chichester and District 1996*, 58. Chichester District Council.

Barton, K. and Holden, E. 1977. Excavations at Bramber Castle, Sussex, 1966-67, *Archaeol. J.* **134**, 11-79.

Blaauw, W.H. 1861. Royal Licences to Fortify Towns and Houses in Sussex, *SAC* **13**, 104-17.

Brandon, P.F. 1974. *The Sussex Landscape,* London: Hodder and Stoughton.

Braun, H. 1936. An early Norman castle site in North Sussex, *SAC* **77**, 251-3.

Brewster, T. and Brewster, A. 1969. Tote Copse Castle, Aldingbourne, Sussex, *SAC* **107**, 141-79.

Burrell, C. 1850. Documents relating to Knepp Castle, *SAC* **3**, 1-12.

Burrell, C. 1852. Documents relating to Knepp Castle, *SAC* **5**, 143-6.

Davison, B.K. 1969. Early earthwork castles: a new model, *Château-Gaillard* **3**, 37-47.

Douglas, D.C. and Greenaway, G.W. (eds), 1953. *English Historical Documents 1042-1189*. London: Eyre and Spottiswoode.

Gardiner, M. 1992. Recent Work on the earthworks at Isfield, East Sussex, *SAC* **130**, 140-46.

Gardiner, M. 1993. An earthwork at Tottingworth, Heathfield, *SAC* **131**, 68-72.

Higham, R. and Barker, P. 1992. *Timber Castles.* London: Batsford.

Holden, E. 1967. The excavation of a motte at Lodsbridge Mill, Lodsworth, *SAC* **105**, 103-26.

Holden, E. 1980. Excavations at Old Erringham, Shoreham, West Sussex: part II the 'chapel' and ringwork, *SAC* **118**, 257-97.

Jones, R.L.C. 1994. *The State of Fortification in Lancastrian Normandy, 1417-50* Unpublished University of Oxford DPhil thesis, 2 vols.

Jones, R.L.C. 1999a. Castles and other Defensive sites, in B. Short and K. Leslie (eds), *An Historical Atlas of Sussex*, Chichester: Phillimore.

Jones, R.L.C. 1999b. Fortifications and Sieges in Western Europe, *c.* 800-1450, in M. Keen (ed.), *Medieval Warfare: A History.* Oxford: University Press.

Magilton, J. 1995. Chichester Castle Reappears, *The Archaeology of Chichester and District 1995*, 23-6. Chichester District Council.

Mason, J.F.A. 1964. The Rapes of Sussex and the Norman Conquest, *SAC* **102**, 68-93.

Montgomerie, D. 1934. Description of earthworks at Isfield, Sussex, *SAC* **75**, 207-8.

Murray, K.M.E. 1960. Park Mound, Pulborough, *Sussex Notes and Queries* **15**, 145-7.

Renn, D. 1971. The *Turris de Penuesel*: a reappraisal and a theory, *SAC* **109**, 55-64.

Salzman, L. 1914. Exploration of the "castle" mound at Hartfield, *SAC* **56**, 201.

Tebbutt, F. 1980. Castle Hill, Hartfield, *SAC* **118**, 377-8.

Thompson, K. 1996. St Ann's Hill, Midhurst: the builders and owners of the castle, *The Archaeology of Chichester and District 1996*, 48-9. Chichester District Council.

Winbolt, S. 1925. Sedgwick Castle, *SAC* **66**, 83-110.

Winbolt, S.E. 1929. Horsham, *SAC* **70**, 219-20.

WINCHELSEA - A ROYAL NEW TOWN

David Martin

Abstract

Amongst English towns Winchelsea is special. A major planned Royal port, the town flourished for half a century from the date of its re-foundation in the1280s following severe coastal erosion of its original site. During this period of wealth Winchelsea can claim to have been one of the principal ports of the realm; its ships ruled the channel, challenging foreign and English vessels alike. Yet, for a variety of reasons, from the middle years of the 14th century it suffered decline, and during the 16th century all but failed, shrinking to the size of a mere village. Over the past 25 years a considerable body of archaeological research has been undertaken within the town. Excavations, earthwork surveys, surveys of standing buildings and documentary research, have added greatly to the picture compiled by Winchelsea's mid-20th-century biographer, W. M. Homan.

Winchelsea as an international port (1280s to mid-14th Century)

Already by the middle of the 13th century the marshlands around the important and prosperous town of Old Winchelsea, located to the south of Rye, were being inundated by the sea. In 1250 a great storm caused the sea to overwhelm "more than 300 houses and certain churches". Two years later yet another great storm broke through the sea walls at Winchelsea and "invaded mills and houses and swept away many drowned men". By 1271 part of the parish church of St. Thomas had been washed away (Page 1937, 63). Because of its importance to the commerce and defence of the realm, in November 1280 Edward I took the first steps to move the town to a new and safer location. Having acquired the manor of Iham on a hill

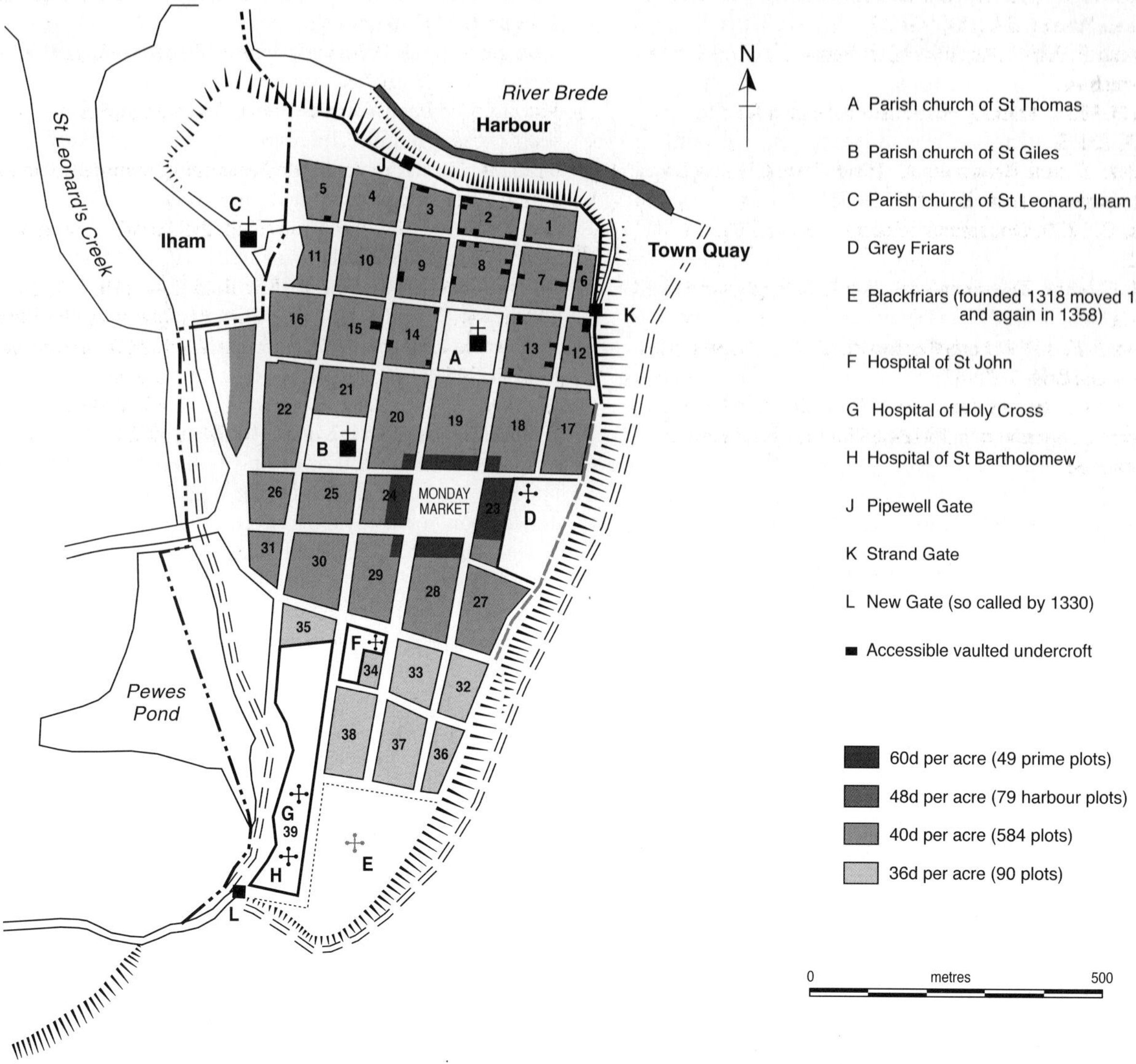

Figure 15.1. *Winchelsea in the early 14th century. This plan is based upon that which appeared on page 45 of* An Historical Atlas of Sussex *(Leslie and Short 1999) and has been adjusted to take into account discoveries regarding the topography of the town made since that date.*

to the west of the estuary, in 1283 Edward instructed commissioners to plan the new town, the old town by then being "for the greater part submerged by inundation of the sea", whilst the remainder was in danger of total submersion. The commissioners were instructed to plan streets, lanes and a market and to set out suitable places for the churches of St. Thomas and St. Giles, to lay out the tenements and to give directions regarding the harbour (Page 1937, 63). The new hilltop site was located overlooking the River Brede some distance inland from the sea, a factor which was later to prove the town's downfall (Fig. 15.11).

The site was handed over to the mayor and jurats in 1288 and in 1292 the town's rent roll was drawn up. Of the lands on the hill the King took over about 150 acres, of which he retained 12 acres for his own use. The remainder of the hill was divided into 39 blocks (called quarters) by a grid of wide, straight streets (Fig. 15.1). In total the new town comprised 802 plots of which 723 were on the hill, and 79 were harbour plots (Homan 1949). Winchelsea's mid-20th-century historian, W.M. Homan noted that the plots within the southernmost quarters of the town commanded slightly lower rents and suggested that this was because they lay outside the town walls. This hypothesis can now be disproved. The lower rents probably reflect nothing more than the distance of these tenements from the commercial centre. In like manner, the plots surrounding the market square commanded a high rent. Recent research has shown that Homan's reconstruction of the town as originally planned placed Quarter 23 too far west, robbing Winchelsea of its spacious market square. Likewise, Quarters 36-38 were each misplaced by one quarter (Martin and Martin 2002)[1].

The commissioners responsible for laying out the new town placed its administrative and commercial centre a surprising distance from the port, being centred on the Market Square two quarters to the south of St. Thomas's church, to the west of the Grey Friars. The Butchery occupied the street leading to the market square from the eastern end of the church.

In addition to the already existing St. Leonard's Church, Iham, at its inception New Winchelsea was planned with two parish churches, St. Thomas (the chief church of the town) and St. Giles, together with a house of Grey Friars and three hospitals. The hospitals were located within the less prosperous southern part of the town, but the other ecclesiastical buildings were sited towards the centre. In 1318 the Black Friars were given permission to set up a house within the southern part of the town. They later moved to a more central, though extra-mural location, and eventually, in 1357 moved yet again to occupy the entirety of Quarter 4, just inside the Pipewell Gate (Salzmann 1907, 94-95; Homan 1942, 127-128; Martin and Martin 2002, Quarter 4 and King's Green)[2].

In 1321 the Abbot of Fécamp complained that the mayor and barons of Winchelsea had, at the King's command, walled the King's town of Winchelsea, and in so doing had enclosed some of the abbot's lands outside the liberty (Homan 1940, 76-77). Of these defences, the Strand Gate and the (later rebuilt) Pipewell Gate survive, as does the New Gate (already so called by 1330) at the extreme southern end of the town (British Library Add. Ch. 18623: Transcript of *c.*1580). Other gates, including a probable principal gate known as the 'Pewes Gate' protecting the landward route from Icklesham, have been destroyed. Fragments of the town wall and two turrets can still be seen to the south of the Strand Gate. These initial defences had a very long circuit, a factor which without doubt favoured the French during their later raids on the town.

From the wealth of documentary information available there can be no doubt that the new foundation was a success - the first 30 or 50 years on the new site represent Winchelsea's greatest period of prosperity. It was regarded as Sussex's chief port and was able to maintain its trade with the Continent and other parts of England at or above its previous level. The most important trade was the importation of wine, in particular from south-west France. During this period many of the most important figures in Winchelsea's history were vintners, including several of the family of Alard (Homan 1942, 43-44; Sylvester 1999). The importance of the wine trade is well substantiated by the large number of subterranean, vaulted undercrofts constructed within the new town: 33 of these are still accessible (Fig. 15.2) and more are known to exist. All the accessible cellars were entered from the street via a wide flight of steps. In most instances this was the only means of access and thus the undercrofts could be leased separately from the houses above. Some, however, have secondary stairs allowing internal access to the house. Most of the undercrofts are barrel-vaulted, being divided into bays by chamfered ribs (Fig. 15.3), though a few are more elaborate and incorporate both cross ribs and diagonal ribs. That beneath The Salutation, at the junction of Castle Street with Mill Road, has elaborately-carved corbels supporting the ribs. During the year 1306/7 15 Winchelsea ships of between 83 and 190 tons were involved in the wine trade with Bordeaux. Over an eight-month period within that year alone 14,400 hogsheads (737,000 gallons) of wine were imported into Winchelsea from south-west France in 21 shipments (Homan 1942, 47-48, 246).

Winchelsea was also important for its fishing. This was not limited to its own fleet, fish being high amongst the town's imports. The port was at this time one of the main sources drawn upon by the royal purveyor. Ignoring the dominance of wine and fish, the import trade was otherwise varied and included the necessities for a large town and its rural hinterland: cloth, corn, wax, pottery, mirrors, cups, leather, fruits, and spices were amongst them. The principal exports were wood, dairy produce and salt (Page 1937, 69-70). Recognition of the town's seaborne strength is found in 1303 when Gervase Alard, a leading citizen and merchant of Winchelsea, was made Captain and Admiral of the southern fleet. Throughout the 14th century the town remained one of the principal ports of embarkation for France, with numerous gatherings of the fleet within its harbour - deemed to be the entire estuary between Rye and Winchelsea (Cooper 1850, 54-55, 67; Homan 1942, 43-44, 156-157; Sylvester 1999).

In addition to the vaulted undercrofts, the remains of at least seven houses survive from the years immediately following Winchelsea's re-foundation. All were substantial stone-built structures and almost certainly represent the homes of leading merchant citizens. In their size and quality they would have been comparable, if not superior, to the homes of the local rural, manorial lords. One of the most complete of these

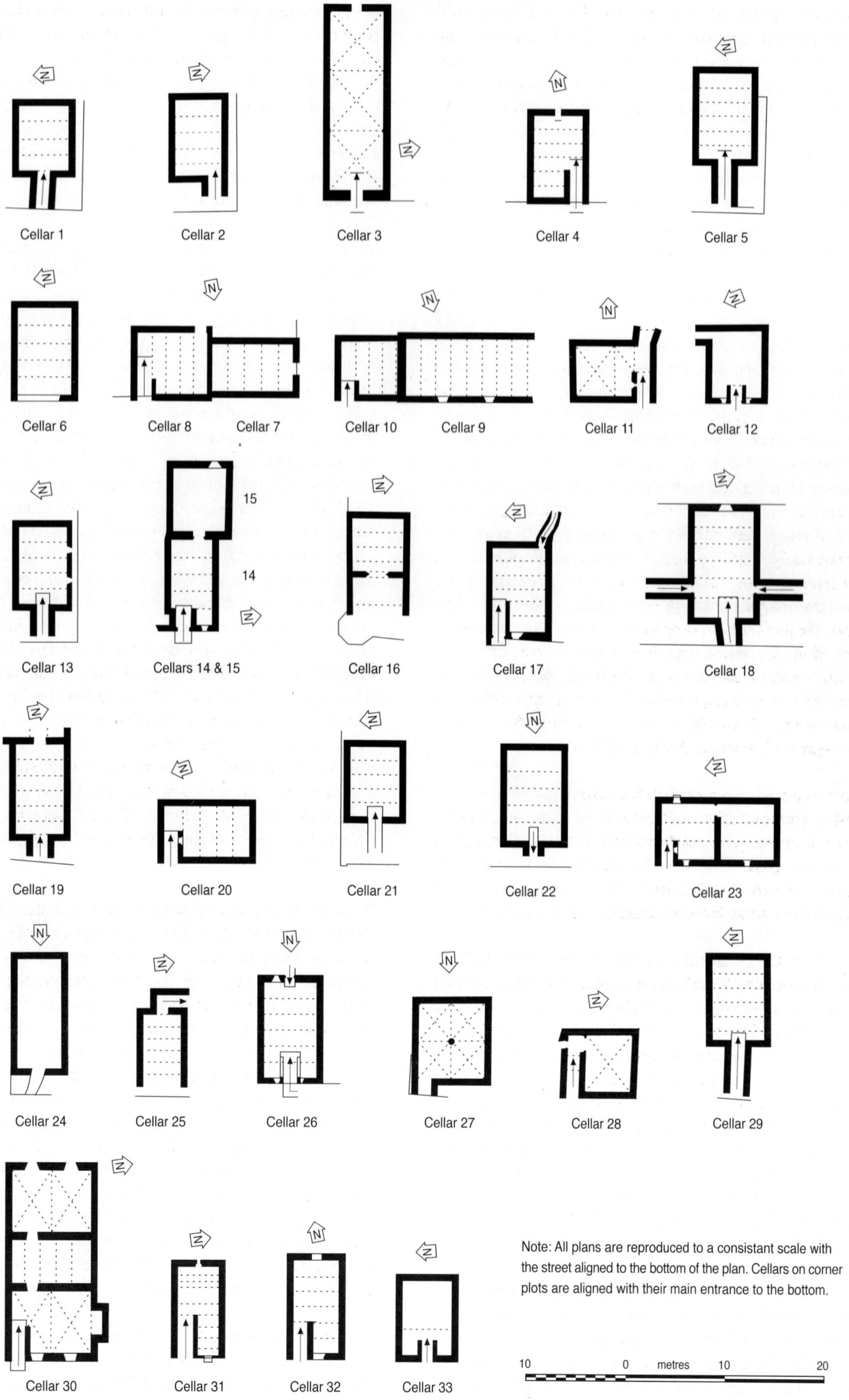

Figure 15.2. *Accessible vaulted cellars*

Winchelsea houses is Firebrand (Fig. 15.4), a substantial house occupying an important corner plot near St Thomas's Church. Only the stonework dates from *c.*1300: the timberwork, including the roof, represents a 15th-century rebuild. Firebrand has a contemporary vaulted undercroft beneath its service rooms, as too does The Armory in Castle Street, another of the better-preserved early houses (Fig. 15.4). Unlike Firebrand, here some original timberwork survives, though unfortunately the roof has been rebuilt. In this instance the rear range represents a *c.*1500 addition, replacing a now destroyed southern rear range (evidenced by a doorway). Although now standing in isolation, when first built The Armory was located within a continuously built-up street frontage. Note how, because of the out-of-square layout of the quarters, the front wall is set askew in order to maintain a flush street frontage. In contrast, most facades along North Street were very deliberately stepped (Fig. 15.5). Here, at the north-western corner of Quarter 2, a 24-metre section of street frontage can be reconstructed by combining evidence from surviving undercrofts and a standing gable, with that recovered by excavation (Rudling and Martin 1981). The undercrofts - three in number - cluster at the corner of the quarter. Immediately to their east stood three houses built using a mixture of timber framing and clay-bedded masonry, neither construction having foundations. The hearth of one of the timber-framed houses was constructed using small yellow 'Flemish' bricks - common in Winchelsea, as too were imported west-country blue roofing slates. The eastern boundary of the easternmost excavated house was formed by the standing gable of a substantial 'L' plan masonry house incorporating the remains of a surprisingly early corner-built two-flue chimney. Beneath its rear range are the remains of what appear to be an inaccessible undercroft.

Of the surviving early non-ecclesiastical buildings the largest is Blackfriars Barn, a ruin standing in the corner of the cricket field beside the A259. Never owned by the Black Friars, the building was only converted into a barn late in its life, though what its original function was is not entirely certain. It may have been the home of a wealthy merchant, but its exceptionally large open hall - set gable towards the street and incorporating a contemporary fireplace - its dearth of domestic rooms and its spacious attached toilet block perhaps favour a more public function, possibly a guildhall (Fig. 15.6). If Winchelsea had a vintners' guild, this building must be a likely candidate for its headquarters, for located beneath the entire building is a three-roomed undercroft, easily the largest within the town. Unusually, the front room of the undercroft has a fireplace. Excavations carried out on the site in 1976 (Freke *et al.* 1977), prior to consolidation of the remains by The National Trust, showed that the building was flanked by other structures and thus only its monumental gable end was visible from the street. The house immediately to the north was excavated during 1977. The results demonstrate vividly the complexity and continual evolution of these urban houses, three major pre-16th-century phases of alterations and additions having been identified (Fig. 15.6). The open hall occupied a position against the street and is clearly recognized

Figure 15.3. *A typical Winchelsea barrel-vaulted undercroft. This example is located beneath Manna Platt on Quarter 2, at the junction of Mill Road with School Hill.*

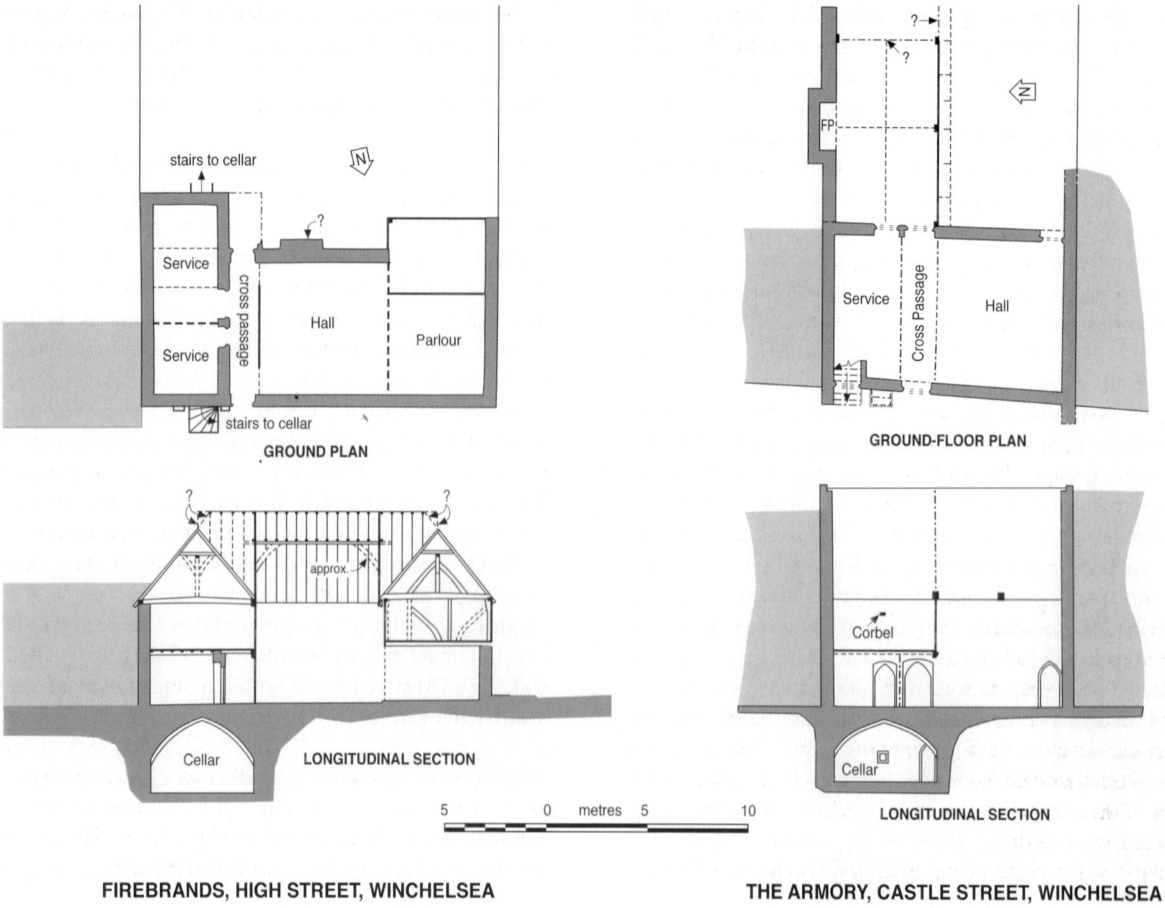

Figure 15.4. *Two early houses - Left: Firebrand, Quarter 13, High Street. Right: The Armory, Quarter 7, Castle Street. Both are here shown as they existed in c.1500, after they had been modified slightly.*

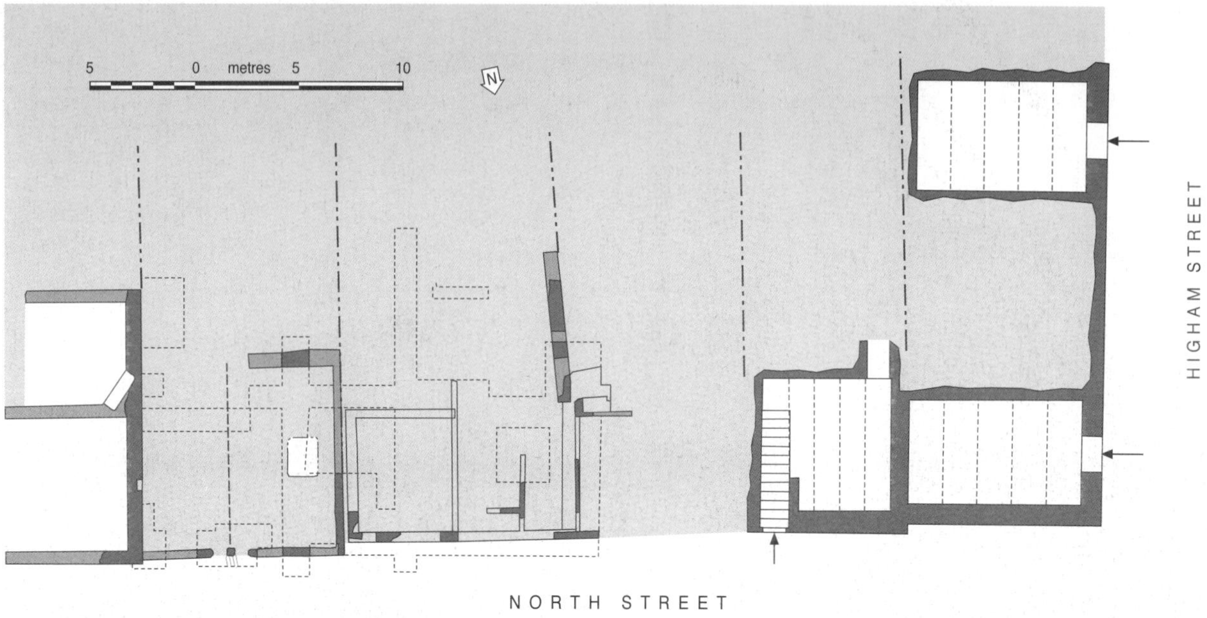

Figure 15.5. *The layout of medieval buildings on Quarter 2, on the southern side of North Street as reconstructed from surviving undercrofts, standing remains and archaeological excavation.*

by its central hearth, again constructed of 'Flemish' brick. One of the 14th-century modifications to the house involved the acquisition of the toilet block serving 'Blackfriars Barn'. The cesspit was filled and the toilet area converted into a kitchen. Unfortunately the backfill to the cess pit was not adequately compacted and as a result the new hearth suffered severe subsidence. At this time the undercrofts beneath 'Blackfriars Barn' were occupied by the owner or tenant of this house, for a new secondary flight of steps was constructed leading down from the house into the central room of the undercroft.

As with the other excavations carried out within the town, those upon the site adjacent to Blackfriars Barn produced a good range of imported medieval pottery. The finding of fine table wares, (such as the polychrome pot shown in Figure 15.7, imported with the wine from south-west France and recovered from an unlined cesspit on the site) was anticipated. More surprising was the large quantity of imported coarse wares recovered, wares which would normally be expected to have been produced locally. The Winchelsea excavations have also produced the remains of six 14th-century glazed ceramic roof louvres, two of which are shown in Figure 15.8. These would have been arranged in a bank of two, three, or perhaps even four, sitting astride the ridge of the roof over the open hall in order to allow the smoke from the central hearth to escape. Note the hoods which protected the openings from the weather.

Of the archaeological excavations carried out within the town so far, only one has been upon a non-domestic site. The church of St Giles, Winchelsea's second church after St Thomas's, occupied the southern half of Quarter 21, immediately to the west of the present A259. It was still standing in 1570, but the site was open ground by 1763. Subsequently a rectory was built in the north-eastern corner of the plot and in 1976 new houses were erected on the south-eastern part of the old churchyard. It had been thought that the site of the church was further to the west and thus no archaeological investigations were asked for. In the event, the foundations of one of the new houses cut through those of the church. A further house has recently been built upon the western part of the graveyard. Limited archaeological evaluation undertaken in 1982 (Rudling and Browne 1993) revealed 17 graves, only one of which was stonelined and vaulted (Fig. 15.9). Its occupant, a male 5'7" in height and 25-35 year-old, was suffering from advanced vertebral tuberculosis, which had caused a deformed spine. Where the stature could be determined the adult males ranged from 5'6" to 5'10" in height, and (with the exception of one 5'7" woman – which it tall for medieval times) the females ranged between 5'1" and 5'3". Only two adults were obviously over 35 years of age. None of the burials could be closely dated.

Now privately owned, the choir of the Grey Friars church is one of the town's most impressive surviving monuments. Dating from the early 14th century, its walls still stand to full

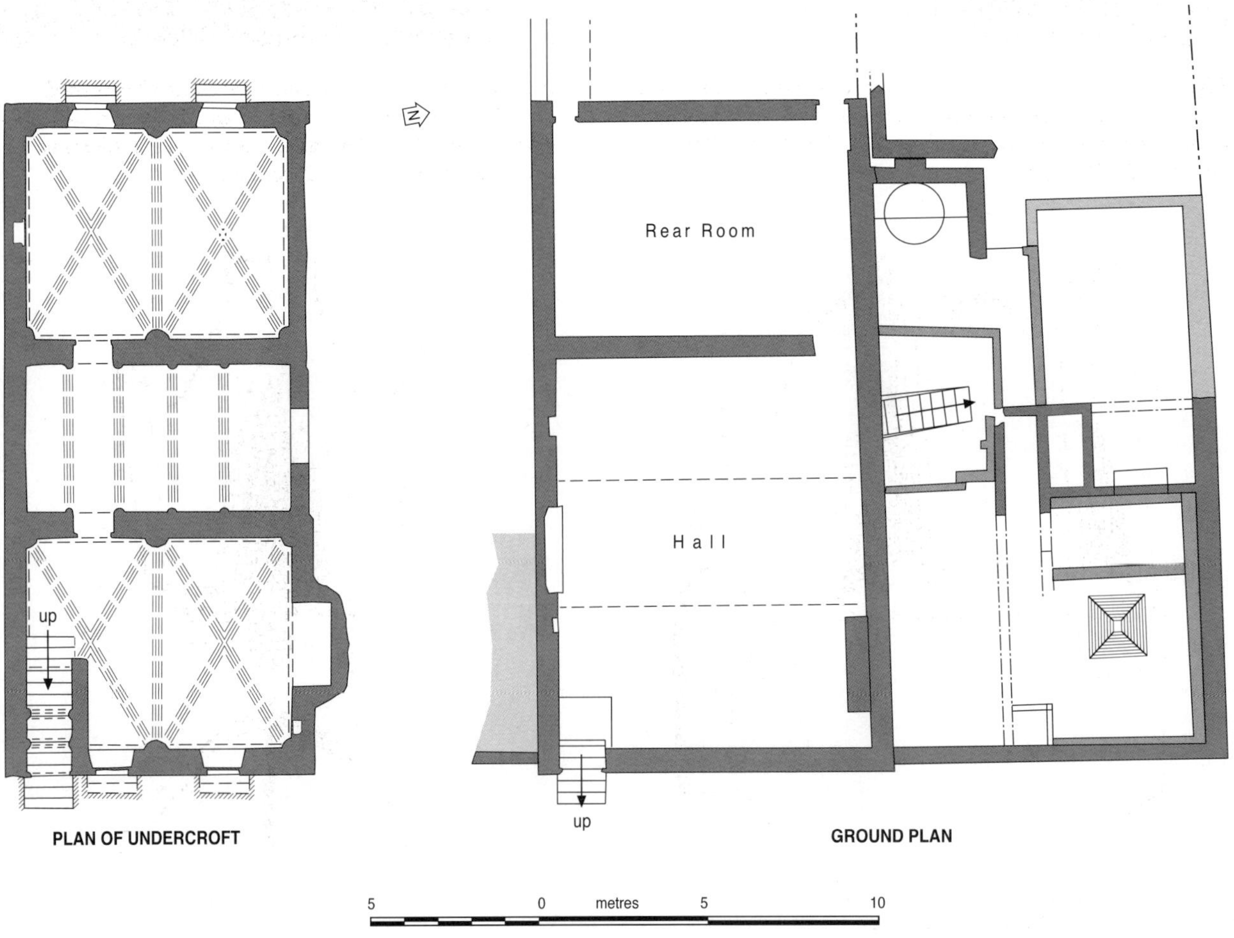

Figure 15.6. Quarter 15. Plan showing the remains of a substantial early 14th-century building and undercroft (now known as Blackfriars Barn) together with the excavated remains of an adjacent building abutting it to the north.

Figure 15.7. *14th-century polychrome-decorated jug imported from S.W. France. This example was recovered from an unlined cesspit upon the site immediately north of Blackfriars Barn, Quarter 15. (Photograph: David Freke).*

Figure 15.9. *Stone-built tomb in St Giles' Churchyard, containing the burial of a male, aged 25-35 years, suffering from advanced vertebral tuberculosis. Scales: 40cm and 20cm. (Photograph: David Rudling).*

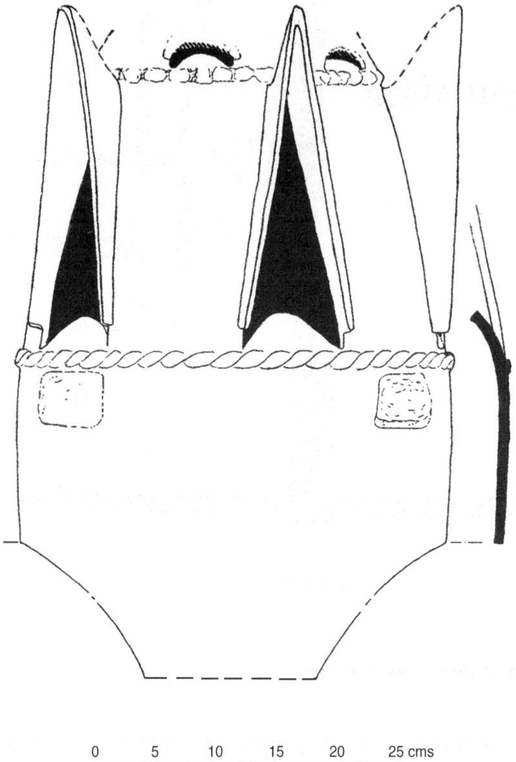

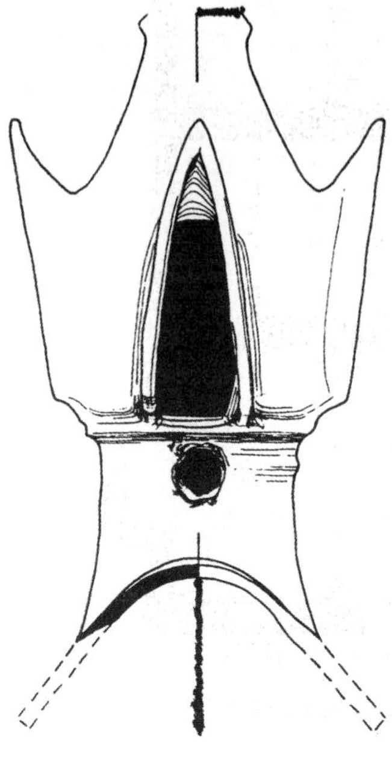

Figure 15.8. *Two green-glazed 14th-century roof louvres recovered from excavations on Quarter 15. The example on the left is attached to a ridge tile, that on the right sat astride the ridge.*

height and are graced by eleven arched windows, four in each of the side walls and three within the three-sided apsidal east end. The remains of buttresses separate the windows. The arch dividing the choir from the walking place still survives, as too does the adjacent stair turret, but the nave of the church has been demolished, as have the other claustral buildings. Even so, what remains gives a good impression of the friary's former splendour. Nothing of the town's other friary, the Black Friars, now stands above ground, but geophysical investigations and scorch marks visible in aerial photographs indicate that these buildings too were built on an impressive scale (Martin and Martin 2002, Quarter 4). The cloister enclosure is easily discernible, as is the outline of the substantial church which occupied the southern range of the cloisters. Apart from their sites, a solitary standing gable which had formed part of St John's hospital is the only physical evidence as to the form and size of the town's three hospitals.

Winchelsea as a local town (Mid-14th Century to Mid-16th Century)

The outbreak of the Hundred Years' War meant interruption to Winchelsea's trade and interference with its shipping. The town's response to this crisis was to take the offensive, a role which was not restricted to action against the King's enemies, but also against its trading competitors. As an example, on 30 September 1321, whilst engaged in a campaign during which they allegedly terrorized the south coast of England, 30 ships commanded by the men of Winchelsea appeared off Southampton, landed and burned 15 ships drawn up on the strand, "contemptuously rejecting the burgesses' offer of two good ships, fully equipped, to help them in policing the Channel". The following day they burned two more ships before sailing off (Platt 1973, 107; Homan 1942, 63). Winchelsea was burnt, probably by the King's enemies, in

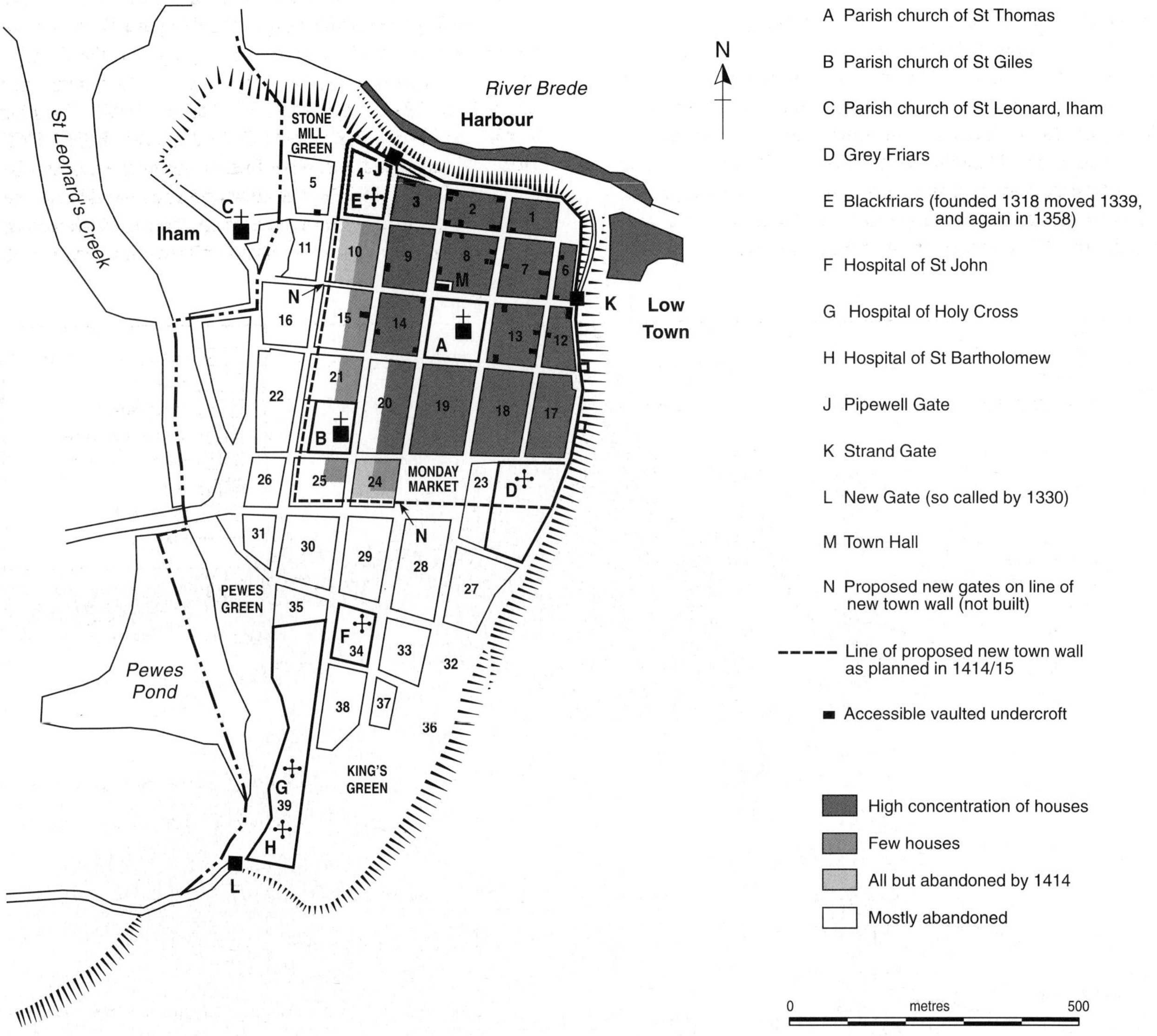

Figure 15.10. *Winchelsea in the early 15th century. This plan is based upon that which appeared on page 45 of* An Historical Atlas of Sussex *(Leslie and Short 1999) and has been adjusted to take into account discoveries regarding the topography of the town made since that date.*

February 1326, but, probably because of its superior strength, escaped unscathed from the French raids of 1339, although neighbouring Rye and Hastings were burnt. Even so, the town was clearly not unaffected by the changed political climate. By 1342 (six years before the Black Death) the bailiff's accounts include a list of 94 tenements within the town lying uninhabited. Almost all were within the southern and south-western peripheral quarters, and in the area of the harbour, suggesting few problems at that date. However, by 1358 a further 90 properties were described as 'in ruins' and an inquiry held early in 1359 reported that there were then within the town many inhabitable houses which were at that time unlet and uninhabited (Cooper 1850, 69; PRO SC 12/15/78; PRO C143/334 (14)). A year later, in 1360, the town suffered a further catastrophic raid by the French. A letter dated 16th March 1360 records that "our French enemies in large numbers of men-at-arms with their horses landed at Winchelsea last Sunday and took the town and inhumanely killed the people found in it". The tide had turned, for until then Winchelsea had largely escaped attacks by the French, despite its ships being at the forefront of English attacks on French towns. Six years after the raid, the bailiff's returns recorded that no fewer than 385 tenements (a little under half of the total) were still "waste, burnt and uninhabited". A further French raid in 1377 was successfully repelled, though only with the aid of assistance from a force mustered by the Abbot of Battle. Even so, the town's decline had become such that in 1378 Chichester supplanted Winchelsea as the chief Sussex port. Just two years later, in 1380, the French again surprised the town and sacked it. A Letter Patent dated 3rd March 1384 records that Winchelsea was "once well inhabited, but by being burnt by the King's enemies and much more by the withdrawal of its burgesses is now so desolate and almost destroyed that the proprietorship of vacant plots and tenements can scarce be known". In consequence, the King ordered that the properties be confiscated unless the houses were repaired and occupied either by their owners or by others (Page 1937, 66-67). To judge from the town's accounts, by 1388 the commercial core of the town had largely been re-occupied. Furthermore, comparison of the town's expenditure records for 1388/1389 and 1399/1400 indicate that the commercial recovery continued throughout the remainder of the century. There are references in the latter accounts to the acquisition and custody of a town clock (Homan 1942, 164-165). During the first decade of the 15th century income was sufficient for the Pipewell Gate (allegedly destroyed in 1380) to be rebuilt.

Although the fortunes of the town were clearly much recovered, Winchelsea now consolidated itself within the north-eastern corner of its original site, the western and southern parts being largely abandoned. That the officials accepted the reduced size of the town as a permanent feature is indicated by their petitioning of the King in 1414 to reduce the defended area of the town. An inquiry into the damage which such a new wall would cause to existing properties was held in 1415 (Page 1937, 67; Homan 1942, 174-175; Martin and Martin 2002; PRO C145/293 (18); ESRO RYE 146/2). From this the precise line of the new wall can be ascertained (Fig. 15.10). The new defences would enclose 21 of the original 39 quarters, placing the parish church of St. Giles (the less important of the town's two churches, which

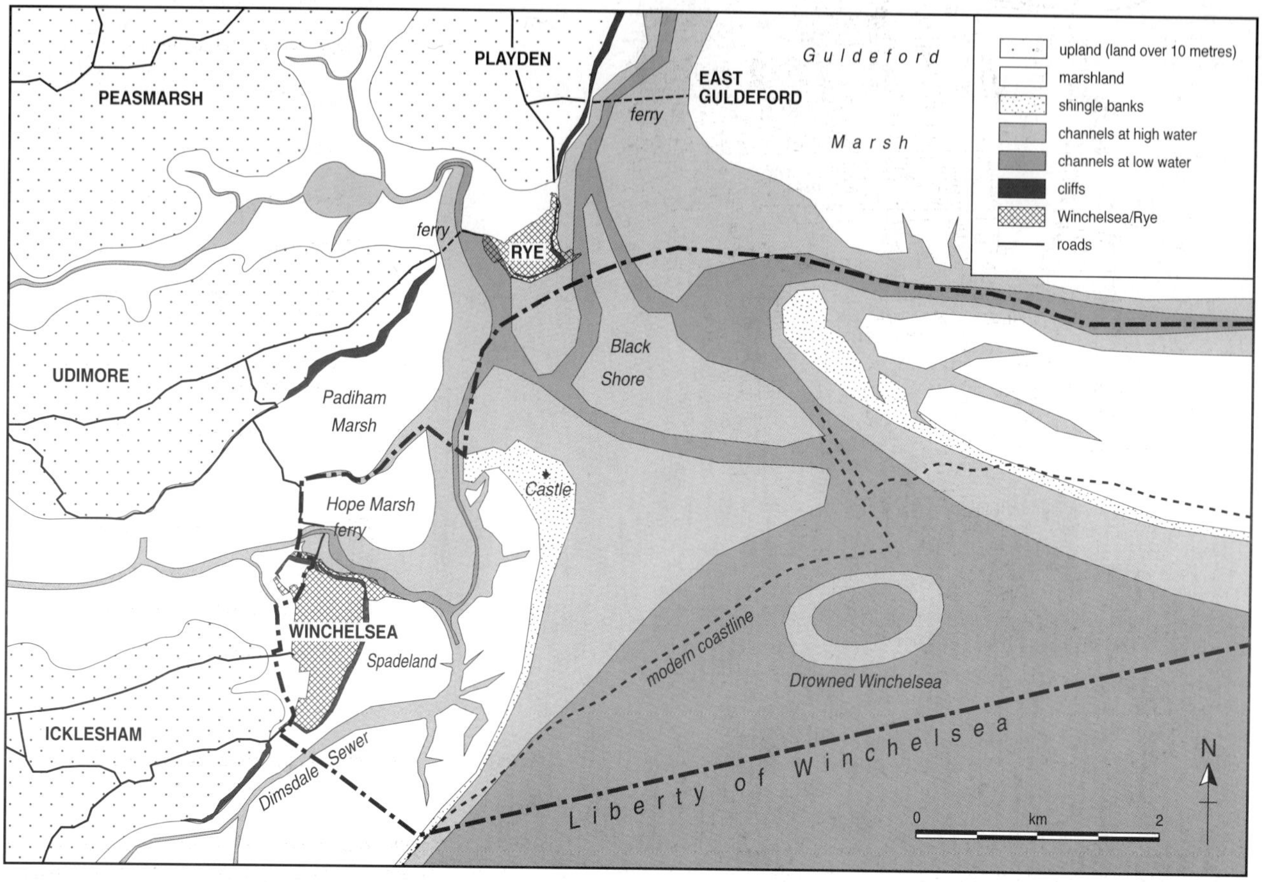

Figure 15.11. The setting of Winchelsea in the 16th century.

had been struck by lightning and burnt in 1413) near the south-western corner of the new circuit. The precinct of the Grey Friars would occupy the site in the extreme south-eastern corner, and that of the Black Friars the extreme north-western corner. St. Thomas's church and the new administrative centre stood almost centrally within the contracted site. Two new town gates were planned to allow access through the new section of wall. Construction of the wall would involve purchasing a strip of land on the edge of those quarters which stood on its route - even so, the inquiry found that only five dwellings would be destroyed by the work, a clear indication of how few houses then stood in these areas of the town. That Winchelsea was still considered of some importance is indicated by the King's grant of 600 marks towards the cost of the works. Payment was made out of the exchequer in 1417, but following a peace treaty with France all further payments were suspended. The work was apparently abandoned after only the northern part of the western section had been started (Homan 1942, 174-175).

Whilst still recovering from the trials of the second half of the 14th-century, yet another threat to the town's prosperity was becoming apparent - the harbour estuary was silting up. Although the port became increasingly choked and less serviceable, it was still able to receive vessels of up to 200 tons in 1433. It was from Winchelsea that Richard Woodville and 1,000 troops crossed to Honfleur in 1438. By the close of the 15th century the silting of the harbour was causing severe concern, though the harbour remained in use during the first part of the 16th century (Fig. 15.11). As late as 1524 the town was called upon to provide four ships of a total of 96 tons, manned by 15 mariners, though this was nothing when compared to their early 14th-century contributions (Homan 1942, 218). Perhaps surprisingly, the town's architecture does not give any indication of reduced prosperity at this time. On the contrary, at least six of the surviving houses date from the years around 1500, whilst others were modified and extended at this same period. One of the new houses was the three-storeyed, fully-jettied Periteau House (Fig. 15.12). Occupying a corner plot at the junction of High Street with Castle Street, the former grandeur of this building is not now immediately apparent, the upper storey having been removed and the external walls rebuilt in brickwork. Internally, however, the boarded ceilings speak of the quality of the original construction work. And it is not the only example of a boarded ceiling within the town, there is another in a house of similar date in Friars Road. It was during this period too that The Salutation was rebuilt above its earlier impressive undercroft.

Winchelsea in decline (Mid-16th Century to 1700)

The spate of building identifiable during the years around 1500 should be seen as Winchelsea's 'swan song'. By 1544 the town could provide but six hoys for the defence of the realm. In 1561 the corporation reported that there were no ships, boats or crayers based at Winchelsea, and only four

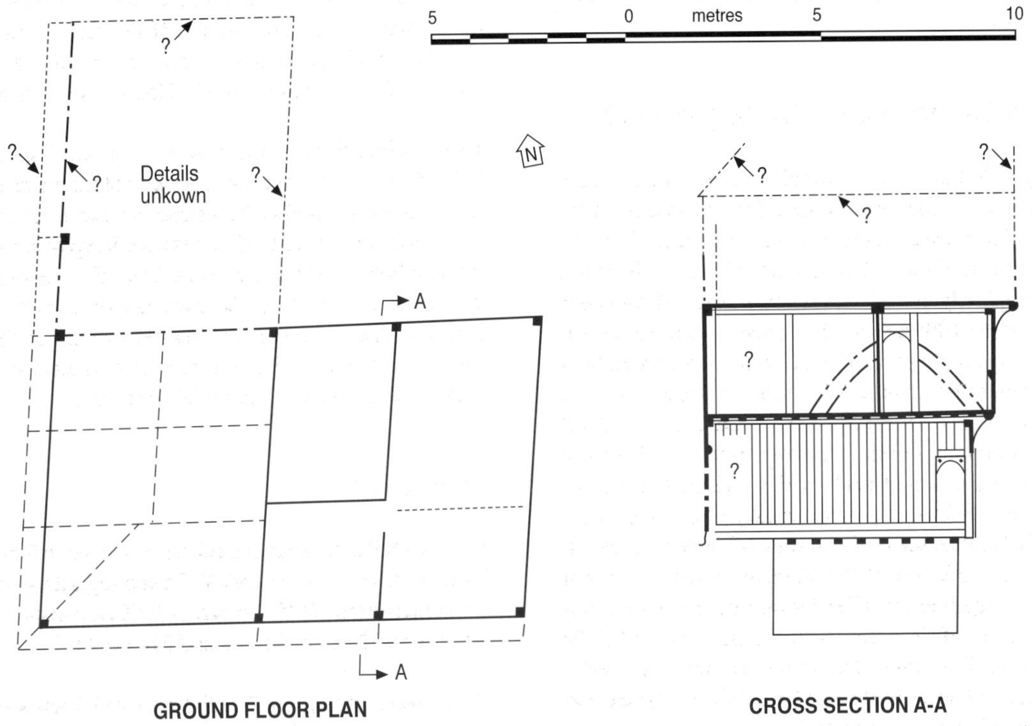

Figure 15.12. Periteau House. A three-storeyed jettied town house of c.*1500 occupying an important corner plot near the church. The exterior of this building is today much disguised*

mariners were resident within the town (Homan 1942, 232; ESRO WIN 52, fo. 146r). Having primarily relied upon its seaborne trade, it was inevitable that during the 16th century the town was to suffer a period of very marked decline. The merchants of Winchelsea increasingly forsook the town. It is probably no coincidence that the 16th century was the period of Rye's greatest prosperity - being located further down the estuary, Rye had not yet been affected by the silting of the harbour. Already during the first quarter of the 16th century decline within Winchelsea was evident: even within the commercial centre houses were being abandoned (ESRO RYE 146/5). The attrition rate accelerated as the century passed. In 1548 the corporation was so impoverished that they were forced to sell both the Great Chalice and the bells of the Great Cross in order to defray debts. In an attempt to stem the tide of demolitions, in 1563 an order was issued forbidding building materials from any buildings within the town from being removed from the liberty, yet already during the same year the corporation was granting a licence for a house in the 12th Quarter to be taken down and transported to Udimore (ESRO WIN 52 fo. 160v). The sites which have been excavated tell the same story: occupation continued into the 16th century, but then ceased abruptly. By 1565 there were only 109 inhabited houses remaining: reputedly by 1575 the number had fallen to just 60. Even so, in 1573 the burgesses were able to entertain the Queen, who referred to Winchelsea - one feels rather tongue-in-cheek - as a "Little London". The 17th century saw no improvement in the town's plight. In 1652 it was described as "all in rubbish . . . . a few despicable hovels and cottages standing" and in another late-17th-century description as "a pitiful spectacle of poverty and desertion". Both descriptions are likely to have been exaggerated for effect, but perhaps not by very much, for in 1676 there were just 91 communicants within the town, probably living within 30 or so houses (Homan 1942, 252; Brent 1975, 36).

Modern Winchelsea (1700 to present)

Although by 1600 the town was nothing more than a village, it still retained its parliamentary seat. Throughout the 17th century the Winchelsea candidates were nominated by the Lord Warden of the Cinque Ports, and by 1700 the borough had fallen completely under Treasury patronage. Throughout the first half of the 18th century the Treasury nominees were returned. By the middle years of the 18th century certain MPs encouraged would-be nominees to invest in property around the town. Two such men were William Belchier and Albert Nesbitt. Belchier, a London banker, had acquired the Winchelsea estate of John Caryll, which included the manor of Iham and some 939 acres, only a small part of which were located within Winchelsea itself. Nesbitt, a London merchant, was a friend and relation of the Pelham family. With that family's encouragement, in 1751 Nesbitt purchased a small Winchelsea estate of 46 acres from the heirs of Arthur St Ledger, Viscount Doneraile. The same year he purchased a further 14 acres adjacent to the last from William Stone and three houses plus ten acres (with other lands not in Winchelsea) from Henry Staffield. Albert died in 1753 and the following year the Prime Minister, Henry Pelham, insisted that Albert's nephew, Arnold Nesbitt, stand at Winchelsea in opposition to Belchier. Nesbitt was the successful candidate. Over the years that followed Nesbitt continued to build up his local estate, his single largest purchase being the manors of Icklesham and Wickham in 1760. The Belchier/Nesbitt rivalry brought about a small revival in the town's fortunes. Belchier built at least four new houses within the town in order to house his principal voting tenants. More importantly, in 1761 Nesbitt (with other promoters) set up within the town a manufactory for cambric. In 1763 this was incorporated under the title 'The English Linen Company'. The industry was supervised by two Frenchmen, Mr Mariteau and Francois-Marie Corbaux (Salzmann 1907, 258; Stevenson 1991). To house the workmen, Nesbitt and his partners converted some existing houses and built a number of new dwellings. A Nesbitt survey of 1767 lists 22 'manufactory houses' at that date, including one new block of five (now The Five Houses) and another new block of fifteen constructed in 1763 (now partly demolished, but partly surviving as 1-10 Barrack Square and bearing Nesbitt's initials and the date) (ESRO AMS 5788/1). When in Winchelsea, Nesbitt himself occupied Periteau House. Cambric manufacture was later replaced by Italian crepe. The industry managed to survive the financial difficulties of various of its proprietors (including Nesbitt) and continued until 1810, when it moved to Norwich. For a long time it was the principal occupation of the settlement. Because of it the town was once more growing, albeit only modestly. The number of houses shown on the 1763 town map (drawn prior to the construction of the new Manufactory houses) was between 49 and 52: by the 1801 census there were 105 inhabited dwellings occupied by 123 families, though it should be stressed that the percentage increase at Winchelsea was no greater than that within most local parishes at this time. The number of houses continued to increase over the following decades. However, the effects of the loss of the linen industry, and of the military barracks which succeeded them, is well illustrated by the 1841 return, which records only 106 inhabited houses within the town and at the Strand: a further 22 were uninhabited. (National Census Returns).

Today Winchelsea remains an ecclesiastical parish, but in 1896 the town suffered the ignominy of being stripped of its status as a civil parish, becoming a ward within the newly constituted civil parish of Icklesham. Despite some infilling by new houses and the construction of three small estates during the 20th century, the town remains, in effect, a small village restricted to the north-eastern corner of the original site. In deference to its historical importance, it retains its mayor and jurats for ceremonial purposes.

End Notes

1. For a full discussion regarding the evidence for the correct location of Quarters 23 and 36-38 and regarding other errors contained within W.M. Homan's (1949) reconstruction of the town as in 1292, *see* Martin and Martin 2001.

2. Homan's note, The Black Friars at Winchelsea, *Sussex Notes and Queries* **5** (1935), 225-229, is challenged by his own unpublished manuscript of 1942 (ESRO AMS 2497).

Acknowledgements

Although based upon the paper presented at the Conference, the final version of this article has been amended to take into account the results of work undertaken and part of an archaeological and historical Re-assessment of Winchelsea, leading to A Quarterly by Quarter analysis of Winchelsea, East Sussex (Martin and Martin 2002) and An Extensive Urban Survey Assessment of Winchelsea, East Sussex (Martin 2002). This research work, which is also intended to result in an academic publication on the town, was principally funded by English Heritage, the National Trust and East Sussex County Council.

References

Brent, C. 1975. Urban Employment and Population in Sussex between 1550 and 1660, *SAC* **113**, 35-50.

Cooper, W.D. 1850. *The History of Winchelsea*. London: John Russell Smith and Hastings: Henry Osborne.

Freke, D.J., Martin, D. and Rudling, D. 1977. VIII. Excavations in Winchelsea, 1976, *Univ. London Inst. Archaeol. Bulletin* **14**, 34-38.

Homan, W. M. 1940. *The Founding of a 13th-Century Town*. Unpublished. East Sussex Record Office AMS 2497.

Homan, W.M. 1942. *The History of Winchelsea.* Unpublished. Copy in the East Sussex Record Office Library, Lewes.

Homan, W. M. 1949. The Founding of New Winchelsea, *SAC* **88**, 22-41.

Leslie, K. and Short, B. (eds). 1999. *An Historical Atlas of Sussex.* Chichester: Phillimore.

Martin, D. 2002. *An Extensive Urban Survey Assessment of Winchelsea, East Sussex.* Unpublished University College London Field Archaeology Unit report.

Martin, D. and Martin, B.J. 2002. *A Quarter by Quarter Analysis of the Town of Winchelsea, East Sussex.* Unpublished. Copy in the East Sussex Record Office.

Page, W. 1937. Winchelsea, in L.F. Salzmann (ed), *The Victoria History of the County of Sussex,* Volume **9**, Oxford: Univ. Press, 62-75.

Platt, C. 1973. *Medieval Southampton, The port and trading community, A.D. 1000-1600.* London: Routledge and Keegan Paul.

Rudling, D.R. and Martin, D. 1981. X. Excavations in North Street, Winchelsea, *Univ. London. Inst. Archaeol. Bulletin* **18**, 42-46.

Rudling, D. and Browne, S. 1993. *An Archaeological evaluation of part of St. Giles' Churchyard, Winchelsea, East Sussex (TQ 9015 1715) and A report on the human remains discovered during the excavations.* Unpublished Archaeology South-East Report No. 22 (1993).

Salzman, L. F. 1907. Industries, in W. Page (ed). *The Victoria History of the County of Sussex,* Volume **2**, 229-271. Oxford: Archibald Constable.

Stevenson, J. H. 1991. Arnold Nesbitt and the Borough of Winchelsea' in *SAC* **129**, 183-193.

Sylvester, D.G. 1999. *Maritime Communities in pre-plague England: Winchelsea and the Cinque Ports.* Unpublished Phd thesis, New York.

WAR AND RUMOUR OF WAR: THE DEFENCE OF SUSSEX 1530-1990

Martin Brown

Abstract

Evidence of works built to counter foreign invasion is plentiful in Sussex where the coast was felt to be particularly vulnerable because of its beaches and its proximity both to the mainland of Europe and to the capital. Despite prolonged periods of warfare, Medieval England had never sought a national defence policy. However, changes both in the government of England and in military technology and strategy during the later middle ages occasioned a change in thinking. By 1536 Henry VIII had created a network of large-scale coastal fortifications, establishing the concept of centrally organised defensive works. From the 16th century onwards the nation maintained its defences, altering, refurbishing and building in response to changes in technology, strategy, tactics and political circumstance.

Archaeology has much to offer in the study of these remains, offering insights into the monuments themselves, the landscapes of war they created, their contribution to the wider historic environment and in recognising the voiceless thousands who built, garrisoned and serviced the many fieldworks and fortifications. Archaeological perspectives can, in their widest sense, seek to consider monuments of war, from trenches to major fortifications, and re-assess their value and contribution to our world: as signifiers of painful history and common heritage; as monuments of our past, as agents of remembrance and as part of processes of mediation of national, political, official, collective and personal discourses.

Introduction

In 1852, the Pre-Raphaelite artist William Holman Hunt was painting at Fairlight, near Hastings. One of the pictures which he developed during his stay depicts sheep straying dangerously close to a precipitous cliff which overlooks the English Channel. This work - *Our English Coasts* - was, according to Fred Stephens, a friend of the artist, an allegory of England, *"a satire on the reported defenceless state of the country against foreign invasion"* (Clark Amor 1989, 101). The sheep represent Victorian society, complacent under the warm imperial sun and unaware of the danger from the cliffs or the Channel below. Hunt was aware that only a few miles away, in France, a new Napoleon, nephew of the infamous Bonaparte, was flexing his muscles and stirring memories. This painting was one of a stream of expressions of concern at the possible threat from France. It raised echoes in Whitehall and caused a review of coastal defences as well as a burst of popular involvement in rifle clubs and militia units. Of course, this was not the first occasion on which there had been a feeling that the coast had been denuded and that England was not ready to resist an invader, nor would it be the last. Another example of this mid-Victorian unease is conveyed in the poem *Dover Beach* by Matthew Arnold, where the author senses decline and fall, audible in the noise of the sea on shingle. France, visible from the English coast, is specifically mentioned. Arnold, like Hunt, is concerned

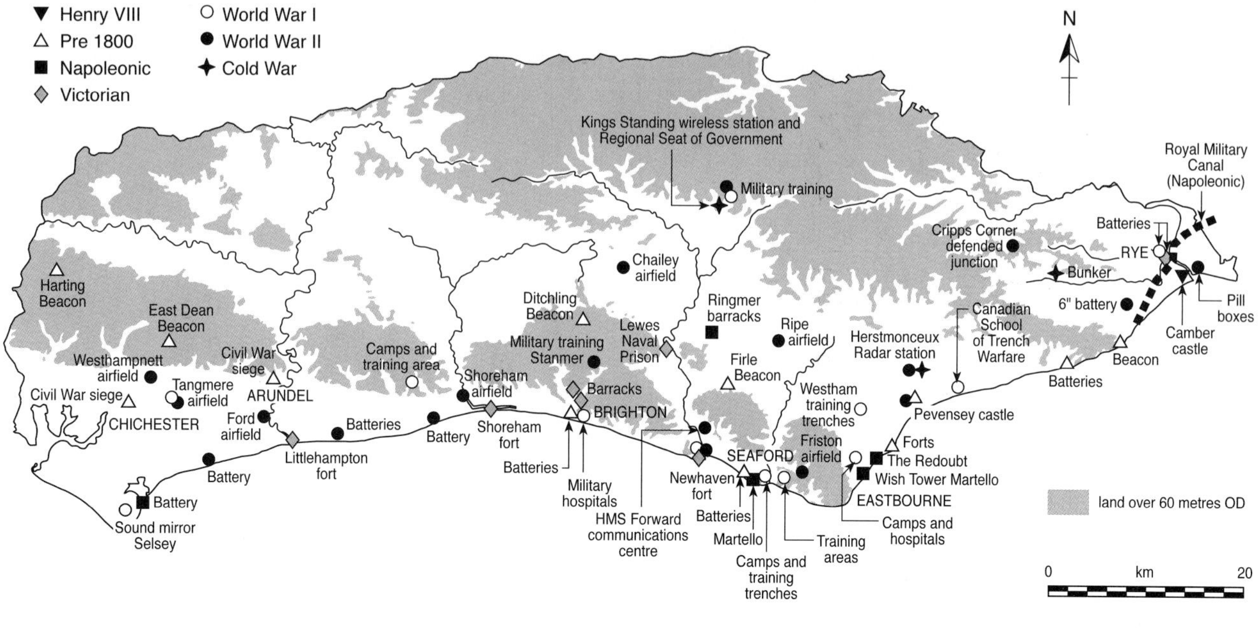

***Figure 16.1.** A selection of key sites and monuments from the military history of Sussex, AD 1500-2000.*

with the crisis of faith and moral decline, but the perceived external threat is also very much in evidence.

These various threats, whether real, or perceived, have left a rich archaeological record across England, but in Sussex the remnants of Post-Medieval defence are particularly numerous. Sussex faces the mainland of Europe, whence the threats were perceived to come. It was in the front line. In consequence the defence heritage is varied and rich, covering more than four centuries, from the ascendancy of gunpowder and the instigation of national defence policy, to the end of the Cold War. The archaeological remains of military works in Sussex reflect different threats, states of preparedness and levels of technology (Fig. 16.1). They also show us something of the world that produced them and, through consideration of their meanings, may offer us pointers to the future.

Three main themes which had an effect on the shape, range and form of military works have emerged in the course of preparing this paper and will be dealt with in turn. They include the technology available to the military and its effect on the strategy and tactics employed in the defence of the realm, as evidenced in Sussex. A final section will consider the theoretical base for this study, exploring some of the reasons for investigating this potentially contentious and painful subject matter.

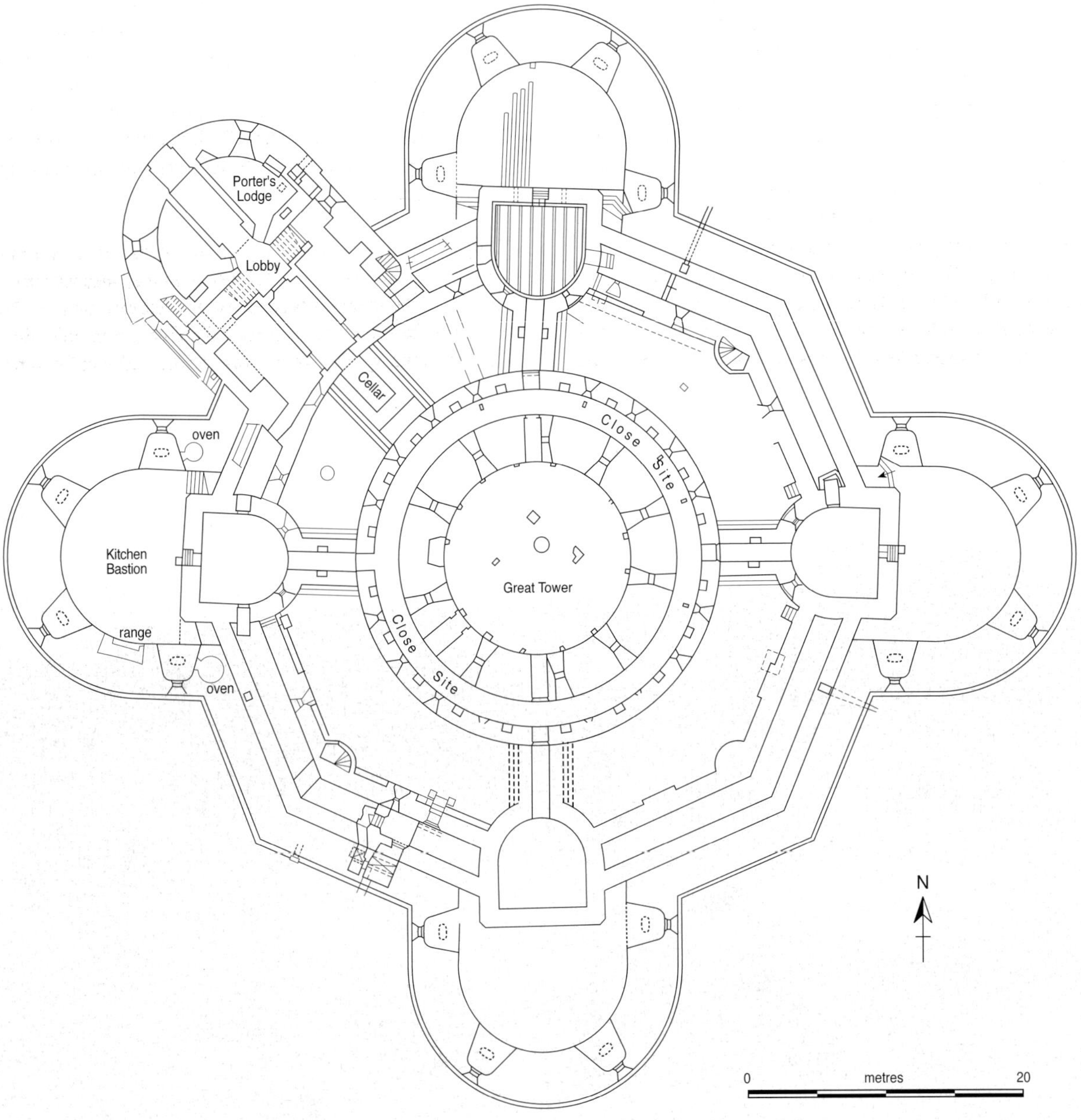

Figure 16.2. *Henry VIII's artillery fort of 1539-40 at Camber Castle. The plan shows the highly developed form of the works, which was built around the earlier Great Tower (1512-14). An intermediate phase with four small "stirrup" bastions was subsumed into the final design, shown here at its full extent. (After Biddle et al. 2001, fig. 3.2)*

Technology

For the first three centuries covered by this study technological development in military hardware was relatively slow: by 1600 the long-bow was obsolete and smooth-bore firearms and ordnance, using gunpowder to fire solid shot, were the principal weapons on European battlefields. Although there were some changes in this situation, such as the introduction of the explosive shell, weaponry of the Napoleonic age is not so different to that of the Spanish Armada, although fire-power and accuracy had increased, and the bayonet had eclipsed the pike as a means of protecting infantry against cavalry attack. Nevertheless, any consideration of these earlier works must consider the improvements in the effectiveness of, for example, gun-casting or the introduction of cartridges or rifling. While the basic forms of smaller works, such as gun batteries, change little, there are huge differences in larger works where ideas of fortification reflect wider military thought and are adapted to respond to technological change. Camber Castle (*c.*1540) is a fine example of a Henrician Device Fort, but its complicated plan (Fig. 16.2) was considered obsolete by 1600 and a greater range of guns available to reduce a fortress, including the howitzer, created a very different fort in Eastbourne's Redoubt (1804), even though both were designed with the same purpose - that of preventing an enemy landing - in mind. Similarly, alterations and rebuilding reflecting new military developments can be seen at some of the longer-lasting sites such as the Gun Garden battery at Rye, where the magazine was periodically refurbished and strengthened in response to the introduction of more effective artillery (James 1997). Camber Castle, the starting point of this study, is a remarkable monument. It was built in response to Henry VIII's need to defend his coast, but is one of the first fortifications to reflect the increasing military importance of gunpowder. The fortification has relatively low thick walls, providing solid gun platforms offering a low profile on which enemy artillery could be brought to bear. Internally, covered galleries allow access around the fort, even when it was under punishing fire. In form, the fortification differs from other fortifications that could mount guns, such as Herstmonceux Castle. Camber is not a home, it is a businesslike structure, designed not to impress with high walls or glazed windows, but to defend Rye and the coast and to resist attempts to reduce it. The effectiveness of this type of fortification can be seen at Mawes and Pendennis castles in Cornwall, both of which were besieged during the English Civil Wars (1642-51) and which resisted both artillery barrage and attempts at escalade. These works show how technology has changed and how government has also altered; the defended home - the traditional castle - is now no longer sufficient as a military structure and, at the same time, Tudor centralisation of power manifests itself in the Device forts rather than in royal support for private endeavour.

Despite the constant, albeit gradual, change manifest in our defences, some features of defence remained almost constant, including the warning beacon, which retained its usefulness until the introduction of more effective communication in the 19th century and which was maintained locally in times

Figure 16.3. *The continuing vulnerability of the coast is demonstrated by the positioning of this World War Two pillbox on top of a battery position on the Napoleonic era Royal Military Canal, near Winchelsea.*

of danger (Kitchen 1986). Elsewhere, developed forms of ancient defences proved very useful in surprisingly recent times. The Royal Military Canal, which could almost have been a Roman work in form and construction, was built to resist Napoleonic invasion, and was re-fortified in 1940 as part of the preparations against Hitler's invasion plans (Fig. 16.3). Such continued usage demonstrates enduring belief in the concept of a linear barrier employing a water-filled ditch and earthen rampart.

It was, however, the 19th century and the Industrial Age that brought about rapid and marked change in warfare and the responses to it. The combination of scientific knowledge, unfettered capitalism and industrial process promoted invention, innovation and development in the field of armaments, while imperialist ambitions amongst European powers not only afforded opportunities to test weaponry and tactics in the field, but also caused friction between the European powers, prompting almost constant military improvement, leading to an arms race. The combination of the introduction of rifled artillery, new explosives and more efficient propellants gave the attacker more effective guns with a longer range. Meanwhile, naval developments, including armour-plating, new methods of propulsion and the introduction of the submarine, increased the maritime threat to England, which was by 1880 at the heart of a global empire reliant on the sea for communication and trade.

Bigger guns and more effective explosives meant that the old batteries were obsolete because they were no longer able to mount effective ordnance or withstand bombardment. Response to this situation can best be seen at Littlehampton where the 18th century battery was replaced by a polygonal fort, or at Rye where the Gun Garden finally came to the end of its full service and was downgraded. Similarly the Martello chain, built to defend the coast against invasion from Napoleonic France, had become now ineffective and several towers were used as targets to demonstrate the effectiveness of the new guns (Sutcliffe 1972). The pace of change in the late 19th century is amply demonstrated at Newhaven where, like Camber Castle three centuries before, designs changed during construction in response to new military thinking, innovative equipment, such as Moncrieff's Disappearing Gun, and the destructive power available to an aggressor (Saunders 1989). This 'progress' culminates in the Great War of 1914 to 1918 which, was very much the product of the first Industrial Revolution - that of coal, steam and steel (Terraine 1996).

One significant development in the 19th century was the introduction of concrete as a building material for fortifications. At Newhaven Fort, built 1862-70, concrete was employed for the first time on a grand scale in British military works (Saunders 1989) (Fig. 16.4). This material was to become a major feature in the military architecture of the late 19th and 20th centuries, where it was used to form bunkers, runways, roadblocks and buildings. From major works to domestic air-raid shelters, concrete has provided an enduring legacy of the defence of Britain and, because it can be inscribed when wet, of some of those individuals involved in the various conflicts. Examples of this type of graffiti (ie recording names and events), can be seen on World War Two

Figure 16.4. *Early use of concrete as a construction material in military works at Newhaven Fort.*

Figure 16.5. *Concrete 'Dragons Teeth' (anti-tank obstacles) at the defended road junction of Cripps Corner, near Rye.*

anti-tank obstacles on the north side of Battle Church and close to the Rye Memorial Hospital.

The war of 1914-1918 demonstrated the limits of land warfare at a time when cavalry and the Maxim Gun were expected to share the same battlefield, but the stalemate in Flanders provided impetus to develop the technology which would shape military thought and planning throughout the ensuing century in terms of conventional, large-scale warfare. These developments included armoured fighting vehicles, including the tank, armoured car and armoured personnel carrier. The legacy of these machines has altered the landscape, since widened downland tracks and hard-standing in Stanmer Park serving training areas survive (John Funnell, pers. comm.), while the threat of mechanised invasion in 1940 has left gun emplacements, including examples on Chailey Common, and anti-tank obstacles such as those at Cripps Corner near Rye (Longstaff -Tyrrell 1998) (Fig. 16.5).

The Great War was also the conflict during which two new battlefields appeared - the air and the ether (Maj. Gen. J.F.C. Fuller quoted in the Introduction to Terraine 1996). Air war soon developed from a matter of reconnaissance to one of full military action, and the archaeology of these developments includes air bases, gun and searchlight emplacements, dirigible tethers, bomb shelters, crash sites and traces of air-raids, including blocks of post-war development amidst pre-war building. At Newhaven Fort the response to air power may be seen in the alteration of gun pits that provided them with concrete canopies intended to provide defence against air-delivered explosives. Other evidence may be seen at Lewes in the form of re-used Anderson air-raid shelters, supplied for personal use in the domestic garden and now used as sheds on the Landport allotments. The 20th century has also been the first age of electronic warfare, employing radio, radar and self-guided weaponry. The archaeology of this aspect of war in Sussex includes radar masts, control bunkers, such as South Heighton (Longstaff-Tyrell 1998), and transmitters, such as Kings Standing, whence information and propaganda where sent to occupied Europe and North Africa during World War Two and to Stalinist Europe during the Cold War (Sussex Police 1996). Nevertheless, despite advances in technology and forms of warfare, some staples of the defence of Sussex were constantly revived, including the coastal battery, from the temporary Tudor earthwork at Pevensey and to a more permanent and heavily built form dating from the Second World War at Pett.

By 1945 the military-industrial complex had produced the Atomic Bomb. Remains of this 'Nuclear period' are scarce in the County, but local Royal Observer Corps posts still survive scattered around Sussex, while the Kings Standing complex (Fig. 16.6) includes a Regional Seat of Government, built between 1988 and 1993 and capable of sustaining life for up to six months following nuclear attack on the UK. Smaller local government bunkers also survive, and it is possible that there are some personal fallout shelters, constructed beneath private dwellings in the 1980s, attached to some of the larger homes in Sussex, as they were elsewhere (Campbell 1982). Such developments rendered most other extant military works obsolete and in 1956 Coastal Defence was abolished and many sites, such as Newhaven Fort, were disposed of by the military. In addition, increased reliance

Figure 16.6. The entrance ramp to the Thatcher era Regional Seat of Government at King's Standing, Ashdown Forest. The complex was built to protect a civil infrastructure in the event of nuclear war at a time of renewed NATO-Soviet tension in the late 1980s. Political changes in both power blocs rendered it immediately obsolete

on the NATO alliance, bases in Western Germany and the nuclear deterrent, caused reorganisation and redundancy of other bases, such as Tangmere.

Strategy

In essence, the strategy for the defence of the realm from invasion has traditionally comprised three strands: the use of the Channel as a barrier; the denial of beaches to the enemy and resistance to and impediment of the advancing enemy forces (Saunders 1989). Of the first strand, little exists in Sussex, except the wreck of the Anne, scuttled at Pett in 1690, following the Battle of Beachy Head (Marsden 1997), but the evidence of terrestrial preparations for the resistance of invasion, both at the shore and inland, is rich and varied.

The first strategic development apparent in the archaeological record in Sussex is also the starting point for this study. In 1540 Henry VIII sent out commissioners to survey the coast and identify locations for permanent garrisons and batteries. A chain of fortifications, with a unity of style resulted. These forts represent a break with medieval practice. No longer was the security of the coast left in the hands of local magnates, now central government intended to maintain a watch on the English shores. They also represent responses to the growing importance of gunpowder on the battlefield.

When Henry VIII formulated the first truly national defence policy he had no large navy on which to rely for the protection of the coast. By 1550, a chain of batteries and artillery towers, reinforced on the south coast by larger fortifications, was complete. At Camber, in the extreme east of Sussex we have a well-preserved example of these device forts, preserved, albeit in a ruinous condition, in its 16th-century state. Excavation has shown how the fort grew around a central tower (Fig. 16.2) and changed in reaction to different ideas of fortification which were developing at the time in response to warfare on the European mainland.

Between the 16th and 19th century the battery continued to be the principal means of coastal defence. The strategic position of some batteries meant that they were maintained, refurbished and developed in response to changes in military thinking, until by the 19th century they had developed into major works. A number of these batteries survive as monuments, such as the Rye Gun-garden, used continuously from 16th to 19th centuries, or Littlehampton. Elsewhere archaeological remains are known to exist, such as Brighton's Great East Street Battery which was recorded in 1892 by Bishop when Markwell's Royal Hotel was built and used its massive walls as foundations. (Carder, 1990) Elsewhere historical records show the historic and geographic range of these works (Hudson, 1984).

The French Revolutionary and Napoleonic wars brought the threat of invasion by a large army motivated by a common ideal. No longer was the French Army looking to inflict defeat and a punitive treaty on Britain, now it was ideologically motivated and its victory meant ruination to the English elite (Saunders 1989). This threat prompted a revision of thinking

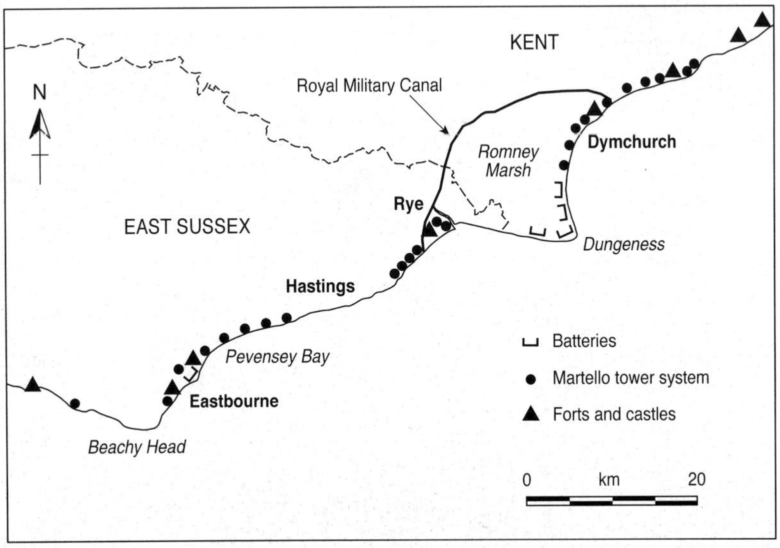

Figure 16.7. Coastal defences in East Sussex and South-East Kent, 1804-1815 (after Brown 1988, fig. 2).

that is evident in eastern Sussex. Although the beacons and batteries continued in use and remains of army camps in the interior provide evidence of preparations to defeat the invader (Margary 1965), it is the coastal strip that reveals the major development.

In order to resist French landings, a chain of brick towers was built between Seaford in East Sussex and Aldeburgh in Suffolk. This Martello Tower chain – taking its name from a tower at Cap Mortella, Corsica - still survives, in parts, with its supporting redoubt fortresses (Fig. 16.7). Although many individual towers have suffered from development, coastal erosion and later military usage - often as practice targets - others still survive in good condition, little changed since their abandonment following the defeat of France (Fig. 16.8). Others, however, display a variety of uses and abuses by subsequent owners, including HM Coastguard and the military during World War Two (Sutcliffe 1972). The towers (Brown 1998, Fig. 1 and Plate 1) were intended to deny the beaches to the enemy, or at least impede any attempt at landing while the Navy harried the invasion fleet and the field army mustered its strength for a pitched battle (Saunders 1997). At the same time a linear defence was created around the landward edge of Pett Level and Romney Marsh - the Royal Military Canal. This work reflects the need to secure a piece of ground with gently-shelving beaches, ideally suited to amphibious landing, without simply flooding it. Flooding would have meant the loss of an important source of food for the capital since grain was grown and sheep were kept on the marshes (Vine 1972). The Canal was a product not only of external policy against the French, but also of an internal desire amongst the politicians of the day to keep an unpredictable and potentially violent London mob fed, thus markedly reducing the likelihood of food riots close to the heart of Government at a time of national danger.

By the mid-19th century, strategy and technology were developing markedly and this can be seen in the surviving remains. Large fortifications now protected key points while the small coastal batteries, so long the mainstay of defence, were allowed to decline and, in some cases, disappear altogether (Aldsworth 1981). Inland, changes can also be seen: the drill hall attests the growth and resourcing of the home forces and an increased reliance on a part-time army home reserve. Outside Sussex, improvements and major defences at naval ports show the importance placed on the Navy at the expense of land forces, while defended mobilisation centres offer an indication of the strategy for resistance to an enemy army (Saunders 1989).

The 1914-18 conflict has left its traces in Sussex. Some such remains include developments at forts such as Newhaven (Dobinson 1997), but others reflect the methods employed in the fighting of the war, despite the fact that Sussex was well away from the main areas of military action, ie of Flanders or the Ottoman Empire. Sussex ports were used for the transportation of troops, war materials and the wounded. In consequence, the surrounding countryside was heavily utilised for training and for the concentration of troops prior to embarkation (Simkins 1988). Training of troops continued while embarkation orders were awaited, and a major feature of training was the building of trenches (MacDonald 1995). This work encouraged fitness, engendered team work and spirit and taught skills necessary for service in Flanders.

Figure 16.8. *Napoleonic Martello Tower, Rye Harbour.*

Figure 16.9. First World War practice trenches dug for training purposes at Seaford. Air photo searches have shown such remains to survive at a number of locations in Sussex, including Thundersbarrow Hill and the Ashdown Forest.

Remains of a number of trench systems can still be found, either surviving as earthworks, as at Seaford Head (Fig. 16.9), or on aerial photographs, such as those at Polegate (Brown 1998, Plate 2). Although no traces of the large army camps remain visible today, the trenches, which are indistinguishable from examples visible in Flanders, survive, demonstrating the presence of troops during the Great War. The location of trenches, often in untenable positions, reveals their educational, rather than defensive nature. While the land war became bogged down, elsewhere mobility increased and new strategies presented themselves to the commanders. This was the first conflict in which the submarine made an impact and counter-measures had to be taken to protect shipping. These included the use of air power, another new military resource. The importance of the Channel in general, and of Newhaven as a port, in particular, can be seen in the presence of a dirigible station at Willingdon and a Royal Naval Air Service seaplane station at the Newhaven Tidemills (Longstaff-Tyrrell 1996). Both types of aircraft were used to spot enemy submarines seeking either to attack shipping or to slip through the English Channel into the Atlantic. The rise of air power during the Great War also presented the first opportunity for offensive action against targets relatively far away from the main theatres. In 1915 there were Zeppelin raids against England and these were followed later in the war by air raids by aeroplanes. The effectiveness of the bombers occasioned the establishment, in 1917, of a section of the Royal Flying Corps given over to bombing strategic targets in Germany. Their bases included Tangmere in West Sussex (Dobinson 1997) where the station was to have a continuing existence through the Second World War and beyond, demonstrating the continuing importance of air-power.

The relics of the 1939-45 war reveal a very definite sense of threat from a mobile invader, as not only beaches, but road junctions and other important points were defended. Meanwhile, phasing of works can show how thinking about the threat and resistance to any invasion changed during the course of the war (Dobinson 1997). The concept of guerrilla action, as a resistance strategy is also discernible from remains of secret shelters, such as the example at Park Wood, Hellingly (Angell 1996). Remains of both World Wars also show the developing importance of aircraft for reconnaissance and combat in the survival of airfields, seaplane bases, balloon stations and anti-aircraft measures. In the Weald, remains of Diver positions - guns located to intercept V1 rockets - mark the introduction of new, remote weapons and the lack of effective new weapons to combat them. Following the defeat of Nazi Germany many of their military innovations were adopted by the allies, including rocket technology. This, coupled with the invention of nuclear weapons, forced a new direction in military thinking and left new classes of monuments reflecting the importance of the new weapons.

The partition of Europe following the defeat of Nazi Germany and the growing reliance on nuclear weapons made coastal defences redundant: Britain's frontier was now the Rhine (Campbell 1982). European Strategy now rested on the concept of nuclear deterrent to prevent war. Nevertheless preparations for war were continued, although the defence of the nation and its population were no longer considered viable. Refuges and shelters were created only for those who would fight massively destructive wars and supposedly emerge to lead post-war governments, as a scatter of bunkers of various sizes reveals.

In some cases the archaeology reveals strategic thinking, but in others there is definite evidence of lack of preparation, as in the Elizabethan and 20th-century phases at Pevensey Castle, where the Roman and Medieval works were hastily reinforced in the face of very real threats from the Spanish in 1588 and Hitler in 1940 (Fig. 16.10). In addition, study of the measures taken at a particular period indicate both the tactics which the defenders expected the enemy to use and the counter-measures which were to be employed against them, however ad hoc these might be. For example, a German attack in 1940 was expected to be highly mobile, as it had been in mainland Europe. Thus, one phase of defensive strategy centred on the blocking of roads and of junctions in particular. At Sedlescombe defences using concrete 'dragons teeth' (anti-tank obstacles) reflect mainstream military architecture, but elsewhere works included concrete-filled oil drums and barriers constructed from tram-lines (Dobinson 1997).

Theory

This study raises some important questions about the past and its study. The first is that of preservation. The relatively long time-frame of this study means that while some older sites, such as Camber Castle, have been preserved and are already conserved and interpreted, others have not enjoyed preservation and arguments against their preservation can be advanced (J. Keegan pers. comm.). As the remains become more recent there is less certainty either of preservation or of the general public valuing them. 20th-century remains are sometimes felt to be too recent and, perhaps, too painful to retain or study. For example, we can happily visit the battlefield at Naseby, have a nice day out and even watch a re-enactment, but how do we feel about the Somme battlefield? It is also said that there is no need for the work of archaeologists in this field since detailed, written records survive. Furthermore, the aesthetic perceptions that argued for the preservation of stone circles and Medieval ruins work against military remains, which are seen as ugly and utilitarian. Finally, the study of this subject could be seen as controversial, even insulting, in modern Europe where citizens are now encouraged to think of their neighbours as contemporary friends rather than as historic enemies. However, those who seek to remove our recent military heritage from the landscape and consign it to the museum and page, if not the rubbish dump, are undervaluing the resource and seeking to avoid important truths about both the past and the nature of history.

Military remains present a particular example of scientific and technological application in each particular period. They reflect political situations and the threats, real or perceived, that a particular society felt. They show reactions to threat, both at national level in the formulation of policy and at a local level in the siting, construction and use of the sites. Meanwhile, non-military archaeological evidence will provide insights into the provisioning and supply of establishments and into the material culture of the garrisons. Archaeology may also show the existence of people who were excluded from official records, including women and children; the presence of such non-military personnel has become increasingly recognised in recent years, although the official histories still tend to ignore them. Indeed the common

Figure 16.10. *Second World War emplacements built into Medieval and Roman walls at Pevensey Castle, camouflaged to resemble the ruins into which they were inserted. This continued re-use of the site illustrates the vulnerability of the Sussex coast in time of war.*

soldier, often thought of as the dregs of Society, may only be identified through his archaeological remains. Social information can also be obtained from these sites. For example, the division of space in a Martello Tower between officers and men demonstrates social attitudes and divisions, both in the military and wider Georgian society. In our own time, the nuclear bunker demonstrates utter disregard for the population at large. The small number of shelters makes it plain that only the politicians and military, who had brought conflict about, and an irrelevant hereditary monarchy were, and probably are, to be preserved, leaving the rest of the world to be abandoned to holocaust, nuclear winter and radiation sickness (Owen 1980; Campbell 1982).

As has been discussed above, these monuments record attitudes within the state in respect of itself and its citizens/ subjects. The formation and pursuit of national defence policy demonstrate the consolidation of central power based, in part, on military strength. Defences manifest the desire of the state to protect its own, but also carry a threat of internal violence against dissident elements. This occured during the 16th century at Kingston-upon-Hull, where the batteries face toward the town as well as outwards into the countryside (Saunders 1989) and in the 19th century in eastern Sussex and Kent, where the Martello chain and Royal Military Canal proved useful in the suppression of the local smuggling trade (Cobbett 1830). Thus some remains reflect the imposition of a social contract from above, offering defence on its own terms. Other works do, however, reflect truly national response to a threat springing from a feeling of common cause (Colley 1992). Such attitudes are revealed by, for example, communally organised and manned 18th-century batteries, local drill halls in the Victorian era and local attempts at defensive works during World War II.

Several factors argue in favour of study and preservation of modern military remains. The great majority of sites are well-documented: government and military authorities kept records, most of which survive and which can be used with the archaeological data. There are other sites which were secret and where local and oral history is a useful source of information (Ellis 1996). There is still a generation which was involved in the construction, supply and garrisoning of such sites, their testimony is invaluable and irreplaceable, but it must be collected soon. One must also recognise that the generations who remember the World Wars are now dying, and in the absence of the actual person it is essential to have the oral testimony, history, monument and archaeology to stand as a witness to and evidence of the past (Chielens 1998).

Some of the concrete defences have now become landmarks in their own right. They contribute to the character of the landscape and are as much part of the historic depth of our environment as the tumulus (Countryside Commission 1996). Furthermore, the experience of seeing the remains of war in context allows a greater understanding of terrain, strategy and threat, to the general public. The remains of a pillbox seen beside a railway line or near to a canal lock convey to the viewer in a way that maps and photographs never can. These contributions, taken with the historic and archaeological value of these monuments, make a strong case for preservation, recording and interpretation. Fortunately, their value has been recognised and there is a British recording scheme involving amateur archaeologists that has sought not only to record monuments, but also to interview those involved in their construction and use (Denison 1995).

The international nature of war means that these remains represent a common heritage shared by England and our neighbours. We should recognise that our archaeological resource and heritage is not only based on Celtic art or Gothic architecture. Joint endeavour in heritage research and conservation should recognise the more painful aspects of our history, since failure to do this would be dishonest and would reduce the scope for fruitful partnerships through failure to confront and build on the past. There are also serious elements of reflection and commemoration in the preservation and presentation of military heritage on both sides of the Channel. It is not enough to record these remains: war and rumour of war has been a common feature of European history since the end of the Roman Empire. If we are to move forward to a more peaceful, more civilised age, then former enemies will need to come to terms with the past, since the past is a foundation of the future. The citizen can be proud of some aspects of that past, but other elements are less laudable. To ignore them is both dishonest and dangerous for it can lead to repetition of past mistakes and to the rise of partial and biased re-tellings of the past (Baker 1987; Uzzell 1989). Here, when some even deny the reality of the Holocaust, History alone cannot tell the whole story and the archaeological evidence is an essential component of the record, providing a wider range of information through study of the physical evidence. Furthermore, there is scope to re-examine responses to combat and the experience of war, as it appears in material culture, including artefacts made and used by the combatants and by those at home. Yet the value of these remains goes beyond academic interest to the point where there is engagement with the general public. The presentation of remains provides particular sites where there can be a connection with the past through place (Schama 1994; Winter 1996). Monuments stand as a physical reminder of past activity: as a memorial to those people who built and garrisoned them. They can also bear witness to the global nature of modern conflict, involving people from countries far removed from the theatre of war, as we see through the India Gate and Chattri (Memorials to Indian troops) at Brighton (Carder 1990). Both in the academic study of the archaeology of warfare and in the presentation of artefacts and monuments archaeology has a moral, as well as an educational purpose, examining human actions and commenting upon them (Carman 1997). Military remains and military history need not present a story of conquest and glory, rather can they acknowledge the human dimension of any conflict, from the General to the refugee, and offer a mediation with the past - an opportunity for the individual to reflect and understand. Mere condemnation of war would be simplistic: it would be preferable to allow the evidence, be it oral history, material culture or physical remains to provide comment on the words and actions of the captains and the kings (Chielens 1998). Whether one finds war abhorrent or sees it as a lamentably necessary evil, the testimony of the monuments is an irreplaceable source of evidence in the study of conflict, its origins, outcomes and resolutions, as well as of those caught up in it. Without such understanding we cannot hope to move toward the end of war as a phenomenon or, until that day comes, to recognise those occasions when warriors and warfare are sadly necessary, neither shall we be able to judge what rules should apply in the pursuit of military objectives (Keegan 1998).

Monuments of war and defence speak of dislocation of everyday life and of fear and confusion. They are a testament to both human ingenuity and human folly, demonstrating what is best and worst about our species. Archaeology is the study of people. It should not shy away from humanity's less palatable achievements or its shameful moments. Archaeology must include such challenging material or else it reduces its relevance to society as a whole and is in danger of reverting to mere antiquarianism, being melancholic and divorced from reality (Shanks 1992). Without responsible, academic frameworks and proper consideration of evidence the past becomes open to misinterpretation. Without proper understanding of the past we cannot effectively consider the present, or make reasoned choices about our futures. The archaeology of defence is part of that past and it may be, that through the retention and study of these remains, large military works can become historic features for study and recreation rather than contemporary, working structures of war and preparation for war.

End Note

Recent research visits to World War I battlefields in France and Belgium have demonstrated the emotional pull of such sites, even for those far too young to have spoken to veterans about the war, the author included. A look around a big cemetery, such as Tyne Cot (Belgium), or a reading of a visitors' book at a Commonwealth War Graves Commission cemetery, will reveal a diverse cross section of society visiting the graves and monuments. Interest in the memorialization of various aspects of 20th-century military sites is demonstrated by various works, including: Winter and Sivian (1999) and Schofield and Anderton (2000). The internet is proving a fertile ground for virtual memorialisation. Searches will reveal not only official sites, such as the Commonwealth War Graves Commission site, but also a host of semi- and unofficial sites, including highly personal memoirs of relatives lost in Vietnam.
(http://members.aol.com/JD2813/Dad.html,http://www.sdit.org/)

References

Aldsworth, F. 1981. A description of the mid-19th century forts at Littlehampton and Shoreham, West Sussex, *SAC* **119**, 181-194.

Angell, S. 1996. *The Secret Sussex Resistance.* Chichester: Middleton Press.

Baker, F. 1987. History that hurts: excavating 1933-45, *Archaeological Review from Cambridge,* 71.

Biddle, M., Hiller, J., Scott, I. and Streeten, A. 2001. *Henry VIII's Coastal Artillery Fort at Camber Castle, Rye, East Sussex: An archaeological, structural and historical investigation.* Oxford: Oxford Archaeological Unit for English Heritage.

Brown, M. 1998. Fire and Water: coastal defence 1530-1945, in X. Delestre and A. Woodcock (eds), *Proximus 2, Publication of the archaeological round-table, Dieppe 17th and 18th September 1996,* 179-184. Rouen: The Association for the Promotion of Archaeology in Haute-Normandy.

Campbell, D. 1982. *War Plan UK.* London: Burnett.

Carder, T. 1990. *The Encyclopaedia of Brighton,* Lewes: East Sussex County Council.

Carman, J. 1997. Interpreting the landscapes of battle, *British Archaeology* **21**, 8-9.

Carman, J. 1996. Giving Archaeology a Moral Voice, in I. Carman (ed), *Material Harm: archaeological studies of war and violence,* Glasgow: Cruithne.

Chielens, P. 1998. *In Flanders Fields,* Ypres: Flanders Fields Museum.

Clark Amor, A. 1989. *William Holman Hunt - The True Pre-Raphaelite,* London: Constable.

Cobbett, W. 1830. *Rural Rides,* London: W. Cobbett.

Colley, I. 1992. *Britons: Forging the Nation,* London: Pimlico.

Countryside Commission. 1996. *Views from the Past.* Unpublished consultation document.

Denison, S. 1995. Tracing the relics of wartime defence, *British Archaeology* **3**, 8-9.

Dobinson, C. 1997. *Twentieth Century Fortifications in England,* York: CBA.

Ellis, G. 1996. The Tunnels of HMS Forward, *Defence Lines* **4**, 3-4.

Hudson, A. 1984. Volunteer Soldiers in Sussex during the Revolutionary and Napoleonic Wars, 1793 - 1815, *SAC* **122**, 165-182.

James, R. 1997. *An Archaeological Investigation at the Gun Garden, Rye, East Sussex,* Archaeology South-East Project **658**. Unpublished. A copy of this report has been deposited in the East Sussex County Council Sites and Monuments Record.

Keegan, J. 1998. *War and Our World,* London: Hutchinson.

Kitchen, R. 1986. The Ghastly War Flame, *SAC* **124**, 179-192.

Longstaff-Tyrell. 1998. *Tyrell's List, The Artefacts of Two Great Wars in Sussex,* Polegate: Gote House.

Lowry, B. (ed). 1995. *20th Century Defences in Britain,* York: CBA.

MacDonald, L. 1995. *1915,* London: Headline.

Margary, I.D. 1965. Military Field Kitchens of the Eighteenth Century, *SAC* **103**, 60-66.

Marsden, P. 1997. *Ships and Shipwrecks,* London: Batsford.

Meades, D. 1991. *Pevensey Castle,* London: English Heritage.

Owen, D. 1980. *Negotiate and Survive,* London: Social Democrat Party.

Pevsner, N. and Nairn, I. 1965. *The buildings of England, Sussex,* London: Penguin.

Saunders, A. 1989. *Fortress Britain,* Oxford: Oxbow.

Saunders, A. 1997. *Channel Defences,* London: Batsford.

Schama, S. 1994. *Landscape and Memory,* London: Harper Collins.

Schofield, A.A. and Lake, J. 1995. Defining our defence heritage, *Conservation Bulletin* **27**, 12-13.

Schofield, J., and Anderton, M. 2000. "The queer archaeology of Green Gate: interpreting contested space at Greenham Common Airbase", *World Archaeology* 32 (2): 236-251.
Shanks, M. 1991. *Experiencing the Past,* London: Routledge.
Simkins, P. 1988. *Kitchener's Army. The Raising of the New Armies,* 1914-16, Manchester: University Press.
Sussex Police. 1996. *Kings Standing,* Unpublished information sheet.
Sutcliffe, S. 1972. *Martello Towers,* Newton Abbot: David and Charles.
Terraine, J. 1996. *The Smoke and the Fire,* London: Sidgwick and Jackson.
Uzzell, D.L. 1989. The hot interpretation of war and conflict, in D. Uzzell (ed), *Heritage Interpretation,* London: Bellhaven Press.
Vine P.A. L. 1972. *The Royal Military Canal,* Newton Abbot: David and Charles.
Winter, J. 1996. *Sites of Memory, Sites of Mourning,* Cambridge: University Press.
Winter, J., and Sivan, E. 1999. *War and remembrance in the twentieth century*, Cambridge.

THE ARCHAEOLOGY OF POST-MEDIEVAL SUSSEX: A REVIEW

Luke Barber

Abstract

Over the last few decades more Post-Medieval archaeology has been undertaken in Sussex than one may at first appreciate. Much of this work, though by no means all of it, has been the result of chance discoveries while excavating for earlier remains. Most intentional work on the period has revolved around standing remains, both domestic and industrial. This has led to a very fragmented and disjointed body of data for the period. The current paper presents an overview of the work undertaken to date on Post-Medieval archaeology in Sussex in order to provide both an easy source for bibliographic reference and help begin to formulate future research agendas for the period.

Introduction

Following the Symposium of Sussex Archaeology held in 1977, Peter Brandon, when writing on medieval Sussex, stated that '...the Medieval period, has, until recently, been very unfashionable in Sussex archaeological circles. Large-scale intensive fieldwork has hardly begun...' (Brandon 1978). Now, some 24 years on, Medieval archaeology is well established in Sussex. However, Post-Medieval archaeology in the county, with a few notable exceptions, still remains peripheral to the main stream of archaeological interest and is often treated lightly, if at all. Despite this, more work has been done on the period in Sussex than may at first be appreciated, even though much of this remains somewhat disjointed. The primary aims of this paper are therefore threefold: to bring together what has been done to date, to use this as a basis on which to identify some of the gaps in the existing data, and to generate further interest in a period paramount to the development of the way we live today.

Archaeologists have often shied away from the period, partly because of its recent time-span and partly due to the huge amount of historical sources and surviving structures available for study. These sources have provided a relatively ridged framework into which the archaeological data must be set (Brandon and Short 1990). Although such sources may hold the archaeologist's enthusiastic imagination in check, they, combined with the excavated evidence, provide a unique and powerful tool for studying the past.

Although various early publications have touched on the period (Wood 1968), the publication of the first standard reference work (Crossley 1990) has brought to the fore the rich archaeological evidence that may be obtained. This book has also highlighted the many gaps in the historical record, particularly with regard to the poorer levels of society and early industry. Within a limited length of text, this paper will unashamedly closely follow the structure of Crossley's work in an attempt to cover most aspects of the period as represented by the Sussex evidence.

Although some 19th-century material is included here, the whole topic of Sussex's rich industrial archaeology has had to be largely omitted. The revolution in transportation, from canals and railways to motorcars and aeroplanes, as well as that of 19th-century industry, are vast topics in their own right and present restrictions of space prevent their inclusion in the current paper. The topics of military and maritime archaeology, which are important aspects of the period, are covered elsewhere (Martin Brown and Peter Marsden this volume).

The landscape

Although the Sussex landscape has been evolving at the hand of man for thousands of years, it is usually the Post-Medieval period which has had the greatest input to its present form (Brandon 1974). The demands of the growing population during this time meant the response from agriculture and industry had a profound affect on the former Medieval landscape. These changes dominate the archaeology of the period and should, where possible, be used to put any excavated site in its original topographical context.

The enclosure of land resulted in a patchwork of hedged and ditched fields which form the familiar landscape around us. These fields are now often being amalgamated for the needs of modern farm machinery, and although often fossilised in the cartographic sources, physical evidence is being lost. Reclamation of marshland, often started in the Middle Ages, continued into the Post-Medieval period, where increased efficiency resulted in more extensive and longer-term benefits. The study of such reclamation cannot be undertaken by archaeology alone: it must rely heavily on documentary and cartographic sources to understand the field evidence (Fig. 17.1). Research, such as that of the Ouse valley and Lewes and Laughton Levels (Brandon 1971; Farrant, J. 1972), show how full reclamation could take many years to complete.

Woodland was also an important economic resource, and although general deforestation took place, especially in the 17th century, there was a marked increase in coppiced woodland, particularly in the Weald, to supply the iron industry. Scant traces survive of woodland industries, despite their importance (Armstrong 1978). However, this may be in part due to the lack of fieldwork that has been undertaken. For example, the remains of a ploughed-out charcoal kiln at Lamberhurst (Barber 1992) and a single charcoal-burner's hut at Fittleworth (Gardiner 1984/5), have been chance discoveries rather than the result of planned research.

Farm buildings

Farms and their associated buildings need to be studied in relation to surrounding housing in order to understand fully

Figure 17.1. *Medieval and Post-Medieval ditched fields in the Brede valley, East Sussex. Infilled boundaries are shown by soil-marks. (Photograph: UCL Field Archaeology Unit).*

the social structure of any rural community. Although farmhouses are generally maintained, many ancillary buildings, from cowsheds and cartsheds to barns and granaries, are either being left to slowly decay or are being replaced by new structures more fitting to present-day agricultural needs. There are too many to preserve and preservation, although the ideal option, is not always justified. However, these buildings represent the very mechanics of a farm unit and offer an insight into the development of agricultural methods and building techniques. As such they ought to be recorded, particularly if demolition/domestic conversion is intended. Perhaps the single largest contribution to this aspect of the Post-Medieval period has been made by the work of the Weald and Downland Museum at Singleton. Other studies, concentrating on both the historical sources and standing buildings have also made a significant contribution (Martin and Martin 1982; Farrant, S. 1983; Caffyn 1983). However, further work is still needed on the many undiscovered/ unrecorded outbuildings which remain.

Less obvious agricultural structures/features are also to be found. For example, the 18th-century stock enclosure on Bullock Down, Eastbourne (Drewett 1982) and a further example, perhaps of 16th- to 17th- century date, on Romney Marsh at Broomhill (Gardiner 1990a). Other studies have included the use of marling pits within the agricultural landscape (Drewett 1982), as well as the excavation of a probable early 19th- century sheep pond at Mill Down (Stevens 1990). Numerous such features still survive, however, although they represent important cogs in the agricultural regime virtually no effort has been made to record them.

Domestic rural buildings and villages

The study of domestic rural buildings can help strengthen the evidence for the growth in prosperity of both the farming and rurally based industrial communities during the period. Many new houses were built or adapted between the later Medieval period and the end of the 18th century. The analysis of standing buildings is perhaps the key to the understanding of this field, and the synthesis of the results of the architectural survey of the Rape of Hastings (Martin and Martin 1987) has shown the importance of studying the houses of a cross-section of the population.

Occasionally rare opportunities have arisen to combine architectural, historical and archaeological surveys at the same site. The Medieval and 17th- century house at Walderton is a good example of such work (Aldsworth and Harris 1982) and resulted in a close understanding of the phases of development at the site. Elsewhere during the 16th and 17th centuries a similar pattern of modification to late Medieval houses was being undertaken. The desire for greater comfort resulted in the insertion of chimneys, stairs, upper storeys and glazed windows to many houses: the excavation of the parsonage house at Hangleton showed a chimney and cellar had been inserted into the existing building during this period (Holden 1963).

One of the fundamental problems for the study of rural buildings, as with urban ones, is that of differential survival. The buildings still extant tend to be those of the wealthier levels of society whose houses were more durable and worth adapting in later periods. Little is known of the humbler dwellings of the labouring class at the beginning of the period as most of these were usually replaced during the 18th and 19th centuries. Those that do survive tend to have been so extensively altered that little of the original structure survives. The documentary sources for these poorer houses is also scarce as the poorer people often left no will and thus no probate inventories were made (Crossley 1990). This is obviously a field in which archaeological research should be directed. Careful excavation, for the structural remains are likely to be slight, should address this issue.

Villages usually offer a good opportunity to study Post-Medieval buildings as redevelopment has often been slow or non-existent. Excavations in Tarring have revealed part of a well-preserved 17th- and 18th- century building (Bedwin 1979), as well as other Post-Medieval foundations (Barton 1964). It is unfortunate that when redevelopment takes place in villages it often does so with little or no archaeological input. As well as living villages Sussex contains many deserted examples. Although these are typically thought of as being Medieval abandonments, many continued into the Post-Medieval period and as such offer the best chances of uncovering undisturbed house plans of all classes of society. Examples range from Aldrington (abandoned post *c.*1700) to Buxted (abandoned due to emparking in the 18th century) (Burleigh 1973).

Houses of the Upper Classes

During the 16th century the increased desire for comfort and its new obtainibility for the more wealthy is demonstrated in the new style of large stately houses being built during the period. Three different types of establishment are worth highlighting.

After the Dissolution many former monastic structures became available for conversion into prestigious domestic residencies. This is frequently seen in Sussex at sites such as Battle and Bayham Abbeys (Hare 1985; Streeten 1983), Wilmington and Michelham Priories (Barton and Holden 1967; Stevens and Stevens 1991), as well as Lewes Friary (Gardiner *et al.* 1996). Despite this, no synthetic work has yet been undertaken to bring together the archaeological and historical evidence in an attempt to study the dynamics of such conversions.

Many moated sites continued in occupation into the Post-Medieval period. However, this is often passed over quickly by the archaeologist in the published report. As with converted monastic sites, this has led to a deficiency in our knowledge of the early Post-Medieval impacts on moated settlements. This problem has been exacerbated by the fact that many sites of this type which continued into the Post-Medieval period are still occupied today and therefore not available for archaeological excavation. One noticeable exception to this general rule is Laughton Place where a 16th- century brick house, with moat walls complete with projections, was built within the existing moat (Fig. 17.2). Excavations of both the moat and part of the interior platform revealed substantial Tudor remains (Rudling 1991a) of both buildings and bridges. Conversely, at Hawksden, excavation only revealed evidence of some late 16th- century, poor quality repairs to the existing building, whereafter it was left to decay (Martin 1990).

Figure 17.2. *Laughton Place, East Sussex. Collapsed brick moat wall with projection. Scale: 40cm. (Photograph: David Rudling).*

Purpose-built houses for the nobility and gentry from this period are frequently still standing, often in the care of the National Trust. These have usually received study to a greater or lesser extent. Many have often been subjected to extensive alterations through the centuries and this can sometimes lead to difficulties in interpretation. Houses which have not continued in use offer good opportunities for archaeological work to obtain unaltered house plans. Unfortunately, the early 17th- century house at Old Buxted Place (demolished 1722) was completely destroyed in 1973 during the enlargement of a lake. The destruction was so rapid that Fred Tebbutt (1975) did not even manage to obtain an accurate ground plan. House shells like that of the early 16th- century Cowdray House (burnt 1793) provide similar opportunities to study relatively unaltered structures. The investigations at the Elizabethan mansion at Ore Place, Hastings, is one of the few instances where actual excavation has been carried out on a house of the 'upper' classes in Sussex (Gardiner 1991; Barber 1998). Unfortunately, the full extent of the building lay outside the excavated area and later disturbance/modification was extensive. A similar situation was faced during an archaeological evaluation at Warnham Place (Barber and Gardiner 1992).

Gardens, parks and estate structures

Recent archaeological trends have expanded the study of upper class dwellings beyond the houses themselves to their associated settings and structures. Perhaps the best known aspect of this expansion is that of garden archaeology. The transition from the formal gardens of the 16th century to the parkscapes favoured in the 18th century is complex and often variable in date depending on the individual house. Archaeological fieldwork can not only establish the layout of the formal garden, but the date of its abandonment in favour of something newer. Little work has been done in Sussex, despite the discipline being frequently used elsewhere. Some limited research, principally from aerial photographs, has been undertaken on the grounds of Petworth House. This shows not only changes of the extensive garden lay-out, but also the site of a substantial stables block (Aldsworth 1980). A stables/ancillary buildings on a similar grand scale are currently being excavated at Herstmonceux Castle (Compton 2001). On a much smaller scale, numerous garden features of 17th- to 19th- century date were located during excavations at Ore Place (Gardiner 1991).

Estate structures are relatively numerous in the county but have seldom been subjected to serious study. Most work in this field has been undertaken by the Sussex Industrial Archaeology Society who have carried out relatively extensive fieldwork. One of the commonest structures on estates are ice-houses. These were used for the storage of ice throughout the year and became common between the late 17th and 19th centuries. A particularly fine, and large, example at Petworth House (built 1784) has been surveyed in some detail (Martin 1983), while others have been catalogued (Martin 1984/5 and 1994). Water-supply to these large houses was often very elaborate. Petworth House had a piped water supply from at least the start of the 16th century (Taylor *et al.* 1979). A beam-pump, driven by a water wheel, was installed in 1782 and similar examples are known from Bignor Park and Uppark (Palmer and Baxter 1989; Eyre and Allnutt 1989). Other estate structures such as pigeon houses, bee-boles (Walker 1988), follies, such as the 18th- century banqueting/viewing house at Uppark (Aldsworth 1983a), and even rabbit warrens have as yet received little systematic study in the county.

Post-Medieval towns

Sussex has seen relatively numerous urban excavations in the last few decades. As elsewhere, these excavations have concentrated on Roman, Saxon or Medieval deposits. This has often been done at the expense of the Post-Medieval layers which are usually mechanically removed with little or no recording in order to reach the earlier horizons quickly. Where Post-Medieval deposits have been recorded they are often not published, or only partly so (Freke 1977/8). It should be borne in mind that urbanization did not stop at the end of the Medieval period; it is an ongoing process with infilling and continual expansion. As such, in order to understand it fully, the study must continue throughout the Post-Medieval period to the present day when the work of the archaeologist can meet that of the urban geographer.

Perhaps the most difficult physical problem for Post-medieval urban archaeology is the heavy truncation of the shallowest deposits suffered at most sites. The best evidence of the period usually comes from negative features such as wells and pits. These have frequently been found during Sussex excavations and examples include Hastings (Fig. 17.3) (Rudling 1976; Rudling and Barber 1993), Lewes (Norris 1956; Rudling 1983, 1991b) and Chichester (Down 1989). These have provided important information regarding diet, but are usually separated from the associated disturbed/destroyed structural remains by the truncation of the linking stratigraphic sequence. A high priority ought to be given to establishing this correlation where deposits allow. Other less 'archaeologically inviting' towns such as Brighton, also played an important role in the period. Although Brighton has yet to produce early Post-Medieval deposits, the potential is good despite a large part already having been lost to the sea (Freke 1979; Farrant, 1993). Chichester is undoubtedly the most intensively excavated town in Sussex and has produced some good indications of housing such as that at Eastgate (Down 1981), and it is commendable that the Post-Medieval deposits from the town have been published, albeit occasionally briefly (Down 1974, 1978, 1981 and 1989; Down and Magilton 1993). It is perhaps time an overview of the Post-Medieval archaeological deposits of Chichester was prepared. This would undoubtedly set the standards for other Sussex towns and go a long way to formulating research agendas for the future.

When dealing with Post-Medieval urban deposits it should be borne in mind that archaeological excavation is slow and expensive and developers cannot always be expected to finance the minute excavation of all features of all periods. Research agendas need formulating between period specialists concerned with urbanisation. These agendas need to be flexible to take into consideration unexpected discoveries and thus resultant shifting emphasis within a costed budget. The current situation within the contracting archaeological world will mean that hard sacrifices may occasionally be needed. The earlier deposits will usually take priority and few would argue against the merits of this: the Post-Medieval specialist has a great many more data above ground in a town to work with than exist in the wildest dreams of scholars of earlier periods. It is also true that the buried Post-Medieval deposits, being the shallowest, are usually more extensively disturbed than those below. This will often make their interpretation difficult, if not impossible, and as such they must be treated accordingly.

The presence of a multitude of standing buildings, plus documentary and cartographic sources must not however be seen as a reason not to study the buried remains. There are elements of the Post-Medieval town that have not survived above ground and of which we know very little. The houses and diet of the poorer majority of the urban population is a case in point, as is small-scale urban industry. If redevelopment threatens, and such research aims are apparent, then appropriate measures can be taken. This will obviously involve pre-excavation research, usually in the form of a desk-based study, to establish what Post-Medieval deposits are likely to be present and whether these fit within a research objective. Suitable provision can then be made within the ensuing excavation strategy to deal with identified remains of interest if they exist. This general strategy need not only be implemented in urban areas known to have Medieval and earlier remains (Aldsworth and Freke 1976), but also in areas of known Post-Medieval expansion.

Churches

For obvious reasons church archaeology has concentrated on the Medieval period. As churches often reflect fluctuations in both the size and prosperity of local populations, they have often proved a good indicator of a changing community. In Sussex Post-Medieval alterations to Medieval churches are often slight. For example at Lullington the nave walls were internally thickened during the 16th century (Barr-Hamilton 1970). Nevertheless, despite this, these alterations are important in the understanding of the evolution of both individual structures and the community they served. Post-Medieval burial practices have also been neglected until recently. This situation is now changing rapidly in Sussex and other parts of the country with the archaeological recording/excavation of both burials and surface funerary monuments (Bareham this volume). The period is also marked by the rise of the Nonconformist population, but to date little systematic study has been carried out in Sussex on such chapels and meeting houses.

Power

Although horse power remained in common use and may be identified today by the often scant remains of horse gins and pug-mills, more effective sources superseded the horse for many tasks. These sources, both wind and water, were themselves to be largely phased out with the coming of steam, electricity and the internal combustion engine.

Figure 17.3. *Phoenix Brewery, Hastings. 16th- century barrel-lined pit. Scale: 40cm. (Photograph: David Rudling).*

Windmills

Although there are still some 88 standing windmills in Sussex (Austin *et al.* 1985) they were once far more numerous. Most of the surviving mills are of 19th- century date: a few 18th-century examples, such as High Salvington (built *c.* 1745), do survive but are often substantially rebuilt. It is important all standing mills be surveyed, and they have generated much interest in the past (Brunnariaus 1979, Fowell 1930, Hemming 1936; McDermott and McDermott 1978a and b). However, no 16th- to 17th- windmills have survived as standing structures and their numerous sites, which can often be gleaned from early historical sources, have received little attention from archaeologists. Perhaps the earliest excavation of a windmill published in Sussex was that at Lodsbridge Motte where 16th- and 17th- century pottery was associated with the cross-trees of a possible mill (Holden 1967). Needless to say, the mill was not the aim of the excavation!

The only archaeological excavation work carried out purposely on windmills in Sussex are the excavation of the 19th- century post-mill at Friston and the 18th- century mill at Pashley Down, Eastbourne (Stevens 1982). At Pashley Down the post-mill had its cross-trees set in a stone-revetted pit and the excavator has suggested this may be an intermediate phase of development between the Medieval tradition of setting the cross-trees in the ground (often in a mound) and the typical Post-Medieval tradition of resting them on the surface, usually on brick piers. The remains of a rectangular 18th- century bolting house (used for sieving the flour from the husks) with an ornate facade was also excavated. It was shown, through using archaeological and historical sources, that this structure had been converted into a horizontal mill (one of only three such mills in Sussex) in 1752.

Perhaps one of the major problems in the archaeological excavations of early Post-Medieval windmills is their location on the ground. Although it may be relatively easy to locate the approximate vicinity of such a mill from historical sources, the small area covered by the base of the mill combined with their often ephemeral nature can make them elusive targets. Once found however, the mill structure itself can be totally investigated using a small excavated area. It should always be borne in mind that the excavated data from any windmill become far more comprehensive if these are combined with survey/excavation of the miller's house, as was the example at Friston (Stevens 1982), and combined with the historical sources (Stevens 1997).

Watermills

Watermills were used extensively in the Post-Medieval period for grinding corn as well as in numerous other types of industry such as iron, gunpowder, fulling and paper. With the exception of the iron industry little excavation work has been undertaken on Sussex mills. This deficit is helped to a certain extent by the analysis of surviving mills, but the majority of these tend to be either of 18th- or 19th- century date (eg Batemans, Burwash and Burton) or have been substantially modified during these centuries (Gregory and Martin 1997). There has been no work on 16th- century cornmills and it is apparent from historical sources that in general watermills are likely to be complex sites, often undertaking more than one operation (ie corn and fulling) either simultaneously or chronologically.

Most of our current knowledge of 16th- and 17th- century mills comes from work on the iron industry. The study of the water-control system, whether it be a bypass system, as at Ashburnham furnace, or a more typical cross valley dam, needs the combination of both excavation and earthwork survey. The study of dams (bays) has shown many slight variations in construction technique. For example, at Panningridge the dam was laid on a log foundation; at Maynard's Gate the only preparation was the prior removal of the topsoil; while at Sheffield Park furnace the dam had a stone built core (Cleere and Crossley 1995). Tailraces, used to transport the water away from the wheel after use, have been shown to be of variable build with stone or timber linings.

The waterwheel was usually placed in a pit, normally set at a right angle to and immediately adjacent, the dam in order to facilitate water control, although there are some notable exceptions such as Kitchenham Forge where the wheel is some 1000m distant from the dam. Most wheels appear to have been overshot, although again there is variation: that at Ardingly forge was undershot (Bedwin 1976). At a number of sites remains of the wheel itself have survived (Fig. 17.4). These were of wooden construction, but vary in both size and build. The degree of variability in watermills associated with just the iron industry is marked and as such more study is desirable. Whether the evidence for the iron industry is representative of other industries remains to be tested by excavation.

Tidemills

The use of the ebb and flow of the tide to provide power has not been common and there are very few tidemills in Sussex. These have received little archaeological attention, such as Emsworth in West Sussex. Perhaps the best known is that of Bishopstone Tidemills between Newhaven and Seaford. Built by 1768, the site also included a large granary and a complete village for the mill workers (McCarthy and McCarthy 1975, 40-51; Farrant, S. 1975; Longstaff-Tyrrell 1996). The site, which is gradually being destroyed by erosion and vandalism, is the subject of ongoing research by the writer and will hopefully be fully recorded in the near future (Fig. 17.5).

The Iron Industry

Most Post-Medieval archaeology in Sussex has concentrated on the Wealden Iron industry. As early as the mid 19th century, the industry had started to receive attention from antiquarians (Lower 1849). This continued and reached its first milestone with the publication of Straker's (1931) work. Since then the tireless work undertaken by the Wealden Iron Research Group, both in the field and record offices, as well as the archaeological excavation of a number of sites, has taken the study a long way forward and culminated in the current

Figure 17.4. Batsford Furnace, East Sussex. Surviving section of timber waterwheel in wheel-pit. Scales: 2m and 20cm. (Photograph: Owen Bedwin).

standard reference work on the subject (Cleere and Crossley 1985) which has recently been revised (Cleere and Crossley 1995). Although much still remains to be discovered, the latest publication includes, in some detail, what is known to date and as such does not need repeating in any detail here.

There are at present in the region of 178 Post-Medieval water-powered sites known in the Sussex and Kent Weald. These roughly divide between furnace and forge sites, although other subsidiary sites, such as boring mills, also exist.

Most excavation has been undertaken on furnace sites. These consist of the 16th- century sites at Panningridge (Crossley 1972) and Batsford (Bedwin 1980); the late 16th- to early 17th- century site at Maynard's Gate (Bedwin 1977/8), as well as the 17th- to 18th- century sites at Pippingford (Crossley 1975b) and Linchmere (Wildman 1989). The Sussex sites have been complemented by those of Scarlets (Crossley 1979) and Chingley (Crossley 1975a) in Kent.

Although these sites have given a representative coverage of furnaces through time, and their general lay-out is now fairly well understood, they have shown much variation in internal organization and construction. There are still obvious gaps in our knowledge regarding details of such sites. For example, the insubstantial nature of the sand casting beds for the production of pigs and objects such as firebacks has meant those that have survived have been badly disturbed. A similar situation is found with the kilns used to make the clay moulds for the casting of cannon and indeed the actual hearths of the furnaces themselves. Future work on well-preserved sites, which have not suffered extensive robbing, will hopefully

Figure 17.5. Tidemills, Bishopstone, East Sussex. Site of mill showing two of the three arches in front of which were sited the waterwheels. (Photograph: Luke Barber).

address such issues. It should also be noted that double furnaces, which contained two hearths in one stack for the casting of large cannon, such as that known from historical sources at Worth, have not received any archaeological excavation to date.

All furnaces producing cannon have an adjacent gun-casting pit. They must also have had a nearby boring mill to bore out the cast guns. These are frequently referred to in the documentary records, but as yet only one, associated with the Pippingford East furnace, has been excavated (Crossley 1975b). The remains of this boring mill were slight and demonstrate the need to study sites which have suffered little later disturbance. Although no actual boring bar was located at Pippingford, one was discovered in a stream at Chiddingly (Butler and Tebbutt 1975).

All iron from the blast furnace that was not directly cast into objects had to be converted into wrought iron by the reduction of the carbon content. This process, which was carried out in a finery furnace, enabled the material to be worked into objects by the smith. Only two such sites have been excavated in Sussex: Ardingly (Bedwin 1976) and Blackwater Green, Crawley (Place and Bedwin 1992), although a site at Chingley in Kent (Crossley 1975a) brings the total to three. The forge often had three waterwheels (to power bellows on the chafery and finery hearths, as well as the tilt hammer) housed in two parallel watercourses. Such water-systems were more extensive than those for a blast furnace.

Unlike furnaces, forges tend to leave little trace of their working area in the archaeological record. This is in the main due to the hearths being raised above the ground. The hearths at Blackwater Green had been totally removed while those at Ardingly were badly disturbed. However, more substantial remains of the anvil base usually survive, at Ardingly, for example, these consisted of a treetrunk capped with a hollow iron cylinder, set in the ground and held in place by a triangular setting of beams. Very little trace of cover buildings has yet been found, although the presence of roof tile demonstrates their existence. Most are likely to have been fairly insubstantial lean-to structures, and as such will require the excavation of well-preserved sites to establish their nature.

Little archaeological evidence has so far been obtained in the county of the early smiths who actually worked the wrought iron from the forges. A possible 18th- century smith's forge was located at Bayham Abbey (Streeten 1983) and the periphery of a 16th/17th-century example was located just across the border in Kent at Brookland (Barber 1995). Others are known of historically, for example at the Eastgate Bastion, Chichester (Down 1974, 59-74), and there are a number of extant 19th- century structures, such as that in North End, Ditchling. This final stage in the production of iron goods needs to be more fully integrated with the work already done on the smelting and forging stages, and future research needs to address this issue.

Despite the work already undertaken on the county's furnaces and forges there are still many aspects that need further research (Cleere and Crossley 1995). For example, it is known that some forges, such as those at Robertsbridge, were producing steel. None of these sites have been excavated and it is not known whether they differ in any way from the conventional forges. Similarly, despite work elsewhere in the country (Crossley and Ashurst 1968), no work has been undertaken on late Medieval Wealden water-powered bloomery furnaces, some of which continued into the Post-Medieval period. Indeed the establishment of the first generation blast furnaces in the Weald at the end of the 15th century was accompanied by an influx of French workers (Awty 1981), but as yet the comparison of Wealden furnaces with those of the continent is still in its infancy.

Research is also needed on the occupation sites associated with ironworks. Blast furnaces had long smelting campaigns, sometimes running continuously for 45 weeks. Workers must have undertaken shifts and lived in nearby accommodation of some form. House platforms were noted at Pippingford (Crossley 1975b) and a 'shanty town' is thought to exist at Linchmere (Wildman 1989). The only excavation on workers' accommodation has been that undertaken on cottages at Ardingly (Worthington undated). Work on this aspect of the iron industry is needed in order to put the sites and their workers into a social framework.

Mining and quarrying

The little archaeological work that has been undertaken in Sussex has barely scratched the surface of this neglected topic. A little work has occurred in relation to the iron industry but even so only three out of a plethora of ore pits have been subjected to excavation: at Herstmonceux and at Rotherfield (two) where both were shown to be 3m deep (Tebbutt 1978; Swift 1982). The excavation of such features is difficult owing to both health and safety considerations and to the general lack of datable material within them. As yet there has been no evidence of bell-pits, but more need excavation before any meaningful comments can be made. Although the preparation of the ore for smelting by roasting is well-known, and indeed slight evidence was found at both Batsford (Bedwin 1980) and Pippingford (Crossley 1975b), there are no excavated Post-Medieval ore-roasting kilns to date.

With the exception of limited historical work (Sowan 1984/5) no serious archaeological attempt has been made to study the quarrying/mining of stone, particularly for building, in the county. Although it is known from historical sources the industry was fairly extensive (eg for 'Petworth Marble'), little work has so far been done (Gardiner 1990b). Although the form of many early quarries may have been destroyed by later working, numerous smaller examples are likely to survive. The most exploited stone in Sussex is probably chalk, which has been used for soil dressing, building (including mortar) and various industries such as tanning. The numerous chalk pits, both large and small, dotted along the downs are a common sight and attest to an important former rural industry. Many of these pits were concerned with the production of lime, and kilns are frequently associated with them (Holt 1971). The smaller pits were often for the individual farmer who produced the lime in small flare kilns for improvements to the more acidic soils on his land. These small kilns became common in the 18th century, such as the one by the Long Man of Wilmington. Although important work has been undertaken listing these kilns (Holt 1971; Martin 1997), only one 18th- century example, at Northiam, has been subjected to excavation (Beswick 1985/6). This example, being located well away from the chalklands, would have used Wealden limestones as a raw material. Larger flare kilns, using mined limestone, were present on the Ashburnham Estate (Beswick 1985/6). Draw kilns, which produced much larger quantities of lime due to their continuous firing, such as those at the Amberley Chalk Pits Museum, were common on commercial quarries throughout the 19th and early 20th centuries. Study of these larger sites has proved rewarding. For example the inclined tramway at Offham shows the ingenuity of many of these establishments (Martin 1985/6).

Textiles

Prior to the 18th century textile production was on a domestic scale. The one exception to this was at the fulling stage which was mechanized from an early period. Fulling involved the woollen cloth being dampened in a solution of fuller's earth and beaten with water-powered hammers. This process both degreased the cloth as well as shrinking it to give it more bulk. Although it is known from historical sources that the Weald contained numerous fulling mills, only two have been excavated. The first of these was at Ardingly, where a late 17th- to mid-18th- century mill had been established on the site of the former iron forge (Bedwin 1976). The mill house consisted of a 'T'-plan brick and stone building with evidence for a few ephemeral ancillary structures and possible drying racks (the tenter ground). Disturbance to the remains was relatively severe. Trial excavations at the site of Darwell fulling mill in 1990 uncovered part of a limestone paved floor with sill walls for a timber-framed building sitting adjacent a probable wheel-pit (Gardiner and Barber 1990). Although some re-use and subsequent robbing was noted, the 16th- to 17th- century site appeared to be in good condition. Further work at this and similar sites in the future will be needed before any conclusive statements can be made. It should also be noted that no direct evidence for fulling was found at either site and historical sources were needed to demonstrate the purpose of each mill.

Tanning

The archaeological potential for tanneries is good in that the process was carried out in numerous pits, frequently lined with clay, timber or brick, set into the ground (Thomson 1981). As a result, such sites will survive a relatively high degree of later disturbance and truncation. Despite the existence of numerous tanneries in Sussex during the Post-Medieval period, only part of one has been excavated. This example, at Brook Street North in Lewes, dated to the 18th-19th centuries and consisted of brick-lined pits with planked bases surrounded by brick paths and drains (Fig. 17.6) (Freke 1975). In order to study the industry, however, complete plans of tanneries are needed. Some later examples may be obtained from cartographic (Barber 1990) and historical (Mead 1989) sources, but complete plans of 16th- and 17th- century establishments will only be obtained through excavation. Large tanneries existed at Chichester and Henfield and development in such areas should be preceded by archaeological investigations. Such investigations should occur prior to, or during, the removal of any 'contaminated'

Figure 17.6. *Brook Street North, Lewes. 18th- to 19th- century brick-lined tanning pits. Scales: 2m. (Photograph: David Freke).*

ground by the developer as such ground will often include all deposits relating to the tannery!

Gunpowder

The production of gunpowder was an important industry which developed rapidly from the 16th century onwards. Water-power was utilized to crush and mix the charcoal, sulphur and saltpetre: the various processes are described in detail elsewhere (Crocker 1986). The industry has undergone historical and archaeological research in Surrey and Kent (Crocker 1984; Philp 1984; Cocroft 1994; Patterson 1995; Percival 1967) but little work has been undertaken in Sussex. The extensive powder works in the Battle area, which began in the late 17th century and consisted of five mills on the Powdermill stream, as well as further mills at Brede and Sedlescombe (Blackman 1923) and the 19th- century mill at Maresfield (Austin *et al.* 1985) are a priority for archaeological fieldwork.

Beer production

Numerous malting houses (for barley) and oasthouses (for hops) survive today, albeit often converted for new uses. As with mills, the conversion to a new use often involves removing all or many of the internal features of historical value and it is thus important that at risk structures are fully recorded prior to modification. Oasthouses, which first appeared in the 16th century, underwent many changes from their appearance to the 19th century. A number of studies have been made of selected standing structures and the related documentary evidence (Jones *et al.* 1988; Cronk 1978, 1979), but archaeological excavations are needed, particularly on the earlier examples, to fully understand their development.

Glass

The glass industry of the Sussex/Surrey border is often overlooked by modern researchers. Very little research has been undertaken on the industry since that of Winbolt in the 1930s. His work, along with that of Kenyon, located some 42 glasshouse sites and culminated in two commendable publications (Winbolt 1933; Kenyon 1967). These summarize both the historical and archaeological evidence for the industry, and through lack of later work, have not been superseded. However, they rely on fieldwork of the 1930s and do not contain any furnace plans to modern archaeological standards. Indeed, of the 42 sites identified, only 26 were investigated and from these only four rough plans of structural elements were produced.

The industry had its roots in the Medieval period. This indigenous industry, which generally produced relatively low-quality glass had declined by the early 16th century. The glasshouses of this early period consisted of a rectangular main furnace with central flue running between two benches (sieges) on which the crucibles were placed. Further furnaces for secondary working were situated close by. This type of furnace was investigated at Alfold (Wood 1982) and Blunden's Wood (Wood 1965), Surrey.

During the second half of the 16th century an influx of immigrant glassmakers from the Lorraine and Normandy regions of France brought new and better furnace types into the Weald which improved the efficiency and quality of production. These consisted of central rectangular structures which housed the main furnace with 'wings' built onto the corners in which the secondary (ie annealing - controlled cooling) and other processes (making crucibles and heating the raw materials for glass manufacture) took place. The wings could be heated from the main furnace or by their own fires. Such early immigrant furnaces were located by Winbolt and Kenyon, eg the Vann Tudor furnace, Hambledon, Surrey, but no detailed plans were made. Such plans will be needed in order to make comparisons between Wealden and Continental sites, as well as the furnaces established in northern England (Crossley and Aberg 1972). Whether the furnace types from the Lorraine and Normandy areas were similar is still uncertain. Although there are modern archaeological plans of immigrant furnaces elsewhere in the country, the earliest furnaces are all in the Weald.

The end of the Wealden glass industry came in the early 17th century. This was due mainly to competition from other industries, particularly iron, for charcoal as fuel. In 1615 the proclamation that wood was not to be used as fuel for glass effectively sealed the industry's fate in the Weald, and with the establishment of coal as a fuel the industry shifted its location predominantly to London and the north of the country.

Although archaeological excavations of glass works to modern standards are needed in the Weald, there are a number of problems. The glasshouses were often built near, or on top of, hills in order to gain adequate draught. As a result the structures tended to rest on the ground surface. These vulnerable remains were usually robbed of their stone once abandoned, leaving little in the archaeological record. Given the natural erosion of hilltop locations, well-preserved sites may prove difficult to find.

Pottery

Ceramics studies of the period can be extremely diverse due to both the increase in vessel types (ie plates and cups) and improved communications increasing the quantity of imported material from the Continent. However, in Sussex there have been precious few groups of pottery from the period which have been fully studied and published. Those that have appeared are often not from closed, well-dated contexts (Backhouse and Backhouse 1977/8; Tebbutt 1968) or have not received the attention of the wider audience they deserve (Child 1990; Vahey 1982). A high priority should be given to good groups in future publications, particularly when in association with closely datable material, such as clay pipes.

Despite the influx of imports, the local ceramic tradition continued to produce utilitarian earthenwares throughout the period in kilns of Medieval types. A number of kiln sites have now been excavated in the county. Perhaps the most interesting is that at Lower Parrock, Hartfield. This early 16th-century single flue kiln, which appeared to have had a short life span despite having two phases, was producing a variety of wares similar to pottery from Beauvais. The proximity of the kiln to an ironworking site, known from historical records to have employed many French workers, suggests the potter may have also been French (Freke 1979). Adjacent to the kiln were other associated features including a waster heap and clay pits. Another 16th- century kiln at Boreham Street has also been excavated, but has as yet to be published.

In West Sussex part of a small 17th- century kiln has been excavated in Crane Street, Chichester (Down 1981, 1989) and a further example, dating to the 17th or 18th centuries and built of brick, has been investigated at Upper Norwood, Graffham (Aldsworth and Down 1990). The latter is situated in an area known to have contained a fairly extensive pottery industry spanning the late 13th to mid-19th centuries. A further seven, as yet unexcavated, kiln sites in the area were located during fieldwork.

Despite the work to date, more kiln sites need to be located and excavated in the county and their plans and products adequately published before detailed study can be made of marketing areas (Streeten 1980). This work should not only concentrate on the earlier part of the period, but should continue the study and development of regional ceramics into the 20th century. Sussex had an extensive industry during this later period (Manwaring-Baines 1980a, 1980b), but no archaeological work has as yet been undertaken on it and where such ceramic groups have been located they have not been published. The development, and close dating, of Sussex ceramic forms from the 18th to 20th century remain obscure and will prove a hindrance for future studies of the period. Further work is also needed to establish the layout/internal organization of production sites. This will entail the excavation of larger areas around kilns in order to locate the clay pits, storage, manufacturing and domestic areas which formed the potter's workshop.

Clay Pipes

The typological development of clay pipes has established them as one of the best dating tools for the period. This has been strengthened still further in Sussex by historical research into the individual makers (Atkinson 1972, 1977). This work has highlighted over 100 pipemakers operating in the county. However, archaeological excavation has, unsurprisingly, been far behind, with only one 19th- century kiln having been investigated in Lewes (Norris 1970). There is a complete absence of excavated kiln plans, particularly for the 17th and 18th centuries. This is a great shame as such sites would also undoubtedly produce wasters which could complement the historical work already undertaken.

Bricks and tiles

The production of ceramic building materials was, and in certain areas still is, a major industry in Sussex. The increase in the use of brick during this time resulted in the establishment of numerous brickfields, many of which were short-lived. A comprehensive survey of the historical sources relating to the industry has now been published (Beswick 1993), but detailed fieldwork is still in its infancy.

The production of bricks in clamp kilns was common in the 16th and 17th centuries, with more permanent kilns becoming more numerous from the 18th century onwards. A late example of a clamp kiln, dated to the 18th century, was fully excavated at East Pallant House, Chichester (Down 1989). The development of more permanent kiln types such as the late 18th- century 'Scotch kiln' at Ebernoe (Aldsworth 1983b) has meant numerous abandoned kilns remain on old brickfields. The opportunity should be taken to record them while they survive. Work by the Sussex Industrial Archaeological Society and the Weald and Downland Open Air Museum has gone some way to helping the situation.

At Ebernoe the brickfield still maintained much of its original layout, and surveys of surviving kilns should take into account the remains of other structures, such as pug-mills (Aldsworth 1989) and drying sheds, that may lie closeby. Other areas with a high concentration of brickworks include Dicker Common in East Sussex, which is known to have seen production from the 17th century. Production here expanded greatly during the 18th and 19th centuries owing to an increase in demand for bricks for military use as a result of the wars with France (Beswick 1983).

Figure 17.7. *Bottle kiln at Piddinghoe, East Sussex. (Photograph: Luke Barber).*

Tiles were frequently produced at the same sites as bricks and their study usually goes hand in hand. Although observations have been made, such as the 17th- century tile kilns at the Slindon Gravel Company pits (Evans 1968), no archaeological excavations have been carried out. The detailed recording and restoration of the 19th- century bottle kiln at Piddinghoe is the most thorough piece of archaeological work done on the Post-Medieval tile industry in Sussex (Fig. 17.7) (O'Shea 1982) and was commendably supported by historical sources (Osborne 1982). It perhaps sets the agenda for other select structures of this nature in the county.

Conclusions

It is hoped that this paper has highlighted the current situation of Post-Medieval archaeology in Sussex and given adequate reference to sources where more detail may be found on the various topics. Although the main lines of research have been highlighted, this paper should not be viewed as an exhaustive study as there are other industries, such as salt and paper production, that have not been covered and it has already been noted that in the main 19th- to 20th- century 'industrial' archaeology has been omitted. Perhaps the fundamental point arising from this paper is the disjointed nature of much of the work undertaken to date. This can be viewed as a direct reflection on the lack of research aims for the period within the county. Much of the work on the period has until now been the result of chance discoveries when looking for earlier remains rather than actively seeking sites which are needed to answer specific questions. At a basic level this paper may be seen as provisionally outlining, by topic, a number of research aims for future work. However, in many instances there has been too little work to contemplate defining specific research aims and in order to do so, initial fieldwork will be needed to test the quantity and quality of the archaeological resource. The systematic location and recording of extant structures of the period is also needed for both the long term preservation of information and to facilitate a secure database from which to formulate future strategies for both the preservation of key examples and in order to safely assess the importance of any archaeological remains.

References

Aldsworth, F. 1980. Petworth House and Formal Garden, *SAC* **118**, 373-377.

Aldsworth, F. 1983a. An Eighteenth- Century Gothic Folly at Uppark, Harting, *SAC* **121**, 215-219.

Aldsworth, F. 1983b. An C18th- Brick Kiln on Ebernoe Common, Kirdford, *SAC* **121**, 219-224.

Aldsworth, F. 1989. A C19th- Brickyard Pug Mill from Barlavington, *SAC* **127**, 263-266.

Aldsworth, F. and Down, A. 1990. The Production of Late and Post-Medieval Pottery in the Graffham Area of West Sussex, *SAC* **128**, 117-139.

Aldsworth, F. and Freke, D. 1976. *Historic Towns in Sussex: An Archaeological Survey*. London: Institute of Archaeology.

Aldsworth, F. and Harris, R. 1982. A Medieval and seventeenth- century house at Walderton, West Sussex, dismantled and re-erected at the Weald and Downland Open Air Museum, *SAC* **120**, 45-92.

Armstrong, L. 1978. *Woodcolliers and Charcoal Burning.* Horsham and Singleton: Jointly published by Coach House Ltd Publishing and The Weald and Downland Open Air Museum.

Atkinson, D. 1972. A new list of Sussex Pipemakers, *SAC* **110**, 37-44.

Atkinson, D. 1977. *Sussex Clay Tobacco Pipes and the Pipemakers,* Eastbourne: Crain Services.

Austin, B., Cox, D. and Upton, J. (eds.), 1985. *Sussex Industrial Archaeology. A Field Guide.* Chichester: Phillimore.

Awty, B. 1981. The Continental Origins of Wealden Ironworkers, *Economic History Review* **2** (Series 34), 524-39.

Backhouse, M. and Backhouse, A. 1977/8. The Old House, Pulborough, West Sussex, *SAC* **116**, 375-392.

Barber, L. 1990. *A resistivity Survey of Tanyard Field, Henfield, West Sussex.* UCL Field Archaeology Unit Report. Unpublished. Copy in the West Sussex County Council Sites and Monuments Record (hereafter SMR).

Barber, L. 1992. *An Archaeological Evaluation of the Proposed Route of the Lamberhurst By-Pass, Kent (A21).* University College London Field Archaeology Unit Report. Unpublished. Copy in Kent County Council SMR.

Barber, L. 1995. *A259 Brookland Diversion, Kent. An Archaeological Evaluation, Stage 1.* South Eastern Archaeological Services Report No. 1994/191. Unpublished. Copy in Kent Council SMR.

Barber, L. 1998. *An Archaeological Watching Brief at Ore Place, Hastings, East Sussex.* Archaeology South-East Report 736. Unpublished. Copy in East Sussex County Council SMR.

Barber, L. and Gardiner, M. 1992. *An Archaeological Assessment, of the Proposed Public Golf Course at Rookwood Farm, Warnham, West Sussex.* South Eastern Archaeological Services Report 1992/57. Unpublished. Copy in West Sussex County Council SMR.

Barr-Hamilton, A. 1970. Excavations at Lullington Church, *SAC* **108**, 1-22.

Barton, K. 1964. Excavations in the village of Tarring, West Sussex, *SAC* **102**, 9-27.

Barton, K. and Holden, E. 1967. Excavations at Michelham Priory, *SAC* **105**, 1-12.

Bedwin, O. 1976. The excavation of Ardingly Fulling Mill and Forge, 1975-6, *Post-Medieval Archaeology* **10**, 34-64.

Bedwin, O. 1977/8. The excavation of a late sixteenth/early seventeenth century gun-casting furnace at Maynard's Gate, Crowborough, East Sussex 1975-6, *SAC* **116**, 163-178.

Bedwin, O. 1979. Excavations at South Street, West Tarring, 1978, *SAC* **117**, 234-237.

Bedwin, O. 1980. The Excavation of a late C16th- Blast Furnace at Batsford, Herstmonceux, East Sussex, 1978, *Post-Medieval Archaeology* **14**, 89-112.

Beswick, M. 1983. Brick and Tile making on the Dicker in East Sussex, *Sussex Industrial History* **13**, 2-10.

Beswick, M. 1993. *Brickmaking in Sussex. A History and Gazetteer,* Midhurst: Middleton Press.

Beswick, W. 1985/6. The Ashburnham Limeworks at Glaziers Forge, Burwash, *Sussex Industrial History* **15**, 18-21.

Blackman, H. 1923. The Story of the Old Gunpowder Works at Battle, *SAC* **64**, 109-122.

Brandon, P. 1971. The Origin of Newhaven and the Drainage of the Lewes and Laughton Levels, *SAC* **109**, 94-106.

Brandon, P. 1974. *The Sussex Landscape*. London: Hodder and Stoughton.

Brandon, P. 1978. Medieval Sussex in P. Drewett (ed), *Archaeology in Sussex to A.D. 1500,* CBA Res. Rep. **29**, 84-86.

Brandon, P. and Short, B. 1990. *The South-East from AD 1000,* London: Longman.

Brunnarius, M. 1979. *The Windmills of Sussex.* Chichester: Phillimore.

Burleigh, G. 1973. An Introduction to Deserted Medieval Villages in East Sussex, *SAC* **111**, 45-83.

Butler, D. and Tebbutt, C. 1975. A Wealden Cannon-Boring Bar, *Post-Medieval Archaeology* **9**, 38-41.

Caffyn, L. 1983. A Study of Farm Buildings in Selected Parishes of East Sussex, *SAC* **121**, 149-71.

Child, D. 1990. *The excavation of a stone-lined pit in the garden of Richmond House, Cooks Green, Winchelsea, 1988-89.* A report of the Hastings Area Archaeological Research Group.

Cleere, H. and Crossley, D. 1985. *The Iron Industry of the Weald. 1st edition.* Leicester: University Press.

Cleere, H. and Crossley, D. 1995. *The Iron Industry of the Weald.* 2nd edition. Cardiff: Merton Priory Press.

Cocroft, W. 1994. *Oare Gunpowder Works,* Faversham Papers **39**. Kent: The Faversham Society.

Compton, J. 2001. Three years at Herstmonceux, *Sussex Past and Present* **93**, 6-7.

Crocker, G. 1984. *Chilworth Gunpowder*. Surrey Industrial History Group.

Crocker, G. 1986. *The Gunpowder Industry.* Aylesbury: Shire.

Cronk, A. 1978. Oasts in Kent and East Sussex, *Arch. Cant.* **94**, 99-110.

Cronk, A. 1979. Oasts in Kent and East Sussex, *Arch. Cant.* **95**, 241-54.

Crossley, D. 1972. A 16th- century Wealden Blast Furnace: A Report on Excavations at Panningridge, Sussex, 1964-1970, *Post-Medieval Archaeology* **6**, 42-68.

Crossley, D. 1975a. *The Bewl Valley Ironworks c.1300-1730.* A Royal Archaeological Institute Monograph.

Crossley, D. 1975b. Cannon-Manufacture at Pippingford, Sussex: The Excavation of Two Iron Furnaces of *c.*1717, *Post-Medieval Archaeology* **9**, 1-37.

Crossley, D. 1979. A Gun-casting Furnace at Scarlets, Cowden, Kent, *Post-Medieval Archaeology* **13**, 235-49.

Crossley, D. 1990. *Post-Medieval Archaeology in Britain.* Leicester: University Press.

Crossley, D. and Aberg, F. 1972. 16th-century glass making in Yorkshire: excavations at furnaces at Hutton and Rosedale, North Riding, 1968-71, *Post-Medieval Archaeology* **6**, 107-59.

Crossley, D. and Ashurst, D. 1968. Excavations at Rockley Smithies, a water-powered bloomery of the 16th and 17th centuries, *Post-Medieval Archaeology* **2**, 10-54.

Down, A. 1974. *Chichester Excavations* **2**. Chichester: Phillimore.

Down, A. 1978. *Chichester Excavations* **3**. Chichester: Phillimore.

Down, A. 1981. *Chichester Excavations* **5**. Chichester: Phillimore.

Down, A. 1989. *Chichester Excavations* **6**. Chichester: Phillimore.

Down, A. and Magilton, J. 1993. *Chichester Excavations* **8**. Chichester District Council.

Drewett, P. 1982. *The Archaeology of Bullock Down, Eastbourne, East Sussex: The Development of a Landscape*, Sussex Archaeological Society Monograph **1**.

Evans, K.J. 1968. Worthing Museum Archaeological Notes for 1965 and 1966, *SAC* **106**, 137.

Eyre, J. and Allnutt, A. 1989. The Water Supply to Uppark, *Sussex Industrial History* **19**, 11-22.

Farrant, J. 1972. The Evolution of Newhaven Harbour and the Lower Ouse before 1800, *SAC* **110**, 44-60.

Farrant, J. 1993. The Making of Francis Grose's Antiquities: Evidence from Sussex, *SAC* **131**, 152-158.

Farrant, S. 1975. Bishopstone Tidemills, *SAC* **113**, 199-202.

Farrant, S. 1983. Marchant's and Hayleigh Farms in Streat and Westmeston (East Sussex): The development of two farms on the Weald Clay *c.*1500 to 1980, *SAC* **121**, 119-127.

Fowell, G. 1930. *Windmills in Sussex.* London: Walker's Galleries Ltd..

Freke, D. 1975. Excavations in Lewes, 1974, *SAC* **113**, 65-84.

Freke, D. 1977/8. Excavations in Church Street, Seaford, 1976, *SAC* **116**, 199-224.

Freke, D. 1979. IX. Excavations in Market Street, Brighton, East Sussex, in P. Drewett (ed), Rescue Archaeology in Sussex, 1978, *Univ. London Inst. Archaeol. Bull.* **16**, 49-52.

Freke, D. 1979. The Excavation of a 16th- century Pottery Kiln at Lower Parrock, Hartfield, East Sussex, 1977, *Post-Medieval Archaeology* **13**, 79-125.

Gardiner, M. 1984/5. A Charcoal Burner's Hut in Fittleworth Wood, *Sussex Industrial History* **14**, 16-18.

Gardiner, M. 1990a. Broomhill Farm, Camber, in Post-Medieval Archaeology in Britain 1989, *Post-Medieval Archaeology* **24**, 194.

Gardiner, M. 1990b. The Archaeology of the Weald - a survey and a review, *SAC* **128**, 33-53.

Gardiner, M. 1991. *Excavations at Ore Place, Ore, Hastings.* University College Field Archaeology Unit Report No. 1991/5. Unpublished. Copy in East Sussex County Council SMR.

Gardiner, M and Barber, L. 1990. *Assessment Excavations at Darwell Fulling Mill and Darwell Forge, East Sussex*, South-Eastern Archaeological Services Report. Unpublished. Copy in the East Sussex County Council SMR.

Gardiner, M., Russell, M. and Gregory, D. 1996. Excavations at Lewes Friary 1985-6 and 1988-9, *SAC* **134**, 71-123.

Gregory, F. and Martin, R. 1997. *Sussex Watermills.* Seaford: SB Publications.

Hare, J. 1985. *Battle Abbey: the eastern range and the excavations of 1978-80,* Historic Buildings and Monuments Commission of England Archaeological Report **2**.

Hemming, P. 1936. *Windmills in Sussex.* London: C.W. Daniel Co. Ltd..

Holden, E. 1963. Excavations at the Deserted Medieval Village of Hangleton. Part 1, *SAC* **101**, 54-181.

Holden, E. 1967. The Excavation of a Motte at Lodsbridge Mill, Lodsbridge, *SAC* **105**, 103-25.

Holt, M. 1971. Lime Kilns in Central Sussex, *Sussex Industrial History* **2**, 23-30.

Jones, G. with Bell, J. and Martin, J. 1988. Oasthouses in Ewhurst Parish: evidence for the history of an industry, *SAC* **126**, 195-224.

Kenyon, G. 1967. *The Glass Industry of the Weald.* Leicester: University Press.

Longstaff-Tyrrell, P. 1996. Bishopstone Tide Mills, *Sussex Industrial History* **26**, 20-26.

Lower, M. 1849. Historical and Archaeological Notices of the Iron Works of the County of Sussex, *SAC* **2**, 64-72.

Manwaring-Baines, J. 1980a. Eighteenth and Nineteenth-century Sussex Ware, *SAC* **118**, 125-128.

Manwaring-Baines, J. 1980b. *Sussex Pottery*. Brighton: Fisher Publications.

Martin, D. and Martin, B. 1982. *Old Farm Buildings in Eastern Sussex 1450-1750,* Historic Buildings in Eastern Sussex Volume **3**. Robertsbridge: Hastings Area Archaeological Papers.

Martin, D. 1990. Three Moated Sites in North-East Sussex Part 2: Hawksden and Bodiam, *SAC* **128**, 89-116.

Martin, D. and Martin, B. 1987. *A Selection of Dated Houses in Eastern Sussex, 1400-1750,* Historic Buildings in Eastern Sussex Volume **4**. Robertsbridge: Hastings Area Archaeological Papers.

Martin, R. 1983. Petworth Ice-House, *Sussex Industrial History* **13**, 15-21.

Martin, R. 1984/5. Ice Houses and the Commercial Ice Trade in Brighton, *Sussex Industrial History* **14**, 16-18.

Martin, R. 1985/6. Offham Chalkpit Tramway and Incline, *Sussex Industrial History* **15**, 11-15.

Martin, R. 1994. Ice Houses in Sussex, *Sussex Industrial History* **24**, 10-23.

Martin, R. 1997. Some Sussex Lime Kilns, *Sussex Industrial History* **27**, 34-39.

McCarthy, E. and McCarthy, M. 1975. *Sussex River Journeys along the banks of the Ouse, Seaford to Newhaven.* Seaford: Lindel Organisation Ltd..

McDermott, R. and McDermott, R. 1978a. *The Standing Windmills of East Sussex.* Worthing: Betford.

McDermott, R. and McDermott, R. 1978b. *The Standing Windmills of West Sussex.* Worthing: Betford.

Mead, G. 1989. The Sussex Leather Industry in the 19th century, *Sussex Industrial History* **19**, 2-10.

Norris, N. 1956. Miscellaneous Researches, 1949-56, *SAC* **94**, 1-13.

Norris, J. 1970. A Victorian Pipe Kiln in Lewes, *Post-Medieval Archaeology* **4**, 168-70.

Osbourne, B. 1982. The Bakers: Brickmakers of Piddinghoe, *Sussex Industrial History* **12**, 24-7.

O'Shea, E. 1982. The Restoration of a Tile Kiln at Piddinghoe, East Sussex, *Sussex Industrial History* **12**, 2-24.

Palmer, R. and Baxter, A. 1989. Water-wheel driven Beam-Pump at Bignor Park, *Sussex Industrial History* **19**, 11-22.

Patterson, E. 1995. *Gunpowder Manufacture at Faversham: Oare and Marsh Factories,* Faversham Papers **42**. Kent: The Faversham Society.

Percival, A. 1967. *The Faversham Gunpowder Industry,* Faversham Papers **4**. Kent: The Faversham Society.

Philp, B. 1984. *The Dartford Gunpowder Mills.* Dover: Kent Archaeological Rescue Unit.

Place, C. and Bedwin, O. 1992. The Sixteenth- century Forge at Blackwater Green, Worth, West Sussex: Excavations 1988, *SAC* **130**, 147-163.

Rudling, D. 1976. Excavations in Winding Street, Hastings, 1975, *SAC* **114**, 164-175.

Rudling, D. 1983. The Archaeology of Lewes: some recent research, *SAC* **121**, 45-77.

Rudling D. 1991a. Archaeological excavations at Laughton Place, 1984, in J. Farrant, M. Howard, D. Rudling, J. Warren and C. Whittick, Laughton Place: a manorial and architectural history, with an account of recent restoration and excavation, *SAC* **129**, 99-164.

Rudling, D. 1991b. Excavations at Cliffe, Lewes, 1987 and 1988, *SAC* **129**, 165-181.

Rudling, D. and Barber, L. with D. Martin. 1993. Excavations at the Phoenix Brewery Site, Hastings, 1988, *SAC* **131**, 73-113.

Sowan, P. 1984/5. Mining and Subterranean Quarrying in Sussex, *Sussex Industrial History* **14**, 25-39.

Straker, E. 1931. *Wealden Iron.* Reprint (1969): Newton Abbott: David and Charles.

Streeten, A. 1980. Potters, Kilns and Markets in Medieval Sussex: a preliminary study, *SAC* **118**, 105-118.

Streeten, A. 1983. *Bayham Abbey,* Sussex Archaeological Society Monograph **2**.

Stevens, L. 1982. Some Windmill Sites in Friston and Eastbourne, Sussex, *SAC* **120**, 93-138.

Stevens, L. 1990. Excavation of a Sheep Pond and Adjacent Lynchet, Eastbourne, Sussex, *SAC* **128**, 256-260.

Stevens, L. and Stevens, P. 1991. Excavations on the South Lawn, Michelham Priory 1971-1976, *SAC* **129**, 45-79.

Stevens, L. 1997. Mills of the Eastbourne Borough Council Area, *Sussex Industrial History* **27**, 22-29.

Streeten, A. 1983. Bayham Abbey. Sussex Archaeological Society Monograph **2**.

Swift, G. 1982. Minepit Surveys, *Bulletin of the Wealden Iron Research Group* **2** (Series 2), 15-21.

Taylor, J., Jerome, P. and Allnutt, A. 1979. Petworth Water Supply, *Sussex Industrial History* **9**, 15-23.

Tebbutt, C. 1968. Sussex: Hartfield, Post-Medieval Archaeology in Britain 1966, *Post-Medieval Archaeology* **2**, 185.

Tebbutt, C. 1975. Old Buxted Place, *SAC* **113**, 51-3.

Tebbutt, C. 1978. The excavation of a 'bell-pit' in Benzells Wood, Herstmonceux, Sussex, *Bulletin of the Wealden Iron Research Group* **14**, 6-7.

Thomson, R. 1981. Leather Manufacture in the Post-Medieval period with special reference to Northampton, *Post-Medieval Archaeology* **15**, 161-75.

Vahey, Z. 1982. *Old Place, Icklesham.* A report of the Hastings Area Archaeological Research Group.

Walker, P. 1988. Bee-boles in Kent, *Arch. Cant.* **106**, 107-27.

Wildman, J. 1989. Linchmere: North Park Furnace, *The Archaeology of Chichester and District 1989,* Chichester District Council, 30-35.

Winbolt, S. 1933. *Wealden Glass, The Surrey-Sussex Glass Industry.* Hove: Combridges.

Wood, E. 1965. A Medieval Glasshouse at Blunden's Wood, Hambledon, Surrey, *Surrey Archaeological Collections* **62**, 54-79.

Wood, E. 1968. *The Collins Field Guide to Archaeology in Britain.* 2nd Edition. London: Collins.

Wood, E. 1982. A C16th- Glasshouse at Knightons, Alfold, Surrey, *Surrey Archaeological Collections* **73**, 1-43.

Worthington, R. Undated. *Archaeology at Ardingly.* Privately produced leaflet.

RECORDING AND INTERPRETING THE CHURCHYARDS OF LEWES

Tristan Bareham

Abstract

This paper covers the recent churchyard recording programme carried out by the East Sussex Archaeology and Museums Project in Lewes. It is intended to give an overview of the fieldwork, its methods and results. A central part of the paper is a discussion of the research implications of this work and what it can tell us about the beliefs of the communities who erected the monuments. This is achieved through a series of case studies. One particular area of research, the study of the significance of the symbolism manifested by 18th century monuments, is considered in detail. Future areas of research are indicated.

Background

Over the last eight years The East Sussex Archaeology and Museums Project (ESAMP) has been recording the churchyards in Lewes. This Lewes Churchyard Programme involves the mapping of the monuments within the churchyards on a scale of 1:100, the recording of all the physical details of the monuments and the collation of the key related historical sources, for example parish registers. This work has had an educational purpose as well as a research objective. The mapping and recording work has formed part of the training programme for ESAMP trainees, and children from local schools have helped with the fieldwork component. Further, ESAMP has run a number of courses, through the Centre for Continuing Education at the University of Sussex, which involved members of the local community with this work.

The Lewes Churchyard Programme is a long-term initiative and this paper forms, in effect, an interim report on the work completed thus far. However, it is not intended to be simply an overview of the details of the physical results of this survey programme, these can be obtained by reference to the individual churchyard reports produced by ESAMP. The paper aims to explore some of the issues and problems associated with this type of investigation and to reveal some of the cultural and demographic issues which can be explored. Three main areas of the work will be considered: the first is a discussion of the patterns of mortality reflected in the monuments, the second is an examination of the developments of local churchyards and finally, the flourishing of carved decoration on monuments during the 18th century is discussed. In each area space is given to examine local examples and also to set any local patterns within the larger regional and national religious, demographic, economic and cultural contexts. This is particularly relevant when considering the patterns of change and development in the usage of churchyards and the formative influence underpinning the symbolism shown on the Lewes monuments. Future areas of development of the research will be discussed at the end of the paper.

Why record?

From an historical perspective the present time can be seen to be the third in a series of periods in which the survival of churchyard monuments has been threatened (White 1988, 6). Following the Reformation, many monuments, particularly those that appeared to encourage idolatry, were deliberately damaged. The situation was so severe that in 1561 Queen Elizabeth I passed a decree commanding people not to break or deface monuments. The Civil War and Commonwealth was also a period in which monuments were defaced, but it is the present period which represents the greatest threat to this fragile and irreplaceable resource. Clearance, erosion, vandalism, neglect and the process of church redundancy all contribute to the threat to churchyard monuments. It is not only the older monuments which are at risk; during our survey work we have recorded damage and removal occurring to monuments of the very recent past as well. This problem may actually get progressively worse. The care and upkeep of individual monuments resides with those who erected them and their heirs-at-law (Burman 1988, 43). The more fragmentary nature of recent societal trends tends to suggest that the past pattern of familial maintenance of memorials will not be sustained in the future. Further, many churches find the cost of looking after churchyards a financial and logistical strain. There can also be conflicts of strategy in maintaining the monuments and encouraging a diversity of habitats and environments within churchyards. So, the present record is both partial in nature and likely to degrade further.

The Recording Programme

The aim of the recording programme is to make a complete record of all the physical data available. Some of the monuments within the Lewes churchyards have already been recorded over the last few centuries, in some cases by several authors. However, these records are not always totally reliable. Commonly, past recorders concentrated on monuments of prestigious individuals or monuments whose methods of manufacture were of particular interest, for example those with Harmer terracottas set into them or those made of cast iron. Further, past recorders were particularly interested in certain specific aspects of the information, for example genealogy, and they therefore tended to be selective in their recording. The programme overseen by ESAMP attempts to create a total record of all the available physical data which can be recovered at this moment in time. During the 1970s, the inscriptions on most of the monuments were recorded by Robert Collingham with a relatively high degree of accuracy and it is therefore possible to attempt to assess the potential rate of loss of surface information since this time.

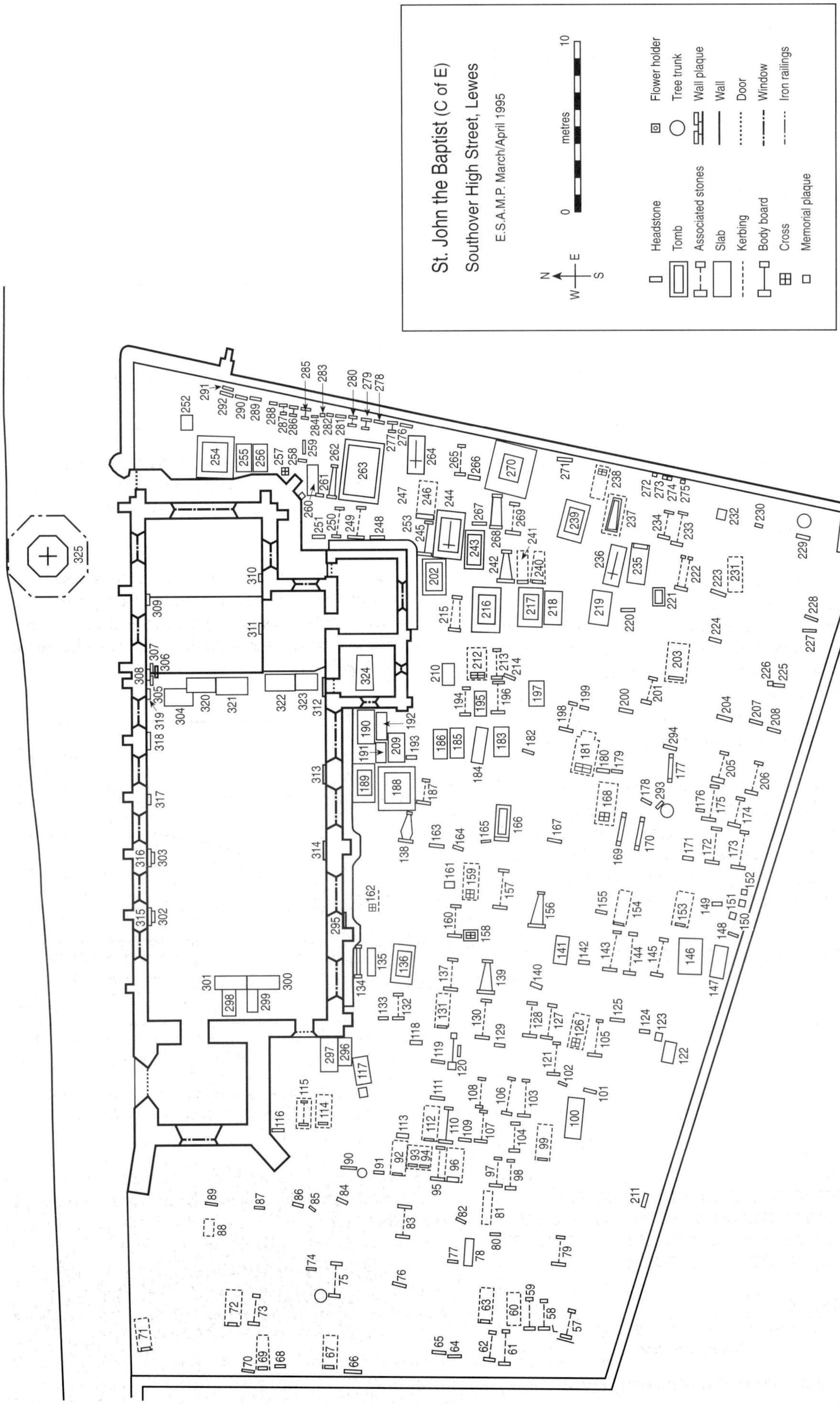

Figure 18.1. *Plan of St. John the Baptist Church and Churchyard.*

Methods

The churchyards are being mapped on a scale of 1:100 (*see* Figure 18.1) and each monument is given a number which is then used on a Memorial Recording Form. The physical mapping is carried out using baselines and offsets as well as a plane table. Where relevant, for example at St Michael's church at South Malling, spot heights are taken with a dumpy level. The monuments are recorded by hand onto a Memorial Recording Form and then entered onto a computer database. The CBA (Jones 1984) and Society of Genealogists (White 1988) have produced recording sheets and we have developed one which meets not only the recording requirements, but which can also be used in a variety of educational contexts. The monuments are photographed in black and white, this is usually a general photograph of the whole monument including a scale, but where the surface detail merits it, more detailed pictures are taken. A broad range of historical sources are used to back up the field record but, owing to limitations of space, it is only the burial registers which are transcribed and included in the finished churchyard report. The value and role of these historical sources will be discussed below.

Mortality Patterns

It is only when we have completely finished recording the data from the fieldwork and historical sources that we shall be able to use them to examine the overall patterns of mortality in Lewes over the period of study (Figure 18.2). The picture gleaned so far is fairly typical of what might be expected from a community of this type. Figure 18.3 shows the numbers of recorded deaths in the churchyard from South Malling. The number of infant deaths is immediately apparent.

When the percentages of all recorded deaths from the burial register is examined, the pattern of infant mortality becomes clearer. Between 1800 and 1850 approximately 30% of all recorded deaths were of children under one year old. Between 1870 and 1925 the percentage had fallen to roughly 17% and it is only after 1925 that it fell below 5%.

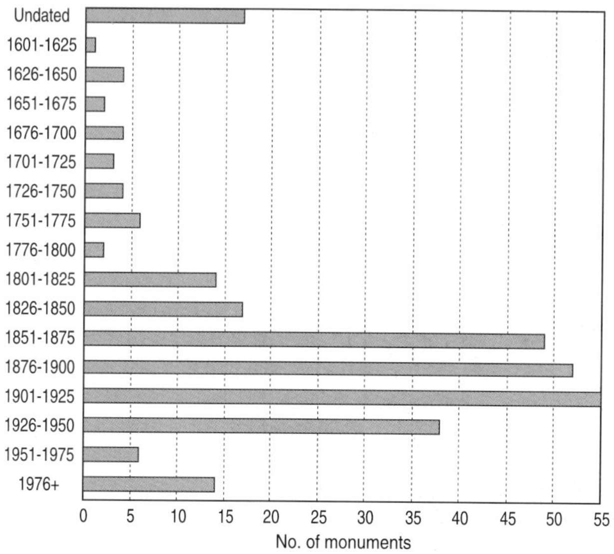

Figure 18.2. Graph of the number of surviving monuments in Lewes by period.

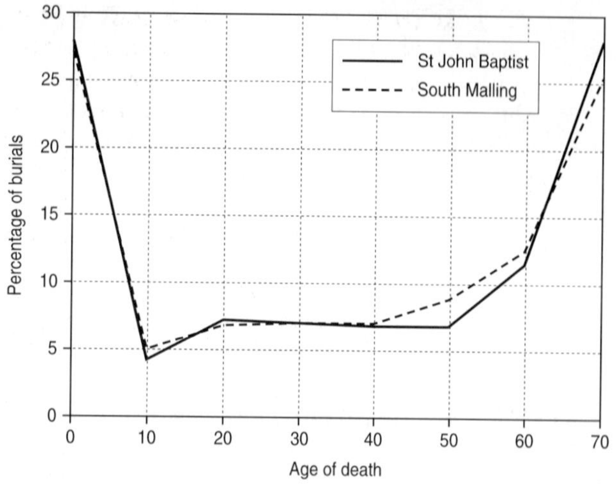

Figure 18.3. Comparison of percentage of burials by age group, 1801-1995, in the churchyards of St. John the Baptist and South Malling.

If we compare the percentage of burials by age group, as shown in Figure 18.3, we can see that the pattern shown by South Malling is almost identical to that of St. John the Baptist.

If we pursue this comparison we can see from Figure 18.4 that the average ages of death from the burial registers of the two churches follow a similar pattern, the main difference being that the average age of death is slightly higher for St. John the Baptist.

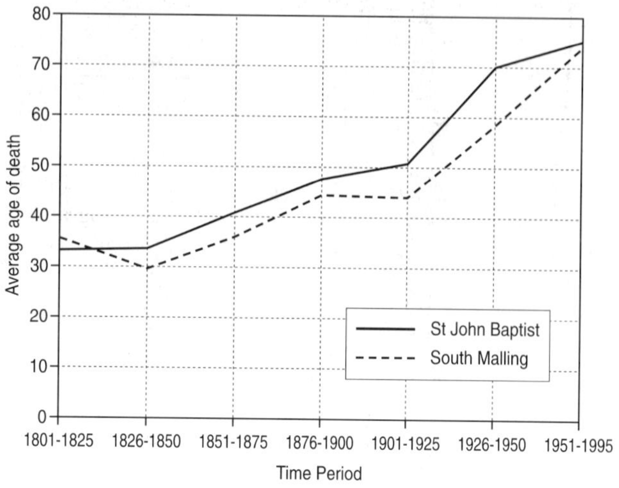

Figure 18.4. Comparison of average ages of death from the burial registers of St. John the Baptist and South Malling.

This may reflect a difference between the two parishes in that for most of this period St. John the Baptist was a relatively prosperous urban parish whereas South Malling was more rural in composition. We have also looked at issues such as seasonality and mortality. The pattern shown in Figure 18.5 from St. John the Baptist is typical of Lewes. It shows that the overall mortality increased notably during the late winter period. Where we have looked more closely at these data we see a definite trend for mortality at this time for those over sixty years of age. However, no clear seasonal pattern of mortality has been established for infants mortality.

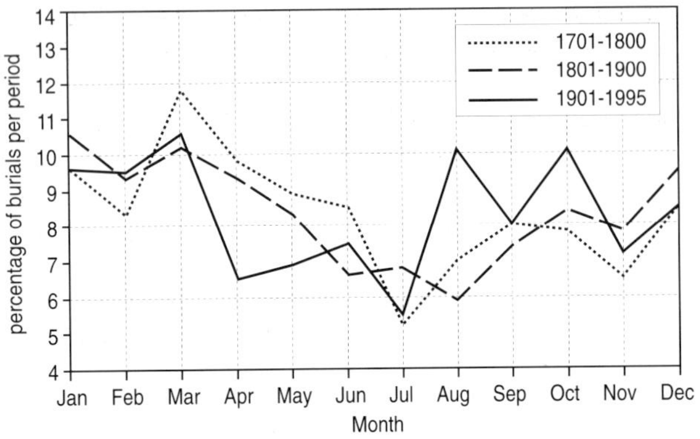

Figure 18.5. *St. John the Baptist burials: months of death, 1701-1995.*

These data give us an insight into patterns of mortality within Lewes, but we need to broaden the scope of this work if we are to gain a fuller appreciation of the health of individual communities. We have examined age at death, but this does not take into account factors such as population size and migration patterns. The burial to baptism ratio is easy to calculate and gives a rough basis for comparisons between communities. We have started doing this for the records from St. John sub Castro and this is tending to give a figure below one. This can be compared to the figure for the marshland communities of eastern East Sussex, where the ratio is consistently over 1.25 (Dobson 1982, 120) for the same period indicating a poorer health pattern. Crude death rates (all deaths per 1000 population), while more difficult to calculate, can give a better cross-community comparison.

We are fortunate in that an extensive amount of data concerning this type of information is available from the work carried out by Mary Dobson and this is now held in the Library of the Wellcome Unit for the History of Medicine. She has carried out a huge amount of statistical work on over 100 parishes in Sussex and Kent and has produced lists of outbreaks of diseases from 1600 to the present day. This is allowing us to set our work within a much larger programme of investigation. However, before being able to explore fully the monumental component in relation to the documentary aspects, it is important to examine the partial nature of the monumental record.

Problems and issues associated with monumental recording

The process of recording the detail on the surface of monuments is by no means straightforward. It can take up to half an hour to record a single badly degraded monument. Many of the Lewes monuments have been subjected to partial or total surface erosion since their erection. While this problem may have been exacerbated by recent atmospheric pollution and its severity may depend on the types of stone used, it is not a new problem. John Eliot, writing in 1778 during his recording work in the churchyard of St. John sub Castro, comments that:

" ...the gravestones of the deceased becoming illegible...as many of the latter in this parish, as are yet legible, which some of them will soon cease to be"(ESRO PAR 4/2/7/4).

Examining the stone when the light is incidental to its surface can greatly increase the detail recovered, as can shining or bouncing light at this same low angle. Even using these techniques, there is still a high level of interpretative skill required by the recorder in such work. In many cases, learning to recognise the patterns of calligraphy being used as well as employing tactile surface examination can greatly increase the amount of information recovered. Nevertheless, while the final record should only be a true representation of what can be observed empirically, it does rely heavily on interpretative judgement.

Case Studies

Three case studies have been taken to show the range of problems and broader research opportunities which can occur when attempting to transcribe the details from monuments and then to cross reference them to other sources. They are typical of many other cases and show the difficulties associated with the physical record. Currently, the earliest Lewes churchyard monument we have uncovered is the headstone of Margaret Cheal at South Malling (Monument no.67). The monument is badly eroded and it is not possible to be definite about all details of the dedication inscription.

Our record is:

> Margarat wife of Thomas Cheal
> died ??? Februar 160(7)

Bax, who recorded many inscriptions in the Lewes churchyards, recorded the inscription in 1888 to Thomas Cheal and gave a date of 1809.

Resolving this discrepancy is not straightforward. The shape and carving of the monument, details of the epitaph and style of lettering are much more redolent of the earlier date we have ascribed. Added to this, we have noted a few cases where Bax has made errors in his inscription recording. The burial registers for the church only start in 1632 and do not record either a Thomas or Margaret Cheal for either period. Even if the date we have ascribed the stone to is correct, we have to be careful in being definite about assuming that the monument has always been in its present location. Any monument near the perimeter wall of the churchyard, as this one is, may have been moved there at some time in the past. Indeed, it is possible that this monument may have been moved from another churchyard at some point in its history.

The Vital Records Index produced by the Church of Jesus Christ of Latter Day Saints gives a christening date for a Margaret Cheal of 28th February 1607. The records for this christening belong to the Church of St. Thomas at Cliffe. It is possible that this Margaret Cheal is the daughter of the Margaret Cheal commemorated on the monument, who may have died in childbirth. Significantly, the date given on the memorial pre-dates the consecration of the present churchyard by some 25 years. The dating of this monument and indeed the whole site is an interesting and important issue. The carved dedication inscription on the porch of the church gives the date of 1628 and we know from John Evelyn's diaries that the church was consecrated in 1632 by the Bishop of Oxford.

Further, we know from the Domesday Book and other sources that there had been a major ecclesiastical site in the area, namely a Collegiate church, which was dissolved in 1547. There are a number of sources of evidence to suggest that the present church was built on the site of an earlier one. In particular, the petition by the parishioners to the Archbishop of Canterbury asks him to consider the:

" ....reedifying of the parish church of South Malling....which is now, accordingly, done upon the ancient foundation in the churchyard, being always, hitherto, our usual place of burial" (Horsfield 1824-1827, Volume **2**, 169).

An 1824 map by Figg shows an unexplained larger black outline projecting out from the present church, and a resistivity survey conducted by John Bleach and Mark Gardiner in 1992 appears to confirm the suggestion that Figg's outline was referring to a masonry feature, now no longer visible. Possibly, Figg was recording the 'ancient foundation' referred to by the parishioners.

The cruciform shape implied by Figg's drawing corresponds to a collegiate form. However, the Sites and Monuments Record held by East Sussex County Council gives the location of the Collegiate church as being further down the river at Old Malling Farm. The sum total of the evidence for this alternative siting is some medieval masonry uncovered at Old Malling. All the other evidence suggests the site_was at the location of the present church. In either case the provenance of the gravestone is still complicated. It is possible that the stone, and maybe the bodily remains, were brought to the churchyard from St. Thomas' Church as it is extremely unlikely that the stone was erected while the churchyard was unconsecrated.

Whatever the reason, it is clear that the monument fits into a much larger, more complex and of the potentially more significant framework of enquiry. Indeed, it was the apparent dating discrepancy which led to our research into the dating of the whole site.

The next earliest stone (Monument no. 12) from South Malling also raises questions concerning a possible link between the two churches. The inscription on the slab is:

'Marie wife of Richard Ikes of ye Cliffe, grocer who died (?) day of September Ano 1632.
She was in life a virtuous wife
A friend and mother dear
Now lies in dust hoping with trust
For Christ to appear.'

No person by the name of Marie Ikes appears in the burial register for South Malling. However, an investigation of records for this period, held at the County Record Office, revealed a Richard Sickes, a grocer in Cliffe. The burial register for St. Thomas' church, Cliffe, makes no mention of Marie Ikes or Sickes. However, in volume 2 of Woolgar's *"Speciligia"*, under extracts from the early registers for Cliffe Parish, there is an entry for the burial of Mary wife of Richard Sykes on September 25th 1631.

Why the memorial slab for Marie Ikes should therefore be in South Malling churchyard is not clear; it is possibly due to the close links between the two churches - they are both in the deanery of South Malling and are both under the auspices of the Archbishop of Canterbury.

The discrepancy between the monumental and register dates of death is not uncommon during this period and this issue will be explored by reference to a further case study, that of the monument to Mary Mantell set in the churchyard of St. John the Baptist.

The monument (No. 292) dedicated to Mary Mantell (and shown as Figure 18.6) is unusual in a number of ways. It is a headstone made of Sussex marble and dated, almost certainly, to 1708: almost all other headstones in Lewes churchyards from this period are made of Portland stone. If the dating is correct, the shape of the monument is also very unusual for the period. Below the inscription dedicated to Mary Mantell is another one dedicated to T.G.C. Kennard. The burial register shows that he died in 1851 aged 31, that is, 143 years later. The surface of the monument is badly worn, but it is possible to decipher the following inscription:

'Here lieth the body of
Mary y wife of Richard Mantell
who died December (?)9th
(?)708'

The details of ESAMP's transcription are confirmed, in part, by the transcriptions of Collingham in 1978 and Bax in the 19th century. However, in 1897 Dunkin lists the memorial inscriptions in the churchyard in great detail and makes no mention of this monument. In the burial register for the church

Figure 18.6. *Headstone of Mary Mantell, in the churchyard of St. John the Baptist.*

there is an entry for December 22nd, 1708, for Avril, wife of Richard Mantell. In 1739, there is an entry in the register for April 12th for "Mary Mantel, widd of Southover". Although it has not been possible to confirm further details of the individual's identity from any of the historical sources, it seems most likely that the Mary on the monument and Avril in the burial register are the same individual. These three examples show the complexity, the difficulty and the value in being able to integrate the archaeological record clearly into the framework provided by the historical sources.

The partial nature of the physical record in the Lewes churchyards

It is only through this careful synthesis of the archaeological and historical sources that we are able to locate the physical record into a larger analytical framework. The partial nature of the monumental evidence is made clear by cross-reference to the relevant burial registers. The burial register for the parish of South Malling lists 2334 burials in the period from 1629 to 1977, the total number of individuals recorded in the churchyard survey is 525 - this figure represents only 22.49% of the total number of burials. Even allowing for the fact that there were 30 monuments, out of a total of 298 recorded monuments (each with an average of 1.8 commemorations per monument), which were illegible, it can be seen how small an overall percentage of the population is represented by the monuments within the churchyard. Again, even when we come to look at the monuments from the most recent period from 1929 to 1977, we find that the number of burials retrieved from monuments as a percentage of listed burials from the parish register is only 60.54%. It is important to bear this in mind when attempting to form frameworks of explanation concerning societal or demographic trends of a given period based on the remaining monuments. If we examine some more comparative details concerning the two sources, we can see from Figure 18.7 that the simple average age of death of those with memorials is higher than those recorded in the burial register.

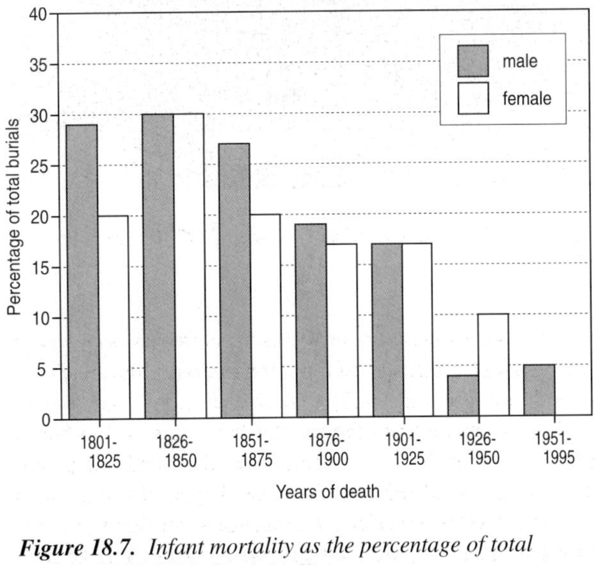

Figure 18.7. *Infant mortality as the percentage of total burials, 1801-1995, South Malling.*

Obviously, a consideration in this discrepancy is that while infant mortality is recorded fully in the burial register, it is largely absent from the monumental record. Even when the effect of this is taken into account, there is still a clear discrepancy between the two groups. The major probable explanations for this discrepancy are economic, aspirational and emotional ones; that is, those people with memorials are mostly of a higher economic standing or they wished to have a memorial for their dead as a statement of the social status of the remaining family members. Further, it has been argued by some writers (Tarlow 1988, 43; Llewellen 1997, 28), that the rise in popularity of monuments in the 18th and 19th centuries was based on an emotional process. In this thesis, emphasis is placed on the greater freedom of individuals to form relationships of their own choice. The longer these relationships existed the stronger the desire to have a memorial irrespective of the purely economic determinants. The corollary to the longevity of any emotional relationship was also the increased ability to be able to afford a permanent memorial.

A constructed landscape

Churchyards are a constantly evolving phenomenon and therefore what is available for us to record now is only a partial record of the total range of monuments that have existed. Prior to the start of the 18th-century many individuals would have had a body mound of soil raised over them and possibly a wooden marker. Such monuments are recorded in Lambert's 18th century watercolours of Lewes churches. These burials have left little trace. In addition to this, older monuments may have been cleared to make way for newer ones. The details of the number of monuments over the last 350 years in the churchyard at South Malling is shown in Figure 18.2. This distribution pattern is fairly typical of the churchyards in Lewes over this time. In addition to the physical factors mentioned above, there are a number of elements that are probably responsible for the substantial increase in the middle of the 19th century.

The population of Lewes increased during the latter part of the 18th century and early part of the 19th century (Brent 1993, 213). Further, monuments became relatively more affordable. We can get an idea of this economic aspect of the cost of a monument from the charges made by May and Parsons, a Lewes-based firm of masons, for a head and foot stone in 1801 at between four and five pounds. This compares with the wages for the craftsmen making these items being on average three shillings per day (Burgess 1963, 272). When we cross-refer burials from South Malling with the details of professions obtainable from the relevant census returns for the middle and late Victorian periods, we see that a wide social range of individuals was being commemorated with a permanent memorial. This was in part due to the fact that the process of mourning and interest in burial was made more fashionable by Queen Victoria's very public mourning of the death of Prince Albert. The subsequent decline in usage can be attributed to a number of factors: the limited availability of space, the opening of municipal and private cemeteries following the introduction of the Burials Act in 1852 and the advent of cremation in 1884 (Hill and Mayes 1987, 14).

Early origins of some Lewes churches

One truism which is commonly proffered about the siting and development of churches is that they were set on earlier, often pre-Christian, sites. Evidence for this is usually extremely hard to establish. However, in the case of Lewes it is possible, from the research undertaken by John Bleach (1997, 131-142), to suggest that a number of the present churches in Lewes were sited in relation to significant earlier monuments. Illustrations of the churchyard at St. John sub Castro show at least one prominent mound in the churchyard and historical records indicate that another one may have existed. These were possibly part of a series of Romano-British burial mounds running down the crest of the spur on which the church is located. St. Anne's Church was located less than a hundred yards away from a rich series of probable Romano-British burials and deposits. The parish register of All Saints church makes reference to a possible early monument of " ye great sand tombstone at ye east side of ye church" (1682). Further, we have seen how the church at South Malling was probably sited on the remains of a much earlier one. The spur of land on which the church sits contains an Anglo-Saxon cemetery and Romano-British burials along its crest (Sites and Monument Record map TQ 41 SW). We also find reference in Horsfield (1824-1827, 273) to a very interesting discovery made in 1748, purportedly from the churchyard at South Malling.

The illustration given shows two blocks of stone with a carved central oval recess in each surface and a carved channel from each of the lower ends of the central cavity. The two halves of the stone fitted together and when found contained a human skull. While due caution must be given to any interpretation of such a putative find, it may fit into the intriguing pattern previously discussed. The siting of churches on sites of existing importance would have obviously had a powerful significance. These sites would already have been areas where communities assembled and would have had an existing legitimisation and status within the ritual lives of the communities using them.

The symbol survey

The churchyard programme has revealed some distinct and striking trends in the development of Lewes' churchyards at the start of the 18th century. There are several related phenomena that can be observed from this survey work. The first is that at the beginning of the 18th century we start to see a relative increase in the number of permanent memorials being erected in the churchyards. The second is that many of these monuments contain a wonderful array of carved symbols and decoration. Thirdly, there is a greater quantity and range of epithetic detail. We have drawn and photographed the decoration of some 85 monuments from the period 1700 to 1830 and we have recorded the epitaphs they contain. After this date the nature of the carved detail appears to become decorative and the range of imagery decreases. So, in the first instance we have focused on the carved detail in the 18th-century. Two headstones (Figures 18.8 and 18.9) from St. John sub Castro are typical of the quality and inventiveness of these 18th century monuments. Figure 18.8 is a photograph of the headstone of John Sharp, 1737.

Figure 18.8. *Headstone of John Sharp, 1737, St. John sub Castro.*

Figure 18.9 shows the set of carpenter's tools on Mark Sharp's foot stone. He was a carpenter and his stone is dated 1747. To understand why we start to find monuments containing such symbols we must attempt to examine the broader cultural context of the whole burial process.

Figure 18.9. *Footstone of Mark Sharp, 1747, St. John sub Castro.*

While it is possible to try and reconstruct the development of the physical landscape of churchyards from the medieval period through to the early modern period, it is much more difficult to reconstruct the mental landscape of the burial process during this time. Throughout the medieval period death was not viewed with the same degree of finality as it was after the Reformation. The idea of a transition of states as represented by purgatory and the means of intercession through prayer and remembrance were devices that helped to make the moment of death and the subsequent burial parts of a more continual process. Even in post-Reformation England we can see that ideas of the boundaries between life and death differ greatly from our contemporary ones. In 1660 William Evans erected a monument to his dead wife in Hereford Cathedral, he was included in the depiction and yet he did not die until 1668. It appears that as many as one third of all monuments in this period, which were intended to commemorate the dead also represent the living (Llewellyn 1997, 17). The process of burial and the erection of the monuments were only parts of a larger process. Medieval burial was a communal event and often many people would attend a funeral and the subsequent feast that went with it, even though they had no real knowledge of the individual concerned. Sometimes their attendance was guaranteed by the dole given out at funerals and the feasting that accompanied such events (Gittings 1988, 155). The monuments we are studying are not the only memorials and images dedicated to the dead. Rings, samplers, woodcarvings and paintings would have also been a part of the symbolic environment in which a deceased individual would have been commemorated.

Imagery and Control

The 18th-century monuments are dominated by symbols and imagery seen as representing mortality and resurrection (Figure 18.10). These themes of death and resurrection would have been omnipresent within Medieval, post-Reformation and early modern society. This imagery had in part been promulgated by the church as a way of centralising its own role in the process of negotiating the spiritual preparation for death. Moralising texts, such as the "Dance of Death", with their explicit imagery depicting the partially decaying corpses in grotesque situations would have been aimed at showing that whatever one's material status when alive, the same physical future awaits us all.

This theme was further developed in the Vanitas style portraits painted in the 15th and 16th centuries (Schneider, 1994, Chapter 5). These would often show the living person on the front of the painting and a skull on the reverse side of the portrait. This duality of portrayal was mirrored in numerous church monuments of the period. These would typically show the decaying cadaver below an effigy dressed in finery (Kemp,1995, 24). This practice was brought to an end by the Reformation when such imagery was regarded as idolatrous. The imagery of church monuments following the Reformation was more constrained and the portrayal of John Donne (1631), wrapped in a shroud and standing on an urn, was influential in the depiction of a resurrection theme. These issues of the depiction of mortality and resurrection were investigated by Deetz and Dethlefsen (1967) in an important survey carried out in New England. Deetz and Dethlefsen studied and recorded 25,000 monuments in and around Boston and observed a marked change in the incidence of the depiction of images of mortality early on in the period and an increase in representations of resurrection imagery, for example cherubs, later on. The distinction was clear and was interpreted as a move from an austere puritanical iconography to a more positive liberal perspective.

Their work has been influential in British studies and according to their thesis, the mortality symbols, for example skulls, bones and sexton's tools, as well as representing puritanical considerations, are seen to have derived from earlier medieval preoccupations with death. These pre-occupations are then seen to have been transcended by a more

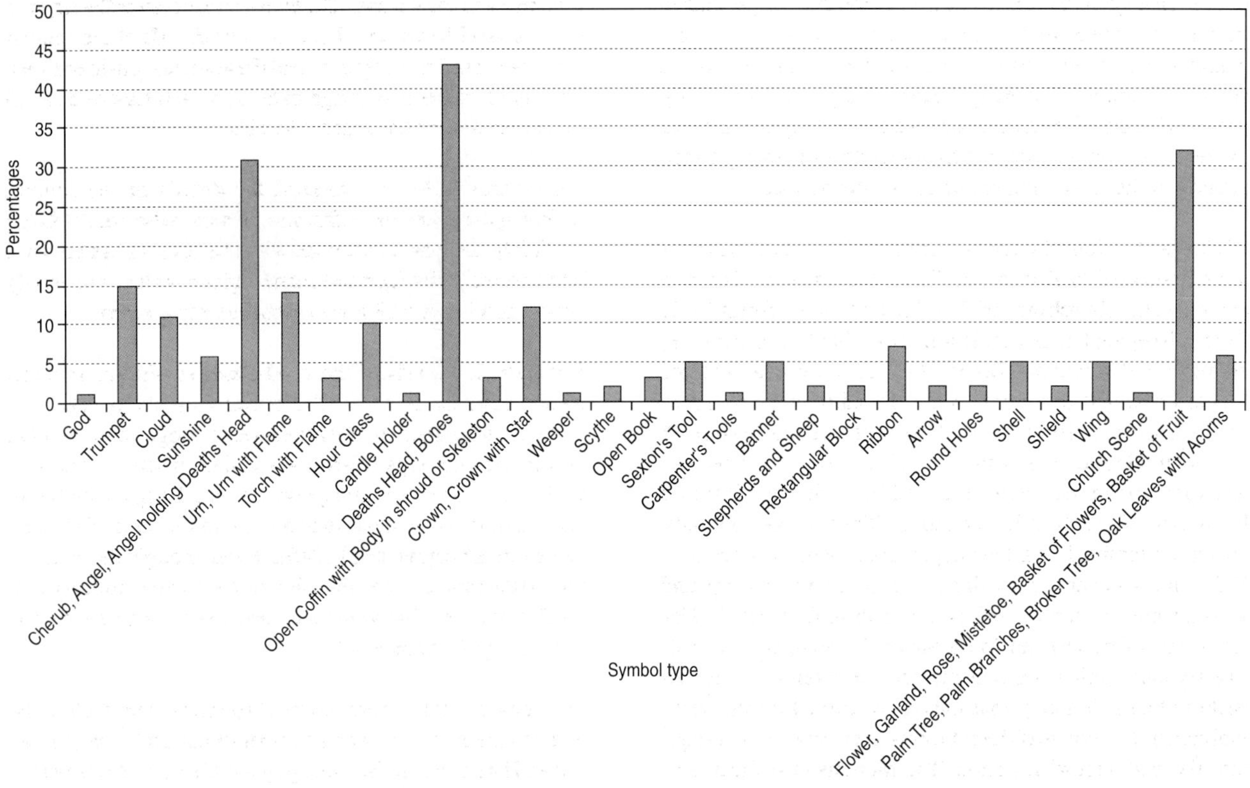

Figure 18.10. *Percentage count of symbol groups from Lewes churches, 1700-1800.*

positive resurrectionist approach, in part motivated by increased rationalist tendencies culminating in ideas based around Methodist-inspired imagery concerning the means of salvation, for example Faith, Hope and Charity and the Cross, the Anchor and the Heart (Burgess 1963, 190).

We can see that the mid-18th century represents a peak in terms of the number of symbols and their occurrence together. The most commonly occurring combination of symbols is the death's head and mistletoe. The sample size is so small that we have to be careful how we view this. It is possible that all the monuments with both symbols are the product of one mason and that the sole significance of this pairing is that it allows attribution, albeit anonymously. It is difficult to make qualitative statements on stylistic aspects of the depictions without these being contemporary value judgements, but certain patterns can be discerned. The general impression of the earlier death's heads is that they are quite realistic and subsequently become more stylised. The earlier realistic depiction of angels gives way in the 1740s to cherubic faces. It has become clear from our survey that the broad trends described by Deetz and Dethlefsen do not apply to the iconography of Lewes monuments. The earliest of these carved monuments is that of Mark Sharp, dated 1703, in the churchyard of St. John sub Castro. The carving at the top of the stone depicts an angel blowing a trumpet.

We also see symbols of immortality and resurrection occurring together and we see symbols of mortality occurring through into the mid-19th century.

There does appear to be a direct relationship between the symbols used and the type of monument on which they are found. However, broadly speaking, the headstones invariably contain the symbols of mortality and resurrection and the tombs have symbols such as urns and flowers. Maybe this is in part a consequence of the different people who manufactured them. While we know that firms of masons such as Parsons and May (later Bridgmans) probably produced many of the monuments we are looking at, the direct evidence of manufacture is difficult to attribute owing to the paucity of the remaining records from the period.

We know that John Morris junior carved the Portland stone tomb dedicated to Robert and Sarah Plummer in 1785 and erected in the churchyard of St. John the Baptist (Brent 1993, 216). The epitaph to his uncle John describes him as a mason, architect and surveyor. (Brent 1993, 210). So, many of the Lewes chest and box tombs were probably made by firms containing architects and therefore the inclusion of architectural relief and symbols, such as urns, can be seen as an expression of the classical revival in architecture inspired by individuals such as Robert Adam. The urn does not only appear on tombs. Its earliest appearance on headstones is in 1753 and it occurs, with flames coming from its top and accompanied by bones, on the memorials of Elizabeth Felder (St. Anne's Church) and Mary Sharp (St. John sub Castro). The stylistic similarities between the two monuments are so striking that it is likely that they were carved by the same individual. The urn, in different forms, then continues through into the mid-Victorian period. The monument dedicated to Edward May, 1803 (All Saints Church), mason and partner of John Morris junior, depicts a tableau including a draped urn, a palm tree, a weeping figure and a broken tree. It is quite possible that May carved this monument himself. Some of the imagery, for example the carpenter's tools shown on Mark Sharp's foot stone, are direct references to actual professions of the deceased, otherwise the imagery seems to be derived from the framework of iconography discussed previously. The potential reasons behind this observed boom in monuments with carved and inscribed detail needs more detailed discussion.

It was not only during the Victorian period that mourning became publicly fashionable. There were complaints in the early 18th century about trades-people imitating the aristocracy in wearing mourning dress (Llewyllyn 1997, 91). We can see this trend for permanent memorial markers as an extension of this process. That is, while previously only a few select individuals could have afforded it and would have been granted the right to a burial in a church, this was no longer true by the start of the 18th century. So, the increasingly wealthy middle classes were able to express their status through the adaptation and development of some material and behavioural traits of the aristocracy. While a memorial within a church was still a desirable social statement, the Reformation and the Commonwealth had remoulded some of the cultural patterns of fashion, orthodoxy and the centrality of the church itself. The symbolism on the monuments and the level of epithetic detail can be seen to be a form of assertion of this new memorial type.

The burial of the dead in many societies can be seen to be an expression of the social hegemony of the living and once any memorial trends had developed sufficiently they probably gained their own momentum. Gittings quotes many cases where executors had ignored the wills of the dead (Gittings 1984, 87) and arranged funerals that they thought were in keeping with the status of the living rather than reflecting the expressed wishes of the deceased. The details of the funeral ceremony itself can help to reveal these social considerations. The burial of Thomas Ridge in St. John sub Castro in 1735 gives a flavour of the process locally.

His brother William organised the details of the funeral including the livery, the coffin and the wine to be drunk (Ridge 1975, 31). Unfortunately, even with this level of background information, no background detail is given of the wonderfully carved headstone which was subsequently erected.

The specific details of the symbolism on the monuments would have been left to the masons involved. There is evidence to suggest that they carved a range of decorative details onto the tops of stones and then when a stone was chosen by a client an inscription was cut. Burgess quotes an 18th-century example of such a stone in the yard of Parsons in Lewes (Burgess 1963, 285). Even though the masons carved the imagery, the selection of the stones probably still resided with the individuals concerned or their executors, usually family members.

The masons, who were often carpenters and architects, selected the imagery from a number of culturally negotiated and validated sources. The imagery must have had a resonance with the people purchasing them and with those viewing them. Even given the reasonable levels of literacy in 18th-century

Lewes, the value of these symbolic markers must have been quite powerful. In some ways these monuments can also be seen as a form of counter-reaction to some aspects of the Reformation and the puritanical attitudes developed during the Commonwealth. The abandonment of certain rites, for example the belief in purgatory, can be seen to have led to a fracturing in the psychological process of bereavement. The establishment of permanent memorials that could be re-visited enabled the bereaved to return to their loved ones and this made the process of death and burial one of transition rather than finality. No two stones are identical from this period and this in itself suggests that these monuments were very much designed to express and emphasise individuality. We can see aspects of this in the epitaphs; during the 17th century we see much more personal detail being included on the monuments than previously. In the case of the Kempe tombs at St Michael's church at South Malling the family relationships are stressed in the inscriptions. Further, we can see from dedications, such as the previously discussed case of Marie Ike, that personal and socially virtuous attributes were being publicly ascribed to individuals. In both these cases the Lewes monuments are conforming to wider national patterns. As discussed previously, the importance of familial affection as a motivating force for the establishment of memorials must be given a central place in any framework of explanation (Llewellyn 1997, 28). Thus we can see a range of causes for a boom in memorials and a complementary development of a symbolic and epithetic language. However, it is important to bear in mind that although we can identify physical similarities within memorials created over a period of time, the ideas, attitudes, fashions and beliefs of the contemporary society within which these monuments were located constantly changed and evolved. So, we have seen how the physical monumental record must be set in the wider, religious, cultural, architectural, economic and social framework in order to gain a full appreciation of the rich learning opportunities these monuments can represent for us today.

Future Developments

The immediate priority is to continue to develop the fieldwork, as the recording work is central to the research programme. It is hoped that one consequence of this work and the published records will be to encourage people to visit their local churchyards and to appreciate the wonderfully rich archaeological landscapes that still exist in the midst of our communities. We shall attempt to refine and develop the research design and to explore further the extensive historical sources available.

Acknowledgements

The churchyard recording programme has involved a huge amount of work on behalf of many ESAMP members. Particular thanks go to Matt Lowerson for his illustrations, to Julian Hills for the photography and to Carl Hogsden and Anouk Freycenon for the symbolism survey work, and to Andrea Grubb, Melanie Parker, Liam Spinnage, Clifford Camp and Tom Burns for all their input and help.

ESAMP would like to thank the relevant church authorities for their help with this work. Our thanks go to the Southover Manor Educational Trust for their continued support for the Churchyard Recording Programme.

References

Bleach, J. 1997. A Romano-British (?) barrow cemetery and the origins of Lewes, *SAC* **135**, 131-142.

Brent, C. 1985. *Historic Lewes and its Buildings.* Lewes District Council.

Brent, C. 1993. *Georgian Lewes 1714-1830, The Heyday of a County Town.* Lewes: Colin Brent Books.

Burgess F.J. 1963. *English Churchyard Memorials.* London: Lutterworth Press.

Burman, P. 1988. *The Churchyards Handbook.* Essex: Church House Publishing.

Deetz, J. and Dethlefsen, E.S. 1967. Death's Head, Cherub, Urn and Willow, *Natural History* **76**, 29-37.

Dobson M. 1982. *Population, Disease and Death in south East England (1600-1800).* Unpublished PhD Thesis: Wellcome Institute Library: ref-EK441.

East Sussex Archaeology and Museums Project. *Church Survey Reports.* Unpublished. Lewes: East Sussex County Council.

Gittings, C. 1988. *Death, Burial and the Individual in Early Modern England.* London: Routledge.

Hill, J.D. and Mays, S. 1986. *Dead Men Don't Tell Tales.* Archaeology and Education **5**, University of Southampton.

Horsfield.T.W. 1824-1827. *The History of Lewes and its Vicinity.* 2 volumes. Lewes: Sussex Press.

Jones, J. 1984. *How to Record Graveyards.* York: CBA/ Rescue.

Kemp, B. 1985. *Church Monuments.* Aylesbury: Shire.

Llewellyn, N. 1997. *The Art of Death.* Victoria and Albert Museum: Reaktion Books.

Schneider, S. 1994. *Still Life.* Koln (Cologne): Taschen.

Ridge, D. 1975. *A Sussex family, The family of Ridge from 1500 to the present day.* Chichester: Phillimore and Co.

Tarlow, S. 1998. Romancing the stones: the graveyard boom of the later 18th century, in M. Cox (ed), *Grave Concerns, Death and Burial in England 1700-1850.* York: CBA, 33-43.

White, L. 1988. *Monuments and their Inscriptions, A Practical Guide.* London: Society of Genealogists.

Other sources

The Parish registers are held in the East Sussex Record Office, as is Eliot's *Notebook of Monumental Inscriptions.* The inscription records of Bax, Dunkin and Collingham are held at the Sussex Archaeological Society's Library at the Barbican House Museum, Lewes.

THE MARITIME ARCHAEOLOGY OF SUSSEX

Peter Marsden

Abstract

Sussex is especially significant in England's maritime history because it borders the English Channel. Its ports and ships have for centuries been linked by trade, transport and warfare with the Continent and other parts of the British Isles. Both local and other shipping was occasionally wrecked on, or close to, the Sussex coast. Yet, despite the county's rich maritime archaeological heritage, its waterfronts and ship wrecks are a generally neglected and unprotected aspect of Sussex archaeology. This paper aims to summarize what little maritime archaeological work has to date been undertaken in Sussex, and to highlight both the potential for, and importance of, future work.

Introduction

The term 'Maritime Archaeology' is not restricted to ships and boats, but applies equally to ports with their waterfront structures such as quays, jetties, cranes and winches, and to the goods that were carried in water transport. It also applies to the vessels themselves wherever they were used, in the sea, on inland waters and even on land, such as when broken-up vessels had their timbers reused in buildings, or when the boats were used in burials (Marsden 1997). To this extent, then, the word 'maritime' is really a misnomer, though a better one cannot be found.

Sussex is particularly significant in England's maritime history because it borders the English Channel. On the one hand its historic ports have for centuries had links with the Continent and with the rest of Britain through its trading ships, whilst on the other hand, the shipping from many parts of the world have voyaged within sight of the land and were occasionally wrecked on, or close to, its coast.

Ports have been created and have failed in every major age since Roman times: some were no longer viable, such as the medieval Cinque ports of Hastings, Rye and Winchelsea. Before them were Roman ports at Pevensey and Chichester, and no doubt there was a base for the *Classis Britannica* somewhere in the Hastings area to serve the ironworking site at Beauport Park. But of all this we know very little since, ancient port waterfront areas have not been investigated in Sussex. It is all very well studying the archaeology of towns and the countryside and reconstructing their history, but to ignore the waterfronts is to create a wholly land-based bias in the interpretation of urban and rural archaeology.

To take Winchelsea, for example. David Martin (*see* Section 15) has described Edward I's planned town that was intended to be a major port replacing the earlier medieval town lost to the sea. The streets and some of the medieval buildings have been not only recorded or assessed through limited excavation, but also the town's documented history has been reconstructed. Included in this documentary research has been a study of its waterfront property owners. That town depended upon trade and shipping, until silting occurred. But has there ever been so much as a trial excavation to examine the waterfront? Sadly, the answer is no. And yet the area is accessible for excavation and evaluation. The same applies to almost every other early port in Sussex. A trench was dug at Pevensey and a medieval waterfront was suggested, but without conviction in the publication (Dulley 1967).

My point is that the waterfront areas of the historic ports form probably the most neglected aspect of Sussex archaeology. And yet at 'The Archaeology of Sussex to AD 2000 conference' the importance of seagoing trade links, as well as the need for defence from seaborne attack, was frequently stated. Archaeologists need to address this matter and give future conferences the benefit of a more balanced view.

Saxon and Medieval

It is not until the late Saxon and medieval periods that we have archaeological evidence for ships and boats in Sussex. A Saxon dugout canoe has been found in the river Arun at South Stoke and has been radiocarbon dated to the 8th-9th-centuries, and a number of others have also been found in the same river, one of which is dated to the 7th century AD (McGrail 1978, 145-147).

These may be the earliest dated boats yet found in Sussex, but however interesting they are to the finders, they have one fundamental failing - they were of very limited economic value in their own time, and contribute very little to our knowledge of the history of water transport. Once plank-built vessels had begun to be built and used over 3500 years ago in southern England, as is found in the Dover boat, the 'logboat' in its various forms (ie dugout canoe, raft or even bark-boat) has nothing further to tell us about the development of boat and ship building. The dugout had become a technological dead-end in history.

So it is with interest that we seek early plank-built boat and ship discoveries in Sussex. They certainly exist, for planked vessels, probably of the Medieval period, have apparently been found at Lewes (Sussex Archaeological Society 1956, 176) and Eastbourne (Gilbert 1964). And no doubt many others await discovery. At present the only plank-built boat to be recorded and published was a strange, undated vessel found at Bexhill in 1888. Unfortunately, Charles Dawson, notorious for his association with the Piltdown fraud, was responsible for its publication, and as he claimed that this boat was a kind of link between primitive and recent vessels, his report must be viewed with caution (Dawson 1894).

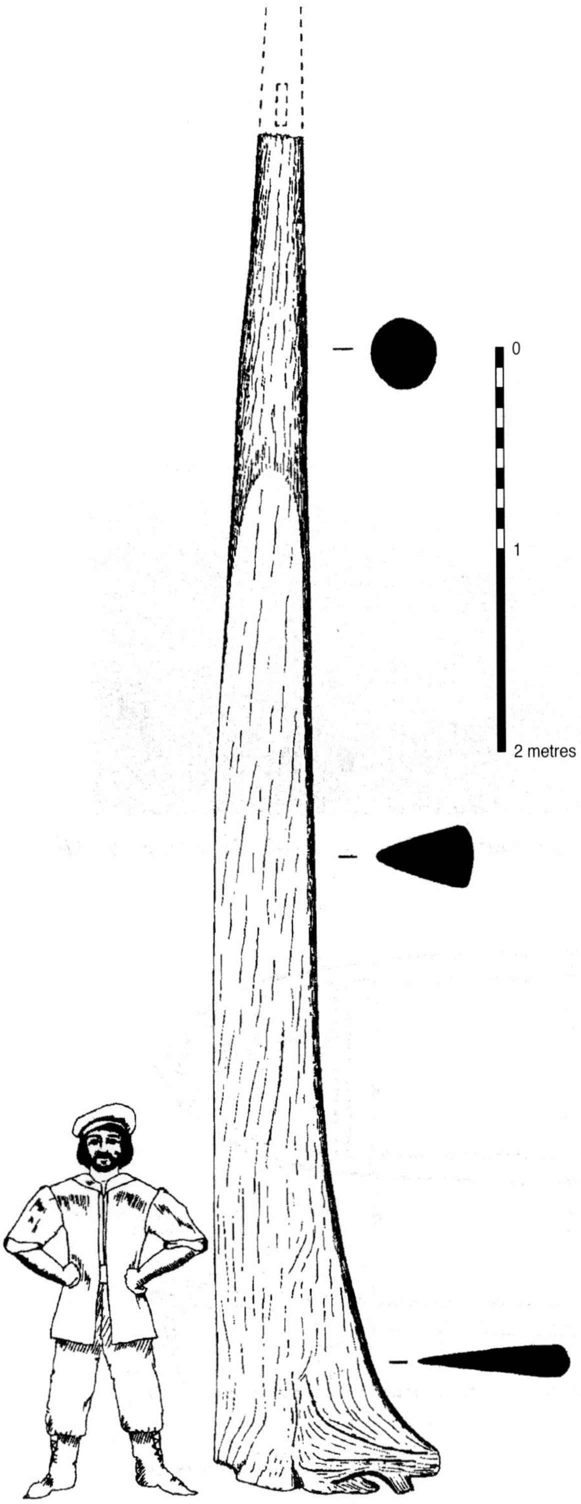

Figure 19.1. An enormous side rudder of the 13th Century trawled up off Winchelsea. The top where the tiller was once located is broken off. It was not completed, but was for a size of ship otherwise unknown in English documentary records. Now preserved at the Shipwreck Heritage Centre, Hastings. (Drawing by Peter Marsden).

Archaeological hints of the size of Medieval ships have now been found in the sea off Rye and Winchelsea. One is a great side rudder 7m long (Fig. 19.1) for a huge ship, and has been radiocarbon dated to the 13th century. This, and a comparable side rudder from Bergen, Norway, is the largest side rudder ever found in Europe and is particularly fascinating, for it gives a clue to the size of probably one of the largest ships of that time. Until then ships in Europe were steered by side rudders, but thereafter the much superior sternpost rudder was increasingly used. It is from the sea off Rye that there is also a sternpost rudder, and this has been radiocarbon dated to the 15th century. It is the only fairly intact Medieval rudder of its type from Britain, and is of great interest because it enables the shape and size of the stern of a small merchant ship, most likely a type known as a 'Cog', to be reconstructed. Both rudders are to be seen at the Shipwreck Heritage Centre, Hastings.

16th century

It is not until the 16th century that we reach more secure ground archaeologically speaking, with the discovery in a former bed of the River Rother at Rolvenden, north of Rye, of a vessel that was thought to be Viking (Figs 19.2; 19.3). It occurred in 1822 and was published in *Archaeologia* (Rice 1824), but the unpublished field notes of the young naval architect, William McPherson Rice, also survive at the National Maritime Museum at Greenwich, together with a scale model of the remains. These and other records include details of pots, shoes and other items that enable the vessel to be dated to about the 1540s. She appears to have been a coastal trader 19.4m long, and may be Dutch. The finding of human skeletons in the wreck is evidence that the vessel had sunk in a storm which rapidly buried the vessel in sea-sand and preserved her. She may also have been an early Rye Barge, a type of vessel known from 16th-century documentary records to be serving the communities beside the local rivers, and even venturing along the coast. They are sketched in an Elizabethan view of Rye, but are only known in detail from two barges built in the late 19th century, one of which, *Primrose,* was rescued from the banks of the River Rother a few years ago and is preserved at the Shipwreck Heritage Centre, Hastings. She is thought to be of similar design and rig to the Rye barges of much earlier times.

Small parts of two other vessels, probably of the 16th century, were also found at Rye whilst laying a sewer, but little detail could be recorded (Lovegrove 1964). Consequently the 1822 discovery is still the best that archaeologists have managed to achieve in recording an early vessel in Sussex.

The earliest known remains of port structures in Sussex also date from the 16th century and comprise the foundations of the stone pier and waterfront of the sea port of Hastings. They were washed away in the 17th century and remained as rows of timber piles and a field of rocks, known locally as 'pier rocks', lying on the beach. In 1833 they were planned in detail and subsequently photographed. The drawing was only discovered recently in the records of Hastings Borough Council (Fig. 19.4).

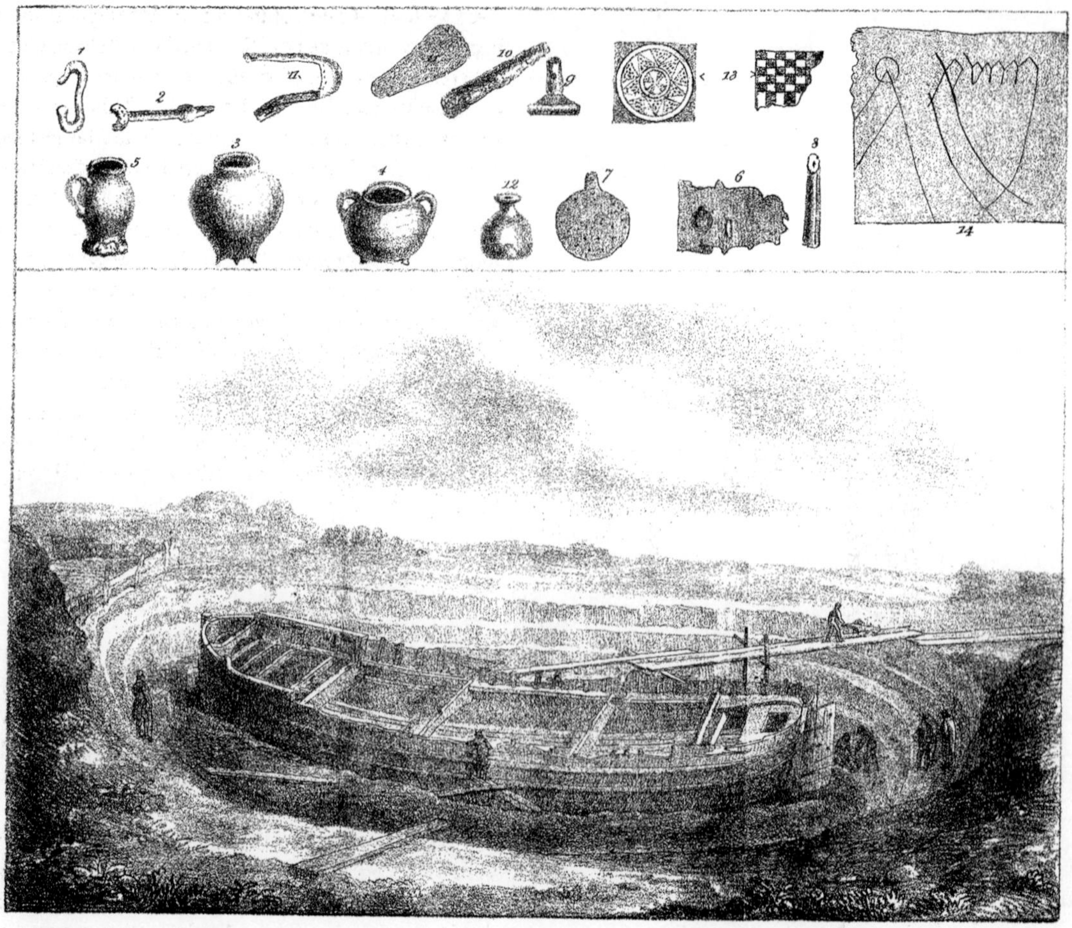

Figure 19.2. *The Rother ship and its contents, found near Rye in 1822, and dating from the 16th century. This is from a booklet published by Mason of London in 1823.*

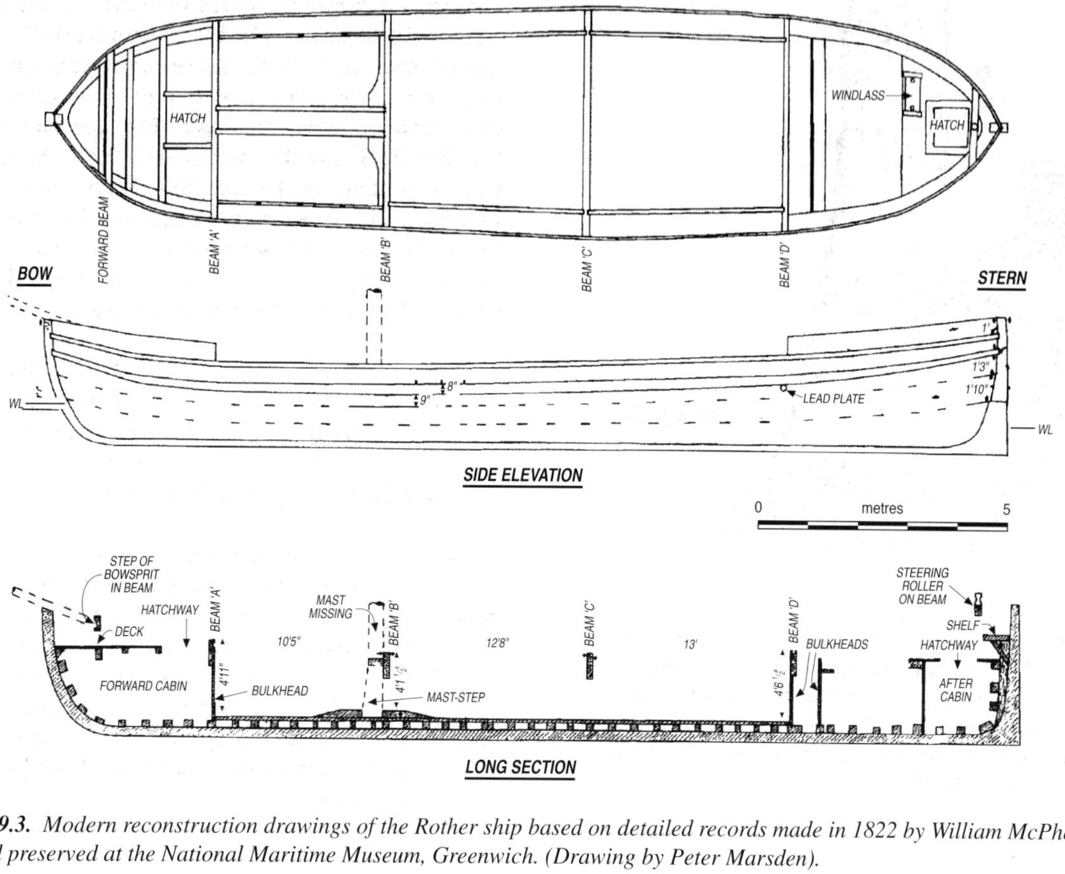

Figure 19.3. *Modern reconstruction drawings of the Rother ship based on detailed records made in 1822 by William McPherson Rice, and preserved at the National Maritime Museum, Greenwich. (Drawing by Peter Marsden).*

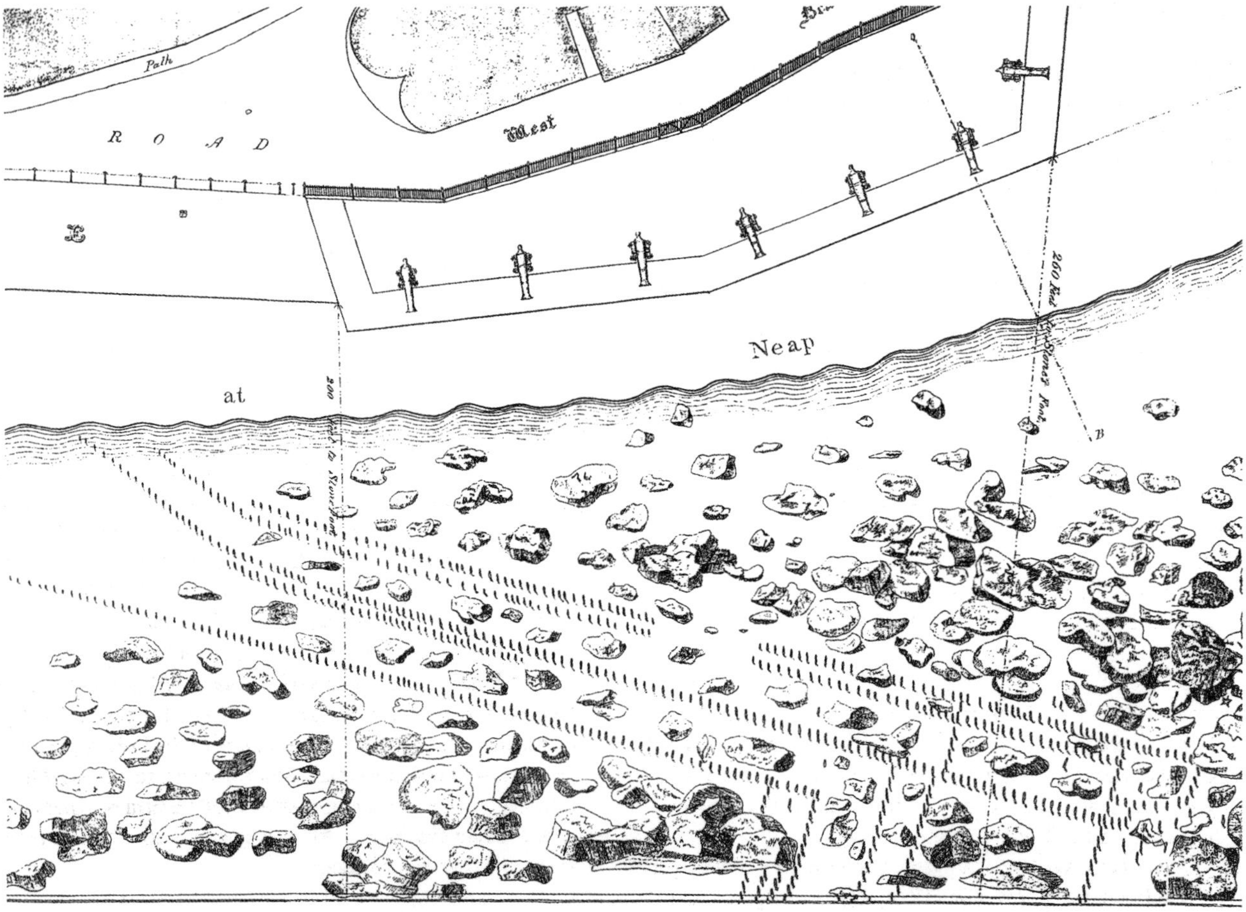

Figure 19.4a. *Timber pile foundations and fallen masonry of a 16th-century harbour wall built in the sea at Hastings. From a plan of 1833 for Hastings Borough Council. This site is now under land forming the seafront.*

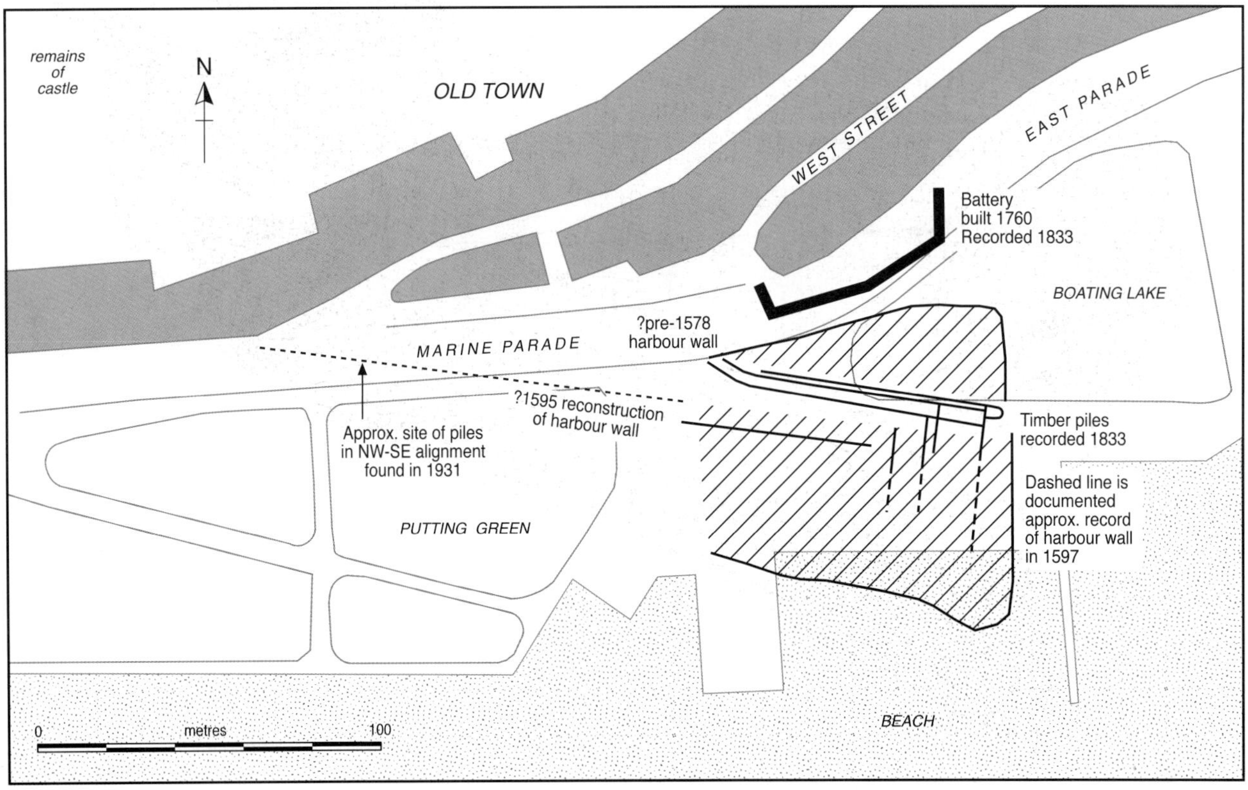

Figure 19.4b.

17th century

The Protection of Wrecks Act was passed by Parliament in 1973, and during the subsequent year a protection order was passed on the wreck of the warship *Anne* (Fig, 19.5), beached and burnt on the Sussex coast in 1690, and attacked by treasure hunters in 1974. The site, off Pett Level, between Hastings and Rye, can be visited at extreme low tide. Sometimes the outline of this important ship is visible in the sands. She was a 70-gun third-rate warship built at Chatham Dockyard for Charles II, on the orders of Samuel Pepys, Secretary of the Admiralty, in 1678. In 1687, under the command of the Duke of Grafton, Charles II's illegitimate son, and Captain Cloudesley Shovell, she carried a young German princess from Rotterdam to Lisbon to marry Pedro 11, King of Portugal. Thereafter the *Anne* visited the Barbary city states of north Africa, Algiers, Tunis and Tripoli, to renew old treaties. The voyage was full of high adventure and is carefully documented in the records of the Public Records Office and the National Maritime Museum. That voyage was directed by James II, who in 1688 fled to France.

In 1690 the French navy of Louis XVI tried to clear away British and Dutch naval opposition to an invasion that would put James II back on the throne, and so replace William and Mary. That summer the great land battle, the Battle of the Boyne, took place in Ireland, and in the Channel off Sussex there occurred the Battle of Beachy Head. The first battle was a success for William, and the second was a loss - though the French did not succeed in destroying naval opposition.

The *Anne,* the only British warship casualty, was beached and burnt by her captain, John Tyrrell. But amazingly, in the few weeks following her loss she sank deep into the clay seabed which here is covered by a submerged forest 5000 years old. Today, the lower 4 metres of the hull, 44 metres long, survives to give us the only substantial part of a warship of the Restoration navy. Eighty-eight years ago, as recorded in a photograph, the hull was a metre higher. Unfortunately, a pilot archaeological investigation in 1997 showed that the ship is being destroyed by the Teredo 'shipworm', by tidal scouring and by waves breaking immediately over her twice a day at low tide.

This ship made history in 1983 by being the first historic warship wreck to be given by the Ministry of Defence to a charitable trust, the Warship Anne Trust, which is based at the Shipwreck Heritage Centre in Hastings. Soon after, the *Mary Rose* was given to the Mary Rose Trust. The *Anne* stands midway between the *Mary Rose* (1545) and HMS *Victory* (*c.* 1800) in preserving the story of Britain's naval history, and the Trust has been advised that she should be preserved if possible. Just as the remains of historic buildings and sites of national importance on land are preserved for public display, so it is believed right that the remains of the buildings of the sea of comparable importance should be preserved. Just how the *Anne* can be saved from certain destruction is a matter of considerable discussion, for it is not easy to create another *Mary Rose* type of project.

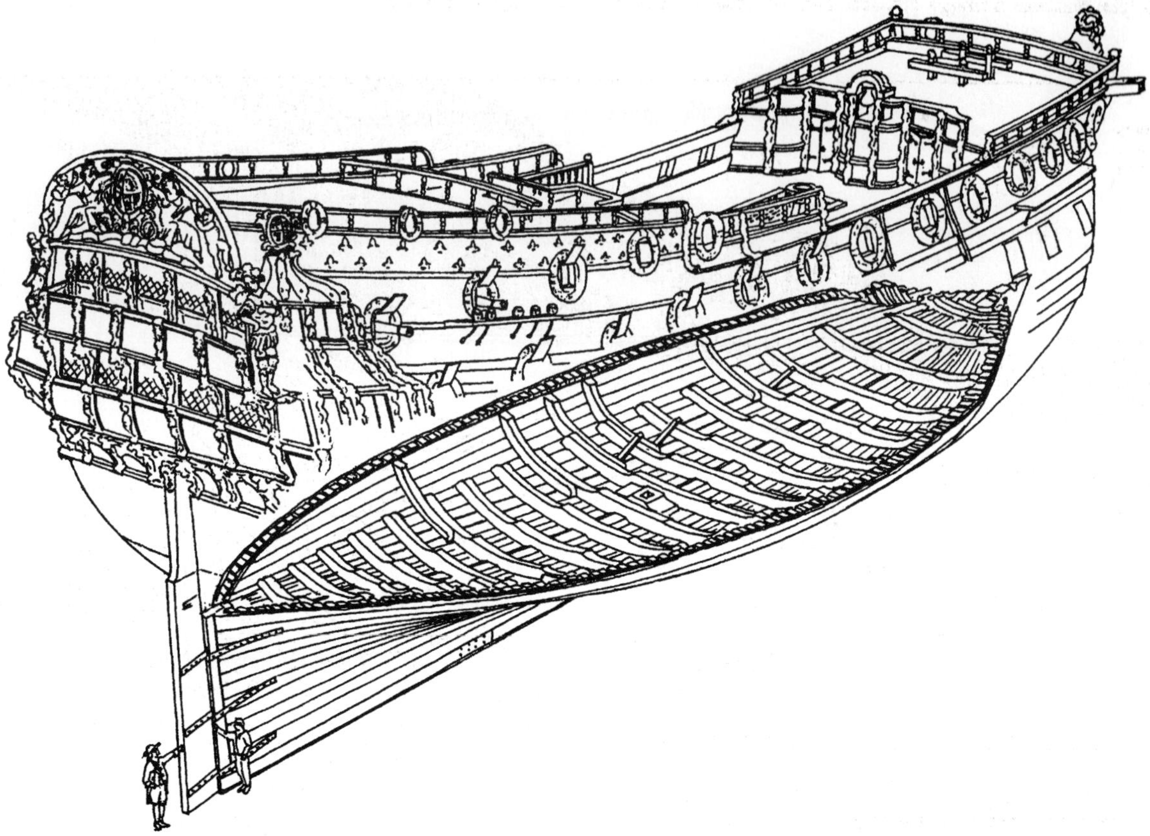

Figure 19.5. *Partial reconstruction of the warship* Anne *(wrecked 1690) and its surviving remains preserved in the seabed off Pett Level, between Hastings and Winchelsea, East Sussex. (Drawing by Richard Endsor).*

18th century

The British warship *Hazardous* lies on her port side in shallow water in Bracklesham, Bay, West Sussex, where she sank in a gale in 1706. She was a third-rate that had been captured from the French in 1703, and had been built by them in 1698. She is a protected historic site because much structure and many objects remain, but there is uncertainty about the fate of the archaeological archive and its full academic publication, because the licensed amateur diving team excavating the site are poorly supported archaeologically (Owen 1988, 1991).

Further east is the wreck of the Dutch East Indiaman *Amsterdam* (Fig. 19.6) cast on the East Sussex shore at Hastings in January 1749. In the following three months she sank about 8 metres so that now two-thirds of the ship, 44 metres long, survives in the beach and is exposed at low tide. Superlatives are rarely used in serious archaeology, but they apply in this case. She is a world-class historic monument, for she is by far the best preserved East Indiaman known in the world, and is of a type that opened up global trade for Europe during the 17th and 18th centuries. Also, she is still filled with her cargo and supplies for the Cape and the Far East, so consequently, she is worthy of being considered as a World Heritage Site, if that status can be accorded to a shipwreck.

The *Amsterdam* was on her maiden voyage from Amsterdam to Jakarta in Java with 333 people on board. Carrying over two tons of silver, and armed with 50 guns she was a formidable vessel. But disease was also on board, and in two weeks 50 men had died, and many more were sick and dying. When she lost her rudder in a severe gale off Bexhill, the men mutinied and ran her ashore on 26 January 1749. The silver was saved, but the cargo and supplies remain in the ship (Marsden 1985).

The site has been stable from 1911, when the earliest photograph exists, to 1969, but since then the ship has been infested by the Teredo 'shipworm' and is now being destroyed. The Dutch government, which owns the ship, will not take action to protect the site because they say that it is the responsibility of the British government, who 'protect' the site under the Protection of Wrecks Act 1973. The British government takes the opposite view and declares that she is the Dutch Government's responsibility. The result is that she is being needlessly lost. When in 1996 the Environment Agency built sea defences nearby, they offered to help protect the site at no cost, but the Dutch government turned this offer down too.

19th century

Many 19th century wrecks exist off the Sussex coast, but two are of particular interest since they have been studied. The first is the Danish wooden sailing ship *Thomas Lawrence* sunk about 10 miles off Hastings in 1863. Found as a 'net fastening' some years ago, it was investigated by divers seeking treasure, but what they found were rusted muskets, machetes, hundreds of bottles of gin and Vieux Cognac', and the tombstone of a woman and her baby, both of whom had died in 1858 at St. Thomas in the then Danish Virgin Islands.

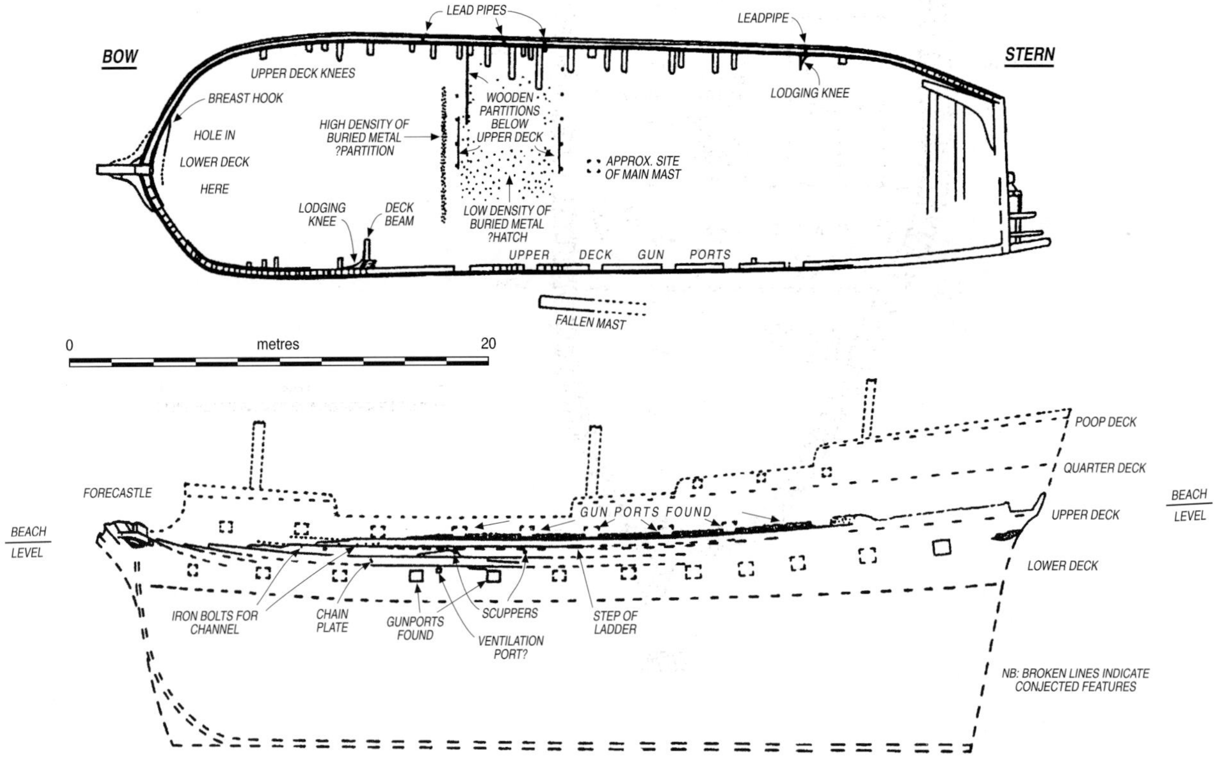

Figure 19.6. *Reconstruction of the remains of the Dutch East India Company ship* Amsterdam *(wrecked 1749) in the beach off Bulverhythe, between Hastings and Bexhill. (Drawing by Peter Marsden).*

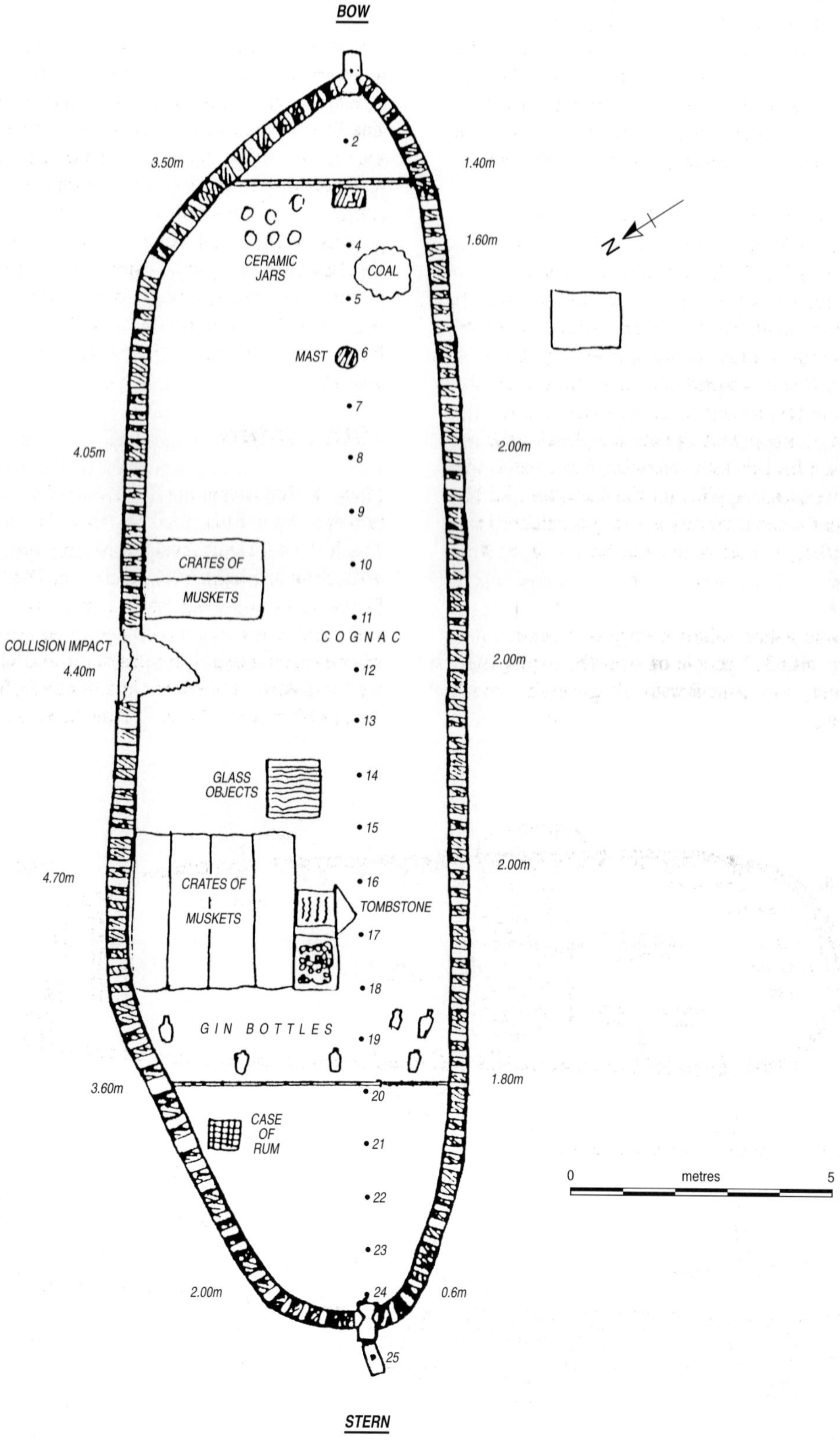

Figure 19.7. *Underwater survey by two Danish archaeologists, Michael Teisen and Gert Normann Andersen, of the wreck of the* Thomas Lawrence, *sunk in the English Channel 10 miles off Hastings in 1863. A German steamer had struck the ship at night, and the V-shaped impact point can be seen on the port side. (Drawing by Michael Teisen and Gert Normann Andersen).*

This wreck (Fig. 19.7) lies in the area proposed for a major gravel extraction scheme and is threatened by serious damage. The Nautical Museums Trust, based at the Shipwreck Heritage Centre, Hastings, has obtained ownership of the wreck so as to help ensure its protection.

The other is the clipper *Coonatto* that was wrecked on the cliffs near Beachy Head in 1876 on her voyage from Australia. The bottom of her hull survives amid the tumble of chalk rocks and can be seen at low tide. She is interesting for the hull is of wooden planks on iron frames, and represents the intermediate stage in construction between wood and iron (Marsden 1987, 27-29).

Conclusions

As we start the new century it is clear that some of the greatest advances need to occur in maritime archaeology, and it is expected that the government will pass responsibility for the historic wreck sites in British waters to English Heritage and so allow the wrecks to cease being the Cinderella of English archaeology - unwanted, unfunded, underprotected, underpublished.

The former Royal Commission on Historical Monuments of England (which is now merged with English Heritage) produced a report on what is known to lie on the seabed in English territorial waters - 30,000 sites, mostly shipwrecks (RCHME 1996). A stupendous legacy from the past, but requiring a huge commitment of resources. The Sussex situation is indicated by a study of wreck sites in Rye Bay. Where the Admiralty chart shows just sixteen wrecks, the local fishermen know also of sixty 'net fastenings' (ie old wrecks that still form obstructions on the seabed) and several extra standing wrecks.

Sussex has a remarkable maritime heritage that needs to be better integrated with the county's urban and rural archaeology. The quality of the maritime sites is best demonstrated by the fact that of the many protected historic wrecks in British waters, only three lie between high and low tide on the shores of the entire United Kingdom. Two of those three, the *Anne* and the *Amsterdam,* are on the East Sussex shore and can be visited by everyone.

References

Dawson, C. 1894. Ancient boat found at Bexhill, *SAC* **39**, 161-163.

Dulley, A. 1967. Excavations at Pevensey, Sussex, 1962-6, *Medieval Archaeology* **11**, 209-232.

Gilbert, R. 1964. Ancient Boats at Eastbourne, *SNQ* **16**, No. 3, 89-92.

Lovegrove, H. 1964. Remains of two old vessels found at Rye, Sussex, *Mariners Mirror* **50.2**, 115-122.

Marsden, P. 1985. *The wreck of the 'Amsterdam'*. London: Hutchinson.

Marsden, P. 1987. *The Historic Shipwrecks of south-east England.* Norwich: Jarrold.

Marsden, P. 1997. *Ships and Shipwrecks.* London: Batsford.

McGrail, S. 1978. *Logboats of England and Wales, pt.* 1, BAR Brit. Ser. **51** (1).

Owen, N. 1988. *Hazardous* pre-disturbance survey report, *International J. of Nautical Archaeol.* **17.4**, 285-293.

Owen, N. 1991. *Hazardous* 1990-1991 interim report, *International J. of Nautical Archaeol.* **20.4,** 325-334.

Rice, W.M. 1824. Account of an Ancient Vessel recently found under the old Bed of the river Rother, in Kent, *Archaeologia* **20**, 553-565.

Royal Commission on the Historical Monuments of England. 1996. *The National Inventory of Maritime Archaeology for England.* Swindon: RCHME.

Sussex Archaeological Society. 1956. Summary of the Research Committee held on 11th January 1956, *SNQ* **14**, Nos. 9 and 10, 176-177.

SUSSEX: FROM ENVIRONMENTAL CHANGE TO LANDSCAPE HISTORY

Elizabeth Somerville

Abstract

Work done since Sheldon's review presented at the conference of 1977 (Sheldon 1978) has shown that any reconstruction of the early to mid-Holocene landscape has to take into account a blanket of loessic soils over both the Downs and Weald. Anthropogenic change to the environment in Sussex started with relatively small, impermanent woodland clearings in the Mesolithic and Neolithic periods, which led to a mosaic landscape with considerable woodland. This was not cleared on a broad scale until the Bronze Age, but, at least as far as the Downland is concerned, there is thereafter little major change in the landscape. Our present understanding is, however, based on a limited spatial coverage of Sussex. A considerable research effort needs to be devoted to understanding environmental change in the historic period.

Introduction

The title deliberately sets a bold agenda, and it must be admitted from the outset that this paper can be no more than an account of work in progress. Therefore, I will first describe the methods which have so far been applied to palaeoenvironmental research in Sussex and then review the information on environmental change which has accumulated since Sheldon's 1977 review. Finally, I want to ask how far we have progressed towards being able to give an account of the landscape of Sussex from the end of the last Ice Age to AD 2000.

For Sussex, as for Lowland Britain as a whole, the general outline of environmental change since the last Ice Age has been long established (eg Bell and Walker 1992). First there is the return of trees to a steppe-tundra landscape, initially birch and pine followed by the re-establishment of a closed canopy deciduous woodland (the original, and only, wildwood), which is subsequently modified by human activity. Finally, agricultural practices, both arable and pastoral, lead to the eventual clearance of woodland and the development of the fully anthropogenic landscape we see today. This is summarized in Table 20.1, together with a listing of earlier periods.

The questions which arise from this thumbnail sketch are "when?", "where?" and "how much?" In an ideal world we would be able to answer these questions by reference to a series of locations which are distributed appropriately over Sussex to cover different underlying geological strata and topographies with an even spread of information from both the prehistoric and historic period.

The map (Fig. 20.1) giving the location of sites referred to in this paper shows that spatial coverage is currently far from even, e.g. most of the information from river valleys comes from the extreme east of the county and much of the information about dryland sites comes from the Downs, most often from the snail faunas found on early prehistoric sites. In Sussex the problem of uneven temporal and spatial coverage is compounded by the difficulties of integrating the

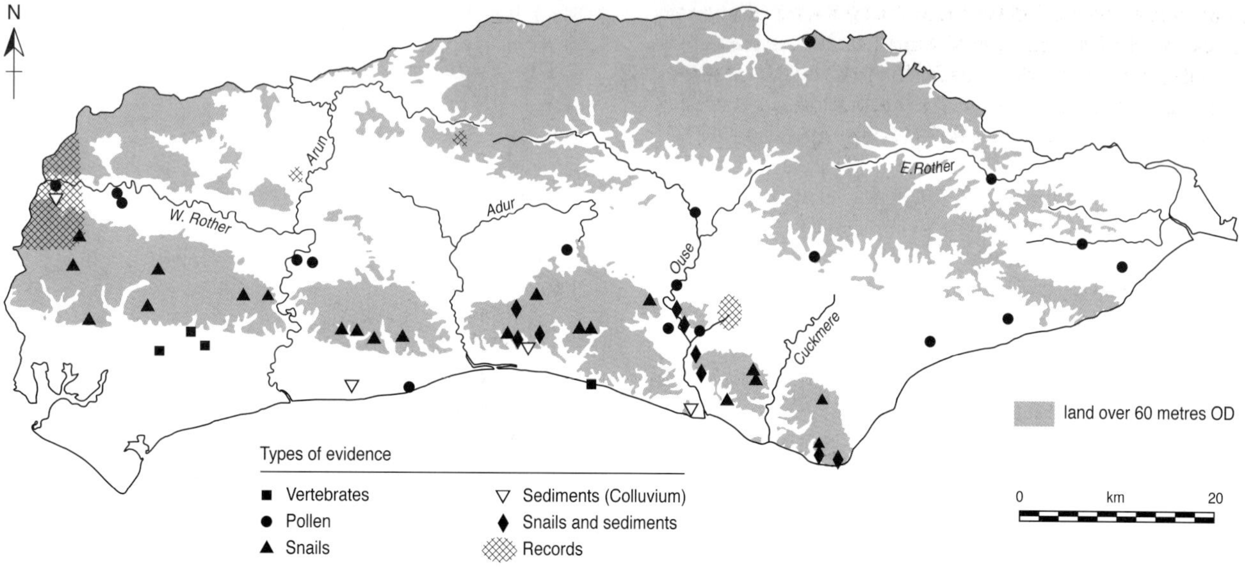

Figure 20.1. *Locations of sites providing information about enviromental change in Sussex.*

different types of information available from different areas in the historic county. Broadly speaking, reconstructions of past environments are largely based on the species of snails present when a Downland site is being considered and on the pollen record for river valleys and the Weald. Evidence from sediments comes from both river catchments and from dry valleys on the chalk. Nonetheless, information from individual sites is slowly building into an increasingly robust data base against which the general regional picture can be tested for specific localities. These different categories of evidence: snails, pollen and sediments, give us a series of different perspectives on past environments in Sussex. It is important to realize the limitations of the methods and to recognize what use could be made in the future of other sources of information.

Evidence for Past Environments

1. Snails

Snail shells are well-preserved in neutral and alkaline soils, and snails themselves are abundant in areas with plenty of calcium carbonate. Thus it is hardly surprising that the presence of shells in buried pits and ditches was noted by the first archaeologists to work in Sussex (eg Lane-Fox 1869). Before the Second World War a number of Sussex sites had samples of snails investigated by Kennard; e.g. the Trundle (Curwen 1929) and Whitehawk (Curwen 1934). This early work is liable to be judged unsatisfactory by today's molluscan specialists (Evans 1970). The shells were simply picked from the excavated areas by eye, biasing the sample towards the larger species and often resulting in very small numbers. Although the inferences made were primarily climatic, the principle used is the same as that used today: if a modern-day snail prefers undisturbed woodland, then it is reasonable to presume that the same species living several thousand years ago had similar preferences, and consequently if you find a lot of this species of snail in a buried soil it is likely that the soil was formed in an undisturbed woodland. Nowadays, bulk soil samples are collected from appropriate contexts. Subsequent extraction is done under laboratory conditions, thereby ensuring the inclusion in the analysis of even the smallest species as well as juveniles of larger species and broken specimens. Based on the work of Evans (1972), the molluscan fauna is usually interpreted in terms of ecological groups relating to conditions such as woodland, shade, open-country, etc. Snails do not move very far or very fast. It therefore follows that reconstructions of the environment based on the changing abundance of the ecologically defined groups of snails can only tell us about the immediate vicinity; how immediate is an important research issue (Thomas 1985). The overall sequence of changes in the snail faunas has been used by Kerney (1977) to establish terrestrial molluscan biozones analogous to those used by palynologists.

2. Pollen

Plants can produce copious amounts of pollen, as any sufferer from hay-fever knows. Pollen grains can be identified at least to genus and often to species. Therefore we can get a picture of the vegetation which has surrounded the point at which the pollen core is taken. As with the snails, but on a considerably larger scale, there are issues about how far the pollen has travelled (*cf.* Williams *et al.* 1998) and how to interpret the pattern of species present in terms of local and more regional vegetation. Some species, eg hazel, can produce so much pollen that they are over-represented in the record, whilst others, eg lime, appear to be consistently under-represented, and both of these possibilities have to be taken into account in interpreting the pollen. Additionally, pollen cores can contain biostratigraphic horizons, such as the elm decline at the very beginning of the Neolithic. For lowland Britain the date of this has usually been found to be about 5000bp. The later lime decline is generally taken as occurring about a millennium later, although there are problems in the secure identification of a drop in lime pollen as a signal of anthropogenic clearance (Waller 1994a). Many pollen cores are taken from peaty deposits which yield sufficient organic material for radiocarbon dating. However, this is sometimes not possible, and the temptation is to use the elm and lime declines as datable biostratigraphic markers. This is potentially dangerous since one of the important current research issues is just how synchronous these declines were. If such a course of action has to be taken, then it is probably better to use the elm decline, as there is quite convincing evidence that this was at least in part due to disease (*cf.* Bell and Walker 1992) and, to judge by the recent epidemic of Dutch Elm Disease in the 1970s, could have been rapid, making it a reliable temporal marker in the pollen record.

3. Sediments

The sediments which have accumulated by colluvial action in the dry valleys found on the chalk were shown by Bell (1983; 1992) to be a source of environmental information in their own right and not just of interest because of what is buried in or below them. Similarly, the great accumulation of sediment in river valleys has been used to document the extent of past erosion within the river catchment (eg Burrin and Jones 1991). In both of these cases the sediment accumulated as a result of erosion from slopes whose vegetation had been removed, presumably by human activity.

4. Other sources of information

The omission of the usual stock in trade of the environmental archaeologist: the bones, seeds and charcoal found on sites may be surprising. These are much less easy to interpret with respect to surrounding environment because they have all probably been brought onto the site by human agency, and therefore constitute a biased record, which may have been brought in from some distance. Straightforward economic inferences can be made when dealing with occupation sites, but to put this information in an environmental framework requires data to be both collected and collated over a broad spatial and temporal range. A good start has been made on the seeds by Hinton (1984), which shows *inter alia* that hulled barley has been known in Sussex from the Neolithic to the present. The relatively poor survival of bone in many parts of Sussex compounds the difficulties of interpretation. Any analyses based on animal bones will also have to contend with the issue of how deadstock (the bones retrieved from the site) relate to husbandry practices (*cf.* Grant 1988) and how these would in turn have affected the environment.

British Quaternary Stages	Oxygen Isotope Stage (OIS)	Main Archaeological Periods in	Climate	Environmental Changes	Major Environmental Events	Date BP (not to scale)
		Modern Medieval Roman Iron Age (700BC - AD43)	Sub-Atlantic: Cooler/Wetter	Mixed farming: later with establishment of "sheep-walk"		Present 2000 2500
		Bronze Age (2000 - 700BC)	Sub-Boreal: Warm/Dry	More extensive clearance of woodland	Lime Decline	*c.*3700
Flandrian/ Holocene	1	Neolithic (4300 - 2000BC)		Deciduous forest with small clearings	Elm Decline	*c.*5000
			Atlantic: Warm/Wet			7000
		Mesolithic	Boreal: Warm/Dry Warming	Return of trees to Britain		10,000
			Younger Dryas: Cold		Loess deposition	12,000
Devensian	2-4		Mainly Cold		Last Glacial maximum @18-20,000	40,000
	5a-d		Mainly Cold			100,000
Ipswichian	5e		Warm			*c.*120,000
Wolstonian complex	6		Cold			
	7		Warm			
	8	Palaeolithic	Cold			
	9		Warm			
	10		Cold			
Hoxnian	11		Warm			
Anglian	12		Cold		Major glaciation of Britain	
Cromerian complex	13	Boxgrove c.500,000 BC	Warm			*c.*500,000

Table 20.1. *Environmental change since the last Ice Age. Based upon information from Gamble and Lawson eds. 1996, fig 1; Bell and Walker 1992; Burrin and Jones 1991.*

Making environmental inferences from bones, seed and charcoal found on ritual sites is an even more difficult procedure.

Obviously, when dealing with more recent change, there are sources of evidence - place names, records, maps, etc. which are not derived by excavation or coring. Work by both historians and geographers in Sussex shows how well this can be used to document landscape change (eg Brandon 1974; 1998; Moore 1965; Yates 1972).

Looking backward to the Pleistocene

Before tackling the task of using the available data to turn the sequence outlined at the beginning of this paper for Lowland Britain into a more detailed account of the environmental history of Sussex, I want to put this history into a broader temporal framework.

The current interglacial follows on from the sequence of approximately 20 cycles which have occurred during the Quaternary in which the climatic pendulum has swung from the cold of the glacial to the warmth of the interglacial. The vegetation in Britain has similarly changed from steppe-tundra to deciduous woodland and back again (Jones and Keen 1993). The animal species present, including humans, have depended both on the climate and vegetation, but also on the existence of a land-bridge to the continent of Europe (*cf.* Preece 1995). The problem with documenting the cycles in detail is that subsequent glacial periods have destroyed much of the evidence about conditions in past cycles.

In Sussex the major site which gives us detailed information about an earlier Ice Age cycle is, of course, Boxgrove, which is remarkable in that it was preserved by the sludging down of gravels over the cliff during the subsequent glacial period (Roberts *et al.* 1994; Pitts and Roberts 1997). It has been excavated during a period when the terrestrial record of the glacial-interglacial cycles has been undergoing considerable revision, with a large measure of success in equating this with the much more complete marine record in the form of oxygen isotope stages (OIS) (Wymer 1988; Pitts and Roberts 1997). The finds from Boxgrove have played an important part in this. However, the interglacial documented at Boxgrove, OIS 13 (approx. 500,000BP), towards the end of the Cromerian complex, does not appear to have been particularly remarkable. The presence of Hazel Dormouse (*Muscaradina avellanarius*) has been interpreted as indicating that the climate was warmer than today's (Roberts *et al.* 1997), but the whole spectrum of the fauna can also be interpreted as more continental than today's (Parfitt 1998).

Palaeogeographical studies of the West Sussex coastal plain (Bates *et al.* 1997) put Boxgrove on the coast of a large embayment. The subsequent breaching of the Straits of Dover must have been one of the most dramatic landscape changes in the history of Sussex.

Boxgrove is the earliest of the Quaternary fossil vertebrate faunas known from the West Sussex coastal plain. Others document some of the later cold and warm phases (Parfitt 1998). The fauna from the Black Rock area at Brighton, together with those from Norton Farm and Westhampnett East, appear to be from periods within the Wolstonian complex: both the warm OIS 7 (approx. 220,000BP) , with a largely grassland fauna; and from the cold OIS 6 (approx. 150,000BP), which has a distinctive steppe-tundra assemblage (Parfitt 1998; Parfitt *et al.* 1998). An interesting feature of the cold-stage assemblage is the small size of the horse, which may indicate differences in the climate at this time compared to other cold stages.

Although Sussex was never glaciated, it has certainly been affected by periglacial processes not just once, but many times. The evidence for more recent periglacial processes can be found when the chalk is exposed by excavation, eg at Newhaven (Bell 1976), as well as being exposed in sections of dry valleys cut by the erosion of the cliffs (Mortimore 1997).

Into the Holocene

Looking backwards in this way, I hope, gives us a sense of the immense forces which have been involved in the formation of the Sussex landscape. A further effect of the last glacial period was to deposit a blanket of loess over Sussex. The extent is revealed by its subsequent loss to erosion (Favis-Mortlock *et al.* 1997) and its reworking into valley and floodplain sediments (Burrin and Jones 1991) as well as into dry valley fills (Bell 1981) and possibly also to the coastal plain. Paradoxically, the presence of this loess during the earlier part of the Holocene may have obscured the regional differences which are so apparent to us today. Blanket both "Downs" and "Weald" with the same soil and their differences will largely vanish under a much more uniform vegetation (Greig 1982).

At one level the answer to why this interglacial is different is almost trivially obvious: the result of the presence and activities of modern people have, quite literally, reshaped the land. However, we can only be confident of this statement in its broadest sense, what remains to be done is to document the detail, the key issues being those of timing and extent. It must also be admitted that the complete chain of events from human activity to environmental impact is also not fully understood, and this is particularly the case for the earlier parts of the record.

Advent of the Wildwood

Within Sussex there is at present relatively little direct evidence for environmental conditions during the late glacial (12,000-10,000BP). Kerney's (1963) work at Cow Gap, and elsewhere on the chalk of South-East England, documents an open-country fauna, which shows a clear peak of abundance coinciding with a fossil soil of this date. An interesting zoogeographical element is the presence this early of relatively warmth-loving species. Investigations of the lowest fills of dry valleys rarely show deposits of this age, but their presence has been demonstrated at Asham Quarry (Ellis 1986), where again the molluscan fauna is dominated by open-country species. A similar assemblage was found by Wilkinson (1993; 2002) at Toadeshole Bottom East, but here it was accompanied by elements more typical of a postglacial woodland fauna. Molluscan assemblages which show the characteristics suggested by Kerney (1977) for the Boreal and Atlantic periods, ie dominated by woodland species, have been described from subsoil hollows, possibly tree-throws, buried below the dry-valley colluvial sequence at Itford Bottom and Kiln Coombe (Bell 1983). Similar assemblages have also been found in the lowest solifluction layers at Asham Quarry and Devil's Dyke (Ellis 1986), as well as at Toadeshole Bottom East (Wilkinson 1993; 2002), and at Southerham Grey Pit (Allen 1995).

Colluvial deposits on the chalk do not yield fossil pollen, so for evidence of the species composition of the vegetation, we must turn to the work done on river valleys. Scaife and Burrin (1983) argue that the earliest local pollen zone at Sharpsbridge, in the upper Ouse valley, is characteristic of the Boreal, being dominated by pine (*Pinus*), together with hazel (*Corylus*), and with very little herbaceous pollen other than that from grasses. There is a marked discontinuity between this zone and the next which reveals a deciduous forest. The lack of dates from the Sharpsbridge core is frustrating, but there is no reason to doubt the general ascription to the lowest zone to the Boreal. Since the deposits at Sharpsbridge are inorganic, the real puzzle is what processes led to so much sedimentation in the valley fill by so early a period. The pollen sequence from Pannel Bridge (Waller 1993), where there is a good series of dates from the organic sediment, which is mainly detrital peat, confirms the presence of pine as a dominant element in the early post-glacial vegetation and also documents the appearance of alder (*Alnus*) by *c.*10,000BP. From this stage to the mid-

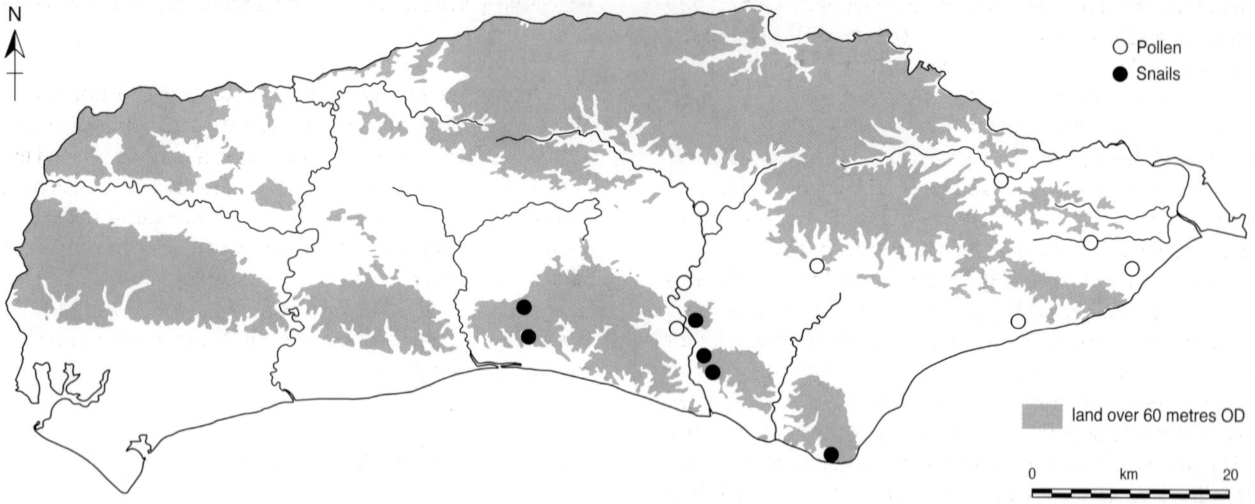

Figure 20.2. *Sites of Mid-Holocene date (approximately 7000BP) which give evidence for woodland.*

Holocene, the pollen records from Sharpsbridge and Pannel Bridge, as well as from Robertsbridge (Scaife and Burrin 1987), Brede Bridge (Waller 1994b), Combe Haven (Smyth and Jennings 1988), the upper Cuckmere valley (Scaife and Burrin 1985) and the lower Ouse Valley at Wellingham (Robinson and Williams 1983), plus the rather scanty record from the Lewes Brooks (Thorley 1981), show the presence of deciduous woodland (see Fig. 20.2). As elsewhere in Britain and Europe, this appears to have been a mixture of lime (*Tilia*), oak (*Quercus*) and hazel, with lime now considered to be an important element (Grieg 1982), although often under-represented in pollen assemblages. Both elm (*Ulmus*) and ash (*Fraxinus*) were also present. It is unfortunate that records for this period all come from the east of Sussex, and predominantly from the Weald, although the broadly similar story from elsewhere in southern England (Scaife 1982), especially the chalklands (Waton 1982), implies that this development of woodland until the mid Holocene is general for inland Sussex. Coastal areas, especially the most low-lying parts of the coastal plain, may well have been marshy (Bedwin 1983). At Worthing there has been one isolated find of peat, with abundant *Tilia* pollen, underlying the brickearth (Barton 1963). Given the likelihood of shifting coastal shingle affecting river drainage, particularly in eastern Sussex (Jennings and Smyth 1990), we probably need to look to the well-documented sequence of events on Walland Marsh (Waller *et al.* 1998), as a guide to the environmental changes near the coast, both in this and later periods.

Clearings in the Woods

It is generally accepted that Mesolithic people manipulated their environment (eg Simmons 1993), albeit on a fairly small scale. Within the last decade there has been a general shift towards thinking of early Neolithic agriculture as utilizing relatively small and ephemeral clearings (Whittle 1996), which blurs the distinction that used to be made between it and the Mesolithic as far as the environmental record is concerned. Since there is little indication in the Sussex pollen record for widespread clearance prior to the lime decline, I will include in this section information from both the Mesolithic and Neolithic periods through to the early fourth millennium BC.

Documenting early woodland clearings in Sussex has proved difficult (see Fig. 20.3). Increased sedimentation in river valleys, prior to the elm decline as found at Sharpsbridge (Scaife and Burrin 1983) and more generally within the Ouse Valley (Burrin and Jones 1991) has been ascribed to clearance, possibly by people, although the mechanism by which such, presumably small-scale, clearance led to increased sedimentation is currently unknown. Loess soils on relatively impervious Wealden Clays would be susceptible to erosion (Robinson and Williams 1983), and much of the sediment in the rivers which cut through the Downs could well have come from the Wealden part of the river catchment, as Burrin and Jones (1991) suggest for the Ouse. As described above, dry valley sediments, as opposed to subsoil hollows, which contain a woodland molluscan fauna have rarely been found. At both Devil's Dyke (Ellis 1986) and Toadeshole Bottom East (Wilkinson 1993; 2002) this fauna is found in colluvium, but in neither case is it clear when the erosion occurred, and so it is probably best to consider the fauna as a relict from the original woodland soils.

Pollen records from river valleys probably sample an area sufficiently large for the postulated small clearings to be difficult to detect, unless coming from the nearby sample site. At Pannel Bridge, Waller (1993) argues that the relatively high values for bracken (*Pteridium*) spores and the presence of herbs such as plantain (*Plantago lanceolata*), dock (*Rumex* sp.) and nettle (*Urtica*) could indicate the presence of woodland clearings in the pollen record between *c.* 8000 and *c.* 6400 BP. Although Mesolithic activity is documented at Pannel Bridge (Holgate and Woodcock 1989), it is unclear whether it is related to any clearances detected in the pollen record. The local nature of the clearance is indicated by the lack of any clear indications of openings in the dryland forest canopy at the nearby site of Brede Bridge (Waller 1994b)

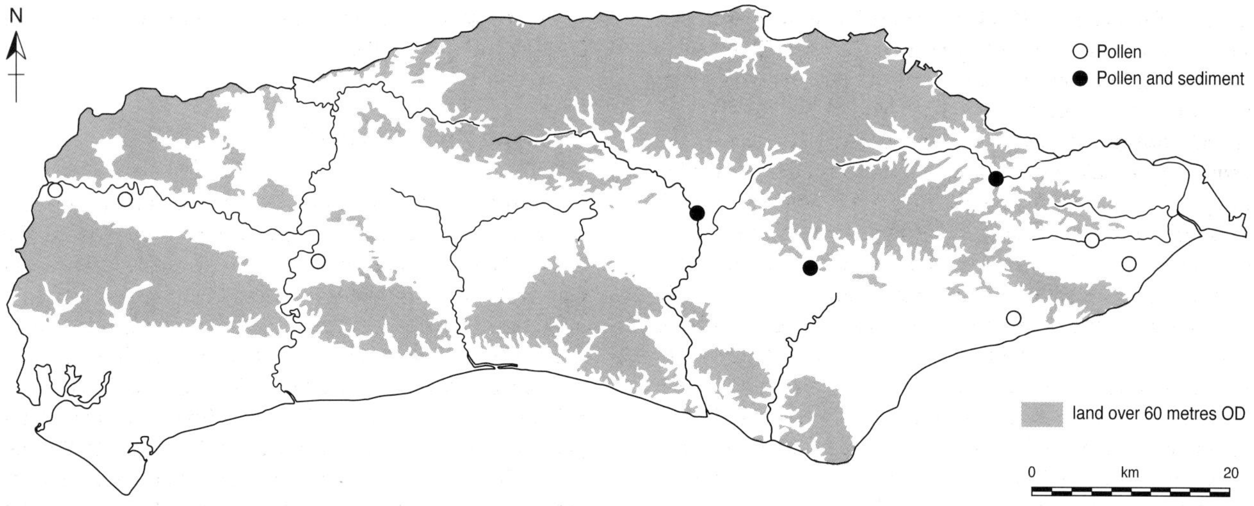

Figure 20.3. *Evidence for early disturbance/clearance (approximately 5000BP).*

until immediately before the elm decline at *c.* 5150 BP. At Pannel Bridge (Waller, 1993) elm is not abundant prior to 5000 BP, but a fall can be detected then, and a single cereal-type grain was found at that level. Elm virtually disappears *c.* 4100 BP, and again, the presence of a single cereal-type grain may indicate that clearings created at this time were used for agriculture. At Brede Bridge (Waller 1994b), the elm decline is dated to *c.* 5150 BP and around this time the pollen record appears to show episodic clearance of woodland. Interpretation of the later lime decline is complicated by changes in the flood plain (Waller 1998), but the continued presence of clearance herbs (especially *Plantago lanceolata*) and cereal grains confirms an anthropogenic clearance at this date within the pollen catchment of Brede Bridge. Combe Haven (Smyth and Jennings 1988), although less securely dated, shows clearance phases at about the time of the elm decline, but after this there is a decrease in clearance herbs whilst there is an increase in local, wetland taxa, showing that the changes in vegetation may have been due to a rise in the water table.

At Sharpsbridge (Scaife and Burrin 1983), there is a hiatus between the early Boreal deposits (*see* above) and the next pollen zone, which is considered to post-date the elm decline, although there is still a good representation of arboreal taxa, including lime. The main evidence for deforestation and subsequent agricultural use of cleared land comes from the presence of both herbaceous pollen and the occasional presence of cereal-type pollen. Similar pollen evidence is found in the short sequence at Robertsbridge (Scaife and Burrin 1987) and also from the upper Cuckmere valley (Scaife and Burrin 1985). All of these sites also provide clear evidence of increased sedimentation from an early date in the Neolithic.

In the lower Ouse Valley at Wellingham (Robinson and Williams 1983), there appears to be a pattern of periods of decline in both elm and lime, followed by recovery, a pattern which can also be seen at Lewes Brooks (Thorley 1981), prior to the disappearance of both taxa from the pollen spectra. Open conditions, marked by the presence of juniper (*Juniperus*) are seen at Mount Caburn (Waller and Hamilton 1998), both before and after the elm decline.

Away from the river valleys, pollen spectra have been retrieved from sites on the acidic sandy soils of the Weald. The Mesolithic site at Iping Common (Keef *et al.* 1965), seems to have been within dense hazel woodland, which shortly afterwards became open heath dominated by heather (*Calluna*). The change in vegetation may well have been anthropogenic, but there is no evidence of continued occupation of the open heath. At about the time of the clearance, ivy (*Hedera*) pollen is present, and this species is also noted from the Mesolithic layers at Minsted (Drewett 1975a), close to Iping and at West Heath, Harting (Drewett 1976; 1985; 1989) also in the same area. It has been suggested (eg Simmons *et al.* 1981) that ivy was collected and placed in clearings to attract wild game. Ivy may also be expected to be a component of open woodland, although it is often poorly represented in the pollen record. At both West Heath (Drewett 1976; 1985; 1989) and Minsted (Drewett 1975a) the Mesolithic levels contain a pollen record consistent with open woodland, dominated by hazel. At West Heath, podzolization may have developed early, and led to the replacement of open woodland by heath (Drewett 1989). At Rackham, ivy pollen is absent. Otherwise the sequence of changes is similar, but the permanent clearance, which resulted in the later domination of the pollen spectrum by heather, appears to be associated with later Neolithic flintwork (Dimbleby and Bradley 1975). In contrast, in the east of Sussex, at High Rocks, near Tunbridge Wells, the on-site pollen record indicates continuous woodland conditions (Money 1960). However, here the presence of beech (*Fagus*) could imply that the pollen record relates more to the Neolithic occupation attested by pottery than the Mesolithic occupation attested by flint tools, although there is not clear stratigraphic separation of these layers.

On the Downland, there are a number of types of sites from the Neolithic which have yielded environmental evidence in the form of molluscan faunas. The Neolithic flint mines at Cissbury, Church Hill, Blackpatch and Stoke Down have produced a primarily woodland fauna (Evans and Jones 1981), although some of the early samples are rather unsatisfactory. These have been interpreted as representing woodland regeneration after abandonment of the site, although the material from Harrow Hill is interpreted as showing that the shaft was opened in a woodland setting (Kerney *in* Ellis 1986). Other Neolithic sites are more difficult to interpret, because their function is unclear, and they are usually described as "ritual". Interpretation of on-site environmental evidence from causewayed enclosures and long barrows is complicated by the possibility that these may have been built in atypical locations in the landscape. In his review of the molluscan evidence from the ditches of five 4th millenium BC enclosures, Thomas (1982) concluded that the snail assemblages from the primary fills of the ditches of Offham Hill, Bury Hill, The Trundle, Combe Hill and Barkhale all had such an abundance of shade-preferring species, that the enclosures must have been sited on land only recently cleared of woods (see Fig. 20.4). This clearance appears to have been rather localized at Offham Hill and Bury Hill, and a similar situation was inferred for Court Hill (Bedwin 1984). Earlier, hand-picked samples of snails from Whitehawk (Curwen 1934) are consistent with the ecological interpretation given for the other sites. However, a recent excavation of the outer tangential ditch at Whitehawk (Russell and Rudling 1996), produced an open-country fauna, implying that here, as at the Trundle, clearance had been extensive, albeit recent. There is no indication at Whitehawk that the environment changed during the time it took for the ditch to fill, but the later Neolithic ditch-fills at the Trundle do show some increase in shade-loving species (Bedwin 1981). A similar sequence of changes can be traced from the enclosure ditch at Halnaker Hill, but it has yet to be firmly established that this site is Neolithic in date (Bedwin 1992). The published snail faunas associated with oval Neolithic barrows in Sussex show open country at or before the time of construction at Alfriston (Drewett 1975b), and North Marden (Drewett 1986), although there is also evidence from both sites of a later return of denser vegetation, possibly scrub or woodland. At Bishopstone (Bell 1977), where Neolithic pits are all that remain of a presumed settlement site, the earliest molluscan faunas from one of the pits indicate woodland conditions, but the later ones show that clearance had started. The samples from a nearby lynchet show open conditions prevailing throughout the Neolithic. A woodland fauna was found in a Neolithic pit remnant at Malling Hill (Allen 1995).

Clearance of Woodland

The strongest environmental evidence for the general clearance of woodland on the Downs comes from the accumulation of sediment in the dry valleys, e.g. at Kiln Combe. Dating this is not always easy, but the artefacts, both in the sediments and in buried soils, as well as occasional radiocarbon dates, all indicate that the bulk of the colluvium has accumulated since the Early Bronze Age (Bell 1983) although general accumulation of sediment was not taking place until the Late Bronze Age/Early Iron Age (Wilkinson 1993; 2002). The molluscan faunas in these colluvial deposits are predominantly open-country, as found at Kiln Combe and Itford Bottom (Bell 1983), as well as in the sites near Brighton studied by Wilkinson (1993; 2002). The frequent lack of any palaeosol or underlying colluvium below these deposits may indicate that this initial erosion was severe (Boardman 1992), a supposition borne out by the nature of some of the earlier deposits in Toadeshole Bottom West, Benfield Valley and Hangleton Bottom (Wilkinson 1993; 2002).

Sediment accumulation in the Ouse valley does not show any marked acceleration at this time (Burrin and Jones 1991), but it is notable that the accumulation of inorganic sediment in the upper Rother valley, and elsewhere in the eastern Weald, shows widespread woodland clearance in the Weald during prehistoric times (Scaife and Burrin 1987).

The pollen records from the river valleys generally confirm this picture of clearance, but with some local variation. At Pannel Bridge (Waller 1993), there is a sharp lime decline at *c.* 3700 BP but this is accompanied by an increase in birch (*Betula*), which could colonize wetland. A further phase of woodland clearance is seen at *c.* 3200 BP, when heather appears, and also cereal grains become more common. After *c.* 2000 BP alder carr is re-established locally. The record for

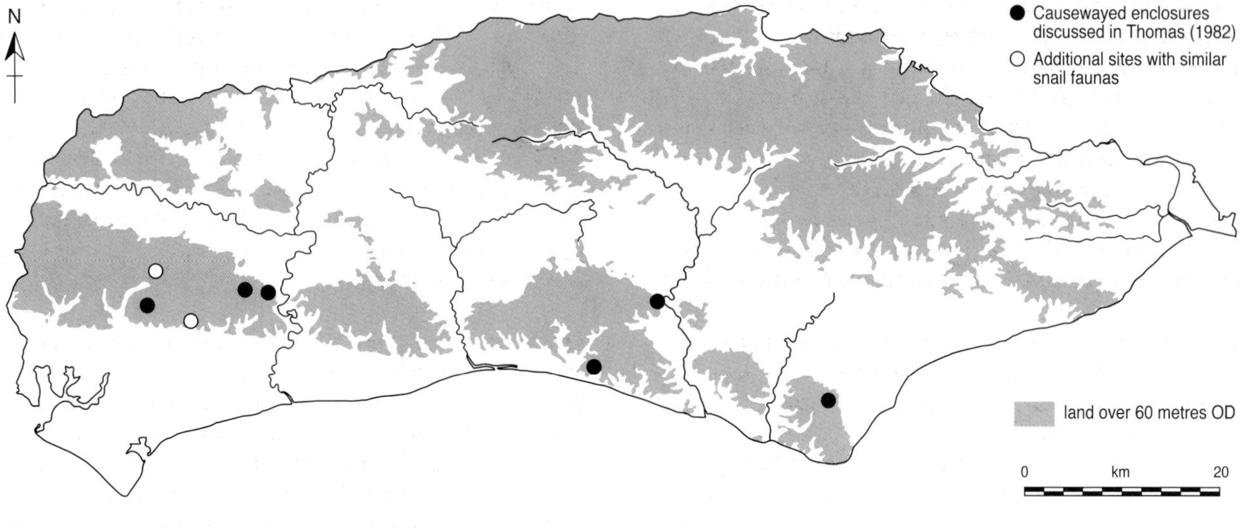

Figure 20.4. *Downland snail faunas from enclosure ditches which indicate recent woodland clearance.*

Brede Bridge (Waller 1994b) also shows the lime decline at *c.* 3700 BP, when it is clearly associated with anthropogenic indicators (cereal-type grains and *Plantago lanceolata*). Little organic sediment has accumulated after this time, but conditions appear to have remained open. At Combe Haven (Smyth and Jennings 1988), the lime decline is associated with a general decline in arboreal pollen and a slight increase in clearance herbs, after which there is a short phase of secondary woodland, albeit with considerable anthropogenic influence, at *c.* 2900 BP, followed by deforestation. At Sharpsbridge (Scaife and Burrin 1983) the lime decline is followed by an increase in herbaceous pollen, including both grasses and plants typical of disturbed ground. In the upper Cuckmere valley (Scaife and Burrin 1985), indicators of agricultural activity increase markedly after the lime decline, as well as increases in aquatic flora, perhaps indicating that anthropogenic activity was affecting the drainage pattern in the valley. In the lower Ouse Valley record the lime decline marks the point at which there is permanent clearance of woodland. At Wellingham, this is followed by clearance herbs and grasses, which attest to subsequent cultivation. More recent work near Mount Caburn (Waller and Hamilton 1998; 2000) shows the expansion of yew (*Taxus*) after the earlier clearances, followed by a phase of further clearance, although this is obscured by the development of brackish communities locally. Thus, the final disappearance of the woodland cannot be well dated in many of the pollen records from the river valleys, but the general interpretation offered is that widespread deforestation is attributable to the Middle Bronze Age (Robinson and Williams 1983). There also appears at this time to be an expansion of beech, possibly replacing lime.

Pollen evidence from Bronze Age barrows on sandy soils in West Sussex show that at both Minsted (Drewett 1975a) and West Heath (Drewett 1976; 1985), there was open woodland at the time of barrow construction. There is little evidence for agricultural activity, and the presence of heather presumably in the clearings may indicate the frequent use of fire in clearance. The construction of the barrows at West Heath itself resulted in substantial soil erosion (Drewett 1989). Although the Late Bronze Age Barrow at Alfriston (O'Connor 1976) appears to have been built from soil whose molluscan fauna is open-country, two recent reports on Downland Bronze Age barrows at Pyecombe (Butler 1991) and Round-the-Down (Butler 1995) also suggest that the molluscan faunas indicate nearby woodland. Putting this together with the evidence from Caburn (Waller and Hamilton 1998; 2000), there seems to be a possible link between sites involving ritual activity in the Bronze Age and woodlands, and an interesting question also arises as to how localized these woodlands were. Allen (1995) describes a colluvial sequence from Southerham Grey Pit where there is evidence of woodland clearance and the establishment of short grassland associated with Beaker occupation in the area. At Malling Hill, an old land surface of Late Bronze Age date buried under a lynchet had a molluscan fauna indicative of grazed grass (Allen 1995).

The Bronze Age settlements at Mile Oak and Downsview (Rudling 2002) and at Varley Halls (Greig 1997), were situated in a cleared landscape, although the use of timber in the buildings must surely indicate its continued presence somewhere nearby. The availability of timber is also shown in the construction of the platform and trackways at Shinewater (Greatorex this volume). In some cases it becomes possible to link occupation and soil erosion, eg at Itford Bottom, the colluvium contains a layer with both an open-country molluscan fauna and pottery sherds which can be linked to similar material found at the Bronze Age site on Itford Hill (Bell 1983). Drewett (1989) links the soil erosion at Ferring rife to the initial occupation of the later Bronze Age enclosure on Highdown Hill.

On the Downland, there seems to be little evidence of any large-scale woodland regeneration after the Bronze Age clearances. At both Southerham Grey Pit and Malling Hill there is no evidence for woodland regeneration in the Iron Age or later (Allen 1995). The extensive archaeological and environmental work at Bullock Down (Drewett 1982) indicates a cleared landscape, which, by Romano-British times, appears to have been grassland and arable. The later molluscan faunas from Downsview (Rudling 2002) show that the landscape remained open after the settlement itself was abandoned. At Bishopstone (Bell 1977) the Iron Age molluscan faunas are typical of disturbed, presumably arable, ground. A cross-ridge dyke at Alfriston (O'Connor 1976) yielded a fauna typical of grassland and a later Romano-British soil contained one which indicated a mosaic of arable and grassland. In West Sussex, the Iron Age assemblage of snails from the Trundle were of an open-country character (Bedwin 1981), as were those from Harting Beacon (Bedwin 1979), although the latter showed a change from moist overgrown grassland, possibly with scrub to open grassland.

North of the Downs, at Friar's Oak, Hassocks, Early Bronze Age waterlogged sediments from a stream bed have preserved a pollen record which shows the presence of woodland, locally dominated by alder. From the same context an ash timber was found to have an irregular bark surface which could have been due to gnawing by beavers (Butler 2000). Pollen samples from Amberley Wild Brooks (Waton 1982) show three successive waves of woodland clearance and partial regeneration during the first millenium BC. Pollen spectra from the Iron Age enclosure at High Rocks (Money 1968) contain arboreal pollen, albeit also traces of cereal pollen and clearance herbs. Later samples from the site indicate that agriculture then ceased and the forest returned. More generally, although speculatively, one might expect managed woodland to be present close to Wealden areas involved in the iron industry (*cf.* Cleere and Crossley 1985).

From Prehistory to the Present

In documenting environmental change after the Romano-British period, there is the general problem that the evidence is often still within the topsoil, especially given the depth of modern ploughing. Further, sedimentation largely ceases in the river valleys after this time (eg Burrin and Jones 1991) and once pasture is established on the Downs the accumulation of colluvium in dry valleys also ceases. Where some arable activity continued, the molluscan faunas in the resulting fill shows open and disturbed conditions. This was particularly notable at Hangleton, which is near to the deserted medieval village (Wilkinson 1993; 2002). At both sites investigated in Toadeshole Bottom there is evidence of a switch during the medieval period from arable to permanent

open grassland (Wilkinson 1993; 2002), and a similar shift in land-use is indicated in the later snail faunas from Varley Halls (Greig 1997). At Bishopstone, snails from two features dated to the Saxon period were typical of short turf grassland, probably intensively grazed and with little, if any, scrub (Bell 1977). These findings are in broad agreement with the documentary evidence for the large numbers of sheep kept on the Downs throughout the medieval and later medieval period (Brandon 1998).

North of the Downs, waterlogged sediment in a stream bed at Friars Oak, Hassocks (Butler 2000) yielded a Middle Saxon pollen sample which shows that the site was then dominated by weedy grassland, with stagnant water nearby. Rather little woodland was left, and clearance was still progressing, to judge from the decrease in arboreal pollen in the successive layers of the sample. The presence of cereal pollen shows that arable farming was established in the locality. Heather pollen and bracken spores may indicate areas of heathland, although these plants could also have been growing as understorey in any local woodland. The pollen profile from Amberley Wild Brooks (Waton 1982), shows woodland regeneration during the Romano-British period and then renewed clearance in the Saxon period, with a peak in arable use of the area at *c.* AD 1250.

On the eastern Pevensey levels, woodland is evident in pollen records from the medieval period (Moffat 1986) although its nature appears to change from forest to secondary woodland *c.* AD 1400, which may reflect changes in woodland management. Clearly, some idea of the productivity of medieval and later woodlands can be obtained from the documentary record, but so far these data have not been satisfactorily married with any environmental evidence (Moffat 1986). Records of 'assarting', which indicates clearance of land, can be informative as Moore (1965) shows at Laughton, where there is a convincing pattern of the better or more easily worked land being taken first. A similar progression in which land was taken into cultivation can also be seen at Harting (Yates 1972), where broad patterns of land-use can be traced back to Saxon times and it can be seen, for example, that the land on the Gault clay was not taken into permanent cultivation until after AD 1400. Further post-medieval woodland clearance in the western Weald at Harting and in St. Leonards Forest near Horsham, was associated with the 16th-century iron industry, and the documentary evidence shows concern about this (Yates 1972; Jack 1997). At the Mens, near Petworth, the medieval glassmaking industry preceded the iron industry in placing a demand for fuel on the woodlands, so that by 1650 documentary evidence shows maximum clearance (Tittensor 1978). In the next two centuries the area was managed in a way that created a woodland pasture landscape, and it is now being allowed to become regenerated woodland as a nature reserve (Tittensor 1978).

Recent reports by the Countryside Commission (1994) on the High Weald and by the Countryside Commission and Sussex Downs Conservation Board (1996) on the Sussex Downs, make it only too clear that there are considerable threats to the quality of the landscape from changes to land-use. It is pertinent to consider what changes would show in a future environmental record. Increased erosion from slopes now ploughed and left bare over winter would be registered in an increase in colluvium in the dry valleys (Boardman 1992); the introduction of new plant species, including both exotic escapes such as rhododendron in the west of the county and the reintroduction of conifers in plantations, would be reflected in the pollen record – that is if increased drainage leaves sufficient wetland to form the necessary mires. Removal of hedgerows, especially the dense shaws, may affect the pollen record more subtly by changing the transport of pollen. The reduction of sheep pasture and the introduction of various management regimes on chalk grassland has the potential to change some of the species composition of the snail faunas, although not necessarily affecting the interpretation of these as "open-country" (Ruesink 1995).

Conclusions

It is obvious from the reference list just how much work has been done since 1977. As ever, the more work done, the more questions there are to answer by further work, e.g. whether there are consistent relationships between site type, landscape use and local environment, a point also picked out by Evans in his 1993 proposal for a regional research strategy for molluscan analysis and archaeology on the chalklands.

The work done to date has shown, *inter alia*, that for the first part of the current interglacial, up to the climatic optimum of the mid Holocene, the whole of the inland part of the county may have looked much more uniform than we think of it now, with the alder carr and other wetland vegetation in the river floodplains and near the coast providing the main contrast. I have been struck by the similarity between my interpretation of the evidence for the first part of the current interglacial and the picture painted for Boxgrove (Pitts and Roberts 1997). This observation leads to the hypothesis that Sussex looked rather similar during most interglacials, which can be tested against the accumulating field evidence.

The elm decline, taken simply as a biostratigraphic marker, can no longer be taken as a marker of the advent of the Neolithic, as it is clear (*cf.* Drewett *et al.* 1988; Whittle 1996) that the material culture associated with the Neolithic starts to appear in the 5th millennium BC, although it is not until the 4th millennium that this archaeological record becomes at all prolific. From an environmental point of view, it is not obvious that there is any immediate qualitative distinction between Mesolithic and Neolithic in terms of the intensity of the anthropogenic impact. Indeed, when looking at the environmental history of Sussex, we need to ask how much it matters whether short-lived, localized disturbances in woodland were made to attract wild-game and encourage the growth of hazel or to grow arable crops and pasture domestic stock? If it is the case that the main differences in the landscape of the current interglacial and previous ones become evident only after the lime decline (i.e. within the Bronze Age), at what point has such anthropogenic change become irreversible?

Answering these questions will require us to put a lot of effort into understanding the ecological as well as the economic base of farming practises in different periods. I hope that the following two examples will show what could be done with this approach. Smith (1984) uses the environmental and settlement evidence from the chalklands around Avebury to show both the similarities between Mesolithic and Neolithic land-use and how clearance of the woodland resulted in difficult secondary environments, particularly an incursion of bracken which in turn affected later patterns of land use. This work sets up a series of hypotheses which it would be instructive to test on the Sussex chalklands. My second example also concerns the Downland, but in the historic period, and draws on Brandon's (1998) documentation of the almost symbiotic relationship in farming between sheep and corn. Certainly as far as the eastern Downs go this was a very long-lived economy, and it would be interesting to see if this model can be applied to earlier landscapes and generate testable hypotheses.

In my view, the continuation of the detailed documentation of environmental change from prehistory to the present is still the biggest challenge. In some ways this could help with interpretations of earlier landscapes. Further work on the relationship between relics of the economy, such as bones, charcoal and seeds, and the documentary evidence, possibly starting from monastic sites (*cf.* Grant 1988; Moffat 1986) may help us to generate mechanisms for using this on-site archaeological information to get at questions of landscape history. The historic period has so far yielded rather little environmental information of the sort which guides us during the prehistoric period. The integration of palaeoenvironmental and documentary information is going to be an essential part of such research, and will be a considerable challenge for both groups of experts, but recent work on the Fenland (Hall and Coles 1994) as well as, more locally, the ongoing research on Romney Marsh (eg Eddison and Green 1988; Eddison 1995), shows that such an approach is indeed fruitful.
Environmental change in Sussex, both natural and anthropogenic, has led to a great diversity in landscape. The challenge for the next millennium will be both to preserve this and to learn how to disentangle the palimpsest which is the result of millennia of interactions between people and their environment.

References

Allen, M.J. 1995. The prehistoric land-use and human ecology of the Malling-Caburn Downs, *SAC* **133**, 19-43.

Barton, K.J. 1963. Worthing Museum archaeological notes for 1961, *SAC* **101**, 20.

Bates, M.R., Parfitt, S.A. and Roberts, M.B. 1997. The Chronology, Palaeogeography and Archaeological Significance of the Marine Quaternary Record of the West Sussex Coastal Plain, Southern England, U.K. *Quat. Sci. Rev.* **16**, 1227-1252.

Bedwin, O. 1979. Excavations at Harting Beacon, West Sussex; Second season, 1977, *SAC* **117**, 21-135.

Bedwin, O. 1981. An excavation at the Trundle, 1980, *SAC* **119**, 208-214.

Bedwin, O. 1983. The development of prehistoric settlement on the West Sussex coastal plain, *SAC* **121**, 31-44.

Bedwin, O. 1984. The excavation of a small hill-top enclosure on Court Hill, Singleton, West Sussex, 1982, *SAC* **122**, 13-22.

Bedwin, O. 1992. Prehistoric earthworks on Halnaker Hill, West Sussex: Excavations 1981-1983, *SAC* **130**, 1-12.

Bell, M. 1976. The excavation of an early Romano-British site and Pleistocene Landforms at Newhaven, Sussex, *SAC* **114**, 218-305.

Bell, M. 1977. Excavations at Bishopstone, *SAC* **115**, 1-299.

Bell, M. 1981. Valley Sediments and Environmental Change, in M. Jones and G. Dimbleby (eds), *The Environment of Man: the Iron Age to the Anglo-Saxon period,* BAR Brit. Ser. **87**, 75-91.

Bell, M. 1983. Valley Sediments as Evidence of Prehistoric Land-Use on the South Downs, *Proc. Prehist. Soc.* **49**, 119-150.

Bell, M. 1992. The Prehistory of Soil Erosion, in M. Bell and M.J. Boardman, (eds), *Past & Present Soil Erosion,* Oxbow Monograph **22**, 21-35.

Bell, M. and Walker, M.J.C. 1992. *Late Quaternary Environmental Change: physical and human perspectives,* Harlow: Longman.

Boardman, J. 1992. Current erosion on the South Downs: implications for the past, in M. Bell, and M.J. Boardman (eds), *Past & Present Soil Erosion,* Oxbow Monograph **22**, 9-19.

Brandon, P. 1974. *The Sussex Landscape,* London: Hodder.

Brandon, P. 1998. *The South Downs,* Chichester: Phillimore.

Burrin, P.J. and Jones, D.K.C. 1991. Environmental Processes and Fluvial Responses in a Small Temperate Zone Catchment: A Case Study of the Sussex Ouse Valley, Southeast England, in L. Starkel, K.J. Gregory and J.B. Thornes, (eds), *Temperate Palaeohydrology,* Chichester: Wiley, 217-252.

Butler, C. 1991. The excavation of a Beaker Bowl Barrow at Pyecombe, West Sussex, *SAC* **129**, 1-28.

Butler, C. 1995. The excavation of a Bronze Age round barrow at Round-the-Down, near Lewes, East Sussex, *SAC* **133**, 7-18.

Butler, C. 2000. *Saxon Settlement and Earlier Remains at Friar's Oak, Hassocks, West Sussex,* BAR Brit. Ser. **295**.

Cleere, H. and Crossley, D. 1985. *The Iron Industry of the Weald,* Leicester: Univ. Press.

Countryside Commission. 1994. *The landscape of the High Weald Area of Outstanding Natural Beauty,* Cheltenham: Countryside Commission.

Countryside Commission and Sussex Downs Conservation Board. 1996. *The landscape of the Sussex Downs Area of Outstanding Natural Beauty,* Cheltenham: Countryside Commission.

Curwen, E.C. 1929. Excavations in the Trundle, Goodwood, Sussex, 1928, *SAC* **70**, 33-85.

Curwen, E.C. 1934. Excavations at Whitehawk Neolithic Camp, Brighton, 1932-3, *Ant. J.* **14**, 99-133.

Dimbleby, G.W. and Bradley, R.J. 1975. Evidence of Pedogenesis from a Neolithic Site at Rackham, Sussex, *J. Arch. Sci.* **2**, 179-186.

Drewett, P.L. 1975a. The excavation of a turf barrow at Minsted, West Sussex, 1973, *SAC* **113**, 54-65.

Drewett, P.L. 1975b. The excavation of an oval burial mound of the third millennium B.C. at Alfriston, East Sussex, 1974, *Proc. Prehist. Soc.* **41**, 119-152.

Drewett, P.L. 1976. The excavation of four round barrows of the second millennium BC at West Heath, Harting, 1973-75, *SAC* **114**, 126-150.

Drewett, P.L. 1982. *The Archaeology of Bullock Down, Eastbourne, East Sussex: the development of a landscape,* Sussex Archaeological Society Monograph **1**.

Drewett, P.L. 1985. The excavation of Barrows V-IX at West Heath, Harting, 1980, *SAC* **123**, 35-60.

Drewett, P.L. 1986. The Excavation of a Neolithic Oval Barrow at North Marden, West Sussex, 1982, *Proc Prehist. Soc.* **52**, 31-51.

Drewett, P.L. 1989. Anthropogenic soil erosion in prehistoric Sussex: excavations at West Heath and Ferring, 1984, *SAC* **127**, 11-29.

Drewett, P.L., Rudling, D. and Gardiner, M. 1988. *The South-East to AD 1000,* London: Longman.

Eddison, J. (ed) 1995. *Romney Marsh: the debatable ground.* Oxford University Committee for Archaeology Monograph **41**.

Eddison, J. and Green, C. (eds) 1988. *Romney Marsh: evolution, occupation, reclamation.* Oxford University Committee for Archaeology Monograph **24**.

Ellis, C. 1986. The postglacial molluscan succession of the South Downs dry valleys, in G. de C. Sieveking and M.B. Hart (eds), *The Scientific Study of Flint and Chert,* Cambridge: Univ. Press, 175-184.

Evans, J.G. 1970. Interpretation of Land Snail Faunas, *Univ. London Inst. Archaeol. Bull.* **8** and **9**, 109-116.

Evans, J.G. 1972. *Land Snails in Archaeology.* London: Seminar Press.

Evans, J.G. 1993. The influence of human communities on the English chalklands from the Mesolithic to the Iron Age: the molluscan evidence, in F.M. Chambers (ed) *Climate Change and Human Impact on the Landscape.* London: Chapman and Hall, 147-156.

Evans, J.G. and Jones, H. 1981. Subfossil land-snail faunas from Grimes Graves and other Neolithic flint mines, in R.J. Mercer (ed), *Grimes Graves, Norfolk Excavations 1971-72. Volume I,* London: HMSO, 104-111.

Favis-Mortlock, D., Boardman, J. and Bell, M. 1997. Modelling long-term anthropogenic erosion of a loess cover: South Downs, UK, *The Holocene* **7**, 79-89.

Gamble, C. S. and Lawson, A.J. (eds) 1996. *The English Palaeolithic reviewed.* Salisbury: Trust for Wessex Archaeology Ltd.

Grant, A. 1988. *Animal Resources,* in G. Astill and A.Grant (eds) *The Countryside of Medieval England.* Oxford: Blackwell, 149-187.

Greig, I. 1997. Excavation of a Bronze Age settlement at Varley Halls, Coldean Lane, Brighton, East Sussex, *SAC* **135**, 7-58.

Greig, J. 1982. Past and Present Lime Woods of Europe, in M. Bell and S. Limbrey (eds), Archaeological Aspects of Woodland Ecology, BAR Int. Ser. **146**, 23-55.

Hall, D. and Coles, J.M. 1994. *Fenland Survey: an essay in landscape and persistance.* London: English Heritage.

Hinton, M.P. 1984. Seeds from Archaeological Excavations: Results from Sussex, *SAC* **122**, 3-11.

Holgate, R. and Woodcock, A. 1989. A later Mesolithic site at Pannel Bridge, near Pett Level, East Sussex, *SAC* **127**, 1-10.

Jack, S.M. 1997. Ecological destruction in the 16th century: the case of St Leonards Forest, *SAC* **135**, 241-247.

Jennings, S. and Smyth, C. 1990. Holocene evolution of the gravel coastline of East Sussex, *Proc. Geol. Ass.* **101**, 213-224.

Jones, R.L. and Keen, D.H. 1993. *Pleistocene Environments in the British Isles.* London: Chapman and Hall.

Keef, P.A.M., Wymer, J.J. and Dimbleby, G.W. 1965. A Mesolithic Site on Iping Common, Sussex, England, *Proc. Prehist. Soc.* **31**, 85-92.

Kerney, M.P. 1963. Late-glacial deposits in the chalk of South-east England, *Phil. Trans. Roy. Soc. Lond. B.* **246**, 203-254.

Kerney, M.P. 1977. A proposed zonation scheme for Late-glacial and Postglacial deposits using land mollusca, *J. Arch. Sci.* **4**, 387-390.

Lane-Fox, A.H. 1869. Further remarks on the hillforts of Sussex: being an account of excavations in the forts of Cissbury and Highdown, *Archaeologia* **42**, 53-76.

Moffat, B. 1986. The environment of Battle Abbey estates (East Sussex) in medieval times; a re-evaluation using analysis of pollen and sediments, *Landscape History* **8**, 77-93.

Moore, J.S. 1965. *Laughton: A Study in the Evolution of the Wealden Landscape.* Leicester University Department of English Local History Occasional Papers **19**.

Money, J.H. 1960. Excavations at High Rocks, Tunbridge Wells, 1954-56, *SAC* **98**, 173-221.

Money, J.H. 1968. Excavations in the Iron Age hillfort at High Rocks, near Tunbridge Wells, 1957-61, *SAC* **106**, 158-205.

Mortimore, R.N. 1997. *The Chalk of Sussex and Kent,* Geologists' Association Guide **57**. London: The Geologists' Association.

O'Connor, T.P. 1976. The excavation of a round barrow and cross-ridge dyke at Alfriston, East Sussex, 1975, *SAC* **114**, 151-163.

Parfitt, S.A. 1998. Pleistocene Vertebrate Faunas of the West Sussex Coastal Plain: their Stratigraphic and Palaeoenvironmental Significance, in J.B. Murton, Whiteman, C.A., Bates, M.R., Bridgland, D.R., Long, A.J., Roberts, M.B. and Waller, M.P. (eds) *The Quaternary of Kent and Sussex,* London: Quaternary Research Association, 121-135.

Parfitt, S.A., Owen, F. and Keen, D.H. 1998. Pleistocene Stratigraphy, Vertebrates and Mollusca, Black Rock, Brighton. in J.B. Murton, Whiteman, C.A., Bates, M.R., Bridgland, D.R., Long, A.J., Roberts, M.B. and Waller, M.P. (eds), *The Quaternary of Kent and Sussex,* London: Quaternary Research Association, 146-150.

Pitts, M. and Roberts, M. 1997. *Fairweather Eden.* London: Century.

Preece, R.C. (ed) 1995. *Island Britain: a Quaternary perspective.* Geological Society Special Publication No. **96**.

Roberts, M.B., Stringer, C.B. and Parfitt, S.A. 1994. A hominid tibia from Middle Pleistocene sediments at Boxgrove U.K, *Nature* **369**, 311-313.

Roberts, M.B., Parfitt, S.A., Pope, M.I. and Wenban-Smith, F.F. 1997. Boxgrove , West Sussex: Rescue Excavations of a Lower Palaeolithic Landsurface (Boxgrove Project B, 1989-1991), *Proc. Prehist. Soc.* **63**, 303-358.

Robinson, D.A. and Williams, R.B.G. 1983. The soils and vegetational history of Sussex, in The Geographical Editorial Committee (ed), *Sussex: Environment, Landscape and Society,* Gloucester: Alan Sutton, 109-126.

Rudling, D.R. 2002. *Downland Settlement and Land-Use: The Archaeology of the Brighton By-pass,* University College London Field Archaeology Unit Monograph **1**.

Ruesink, J.L.1995. Snail faunas on chalk grassland: site comparisons and implications for management. *J. Moll. Stud.* **61**, 9-20.

Russell, M. and Rudling, D.R. 1996. Excavations at Whitehawk Neolithic enclosure, Brighton, East Sussex: 1991-93, *SAC* **134**, 39-61.

vegetation changes in southern England. in M. Bell and S. Limbrey (eds.), *Archaeological Aspects of Woodland Ecology,* BAR Int. Ser. **146**, 57-74.

Scaife, R.G. and Burrin, P.J. 1983. Floodplain Development in and Vegetational History of the Sussex High Weald and some Archaeological Implications, *SAC* **121**, 1-10.

Scaife, R.G. and Burrin, P.J. 1985. The environmental impact of prehistoric man as recorded in the upper Cuckmere valley at Stream Farm, Chiddingly, *SAC* **123**, 27-34.

Scaife, R.G. and Burrin, P.J. 1987. Further evidence for the environmental impact of prehistoric cultures in Sussex from alluvial fill deposits in the eastern Rother valley, *SAC* **125**, 1-9.

Sheldon, J. 1978. The Environmental Background, in P.L. Drewett (ed). *Archaeology in Sussex to AD 1500.* CBA Research Report **29**, 3-7.

Simmons, I.G. 1993. *Environmental History: A Concise Introduction.* Oxford: Blackwell.

Simmons, I.G., Dimbleby, G.W. and Grigson, C. 1981. The Mesolithic, in I.G. Simmons and M. Tooley (eds), *The Environment in British Prehistory,* London: Duckworth, 82-124.

Smith, R.W. 1984. The ecology of Neolithic farming systems as exemplified by the Avebury region of Wiltshire, *Proc. Prehist. Soc.* **50**, 99-120.

Smyth, C. and Jennings, S. 1988. Mid- to late-Holocene forest composition and the effects of clearances in the Combe Haven valley, East Sussex, *SAC* **126**, 1-20.

Thomas, K.D. 1982. Neolithic Enclosures and Woodland Habitats on the South Downs in Sussex, England, in M. Bell and S. Limbrey (eds), *Archaeological Aspects of Woodland Ecology,* BAR Int. Ser. **146**, 147-170.

Thomas, K.D. 1985. Land snail analysis in archaeology: theory and practice, in N.R.J. Feiller, D.D. Gilbertson and N.G.A. Ralph (eds), *Palaeoenvironmental investigations: research design, methods and data analysis,* BAR Int. Ser. **258**, 67-92.

Thorley, A. 1981. Pollen analytical evidence relating to the vegetational history of the Chalk, *J. Biogeog.* **8**, 93-106.

Tittensor, R.M. 1978. *A history of the Mens: a Sussex woodland common. SAC* **116**, 347-374.

Waller, M.P. 1993. Flandrian vegetational history of south-eastern England. Pollen data from Pannel Bridge, East Sussex, *New Phytol.* **124**, 345-369.

Waller, M.P. 1994a. Paludification and pollen representation: the influence of wetland size on *Tilia* representation in pollen diagrams, *The Holocene* **4**, 430-434.

Waller, M.P. 1994b. Flandrian vegetational history of south-eastern England. Stratigraphy of the Brede valley and pollen data from Brede Bridge, *New Phytol.* **126**, 369-392.

Waller, M.P. 1998. An Investigation into the Palynological Properties of Fen Peat through Multiple Pollen Profiles from South-Eastern England, *J. Arch. Sci.* **25**, 631-642.

Waller, M.P. and Hamilton, S.D. 1998. The vegetational history of the South Downs: Mount Caburn, in J.B. Murton, Whiteman, C.A., Bates, M.R., Bridgland, D.R., Long, A.J., Roberts, M.B. and Waller, M.P. (eds), *The Quaternary of Kent and Sussex,* London: Quaternary Research Association, 115-120.

Waller, M.P. and Hamilton S.D. 2000. Vegetational history of the English chalklands: a mid-Holocene pollen sequence from the Caburn, East Sussex, *J. Quartenary Sci.* **15**, 253-272.

Waller, M.P., Long, A.J., Long, D.J. and Innes, J.B. 1998. Walland Marsh: wetland vegetation dynamics, sea-level change and coastal evolution. in J.B. Murton, Whiteman, C.A., Bates, M.R., Bridgland, D.R., Long, A.J., Roberts, M.B. and Waller, M.P. (eds), *The Quaternary of Kent and Sussex.* London: Quaternary Research Association, 70-115.

Waton, P.V. 1982. Man's impact on the chalklands: some new pollen evidence, in M. Bell and S. Limbrey (eds), *Archaeological Aspects of Woodland Ecology,* BAR Int. Ser. **146**, 75-91.

Whittle, A. 1996. *Europe in the Neolithic,* Cambridge: Univ. Press.

Wilkinson, K. N. 1993. *The Influence of Local Factors on Palaeoenvironment and Land-use: Evidence from Dry Valley Fills in the South Downs.* Unpublished Ph.D. Thesis, University of London.

Wilkinson, K.N. 2002. The Excavation of Six Dry Valleys in the Brighton area: The Changing Environment; Appendix 1: Sweetpatch Valley Bottom, *in* D. Rudling (ed) 2002.

Williams, M., Dunkerley, D., De Deckker, P., Kershaw, P. and Chappell, J. 1998. *Quaternary Environments.* Second Edn. London: Arnold.

Wymer, J.J. 1988. Palaeolithic archaeology and the British Quaternary sequence. *Quat. Sci. Rev.* **7**, 79-98.

Yates, E.M. 1972. *A history of the landscapes of the parishes of South Harting and Rogate,* The Harting Papers **3**, Chichester: Phillimore.

Index

Note: Bold page numbers refer to Figures and Tables

A

B

D

E

H

I

J

K

L

N

O

P

Q

R

S

T

U

V

W

Y